ORAL COMMUNICATION

SPEAKING ACROSS CULTURES

Eleventh Edition

Larry A. Samovar
San Diego State University

Roxbury Publishing Company
Los Angeles, California

Library of Congress Cataloging-in-Publication Data

Samovar, Larry A. 1935–
Oral communication: speaking across cultures / Larry A. Samovar.—11th ed.
 p. cm.
 Rev. ed. of: Oral communication / Larry A. Samovar, Jack Mills.
 10th ed. Boston, Mass.: McGraw Hill, c1998.
 Includes bibliographical references and index.
 ISBN 1-891487-28-0
 1. Public speaking. 2. Oral communication. 3. Intercultural communication. I. Title.
PN4121.S188 1999
808.5'1—dc21   99-34763
                                                                    CIP

Publisher and Editor: Claude Teweles
Copy Editors: Arlyne Lazerson, Jackie Estrada
Production Editor: Jim Ballinger
Production Assistants: Dorie Kelly, Josh Levine, Raoul Limeres
Typography: Synergistic Data Systems, Evans and Associates
Cover Design: Marnie Kenney

Printed on acid-free paper in the United States of America. This paper meets the standards for recycling of the Environmental Protection Agency.

ISBN: 1-891487-28-0

Roxbury Publishing Company
P.O. Box 491044
Los Angeles, California 90049-9044
Tel: (310) 473-3312 • Fax: (310) 473-4490
Email: roxbury@crl.com • Website: www.roxbury.net

To Jack Mills

My friend and mentor for thirty years.

"Memory is the treasure-house of the mind wherein
the monuments thereof are kept and preserved."

—Thomas Fuller

Brief Contents

Table of Contents

Part Two: Your Ideas

6. Evidence: The Foundation of Your Ideas 147

Part Three: Having an Influence

Part Four: Changing Environments

Preface

In a culture that is so very fond of novelty, it is indeed rewarding to be asked to prepare an eleventh edition of this text. My late co-author and I took great pride in the fact that over the years hundreds of schools selected our text. The message of this longevity and our success, at least as read by our egos, is that we had something basic and worthwhile to say for the last 33 years. However, our feelings of exhilaration were tempered by the realization that we survived not only because we have always preserved some fundamental precepts from previous editions, but because we welcomed alterations when we believed change would assist us in our efforts. In approaching this current edition, I have once again endeavored to retain the basic framework and philosophy that sustained prior editions while at the same time offering new materials to help readers improve their communication skills in a changing society.

As you would suspect, tampering with a book that apparently has met the needs of students for such a long period of time is not an easy assignment. I know it needs to strike a balance between what represents the core of the discipline and what is new and innovative. Accordingly, this edition aims to make changes that take into account the new complexities of communicating in the twenty-first century. This era, I believe, will be marked by three significant developments that all influence the manner in which we communicate with other people. First, *new technological advancements have had a major impact on all phases of human communication.* Second, *the shifting ethnic and cultural composition of our communication partners means that intercultural adaptation is now a necessity if one is to be an effective communicator.* Finally, *as intercultural and interpersonal conflicts become more commonplace, there is a pressing need to consider the ethical implications of our communication behavior.* While these three cultural changes are commonplace and well documented by the media, their specific impact on public speaking may not be as transparent. Yet these three phenomena serve as the major motivation for most of the significant changes in this current edition. In short, a great deal of time is spent in this new edition talking about the roles of technology, culture, and ethics in the study of public speaking.

Rationale

The freedom to speak, and the ability to speak effectively, has long been recognized as an asset to the citizens of a democracy. The utility of this skill is seen in both our personal and professional lives. In the United States, even the success or failure of our relationships and careers is often linked with our ability to speak well. In this book, I hope to present material that will assist you in understanding communication principles and in mastering the techniques of speaking that are instrumental to the achievement of success in our society.

Philosophy

A dual philosophy has guided us in the preparation of every edition of this book: first, a recognition of the individual's need to know how to speak well and, second, a conviction that a person's speaking ability is something that can always be developed and improved. We have maintained that speech improvement does not begin and end with a single course or with the reading of one textbook. It is the study of a lifetime. Each attempt at sharing an idea or feeling with another person offers us yet another new learning experience, the result of which can teach us something about the principles of social adaptation. Your course, and this book, represent a first step in that adaptation process. As you complete the course and the book I would urge you to seek out as many of these experiences as possible.

Approach

Fundamental to the book's approach to communication is the belief that communication is a social activity; *it is something we do with and to other people*. Since it is a behavior, it can be approached from a practical viewpoint. Therefore, I have put into this book information and advice that I feel will be usable—*ideas that can be translated into action*.

Organization

Determining the sequence of chapters for this book might well have been one of my most difficult assignments, for any arrangement selected would have been linear. The nature of language forces people to employ words and ideas one at a time. However, the act of communicating, because it is a dynamic, holistic process, has many things going on at the same time. For example, you are using evidence, vivid language, interesting material, and clear organization while you are talking, looking at your audience, and moving. Ideally, one would offer advice on these six or seven concepts all at the same time. But I cannot. Again, there is the dilemma. Which of these many skills do I treat first? Which second? Which last? Forced to make the choice of which skills to discuss first and which to discuss later, I based the decisions on one of the philosophies behind this book—students need information that meets their current stage of communication development. That development, like most evolutionary stages or learning processes, reflects movement from the simple to the complex. In short, as you progress from the first simple speeches to the later complex presentations, you will experience a need for a steadily growing supply of information. This book is organized with that need in mind. Acquiring information in manageable increments enables you to move smoothly from simple to more advanced principles, taking along the accumulated learning from one experience to the next. Each chapter builds upon the preceding chapter.

The book is divided into four major parts, each part encompassing a group of closely related chapters. Part 1, "Preliminary Considerations," encompasses chapters 1 through 5, which collectively introduce you to some of the basic concepts of oral communication. Chapter 1 looks at the communication process in general, then focuses on public speaking, comparing it to writing and to conversation. The topic of intercultural communication, and its relationship to public speaking, is also discussed. The ethical responsibilities of both the speaker and listener, although treated throughout the book, are introduced and described in this first chapter. Some rudimentary skills and techniques are offered at the conclusion of the chapter so that you can begin speaking during the first days of your class. Chapter 2 further develops the principles already set forth and adds information about selecting a speech topic, formulating a general and a specific speech purpose, choosing a method of presentation, using notecards, and practicing the speech. Some guidelines for gaining confidence and reducing apprehension are also in this early chapter. Chapter 3 examines the process of audience analysis. The advice offered here focuses on individual, group, and cultural differences. Methods of analyzing the occasion and developing empathy are also presented in chapter 3. Chapter 4 deals with speech delivery. Suggestions for improving both the visual and aural dimensions of communication are offered. Chapter 5 examines ways to improve both informative and critical listening.

Part 2, "Your Ideas," moves to more advanced principles. It begins with chapter 6, which offers explanations and suggestions regarding the various forms of evidence needed to prove and clarify your ideas. A discussion of the ethical uses of evidence is also included in this chapter. In chapter 7, the focus is on visual aids: how to gather, prepare, and use them. Gathering speech materials from personal, written, and electronic sources is one of the topics in chapter 8. Ethical considerations in collecting data are also covered in this chapter. Ways to critically evaluate your speech materials are treated in chapter 9. In chapter 10, the discussion is primarily concerned with the proper ways of organizing materials for oral presentation. The subject of speech introductions and conclusions occupies chapter 11. Chapter 12, the final chapter in part 2, examines the details of language usage. Various devices for making language clear and vivid are presented. The ethics of appropriate word choice are also discussed in this chapter.

Part 3, "Having an Influence," shows you how to move on to more complicated speech forms. Advice on how to prepare and deliver a speech to inform is offered in chapter 13. Advice regarding persuasive speaking is set forth in chapter 14.

The last section, part 4, "Changing Environments," is composed of two chapters dealing with unique communication situations. Chapter 15 examines impromptu speeches, manuscript speeches, entertaining speeches, television speeches, speeches of introduction, and answering questions. Chapter 16 deals with communication in small groups. This chapter also includes a section on teleconferencing (or videoconferencing) as a potential small-group context.

New Features

New Design of the Book

Perhaps the most obvious new feature of the eleventh edition, at least for those who are familiar with the previous editions, is the new design of the book. The book has been visually altered with the addition of color, new display type, and 51 new photographs. We have also "opened up" the pages of the book and highlighted key concepts.

Ethical Considerations

Because of the requests from our readers and reviewers, I have added material on ethics throughout the book. Rather than having a single chapter on this important topic, we have included material on ethics in nearly every phase of the communication process. The appropriate ethical considerations are examined in each chapter, ranging from those related to gathering material, to using material, to listening, to appearing on television, to preparing and delivering the persuasive speech. Throughout the book, the various ways in which stereotyping and prejudice hamper successful communication are pointed out.

The chapter on critical thinking (chapter 9) has also been updated to include new information that will enable you to test the validity of your ideas and to recognize the false premises advanced by others.

New Technology

A far more detailed analysis that directly relates to one of the cultural developments we alluded to earlier in the preface—electronic technology — has been added. Guidance in dealing with the link between the new electronic technology and speech communication is found throughout the book. For example, chapter 7 has current information concerning the use of such audiovisual aids as computer graphics and video equipment. In chapter 8, there is an expanded section on employing new technology to aid you in your research. Advice on conducting computer searches using the World Wide Web and CD-ROMs is included in this chapter. Because of the widespread use of television and video, chapters 15 and 16 have been enlarged to include new information on television speaking (chapter 15) and teleconferencing (chapter 16). Throughout the book, I have offered advice and encouragement intended to stimulate readers to use personal video equipment to practice, gather information, present information, and evaluate performance.

Intercultural Communication

New material in the area of intercultural communication is so infused into the book that it would be impossible to indicate each and every place the concept of cultural adaptation appears. Instead of designating one chapter to look at culture, we have woven this topic into all aspects of communication. For example, the discussion of ethics, feedback, ethnocentrism, empathy, values, language, small groups, stereotyping, listening, credibility, humor, forms of reasoning, conflict, audience analysis, delivery, and persuasion are just a few of the places where culture is included. It is not my intent to write a book on intercultural communication but rather to raise readers' consciousness of the place of culture in human interaction. As stressed in each chapter, we are now in a period of history that sees us doing business, going to school, socializing, and giving speeches to people from cultures other than our own. I simply want students to be aware of and adapt to those differences when they are engaged in a communication event.

Audience Analysis

The chapter on audience analysis (chapter 3) has been significantly altered. New material on cultural values has been added, as well as a new section on how to use the material gathered in the audience analysis. Practical advice is offered on various ways to adapt to an audience before and during the speech.

End-of-Chapter Pedagogy

In this edition, there is material at the end of each chapter that encourages the reader to rethink and to use the material in each chapter. All chapters now conclude with two new pedagogical devices. I have added a section called "Concepts and Questions" and another labeled "Activities and Exercises."

Other Features

Other features that have been added or expanded upon include the following:

- An analysis of inappropriate and offensive words as they relate to culture and gender.
- A detailed listing of new computerized reference works to assist research.
- An expanded section on gaining confidence and overcoming communication apprehension.
- An enlarged section on credibility.

- Additional proverbs and quotations from a variety of cultures to stimulate interest and discussion.

- New material discussing the components of humor.

As with prior editions, there are fresh new examples throughout the book. In addition, I have increased the number of examples as a way of responding to some of the feedback we received from past readers.

Supplementary Material

Instructor's Manual

An enlarged *Instructor's Manual* is available with *Oral Communication: Speaking Across Cultures* that offers guidelines for organizing the structure of the course while providing goals, overviews, classroom activities, and examination questions for each text chapter.

MicroTest (Computerized Test Bank)

The MicroTest is a computerized system that enables the instructor to make up customized exams quickly and easily. Test questions can be found in the Test Item File, which is printed in the Instructor's Manual or as a separate packet. For each exam, the instructor may select up to 250 questions from the file and either print the test or have the publisher print it. Printing the exam requires access to a personal computer—an IBM that uses 5.25- or 3.5-inch diskettes, an Apple IIe or IIc, or a Macintosh. MicroTest will work with any printer. Diskettes are available through the publisher (310-473-3312).

Acknowledgments

A number of individuals have helped, in very different ways, with this project. First, I want to thank my new editor and publisher, Claude Teweles. He has offered me support, sound advice, and most important, the freedom to stake out new territory. Second, I wish to express my appreciation to Professor Susan Hellweg, who has agreed to prepare the *Instructor's Manual* for this new edition. Professor Hellweg is coordinator of the Basic Course at San Diego State University. In that capacity she has trained and mentored hundreds of people on how to teach public speaking.

Finally, I want to thank my two "bosses"—Dr. Al Weitzel and Dr. Mike Real. They are part of a university system that has, for 36 years, created an atmosphere that encourages both teaching and writing.

I cannot hope to list all the reviewers and other people who have provided invaluable insights and suggestions over the ten previous editions of the book. Their feedback has made each edition a more useful teaching and learning tool than its predecessor.

Finally, I want to thank the nearly 700,000 users of prior editions of *Oral Communication*. They are the ones who have given me a chance to "talk to them" about communication. While it may have been a rather intangible link, I have greatly appreciated it.

—Larry A. Samovar ✦

Part One

Preliminary Considerations

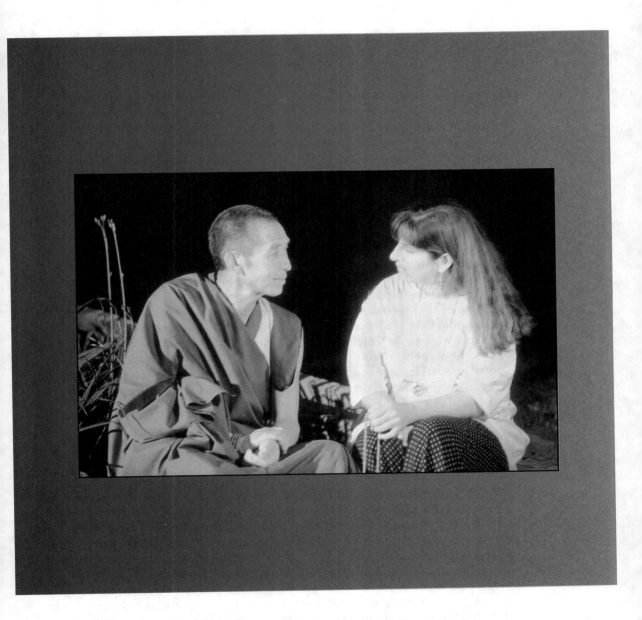

CHAPTER ONE

Communication: Overview and Preview

> The seeds of knowledge may be planted in
> solitude, but must be cultivated in public.
>
> —*Edgar Johnson*

If you are even remotely like the millions of other students who have had to register for a required course in oral communication, it is likely that you have already asked yourself or your instructor the following question: "Why do I have to take this course?" As a history, chemistry, computer science, art, or engineering major, you are justly concerned with the question of taking a course "outside" your special major. In this age of specialization most college students, regardless of their major, realize how vast is the amount of knowledge they need to master in their selected area of study. So the query remains: *"Why a speech class?"* The answer, at least in its stating, is quite simple: *We are born into and live in a society that we share with other people, and it is communication that enables us to function in that society.* We are social creatures who operate in a social world, and communication links us to that world. We need to add at this point that one of the major themes of this book is that although we may be in contact with many people who share a somewhat similar view of that world, we are now communicating more than ever before with people from cultures that do not perceive the world or interact with it in the same way we do. International business, global conflicts, worldwide pollution, new immigration patterns, affirmative action rulings, and calls for "equal justice" have put us in contact with a great number of people who communicate differently than do members of the dominant culture of the United States.

The Importance of Communication

We begin our discussion on the significance of communication by making two points that underscore the importance of communication as an integral part of every person's life. First, *our communication behavior has an influence on other people*. Put in slightly different terms, communication is an activity that produces a result. Although this activity may originate in the mind, communication is first and foremost something people do with and to each other. When you smile and someone sees your smile, you have done something to that person. If your best friend is smoking and you suggest that she terminate this habit, you have done something to her—whether or not she discontinues smoking. If you are successful in getting an audience of 300 people to sign a petition opposing the use of animals for testing cosmetics, you have done something to that audience. As you can see from these three simple examples, communication has a consequence—sometimes subtle, sometimes powerful, but a consequence. Second, *because communication is something we do (an activity), we can alter the way we engage in that activity; we can improve.* Thus,

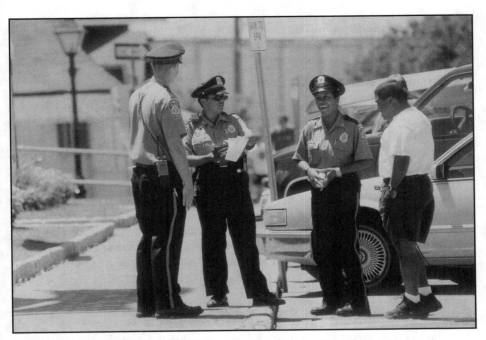

In the workplace you may communicate in a variety of ways. (Photo: Mark C. Ide)

this book can help you improve your communication ability—your ability to influence your environment in a way that benefits both you and the people you come in contact with.

You need only take stock of your waking hours to see the importance of communication in both your professional and private life. Reflect on what you consider a normal day, and you will discover that you spend most of that day in communication. Studies estimate that humans spend up to 80 percent of their waking hours engaged in communication. Let us pause for a moment and discuss how some of those hours are spent and how, with practice, you can improve the quality of those hours.

Communication and Democracy

For anyone who has ever studied government, the link between communication and democracy is crucial and clear. Thomas Jefferson eloquently told us of this link when he wrote, "Democracy is cumbersome, slow and inefficient, but in due time, the voice of the people will be heard and their latent wisdom will prevail." The key words in Jefferson's dictum are "the voice of the people." What he was telling us is that the people must be heard if democracy is to succeed. And to be heard they must speak. However, the gift of human speech cannot benefit us unless we have the ability to speak effectively. For democracy to work, each citizen must take part in the process of governing. A philosopher once said that democracy is the only form of government in which the free are rulers. To help "rule," you need to speak in a lucid manner, you need to put words in their proper place, and you need to promote and defend your ideas in a clear and persuasive fashion. It is not enough simply to imagine that you do not want a trailer park built in a surrounding wilderness area; you must speak before the County Board of Supervisors and articulate your position clearly and concisely. Although it may sound hackneyed and simplistic, that is the way democracy works.

Communication and Careers

Effective communication is an important part of nearly all your professional life. According to one study, oral communication competence was ranked as the skill most necessary for college graduates' career success. The reason is obvious—in the workplace you use communication in many different ways. You may need to complete a sale, take part in an important meeting, negotiate a contract, demonstrate a product, be a participant of an international teleconference, teach a lesson in a class, appear before a judge and jury, or explain company procedures to a new employee. In each of these instances, among countless others, communication is crucial. And as more and more careers focus on "service industries" instead of manufacturing, the importance of effective communication skills for job success will become even more evident.

Communication and Social Relationships

The personal uses for communication can range from the therapeutic to the pragmatic. You might tell a friend how much you are suffering because you failed an important examination, knowing full well your friend cannot change the results of the test. Nevertheless, sharing the information about the examination seems to have a therapeutic effect. As trite as it sounds, talking usually makes us feel better. Whether that talk is about our spiritual life or our social life, using communication to make contact with other people seems to be a basic human drive. Much of what we know about chronic depression suggests that it is often caused by a lack of human contact. We also know that our relational contacts are more profitable if we understand the communication process. Knowing how to listen and how to talk in a sincere and competent manner to a family member or a close friend can offer a great deal of satisfaction to both parties.

Communication and Culture

As indicated earlier, being able to communicate effectively with people from different cultures has taken on added significance during the past few decades. Events both abroad and at home have radically changed intercultural communication. At one time, the international arena was reserved for a small proportion of the world populace. Government officials, selected merchants, missionaries, and a few tourists were primarily the people who visited with "strangers." Today, this is not the case. A combination of circumstances has created a world in which we are constantly meeting with people from diverse backgrounds. These people may live and work thousands of miles away or right next door. What is certain is that Marshall McLuhan's global village prophecy has become a reality. The causes of this increased contact are almost as divergent as the contacts themselves. Knowing what has brought about the increase in intercultural contact might well be the first

Culture teaches us everything from what language to speak to what life is and how to live it. (Photo: indexstock.com)

step in arousing interest in this important development. Hence, to better understand the role of intercultural communication in all of our lives, let us look at some of these new "contact points" on the international as well as the domestic level.

International Contacts

Internationally, there are a number of reasons why we may find ourselves communicating with people from various cultures.

New Technology. *New technology in transportation and information systems places us in instant and constant contact with people all over the world.* Air travel to "foreign" places is now relatively inexpensive and rapid. Through communication satellites, the Internet, sophisticated television transmission equipment, and digital switching networks, we are now sharing information and ideas with people whose cultures are far removed from our own.

Global Conflict. The past few decades have given credence to the axiom that *violence and conflict in one part of the world influence the entire planet.* Staying aloof from global disorder is no longer an alternative. From the Middle East to Eastern Europe, from North Korea to South America, we are learning that distant places can be as troublesome as next-door neighbors.

Worldwide Pollution. Intercultural "conversations" have also increased because people all over the world have started to realize that the earth cannot continue to yield its current bounty unless all people work together. *People now realize we need to talk to each other so that we can avoid world hunger, learn to share natural resources, and combat global pollution.* As simplistic as it sounds, intercultural communication is being used to deal with these and other universal problems.

Economic Developments. It is now a fact of life that *the economic arena includes the entire world.* In the 1990s, 75 percent of all North American

❖ ❖ ❖ ❖   industries faced international competition. Today, nearly all major U.S. companies have offices in foreign countries. More than a third of the profits of U.S. companies are generated by overseas operations. There are more than 37,000 transnational corporations, with 207,000 foreign affiliates. The foreign presence in the United States has also increased; more than 6,500 foreign firms now operate in the United States. Foreigners have invested billions of dollars in joint ventures with U.S. entities, ventures such as those found in the maquiladora plants along the Mexican-American border; these often have representatives of three different cultures working in the same factory. Whether we stay home or leave the country, we are doing business with, working for, or sharing work space with someone from another culture.

Domestic Contacts

As changes throughout the world began to alter our communication patterns and even reconstruct life in the United States, a kind of cultural revolution was also affecting our need to interact with people who had, until this time, remained silent and/or invisible. It seemed that the word "American" could no longer be used to describe a single group of people. Americans were now coming in different colors and from different ethnic backgrounds. Alterations in birth rates and legal and illegal immigrations into the United States have significantly transformed the demographics of this country. The United States permits more legal immigration than the rest of the world combined. This fact is clearly reflected in the following set of numbers: the population of this country annually increases by a net figure of 3 million people. Of these, between 1.4 million and 2 million are immigrants—both legal and illegal. These figures only confirm what we can all observe—ethnic groups are the fastest-growing segment of the population. Nearly 9 percent of Americans were born in other countries. Most of these people have cultural characteristics that they are proud of and that influence the way they communicate with the European American dominant culture. When we add groups such as Native Americans, homosexuals, the disabled, and the elderly to the dominant culture, we can see that members of the dominant culture are interacting with people from different cultures with greater regularity and in a variety of settings. Schoolteachers, politicians, employers and employees, and parents and students are having daily interactions with people who, because of their backgrounds, often communicate in a manner that is different from that of the dominant culture of the United States. This book seeks to increase your understanding of those interactions so that your encounters, whether one-to-one or in the public-speaking setting, will be more rewarding and more successful.

Improving Communication

From all the instances cited in the previous pages, it should be clear that your chances for success as a speaker are greatly increased if you have acquired some specialized skills in communication. These skills are so essential in today's society that most universities and corporations offer courses in effective communication to their students and personnel. The assumption behind this training is that by learning about communication, you will be able to acquire the skills necessary to think critically, solve problems, manifest high levels of personal credibility, adapt to social changes, develop self-confidence and poise, present creative and important ideas, and communicate interculturally. The main point should be clear: without communication skills, we are isolated from one another, unable to share thoughts and feelings with family, friends, and foes.

Because of the significance of communication and because communication can be improved, this book is about how to communicate. It is primarily concerned with the efficiency with which you share your opinions and ideas with other people. However, understanding the processes involved is the first step toward improvement. Therefore, this chapter is based on the assumption that understanding and doing are two sides of the same coin. In this chapter, we seek to explore that relationship by examining what communication is and how it works. We will also discuss the ways that communication and public speaking are both alike and different.

The Communication Process

To understand the nature and function of speech, we must examine the process of communication, of which speech is but one manifestation. This text uses the terms "communication," "speech communication," "public speaking," "oral communication," and "speech" synonymously, simply because a speaker is primarily engaged in communication whenever he or she is, consciously or unconsciously, affecting the behavior of others. We ask and answer questions, we take part in conversation, we exchange ideas in committees, we take part in class discussions, we deliver formal speeches, and we participate in situations for which we are prepared and in some for which we are not prepared. In short, the text uses "communication" and "speech" interchangeably because, in most instances, the same principles and concepts apply to both. In fact, someone once referred to *public speaking as a kind of expanded conversation; the components of communication are essentially the components of public speaking.* In both cases, factors such as credibility, culture, interest, motivation, organization, clarity, feedback, and delivery come into play. Even the differences we will discuss later can be taken into account in nearly all instances. For example, although usually only one person talks during public speaking, the "other person" is still sending messages. Nonverbal communication is present in all public-speaking situations. The way the audience responds is a type of message. There is even commonality in that in both public and private interaction, a person has a purpose that triggered his or her role in the communication process; people seldom engage in random behavior. Thus, although the number of people involved may vary and the time allowed for preparation may differ from occasion to occasion, public speaking and communication basically include the same elements. In short, *you will find it useful if throughout this book you can transfer your newly acquired public-speaking skills to various situations and settings.* To help you understand the relationship between the general concept of communication and the public-speaking setting, the next few pages will (1) define communication, (2) discuss the ingredients of communication, and (3)

❖ ❖ ❖ ❖   explain in what specific ways public speaking and communication are both
similar and different.

Defining Communication

Defining communication is one of those assignments in life that is analogous to having to explain to someone why you love him or her. In both instances, it is often easier to remain silent and hope that you and your partner have similar meanings. The difficulty in both instances is that definitions of concepts as complex as love and communication are bound to be incomplete. The reason, of course, is that both can take so many different forms. With regard to communication, actors, artists, writers, and musicians communicate with their audiences by diverse methods, including spoken or written words, sounds, actions, forms, and colors. Audiences participate in the communication process by responding to the symbols sent by each communication source. Not only are the sources and symbols different, but so are the messages. A tired student who yawns in an early-morning class communicates something to the professor and to those who sit around her. A smile is a communication act, and so is a frown. The term *communication* is enigmatic; although it is something we all do, communication is so capacious a concept that it is difficult to define. An article in the *Journal of Communication* presented no less than 15 working definitions of human communication.

The problem of defining communication becomes even more difficult when we realize that in one sense, inanimate as well as animate objects can communicate. Therefore, in any definition, we must allow sufficient latitude to include the processes as well as the functions of the act. Perhaps the most useful of all definitions suggests that **communication** *is the process of verbally and nonverbally sharing with another person or persons one's knowledge, interests, attitudes, opinions, feelings, and ideas.*

Add to Encoder→ Sender

The Ingredients of Communication

Although each communication event differs in some ways from every other one, we can isolate certain elements that all communication situations have in common. Every time you talk to your neighbor, deliver a speech, or act as a member of a group composed of people from various cultures, certain ingredients of communication are present. Understanding those ingredients can help you place public speaking into the larger context of human communication. Before I begin the explanation, I need to mention two limitations of any discussion of communication ingredients.

First, the enumeration of communication ingredients could extend for the remainder of this book, for communication is highly complex and multidimensional—it is not subject to simple analysis. Factors such as perception, gender, culture, motivation, communication skills, knowledge level, and social systems all play a role in the process. I have merely isolated the factors that are common and dominant in the response made by the receiver of the message.

Second, although at times it may appear that the ingredients describe a linear process by placing one item ahead of another, communication is not linear, but language is. Hence, only one element can be discussed at a time, even though this distorts the way communication actually operates. In "real life," things happen all at once, not one after another. In most communication encounters, both parties simultaneously are using feedback, are encoding and decoding, and are aware of the context and the relationship.

Source. The communication act has to originate from a **source**. You, as the source, want to express yourself—to pass on your feelings, to convey information, to give directions, to obtain agreement, to get something done, or to relate an idea. You have something that you want to share with others.

Encoding. The source of the message must translate his or her ideas and feelings into a verbal (words) or nonverbal (actions) form. This translation process is called **encoding**. It is simply the process of putting feelings and ideas into a set of symbols that can be sent to another person. While symbols can take the form of art, dance, and even architecture, in most human interaction we think of symbols as being either words or actions.

Message. Your original idea, now represented by a set of symbols, is the **message**. This is the essential part of the communication process—the subject matter to be communicated. Your message, in written or spoken language or in nonverbal actions, is the symbolic representation of your idea. Regardless of the language system employed or the meaning given to various nonverbal actions, all of us use symbols as the primary means of sharing our internal states. Because our messages can be intentional or unintentional, it is very important for you to be conscious of the words you select and actions you generate.

Channel. You send your message through a carrier, or medium, called a **channel**. Channels take various forms, such as wires, graphic signs, light vibrations, and air vibrations. Channels should be thought of as the vehicles that carry the message. For the public speaker the primary channel is the voice, in combination with the visual channel that carries your gestures, facial expressions, movements, and visual aids.

Receiver. Even though you have sent your message, communication has not yet taken place, for there must be another ingredient, someone to whom your message is directed—a **receiver**. For the receiver to understand and react to your message, *he or she must engage in decoding your message—translating it into a code that he or she can use.* This operation (the converting of external energies to meaningful experiences) is once again a private matter—the initial response to the message happens inside the receiver. The receiver's (listener's) response to your message will, of course, be dependent on a number of factors. Variables such as the receiver's past experiences, culture, attitudes, beliefs, age, gender, values, and fund of knowledge will come into play as he or she searches for the meaning of your message.

Context. Communication takes place within a particular **context**, or setting. As you know from personal experience, the place of an act controls many aspects of that act. The same words spoken at a party may take on different meanings if uttered in a classroom. The locale of communication, whether in a classroom, large auditorium, television studio, hallway, or church, influences the channels we use (speaking, writing), our purpose for communicating (persuasion, information, enjoyment), and the roles we play (student at school, nurse at hospital, boss at work). The effective communicator is well aware of the specific setting he or she is in and adapts accordingly. The adaptation might include all behaviors, from volume level to the selection of clothing.

Number of Participants. The number of people receiving the speaker's message is also an issue when considering the subject of context. The four most common contexts we find ourselves in are *dyadic, small group, mass (often referred to as mediated),* and *public.*

Dyads. When our encounter involves one other person, we are engaged in a dyadic situation. These events are usually more intimate than the other three settings and because we are close to our communication partner, they allow us an opportunity to monitor the other's response to us and our message.

Small groups. The small group context, because we are sharing ideas and information with six to ten other people, influences everything from the amount of time an individual gets to talk to the type of feedback we receive and send. The popularity of this context demands that we treat it in detail in chapter 16. In fact, that entire chapter examines how communication can be improved in a group situation.

Mass communication. Mass communication refers to those situations when we communicate via some electronic device. As is the case in all four settings, adjustments are required when we engage in mediated communication. Television, for example, will influence everything from the feedback we receive to the clothes we wear. In chapter 15 we spend some time discussing how you tailor your presentation when you are confronted with a mass communication context.

Public speaking. Public speaking is yet another context that makes specific demands on the speaker. This form of communication, as explained later, is usually more planned, formal, and structured than casual conversation. However, what is important to keep in mind is that you do not have to develop an entirely different set of skills to speak in public; rather, you have to adapt the ones you learned in other settings to the public arena. Throughout this book, there is specific advice that will allow you to expand and develop those basic skills.

Feedback. As senders of messages, we usually perceive the response people make to our messages. The response may be words, silent actions, or both. It matters little; what is important is that our message, as a stimulus, produces a response that we take into account. *Our perception of the response created by our message is called* **feedback**.

The term *feedback* applies directly to (1) the reactions you obtain from your listeners and (2) your efforts to adapt yourself to these perceived reactions. The term was originally used only in the literature of engineering and cybernetics to designate the return of information to a machine so that the machine could adjust itself to changing conditions. A thermostat is an example of a device that uses feedback. As information related to the original message (a certain degree of heat) is returned to the machine, the machine readjusts—it shuts off the heater when the air reaches the specified degree and turns it on when the air is cooler than the thermostat's setting. The source makes adjustments because of the information it receives.

Feedback provides a communicator with essential information concerning his or her success in accomplishing the desired objectives. In so doing, feedback controls future messages. Whether talking to one or 100, a speaker has the twofold task of (1) observing and interpreting audience reactions (people look as if they are losing interest) and (2) readjusting the next message in light of his or her observations and interpretations (adding more "life" to a delivery).

Competing Stimuli. If the list of ingredients is to accurately describe how communication operates, we must include the role of **competing stimuli**. The source is not the only one sending messages to the receiver. Each situation is also characterized by competing stimuli; all those other messages vying for the listener's attention are a form of interference, or "noise." In most situations the speaker must be aware of the three most common distractions that can interfere with successful communication. First, there are *external distractions*. External distractions can be someone in the audience coughing, loud talk coming from another source, or even an obnoxious-sounding air conditioner. All these are external to the speaker and become competing stimuli. Second, listeners' "talking to themselves" is also a form of competing stimuli. These *internal distractions* range from daydreaming to mentally debating what is being said by the speaker. Finally, interference with the message can also be generated *by the speaker*. If your mannerisms are clumsy or if your unusual attire calls attention away from your message, you are the source of the interference.

Levels of Response. A careful description of human communication must allow for the fact that the responses people make to messages do not occur as single, one-dimensional acts. There are **levels of response**; people usually respond in more than one way. Let us assume that someone tells you that driving a motorcycle is dangerous and that you should not purchase one. At one level—the cognitive level—you agree with the person, yet, while that person is talking, you discover that you have some bad feelings about him or her, which you keep to yourself. This is a type of conscious, unstated response. When the person is finished speaking, you reply that perhaps you will think over the entire issue—a verbally expressed response. A few weeks later, you find that you have still other feelings about motorcycles. This is another level of response—your subconscious is reacting.

Communication and Public Speaking

Thus far, we have talked about communication in general terms, lumping all the ways people share ideas and feelings into a few broad categories. This view, although useful as an introduction, does not make important distinctions that you should be aware of as you begin your training in public speaking. Consequently, we will now turn our attention to the differences between public speaking and other forms of communication. We will then conclude this section by examining a number of ways in which public speaking resembles other forms of communication. An awareness of these differences and similarities will help you adapt your message to the unique situation you find yourself in.

Public Speaking and Writing

Although oral and written discourse have a great deal in common (they both employ symbols) and have the same primary goal—to assist us in sharing internal states with others—they have some obvious differences that

❖ ❖ ❖ ❖   affect all phases of the communication process. Let us look at some of the most obvious distinctions and briefly discuss how these differences influence the way you prepare and present your message.

Different Channels. The most obvious difference between oral and written discourse is that they use *different channels*. You will recall that a channel is a carrier, or medium, for moving the message from person to person. For example, an essay requires writing devices (paper, computer keyboard and screen, blackboard), while a speech uses aural (hearing), oral (speaking), and visual (seeing) channels.

Personal Contact. Another major difference between written and oral channels is *personal contact*. Because of the face-to-face nature of oral communication, the entire personality comes into play. This, of course, makes oral communication more informal than written communication. You are being heard and seen at the same moment. Not only is everything about you being evaluated on the spot, but you often have to adapt to this live setting. If people begin to show a lack of interest or ask a question you did not expect, you may find yourself altering your planned presentation. Although at times personal contact may be unnerving, it gives oral discourse a greater sense of immediacy than written communication has.

The differences described often require the speaker to make a series of adjustments to both the content and presentation of the message. For example, if a writer makes a point that a reader does not immediately understand, the reader can go back and reread that section. With oral communication, the participants are not afforded that luxury. Hence, the speaker has the added burden of being clear at the first hearing.

The difference in the two styles often means that oral language demands more elaboration. Successful speakers learn how to orally develop, underscore, and repeat key and/or potentially confusing ideas and information. It is also important for you as a speaker to learn an entirely different set of organizational and "punctuation" devices. As a speaker, you do not have paragraphs, bold print, quotation marks, underlining, and other devices. This fact, then, requires you to replace these writing or printing devices with vocal nuances, body movements, glances, and other nonverbal substitutes. It also means using a series of verbal transitions to replace paragraphs, periods, and the like. Throughout this book, I will present specific speech techniques that can be used as public-speaking "punctuation" devices.

Other alterations need to be made when you move from written to spoken discourse. For instance, oral style asks for a greater variety in sentence length, sentences that are less involved, more personal pronouns (I, we, you), and more use of rhythmic phrasing. Once again, remember that all these techniques, capable of changing your style, will be expanded upon later in the book.

Public Speaking and Conversation

Although public speaking and conversation are basically both concerned with sharing information, ideas, and feelings, they are not identical. There are some major differences that help explain why an effective public speaker does not simply "talk as usual" when thrust into a speech-making situation. To be successful, he or she must take the following 10 differences into account.

❖ ❖ ❖ ❖

Public Context. Public speaking, as the words suggest, is **public**, while everyday conversation is often private. This difference has a number of spin-off effects that help define the boundaries of public speaking. In a one-to-one situation, you have to interest only one other person. In the public context, the need to be interesting and relevant is much more complicated. Not only are there more people, but they are apt to come from a variety of backgrounds and cultures. As you might suspect, the more heterogeneous your audience, the more difficult is your task of locating a "general level" on which to speak. For example, there are major cultural differences in what constitutes humor. In cultures that value the elderly, humor that makes old people the butt of a joke is in poor taste. Because this need to adapt to an audience instead of to an individual is of such importance, an entire chapter is needed to treat this topic (chapter 3).

Feedback. In the public-speaking context, **feedback** from the listener is primarily nonverbal. Although on some occasions your listeners will ask questions, in most instances feedback comes from nonverbal actions such as head nods, smiles, yawns, aimless movement, and even someone falling asleep. In face-to-face meetings, your partner sends both words and nonverbal codes in response to your message.

Clearly Defined Roles. In the public-speaking situation, **roles** are clearly defined and are not subject to the shifting patterns found in conversation. The speaker realizes his or her responsibility to do the talking, and the audience members are aware that they are the listeners. In conversation, roles usually change each moment and with each topic.

Clearly Defined Purpose. One of the most important differences between conversation and public speaking is in the area of **purpose**. For example, the purpose and content of conversation grows out of what is going on at that instant. This often contributes to a constant shifting of purpose. However, in public speaking you know in advance what you want to accomplish and how you plan to accomplish it. Whether you decide on your purpose or someone selects it for you is not important at this point. What is important is your realizing that public speaking is not aimless chatter; it is goal directed. Even impromptu speaking, or getting up before a group to speak with little or no preparation, has a specific purpose. In chapter 2, we will discuss in detail the various types of speech purposes and how to select them.

Level of Preparation. Because public speaking is purposeful, it is characterized by **preparation** before the communication begins. Your plan to influence your listeners demands that you prepare your material before you see the audience. Conversation is usually spontaneous—with both people responding to what is happening. The topic of how to prepare for a public-speaking situation will be examined in nearly every chapter of this book.

Time and Space. Public speaking is bound by **time and space**, but conversation is not thus constrained. As a speaker, you have a set amount of time to accomplish your purpose. It matters little whether you or someone else sets the time limit, because in either case the clock must be taken into account. Being aware of the time constraints imposed by public speaking means that your speech must be structured and well planned. In addition, you must keep the time limit in mind because if you go on and on, you may lose the attention of some or all of your audience. In conversation, as you know from experience, people can engage in communication acts for long periods of time.

When I speak of being space bound, I am not talking about science fiction but am referring to the idea that a public speaker is confined to a location. It can be a conference room, a television studio, a classroom, or an auditorium. When we take part in a conversation, we can walk on the street or move from room to room. As you would suspect, this lack of mobility is yet another reason why successful speakers strive to be interesting and to motivate their listeners.

Delivery. Both conversation and public speaking involve sending messages to other people, but the **delivery** of those messages is influenced by the setting. For example, in conversation, you have eye contact with just one person; in public speaking, you need to look at many more people. In conversation, your voice level may be low when someone is sitting or standing next to you. In public speaking, your voice level must be adjusted to the context. Are you in a large hall or a small room, or are you using a microphone? The answers to these questions affect your volume, rate, and pitch. Because your presentation is under greater scrutiny during public speaking, you must also try to avoid vocal distractions such as "uh," "er," and "um." Even your body must reflect the differences between conversation and public speaking. The added distance between you and your listeners demands that your gestures be clearer and larger. Posture and movement must also be tailored to the situation. The adjustments necessary for successful public speaking are important enough to occupy an entire chapter (chapter 4).

Language. As you move from conversation to public speaking, you also modify your **language**. With one person, you can be very personal in your use of language. Slang and jargon might be appropriate. In the public-speaking context, however, you should be flexible in your language use. A speech before the county board of supervisors might require you to be formal, yet a speech to your peers explaining a new piece of office equipment would require less formality. The requirements of language for public speaking will be treated in chapter 12.

Control. Public speaking differs from conversation in regard to the amount and **control** of distraction found in each. When you talk with one person, the two of you are focused on each other, sharing a common topic, and taking turns as speaker and listener. Conversation tends to produce very few distractions, and, if they do arise, the two of you can probably reduce them. If the distractions are serious, you can even change the location. In the public-speaking setting, there is a greater chance for distractions—there are more people to create "noise." These distractions are also harder to overcome. In most cases, the speaker cannot tell someone to stop talking or move the entire audience to another location.

Influence. The potential for influence is greater for public speaking than for conversation. We are not diminishing the power of face-to-face persuasion but are only pointing out that in public discourse you reach more people and, hence, affect more lives. Telling one person the dangers of driving without wearing a seat belt does not have the same impact as giving this message to 60 or 6,000 people. The ethical responsibility that this places on the speaker is important enough to make it a topic of discussion later in this chapter.

Although we have just spent some time differentiating public speaking from conversation, we need to end this section by noting that in most instances the skills that mark a successful public communicator are the same skills that distinguish the person who is a good conversationalist. Reflect for a moment on the people who are most captivating and persuasive even in a one-to-one situation. They are people who are organized; who tailor their message to a person or setting; who adapt to what is going on at the moment (using feedback); who are interesting, attentive, credible, and knowledgeable; and who use language effectively. These, and other traits, represent the major components of this book. Hence, as noted earlier, becoming a good public speaker also means becoming a good communicator.

Ethical Responsibilities of Communication

We now come to one of the most important topics in this entire book—**ethics**. These are the judgments we make all day long concerning the degrees of rightness and wrongness and of virtue and vice. Ethics is a subject that, for most of us, is often easier to talk about than to put into practice. For when we speak of ethics, we are talking about the standards we employ to judge human behavior—our own and that of other people. Because all cultures and societies need ethical standards, philosophers and religious leaders have been trying for thousands of years to offer us guidelines by which we can evaluate our actions and the actions of others. In the sixth century B.C. Confucius told us, "If language be not in accordance with the truth of things, affairs cannot be carried on to success." Nowhere is the notion of truth more profound than in the public-speaking arena. When you occupy the role of the "speaker," you are asking other people to believe you, to trust you, and to adopt the actions you are recommending. These are indeed ethical issues. As George Horne reminds us, "Words may safely guide us in the direction of truth or they may lead us into swamps where there is no solid footing." This next section seeks to offer you the needed "footing."

Some Working Principles

The topic of ethics is of such great importance that it is discussed in nearly every chapter of this book. However, because you are preparing to give your first speeches, you need to be introduced to some of the issues related to ethics and to be provided with some guidelines for judging your own actions and the actions of others.

Earlier, the book alluded to three principles of human communication that directly relate to this important section on ethics. Let us crystallize these three ideas so that we can use them as the basis for our analysis of the ethical dimensions of human communication.

Social Creatures. Early in the chapter it was noted that regardless of our culture, *we are all social creatures.* What this means is that from the moment of birth until we leave this earth we live among other people. We need others for reasons as basic as receiving love and as pragmatic as gathering material comforts. English essayist Samuel Johnson expressed the same idea in a rather impassioned way when he observed, "In civilized society we all depend upon each other, and our very happiness is owing to the rest of mankind." Hence, our first point is that a symbiotic relationship exists between all people and that this relationship and interdependence are negotiated through communication.

We Have Free Choice. Even at this early stage of the book, you have seen how you can select material that enables you to adapt to both person and place. Embedded in this idea is a fact about human life that is both elementary and profound: we have *free choice*. From selecting a mate to deciding on a specific word when we talk, in most instances we exercise our free will. Even though many of our actions are habitual, when we greet a stranger we can still decide to smile, frown, look the other person in the eye, or glance down. The choice, like thousands of others we make each day, is ours. As a philosopher once remarked, "The difficulty in life is the choice." *The study of ethics asks you to think about that choice.*

Communication Produces a Change. From our first two points, it should be evident that our choices influence other people—the very people we need so that we can accomplish our physical and social goals. Put in slightly different terms, communication is something that persons do with each other, and this behavior produces a response that has an effect. Because of the nature of the complex human nervous system, the perception of any message involves varying degrees of behavioral change in both sender and receiver. Each party gains entry into the other's life. This entry may produce only a temporary alteration in body chemistry, or it may change the person forever. In either case, the link between communication and ethics should be clear. Whether we accept the responsibility or not, we are invading the personality of our communication partners. Remember, we have free choice, and therefore in nearly all instances have made the decision to influence another person. The significance of affecting another person's personality is clearly confirmed by Ordway Tead in his book *Administration: Its Purpose and Performance*. His observance:

> Tampering with personal drives and desires is a moral act even if its upshot is not a far-reaching one, or is a beneficial result. To seek to persuade behavior into a new direction may be wholly justifiable, and the result in terms of behavior consequences may be salutary. But the judgment of benefit or detriment is not for the communicator safely to reach by himself. He is assuming a moral responsibility. And he had better be aware of the area with which he concerns himself and the responsibility he assumes. He should be willing to assert as to any given new policy, 'I stand behind this as having good personal consequences for the individuals whom it will affect.' That judgment speaks a moral concern and desired moral outcome. (p.52)

Ethics and Public Speaking

In the foregoing quote, Tead is talking about ethical standards related to the production of messages that influence other people. Ethics, as we noted earlier, is a mode of conduct based on high moral standards. As members of a culture that has given us various moral values and principles, most of us are aware of the constituents of these high standards and of our moral responsibilities to our fellow humans. *These responsibilities are compounded as the group we are addressing grows in size.* Our audience may range from a handful of friends to a large conference or convention. This social responsibility has never been more important than it is today, when television and radio make it possible for a single speaker to influence the actions and thinking of millions of persons.

For centuries, the power of speech to influence minds has caused grave apprehensions. The crux of the fear is this: the means of changing behavior are so potent that a malicious person may use them to induce an audience to act unwisely or unjustly. One of the most astute rebuttals to this position was written by Aristotle over two thousand years ago. In *The Rhetoric*, Aristotle asserted that the art of persuasion (changing behavior) is good in itself but can be used either for good or bad ends:

> If it is urged that an abuse of the rhetorical faculty can work great mischief, the same charge can be brought against all good things (save virtue itself), and especially against the most useful things such as strength, health, wealth, and military skill. Rightly employed, they work the greatest blessings; and wrongly employed, they work the utmost harm.

Because communication is so powerful, we must consider the ethical implications of our messages on other people. In the communication context, the study of ethics embraces an analysis of the conscious choices people make about their intentions toward and strategies for influencing other people. To better appreciate the need to consider our motives and tactics, we should examine our role as the sender of messages, as well as our responsibilities as the recipient of messages. In addition, because culture greatly influences our view of ethics, we should also examine cultural differences in perceiving ethical behavior.

The Sender's Responsibilities

Recall the quotation from Aristotle. Understand that the evils, if they occur, are brought forth by humans, not by the processes of communication. The devices and means used by speakers are indeed their own responsibility. The issue is one of speakers realizing that they have an obligation to their listeners as well as to themselves. In short, all of us need to be aware of the potential power of our communication behavior. It is imperative that we think about this power before we speak, before we influence another person. As noted in a Chinese proverb, "A harsh word once dropped from the tongue cannot be brought back again by a coach and six horses." Accordingly, you should consider the following questions each time you initiate a communication act.

Examine Motives for Speaking. *What are my motives for giving this speech?* An ethical speaker begins by examining the motives behind her or his speech. The audience's perception of you as a good person greatly influences the success of your communication act. Volumes of research indicate that what the audience thinks of you as a person can either hinder or aid your cause. Aristotle, Quintilian, and Cicero, the great speech theorists of classical Greece and Rome, agree—a speaker whose prestige is high in the eyes of the audience has a better chance of gaining acceptance for ideas presented than does a speaker whose credibility is low.

Part of examining your motives is being able to constantly remind yourself of the power you have as a public speaker. Do you realize that you are altering the attitudes, the feelings, and perhaps even the health of others? A constant awareness of such alterations allows you to reevaluate your content and your intent. Realizing that you are altering the thinking and behavior of other people compels you to continuously ask yourself if your purpose is responsible, reasonable, and honorable. Are you advocating ideas that will benefit others or only yourself? Being always aware of the notion of speech consequences also reminds you of the power of a single word and the impact of your overall message. When you think of this power, consider both the short-range and long-range effects of your speech. For example, the short-range purpose of a persuasive speech on the advantages of vegetarianism may be ethically sound, but if you fail to inform your listeners about the need to supplement their diets with foods high in protein, you are ignoring the long-range effects.

Being conscious of your responsibilities should also encourage you to make sure that all sides of the issues are heard. Notice in the example on vegetarianism how important it is for the speaker to identify some of the other issues surrounding this subject. Although none of us has the duty to solicit contradictory arguments on every idea we express, to suppress essential information diminishes us and our listeners.

Investigate and Analyze the Topic Thoroughly. *Have I investigated and analyzed the subject fully before expressing opinions about it?* In your speech class and in this textbook, you will discover that serious research and preparation are important parts of successful, effective, and ethical speaking. Anyone can "make up" facts and figures, but common sense and good judgment tell you that is not proper behavior. Because you should speak only from a sound background, you have an obligation to be silent if you do not understand what you are called on to discuss. "I don't know" is a valuable and too rarely used phrase. When you do speak, you have a duty to be morally thoughtful—to know what you are talking about before you try to influence the thinking of your associates. The idea of investigation is of such importance that chapters 6, 8, and 9 are set aside to assist you in developing the skills necessary to inquire into any topic.

Avoid Plagiarism. *Have I avoided all types of plagiarism?* Presenting information that is not your own or repeating entire paragraphs without citing sources are just two of the ways plagiarism occurs. Use of another's words or ideas without attribution is both insulting to an audience and highly unethical. Plagiarism can be as blatant as stealing an entire speech or as subtle as offering a witty quotation as if it sprang from your own creative imagination. Some simple guidelines should be followed as a means of avoiding plagiarism:

1. Take careful and complete notes when gathering your material.

2. Identify and/or cite any ideas, words, or examples that are not your own.

3. If you paraphrase ideas, words, or examples, you should also acknowledge the source of the information.

Be Accurate in Your Presentation. *Have I presented my material in an accurate and ethical manner?* This means avoiding half-truths, outdated information, lies, and unsupported assertions. Not being accurate can also include withholding important information from your audience. If you are offering statistics about traffic accidents on a certain street in your town but fail to tell your audience that the statistics only reflect accidents that took place at night, you are not being accurate or ethical in your presentation of material.

Show Respect. *Do I respect the intelligence of the people to whom I am speaking?* You should never amplify, oversimplify, or "adjust" the truth because you think the listeners are not knowledgeable on the topic and will not notice the distortion. Nor should you use the assumption that listeners are not capable of understanding your message as a justification for withholding or altering information. This lack of respect for people is insulting and unethical. Respect the worth of each individual and allow each person to think for himself or herself.

When speaking to members of cultures other than your own, you must guard against the tendency to make decisions without respecting the audience's point of view. It is wrong to assume that because the listeners are unacquainted with the material, you can leave things out and alter the truth. Any misrepresentation is unethical and can easily lead an audience to reject you and your cause; once audience members perceive you as being a dishonorable person, it will be nearly impossible to recapture their confidence. An Ashanti proverb admonishes us with the following warning: "One falsehood spoils a thousand truths."

Be Clear. *Is my material clearly presented?* As a speaker, you have the obligation not only to be accurate, but also to make sure that your speech is understandable to your listeners. It is an unethical practice to intentionally use words your audience does not understand or to advance ideas you do not fully explain. In addition, you need to avoid using emotional appeals that are intended only to frighten your audience. For example, recently a speaker stated that if people who have tested positive for the HIV virus were allowed to enter the United States, it would cause a major AIDS epidemic. This is a vivid example of using hysteria to accomplish a purpose.

Do Not Engage in Personal Attacks. *Is my speech free from personal attacks?* To slander another person or culture is yet another example of poor ethical behavior. If you opposed the North American Free Trade Agreement, it would have been far more ethical to point out the weakness of the treaty than to attack the people involved with it, the people of Canada and Mexico. Also avoid "name calling" and other forms of demagoguery—appeals to prejudice or passion. The word is a commanding instrument and should be used with great care. A Native American proverb can remind us of the power of communication: "Talk is but wind, but wind can break a tree."

At times the issue of right and wrong speech may seem complex and difficult, but for most of us common sense is often the best guide. We all know deep down, because of the way we feel, whether we have been ethical or unethical in our actions. Although he was talking about morality, the American author Ernest Hemingway said much the same thing when he wrote, "I know only what is moral is what you feel good after and what is immoral is what you feel bad after."

The Receiver's Responsibilities

Give the Speaker Your Full Attention. Because communication is a two-way process, ethical responsibility in the communication situation is not borne by the speaker alone. The listener also has a share of moral issues related to the speech act. Much ethical responsibility lies in listening itself. If one is to evaluate, accept, and respond to the remarks of others, one must first hear and understand those remarks. It is unfair, as well as unethical, for us, as listeners, to act on a message to which we have not given our full attention. Therefore, *a listener's first commitment is to offer full attention to the speaker*. Each communication act is characterized by countless distractions, but the listener must overcome them to analyze fairly what is said. We will discuss much more about listening in chapter 5.

Create a Positive Communication Atmosphere. In addition to paying attention, *ethical listeners create a listening atmosphere that encourages speakers to do their best job*. As a listener, if you send speakers negative feedback (looking out the window, doodling, or yawning), they are bound to be tense when delivering their talks. By sending positive feedback (leaning forward, smiling, making eye contact) and being attentive, you help speakers relax. It follows that their speeches will be better delivered and much more accurate. In short, remember the circular nature of the communication act. Speaker and listener are interdependent—touch one and you touch the other.

Be Open Minded Yet Skeptical. Ethical listeners are discriminating. Since listeners are changed, in one form or another, by the speaker, *they must not accept everything that is said without questioning key assertions*. There is nothing wrong with some degree of measured skepticism when someone is asking you to behave in one way or another. Your ethical obligation is to be open minded, and at the same time to question what you hear and hold off making conclusions until all the evidence has been presented.

Suspend Conclusions. An ethical listener will hold off reaching any hard-and-fast conclusions until the speaker has finished his or her speech. This ability to listen without prejudging is not only the fair thing to do, but it can contribute to greater understanding. The listener who stops listening too soon might well miss an opportunity to learn some new and useful information.

Culture and Ethics

To this point, we have talked about the role of ethics in human communication and how each of us must be aware of the ethical decisions inherent in asking someone to think, feel, or respond according to our wishes. We are now ready to talk about how those decisions transcend a single culture. The need for this discussion should not surprise you, for it is evident even at this early juncture in the book that we will be talking about the role of culture in nearly every phase of the communication process. Therefore, we need to pause for a moment to discuss how ethics and culture are linked. When we examine ethical issues in intercultural communication, we are immediately confronted with a dilemma: cultures, when compared with one another, are like people; they differ on some characteristics and share others. The members of one culture may believe in animal sacrifice as a religious ritual, while the members of another bury their pets in animal cemeteries. The people of one culture may believe in multiple spouses, while those of another believe in monogamy. Thousands of other examples demonstrate that cultures differ from one another. As you would suspect, many of these differences make it difficult to arrive at a universal set of truisms or a metaethic. Yet ethical speakers can find some ethical guidelines that transcend all cultures. Let us look at three of these omnipresent principles.

Learn About Other Cultures. It is crucial to learn all you can about the cultures of the people you will be addressing. You need to discover whether the

❖ ❖ ❖ ❖

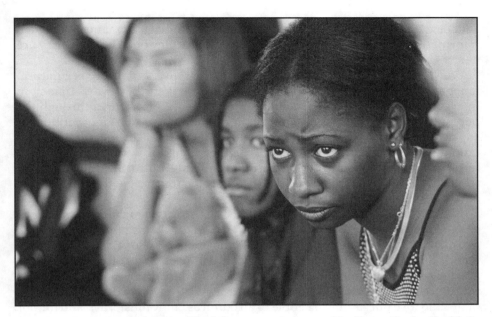

A listener's first commitment is to offer full attention to the speaker. (Photo: Charles Kuo/Daily Bruin)

changes you are requesting are consistent with the values and norms pervasive in that culture. From judgments of beauty to attitudes about birth control, to dietary habits, to the perception of women, cultural variations need to be taken into account.

Avoid Stereotypes. *The ethical speaker seeks to avoid stereotyping.* Stereotyping is a complex form of categorization that mentally organizes our experiences and guides our behavior toward a particular group of people. Stereotypes organize our images into fixed and simple categories that we mistakenly use to characterize an entire collection of people. Some degree of stereotyping is found in nearly every intercultural situation. The reason for the pervasive nature of stereotypes is that human beings have a psychological need to categorize and classify. The world we confront is too big, too complex, and too transitory for us to know it in all its detail. Stereotypes, because they tend to be convenient and expeditious, help with our classifications. And even though it is unethical to place entire groups of people into negative, rigid categories, stereotypes continue to endure. However, regardless of how much time stereotyping may save us, they are unfair and hamper intercultural communication. There are a number of reasons why stereotyping is damaging to the target of the stereotype. Let us look at three of these reasons, to help you to avoid engaging in this negative activity.

First, *stereotypes are oversimplified, overgeneralized, and exaggerated.* They are based on half-truths, distortions, and usually untrue premises.

Second, *stereotypes fail to specify individual characteristics.* They assume that all members of a group or culture have exactly the same traits. And, as we indicated, the traits described are usually negative and unfavorable ones.

Third, *stereotypes are repeated and reinforced beliefs that over a period of time are taken by some people to be "true."* This unethical practice creates misguided perceptions that lead to prejudices and even to outright hostility. In all your communication practices avoid engaging in behaviors that foster and

❖ ❖ ❖ ❖   encourage stereotypes. They are products of limited, lazy, and misguided information. Or as the English statesman John Morley once noted, "They are devices that save us from thinking."

Respect Diversity. An ethical speaker respects diversity. There is a natural tendency among all of us to believe that "our way is the best way." In fact, in intercultural matters, this penchant to judge all other cultures through the perceptual lens of one's own culture, and to conclude that one's culture is superior to others, is called **ethnocentrism.** Respect for diversity is an orientation that sees cultural differences as neither right nor wrong, simply as different. This sort of cultural sensitivity and intercultural ethic not only respects the rights of others but is also a first step toward overcoming racism and prejudice.

Seek Similarities. Although differences exist between cultures, *people of all cultures share many characteristics that help determine and define an ethic for intercultural communication.* As famous photographer Edward Steichen noted, "I believe that in all the things that are important, in all of these we are alike." Reflect for a moment about just a few of the universal characteristics that unite people. We all sense the thrill of a new birth, crave freedom, desire a mate, and love our families. People of all cultures enjoy music, art, and humor and believe in being civil to each other. Finally, all of us must face old age, death, and the suffering that can go with both. Hence, Steichen is right—as humans we are more alike than we are different. And those likenesses can serve as the basis for an intercultural ethic.

Follow the Golden Rule   (Consider the Platinum Rule)

Our preceding discussion of commonalities is perhaps the single most important guide to developing an ethical code that can go beyond any differences found among people and cultures. That code, as simple as it sounds, is *the Golden Rule.* Although many Westerners have been exposed to the phrase "Do to others what you would have them do to you" through Christianity, the same concept is found in every culture and religion. Buddha said, "Hurt not others in ways that you yourself would find hurtful." In Islam we find these words: "No one of you is a believer until he desires for his brother that which he desires for himself." And the Hindus are told, "This is the sum of duty: do naught unto others which would cause you pain if done to you." If it were not for space constraints, we could have included an even longer list of traditions that exhort their members to the "oneness of the human family."

When applied to speech making, the Golden Rule reminds us that it is unethical to send messages that demean or belittle another person if we would not welcome the same messages to be directed at us. The canon also tells us something we discussed earlier in this section—that all of us, regardless of our culture, are linked. The great humanitarian Albert Schweitzer made this same point when he wrote, "The first step in the evolution of ethics is a sense of solidarity with other humans." We urge you to take that step and to appreciate the fact that while each of us is unique, we also share a common humanity.

I conclude this section on the ethics of communication by once again exhorting you to think about your intentions and your actions. Once you send a message to someone, it will have an effect, and it is almost impossible to

undo that effect. An Arab proverb captures this idea in a more poetic manner:
"It is with a word as with an arrow—once let loose it does not return."

Preview of Principles

Although it may appear that I am making a rather sudden shift in emphasis as this chapter now moves from theory to practice, it is important to remember that we are still talking about communication. Up to this point, we have examined some of the theory behind human communication—what communication is, how it works, and how to employ it in an ethical manner. On the other hand, *communication is an activity that persons engage in; it is something we do.* Because communication "is something we do," theory and practice can never be separated. Therefore, we shall now focus our attention on the "*doing.*" We shall look at the aspects of communication concerned with the practical phases of human communication. Everything we have discussed thus far about communication and ethics leads to the conclusion that becoming a more effective communicator should be the goal of everyone who shares ideas and information. In short, we take part in communication so that we can have an influence. Let us now talk about how you can develop the skills that will contribute to your greater efficiency in exerting that influence.

I want to introduce some of these skills in chapter 1 so that you can start to practice them early in your training. In every instance, what is discussed in the next few pages will be expanded in subsequent chapters; however, it is important that you begin at once. What follows is some advice to assist you in your initial efforts.

Organizing Ideas

In your speech class, you may face the issue of having to give speeches in the first few days of the semester, before you have had an opportunity to study all the principles treated in this book. For this reason, we shall briefly look at some steps you should take in preparing your first speeches. The order of the steps is not nearly as rigid as the list might suggest. For example, you may discover situations in which audience analysis precedes the analysis of the purpose of the speech. Regardless of the order in which you consider the six items, however, a thorough preparation should include them all.

1. ***Determine the purpose of your speech.*** Nearly all communication is purposeful—it seeks to elicit a response from the person receiving the message. We smile at someone because we are glad to see them. We give someone specific directions on how to find the library so that they will not get lost. We tell good friends to stop eating so many potato chips because we are concerned about their health. As you can see, the reaction we want from the other person can range from enjoyment (the warmth of a smile being returned) to direct, specific action (stop eating those potato chips). So ask yourself, do you want your listeners to understand how to select the best methods for preparing a term paper? Do you want them to sign a petition outlawing the sale of cigarettes in the college cafeteria? Do you want them to

believe that teenage suicide is a serious problem? Think of your speech as an instrument of utility—a means of getting a reaction—and think of that reaction as your first step of speech preparation.

When analyzing the reaction you want from your audience, you should begin with your **general purpose**. The next chapter will introduce three kinds of general purposes and discuss each of them in greater detail; however, for now it is important for you to know that these purposes are: *to inform* (increasing your listeners' fund of knowledge), *to persuade* (changing the thinking and/or behavior of your listeners), and *to entertain* (eliciting a pleasurable response from your listeners). Although these purposes often overlap each other, you nevertheless need to decide on the general response you hope to elicit. You should also think about the **specific reaction** you hope to produce. For a speech to inform, your specific purpose might be to have your listeners understand the operation of the campus general store. A speech to persuade could have the specific purpose of asking the audience to support a law to make it illegal for anyone to transport a dog unattended in the back of an open pickup truck. A specific purpose for a speech to entertain might be to have the audience laugh while you explain how to pick a winning horse at the racetrack simply by examining the horses in the paddock.

2. **Choose and limit the topic of your speech.** In speech class, you may be assigned a subject area, but in most cases your instructor will let you make your own selections. You will find that, in speaking situations outside the class, circumstances are much the same. Observing a few basic principles will enable you to choose the proper subject and to limit its scope to meet the demands of the audience, the occasion, and your purpose.

    a. *Select a topic worthy of your time and the time of your audience.* No listener enjoys hearing about a subject that is insignificant. Although it might make an excellent humorous speech, very few college students would like to hear you give a ten-minute informative speech on how to sew a button on a shirt, yet that group might find a speech on using campus health services very informative. In short, talk about subjects, issues, and controversies that affect the lives of your listeners.

    b. *Select a topic that interests you.* Unless you are interested, you will not be sufficiently motivated to accomplish your purpose. Pick a topic that you are or can become interested in, and you may find that your enthusiasm is contagious.

    c. *Select a topic you can deal with adequately in the time at your disposal.* It is apparent that subject areas such as "Peace in the World" or "The Meaning of Life: Part II" cannot be intelligently discussed in a five-minute speech.

3. **Analyze the location of your speech, the occasion of your speech, and your audience.** By knowing the impact of these three factors, you will be able to adapt your material and your preparation to the situation you meet.

The process of analyzing the audience and the occasion is discussed more thoroughly in chapter 3. However, following are a few guidelines to assist you in your early speeches.

a. *Learn all you can about the place where the communication will occur.* Interaction is influenced by your location in regard to that of other members of the gathering, the size of the room, its shape, and other physical conditions. If you are being interviewed by the school newspaper regarding your beliefs on the use of animals in research and later will talk on the same subject on television, you would need to adjust to these two very different locations.

b. *Learn the occasion for the gathering.* Is it a regular weekly meeting, is it a special meeting, or is it a spontaneous gathering? Are the people going to listen to you because they are interested in the topic, or are they meeting for another purpose? If the occasion is a festive celebration and you talk about the menacing effects of acid rain, the audience is apt to find your observations rather inappropriate.

c. *Learn as much as you can about the people to whom you will speak.* Knowing the age, gender, educational background, occupation, interests, ethnic and cultural background, values, and attitudes of each listener will enable you to adapt your remarks to the needs of the listeners you will face. For example, an audience of Chinese and Native American students, whose culture has taught them to value harmony in interpersonal relationships, might not be receptive to your speech on the advantages of being assertive, unless you were to adapt your message to point out the benefits of being assertive while maintaining or promoting harmony in relationships.

4. ***Find the material for your speech.*** There are basically two places to look for materials: within yourself for what you already know and outside yourself to discover what you do not know. Start your preparation by looking in your private, internal "library." What you already know, however, may not be enough to accomplish your objective. In most instances, it is necessary to augment your observations and opinions with those from other sources. In chapter 8, we talk about finding materials in books, magazines, newspapers, through computer searches, and other storehouses of information. At this point, it is important to remember that successful speakers are seldom the ones who think they know everything there is to know on all subjects.

5. ***Organize and arrange the speech.*** Now that you have the ingredients of your message—the materials—you must arrange them so that they make sense to your listeners. Chapter 10 presents a number of organizational sequences, but for now you should arrange your material around the following three parts of a speech—introduction, body, and conclusion.

   Introduction. The main purpose of the *introduction* is to gain the attention and interest of the listeners, to put them at ease, to help them focus their attention on your speech, and to begin to establish your credibility. The material you select should accomplish those objectives.

Body. It is the *body* of your talk that contains the majority of your message. The body of the speech should be planned first. This includes marshaling all the supporting material designed to establish the central idea of the speech. You also need to think about keeping your material interesting if you expect to hold the audience's attention for any period of time.

Conclusion. The *conclusion* ends the speech gracefully and in a compelling manner. It may take the form of a summary, an illustration, an appeal, a challenge, or several other endings that are discussed in chapter 11. As you might suspect, issues such as your specific purpose and the amount of time at your disposal will influence the concluding device you select.

An outline is one of the chief organizational aids. It enables you to see what materials you have and assists you in sorting the relevant from the irrelevant. An outline helps you avoid the aimless, disorganized thinking characteristic of many speeches.

6. ***Practice your speech aloud.*** If you hope to have your message understood, to accomplish your purpose, and to feel relaxed, you must practice aloud. You should deliver your speech three or four times before you present it to the audience. In the next chapter, we will examine some ways to make your practice session more productive. For now, try to keep these few ideas in mind as you prepare and practice:

    a. *Avoid memorizing while you practice.*

    b. *Learn the main ideas of the speech; do not try to memorize every word.*

    c. *Practice your speech aloud and allow time for changes if, after hearing it, you decide that you need to make alterations.*

Presenting Ideas

Of all the aspects of public speaking, it is delivery that makes people most anxious. Although delivery is important, it certainly does not warrant the amount of energy we give it or the degree of stress it produces. An entire chapter deals with the topic of speech delivery (chapter 4); however, you will need a few general suggestions at this time so that you can present your first speeches in a natural, relaxed manner.

1. ***Have a good mental attitude.*** A good mental attitude toward the presentation of your ideas will make the job of delivering your speech much simpler and much more pleasurable for you and your audience. Do not be unduly alarmed about stage fright. The following suggestions may help allay your apprehensions.

a. *Realize that some nervousness is normal.* This realization may, in itself, help reduce your nervousness. You are not odd because your body is not enjoying the prospect of having to talk in front of a group of strangers.

b. *Recognize that, in most instances, the audience is your friend, not your enemy.* This is particularly true of your speech class, where you can be assured that everyone is wishing you well. Your classmates will also get a turn in front of the class and will welcome the same support.

c. *Come before your audience fully prepared.* If you have doubts about your speech and your preparation, you will likely appear nervous.

d. *Try to feel confident.* Your attitude toward yourself is the single most important variable in successful communication. Do not rush through your speech; remember that you are talking with your audience. Feel free to pause whenever you desire. Do not be embarrassed if you find that some of your words are not coming out as you wish. In many instances, you may be the only one to realize what is happening. There are even occasions when acknowledging a "flub" will relax you and your audience.

e. *Nervous tension can be reduced by having some meaningful physical action in your speech.* Try walking during your talk as a method of relaxing and releasing nervous strain.

f. *Remember, even if you are nervous, you will be able to finish your speech.* Everything in life has a beginning and an end. Whether it is sitting in the dentist's chair, reading this sentence, or giving a speech, eventually it will be over. Too many speakers tell themselves during their speech that they are just too nervous to go on, only to find out at the conclusion of their talk that the presentation went very well. So keep going.

g. *Take comfort in the fact that there is a relationship among improvement, practice, and nervousness.* Students say that as they become more proficient in speech making, their nervousness and all its outward manifestations seem to lessen. In short, the more you speak, the less you will be nervous.

2. **Be direct.** Looking directly at your audience serves two vital functions. First, directness adds to a lively sense of communication. It tells your listeners that you care about accomplishing your purpose and that you are interested in them. Second, by looking directly at the audience, you gain valuable insight into how your message is being received. Successful communicators use the information they receive by observing their audience and making adjustments based on audience reactions.

3. **Be physically animated.** Try to avoid a rigid appearance. Your posture should be comfortable and natural. Gestures are quite useful in conveying thought or emotion or in reinforcing oral expression. They increase your self-confidence, ease nervousness, aid in the communi-

cation of ideas, and help hold attention. Relax and be yourself, and you will learn that gesturing comes naturally.

4. ***Use vocal variety.*** Just as movement and gesture help reinforce ideas, so does an animated voice. If there is a sameness of rate, pitch, loudness, and quality, there is monotony. Vary as many of these elements of voice as you can, consonant with conveying the full meaning of your ideas and emotions.

   Avoid unpleasant and distracting vocalizations such as "and a," "like," "ya know," "well," and "uh," which call attention to themselves and detract from your message.

   Competent delivery is simply direct, friendly, natural, conversational, animated, and enthusiastic. Good luck with your first few speeches.

Summary

This chapter began by indicating to you the importance of human communication in every aspect of your life. It was pointed out how both internationally and domestically it is important to learn how to communicate with people from cultures different from your own. This chapter also introduced the fields of communication and public speaking and presented a few elementary principles, the essential tools of effective speech making.

In its broadest sense, communication is the process of sending and receiving messages. All communication involves the following ingredients: a source, encoding, a message, a channel, a receiver, decoding, and feedback. Communication also takes place in a specific context. This chapter looked at the similarities and differences between public speaking and other forms of communication—specifically, how public speaking differs from writing and casual conversation.

The responsibility and seriousness of communication are so great that communicators must be of the highest ethical character. They should know their subject, respect the intelligence of their listeners, treat their content honestly, and realize that they are changing behavior—both theirs and the receivers'.

In preparing speeches early in your course, remember to determine the purpose of the speech, choose and limit the topic, analyze the audience and the speaking occasion, gather material, organize and arrange the material, and practice aloud.

In delivering speeches, it is essential that you have a good mental attitude, that you be direct, that you be physically animated, and that you use vocal variety.

Concepts and Questions

1. How do you believe that training in communication will help you in your specific career choice?

2. What do you find most troubling when you are called upon to give a speech?

3. What public figures do you regard as excellent public speakers? Why?

4. How often do you communicate with people from cultures different from your own? What are these cultures?

5. Do you ever find it difficult to be an ethical speaker? Why?

6. Why is it important to be an ethical speaker?

7. What was your image of a public-speaking class before you enrolled in this class?

8. What do think are the major differences between public and private conversation?

Activities and Exercises

1. Locate a story from a current newspaper, a magazine, or Internet sources that demonstrates a problem arising when people from different cultures attempt to communicate. Try to identify the problems and offer some solutions.

2. Prepare a three-minute talk to deliver in class that mentions the intercultural experiences you have had at work, at school, or during your travels. Tell the class what you have learned from these experiences.

3. Listen to a speech by a public figure and write a review of the speech. Discuss both strengths and weaknesses.

4. Interview a member of the class. During the interview try to gather information about your interview partner that will aid the other members of the class in getting to know that person.

5. Bring a picture or object belonging to you to class and explain how that item offers insight into one of your personality characteristics.

6. Give a short talk that discusses why you believe so many people have a fear of public speaking. ✦

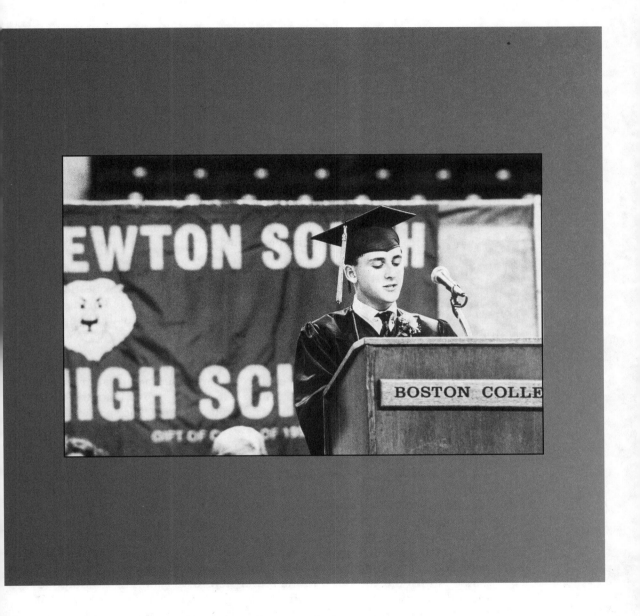

CHAPTER TWO

Your First Speeches: Getting Started

The beginning is the most important part of the work.

—Plato

In Aesop's fable "The Crow and the Pitcher," the reader is offered the following advice: "Little by little does the trick." We begin this chapter with that same counsel. That is to say, start the process of improving your communication little by little. One of the philosophies driving this book maintains that communication is something we *do*. Although it takes shape in our minds, the act of communicating demands some outward behavior. This book is organized so that you can start working on that behavior now instead of having to wait until you have turned the last page of the final chapter. In short, now that you have finished reading chapter 1, and have encountered a preview of the basic principles of oral communication, you can begin to apply those principles in an actual speech.

You probably have questions running through your mind such as, Where do I go from here? and, How do I get started? Answering those questions is the principal objective of this chapter. Nearly all the ideas offered in this preliminary chapter will be developed in much more detail later in this book, but for now you should begin practicing so that "little by little" you will become a more effective communicator.

Chapter 1 noted that most communication is initiated because someone wants to fulfill a purpose. In the specialized form of human communication called public speaking, the speaker wants a *specific response* from the audience and communicates in order to secure that response. The speaker has a *preconceived purpose*, which he or she has chosen *before* the talk. In fact, that characteristic often distinguishes public speaking from other, more random communication activities. Trying to talk to an audience without having a clear idea of what you want them to hear and learn would be an unnerving experience, to say the least. The audience (and you) would be frustrated and confused as you drifted aimlessly from point to point. What is needed, then, is a unifying thread to weave all the pieces together, and that thread is the preconceived purpose. By deciding on the response you want from your audience, you can more wisely select the materials, organizational patterns, language, and delivery methods that will enable you to reach your goal.

Let us turn our attention to the initial steps of speech preparation and look at the processes of (1) deciding on a topic, (2) narrowing the topic, (3) formulating a general purpose, (4) formulating a specific purpose, (5) choosing a title, (6) choosing a method of delivery, (7) using notecards, and (8) practicing the speech. Also included in this chapter is a large section on various methods of gaining confidence and overcoming nervousness. I include this material early in the book to deal with any questions or fears you may have concerning stage fright and other forms of communication apprehension.

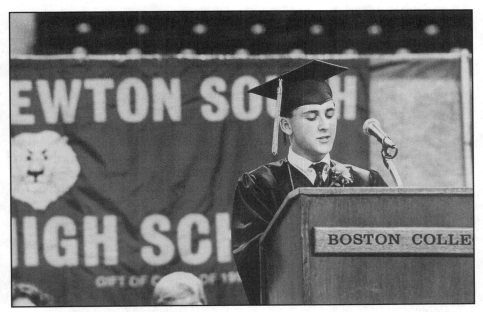

There will be speaking situations when the occasion dictates the subject area. (Photo: indexstock.com)

Selecting a Topic

An inevitable question facing the speaker is, "What shall I talk about?" There are, of course, several ways of answering this question. First, in many instances, *you are asked to speak on a particular subject*. On those occasions, subject selection has been done for you. If your history professor asks you to give a speech on the history of impeachment, or your employer tells you, "Explain the company's new computer system to the rest of the staff," your questions regarding subject selection are answered—someone has influenced what you will talk about. On those occasions your assignment, even before you start the other steps of speech preparation, is to narrow the subject to fit the specific audience and the various constraints imposed by time.

There will also be speaking situations *when the occasion dictates the subject area*. A political rally for a specific candidate, a toast at a friend's wedding, a eulogy, or a graduation ceremony are such occasions.

In most instances you must select the subject. As pointed out in detail in the next chapter, you should screen potential subjects with an eye to their value and interest to the audience and their appropriateness for the occasion. Specific time limits should also be kept in mind.

Where do you locate those potential subjects in the first place? Many beginning speakers are overwhelmed at the prospect of talking on any subject they want. Most speech instructors spend many office hours trying to help students pick a topic, yet, if students would not panic, would slow down, and would reflect for a little while, the task of topic selection would not be such drudgery. Let us suggest a few procedures to follow that will help you make intelligent choices regarding the general subject of your talks.

Begin With Yourself

If you are going to enjoy researching and delivering the speech, it is obvious that you should try to locate a subject that interests you as well as the audience. The first step in this process is to begin your search for a topic by reviewing what you already know. Examine your personal interests, experiences, and convictions. Consider any special knowledge you have acquired, places you have traveled, or jobs you have held. Many students find it helpful to start the process of topic selection by taking an inventory of their fund of knowledge and personal beliefs. When students make their inventories early in the semester, they develop a list of possible topics to draw on for future speeches. An inventory works best when it is developed in a systematic manner. The following is a sample inventory:

Personal Experiences	***Abilities***
cultural background	artistic
vacations	athletic
summer jobs	intellectual
interesting elective classes	educational
Hobbies	***Beliefs and Attitudes***
tennis	student loans
politics	value of health food
sculpture	funding the arts
rock hunting	health care costs
computer graphics	crime victims' rights
sport cars	insurance rates
skydiving	housing the homeless
musical instruments	judicial caseloads
hot-air balloons	sex and violence on TV
hang gliding	private education
writing	military reduction
gardening	future of the family
sports cars	new European alliances
astrology	welfare
rodeos	animal rights
camping	public transportation
drama	underage drinking
horse racing	gun control
calligraphy	trade investments
Personal Knowledge	drug abuse
animal handling	immigration quotas
appliance repair	advertising abuses
fitness equipment	beauty contests
foreign languages	gangs
automotive upkeep	labor unions
Native-American folklore	vegetarianism
first-aid training	genetic engineering
religious studies	herbal medicine

Looking Elsewhere

In addition to your personal inventory, you can probe other sources for possible speech topics. Newsmagazines, newspapers, reference books, computer searches, and newscasts can enable you to assess current events. Questioning your friends and professors can also yield useful topics. Most college campuses have a variety of activities that can help generate still other topics: Guest speakers, controversial debates, and career opportunity lectures are just a few events that can produce subjects.

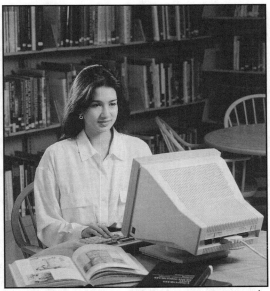

In addition to your personal inventory, you can probe other sources for possible speech topics. (Photo: indexstock.com)

The World Wide Web, via the Internet, is also an excellent source to employ in your search for a topic. By using the Web you can contact a host of subject-based search engines. Some of the most popular sites are Yahoo!, Britannic, Leeks, Alta Vista, and Magellan. What is helpful about these sites is that once you select a general category, such as religion, you can then follow up on this initial request with hundreds of subcategories. This will offer you countless subjects from which to choose.

You can also use the Internet to access newspapers, magazines, and television stations. For example, *Newsweek*, *Time*, the *New York Times*, and all the major networks can be accessed via the World Wide Web.

Important Considerations

In the final analysis, it is usually your personal decision and your perception of your audience that serves as the stimulus for your talk. You must determine, and eventually formulate, your reason and purpose for engaging in communication.

There are five categories of topics that normally do not lend themselves well to the public-speaking situation. First, *some topics are too technical for your audience*. A speech dealing with the stress requirements of materials used in fashioning artificial knee joints might be appropriate for a group of orthopedic surgeons, but most other audiences would find it boring and confusing. Likewise, while everyone might be interested in Alzheimer's disease, a speech that talks about the role of the cerebral cortex, basal forebrain, and hippocampus might be too technical for the average audience.

Second, some topics are *too broad to be covered adequately in a single speech*. Trying to offer a detailed explanation of the social, political, and economic causes of the collapse of Communist rule in Eastern Europe is too ambitious an objective for a single speech. A speech looking at all the causes of global warming, including the ten steps to reduce global warming, is yet another example of a speech that attempts to do too much at one time.

Third, subjects that are trivial are risky material for a speech because the listeners may feel that *the speaker is insulting their intelligence.* Shallow topics can be used in some humorous speeches, but in most cases you should not ask adults to listen to a speech, for example, on how to heat a frozen TV dinner in a microwave oven or how to wind a watch. There are times when even a technical topic can be superficial if presented to the wrong audience. For example, a group of trained nutritionists would not be impressed with a speech on what foods contained high levels of beta-carotene and vitamins C and E.

Fourth, there are topics *too personal to be suitable for public airing.* For example, confidential and intimate self-disclosure is ordinarily out of place in speaking to anyone other than a group of very close friends. Most audiences would be embarrassed if you were to offer intimate details regarding how your father's bout with alcoholism caused you great mental anguish.

Finally, you need to decide whether *there will be adequate material available on your subject.* Too often, speakers select topics that cannot be researched and developed because there is not adequate information on the subject. Although it might be interesting to look at the behind–the–scenes operation of the United States Supreme Court, if that information were not available it would not make much of a speech.

Once you have completed your personal inventory, you are in a much better position to narrow your focus and start the process of speech preparation. The steps of preparation were briefly introduced in the last chapter; now we will return to those preparatory phases and examine them in much more detail.

Narrowing a Topic

After you have chosen your general subject area, you must determine what aspects of that subject will be relevant to your audience, offer them something new, and be of greatest interest to you. Some serious paring of the subject is necessary if you are to accomplish your goal. Most subjects need to

Figure 2.1 Narrowing a Topic

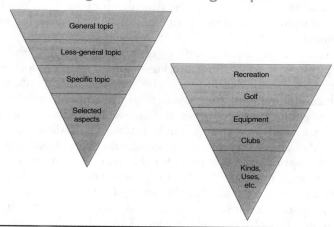

be limited to meet the demands imposed by both time and purpose. Try to visualize the narrowing stage as an inverted pyramid—wide (genereal) at the top and narrow (specific) at the bottom (see Figure 2.1).

As you can see from the pyramid, the scope of the subject is reduced so that it can be researched in a specific amount of time and presented in an intelligent manner. Regardless of the subject, you must concentrate your focus. It is best to remember that you are treating only part of the whole. An audience doesn't expect you to cover a broad subject in its entirety. Consider, for example, how much more manageable the following subjects are after they have been narrowed:

General Topic	*Narrowed Topic*
Environmental issues	Home recycling procedures
Gambling	Native-American gaming casinos
Cambodian culture	Games Cambodian children play
Japanese management practices	Treatment of American workers in Japanese-managed automobile plants
Environmental Issues	Home recycling procedures
Health	Finding meat substitutes
Consumer electronics	How high-definition television will affect your viewing habits
Professional athletes	Basketball's greatest star
Nuclear energy	Problems in nuclear waste disposal
Native Americans	Native-American medicine
Advertising	Subliminal advertising
Weight loss	Fat reduction in diets
Animal rights	Animal testing for cosmetics
Folk art	Handmade African masks
Education	Teaching English as a second language
Current events	Balancing the national budget
Court reform	Eliminating trial by jury
Financial planning	Establishing a trust fund
Music	The history of jazz in the United States
AIDS	Sexual precautions
Hinduism	Karma
The elderly	Elderly parents lving with their children

In many instances, these topics could be narrowed even further. The time spent in thoughtful consideration of the many aspects of a subject will pay dividends when it comes to selecting the approach that will be most stimulating to you and your audience.

❖ ❖ ❖ ❖   ## Formulating a General Purpose

The next step of preparation is perhaps the most crucial phase of all, for it is in this stage that you determine your *general purpose*—why are you speaking? The classification of speech purposes has long been a subject of controversy among rhetorical scholars and teachers of communication. Since ancient times, disagreements have arisen over the number and nature of these purposes. However, critical study of the historical arguments indicates that there are three general speech purposes—*to inform, to persuade, and to entertain*. These three purposes apply equally to public and private communication.

You should remember as we discuss these speech purposes that in reality we are talking about responses you desire from your audience. You must take into account the obvious fact that individuals are all different and, therefore, what is intended by the speaker as a speech to inform may well persuade or entertain certain audience members. For example, it is possible that while you are "informing" an audience about the hiking trails within the Grand Canyon, someone might be "persuaded" to go camping there. This does not mean your general purpose was altered but, rather, that there were multiple responses to that purpose. Once again, think of *general purposes as targets that you aim at so that your arrow will have some direction and purpose*.

Although all three types of speeches are treated in later chapters, they are introduced now to offer you some working principles early in your speech training. You need some information and skills now so that you can start practicing the art of speechmaking without delay. As William Shakespeare said so eloquently, "In delay we waste our lights in vain, like lamps by day."

Speech to Inform

The purpose of informative communication is to increase a receiver's knowledge and understanding of a subject. As already indicated, it is possible that a speech to inform may also entertain or change listeners' beliefs. A speaker whose immediate purpose is to impart information may use amusing or dramatic illustrations to entertain the audience members, thus holding their attention. Moreover, information may lead to changes of belief and eventually to physical action, although such results may not be a part of the speaker's purpose.

An informative speaker's main concern is to have the audience understand, learn, and remember the information presented. You are trying to teach. You attempt to convey this information in an objective and impartial manner.

A librarian leading a group of students on an orientation tour of the library, a teacher demonstrating how to study for an examination, and a personnel officer explaining the duties of a job to new staff members are all engaged in informative speaking. How much the listeners know at the conclusion of a talk is the test of the speech to inform.

Following are some examples of informative subjects:

- Gender differences in ways of speaking.

- An explanation of Canada's health care system.

- Unusual uses for a microwave oven.

- How to use a videocassette recorder to tape FM musical programs.

- The workings of a pollution-free engine.

- An analysis of the federal drug interdiction program.

- A description of a proposed student activity center.

- The major causes of crime in the downtown area.

- Cures for a computer virus.

- How to install a simple home security system.

In all these examples, the apparent aim is to have the listeners acquire or improve on a skill or gain new knowledge. In short, after the speech, the listeners should know something they did not know before the speech.

Speech to Persuade

A persuasive speech seeks to induce the audience to believe, feel, or act in a manner selected by the speaker. Perhaps you want your listeners to discard old beliefs or form new ones, or perhaps you just want to strengthen opinions that they already hold. You may even want them to take an action. Persuasive speech topics are normally more controversial than topics selected for speeches to inform, because in most persuasive situations there are opposing points of view. A salesperson uses a speech to persuade as a means of getting a customer to buy a word processor. A worker asking for a raise, a college student asking a professor to extend a deadline for submitting an assignment, a parent trying to get a child to practice the piano, a motorist asking a traffic officer for leniency, and a telephone solicitor asking a homeowner to subscribe to a magazine are all attempting to persuade someone to do something. Your own daily routine probably requires you to use persuasion from time to time.

The following are examples of persuasive subjects:

- Newspaper recycling bins should be placed on campus.

- Library hours should be extended to ten o'clock on weekend evenings.

- High school students possessing knives on campus should be expelled immediately.

- The city should rent vacant commercial buildings for use as temporary shelters for the homeless.

- The police department should double its staff of multilingual patrol officers.

- All new-car dealerships should be required to provide on-site air bag installation.

- The use of wooden shingles on residences in drought-prone areas should be prohibited by law.

- Women should be allowed to join military units that might be involved in combat.

- You should reduce your intake of fat.

- All cigarette advertising should be prohibited.

In each of these examples, a persuasive purpose is apparent. The speaker wants the audience to modify a behavior, an attitude, or an opinion.

Speech to Entertain

The third major type of speech has the purpose of entertaining the audience. We are using the word "entertainment" in its broadest sense, to include anything that stimulates a pleasurable response, whether humorous or dramatic.

The speaker's objective is simply to have the listeners enjoy themselves. There is no concern that they learn a great deal or that they change their minds in one direction or another. Many after-dinner speeches have entertainment as the principal aim, and it goes without saying that the speech to entertain is a comedian's favorite type of speech.

Following are some subjects that lend themselves to humorous treatment:

- Popular alibis for being late to work.

- Trying to order a meal in a foreign restaurant.

- How to occupy your time when waiting in a line.

- Cloning as a way of life.

- The case for procrastination.

- Twenty-four hours in a shopping mall.

- How to keep smiling when the computer erases your term paper.

- Proven methods to promote falling asleep easily at night.

- How I live with a talking dog.

- Backpacking through the university library.

The speaker's goal in all these instances is to provide a view of the subject that the listener will find amusing and pleasurable.

Formulating a Specific Purpose

Whereas the general purpose of a speech may be stated in terms of informing, persuading, or entertaining, the specific purpose describes the exact nature of the response you want from your audience. The specific purpose is a one-sentence summary of what you want your audience to know, feel, believe, or do by the end of your talk. Some speakers even find it useful to use the phrase "At the end of my speech my audience will . . ." as a means of visualizing their specific purpose. In this way the specific purpose becomes the precise spot on the target they are aiming at.

When your general purpose is to *inform*, your specific purpose might be:

1. To have the audience understand how the magnitude of earthquakes is measured.

2. To have the audience understand the tutorial services available on campus.

3. To have the audience understand how to find the best air travel bargains.

4. To have the audience understand the dietary habits of vegetarians.

5. To have the audience understand the economic impact of military base closures on the local economy.

6. To have the audience understand the procedure for applying for student loans.

7. To have the audience understand the concept of "saving face" in the Chinese culture.

8. To have the audience understand how to protect themselves from the harmful rays of the sun.

9. To have the audience understand the best ways to use an Internet search engine to do research.

10. To have the audience know the steps Congress must go through to impeach a President.

If your general purpose is to *persuade*, your specific purpose might be:

1. To get the audience to contribute money to the Special Olympics Fund.

2. To get the audience to believe that caller-identification devices should be prohibited in all telephone systems in the United States.

3. To get the audience to sign a petition calling for a mandatory ceiling on student activity fees.

4. To get the audience to support a ban on the possession of alcoholic beverages on public beaches.

5. To get the audience to register for a course in cardiopulmonary resuscitation.

6. To get the audience to request that their supermarket purchases be placed in paper bags rather than plastic bags.

7. To get the audience to support a federal bill that outlaws the sport of boxing.

8. To get the audience to support a plan to keep the campus tennis courts open at night.

9. To get the audience to support a plan to drop all economic sanctions against Cuba.

10. To get the audience to join Mothers Against Drunk Driving.

If your general purpose is to *entertain*, your specific purpose might be:

1. To have the audience enjoy hearing about your trip through a merchants' bazaar in Tunisia.

2. To have the audience enjoy your predicament in finding yourself going in the wrong direction when on a nonstop high-speed train trip.

3. To have the audience enjoy the absurdities of manufacturers' claims for their products.

4. To have the audience enjoy hearing about your experience in trying to crash closed classes.

5. To have the audience enjoy your account of a day in traffic court.

6. To have the audience enjoy hearing about the hazards of caring for your vacationing neighbor's pets.

7. To have the audience enjoy the thrills associated with a day of hang gliding.

8. To have the audience enjoy hearing about the first time you went skiing.

9. To have the audience enjoy hearing about the best ways to shop for a used automobile.

10. To have the audience enjoy hearing why you do not like attending meetings.

In selecting and wording your specific purpose, there are a number of important considerations. First, you should remember that a *well-phrased specific purpose contains one central and distinct idea*. A specific purpose that contains too many points is confusing to both you and your audience. In the following specific purpose, notice how many ideas are being expressed: "To persuade my audience that teen-age pregnancy is a serious problem as more and more young girls experiment with sex, hence we must advocate sex education by the sixth grade." The speaker should have had a specific instance that said, "To persuade my audience that sex education should begin in the sixth grade."

Second, *begin with an infinitive* (to explain, to inform). The infinitive represents yet another way to focus you on the goal orientation of public speaking. The sentence "Exploring the greenhouse effect" is not nearly as useful as a specific purpose that states, "To have my audience understand the results of the greenhouse effect on the environment."

Third, the specific purpose should *be worded in terms of the response you want from the audience at the end of the speech*. Although it might appear to be a minor matter, your specifying the desired response reminds you that all your preparation is aimed at a specific audience response. Hence, a typical specific purpose would say, "To have my audience sign a petition allowing Native-American gaming in California."

Finally, the specific purpose should be *worded as a statement not a question*. While questions might make good titles, they do little to point you in the direction of the exact response you want from your listeners. Notice the difference in the following two specific purposes: "Do we need capital punishment?" "To persuade my audience that the Supreme Court should rule that all capital punishment is illegal."

I recommend that you begin the process of speech preparation by writing your specific purpose down on a sheet of paper. Its formulation will give you a constant target at which to aim. It allows you to see, at a glance, whether the material you have gathered and its organization relate directly to your specific purpose.

Choosing a Title

On certain occasions, you may be asked to provide a title for your speech. Ideally, a speech title should be (a) short, (b) provocative, (c) suggestive of your purpose, and (d) appropriate to the target audience and occasion.

A few examples might illustrate how these characteristics can be brought into play in phrasing a speech title. A student speech reviewing the growth of credit-card buying and high interest rates in the United States was entitled, "Credit Cards: Bankruptcy Made Easy." The title stimulated interest in the talk even before the presentation began. A student giving a talk on world religions used the following title: "God Comes in Various Shapes and Colors." Titles such as "Killer Bees: Is the Name Justified?" "Are Headphones Music to Your Ears?" and "Term Papers: A Growth Industry" are others that capture attention and steer the listener toward the content of the speech.

Choosing a Method of Speaking

Regardless of your background, knowledge, and skill, each time you speak it is a unique experience. An effective communicator recognizes this fact and prepares specifically for each occasion. Included in his or her thought and preparation is an analysis of the type of delivery best suited for the subject, audience, and occasion.

There are four fundamental ways of presenting a speech: (1) reading it from a manuscript, (2) reciting it from memory, (3) giving it in an impromptu manner, and (4) delivering it extemporaneously. Three observations are in order before we examine each of these methods of speaking. First, many speaking situations call for a combination of two or more of these types. You might begin by reading your introduction from a manuscript and then move to notecards as you use an extemporaneous style. Second, because all four of the methods are concerned with the act of communicating, you will find that they have a great deal in common. For example, in each instance, issues such as credibility, interest and attention, eye contact, vocal variety, posture, and organization need to be taken into consideration. Finally, because our focus at this point is on delivery, we will discuss only the presentational aspects of these four methods of speaking. Other considerations, such as organization, content, and the like, are reserved for later chapters.

Speaking From a Manuscript

In the manuscript form of delivery, you read your speech directly from a manuscript. In some instances, this type of delivery is essential and appropriate. For example, on radio and television, and at conferences and conventions, speakers are often accountable for their remarks and must be extremely accurate in what they say. Indeed, all speakers should be accountable and accurate, but a mass media speaker has to be able to make instant referrals to sources and materials. At conventions and business meetings, a manuscript is helpful for a speaker who wishes to have the speech circulated.

There are certain advantages to manuscript speaking, in addition to those just cited. The obvious advantage is that it puts no strain on your memory. Your speech is before you and you need only read it. A second advantage is that the manuscript, having been written well in advance of the speech situation, enables you to be very selective in your choice of materials and equally meticulous in your style of delivery. Hence, a manuscript speech should be free of vague phrases, rambling sentences, and inappropriate colloquialisms. Because the manuscript speech is usually written well in advance of the actual speech, it also affords ample opportunity to work on all aspects of delivery. Some speakers even mark their manuscripts with cues to pause, use emphasis, and the like. Third, the manuscript mode of delivery and preparation is also useful for situations in which time constraints demand that your speech fit into a specific time period. Using a manuscript allows you the luxury of keeping your speech within the assigned limits. The importance of staying within time limitations is perhaps best illustrated by the demands of television. If you are allotted 10 minutes on television, you usually cannot take 11. If you attempt to take the extra time, you are apt to be cut off the air. Therefore, a manuscript speech, because it is prepared, practiced, and timed in advance, can easily meet time requirements.

This type of delivery also has serious disadvantages. One marked disadvantage is that you can easily lose sight of the importance of communication. You read your remarks and may fail to establish rapport with your listeners. The manuscript becomes more significant than the audience. When this happens, you forget eye contact and lose all sense of spontaneity. Because each word and phrase is decided on in advance, a manuscript speech does not allow for immediate and specific adaptation of its content to the changing moods and needs of the audience. About all you can do is modify an aspect of delivery. For example, if some people in the audience appear bored or uninterested, you cannot make major changes in the content of your speech; you can only speak louder, pause in a dramatic way, or intensify your gaze.

Although we will have much more to say about manuscript speaking in chapter 15, for now you should remember to (1) write your speech for listeners and not for readers, (2) practice reading aloud, (3) use eye contact and other techniques of effective delivery, (4) concentrate on getting your ideas across, not just the words, and (5) use clear, large type so that you will have an easy time reading your manuscript.

Speaking From Memory

A memorized speech, much like a manuscript speech, provides you with the advantage of a carefully thought-out and well-worded speech. Every word is committed to memory and this, of course, frees you from the manuscript. One problem of the memorized speech is that this "freedom" often leads to a mechanical delivery, the presentation of a so-called canned speech.

A memorized speech is also dangerous because you are apt to forget the entire speech. It is often difficult to recall the exact wording, and if you forget one word, you may forget the entire speech. As English writer Thomas Fuller warned, "We have all forgot more than we remember."

Even though a memorized speech permits a careful ordering of your thoughts and materials, you should avoid it. Training in the other methods will offer you and other beginning students practice in speech situations that more closely resemble real-life occasions.

We should discuss two important points before we conclude our treatment of the memorized speech. First, the phrase "speaking from memory" refers to word-for-word memorization, not remembering key ideas and phrases. That is to say, a vast difference exists between word-for-word memorization and knowing in advance what points you want to cover and the general phraseology you want to use. We will examine this distinction in more detail when we discuss extemporaneous delivery. Second, although I have attempted to discourage you from using the memorized method of delivery, I should point out that there might be certain sections of your talk (the introduction, for example) you want to memorize. Third, many cultures prefer the memorized speech. For example, in Korea, Japan, and China, students study and learn by memorizing. People in these cultures also feel uncomfortable with direct eye contact. Hence, it is logical and comfortable for them to use a memorized or manuscript speech.

Impromptu Delivery

When you speak on the spur of the moment, without advance notice or time for preparation, you are engaging in impromptu speaking. Much of your daily conversation is nothing more than a series of short, impromptu talks.

As was the case with manuscript and memorized delivery, impromptu speaking also has advantages and disadvantages. The main advantage of impromptu speaking is that it is spontaneous. This, of course, makes it very natural. The chief drawback of this form of delivery is its lack of preparation, which often encourages a speaker to ramble. In facing an impromptu situation, (1) try to tie together all of your thoughts quickly—in a few seconds or minutes, (2) attempt to relate the topic to something you are familiar with, (3) think in terms of an introduction, body, and conclusion, (4) be brief, and (5) do not go off on tangents.

The best preparation for impromptu speaking is being well informed and having practice in prepared speaking situations. A speaker who knows how to prepare a speech when time is not a factor in preparation will have little trouble in making the transition to the spur-of-the-moment occasion. Because impromptu speaking is a very common form of delivery, a large part of chapter 15 is devoted to some of the principles and skills of this form of speaking.

However, because many speech classes start with some impromptu speaking, you may need to turn to that chapter early in the semester.

Extemporaneous Delivery

Extemporaneous delivery is often referred to as the "middle course." This speech form is by far the most desirable of the four. It allows the speaker to prepare in advance of his or her speech, and, more importantly, it has the added advantage of what we might call "communication flexibility." What this means is that adjustments can be made *during* the talk.

If the audience seems confused, the speaker can put his or her notecards aside for a few moments and take time to explain an idea in more detail. In short, extemporaneous delivery encourages adaptation and spontaneous adjustments at the same time it demands thorough preparation.

Because extemporaneous speaking is the method recommended for most occasions, we will examine it in the most detail.

Extemporaneous speaking has a number of characteristics that help explain both its uniqueness and its attractiveness. Extemporaneous speaking calls for a speech to be (1) researched, (2) outlined, (3) practiced, and (4) delivered in a conversational manner.

Research. When you choose the extemporaneous method, you are also making a decision concerning research and preparation. Because you know about your speaking purpose beforehand, you have time to gather the necessary information. Remember, you do not have to spend time memorizing or writing out your speech word for word. I will have much more to say about the entire process of gathering material and doing research in chapter 6.

Outline. After you have gathered the data, you must organize and outline the material in a clear and systematic pattern. A major advantage of an extemporaneous speech is that it is prepared in advance and therefore can be well organized. You are not asked to speak "off the top of your head" but, instead, are usually granted ample time to prepare and make adjustments in your talk.

The delivery style of the extemporaneous approach is conversational. (Photo: indexstock.com)

Practice. The time factor in extemporaneous speaking not only gives you an opportunity for research and organization, it also means that you can practice the speech. Keep three points in mind as you practice your talk. First, read over your complete outline a number of times so that you become familiar with your material. Do not memorize the exact language for delivery; instead, learn your organizational pattern, main points, subpoints, opening, and closing. The focus during practice is on ideas, not on specific words. Too much practice can give your speech the appearance of a formal stage performance rather than a conversation with your audience. "Canned" speeches lack sincerity, and often the artificiality detracts from the content of the speech. Again, learning your outline does not mean memorizing your speech.

Second, when you think you have learned your outline, you are ready to determine the approximate amount of time needed to deliver your speech. This can be accomplished by putting aside your outline and timing your talk as you deliver it aloud. Timing your speech will help you decide how much material to delete or how much more detail to add.

Third, after you have made the necessary adjustments to your outline, you are ready to determine what notes to write down on the cards that you will use when you present the talk. You will learn more about notecards in the next section of this chapter, but for now try to remember that you should learn your outline, not memorize it.

Delivery. The delivery style of the extemporaneous approach is conversational, and it is this characteristic that is one of its most attractive features. Because preparation stops short of memorization and because notecards may be used, you do not have to worry about forgetting key sections of the talk. Instead, you can give attention to establishing rapport with the audience—directness, eye contact, spontaneity, and a general conversational tone. If you think of extemporaneous delivery as expanded conversation, you can develop delivery techniques (chapter 4) while still being relaxed, friendly, and natural.

Extemporaneous delivery also enables you to make maximum use of feedback. That is, the flexibility of this method lets you adapt to the responses being produced by your talk. If you observe some confusion on the faces of your listeners while you are offering your statistics, the extemporaneous style will let you deviate from your outline and explain the statistics in a slightly different manner. For example, the extemporaneous method would allow you to say, "If these comparisons seem to be a little bewildering, I can explain them in yet another way." Memorizing or reading does not allow for this sort of adaptation to feedback.

The shortcomings of the extemporaneous method are probably obvious to you now that we have discussed the other three styles. The extemporaneous method takes time—research, outlining, and practice cannot be done in haste. Also, because the speech is not written out word for word or memorized, the beginning speaker often becomes careless in his or her choice of language—there is a tendency for these speakers to rely completely on inspiration for their vocabulary. This indictment is really directed more at the misapplication of the method than at an inherent weakness in the method itself. There is, after all, nothing in the explanation of this form of speaking to suggest that language is unimportant. In fact, the notion of preparation and practice implies that all phases of the communication process are of equal significance.

❖ ❖ ❖ ❖   This section on the four methods of delivery concludes with two final thoughts. First, although we have treated the four methods of speaking independently, in most instances you will find yourself using more than one at a time. For example, following this chapter's advice, you may decide to deliver your talk by means of the extemporaneous method. However, because you wish to quote some very important expert testimony, you write down the complete quotation on a card, expecting to read from it when you deliver the speech. In addition, you are so pleased with your clever introduction and conclusion that you decide to commit them both to memory. Now you are ready to give your speech—a speech that combines bits and pieces of the extemporaneous, memorized, and manuscript methods. And once you start giving your talk, you find that you are momentarily thrust into an impromptu situation—someone stops you to ask a question. You now prepare and respond on the spur of the moment.

Second, throughout, this book continuously looks at the link between culture and communication; much of what we discuss about speechmaking has a North American tone. The area of speaking methods is an excellent illustration of these two points. For instance, not all cultures would agree about the advantages of the extemporaneous style. In cultures such as the Japanese and the Chinese, where there is a lack of a rhetorical tradition and where direct eye contact often makes people feel uncomfortable, the manuscript speech is usually the preferred method of delivery. However, in the Arab and Mexican cultures, in which rhetorical artistry is admired, most people enjoy speaking and are not the least bit bothered by the impromptu situation.

Although these two concluding comments might be somewhat overstated, they do illustrate one of the major themes of this book—that a successful speaker does not get locked into any single technique but, instead, is able to adapt his or her preparation and presentation to a variety of topics and situations.

Using Notecards

"When out of sight, quickly also out of mind." Why is it we all know those famous few words written over five hundred years ago by German philosopher Thomas à Kempis. The reason is obvious—our memories cannot be trusted. It is very easy to forget something, even if we concentrate and are motivated to remember. Hence, this is one reason why people use notecards—but there are other reasons as well. Cards serve at least two purposes. First, they assist you in recalling what you want to talk about in your speech. Notecards contain the key words and phrases that trigger the speaker's memory. Second, they also have the advantage of offering a sense of security. It is reassuring to know that if you draw a mental blank during a speech, your notecards are there to rescue you. You can pause, look at your cards, and quickly resume speaking. Moreover, the audience doesn't have to worry about the embarrassment of seeing a speaker flounder because of memory failure. One additional advantage of notecards is that they are more effective than entire sheets of 8-1/2 by 11-inch paper. When using sheets of paper, speakers often have a tendency to include too much information. Large sheets of paper can also cause a speaker to read his or her speech instead of trying to deliver it in an extemporaneous manner. And, finally, if you bring sheets of paper to a particular room and find that a lectern is not available, then you are forced to juggle the papers from hand to hand.

Although most people like the idea of using notecards, they often have difficulty in both constructing and using their cards. Let me therefore offer some guidelines that will help you use notecards to the best advantage.

First, *put your notes on stiff cards, preferably the 3–by–5-inch size*. Cards this size are easy to hold in your hand and do not impede your gestures. Larger cards or sheets of paper can be rather clumsy to handle, thus causing a distraction.

Second, *you should keep in mind that you are preparing notes, not a manuscript*. You should not write the entire speech on your cards. A good rule of thumb is to write down only what it takes to remind you of your main points and subpoints. For example, if your topic is recycling, one of your notecards on the need for recycling might read:

> *Recycling—Need For*
>
> 1. Conserve limited resources
>   - a. Minerals
>   - b. Forestry
> 2. Avoid waste build-up consequences
>   - a. Limited landfill space
>   - b. Costly disposal methods

In the sample notecard, notice that an outline form is used. In fact, it should be the same outline form and structure as the larger speech outline. However, now the outline is only highlighting key points that will trigger your memory. Notecards are based on the premise that you have practiced your speech and that certain words and phrases will serve as a stimulus for what you have stored in your head.

Third, *you might want to completely write out any long quotations, expert testimony, and statistics you plan to use in your talk*. This will relieve you of having to memorize long and complex portions of your speech. It will enable you to be more accurate when presenting these three types of support. If you try to remember long passages or series of numbers, you may present them in a confusing or misleading fashion. It is always a good idea to write down completely anything you deem too crucial to be left to memory. This rule applies to your introduction and conclusion as well. At the very least, you should consider writing out the first sentence of each of these two crucial sections of your speech.

Fourth, *the printing or writing on your notecards should be clear, easy to read, and confined to only one side of the card*. Many speakers have found themselves unable to use their cards simply because their writing was illegible. Some speakers have also made the mistake of writing on both sides of their cards, which requires flipping cards in a distracting manner during their presentation.

Fifth, it is also distracting if you happen to get your notecards out of their correct sequence. Therefore, *number your cards in the upper right-hand corner*.

❖ ❖ ❖ ❖   Sixth, *you may find it useful to insert a card containing a helpful hint or an important reminder*. For example, speakers who talk too fast might include a card that says "Slow down!!!"

Seventh, *while practicing your speech, you should use your notecards in the same way you intend to use them during the actual speech*. This means placing them on a table if one will be available when you talk or holding them in your hand if the room does not have a table or speaker's stand. Practicing with your cards will help you keep them from becoming a distraction to you or the audience. As noted earlier, you might have a tendency to spend too much time looking at your notes. You should also avoid randomly shuffling cards or moving them from hand to hand in a purposeless manner. Remember, your cards should aid communication, not hinder it.

Eighth, as a general rule *you should plan on two to four cards for each five minutes you plan to talk*. As you might suspect, this number is very tentative. Issues such as the subject matter and preparation time will influence the exact number of cards you end up with.

Finally, when using your notecards, do not try to hide them from your audience. There is nothing wrong with using notecards. What is most important is that you remember to speak directly to your audience while having the security of using notecards. In time, you will gain the confidence and poise to use your cards in a variety of ways. You will be able to glance at them, pause, read from them when appropriate, walk around with them, set them down on a table, use them as cues, and still not have them inhibit your delivery.

Although I have concentrated primarily on notecards as a means of helping you remember your talk, I need to add one additional note system that is used by some speakers. This technique uses the speaker's visual aids as a prompting device. For example, if you are using transparencies (which will be discussed in detail in chapter 7), you might find it helpful to let each aid contain some of your speech content. As you move from aid to aid, you are automatically being reminded of the points you plan to cover.

Practicing the Speech

The Persian poet Sa'di once noted that "However much thou art read in theory, if thou hast no practice thou art ignorant." I would reword this advice to say that without adequate practice, all your research and preparation will not produce the results you desire. It would be great folly not to believe that practice is essential for successful public speaking. To help with that practice, let me offer a few suggestions as you move into these final stages of your speech preparation.

1. *Have a systematic sequence for practicing well in mind*. You should start by taking your complete-sentence outline and talking from it two or three times. This will help you to think about transitions and to identify difficult passages. You should then abridge the outline to a smaller version that you will eventually place onto your notecards. You are now ready to start practicing your speech.

2. *Have a positive attitude toward practice*. The preceding sentence is easier to write and read than it is to put into action. We all know from personal experience that, whether it is baseball or the piano, it is more fun to play than

If possible, rehearse your speech before an audience and use any available electronic equipment to record and play back speech assignments. (Photo: indexstock.com)

to practice. This analogy is also true of speechmaking. Just as a professional baseball player and a concert performer have accomplished their goals through study and training, you, too, must practice if you want to deliver a successful speech. Seeing the bond between practice and achievement should help you develop a positive attitude. In short, see your practice sessions as times to sharpen your skills so that the actual speaking event will be smooth and free from tension.

3. *Practice early and often.* Author Henry Miller was talking about all of us when he wrote, "Life for most of us is one long postponement." We are all practitioners of procrastination from time to time. Putting things off can be a great hindrance, however, when it comes to developing your proficiency as a speaker. You can reap a number of benefits from avoiding this fault and starting your practice sessions early. First of all, the extra time spent in practice will help you master your ideas. It takes time to secure the delicate balance between knowing what you want to say and falling into a pattern of memorization. Trying to accomplish this balance in only one or two sessions is nearly impossible, particularly if your only rehearsal is behind the steering wheel of your car as you drive to class to present your speech. Last-minute practice in the car will most likely make you a candidate for failure and, perhaps, for an accident as well.

Second, by allowing yourself ample time for practice sessions, you will reduce your chances of forgetting the speech once it comes time to deliver it before an audience. These practice sessions should also help you build confidence. Sometimes a nervous presentation signals a lack of preparation, a fear of forgetting parts of the speech. By starting practice early, you will have one less thing to worry about.

Third, by starting your practice sessions early, you will allow yourself sufficient time to identify and correct any flaws in your speech content or delivery. In addition, if the speech is too long, you will have time to do some editing, and if it is too short, you can add some material.

4. *Start by practicing with your main outline.* Once you learn the key points of your outline, it will be easy to move to your notecards. This weaning process will lead you smoothly from your detailed outline to your notecards, to the words and phrases you use during your talk.

5. *Work to remember ideas, not words.* Your practice sessions—and you should try for five to seven of them—should focus on your learning the main points of your speech, the ideas and sequence. Again, do not try to remember exact words.

6. *Practice your complete speech at least four times.* There is, of course, nothing magical about the number "four." Factors such as time constraints, complexity of the material, and the length of the speech will all influence the exact number of times you practice the complete speech.

7. *Time your talk.* By timing your talk during the practice sessions you will be able to add or delete material to accord with the time you have been allotted for your talk.

8. *Make your practice sessions as realistic as possible.* Practicing your speech by "running it through your head" as you lie flat on your back in bed may not be much help when you face the actual speaking situation. Experience has shown that practice sessions should be as realistic as possible. What follows are a few suggestions to increase the realism.

First, practice the speech standing up. You will not deliver the speech from your bed or your desk at home, so do not practice at those places. Instead, try to get your body and mind accustomed to the position and posture that you will use when you deliver the speech before an audience. If at all possible, try to rehearse in a room that approximates the type of room in which you will present your talk. Ideally, you should rehearse in the room, studio, or auditorium where you will give the speech.

Second, practice the speech in a realistic manner. Visualizing your speech in your head can create a false feeling of security. Silently responding to thoughts is not the same thing as actually producing the sounds. You need to speak many, but not all, of the same words you plan to use in the talk.

Third, practice using whatever memory aids (cards, outline, cue cards, Teleprompter) and audiovisual aids (posters, models, films, tapes) that you will use in your final presentation. Many public speakers have spoiled all their research and preparation by not having practiced with their aids prior to their speech.

Fourth, develop the habit of not stopping your speech when you are saying it aloud. The reason behind this suggestion should be clear—when you give the speech, you will not be able to stop every time you select the wrong word or make a mistake. In addition, too much stopping during your rehearsals works against the impression that your speech is a smooth, continuous flow from start to finish.

Finally, if possible, rehearse your speech before an audience. That audience can be your roommate, parents, fellow class members, or secretary. Talking to people is a very different matter from talking to tables, chairs, or pets. Not only will you get the "live" feeling, but you will be able to solicit suggestions from those present at your practice sessions. Depending on their qualifications as critics, they can comment on content and delivery.

9. *Try to locate a videocassette recorder and camera*. A speaker makes a big mistake if he or she does not take advantage of all available electronic equipment. Most campuses have media centers that provide students with video equipment allowing them to record and play back speech assignments. Seeing and hearing yourself enables you to make adjustments to your presentation and content.

10. *Allow time for one final run-through*. We have already mentioned the importance of budgeting your time; allow yourself a few quiet minutes before the speech has to be delivered. This private time can serve two purposes. First, you can practice your speech one final time. Second, you can put your mind and body into a relaxed mood. If you have taken time to prepare and practice, you should have little trouble with your mental attitude—your confidence should be high. If your body has not gotten the message and you seem physically nervous, you can try some of the following tension-relieving techniques: (1) walk around (it releases nervous energy), (2) take deep breaths or yawn (it increases your supply of oxygen), and (3) take a drink of water (it keeps your mouth from going dry).

Gaining Confidence

Ralph Waldo Emerson noted that "all the great speakers were bad speakers at first." He might also have added that all speakers, regardless of their ability, have experienced at least some of the conditions associated with stage fright. In fact, someone once remarked that the mind is a wonderful thing—it starts working the instant we are born and never stops until we get up to speak in public. It is because these kinds of attitudes toward public speaking are so common that I have decided to examine the issue of stage fright during the early stages of this book. The rationale for this early placement is buttressed by the fact that you be will giving speeches at the start of the semester, and therefore you should immediately begin the process of building your confidence. This text aims to help build that confidence by explaining speech anxiety and then suggesting some ways to deal with it.

Understanding Communication Apprehension

Picture the following scene:

> The voice quavers or becomes very tense. The rate of speaking becomes unusually rapid or agonizingly slow. The voice lapses into a monotone and emphasis is neglected. Breathing becomes labored. There is an urge to swallow or clear the throat frequently. Stammering sets in. Every pause is vocalized with an 'um' or 'er' or other meaningless sound. There is a fumbling for words. Eye contact with the audience is lost. The face becomes expressionless. The hands and arms become rigid and start to tremble uncontrollably. The body begins to sway back and forth and the feet begin to shuffle restlessly.

According to communication researchers Anthony Mulac and Robert Sherman, the conditions just described are those typically associated with speech fright. Although as a whole they may sound frightening, they are experienced by nearly everyone who speaks before a group. In short, whether we call it speech fright, stage fright, communication apprehension, or speech anxiety, it is well known to anyone who has been at a party composed of strangers, had a "blind date," attended a crucial job interview, or appeared before the public, whether as a theatrical performer, a product demonstrator, a teacher, or a student in a speech class. Even the most experienced platform artists are not totally immune to stage fright, although some hide its effects more skillfully than do others. You can take comfort from The Bruskin Report, which claims to have discovered that Americans fear speaking before a group more than they fear flying, deep water, snakes, heights, and even death.

Speech Anxiety Defined. We begin our discussion of speech anxiety with these two key questions: What is speech anxiety and why is it so prevalent? Basically, speech anxiety is your body reacting to a fear-producing situation. In many ways, the reaction is no different from the feelings you would experience if you were to see a car coming directly at you as you were driving on the freeway—your body would want to flee the situation. In speech anxiety, it is not an approaching car that your body is responding to but, rather, the idea of having other people evaluate you and your message. However, just as you can control the situation of the advancing automobile by manipulating your car, so can you control speech anxiety.

Speech anxiety is but one of a number of related conditions that are referred to collectively as **communication apprehension**. A person suffering the most severe degree of communication apprehension may try to avoid communicating with anyone other than relatives and close friends. He or she may even seek out an occupation that does not require much interaction with other people or may find housing that is remote from others.

Speech anxiety may be generalized—that is, experienced in any or all public-speaking situations—or it may be situation specific—that is, experienced to a greater degree in certain public-speaking contexts. For example, one might experience very little anxiety when contemplating or presenting a speech before friends but a great deal of anxiety when faced with the prospect of appearing before an audience of total strangers. At any rate, this mild form of communication apprehension—speech anxiety—is what the majority of us experience.

Causes of Communication Apprehension. The causes of communication apprehension are not clearly established. Some scholars theorize that a genetic predisposition to shyness might be operative. Others see communication apprehension as essentially a learned behavior, perhaps stemming from childhood communication experiences that had negative outcomes. For example, a child might have been punished for talking too much or rewarded for staying quiet. Perhaps the child chose to imitate the quiet behavior of an adult role model. We shall not debate the merits of these theories but shall deal, instead, with the reality of the anxiety that is clearly present.

What is there about the public-speaking situation that might trigger an attack of anxiety? The following list of answers might explain why the speech context can be the stimulus for feelings of anxiety. First, *it may be the sheer strangeness of suddenly being thrust into the spotlight*. After all, giving a public speech is not an everyday activity for most of us, so it is natural for us to experience anxiety about the unfamiliar role we are being called on to play. People don't seek out situations where they can make fools of themselves. You need to remember that while the public-speaking situation might be unfamiliar, communicating with other people is common.

Second, *sometimes the physical setting can be intimidating*. If the speaker's platform is elevated several feet above the seated spectators, we may feel vulnerable and ill at ease. If we are obliged to use a microphone, stand in a spotlight, or face a television camera, we may be unnerved. The strangeness of the physical environment can induce anxiety. If possible, you should become familiar and comfortable with the setting *before* you give your speech.

Third, *the fact that many eyes are staring at us can make us feel terribly uncomfortable*. This seems to be entirely normal behavior in both humans and animals. Most of us do not like to be conspicuous, and we may actually fear being stared at. Part of the fear associated with people looking at us is not knowing what they are actually thinking. It is sad that too many speakers imagine that the audience is engaging in negative conclusions and therefore are fearful of making fools of themselves.

The sheer uncertainty of how our listeners will perceive us and our ideas is at the heart of communication apprehension. This apprehension is very natural when we feel we are being evaluated: I wonder if they will like me? Will they notice my knees shaking? What will they think if I forget part of my speech? Suppose they disagree with my arguments? What if they misinterpret my meaning? What if they think I'm being presumptuous? What if my voice fails me? These are all questions that can flash through our minds when we face an audience, particularly an audience of strangers. Our anxiety seems to grow or diminish, depending on the degree to which we think we are being evaluated. The reality of the situation is that most people are basically curious and eager to hear what others have to say; therefore, most such fears are without merit.

Fourth, *having a strict time limit placed on a presentation can cause anxiety*. Such limits are apt to be applied in a speech class, where the instructor may limit a speaker to, say, five minutes for a presentation. Worrying about finishing on time or, conversely, about not talking long enough can aggravate one's anxiety. If you practice your speech, and time it, there should be no reason for the issue of time constraints to impede your delivery.

Finally, *for people who have English as their second language, anxiety might be aroused by having to speak in a language that they are not yet comfortable with*. Imagine for a moment how any of us would feel if, wanting to do a good job with our speech, we were asked to deliver that speech in a language that was not the one we normally speak. We would be very nervous indeed. Ways of overcoming these feelings of apprehension are discussed in the following section.

All of these conditions—unfamiliar role, strange environment, time constraints, uncertain reception, English as a second language—are potentially anxiety arousing. It is understandable that we react to them as we would to any unnerving stimulus. Now the question is: How shall we deal with our anxieties?

Dealing With Communication Apprehension

With this background in the symptoms and causes of speech anxiety, you can begin to understand the problem. Actually, you are already on the road to coping with speech anxiety if you have read and followed the advice provided in chapter 1. Let us recall a few of the principles that can help build your confidence. First, we will talk about some things you can do before the speech and then what you can do during the actual presentation. Finally, we will examine some measures to be taken in the future that can help you maintain control over those natural anxieties that arise whenever you face the prospect of speaking in public.

Before the Speech. The measures to combat speech anxiety should be set into motion well before the time the actual speech is presented.

First, although it seems somewhat apparent, *you need to develop a positive attitude*. If you dread the speaking experience, you will find that it can develop into a minor phobia and you will never enjoy the public-speaking arena. Shakespeare said much the same thing when he told us "In time we hate that which we often fear." To keep you from abhorring public speaking, I will suggest some ways to promote a positive attitude.

One way to develop a positive attitude is by *selecting a subject that interests you*. If you have strong feelings about your subject and you want others to feel the same way about it, you are apt to commence your preparation with a greater sense of confidence. Since fear and confidence can hardly be experienced at the same time, you have put fear on the back burner right at the outset. If a condition in your community makes you indignant, talk about it. If you are interested in necromancy, talk about it. Feeling strongly about something—whether the feeling is anger, indignation, love, pity, or mirth—can help you forget about being frightened, so give careful thought to your subject selection. Being preoccupied by your topic will keep you from being preoccupied by speech anxiety. On those occasions when your subject is selected for you it is important that you try to locate some redeeming feature in the assigned topic. In short, if you dislike the topic you will dislike the entire speaking experience.

A confident point of view can also be accomplished if you *openly discuss the upcoming speech with yourself*. Try telling yourself such things as:

'These are my classmates, they want me to do well.'

'Countless other students have given speeches and managed to get an
    A in the course.'

'The speech will eventually end and I will be able to sit down.'

Although these three examples may at first blush appear frivolous, years of experience and countless student observations have taught that me they do work.

A positive attitude can also be encouraged by *visualizing the communication experience in an optimistic and upbeat manner*. Run a movie in your head that shows you being calm, relaxed, and successful. There is evidence that this sort of positive image making can be helpful. I repeat—be optimistic. The American writer Elbert Hubbard is right, "Optimism is a kind of heart stimulant."

You might also find that *wearing one of your favorite outfits can also help build a positive attitude*. Although it is somewhat of a cliché, when we think we look good, we tend to feel good.

Second, *be thorough in your audience analysis*. By taking more-than-ordinary pains to find out who your listeners will be, what their probable attitudes will be toward you as an individual and as an authority on the subject matter, what their beliefs are on your topic of discussion, and what their expectations are likely to be, you can dispel some of the mystery surrounding the reception you are likely to get from your audience. You can use that information to plan and prepare your speech more intelligently.

Third, as noted in the first suggestion, *think of speech anxiety as short-lived*. The degrees of anxiety experienced by the average speaker tend to vary greatly. Anxiety is probably at its highest level in the moments before one stands up to speak. If one gets through the speech opening satisfactorily, anxiety usually starts to dissipate. By the time the speech is in full swing, the last traces of anxiety may be gone. In certain cases, the anxiety is connected with a controversial point the speaker must address. Once that point is successfully concluded, the anxiety subsides.

Knowing that speech anxiety is usually short-lived not only serves as a source of comfort, but it also enables you to pay particular attention to the preparation of the materials you will be presenting during those parts of the talk you anticipate will produce the most anxiety.

Fourth, *start your preparation early*. Although this idea is stressed elsewhere, it is worth repeating, for to start preparing your speech the night before you have to give it is inviting trouble. My years of teaching experience and conversations with thousands of students has convinced me that lack of preparation is a major cause of speech anxiety. So start early. By allowing yourself ample time to prepare and practice and making yourself knowledgeable about your subject, you can tell yourself, "I know what I'm talking about." By making yourself more of an expert than your listeners, you are less likely to feel intimidated by them.

Fifth, *rehearse your speech, but do not memorize it unless the situation demands it*. Beginning speakers often make the mistake of writing down their speeches and attempting to commit them to memory. If anything can contribute to speech anxiety, it is the fear of forgetting words that have been memorized. It is a better idea to rehearse your speech extemporaneously, varying your word choice from rehearsal to rehearsal. In that way, you are focusing on the ideas, not the words. Prepare your speaking notes on small, stiff cards, as suggested earlier in the chapter.

Sixth, *inspect the physical environment in which you will be speaking*. By knowing in advance the peculiarities of the physical environment and its limitations, you can make necessary adjustments and thus remove another uncertainty from the speaking situation. Perhaps you will be afforded the luxury of controlling the seating arrangements, placement of the speaker's stand, adjustment of the microphone, and so on. Control over these variables helps build your confidence.

Inspecting the setting before the speech also helps reduce anxiety associated with the unknown. As noted elsewhere, the unknown, whether with regard to the audience or the location of the speech, is a major cause of nervousness.

Finally, *try to engage in some relaxing behaviors just before your speech*. Some common relaxing techniques have proven to be effective when applied to speech anxiety. Some of these techniques can slow breathing, lower your pulse rate, ease muscle tension, and help you focus on your speech, not your nervousness.

1. *Excessively yawn a minute or two before you begin*. This not only gives you more oxygen, but it relaxes your throat muscles.

2. *Try stretching as many parts of your body as you can without calling attention to your strange acrobatics.* This stretching relaxes the muscles that are apt to be tensing up as you wait for your speech to begin. You can tighten and relax your leg muscles or even press the palms of your hands against each other.

3. *If time allows, you might also try to sit quietly, close your eyes, and concentrate on relaxing your entire body.* Take slow deep breaths and imagine oxygen slowly flowing throughout your entire body.

4. *If possible, try to walk and/or engage in some other movement before the talk.* This movement will help relax your entire body.

5. *Take a small drink of water* so you can avoid the "dry mouth" feeling that makes talking seem impossible. A word of warning—be careful of too much water; you know the results of consuming too much liquid in a short period of time.

During the Speech. When it is finally time to give the speech, you can adopt some behaviors that should help you maintain good control over your anxieties about speaking. Let us examine these behaviors.

First, do not begin as soon as you find yourself in front of the audience. *Take a moment or two and pause before you begin speaking.* This brief interlude before you begin will let you get oriented to the situation, appear poised, and arouse audience interest; also it will calm you down and give you a chance to look at your notes. In short, do not rush into your speech before you are ready.

Second, *use relaxation techniques while you are before the audience.* The value of deep breathing for nervousness has already been stated, so now I simply urge you to take some final breaths before you utter your first words. In order to benefit from deep breathing, you should position yourself so that you can make full use of your diaphragm, the muscle that separates your chest cavity from your abdominal cavity. You should be able to feel your waistline expand as you inhale and contract as you exhale. Deep, regular diaphragmatic breathing will soon make you feel more relaxed. You might even pause one final time and take one last breath just a few seconds before you begin. If you feel some tension in your upper torso, let your shoulders slump down and allow your arms to hang loosely at your sides. This will help further promote the feeling of relaxation induced by your deep breathing.

Third, *immediately adopt behaviors associated with confidence.* Before you rise to speak, sit "tall," with your shoulders relaxed, and lean slightly forward. After rising, walk with a confident stride to the podium. Arrange your notes on the lectern. If you choose, let your hands rest lightly on the lectern, but do not grip it; you may let your arms hang comfortably at your sides. And, as just mentioned, pause before you begin to speak.

Fourth, *focus your mind on your audience and your speech.* Are my knees shaking? Is my face red? and Am I making a spectacle of myself? are thoughts that can serve no useful purpose. If your mind does drift to self-evaluation while you are talking, simply remind yourself that the audience is there to hear what you have to say, not to see you fail or to ridicule you. You might also, during the "visit" with yourself, offer a short "pep talk" and tell yourself how well you are doing.

Fifth, *use effective delivery techniques.* Hand gestures, bodily movement, and walking ought to be used as fully as possible. They will help dissipate the natural tension that you are feeling and will reinforce your verbal message at the same time. If you have an opportunity to use visual aids, the movements involved in manipulating the aids can give a healthy outlet to the nervous energy crying for release.

Using positive delivery skills also means making proficient use of your voice. Too many beginning speakers use a delivery rate that is much too rapid. A hurried pace is not only a sign of nervousness— it also contributes to anxiety. So slow down and pause often.

Sixth, *seek out receptive faces and talk to them*. Once you establish one-to-one eye contact with friendly persons, you may soon stop thinking of your listeners as a mysterious crowd and start treating them as friends engaging in a one-sided conversation with you. After all, a public speech is essentially an enlarged conversation, with you doing all the talking.

Seventh, *if you should make a mistake, do not apologize, simply go on with your speech*. In most instances the audience will not even know that you made a minor error or left out one of your illustrations. However, if the mistake involves a major distortion of the facts, you ethically must pause and correct the misunderstanding.

Finally, *try to keep in mind that your audience will not know you are nervous*. That is, most of the symptoms associated with speech anxiety are not even seen by the listeners. You will only add to your apprehension if you tell yourself that everyone is observing your nervousness. In reality, you are the only one who knows.

After the Speech. Once you have completed your speech and have regained your composure, you should congratulate yourself for a job well done. You will also find that each time you talk, the task gets easier. To alter an old expression, "Familiarity breeds confidence." Look for further opportunities to speak in public, thus changing an unfamiliar role into a familiar one by sheer repetition of, and exposure to, the act of speaking. As already indicated, experiencing the act of speaking over and over again is one of the best ways to calm needless fears. You will probably find that you will experience a lessening of anxiety in your classroom speeches with each successive speech, especially if you maintain a consistent level of preparation.

Perhaps the single most important key to reducing speech anxiety is remembering the words of poet T. S. Eliot: "Every beginning has an end." This applies to both your speech and your anxiety.

Summary

Communication normally takes place because the speaker wants to achieve a preconceived purpose. Thus, the purpose must be clear in the speaker's mind. Public speakers usually prepare and give speeches that fulfill three general speech purposes—to inform, to persuade, or to entertain. In addition to selecting a general purpose, a speaker must formulate a specific purpose that describes the immediate and exact nature of the response wanted from the audience.

Speakers may encounter situations that make it necessary for them to provide titles for their speeches. In these cases, it is important to remember that a good title is brief, is appropriate, is provocative, and suggests the purpose of the speech.

In deciding on a method of preparation and delivery, a speaker can use any one of the following procedures: (1) speaking from a manuscript, (2) speaking from memory, (3) speaking impromptu, and (4) speaking extemporaneously. The extemporaneous method is recommended for beginning speakers.

When using notecards, it is important to (1) use stiff cards, (2) keep notes brief, (3) write out direct quotations, expert testimony, and statistics, (4) write clearly, (5) write yourself personal reminders, and (6) practice with the cards.

When practicing, speakers should start early, make practice sessions realistic, use video equipment, and allow time for one final run-through.

Fear of speaking, or communication apprehension, is a common condition experienced even by seasoned speakers. While its causes are not fully understood, it seems to surface particularly when a speaker is faced with an unfamiliar role in an unfamiliar environment before an unfamiliar audience. The control of communication apprehension lies in removing as many of the areas of uncertainty and unfamiliarity as possible. Thorough preparation and practice, coupled with a good mental attitude, will help guard against the disabling effects of communication apprehension.

Concepts and Questions

1. What are some major considerations when selecting a topic?

2. What are the four main ways someone can deliver a talk? What are the advantages and disadvantages of each?

3. Why do certain people become anxious when called upon to give a talk?

4. Why is practicing a speech such an important element to successful public speaking?

5. What are some guidelines in preparing and using notecards?

6. What are the major differences between a general purpose and a specific purpose?

Activities and Exercises

1. Prepare a short speech on your main hobby. First deliver the talk by means of a manuscript. Then change the speech so that it can be delivered in an extemporaneous fashion. What major differences did you see?

2. In class deliver an impromptu speech. Once you have delivered the talk, take the same topic and develop it into a more detailed extemporaneous speech. What differences did you notice in both content and delivery?

3. Formulate a general and a specific purpose for the following topics:

    a. The World Wide Web

❖ ❖ ❖ ❖

   b. Globalization

   c. Good health

   d. Interpersonal conflict

   e. Race relations

4. Interview someone who you believe is a good public speaker. Ask the person to share with you her or his personal philosophy for coping with communication apprehension.

5. Decide for yourself how you can be less apprehensive the next time you give a talk. Share your specific plan with your classmates. ✦

CHAPTER THREE

Audience Analysis: Understanding Your Listeners

> If we would consider not so much wherein we
> differ, as wherein we agree, there would be far less of
> uncharitableness and angry feeling in the world.
>
> —*Joseph Addison*

The lyrics of a song by Scottish poet Thomas Campbell lament

> Oh, how hard it is to find
> The one just suited to our mind!

These words could easily apply to a speaker in search of a sympathetic audience. Trying to get a diverse group of people just to listen may seem to be an impossible task at times; what interests one individual may not interest another. Any individual's reasons for believing or acting in a certain way are the product of many and varied influences. Our ethnicity, the neighborhoods we grew up in, the groups we hold allegiance to, our gender, and other factors all help produce an individual's unique outlook on a host of topics. In short, we are the product of countless affiliations, and these affiliations shape our view of world. Yet in spite of the problems we face when trying to adjust to the people around us, we have all, very early in life, learned to adapt our messages to the diverse populations we confront on a daily basis. Think back to your own childhood, when you had to convince several people—perhaps family members—to let you do something. Maybe you wanted to go on a vacation with a friend, buy a certain car, or get a special kind of haircut. Chances are that when you approached your father, you employed a different set of arguments than the ones you used on your mother. Experience had taught you that there were vulnerable spots in each person's make-up, so you tailored your arguments accordingly. You knew your mother's first concern was with your personal safety, so when you asked to go to camping alone for the first time, you stressed all the points that underscored the safety aspects of the trip. You knew your dad was concerned with how you spent his money, so you told him that you and your friends were going to share expenses of food and gas and that sleeping outside under the trees would be free. You knew your success depended on how accurately you had forecast the responses of your mother and father and how well you could adapt your message to meet those potential responses. This chapter, in principle, is about your adapting not to a single person but to an entire audience composed of many individuals. The basic premise seems rather simple—*people are different and they are alike. When you are a public speaker, you must try to locate likeness if you are going to accomplish your communication.*

The configuration of an audience can take a variey of forms. (Photo: Gloria Thomas)

The Importance of Audience Analysis

The interrelated concepts of **prediction** and **adaptation** are perhaps two of the most basic principles of human communication. Let us briefly look at these two concepts so you will be able to better appreciate the importance of audience analysis to the study of human communication.

In nearly all of your communication experiences, you take the other person into account; you make some predictions about who he or she is. Even in your initial encounters with strangers, you note some features that affect the image you form of each person. You know rather quickly if that person is old or young, African American or Caucasian, male or female, neat or sloppy. You know if he or she is wearing a uniform, western clothing, or a three-piece business suit. Once you make these observations, you automatically begin to adapt your message to the person. As you get more information about your communication partner, you make further predictions about how he or she is apt to view you and your message. When your predictions and resultant adaptation involve a collection of people, you are engaging in audience analysis. **Audience analysis** *means finding out all you can about the people you are talking to or will be talking to so that you can adapt your material to their interests, needs, attitudes, fund of knowledge, beliefs, values, and backgrounds.*

Central to this idea of adaptation, and to the entire process of communication, is the concept of **identification.** In *Rhetoric of Motives*, Kenneth Burke suggests, "You persuade a man only insofar as you can talk his language by speech, gesture, tonality, order, image, attitude, idea, identifying your ways with his." Successful communication must ask the speaker to "talk the language" of those he or she hopes to influence. Audience analysis allows you an opportunity to learn the "history" and current "language" of your receivers so that you can fuse your goals and purposes with theirs.

Failing to take your listeners into account can produce embarrassing results. A student from San Francisco who was attending a university in San Diego was so enamored of San Diego that he decided to give a speech to inform about the sight-seeing attractions within reach of the university. However, he failed to take into account the knowledge level of his potential audience. The majority of his classmates were local residents. Although his speech provided interesting and useful information to the handful of nonresidents in the class, the rest of his classmates were bored by hearing information about places they had already visited.

The importance of audience analysis should be clear. Information about your audience can help you forecast how that audience is likely to perceive you and your topic. For example, suppose you are a young male speaking about preventing sexually transmitted diseases to an audience composed of older women; then later that day you are also scheduled to give the talk to a group of sixth-grade students. The arguments you use, the evidence to support those arguments, the language of those arguments, the amount of time you spend establishing rapport, the content of your emotional appeals, and the ways in which you define new concepts are all touched by what the audience members believe before you begin. Likewise, knowing in advance that your audience has little or no information about your subject or are opposed to the stand you will be taking will enable you to cope with the situation more intelligently. Such knowledge helps you control future events. As philosopher Eric Hoffer wrote, "The only way to predict the future is to have the power to shape the future." Audience analysis enables you to shape your speech.

Assessing the Audience

There are very few pages in this text that do not contain a reference to "the audience." Remember, however, that the concept of "the audience" is an abstraction. No such creature exists. When you present a speech, you are facing a group of individuals, who together make an audience. And just as no two people are alike, no two audiences are *exactly alike*. Therefore, you need to ask yourself a series of questions at the beginning of your audience analysis. Your answers to these questions will help you in each and every phase of your preparation process.

Although the list of questions is by no means exhaustive, it does represent a general sampling of the types of questions that will help point you toward your specific audience and will tell you a great deal about the information that should be included in your talk. You will notice that each of these questions is placed on a visual continuum. I recommend you do the same, for the audience's location on the continuum will make different demands on your level of preparation.

What is the attitude of the audience toward my purpose?

Enthusiastic   Neutral   Apathetic

What is the attitude of the audience toward me?

Favorable   Neutral   Unfavorable

What type of audience will I be facing?

Voluntary	Neutral	Captive

What do my listeners have in common?

A Great Deal	Very Little	Nothing

What does my audience already know about my subject?

A Great Deal	Very Little	Nothing

What Listeners Bring to Communication

The American playwright Eugene O'Neill was right when he wrote, "The past is the present, isn't it? It's the future too." What O'Neill was telling us is that our past experiences, to a large extent, determine our response to the present and the future. Yet deciding on the impact of past experiences is a very difficult task. That is to say, there is no escaping the fact that it is at times very puzzling to investigate the impact and influence of what each of us brings to a communication experience. For example, a person receiving bad news just before entering a classroom will react to a classmate's speech differently than will those who are untroubled. This "mood of the moment," as well as what happened to the person 10 years ago, could affect his or her reaction to a speech.

We need to focus our discussion of audience analysis on two rather obvious points. First, it is impossible to know everything about each audience member. All of us are extremely complex individuals. We have had millions of experiences that have shaped our character and personality. It would be impossible for any speaker to know even a small fraction of those specific experiences. Second, because each of us is unique, a speaker's conclusions about an audience might not apply to every member of that audience. Therefore, what a speaker has gathered at the end of an audience analysis is some general information about cultural background, group affiliation, educational level, occupation, gender, age, and the like. If we know how to use it, this general information can tell us a great deal about the people we will be addressing. The usefulness of this information is based on the assumption that as *members of a culture or group, listeners share a set of norms, perceptions, attitudes, motives, needs, values, and interests.* As speakers, our job is to discover the affiliations of our listeners, to make some valid generalizations about those affiliations, and to adapt our material to accommodate those generalizations.

What do listeners bring to a speech that will influence how they respond to the speaker and the specific purpose? As we have seen, this is a rather difficult question to answer, for, in essence, what listeners bring is both general and specific and falls into four broad categories: (1) *a fund of knowledge* (what they know about a countless number of subjects), (2) *attitudes* (their feelings about a topic), (3) *beliefs* (what they believe to be true or false about the world), and (4) *values* (how they believe they should act in the world). In subsequent chapters, we will examine these categories in more detail, but for now you need to understand how those four elements influence listeners' responses to your ideas and information. Your understanding can be increased if you discover what is often called *the demographics of your audience*, the salient characteristics of the people you will be addressing. The study of these characteristics—whether age, gender, or culture—is based on two simple assumptions. First, *although we are all unique individuals, we are also members of countless groups that supply us with our fund of knowledge, attitudes, beliefs, and values.* Second, *if you know something about the group and cultural affiliations, you can make some important choices about your speech content and delivery.*

Cultural Characteristics

During the past thirty years, the United States, and indeed the world, has undergone a series of cultural changes. In fact, the phrase "cultural diversity" has now become a common term. In the United States, large populations of people are from various ethnic and cultural groups whose experiences make them perceive the world very differently than do members of the dominant culture. Also, if you leave the United States, you will interact with people whose cultural composition most likely will not be the same as your own. It is because of this increase in cross-cultural contact that we begin our discussion of audience analysis with the topic of culture.

Culture *has been described as the totality of learned and accumulated experience that is socially transmitted from generation to generation.* Our culture gives each of us, in both conscious and subconscious ways, modes of behavior, patterns of thought, beliefs, attitudes, ideas, values, and many of our habits. To understand those with whom we attempt to communicate, we must know something about the culture that they bring to a communication event.

Two important points need to be made before we proceed with our discussion. First, a person must be careful not to rely too heavily on preconceived notions about another's culture. All too often, those notions are based on limited experience and unrealistic images of a culture as portrayed in movies, novels, and the remarks of biased observers. Moreover, we must remember that our perceptions of other cultures might be influenced by a feeling of **ethnocentrism.** As mentioned in chapter 1, *ethnocentrism is a tendency to judge all other cultures by the standards set in one's own culture.* The danger of ethnocentrism is that it can obstruct an individual's perception of another culture.

Second, when we speak of the "dominant culture of North America," it is with the realization that the United States is composed of many cultures. However, when we refer to the "dominant culture," we are talking about that part of the population that controls and dominates the major institutions, determines the flow and content of most of the information, and is consequently white, male, and of European heritage.

still true?

North American Values. The list that follows briefly summarizes some key values as they apply to the dominant North American culture. The list and discussion of these values will not only help you understand members of the dominant culture and how to aim your material at these values but will also serve as a backdrop and reference point for looking at how values function in other cultures.

Individualism. The value of individuality is perhaps the most sacred of all values in the United States. Individualism refers to the doctrine that each individual is unique and special. With this as a starting premise we can see how, for most Americans, the interests of the individual are, or ought to be, paramount, and that all values and rights originate in individuals. Whether it be in sexual, social, or ethical matters, the self for Americans holds the pivotal position.

This key value manifests itself in a variety of ways. It stresses individual initiative ("Pull yourself up by your own bootstraps"), independence ("Rules are for fools"), individual self-expression ("My way or the highway"), and even privacy ("A man's home is his castle"). Each of these beliefs needs to be considered when trying to persuade people who value individualism.

Materialism. People in the United States value materialism. Americans consider it almost a right to be materially well off and physically comfortable, and often judge a person's success by his or her material possessions. There is even a popular bumper sticker that proclaims, "The person with the most toys wins."

Work. Hard work is an important value in the United States. Whether motivated by ego gratification, material possessions, or the Puritan ethic, Americans believe that work is something important. When people meet each other for the first time, a common question is "What do you do?" Embedded in this simple question is the belief that "what we do" even contributes to our personal identity.

Humanitarianism. People in the United States have a long history of being highly humanitarian. They give more to charity, both at home and abroad, than any other country in the world. Americans act swiftly, both as individuals and as a government, to help those in need.

Progress. People in the United States progress. In the name of progress Americans emphasize adaptability, technological innovation, economic expansion, and change. Almost since the founding of the country, people have railed against stagnation and the status quo. While conquering the land, seas, airways, and finally space, progress and change have been prime articles of faith for most Americans. They enjoy what is new and different. It is also important to remember that each generation seeks to stake out new territory and contribute to change.

Democracy. Democracy, while perhaps closely linked with the value of individual freedom, is important enough to have its own enumeration. Since the founding of the United States, Americans have rejected aristocracy and authoritarianism. From the Declaration of Independence to an insistence on majority rule, Americans pride themselves on being the most democratic people in the world. Americans believe that all people have a right to succeed in life, and the state, through laws and educational opportunities, should ensure that right.

Competitiveness. The culture of the United States is marked by competitiveness. Whether in sports, business, or personal life, Americans are taught to strive to be "number one." The U.S. economic and social systems thrive on perceiving life as a contest that categorizes people as winners or losers.

Cross-Cultural Values. The influence of cultural attitudes, beliefs, and values on communication is of immense importance. A culture gives its members a world view that enables them to deal with the large issues of life and death, suffering and happiness, heaven and hell. It also provides them with certain ways of perceiving and responding to such events and ideas as work, leisure, violence, change, conflict, sex rules, the elderly, and self-worth. The cataloging of cultural values and characteristics could, of course, fill an entire

❖ ❖ ❖ ❖   book. Therefore, what is offered in the next few pages is a list of some important cultural values and characteristics that need to be considered when speaking to diverse audiences.

Nature. The differences in conceptions of the relationship between humanity and nature and the environment produce distinct frames of reference for human desires, attitudes, and values. Many cultures (Asian, Native American) affirm that people should live in harmony with nature. The philosophy holds that a "power" links all things and creatures together. If you planned to speak in favor of strip mining, and you knew that your audience would be composed of many Native Americans, you would have to explain how what you are recommending would not exploit nature. If you were to use the Western view that it is both a right and a mandate for human beings to control nature, you would be employing an unsuitable premise on which to base arguments for that audience.

Collectivism. Earlier in the chapter we noted that for most Americans individualism is a strong personal value. However, in many other cultures, and in nondominant American co-cultures, collectivism is the orientation that helps determine a person's view of the world. Look at the words of Confucius for a clear, simple example of collectivism: "If one wants to establish himself, he should help others establish themselves first."

A speaker can profit from knowing how the Asian and Latin outlook on individualism versus collectivism differs from the view found in the dominant North American culture. Whereas North Americans tend toward individualism, stressing self-motivation and competition with others, Eastern cultures give primacy to the group. Hence, a speaker addressing Japanese business executives might say, "This product will benefit all the members of your firm."

Family

One result of collectivism is the strong emphasis on family. In the Middle East and Latin America, the family is seen as the most important social unit. Middle Easterners are so protective of their families that they would never berate a family member, even in jest, in the presence of an outsider. Moreover, if one were to boast of being a "self-made man," it would be seen as an affront to the family—that the family had been derelict in its responsibility to the man.

Uncertainty. Cultures also differ in the degree to which they tolerate uncertainty and ambiguity. That is to say, people from cultures such as the Greek, Japanese, French, and Portuguese do not like the unknown and function much more efficiently when the uncertainties they face are reduced. There is, in these cultures, a need for rules, a wish for specific proposals, a strong respect for the view of experts, and a dislike of risk taking.

Some cultures have a very high tolerance for the ambiguous nature of life. People from the United States, Denmark, Sweden, Ireland, and Great Britain do not suffer great feelings of stress when some issues are left unresolved. Knowing a culture's view of ambiguity can enable you, as a speaker, to decide how specific your proposals must be.

Formality. Part of your audience analysis should include a consideration of a culture's value regarding formality or informality. This value has an impact on issues such as status, language, content, and delivery. For instance, the United States is a rather informal culture, while Germany, Japan, Egypt, and Great Britain are cultures in which correct protocol and conventional behavior are appreciated. The manifestations of formality are seen in many ways. For instance, in most formal cultures last names are used instead of first, dress style is conservative, and correct language is stressed. Violation of these norms might keep you from accomplishing your specific speech purpose.

Time. Cultures also perceive time differently. Whether or not a culture places emphasis on past, present, or future will influence how people in that culture respond to messages and even how they will concentrate on the speech itself. For North Americans, what is yet to happen—the future—is of great importance. We are always planning and thinking ahead. Buddhists believe in "mindfulness"—the complete focus of all senses on the present.

Past-oriented cultures believe in the significance of prior events. History, established religions, and traditions are extremely important to these cultures, so there is a strong belief that the past should be the guide for making decisions and determining truth. We see this orientation among the Chinese, who, because of their long and resplendent history, continue to respect the past. For the Japanese, Shintoism is strong and ancestor worship important, so the past remains paramount. The English, because of their extensive devotion to tradition, continue to resist change. Knowing how these three cultures venerate the past can help speakers in preparing and presenting their arguments.

Credibility. Although a lengthy discussion about credibility appears in chapter 14, it is important at this juncture that you understand how important cultural influences are in shaping an audience's view of the speaker's credibility. A speaker who is perceived as dynamic, outgoing, and articulate by an American audience will have high credibility. Yet this same person is apt to be viewed as aggressive or presumptuous by a Japanese or Chinese audience. These cultures are more accustomed to a quiet, humble, pensive, reserved approach to communication. American diplomats and executives dealing with the Japanese or Chinese can attest to the advisability of downplaying the demonstrations of enthusiasm and persuasiveness so admired by many Western audiences. On the other hand, for an Arab audience, signs of ebullience and energy in both content and delivery add to a person's credibility.

Age. There are also major cultural differences in the perception of age. It does not take a great deal of documentation to justify the assertion that the dominant American culture prefers youth to old age. This condition does not exist in all cultures. In the Arab culture, for example, children kiss the hands of older people and respect their views and opinions. We find this same view in most of the cultures of Asia. Both the Japanese and Chinese show great respect to the elderly. Think for a moment about the view of age expressed in the simple Chinese proverb, "To succeed, consult three old people." Filipinos and Native Americans are two additional cultures that greatly value old people. Knowing this type of information might prevent you from telling your audience, if it was composed of members of these five cultures, that something should be rejected just because "it is old" or "out of date."

Harmony. The final value discussed here deals with cultural differences as they apply to assertiveness versus interpersonal harmony. Because Americans value individualism and freedom of expression, our culture is known for its assertiveness and aggressive style. We learn very early in life that the "squeaky wheel gets the grease." We are expected to "stand up for our rights" and even be confrontational should the situation call for such action. The notion of argumentation and debate is very much a part of Western history.

There are, of course, cultures that have a very different communication style from the one found in the United States. The Thais, Filipinos, Chinese, and Japanese stress harmony and a lack of direct confrontation. Staying calm is valued, not outward aggressive action. There is even an Asian proverb that states, "The first man to raise his voice loses the argument." And for the Japanese the same view toward "speaking up" is expressed in the saying, "It is the quacking duck that is the first to get shot."

It is difficult to overemphasize the role of culture in human communication—cultural and ethnic affiliations influence how members of a particular audience will respond to you and your ideas. Although there are individual differences among the people within each culture, it would not be surprising to learn that an audience of Jewish Americans is pro-Israel, that Native American listeners do not view Christopher Columbus as a great hero, or that most Hispanic Americans support bilingual education.

Let me add a cautionary note at this point. One must be careful in generalizing about foreign nationals now residing in the United States. Some are more assimilated into the dominant North American culture than others. Some still observe the traditions of their homeland, while others have adopted the ways of their new land. The more heterogeneous a group is, the more difficult it is for a speaker to make reliable assumptions about the viewpoints and probable reactions of the individuals within that group.

Religious Characteristics

Religious orientations, much like culture, have a strong influence on how people perceive and live in the world. Former Supreme Court Justice Oliver Wendell Holmes, Jr. said much the same thing when he noted that "Religion is at work on those things that matter most." For thousands of years people have turned to religion for guidance, whether the teachings are those of the Bible, Vedas, Koran, Torah, or I Ching. In a host of ways, religion has provided the peoples of the world with advice and values on how they should live their lives. Therefore, knowing the religious views of your audience is an essential part of any audience analysis. If you plan to discuss nutrition, you should know that some Hindus don't eat meat and most members of the Islamic faith don't eat pork. If you plan to talk about a technological breakthrough in climate control, you should know that the Shinto religion has a strong emphasis on nature. You need to examine how religion gets translated into an individual's value system. Knowing the ethical underpinnings of Karma would enable you to discuss the consequences of your proposal as it applies to the notion of "good deeds." Having knowledge about the Hindu view toward reincarnation would help you in your selection of arguments for a persuasive speech dealing with cloning.

As we have just noted, religious alliances can influence one's thinking on a number of matters. Obviously, we all have values and attitudes that are more grounded in religion, but, all things considered, you could expect a Pentecostal to be upset by your employing words such as *hell* and *damn*. You could also expect Quakers to oppose all types of violent activity and be in favor of human rights. Someone who is Catholic is likely to oppose abortion and most types of birth control. Jews, for thousands of years, have historically valued education and are more inclined than others to support a tax increase if the money is earmarked for colleges and universities. Mormons have a

strong commitment to self-help and see the church as part of the family. They
believe that these two institutions, church and family, not the government,
should take care of individuals who have financial problems. Therefore, they
are not strong supporters of the current welfare system.

We conclude this section on religion by once again reminding you that all
your generalizations, whether about culture or religion, cannot always be
reliable. People are complex and are shaped by a variety of forces—religion is
just one of those forces. In addition, not all members of the same religion have
similar beliefs. Your own experience tells you that not all Catholics oppose
abortion, nor do all Muslims follow the Five Pillars of Islam. In short, your
audience analysis must include as many areas as possible so that when you
draw the profile of your listeners, it will be composed of a great many
characteristics.

Age-Level Characteristics

The Spanish writer Baltasar Gracian once noted that "at twenty the will
rules, at thirty the intellect, at forty judgment." Although this commentary is a
generalization, it nevertheless calls our attention to the notion that, at different stages of life, individuals are apt to have different concerns and interests.
As we accumulate a personal history, naturally we change. Knowing about
those changes and how they influence listeners should be part of audience
analysis.

Persuasive Issues. A great many research studies and public opinion polls
have revealed the impact of age on a number of issues. That is to say, studies
confirm that older people are more inclined to become entrenched in their
opinions and, hence, are much harder to persuade, while younger people are
much more open to persuasion. Growing older also tends to make one more

*The age of an audience will help determine what subjects it is interested in. (Photo:
corbisimages.com)*

conservative. Hence, it is not surprising that many older people differ with the younger generation on subjects such as Social Security, Medicare, defense spending, pornography, censorship, and prayer in school.

Fund of Knowledge. The age of an audience will also help determine their fund of knowledge and what subjects they are interested in. An older audience will know more about John Wayne, Frank Sinatra, "Howdy Doody," the AARP (American Association for Retired People), "Watergate," and "boat people" than will a group of high school students. Therefore, in selecting examples you need to take the age of the audience into consideration. References to MTV and the people who appear on that channel might well be confusing to older adults, who seldom watch that channel. On the other hand, analogies and examples that refer to "the folly of the Tet offensive" and "similar to the long lines to purchase gasoline in 1973" would be baffling to most young people.

Use of Language. The age level of your audience can be an important determinant of the kind of language most appropriate in your speech. The meanings attributed to words such as "chill out," "blast," "cool," "stoned," "pits," "awesome," "wasted," and "don't have a cow" are clearly related to age.

Needless to say, there can be many exceptions to any generalization about a given age group. By and large, however, a group of older persons differs in attitudes and experiences from a group of young persons. After all, there is an old saying that a forty-year-old has been sixteen, but a sixteen-year-old has not been forty. Put in slightly different terms, someone who served in the military in World War II might have a difficult time understanding why some young people refused to "serve their country."

Gender Characteristics

In recent years there has been a growing awareness that gender plays a key role in how people perceive and interact in the world. While men and women share many common experiences, goals, values, and the like, they are different in many ways. This condition has important implications for public speaking. A speaker who fails to consider the ratio of males to females in the audience when preparing and presenting a speech may not succeed in achieving his or her purpose. Thus, it is crucial to ask yourself these questions: Will my audience be an all-male or an all-female group? Will it be made up of mostly one sex, or will it be equally divided between the sexes?

Values. The answers to the two foregoing questions govern everything from your choice of a subject to the examples you decide to place in your speech. As indicated, the two sexes, although living in the same country, are often socialized in different ways. A person's gender propels her or him in both subtle and manifest ways, to behave according to certain cultural patterns. A few examples will emphasize this idea. Studies show that the sexes differ in how they rank certain cultural values. For example, women hold more traditional values regarding family and religion. Polls show that women often hold different attitudes than men on social issues such as the homeless, rape, defense spending, poverty, unwed mothers, child care, the death penalty, contraception, equal rights, affirmative action, and sexual harassment.

Stereotyping. Changes in our culture over the last 50 years have not only enabled women to share a wider range of experiences but have made many

❖ ❖ ❖ ❖

women highly conscious of the problems inherent in our culture's perception and treatment of women. For example, most women would be offended by a male speaker who referred to them as "girls." A speaker's credibility could also suffer if, by his or her examples and illustrations, female roles were portrayed in a demeaning light. Imagine how offended most women would be if a speaker, talking about the need to exercise, used the following appeal:

> It is time for all you little ladies to get out of the kitchen. Take off those high spiked heels and get yourself some running shoes. Exercise will not only give you the girlish figure, but it will help you get a man.

There are, of course, other examples that demonstrate a lack of awareness with regard to gender issues. To speak as if only men were governors, judges, engineers, or corporation heads while only women were schoolteachers, nurses, or homemakers is an example of insensitivity that could lower a speaker's credibility. Also, humor that returns to old stereotypes that characterized women as vain and "empty headed" is insulting and must be avoided. I recently heard a speaker make the following attempt at being humorous:

> You know how you can tell men from ladies now that they both wear pants? It is easy. The one doing all the talking is the woman.

Even though a speaker must be aware of differences in experiences shaped by culture, he or she must also be aware of similarities and try to avoid stereotyping. In recent years, the behaviors and attitudes of women have undergone a major transformation. In areas of sexual relations, education, and employment, the sexes have grown closer together. They now share a number of common experiences in sports, language, occupations, and politics. In short, be careful when making sweeping generalizations regarding gender.

An effective speaker must be aware of gender differences and consider the ratio of males to females in an audience. (Photo: indexstock.com)

Occupational Characteristics

A speaker can often gain clues to a listener's values, attitudes, and even sense of humor from what he or she does for a living. The rationale behind the importance of occupation is based on two closely related assumptions. First, *people have certain personality characteristics that draw them to one career over another.* The traits that make someone a good engineer are different from the attributes associated with being a divorce attorney or welfare worker. Second, *being a member of an occupational group usually means adopting, either consciously or unconsciously, many of the values associated with that profession.* Remember, most people spend eight to ten hours a day on the job. Someone who is a teacher might see things differently than a doctor, professor, steelworker, restaurant owner, rancher, computer programmer, or fashion designer.

Whether you are preparing an informative or a persuasive speech, you should ask yourself this question: Is the occupation of my audience related in any way to what I am going to talk about? For example, a construction worker would most likely know about framing a house, while a genetic engineer might have little experience with the terms, tools, and mechanics of construction. It should be remembered that occupation often influences much more than a listener's fund of knowledge. Polls show that there is a direct link between occupation and current events. Business executives are apt to be concerned with tax regulations, government controls, and unemployment. Schoolteachers are interested in issues related to class loads, community funding, academic freedom, literacy, and multicultural education.

In many instances, audiences are made up of people from a variety of occupational backgrounds. Knowing those backgrounds enables a speaker to locate the points shared by the majority of the listeners. Remember, however, that in times of national economic distress many people are not fortunate enough to work at the job for which they were trained. Making generalizations about them based on their temporary jobs, or jobs they have been forced to take, may be misleading.

Educational Characteristics

Suppose you were invited to talk about your college or university at an assembly of "students." Very likely, you would ask, What is meant by "students"? First graders? Seventh graders? Graduating seniors? Graduate students? Their educational level would dictate your approach to language, examples, evidence, interest factors, and the like.

Like so much of the demographic data we have discussed in this chapter, the educational level of your potential audience can be reflected in a number of ways. First, polls have demonstrated a link between an interest in current events and a high level of education. For example, well-educated people tend to be more health conscious and more interested in environmental issues than are people who have not gone to college. Second, the educational level of your listeners might also influence how much they know about your topic. In most instances, the more education one has, the larger is one's fund of knowledge. You know from your own experience that the more you go to school, the more you learn. Finally, your choice of ideas, concepts, and people you allude to must be modified according to your listeners' levels of education. Nearly

❖ ❖ ❖ ❖

everyone has heard of poet Bob Dylan, but recognizing poet Dylan Thomas may take some formal education. The same discernment may be called for with countless other specific references. We all know that for Muslims God is Allah, yet it is only through education that we learn the importance of the Five Pillars of Islam and the specific role Muhammad plays in this religion. In short, with education comes information.

The type of education your audience has should also be considered. Someone with a Ph.D. in physics has a different pool of information than does an individual with a degree in English literature. These types of data will help you decide what words need defining and what words the audience will automatically understand.

Educational levels might also influence the types of arguments you present to support your assertions. For example, some evidence suggests that for highly educated people it is best to offer both sides of the argument when delivering a persuasive speech. It is important not to overestimate or underestimate the education of your listeners. In either case, the cycle of communication can be broken if there is a lack of understanding. Moreover, it is good to remember that education acquired through practical experience, as well as through formal schooling, helps determine what your audience members think about and how they tend to react.

Before ending this section on education, we need to note the link between culture and education. For instance, when compared with students in the United States, students in Korea, Japan, and Germany have almost three more years of education by the time they graduate from high school. In addition, cultures often stress different subjects as part of their educational curriculum. In much of Europe, the emphasis is on history, language, and literature. In Japan, China, and other Asian cultures, the accent is on science. In Mexico, education focuses on folklore and the arts. In short, finding out what your audience knows, or does not know, needs to be part of your audience analysis.

Group Characteristics

A Spanish proverb notes, "Tell me with whom you live and I will tell you who you are." We might alter this maxim to read, "Tell me with whom you associate and I will tell you who you are." The point is obvious: the people with whom we affiliate, whether family members or fellow members of a group, can be a reflection of who we are, what we believe in, and what interests us. Hence, part of audience analysis should include an examination of the civic, social, political, and professional groups that hold sway over listeners. We see ourselves and others in terms of the roles we play, and the groups to which we belong contribute to the creation of these roles. As indicated, group membership suggests, in a general way, types of people, their points of view, their interests, their attitudes, and even their vocabulary.

The information you secure about your listeners' group affiliations has important implications for both informative and persuasive speeches. A member of Greenpeace is likely to know more about the harmful consequences of using driftnets than would a person belonging only to the Radio Amateur's League. A person's general fund of knowledge seems to be directly related to how he or she spends time. Whether we belong to the American Society of Mechanical Engineers, the National Organization for Women, the

Sierra Club, the National Rifle Association, the International Backpackers' Association, or the Young Republicans, our group affiliation tells other people something about us and what we deem important.

In your class, you must also attempt to discover the groups that your colleagues affiliate with. You might try to determine what clubs they belong to (Ski Club, Campus Crusade for Christ, Debate Team, International Students Society, etc.) and what college majors are represented in class (psychology, education, computer science, etc.).

Geographical Characteristics

If you have traveled throughout the United States, you know that where people were raised and where they live can help mold their beliefs, values, and actions. The Deep South is as different from New York City as Montana is from Beverly Hills. Whether you live in a location by design or by chance, the place of your residence will expose you to certain topics and deny you others. A small rural high school, with its 4-H programs and agricultural classes, offers experiences quite different from those of students attending a large high school in a densely populated urban area. Interests and attitudes—and what you know and do not know—are partly shaped by geographic circumstances. A person from a fishing village in Maine, who makes a living by catching fish, might well have a different concept of the ocean than a person who rides a surfboard in Malibu Beach in southern California. When an Oklahoma rancher refers to "my neighbors," he or she may be thinking of distances that would seem anything but neighborly to a person living in the middle of Manhattan Island. The notions of gun control and farm supports certainly have different meanings in Texas than in San Francisco. People in San Diego, California, have a different view of military base closures than does someone from an area that does not have a military garrison. And if you are from a small town in Indiana, your view of unemployment might be significantly different from that of a person from a larger city.

Special Characteristics

Homogeneous Groups. You might face some occasions when your listeners are, for the most part, a homogeneous group, having the same age, gender, college major, vocational background, religion, and the like. In these instances, the content of your speech might be accepted by the majority of your audience. You could also find yourself in situations in which one common interest unites the audience. That shared special interest may be a passing one (wanting to learn about treating snake bites prior to a camping trip), or it may be something permanent (wanting to know the best ways to maintain good health). In any case, as part of your audience analysis, you should locate that area of common interest and adapt your speech to it. The audience may consist of residents of the same dormitory. To disregard this type of information—especially if the audience deems the affiliation to be important—might be perceived as an insult to the group.

Groups With Disabilities. In recent years it has become apparent that disabled persons are an active group in our society—a group that is not only large (7 percent of the population) but vocal and dynamic. The passage of the Americans with Disabilities Act was a sort "bill of rights" for this group of people. This act made it much easier for people with disabilities to take part in of many activities that they had previously been denied, including having access to certain facilities. When you are going to speak in a situation where people with disabilities will be present, it is important to be sensitive to their specialized needs. Keep the following two points in mind. First, do not make the mistake of treating someone's disability as a mental limitation. Too often members of the general population treat people with disabilities as if they were little children or mentally impaired. I have even seen speakers using an abnormal voice when speaking to people who are blind. Second, if there are going to be deaf people in the audience, try to have someone who knows sign language at your side so that she or he can serve as an interpreter during your talk.

Gathering Information About Your Audience

Now that you are alerted to some of the factors that influence an audience, factors that you need to consider before you make your predictions about how the audience will respond to you and your message, you are probably wondering, *how do I gather the information to make those predictions?* Before we explore some sources of information, we should examine two factors that will direct the way you gather data. First, *there are time constraints that limit your efforts to identify your audience's beliefs and values.* The amount of time you are given to prepare your talk—whether one minute or one month—is often out of your control. Second, *the availability of information obviously has an impact on your investigation.* At times data about your audience will be available from a number of sources, yet on other occasions you might be talking to complete strangers. When information is not accessible you might have to rely heavily on educated guesses, common sense, and speculation. If you are fortunate enough to have sufficient time to conduct your analysis, some of the following sources will help you discover the composition of your audience.

Before the Speech

Shared Affiliations. If you share membership in some of the same groups as the audience, you can gather information directly. For instance, if you are active in environmental issues, you can understand some of the topics that interest an audience of the college recycling club. If you are talking to members of your class, you also share common experiences that you can call on. Being a member of a specific ethnic group also enables you to understand the backgrounds of an audience should the majority of your listeners be from this same group. Speakers addressing members of their company or organization are yet another example of sharing mutual interests and experiences that can help in the construction of the audience profile.

Public Opinion Polls. Published opinion polls yield information about your audience's interests, beliefs, attitudes, values, needs, motives, and the like. Results of polls such as the Gallup Report, CBS/New York Times, Harris, CNN/USA Today, and Roper appear regularly on television and in newspapers and magazines. They offer information regarding specific groups' views on issues such as inflation, welfare, race relations, military spending, capital punishment, federal aid to education, term limits, gun control, drugs, and teenage pregnancy. These polls are often categorized by specific characteristics such as education, race, gender, age, and the like. By using these polls, you can learn a great deal about prospective audiences.

Attitude Scales. There might be some special occasions when you can find out about your listeners by giving them an information or attitude pretest. This is a questionnaire or attitude scale that tries to determine what an audience knows and/or believes before you start your speech. These tests and scales can be administered minutes, hours, or even days before you give your speech. In most cases, the tests can tell you a great deal about your audience, making adaptation much easier.

The three most widely used questionnaires (forced-choice, scale, and open-ended) are actually rather easy to construct.

Forced-Choice Questionnaire. This type of questionnaire offers fixed choices.

Have you ever considered donating an organ to another person?

Yes_____

No_____

Not sure_____

Scale Questionnaire. Scale questionnaires allow for more latitude in responses given to the question.

Have you ever considered donating an organ to another person?

Never _____   Occasionally _____   Often _____

Open-ended Questionnaire. This particular form allows the person an opportunity to write down their specific response.

What is your opinion concerning organ transplants?

_____

_____

_____

Interviews. An interview can produce valuable information concerning your audience. Information-gathering interviews are useful because you can directly question the people to whom you will be talking. You can ask individual members or a group of members about their views on various topics. You can also interview various individuals who may not be potential audience members but are familiar with the audience. Their observations could help you harmonize your information with the audience's fund of knowledge and belief system. The chapter on conducting research (chapter 8) offers you some specific advice on how to conduct effective information-gathering interviews.

During the Speech

All the methods just described deal with gathering information before the speech begins. However, there are many instances when you can collect information about the audience during the speech. Because being able to

It is important to analyze the occasion and the setting as well as the audience. (Photo: Gloria Thomas)

adapt to the speaking situation is one of the hallmarks of a successful communicator, it is important that you develop this skill. To help you, let us briefly look at (1) gathering verbal information, (2) gathering nonverbal information, and (3) using the information you have collected.

Verbal Information. You might find it useful to conduct your audience analysis during the speech by simply asking questions. For example, you might ask for a show of hands as a means of detecting audience attitudes toward your topic. The question "How many of you believe admission requirements at this university are too restrictive?" would reveal how some members of your audience feel about this issue. You could also ask for verbal responses to the same question. This information, whether through raised hands or verbal answers, lets you tailor your talk to the group.

Nonverbal Information. Experienced speakers also use very subtle nonverbal messages during the speech to help them with their audience analysis. They interpret listeners' eye contact, facial expressions, restless movement, and the like and can decide if these behaviors are indicating confusion, disinterest, lack of understanding, anger, frustration, or some other emotion.

Using Audience Responses. Sensitivity to the mood of the audience gives experienced speakers the information to make the necessary changes in their speech. They might employ some of the following techniques when trying to adapt to what their "on-the-spot" audience analysis discovered:

- Adding interesting examples and stories.
- Directly arousing the listless members of the audience.
- Altering the rate of delivery.
- Using more humor.
- Walking toward the audience.
- Pausing in a dramatic way.
- Personalizing their information.

- Changing the organizational sequence during the speech.
- Repeating key ideas.
- Writing important points on the blackboard.

In conclusion, you should beware of potential pitfalls associated with conducting an audience analysis. Speakers must be vigilant when making demographic generalizations. People are complex and unique. We are all much more than our gender, race, age, culture, profession, religion, education, and the like say about us. Thus, although speakers can benefit from doing a detailed audience analysis, they must also remember that no single characteristic defines who and what a person is.

Analyzing the Speaking Occasion

In our attempt to discover as much information as possible about our listeners, we must not lose sight of the fact that the circumstances under which we will be presenting the speech will play a vital role in determining its outcome. As was pointed out in chapter 1, communication does not take place in a vacuum. The role and influence of the (1) occasion, (2) setting, and (3) time constraints must be considered. Common sense tells you that your attire, topic selection, language, and overall demeanor are partially controlled by the occasion, in which you share a time-space continuum with other people. In addition, the cultural make-up of the audience must be taken into account when analyzing the occasion and setting.

Kind of Occasion

When considering the occasion that brings forth your speech, you should ask yourself some of the following questions:

- Have the people gathered only to hear my speech, or do they meet on a regular basis?
- What will the audience be doing before I talk? After I talk?
- Is it a spontaneous gathering?
- Will the procedure follow certain well-established traditions?
- Will the occasion be formal or informal?
- Will the occasion be a panel discussion or a "stand up" speech?
- Will the audience be permitted to respond to me?
- How many people will be present to hear my talk?
- Are there certain rituals and protocols that I should be aware of?

Physical Surroundings

Analyzing the physical setting involves being able to answer the following questions:

1. Is the speech being delivered indoors or outside?

2. Will I need an extension cord for my slide projector, VCR, or other electronic visual aids?

3. Will there be a table and/or a podium?

4. Will the speech be in a very large auditorium or a small room? In a television studio or before a "live" audience?

5. Will people be sitting in circles or in rows?

6. How effective are the acoustics of the room or hall?

7. Will there be a public-address system?

8. What will the lighting arrangements be like if I want to use a VCR, transparency projector, or other visual tool?

9. How close will I be to my audience?

10. Will there be noises or outside distractions that might disturb my audience?

11. Will there be barriers that I must remove so that people in wheel-chairs can have access to the facility?

Answers to questions like these also influence the way you deliver your talk. For example, if there are only a few people in the audience and it is an informal gathering, you do not need to use the same volume level as if it were a large room with many people. Even your gestures and movements have to be adjusted to the physical surroundings. Also, if you use a microphone to amplify your voice, it will restrict your ability to move around the room or the platform. (Later chapters discuss the constraints imposed by microphones and television cameras.)

Time

What time of the day or night will the speech be delivered? Personal experience tells you that most people are more vigorous and energetic in the day than they are at night. Hence, ask yourself if the listeners will be tired or alert because of the clock. In addition, part of analyzing the occasion means that you discover how long you are excepted to talk. You might be assigned an amount of time or you could face an "open-ended" situation. In either case, you need to deal with questions concerning time long before you start conducting your research or preparing your outline.

Culture and the Occasion

The audience's culture might also have impact on the occasion and setting. For example, people from cultures that are very ritualistic and formal, such as the Japanese and German, perceive a business meeting very differently than does someone from the United States. Mixing business and pleasure is the exception, not the rule, in formal cultures. Knowing these and other cultural differences will enable you to make the necessary adjustments to your delivery and content should you be speaking to an audience composed of people from these cultures.

Adapting to Your Audience

Plato once wrote that "No law or ordinance is mightier than understanding." He, of course, was talking about understanding other people. This same point weaves in and out of every chapter in this book and will continue to be a major theme. The idea is a simple one: human communication demands that the sender of a message knows the receiver so that he or she can predict how that person will respond to a particular message. In our everyday encounters all of us carry around in our minds images of other persons, and we take these images into account whenever we speak. This idea, as we have stressed in this chapter, applies as well to a public-speaking situation: *You need to understand your communication partners, whether those partners are two in number or two million.* If you can understand the ideas and feelings of your listeners, you greatly increase the chance that you will be able to find out their attitudes, desires, backgrounds, interests, and goals.

As mentioned previously, to project yourself into others' personalities requires having a correct image of each person. Who is he or she? What are they like? What are they feeling? How can I better understand them? As emphasized during this entire chapter, to answer these types of questions you need to gather data about the other person or persons. As you would suspect, once you have gathered that information, there are certain behaviors that can help you adapt your material to specific audiences. The paragraphs below mention a few positive actions you can take that will demonstrate to the audience that you understand who they are.

Ask Rhetorical Questions

Although rhetorical questions are discussed in detail later in the book, they need to be introduced at this point because they represent an excellent means of adapting to your audience.

Rhetorical questions are worded in such a manner that they call for a mental response but not a vocal one. If I were to write "Have you ever wondered what it would be like to travel in a space vehicle?" your mind would almost automatically think about the answer to the question. As a means of fitting your rhetorical question to your immediate audience, you would phrase the questions to show that you were aware of their experiences and background. For example, if you were speaking to a group of students about parking problems on campus, you might involve them mentally by asking some of the following rhetorical questions: "How many of you often arrive on campus only to find that all the parking spaces are filled?" "Do you ever find yourself entering a class after it has already begun simply because you could not find a place to park your car?"

Focus on the Audience

❖ ❖ ❖ ❖

It is wise for a speaker to be sensitive to the factors that can make an audience feel comfortable. If you are thinking constantly about yourself, it is difficult to concentrate on cues from other persons. A successful communicator is aware of others, cares about them, and is not preoccupied with thoughts about himself or herself. This is indeed a very difficult assignment, for, as the German proverb states, "Everyone thinks that all the bells echo his own thoughts." In short, constant self-focus hinders the adaptation process.

Use Personal Pronouns

You can demonstrate a direct link to your audience by using personal pronouns. You distance yourself from your listeners when you use words such as "they" or "people." For example, to say "People realize campus parking is a serious problem" is not nearly as personal as saying "All of us know that parking on this campus is a serious problem." Therefore, learn to speak in terms of "you," "us," "we," and "our."

Use the Experiences of the Audience

One of the most effective ways to use the data from your audience analysis is to have your examples come directly from the experiences of the listeners. For example, when you use hypothetical illustrations, the audience and what you have learned about them should be woven into your stories. If you were going to give a speech on interviewing techniques and you learned that the audience was composed of graduating seniors who were about to search for jobs, you could use the following hypothetical illustration:

> Well, now is the big day. You start by putting on the new outfit you bought for this special occasion. After you finish dressing you look in the mirror and decide you look pretty good. You now leave your house and drive downtown for the job interview that means the most to you; this is the position you have been after since you started college. As you are sitting in the outside lobby waiting to be called into the office, you begin to ask yourself some questions about the upcoming interview—questions ranging from what is correct protocol for a job interview to what sort of questions you will be asked. As the moment for the interview draws closer, your anxiety increases. I am here today to relieve some of that anxiety. That is, I want to talk to you today about the employment interviews you will all be facing in the next few months.

Summary

The process of adapting one's speech purpose to a particular group of people calls for very careful analysis of the target audience. Such an analysis will help a speaker make reasonable predictions about how the audience will respond both to the speaker as a person and to the speaker's message. Valuable insight into the audience's values, beliefs, attitudes, needs, wants, and desires can be gained from information about each listener's cultural background, religious characteristics, age, gender, occupation, education, group affiliations, geographical experiences, and special interests. Information about these matters can be derived from such sources as published opinion polls, reference books, computer searches, information and attitude pretests, and interviews. Interviews are especially useful for yielding crucial information. Useful information about the audience can also be gathered while the speech is being given. The speaker can use both verbal and nonverbal information to assess how the audience is reacting to his or her presentation.

An experienced speaker should also take time to analyze the speaking occasion. This investigation consists of questions related to the kind of occasion the speaker will be facing, what the physical surroundings will be, and what will precede and follow the speech.

By implementing the material gathered through an analysis of the audience and the occasion, a speaker can use the data collected to adapt to her or his listeners.

Concepts and Questions

1. As applied to public speaking, what is meant by the terms "audience analysis" and "adaptation"?

2. What special factors should be taken into consideration when speaking to members of a culturally diverse audience?

3. In what ways can you use your audience analysis during a speech? Be specific.

4. What are some ways you can gather information about a specific audience?

5. Why are cultural values an important area of consideration when you are conducting your audience analysis?

6. Explain how being aware of the audience's age might be an important consideration when gathering and presenting your information.

Activities and Exercise

1. Make a list of what you believe to be your most important values. Conduct an interview with someone from another culture and ask that person to discuss what he or she deems important. Then make a comparison of the two sets of values. How are they alike? How do they differ?

2. Listen to a speech given by a political figure. After the speech write a short essay that discusses how you believe the speaker used or did not use an audience analysis.

3. What factors would need to be considered if you were going to give the same speech to the following audiences?

   a. A group of high school seniors.

   b. Members of the city council.

   c. Your classmates in your speech class.

d. A group of senior citizens.

e. A group of local business leaders.

4. Design a survey that you could use to assess an audience's view of capital punishment.

5. Visit four settings that would all make different demands on a speaker's adjustment. Write a short essay discussing how you would adapt to each of these settings.

6. Attend three different speech situations (formal business presentation, classroom lecture, church sermon, political rally, award banquet, etc.). Write a short essay that discusses your view on how each speaker adapted to his or her audience and occasion. ✦

CHAPTER FOUR

Sound and Action: Presenting Your Ideas

❖ ❖ ❖ ❖

Suit the action to the word, and the
word to the action; with this special observance,
that you o'erstep not the modesty of nature.

—*William Shakespeare*

[handwritten margin note: Especially if not known to your audience]

The French author Paul Lorain once noted that a printed speech is like a dried flower: the substance, indeed, is there, but the color is faded and the perfume is gone. What he is telling us is rather simple—it is the presentation of your ideas that brings your speech to life. Regardless of how much research you conduct or how noble your mission, your delivery must be skillful or it can hinder your overall message and keep you from accomplishing your purpose.

The importance of speech delivery is obvious for a number of reasons. First, and perhaps most obvious, *the components of voice and body carry your ideas to your listeners.* As we noted in chapter 1 when we described the process of communication, your voice and your actions are the channels that move your thoughts to another human being. A famous American preacher, Alexander Gregg, once said that there are three things to aim at in public speaking: first, to get into your subject, then to get your subject into yourself, and lastly, to get your subject into your hearers. As we just mentioned, it is your delivery that "gets your subject into your hearers."

[handwritten margin note: Bring a pen w/ opinion piece to Read]

Second, *the manner in which you use the nonverbal elements of voice and body influences the audience's perception of you as a credible person as well as an effective speaker.* As pointed out in detail in chapter 14, in assessing credibility, personal image and delivery are directly linked. Nothing hurts a speaker's image more than a dull voice and listless bodily activity. If you appear to lack enthusiasm, you cannot expect an audience to be zestful about you or your topic.

Third, *your presentation is important because of the power of first impressions.* Remember, the audience makes a rapid judgment even before they hear you utter your first word. Part of their decision will be based on your posture, dress, accessories, poise, and the like. Should they, justly or unjustly, reach an unfavorable conclusion, your words might "fall on deaf ears."

Fourth, *your nonverbal behavior carries a strong emotional message.* Your face and body are perhaps better indicators of your emotional state than are your words. Even the sound of a voice carries important messages. The tenth century philosopher Tancred said much the same thing when he wrote, "There is no index of character so sure as the voice."

Finally, because nonverbal communication is far more universal than verbal communication, *cultural barriers can be crossed with actions such as smiling, pointing, waving, and the like.*

One important observation is in order before we begin dealing with the specifics of speech delivery. Because language is linear, this discussion treats the elements of delivery as separate entities, looking first at the visual aspects of presentation and then moving to the oral. This organization is of course misleading, for in reality your ideas are expressed by all parts of your body at the same time. Your tone of voice, volume, pitch, and rate are in operation at the same instant you are moving, gesturing, using eye contact, and using many other nonverbal elements. Therefore, even though we discuss the variables of delivery one at a time, it behooves you as a speaker to see to it that these elements blend harmoniously.

This chapter talks about the speaker's nonverbal behavior and the messages such behavior conveys largely from a North American point of view. Nonverbal behaviors carry different meanings for different cultures. This is especially true of learned behaviors such as gazing, gesturing, moving, using space, and manipulating the voice. Everyone learns when, where, and before whom they can show certain emotions according to the rules of their culture. The meanings we assign to another person's nonverbal behavior are influenced by what our culture says that behavior means. It is easy to see that misunderstandings can arise when people from different cultures interact in a communication situation. Therefore, be aware that we are going to talk about nonverbal behaviors as they tend to be viewed from a North American perspective. During the course of this chapter, we will explore some cultural variations that apply to nonverbal communication. This information will serve two purposes. First, it will allow you the option of adapting your delivery to culturally diverse audiences. Second, having a fund of knowledge on cultural differences in nonverbal communication will enable you to appreciate these differences when you are a member of the audience.

Let us turn now to an examination of the visual and aural dimensions of speech delivery.

Visual Dimensions of Presentation

As you give voice to your words, you also send a number of visual signals to your audience that may profoundly affect the way they react to your words. Your (1) general appearance, (2) facial expression, (3) eye contact, (4) movement, and (5) use of space all play key roles in determining the quality of the message the audience receives. Your awareness of each element's unique role in influencing listener reaction to your verbal message may help you avoid placing barriers in your path to effective communication.

General Appearance

Although you may not approve of the emphasis I place on appearance, it is nevertheless true that how we look influences what people think of us. The West African proverbs says the same thing a little differently when it tells us "A chicken with beautiful plumage does not sit in a corner." The person whose appearance is convincing is contributing to his or her chances of success. Remember that, in most instances, the audience will see you before they hear you. The way you are standing, the clothing you are wearing, the jewelry and accessories you are displaying, and your general grooming all contribute to that vital first impression. Let us examine some of the ways in which these elements of general appearance exert an influence.

Posture. Perhaps you have seen speakers who fit into the following categories. One speaker looks like a soldier standing rigidly at attention; another slouches as though all the burdens of the world have fallen on her shoulders; still another stands with feet placed comfortably apart and shoulders held straight (but not rigidly so). The first speaker's posture probably communicates tension, anxiety, and uncertainty; the slumping posture of the second speaker probably suggests resignation or a woeful lack of enthusiasm or energy; the posture of the third speaker may suggest a comfortable alertness. North American audiences are likely to react most favorably to the third posture, at least at the moment before the speaker utters the opening words of the speech. Before rendering a final judgment on what is the "right" posture, we need to account for the circumstances prompting the speech, the audience being addressed, the speaker's purpose, and the verbal message that accompanies the unspoken message of the speaker's posture. There is no single posture that is always right for all speakers on all subjects on all occasions; however, as a general guideline try to avoid the extremes of being too rigid or too sloppy. On the positive side you should aim for an even distribution of your body weight so you appear both poised and relaxed at the same time.

We explore the topic of posture later in this chapter, when discussing its relationship to the speaker's movements, but for now it is important to keep in mind that whatever posture you assume should be comfortable and natural without being too nonchalant. As noted earlier, public speaking is "extended conversation." Even though you are "only talking" to your audience, nevertheless you have to make some alterations because of the situation—posture is one of those alterations.

Apparel. Benjamin Franklin once offered the following advice: "Eat to please thyself, but dress to please others." Although this caveat might be a slight overstatement, nevertheless it indicates the importance of apparel in human interaction. In fact, in every culture, the way people dress plays a role in how others perceive them. We all make generalizations about speakers from the clothes they wear, the objects they keep on their person, and their general grooming habits. Rightly or wrongly, we judge people by their appearance. "His head's shaved and he's wearing heavy boots; he must be one of those skinheads we've been reading about." "That person over there is wearing a Brooks Brothers suit; must be an executive." "Guess she's really concerned about physical fitness; she's wearing a health club sweatshirt." Once the person begins speaking to us we often have to reexamine our tentative label—although this initial reaction was part of our first impression. We often find out that the label doesn't fit after all. "Well, I'll be darned! She doesn't look like a ship's captain." "He's a college president? You've got to be kidding. He's wearing an old T-shirt, ragged jeans, and sandals." Regardless of the validity of generalizations drawn by listeners on the basis of the speaker's apparel and grooming, the point is that generalizations are drawn, and the speaker should be ready to accept the consequences.

Throughout, this book stresses the idea that a successful communicator is able to adapt to the audience, the occasion for the speaking event, and the particular setting. Therefore, it is difficult to prescribe dress or grooming that is appropriate for all situations. Common sense, however, tells you that in general terms you should be well groomed and neat. For specific standards of appearance, it is up to you to become familiar with the audience's expectations. Also remember that the standards the audience sets, and the judgments audience members make about the speaker's compliance with those stan-dards, are subject to cultural variations. In one culture, robes and a veil might be the correct attire, while in another a black formal suit would be considered proper dress. In short, your grooming and apparel, like your posture, should be compatible with your subject, purpose, audience, and occasion.

How we dress not only sends numerous messages to our audience, it also contributes to our self-image and self-confidence. You know from personal experience that when you feel good about the way you look, it usually puts you in a positive mood. This mood will be transmitted to the audience and help you accomplish your overall purpose.

Facial Expression

Because this is a book about public speaking and not about acting, it is somewhat awkward to talk about facial expressions. Yet some of the most revealing visual signals come from the face. From a speaker's facial expres-sion, be it a warm smile or a serious grimace, we listeners form impressions of the speaker's attitude toward us, toward himself or herself, and toward the subject matter. The expression may tell us, "I like you people," "I'm really enthusiastic about my topic," and "I believe what I'm saying," or it may tell us just the opposite. It may depict a wide range of emotions from fear to confi-dence, from joy to sadness. Tiny subtleties of expression, of which we may be unaware, tell us that one speaker's animation is sincerely motivated but that another's is feigned. It is probably no coincidence that a speaker who lacks facial expression generally lacks visual and vocal animation. If this paucity of animation stems from apathy toward the ideas being expressed, the solution would seem to be to abandon the speech rather than to fake a display of ani-mation. For although the affected or counterfeited animation might tempo-rarily gain the listeners' attention, they would probably become conscious of the affectation rather than the ideas of the speech. On the other hand, if the lack of animation results from inhibition rather than from apathy, then the answer lies essentially in placing oneself in the proper psychological attitude. What is important to keep in mind is that if the setting of your speech and your ideas warrant it, you should not keep the same facial expression throughout your talk. Your face is capable of many "expressions." As the poet Rainer Maria Rilke once noted, "There are quantities of human beings, but there are many more faces, for each person has several."

Eye Contact

The importance of eye contact was eloquently captured by Ralph Waldo Emerson when he wrote, "One of the most wonderful things in nature is a glance of the eye; it transcends speech; it is the bodily symbol of identity." Some writers in the area of human communication maintain that eye contact with our communication partners is the single most significant of all the com-ponents of delivery. Their rationale is a simple one. Our eyes are capable of sending innumerable messages. They tell others when our communication channels are open and when we wish to terminate or avoid communication. They say something of our emotional state, be it elation or depression, interest or boredom, trust or suspicion, love or hatred. The quality of interpersonal relationships is often signaled by the kind of eye contact taking place. Eye

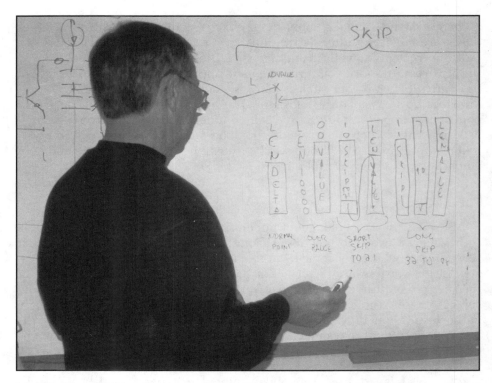

It is difficult to establish and maintain rapport with your audience if you avoid eye contact. (Photo: Gloria Thomas)

contact also reveals information concerning status, relationships, interest, motivation, anxiety, and many other factors that are in operation during communication.

In using eye contact, you should try to keep three simple ideas in mind. First, establish eye contact with your audience *before* you begin talking. Second, look at *everybody*. Finally, *sustain your eye contact* for a few seconds before you move on to another member of the audience.

We conclude our discussion of eye contact by once again reminding you to "keep in touch" with your listeners by looking at them. As indicated, this allows you to show interest and enthusiasm. And, of course, eye contact is essential if we want to monitor the audience's reaction to our message. By "seeing" their reaction, and adjusting to it, we can alter both our presentation and our content.

Movement

There are two important yet often overlooked points regarding people's use of nonverbal communication. We all engage in some bodily actions that are intentional and some that are unintentional or spontaneous. Intentional movements are those that we use consciously and with purpose. A gesture that sees you pointing your arm and finger toward the window in your classroom while you say, "I ask you to notice how polluted the sky over our city looks at this time," is an example of intentional movement. Being animated while you talk, without even being aware of your enthusiasm, would be an instance of employing unintentional movements. The following section talks

❖ ❖ ❖ ❖

Dynamic speakers often move around their audience.

about both types of movement. Although the text often discusses one movement or gesture at a time, they usually work in combination, not in isolation.
Therefore, as you read the discussion of movement in the next few pages, try
to think of your entire body, including your voice and your words, working as
a single integrated unit.

   Movement and Attention. Imagine that you are gazing at a serene lake
somewhere far from the city. Your eyes take in the glassy smoothness of the
water but do not focus on any particular object. Suddenly, the placid surface
of the lake is broken by a leaping fish. Instantly, your eyes are riveted to the
spot. The motion of the fish and the splashing of the water have captured your
complete attention. Now try an experiment. Look up from this page for a
moment. Is there anything in particular that immediately seizes your attention, or does your gaze rove about at random? There is a good chance that if
something in your field of vision were to move, you would notice it, and you
would probably continue to look at it until a more powerful stimulus drew
your attention elsewhere. The point is simple—movement draws and holds
attention.

   Many applications of this attention factor are obvious. A motion picture
attracts attention more quickly than a still picture. A blinking image on a
computer screen displaying a web page gets our attention before printed
words. A still picture that depicts action attracts attention more quickly than
one that depicts a static situation. A flashing neon sign attracts us more
quickly than a steadily glowing sign. The movement causes us to focus our
eyes and, thus, our attention on the object.

   Given the speaker's power to intensify listener attention through appropriate bodily action, we are unwise not to use it. In fact, our natural impulse is
to use it. Bodily movement during the communicative act is a natural, spontaneous response to our own uttered thoughts, the reactions of the listener, and
the impact of the occasion. In most informal, unstructured communication
situations, we use movement freely, without inhibition. We are not even con-

scious of using it because it accompanies our utterances so naturally. Public-speaking situations, on the other hand, frequently impose restraints that inhibit us from our natural impulse to move. We root ourselves in one spot (usually behind a lectern) and remain there for the duration of the speech. We grip the lectern or thrust our hands in our pockets or otherwise immobilize them so that they cannot be used for meaningful, spontaneous gestures. Thus, we deprive ourselves of an important means of reinforcing our verbal message and of successfully competing with the other stimuli fighting to gain the listeners' attention.

Facilitating Movement. When circumstances suggest that meaningful bodily action will add impact to your verbal message, you should adopt a bodily position that encourages (or at least does not inhibit) easy, spontaneous movement. If the occasion calls for a formal stand-up speech, your movements are likely to be largely gestural. When you and your audience are in proximity, changes in your facial expression may be the only movements needed. Whatever the case, you would do well to place yourself in a position that does not immobilize the muscles you need for easy use of your hands and arms and that does not inhibit facial expressions.

Perhaps we can determine the characteristics of an appropriate stance for a stand-up speech if we reexamine the postures discussed earlier. A slouch tends to inhibit movement of the entire body from one location to another within the speaking area because you must first return to a position of equilibrium before you can move easily to the right or left, toward or away from the listeners. Thus, you take the path of least resistance and remain in the slouch. The "soldier at attention" posture encourages movement but of the wrong kind, a nervous, rocking motion that can call so much attention to itself that it overrides the verbal message. The last posture we discussed, the alert posture, probably provides the best starting point for meaningful movement. Many speakers find it easier to move from that posture when they feel it necessary. However, the best advice is to experiment with a variety of positions and make an honest appraisal of each.

Types of Movement. The number of movements involved in nonverbal communication can be staggering. It has been estimated that people are capable of using over half a million physical signs. To examine each of them individually in this book is an obvious impossibility, so we have to talk about them in terms of major groups. For purposes of analysis, I am going to group them into (1) those that involve movements of the whole body from one location to another on the speaking platform and (2) those that involve motions of the arms, head, and shoulders.

Movement of the entire body. Have you noticed that when speakers make a verbal transition from one point to another in a speech, they often move from one location on the platform to another? Picture yourself saying, "Now that we've examined the causes of the problem, let's take a look at some of the possible solutions." Doesn't such a statement beg for an accompanying movement of the body to reinforce what is being said? Very likely such a transitional movement would be to your left or right because, in the North American culture, lateral movements tend to be associated with a change from one group of related ideas to another. Sometimes, this transitional movement is as subtle as a shift of weight from one foot to the other.

When you move toward the audience, you seem to be suggesting (nonverbally) that you want to emphasize what you are saying or that you wish to take the listeners into your confidence. "Now listen to this," you say as you lean toward a companion in conversation or as you take a step toward the audience in a public-speaking situation. Feelings of warmth, friendship, and rapport tend to be suggested by such actions, especially when the speaker appears to be relaxed rather than tense or stiff.

Movement of the upper body. Almost daily, we make use of hand gestures, sweeping movements of the arms, shoulder thrusts, and head nods, which carry standardized meanings for the majority of our population. A wave of the hand substitutes for "hello" or "good-bye." We signal disapproval by folding our arms across our chest and shaking our head from side to side. We shrug our shoulders while we turn our palms upward to communicate "I don't know." Such conventionalized behaviors, called emblems, are a part of our everyday interactions with others of our culture. However, although such signals are common to one culture, they may carry different meanings (or no meanings) for other cultures. One study revealed that 20 common hand gestures carried different meanings for each of 40 cultures. The gesture made in the United States to signal "everything is fine" or "OK" (an "O" performed with the thumb and index finger) is likely to be interpreted as a sign of hostility in the Arab world, as a vulgar expression in Mexico, as an indication of monetary significance in the Far East, and as a way of saying "I'll kill you" in Tunisia. Sensitivity to cultural variations in the interpretation of gestures is important as you move into speaking situations involving audiences composed of mixed cultures.

It is reassuring to note that there are thousands of gestures and movements that hold a common meaning for all people. The simple fact that we can usually understand the behaviors of the actors in a foreign film shows the extent to which body language is universal; it has the power to heighten attention and to intensify the meaning conveyed by the spoken word.

Most of us acquire a number of inhibitions when we have to appear before an audience. These inhibitions are simply the manifestation of a response to a strange situation. We become tense, as we do in any fearful situation. The same hands that move about so freely and effortlessly when we converse with a friend suddenly are bound by an invisible force. Our first impulse is to get them out of sight, so we thrust them into our pockets (where they will probably jingle coins and keys), we lock them behind our backs, we clasp them together in front of us in the so-called fig-leaf position, or we grip a lectern until our knuckles whiten. This may well be one reason why it does not feel natural to gesture at such times: we have placed our hands and ourselves in a position that inhibits free, spontaneous movement.

Just as it is wise to adopt a posture, or stance, that will not inhibit you from moving from one location to another on the platform, it is also wise to adopt a "starting position" for your hands and arms that does not inhibit their movement. The best thing to do is to keep your hands and arms unencumbered. Then, when you feel a spontaneous urge to gesture, your hands and arms can move naturally into motion.

Some Guidelines in the Use of Movement. We examine here a few guidelines for using movement in public speaking.

Bodily action should be sincerely motivated. To gesture effectively, we must feel like gesturing. That is, our movements should be natural and sincere. If we force ourselves into action, the listener can usually detect the artifice, equating it with insincerity. If we perform planned actions, we run the

Bodily action should be sincerely motivated. (Photo: Jon Ferry/Daily Bruin)

risk of concentrating on the actions rather than on the ideas we are explaining. The conscious use of movements, gestures, and facial expressions should be reserved for practice sessions.

Bodily action should not be overused. Most of us habitually use certain actions for emphasis, but, if we are not careful, we overwork those actions to the point that the listener begins to notice the actions rather than the ideas they are supposed to emphasize. By cultivating a greater variety of actions during practice sessions, we will be less likely to overwork any one spontaneous action.

Bodily action should be appropriate for the occasion. A speech can be delivered in several ways, depending on the circumstances and the occasion. For example, if you are speaking in a large room where there is some distance between you and the most remote section of the audience, you will have to make your actions more pronounced so that they can be seen clearly. If you speak in a small, intimate room, your actions will be subtler (and probably fewer in number).

Bodily action should be appropriate to the audience. Later, this chapter talks about cultural differences as they relate to all aspects of nonverbal communication; for now it is important that you appreciate the idea that not all cultures use and interpret movement in the same manner. Therefore, you need to return to your audience analysis when you think about using movement. For example, if you know that a culture values a calm demeanor, then it would behoove you to show some constraint when gesturing.

Bodily action should not be random. The wrong kind of movement may impair the effectiveness of your verbal message. If you continually tap your pencil or drum your fingers on the speaker's stand, tug at your sleeve or collar frequently, rub your nose, or stroke your hair very often, these movements may eventually call attention to themselves and away from what you are saying. It is probably better to have no movement at all than to have such distracting movements. They are, after all, manifestations of nervous tension seeking release. The best way to avoid the buildup of this tension may be to use message-related movements, thus giving the tension a constructive outlet.

Bodily action should not be one-dimensional. You need to strive for variety in your movement. This means that you attempt to vary your gestures and that you try to alternate between walking and standing still.

The Use of Space

The silent messages conveyed by the physical distances separating communication partners are many and varied. As onlookers, we make judgments about the quality of a communication encounter partly on the basis of spatial cues. We surmise that there is cordiality or hostility, interest or disinterest, acceptance or rejection, depending on how close one person is to the other. We judge that people are lovers, enemies, close friends, strangers, bosses, or workers by the way they use space.

The study of using personal space as a means of communication is often referred to as **proxemics.** Proxemics is primarily concerned with how the distances between people send various messages. The distance you set up between you and your audience is contingent on a number of factors. For example, if you find yourself in a very small room, you will be much closer to your listeners than if you were in a large auditorium. It is important to remember that formality and "coldness" increase as you get farther away from your audience. On the other hand, getting too close to your listeners could make them feel uncomfortable. We all have personal space that surrounds us like an invisible bubble. If someone gets inside that bubble uninvited, we feel uneasy and even hostile.

This section's primary concern is how considerations of space relate to public speaking. The physical distance that separates you from your audience affects you in several ways. First, *it has an impact on your use of movements, hand gestures, and facial expressions.* If these nonverbal elements are to serve you properly, they must be seen. Therefore, the greater the distance between you and your listeners, the more exaggerated these visual factors must be. Second, *physical distance affects your use of voice.* If there is no public-address system available, you will probably have to talk louder and enunciate more distinctly as the distance increases between you and your audience. Third, *physical distance may affect your feeling of mental proximity to the audience.* It is more difficult to get mentally close to your listeners when a large space looms between you and them. Imagine trying to get an audience to enjoy your favorite joke when 20 rows of empty seats separate you and them. The audience also may feel alienated if too much distance separates them from you. Rapport, then, can be affected by spatial relationships. Remember that your management of spatial cues provides the audience with information by which to judge how you feel, your degree of confidence and authority, and your sincerity and enthusiasm.

❖ ❖ ❖ ❖   ## Visual Dimensions and Culture

Culture is all-pervasive. It influences our behavior in both obvious and subtle ways. The same is true of the nonverbal influences that are part of one's cultural heritage. Let us examine how some of those influences can be reflected in the public-speaking arena.

Posture. The effect of culture on posture during communication can be seen in a variety of ways. In North America, being spontaneous and casual is highly valued. It is not uncommon to see speakers reflecting these values in the way they stand. However, in cultures that are more formal (German, English, Swedish, Japanese), being too loose can result in an attitude of disrespect and can even lower one's credibility. In the four cultures just noted, even the simple act of placing one's hand in a pocket can be perceived as a sign of indifference.

Cultures also differ in the body orientations they assume during communication. Anyone who has interacted with Arabs realizes that they use a very direct body orientation when communicating. The Chinese, on the other hand, tend to feel uncomfortable with this style and will usually communicate, particularly with strangers, in a less direct stance.

Apparel. Clothing is also a reflection of both cultural values and a culture's approach to communication. In the United States, as we have already mentioned, being informal is highly valued. This value is often reflected in how people dress. It usually takes a very special occasion for men to wear suits and women to dress in clothes that call for high heels and hose. In other cultures, where formality is valued, such attire is worn on most occasions. In the Arab, Spanish, English, and German cultures, formal attire is appropriate even in very warm weather. If your audience is composed of members from these cultures, it would behoove you to dress in a rather formal and conservative manner.

Facial Expressions. It is good to remember that when and how facial expressions are displayed is subject to the dictates of one's culture. For example, Koreans, Japanese, and Chinese do not usually show outward signs of emotion through their faces. In fact, in these cultures people have learned to mask their emotions. Japanese men will even go so far as to hide expressions of anger, sorrow, or disgust by laughing or smiling.

In many Mediterranean cultures people take a very different view of facial expressions. In these cultures both men and women will be very animated when they speak and expect others to be expressive in their emotions. Within the United States, there are groups that use facial expressions in ways that differ from that of the majority of the population. Some Native American groups, for example, use far less facial animation than do other North Americans. Evidence also suggests that men and women use facial displays differently, with women displaying more facial animation and smiling than men do. Thus, in your role as either speaker or audience member, take into account the cultural norms of your communication partners.

The smile is yet another nonverbal expression that is rooted in culture. Even though smiling is a universal facial expression, the amount of smiling, the stimulus that produces the smile, and even what the smile is communicating often shift from culture to culture. In America, a smile can be a sign of happiness or friendly affirmation when used as a greeting. In Korean culture, too much smiling is often perceived as a sign of a shallow or insincere person.

In the Japanese culture the smile can mask emotion. What is important about these examples is that they call your attention to the idea that you must know something about the culture of the people you are speaking to so that you can adapt and adjust your delivery to meet specific cultural characteristics.

Eye Contact. Although people everywhere use eye contact for similar reasons, cultural norms govern the amount of eye contact a person can engage in and with whom. In the United States people expect direct eye-to-eye contact with their communication partners. In fact, we tend to hold suspect anyone who does not look directly at us; however, in certain other cultures, such directness of eye contact may be interpreted as a sign of disrespect. The Chinese, Koreans, and Japanese usually avoid sustained eye contact. Some Nigerians and Puerto Ricans also have been raised to think it is impertinent to have prolonged gazes. The same sort of socialization process often has Latino children avoiding eye contact as a sign of respect. At the other end of the spectrum, Arab culture subscribes to direct and prolonged eye contact as a sign of showing interest in the person with whom one is communicating.

The way in which the men and women of a culture relate to one another also has implications for eye contact. In some Middle Eastern cultures, women are not expected to look directly into the eyes of men. Accordingly, the men of those cultures respectfully avert their eyes from the women, in contrast to the directness of their gaze at other men. French and Italian men have no inhibitions about staring openly at women. Studies indicate that American women maintain more eye contact and hold eye contact longer with their communication partners than do American men.

So delicate is our use of eye contact that we seldom realize the modifications we make. For example, the next time you are talking to a disabled person, perhaps someone in a wheelchair, notice how little eye contact you make with him or her as compared with someone who is not disabled. As a speaker you must be aware of these nuances in eye contact so that you can include everyone in the audience in your gaze.

Movement. When we talked about movement earlier in the chapter, we were discussing the subject as it applied to the dominant culture in the United States. As discussed throughout this book, the influence of culture is echoed in nearly every aspect of human communication. For example, there are cultures (Arab, Jewish, Italian) in which a great deal of activity and animation is the norm; however, in many other cultures (Japanese, English, German), people are expected to be reserved in both manner and movement. There are even cultural differences in greeting behavior. Someone from Japan might bow as a way of first addressing an audience, while a person from India would find it appropriate to place both hands together just in front of his or her chest. It is important for you to become aware of some of these cultural variations so that you can adapt your delivery as you move from audience to audience.

We can also observe significant differences in the use of gestures by looking at co-cultures in the United States. For example, as compared to males, women tend to use fewer and smaller gestures. African Americans, because they value a lively and expressive communication style, display a much greater variety of movements than whites when communicating.

Space. The way we use and respond to space is colored by our cultural orientation. The people of cultures that stress individuality, for example, demand more personal space than do the people of cultures that are more communal. Thus, two friends conversing in the United States, Germany, Scotland, or Sweden might sit or stand farther apart than their counterparts in Israel, Greece, Mexico, Italy, and Brazil. It is not uncommon for students in Asian cultures to place themselves farther away from their teachers than do North American students. This added distance reflects their respect for teachers. The successful public speaker must be aware of these differences as he or she walks around the room and moves toward the various members of the audience. Some people may welcome the closeness while other might feel uncomfortable.

Aural Dimensions of Presentation

The classical rhetorician Aristotle wrote that "it is not enough to know what to say—one must know how to say it." He was, of course, referring to the importance of the vocal aspects of communication. We have already seen how part of the message you send to an audience is visual; however, it is ultimately by vocalized sound that the linguistic elements of your message are carried. Your voice does a lot more, though, than simply make your words audible to the audience; it enables you to impart different shades of meaning to those words. Your voice, like your posture, gestures, facial expressions, and movements, tells things about you quite apart from the verbal message you are uttering. Thus, you need to be aware of the voice's potential to help or hinder you in each communication endeavor.

The sound of your voice affects the audience's impression of you as a person. Your voice may tell the audience that you are from a particular socioeconomic class, that you hail from a particular part of the country, that you have a certain educational background, that you are in a particular emotional state, or that you have a specific attitude toward those being addressed.

As you read earlier, body movements and gestures can help hold an audience's attention. In like fashion, vocal movements—vocal variety—can help keep an audience attentive. If you fail to vary the pitch, loudness, rate, or quality of your voice, you may have difficulty sustaining audience attention for any appreciable length of time unless your verbal message is especially compelling. Naturally, your vocal variations should be properly motivated. It would be ludicrous, for example, to alter your rate of speaking just for the sake of gaining attention. That would only call attention to the artifice itself, not to your verbal message. No delivery technique should call attention to itself—it should direct attention to the message.

Whenever a speaker's vocal behavior fails to gain and hold attention, fails to enhance word meaning, or conveys an inaccurate impression of the speaker's personality, there is always the temptation to blame these shortcomings on nature. A popular lament is, "I just wasn't born with a good voice." To be sure, nature does impose limitations on us, and our vocal equipment may be inferior to that of someone else, but it is in the use of the vocal apparatus that we are more apt to find the cause of success or failure. Much of our vocal effectiveness depends on the way we control the (1) loudness (volume), (2) pitch, (3) quality, (4) rate, (5) distinctness (articulation), and (6) correctness (pronunciation) of the sounds we produce.

Loudness (Volume)

The first requisite of vocal sound is that it be loud enough for comfortable hearing. Listeners may be willing to exert extra effort to hear a person with a weak voice if that person has something compelling to say. Even so, it is likely that the sheer physical exertion of straining to hear the speaker will ultimately cause the listeners to abandon further effort.

Although attaining a comfortable volume should be our first concern, we must not overlook the need for changes in loudness level. By varying our loudness, and having a great deal of vocal variety, we enhance word meaning and sustain attention. A speech delivered without variations in loudness is analogous to a symphony played without crescendo or diminuendo. Without variations, the symphony and the speech would be boring and lifeless. Not only do changes in loudness give your speech vitality, they can be particularly helpful in giving emphasis to words or phrases. Uttering a word at an intensity level different from that used with the other words in a sentence directs audience attention to the word's importance. Such emphasis may be attained either by making the sound suddenly louder or by making it suddenly softer; recent research suggests that a sudden change to a softer level is apt to be the more effective means of emphasis.

Pitch

The musical scale of a piano ranges from very low notes, called bass notes, to very high notes, called treble notes. A piccolo, however, is much more limited in the spectrum of notes it can produce. Like a piano and a piccolo, your voice has its own pitch range. If someone tells you that you are a tenor, baritone, or soprano, he or she is referring to the pitch range of which your voice is capable.

Changes in pitch level (inflection in upward and downward movement of your pitch) provide you with a very effective means of giving different shades of meaning to your spoken words. Moreover, such changes tend to help hold audience attention. Upward inflectional patterns are thought to convey feelings such as enthusiasm, sincerity, and excitement. Under the duress of a formal speaking situation, however, you might become tense and inhibit your natural tendency to vary your pitch level. The resulting effect, monotony, robs your words of much meaning and deadens the listeners' attention.

Rate

Television advertisements occasionally feature an actor who specializes in delivering his lines at an incredible rate of speed. He seems to be enunciating clearly, but his words go by so fast that it is difficult to keep up with him. His routine is very amusing but not very enlightening.

Intelligibility, meaning, and attention are all affected by a speaker's rate of utterance. If the rate is too fast, intelligibility suffers. If the rate is slow when it should be fast or fast when it should be slow, meaning may suffer. If the rate is not correctly varied, attention may wane.

Rate is measured in terms of the number of words uttered per minute. It is generally agreed that 125 to 150 words per minute constitute a satisfactory rate for public speaking, but modifications must be made to adapt to room acoustics, audience reactions, the atmosphere of the occasion, and the speech material.

Variety of rate is as important as variety of pitch or loudness. A speaker who seems to be following a metronome in his or her rate of utterance can cloud meaning and diminish attention almost as quickly as a person with a monotone. Emphasis and mood changes can be effectively expressed by variations in rate. For example, when a speaker wishes to emphasize one particular statement of a paragraph, he or she tends to utter it more slowly than the sentences that precede or follow it. A mood of excitement is usually accompanied by an acceleration in rate; a mood of sobriety, with a slowing down in rate.

Your use of a **pause** is yet another way rate can be put your advantage. Great musical conductors and dramatists know about the power of the pause. The English playwright W.J. Lucas wrote, "It is the wise head that makes still the tongue." A pause, when used effectively, is an excellent vocal device. However, most novice speakers are reluctant to use silence as a form of communication. This is a mistake, for a pause, like other vocal techniques, can serve a variety of functions. First, the silence inherent in a pause allows the listeners an opportunity to think about what has been said. Second, a pause can dramatize and emphasize key points. Imagine how startling it would be if someone talking about violence in the United States were to pause in some of the following places: "Think about this (pause)—more than 2 million Americans are beaten (pause), knifed (pause), or shot each year, 23,000 of them fatally (pause)." Third, a pause can serve as a transition as you move from point to point. It is a type of "oral punctuation" that can take the place of a comma, a colon, parentheses, or a dash.

Many inexperienced speakers use a pause as an unconscious excuse to use what are called "vocal interferences." These interferences take a variety of forms and should always be avoided. A few of the more common sound hindrances are "uh," "ah," "er," and "um." Vocal clutter to fill silence and the uneasiness of the pause can be "well," "OK," "like," and "you know."

I conclude this brief section on rate of presentation by repeating a message that has been mentioned throughout this chapter—balance. Too many novice speakers talk too fast, yet speaking too slowly can make your message seem flat, so the key is locating the balance between the two extremes.

Distinctness (Articulation)

You already know that the manner in which you speak is directly related to how you are perceived. If your language is coarse, impudent, crude, and riddled with slang, you will not be viewed as a highly credible source. What is true of the words you use is also true with regard to how you say those words. Simply put, your success as a speaker is directly linked to the clarity, or distinctness, of the sounds you produce. We are, of course, referring to the manner in which you articulate and enunciate your words.

Although some articulation problems are serious enough to warrant work with a speech therapist, most are caused by the way a person manages his or her organs of articulation. Some sounds depend for their clarity on precise lip movements, others on critical placement of the tongue, and still others on full mobility of the jaw. If you use these three organs with care, you can overcome most of the problems associated with poor articulation.

Poor enunciation of consonants such as *p, b, v,* and *f* is usually the result of lip laziness. For example, the distinction between *have* and *half* depends on your lip movements. Your tongue placement must be correct for the clear production of consonants such as *t, d, k,* and *g,* as in *cat* and *cad* or *dock* and *dog.* The part that jaw mobility plays in clarity of enunciation is apparent when you try to recite the alphabet through clenched teeth. As you strive for greater precision, however, avoid becoming overly precise, because your audience might interpret that as a sign of affectation.

Your instructor may offer suggestions for improving your enunciation. If so, get into the habit of implementing those improvements in your everyday conversation; then the demands of other speaking situations will be much easier to fulfill.

Because poor articulation can harm both your message and your credibility, let us examine a brief list of words and phrases that tend to call forth deficient enunciation. As you practice the following list, remember that most articulation problems stem from sounds that are left out, added, distorted, or run together.

Incorrect	Correct
wanna	want to
soun	sound
otta	ought to
dint	did not
comin	coming
I et	I eat
nuthin	nothing
swimin	swimming
gimme	give me
hafta	have to
seeya	see you
wilya	will you
didja	did you
gonna	going to
whadayado	what do you do
lemme	let me
mornin	morning
wep	wept
skien	skiing

Correctness (Pronunciation)

While enunciation has to do with the distinctness of a spoken word, pronunciation has to do with its correctness. It is possible to enunciate a word with the greatest clarity while grossly mispronouncing it. Listeners are less likely to forgive faults of pronunciation than faults of enunciation, because faulty pronunciation seems to reflect the speaker's intelligence and educational level rather than just his or her muscular dexterity in manipulating the organs of speech. The negative connotation of poor pronunciation is usually detrimental to a speaker's credibility. To avoid faulty pronunciation, become familiar with the following words, which are often mispronounced.

Incorrect	Correct
uh–crost	a–cross
burg–you–lur	bur–glar
pur–fess–ur	pro–fes–sor
rev–uh–lant	rel–e–vant
deef	deaf
Feb–u–ary	Feb–ru–ary
De–troit	Detroit
gun–u–wine	gen–u–win
wit	with
ath–a–lete	ath–lete
thee–a–ter	theater
then	thin
nu–cu–lar	nu–cle–ar
pich–er	pic–ture
hunnert	hundred
ly–ber–y	li–brar–y
git	get
worsh	wash

If you have any doubts regarding the correct pronunciation of any word, look up that word in a standard dictionary, which offers guidelines for pronunciation.

Dialects

A dialect represents a language variant used by a collection of people from a similar geographic region and/or ethnic background. Dialects can be troublesome in public speaking because many listeners use dialect as a variable in personal perception. Although such reactions are unavoidable, it is important to remember that there is no such thing as a correct or incorrect dialect, or accent. This is especially true in the United States, where so many dialects are spoken. First, there are dialects peculiar to a geographic region. Someone from the Midwest, for example, pronounces the word *hard* with the *r* sound uttered prominently. A Southerner drops the *r* sound and the word becomes "haahd." A New Englander may even pronounce that same word as "had." What is acceptable in New Orleans might not be acceptable in Milwaukee or Seattle.

Then there are dialects peculiar to people who share a common cultural background. Not only is their pronunciation of some words different from that of the majority of the people in a geographic area, but their grammar and syntax may differ as well. The dialects of Hispanic Americans, African Americans, and Asian Americans are cases in point. Each group has its own standards of pronunciation, grammar, and syntax for communication within the group. When group members interact with members of the larger community, which has other standards, they face the problem of deciding which set of standards to follow—the ethnic standard or the majority standard. In such communication encounters, to follow the ethnic standard is to run the risk of being perceived by some members of the majority culture as deficient in language development. But then if you follow the standards set by the majority, you are apt to be perceived by some members of your own culture as disloyal. As intercultural understanding increases, respect for the speech patterns of others is also growing. Moreover, with the increasing mobility within our society and the pervasiveness of mass communication, regional and cultural differences in pronunciation are becoming less evident; hence, most people are not using dialects as badges of power and prestige. It is important to remember that your dialect will most likely not interfere with effective communication if it is natural and correct.

Aural Dimensions and Culture

As listeners, we should not be hasty in equating a speaker's voice with his or her character or emotional state. We need to consider the possibility that the speaker's voice may be part of a "mask" hiding his or her real identity or that the speaker may be observing cultural norms that differ from our own. For example, the people of some cultures speak in a loud voice because loudness is equated with strength and conviction, while people of other cultures speak softly because they regard that practice as a sign of politeness and intelligence. You can imagine the possibilities for misunderstanding that can occur when people of diverse cultures attempt to interact. When a soft-spoken Thai hears a louder North American speak, he or she may think that the North American is angry or disturbed about something. In Japan, laughter is not always a sign of mirth, because the Japanese often use laughter to mask embarrassment, sadness, disapproval, and even anger. Thus, we need to be wary of making snap judgments about others on the basis of their vocal behavior. At the same time, we should remember that, as we speak, our listeners form an impression of our personality and character on the basis of the words we utter and the sound of our voice.

As said elsewhere in this text, it is important that you become aware of cultural differences in how people use their voices. Volume, either loud or soft, is a case in point. For example, Jews, Italians, and Arabs tend to speak louder than North Americans and can even give the impression, at least to those who do not understand these cultures, of shouting. This intensity of volume is in stark contrast to that of the Native American population and to that of East Asia. People in these cultures speak in much softer tones. Women, at least in the United States, also tend to employ less volume when speaking than do males. Discovering the cultural composition of your audience will assist you in adapting your volume to the people in your audience.

Pitch is yet another vocal characteristic that is influenced by culture. For example, Arabic speakers are often perceived to speak in an unusually high pitch, which often carries the unintentional meaning of intense emotion. Be careful not to apply North American standards to other cultures; this can lead to misinterpretations and misunderstandings.

There are cultural differences in the use and perception of long pauses. For many North Americans, an extended pause can cause tension and anxious feelings. Hence, your pauses should not be drawn out. In India and Japan, there is less uneasiness with silence and long pauses. For members of these cultures, a prolonged pause is perceived as a time for reflection and the gathering of one's thoughts—it is a positive message, not a negative one.

Improving Your Speech Delivery

Now that we have discussed the factors that combine to form speech delivery, let us explore some ways in which you can use this information. Many of these ideas have been presented elsewhere; however, they are all important enough to be cited one more time.

Your Body

Although I will arbitrarily begin with the behaviors that the audience sees, it is important to keep in mind that skillful delivery involves the body as a whole. As we noted at the outset of this chapter, because we can talk about only one idea at a time, our discussion of delivery has had to separate the visual from the oral. However, in reality, the body works as a single unit, and therefore delivery involves the whole person.

Practice good posture, and you will find it easier to move spontaneously from one point to another on the platform. Moreover, the audience will view good posture as a sign of your being alert and at ease.

Dress in such a way that your apparel does not call attention to itself. Avoid gaudy colors and T-shirts that have logos or slogans, and avoid wearing any kind of distracting jewelry or ornamentation.

Be enthusiastic. Enthusiasm gets transmitted; therefore, if you are involved with your subject in both body and voice, you will find that the audience feels that it is included in the excitement.

Do not wear a dispirited face. Give your audience a friendly smile from time to time and let your feelings be reflected in your facial expressions.

Establish and maintain good eye contact with your audience. You might start by picking out a friendly face and talking to that person for a moment, then switch to another friendly face somewhere in the room. Soon you will find it easier to look at more and more people. Remember, not only does eye contact let your listeners know you are aware of them, but it provides you with invaluable feedback on how they are responding to your speech.

Try to use meaningful gestures to reinforce your points. If you avoid gripping the lectern or otherwise immobilizing your hands, you are more likely to gesture spontaneously. It is best not to plan your gestures, because they will probably look planned. Instead, keep your hands free and they will likely work for you.

When you want to emphasize a point or make a transition, consider moving from one location to another on the platform. A good posture, with weight evenly distributed on both feet, makes such movements easier to execute spontaneously.

Avoid letting physical remoteness come between you and your listeners. Try to get your listeners seated close to one another near the front of the room, where you are standing. Such physical closeness tends to promote a feeling of mental closeness and helps establish rapport between you and your listeners.

Your Voice   ❖ ❖ ❖ ❖

The following is a review of some ways in which you can make optimal use of your speaking voice.

Cultivate vocal variety. Remember, a voice that features meaningful variations in pitch, rate, and loudness tends to hold a higher level of attention than does a monotonous one. Using vocal variety also means not being afraid of silence. Remember the African proverb, "Silence is also speech."

Work to enunciate your sounds clearly, avoiding slurring your words or mumbling because of lip laziness. If you keep your jaw relaxed, you will avoid the clenched teeth tightness that muffles sound; however, remember to avoid being overly precise as you enunciate, because listeners may perceive it as an affectation.

When you are in doubt about the pronunciation of a word, find out how it is pronounced by the educated speakers in your area. Remember that there are regional standards of pronunciation rather than one universal standard. You can always use the dictionary's recommended pronunciation.

Finally, you should carefully take an inventory of your current delivery practices in various communication situations. Ask friends to offer candid views of your assets and liabilities in informal conversation, discussions, and conferences. Ask your speech instructor for an analysis of your needs in public-speaking situations. Try to find answers to questions such as these:

To what degree do I use bodily action and effective vocal variety in each of the various communication situations: to an insufficient degree in public speaking, a sufficient degree in conversation? to a distracting degree in some cases?

What is the quality of the action I use? Does it help or hinder the communication of my ideas? Is it meaningful action? Does it call attention to itself? If so, why?

Does my posture communicate a positive impression? Does it combine ease with alertness? Are my movements and gestures graceful and decisive, or are they hesitant, tentative, and lacking in vigor and enthusiasm?

Do I have any annoying mannerisms that should be curbed? Does my use of my voice add to or detract from the communication situation?

Securing answers to these and other pertinent questions will enable you to chart your course toward greater effectiveness in the use of the visible and audible aspects of communication.

Your Confidence

Perhaps the best way to improve your delivery is to follow the words of the Roman poet Virgil when he wrote, "They can do all because they think they can." Virgil was, of course, talking about having self-confidence and believing in oneself. Although it may sound somewhat simplistic, it is nevertheless true that if you deem yourself a failure, you will be. On the other hand, if you believe that delivery is something that can be controlled (and it can), you can develop poise and manipulate your delivery. Gaining control over your actions will improve the manner in which you deliver your speeches and add to your self-confidence. As we noted in chapter 2, your confidence level can be greatly increased if you (1) know your subject and your outline, (2) allow sufficient time to practice, (3) develop a positive mental attitude toward the speaking situation, and (4) are enthusiastic about your topic.

Summary

For effective oral communication, it is essential that the verbal and nonverbal elements of the message work in harmony. The nonverbal elements of the message are visual and vocal. The visual constituents include the speaker's general appearance (posture and apparel), facial expressions, eye contact, movements, and spatial relationship to the audience. The speaker's appearance should provide nonverbal cues that are compatible with the verbal message being uttered. Movements help convey meaning and sustain audience attention. The speaker should adopt a bodily position that does not inhibit spontaneous movement. Movement on the platform is generally motivated by a desire to make an idea emphatic or to suggest a transition from one idea to another. The speaker's action should be sincerely motivated; should be appropriate to the subject, to the audience, and to the occasion; and should not be overused. The amount of space between the speaker and listener can affect the quality of the communication encounter. The speaker should use spatial cues in a manner consistent with the speech purpose.

The voice does more than simply render a word symbol into audible form. It enables a speaker to impart various shades of meaning to the spoken word; it transmits an impression of the speaker as a person; and it acts as a factor of attention. The controllable elements of voice are loudness, pitch, and rate. These elements should be varied in a manner consistent with the sense of the verbal element of the message. Faults in distinctness of vocal sounds (enunciation) are more readily forgiven than are faults in the correctness of the sounds (pronunciation). Acceptability of pronunciation varies from region to region. You are advised to emulate the pronunciation of the best-educated speakers in your geographical area.

A successful speaker needs to be aware of the influence of culture on all aspects of nonverbal communication. For both bodies and voices, our culture affects our delivery. A successful speaker also seeks a variety of methods that lead to improved delivery and greater self-confidence.

Concepts and Questions

1. How can body movements help or hinder your presentation?

2. What elements of your voice are controllable?

3. Why is good delivery such an important element in public speaking?

4. How would you relate credibility to effective delivery skills?

5. What methods would you use to remain calm and relaxed while you are
    delivering your speech?

6. Why is eye contact such an important aspect of successful delivery?

Activities and Exercises

1. Attend a public event where a speaker is addressing an audience. Write a
    short report analyzing the speaker's delivery.

2. Locate a video recorder and make a videotape of your next speech. Play
    back the tape and write an essay discussing the manner in which you
    delivered the talk. Try to have your analysis include some of the elements
    discussed in this chapter.

3. Obtain a recording (video or audio) of a speaker who you believe pos-
    sesses good delivery skills. Make a list of what specific techniques the
    speaker used that you might be able to incorporate into your own
    presentations.

4. Prepare a five-minute speech that discusses cultural differences in non-
    verbal communication. ✦

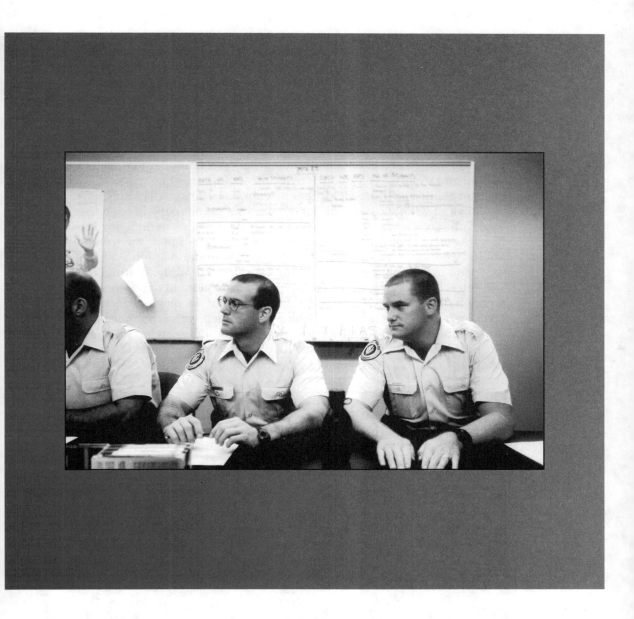

CHAPTER FIVE

Listening:
Evaluation
and Criticism

Listen carefully and you will learn.

—*Kikuyu Proverb*

"Most people are not very good listeners."

"What did you say?"

This simple two-line conversation tells us a great deal about the topic of listening. What it says is something most of us probably already know—that it is often difficult to pay attention, comprehend what we hear, and remember that information at a later date. It seems that even though listening is a fundamental and significant human activity, most of us are not very good at it. The irony of being a poor listener is that listening is an extremely important activity. Much of what we know about the past has come to us through listening. Small children learn about their new world through listening, for it is their first means of acquiring information and ideas about their environment. As adults, we use listening more than any other communication skill. The time we spend listening far exceeds the time we spend reading, writing, or speaking. It has been estimated that we spend 40 to 50 percent of our total communication time engaged in listening. In fact, one of the original authors of this text conducted a research project that concluded we spend more than one-third of our waking hours listening. Stop in the middle of what you are doing a few times during the day, and you will discover that the statistics concerning listening are valid. We listen at home, on the job, at school, and at play. The

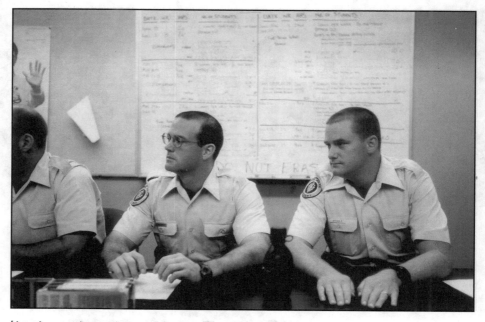

Listening requires active participation. (Photo: Mark C. Ide)

outcome of these listening experiences can influence everything from how much money we earn to the success or failure of our most intimate relationships. We all know from personal experience that poor listening habits can cost us both time and money. And reflect for a moment on the strife and conflict created in interpersonal relationships when people fail to understand each other simply because they were not listening to one another.

Inherent in our earlier definition and explanation of communication was the idea that speech is a *two-way process. Speaking and listening are two indispensable ingredients of communication:* there can be no effective transaction without someone on the other end. If our discussion of oral communication is to have real meaning, we must give a proper share of attention to listening.

The Rewards of Listening

The rewards of effective listening are numerous. First, listening carefully can make a speaker's remarks more informative and interesting. You are apt to discover things you never knew before—things you would have missed had you not been fully focused on the interaction. In this sense, *listening adds to your fund of knowledge.* It also lets you update your collection of facts, attitudes, and beliefs. On many occasions this fund of knowledge is crucial to your well-being. If your doctor is giving you advice on how to cope with a current illness, and your mind is pondering other matters, you will fail to receive an important message.

Second, becoming a more effective listener *can make you more critical* of the thousands of messages that are sent your way each day. This need for improving listening, as part of the communication process, has gained importance with the onset of the "era of communication." Most of us are confronted with about a million advertising messages each year—messages that ask us to take certain actions. Not only do we have to listen to more advertisements, but we are confronted with a large variety of individuals making specific demands on our actions and thoughts. Some of these individuals rely on the supposition that we are poor listeners. Cult leaders want our minds, politicians want our votes, and hucksters want our money. Listening is extremely important in a time when the mass media attempt to determine our tastes and to run our lives. In short, improved listening is good protection against the devices and techniques of an unethical yet plausible speaker. There is a Spanish proverb that makes the same point: "Though the speaker be a fool, let the hearer be wise."

Third, an improved listening attitude can also help us cope with those countless situations when *the person we are communicating with is not fluent in English.* Throughout this book, we have stressed the idea that many of our communication encounters are with people from different cultures and that these individuals may speak English as their second language. It may be difficult to understand certain dialects; however, if you try to be a conscientious listener, you greatly enhance your chances of comprehending such messages.

Fourth, we are apt to find that with *improved listening skills we can appreciate and enjoy what we hear with greater intensity.* Even though much of our time is spent listening, we often miss the little nuances of what we hear. How very different the sound of singing birds can be when we give this simple plea-

❖ ❖ ❖ ❖   sure our full attention. This chapter seeks to help you direct and control that attention.

Finally, *good listening helps improve your speaking.* By listening to the speeches of others, you will be able to distinguish the characteristics of content and delivery that ought to be emulated. As the English author Lord Chesterfield noted, "We are, in truth, more than half what we are by imitation." Therefore, learn how to listen so you will know both what to imitate and what not to emulate.

You will discover that most of your time in speech class is spent listening to student speeches and to the instructor's remarks. In fact, you may listen to over one hundred speeches in your class, although you will deliver only five or six. Take full advantage of this listening time to sharpen your perceptions, and you will be a better speaker, as well as a better listener, for the experience.

The first question to ask is, What kind of listeners am I? There is sufficient evidence to support the generalization that, as a whole, people are poor listeners. Countless studies have concluded that a large percentage of those tested could not locate a central idea after listening to an exposition that had been designed for clarity and simplicity. Other research results say that listeners comprehend only a small percentage of what they hear. Perhaps you can provide the best proof for these assertions with some serious introspection. Simply ask yourself these two questions: Do I pay attention when other people talk? Do I remember very much of what I hear? If you have been honest in your response, you most likely answered "no" to both questions.

Fear not, for one of the most gratifying aspects about listening is that with motivation and hard work you can substitute good listening habits for poor ones. This improvement is possible for one simple reason; as stressed in chapter 1, human beings have free choice. You can choose what you pay attention to. You can decide to focus on the speaker and the message or to let your mind dart from daydream to daydream. Again, you have free choice. Because of this freedom, people have the power to listen or not to listen. The central message of this chapter is to urge you to use that power. As poet Oliver Wendell Holmes (father of the Supreme Court Justice) noted, "It is the province of knowledge to speak and it is the privilege of wisdom to listen."

The Process of Listening

One of the major reasons people are poor listeners is that they fail to understand the complex nature of listening. Because the act of hearing sounds is such a simple process, they often assume that hearing is listening. This belief is wrong. In actuality, listening involves six interrelated steps. Knowing these processes, and the choices a listener makes at each stage, will help you improve the manner in which you listen. Before briefly identifying these six steps, we should note that although all six steps are listed separately and are described in a linear fashion, in reality the time between steps is often less than a millionth of a second. The six steps can even work in combination:

1. *Hearing* (physiological process of listening—the reception of sound waves),

2. *Attending* (focusing on a specific sound or series of sounds and rejecting others),

3. *Understanding* (the brain interpreting the message and assigning meaning),

4. *Remembering* (storing the message for later use),

5. *Evaluating* (making a judgment about the message), and

6. *Responding* (giving an overt response to the message).

As you can see, this description incorporates much more than simply hearing sounds. It includes focusing on certain sounds, excluding others, making sense out of what has been selected, and using what is remembered. What should emerge from these six steps is the impression that listening is a highly active process that demands concentration and attention.

The Purposes of Listening

You will recall that there are different reasons for speaking and that, by identifying your reason for speaking, you can better accomplish your goal. The same is true with regard to listening. We all listen for a variety of reasons and for different purposes. By knowing why you are listening, you can adapt to each communication situation. Listeners as well as speakers must alter their behavior as they move from encounter to encounter. Although the purposes for listening often overlap, they generally fall into four basic categories: (1) empathic, (2) informational, (3) evaluative, and (4) appreciative.

Empathic Listening

Empathic listening occurs in countless communication contacts when we share feelings and build and maintain supporting relationships. For example, imagine that a close friend has just had a major accident involving his new car and tells you how frustrated and upset he is. In this circumstance, there might be nothing you can do, yet your friend feels better because you have listened and offered moral support. If you are going to respond, and not only listen in an empathic manner, it also behooves you to listen carefully. Then your response will reflect the fact that you have heard your friend and thought about your response. This kind of emotional sensitivity demands that you listen carefully so that the other person will know you appreciate and understand his or her dilemma. Although the following suggestion may seem simplistic, I would suggest that each us has an obligation to listen carefully to those who need "our ear." Nikki Giovanni, an American poet, said much the same thing: "I'm glad I understand that while language is a gift, listening is a responsibility."

Informational Listening

The human mind is a marvelous and amazing instrument. It is capable of receiving and remembering an endless amount of information. Think for just a moment about how much of your day is taken up with listening to things that in some way teach you something. Listening for learning is listening that has you gathering information. If you are like most people, these occasions range from the superficial to the significant. You may ask directions and listen to the words to keep from getting lost, or you may listen to a lecture in class so that you could receive an A on the next examination. Perhaps you listen in order to learn how to saddle a horse, change the oil in your car, repair your computer, or make an intelligent choice in the voting booth. In all these instances, your purpose is to gather information. Knowing that your purpose is informational will enable you to make the necessary decisions regarding how you want to listen. Decisions about taking notes, watching for nonverbal cues, asking questions, and answering questions are all related to informational listening.

Evaluative Listening

We also listen to a great deal of material intended to persuade us. On these occasions, our purpose for listening is to evaluate what we hear. Whether the mayor is asking for our support, someone is asking us to buy a certain car, or a friend is wanting a loan, we are always confronting people asking us to believe in their messages. In these situations, we assume a listening attitude that is critical yet fair. Later in this chapter, we will look at some specific guidelines for critically evaluating what we hear.

Appreciative Listening

The appreciative aspects of listening are rather obvious. We listen to music, watch television, go to movies and plays, and engage in a great deal of social conversation. In all these situations, the experience is greatly enhanced and more appreciated if we listen carefully. As we noted earlier, even the sounds of nature take on new meaning when we learn to be mindful of what we are taking in.

Misconceptions About Listening

It should be clear from the last few pages that listening is not the simple matter that some people believe it to be. Having a number of misconceptions regarding listening can cause problems. Since these misconceptions can seriously affect the quality of one's communication behavior, it might be helpful to look at five of the more common myths that influence what we hear and what we remember.

Hearing Versus Listening

Many people believe that listening is a natural activity and that hearing is the same as listening; it is not. Hearing is a physical act, while listening is the process of giving meaning to electrochemical impulses. You can, therefore, hear without listening. Do not be misled into believing that because you are receiving sounds (voices, music), you are listening.

Objectivity Versus Subjectivity   ❖ ❖ ❖ ❖

The belief that once sound is produced, everyone receives the same message is also false. Communication is first and foremost a subjective activity. It is what happens inside of us. Each person responds in a unique and highly personal manner. Think for a moment about the words *Doberman pinscher*. For a person who raises and trains these dogs, the internal response will differ greatly from the response of a person whose only experience with Dobermans is seeing them, teeth exposed, being used by local police to control an unruly crowd. Obviously, both parties hear the same five syllables, but their internal responses contrast sharply.

Active Versus Passive

Many people make the mistake of believing that listening is a passive activity. They feel that one merely has to sit back and relax, and listening will take care of itself. This is simply not true. Listening requires active participation. To be a good listener, you must stay focused on the moment; you cannot remain passive and expect to retain much of what is said. The notion of being alert and concentrating on what is transpiring is eloquently stated by Lord Chesterfield: "One should always think of what one is about; when one is learning, one should not think about play; and when one is at play, one should not think of one's learning."

Listener Versus Speaker

People are often deluded into believing that effective interaction is the exclusive responsibility of the speaker. Think of how often you have left a college classroom believing that if you did not receive very much from the lecture, it had to be the professor's fault. Although in some instances this excuse may be a valid one, too often it is a reflection of the misconception that the burden for success resides solely with the sender of the message. Again, this is not true. As we have said throughout this book, communication is a circular process involving both the sending and receiving of messages.

Change Versus Static

There is a myth that people are born either good listeners or bad listeners and that there is very little they can do about it. This false idea often gives people an excuse for not trying to improve their listening ability. Listening skills can be developed, like any other skill; however, improvement comes only if one is willing to practice and work hard. You may have heard the saying, "He that would have the fruit must climb the tree." Climb the tree; the rewards are worth it.

Barriers to Listening

By now, you should know that listening is a complex activity and that being a good listener is not a simple matter. Effective listening can be impeded by many factors. Some of these factors are worth examining in detail, for if you can identify what you are doing wrong, you are in a better position to take the next step and start to improve your listening behavior.

Over two thousand years ago, the Roman poet Ovid indirectly offered us an excellent introduction to our first barrier when he wrote, "Nothing is more powerful than habit." Like so much of human behavior, listening tends to follow consistent patterns in individuals. Most of us fall into listening patterns that become so habitual that we fail to realize fully that we are creating a listening barrier. Although all the barriers discussed in this section can become subjects of habit, Ralph G. Nichols and Leonard A. Stevens suggest that there are six bad listening habits that are the most common. Although Nichols and Stevens prepared their list many years ago, these problems seem to persist. This persistence, of course, adds credence to the notion that bad listening behaviors are indeed habitual.

Faking Attention

Most of us have probably learned to fake attention from time to time so as not to appear discourteous or to make a teacher think we are interested in learning. All cultures teach their young people to have good manners and therefore place a very high premium on politeness. The result is that we look as if we are listening when we are actually faking attention. The danger of such action is that it may become habitual.

Listening Only for Facts

Because North Americans value time and are impulsive, they view many communication encounters as situations where something has to be done. This attitude often translates into a listening habit that only seeks specific facts. Even the overused expression "Just give me the bottom line" is actually saying that all I want is the specific point. This habit, when carried to an extreme, often leads to a listening personality that is narrow, because once the so-called "facts" are obtained, the person stops listening.

Avoiding Difficult Material

Most of us feel comfortable with what we know and avoid what is unfamiliar or difficult. We turn off those listening situations requiring too much energy. Such avoidance becomes a habit; whenever the material becomes slightly difficult, we drift away mentally, if not physically. We approach the communication situation without being in the right frame of mind. Not only do we avoid difficult material, but we take a casual attitude toward listening in general. All day long, we move in and out of listening situations that have different purposes. We listen to music or talk to friends in a very relaxed and casual manner, and then quickly go to, say, a history class, where we need to pay close attention to each word so that we can receive an A on the next examination. Without even realizing it, we slide from situations that demand very little concentration to informational encounters that call for high levels of commitment. Although a casual listening attitude is permissible in a pleasurable encounter, it is a serious barrier to listening for information.

In the United States in the 1990s, avoiding difficult material has become a very serious problem. More and more we find ourselves interacting with people whose primary language is not English. As they attempt to speak their "second language" (English), your listening skills will be challenged, for on many occasions you will have to strain to understand them. If you give in to the habit of avoiding arduous listening situations, you will not receive much from experiences that contain some element of cultural diversity.

Avoiding the Uninteresting

We often make the mistake of equating "interesting" with "valuable" and, hence, stop listening too soon. Our culture puts a premium on being entertained, and because of this we tend to listen only to what is "fun." If the messages we are confronted with do not immediately seem to be fun or interesting, we habitually stop listening. Television viewing, of course, contributes to the speed with which we are willing to stop listening. From the MTV channel to the action films that fill our screens, we have come to demand rapid activity and short bits of information. When asked to pay attention to what may not be lively, funny, or interesting, we tend to cease listening.

Not only do we often show a lack of interest in the topic, but on many occasions we do not listen because we find the speaker uninteresting. Without even giving the other person a chance, we decide early in the conversation that he or she "is not our type." Notice how you pay attention to your friends because you share a common interest with them. If you would apply this level of interest to everyone you are confronted with, your listening habits would be greatly improved.

Criticizing the Speaker

One of the most common problems in listening is that too many of us reject speakers on the basis of how they look or how they deliver their messages. This rejection or acceptance of what a speaker says, however, goes beyond how that person delivers the message; it also includes our perception of his or her role, culture, and status. We know that when we like and respect someone, we tend to listen to that speaker more attentively. Unfortunately, in these circumstances we may become overly concerned with the speaker as a person and neglect to think critically about what is being said.

We can also be so critical of a speaker that we prevent ourselves from processing his or her message. This barrier is perhaps most manifest in the area of gender, cultural, and ethnic stereotypes. Too often, people see the gender, skin color, hairstyle, or traditional attire for a specific culture, or hear a dialect or accent they are not familiar with, and immediately experience an unfavorable reaction. These responses keep us from listening to the content of the message.

A good listener must recognize that culture, gender, race, status, and the like are factors present in all communication situations and must not let these considerations prevent maximum comprehension.

Yielding to Distractions

The English writer Thomas Fuller once remarked that "If you run after two hares, you will catch neither." He may well have been talking about how easy it is to become distracted. In a sense, all the bad habits we have discussed thus far are a kind of yielding to distractions, chasing that second rabbit, but there are some additional distractions that merit special consideration. These are the distractions that fall into three broad categories—mental, semantic, and physical.

Mental Distractions. *Mental distractions* are perhaps the most common of all the distractions and the most difficult to overcome, for they occur when we talk silently to our favorite companion—ourselves. It is a very natural tendency to make ourselves the central character in our daydreams and fantasies. However, when we "visit" with ourselves we often forget about the speaker. Ask yourself how many times a day you are supposed to be listening but, instead, find yourself thinking about your next meal, planning tomorrow's activities, or evaluating what you did yesterday. Throughout this chapter, we will return to the advice that you need to *learn* how to stay in the moment and concentrate on what the other person is saying.

Semantic Distractions. Listeners also yield to semantic distractions. Individuals often have different meanings for the same word, and if these differences are too great, a semantic distraction can occur. For example, if a speaker and listener are from different generations and cultures, a phrase such as "Man, that is bad" could cause a semantic distraction. What usually happens is that the listener must stop to think about the term's specific meaning while the speaker continues his or her presentation.

As you listen to more and more speakers who have English as their second language, you must work very hard not to allow semantic distractions to keep you from staying focused. If a word fails to make sense to you, try to place it in the context of the moment and see if you can define it in that man-

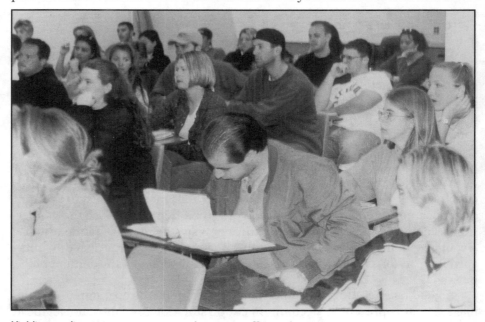

Yielding to distractions is a common barrier to effective listening.

ner. You may also be given an opportunity to ask the speaker how the word is being used.

Physical Distractions. As listeners, we can also experience a number of physical distractions that make demands on our attention. A cold auditorium, the wind howling outside the window, a man next to you tapping his finger on a desk, someone entering the room when the speaker is talking, odor from someone's strong perfume, and an uncomfortable chair are all distractions to which we often yield. The real danger of physical distractions is that listeners use them as an excuse for tuning out the speaker. We all know from personal experience that we can yield to any distraction quite easily and thus make the distraction more important than what is being said.

Having examined the six poor listening habits advanced by Nichols and Stevens, we are now ready to discuss a few additional barriers to listening.

Defensive Listening

In *defensive listening*, a person selects only the negative aspects of what is being said and fails to listen to what else the speaker is discussing. None of us delights in being criticized or attacked, so it is quite easy to adopt a defensive attitude when we perceive that what the speaker is saying is challenging some of our beliefs and values. However, this defensive attitude usually keeps us from listening and, in many instances, from learning. A good example of this barrier might be drawn from your speech class. If your instructor were to be critical of your use of evidence and were to say so, you would probably become defensive and stop listening. However, while you were responding defensively, she might go on to offer you some excellent advice about how you could remedy the problem. By being defensive, however, you would allow the negative comments to represent the entire transaction.

Prejudice

A prejudice is an unfair, biased attitude toward a group of people or an individual. These attitudes are usually deep-seated; they have developed over a long period of time; and they are barriers to listening. For instance, persons with predetermined negative views toward Arabs would be less likely to give their full attention to a speaker who is talking about Islam. The speaker is not receiving a fair hearing because of the listeners' preconceived attitudes. To break this barrier, we listeners must try to exert some command over our emotions and initial responses. We must try to withhold judgment until we have listened completely and objectively to what has been said. Remember, it is easy to be critical of others and their ideas. If we want to be prejudiced and negative, there is always something to focus on. As an old Yiddish proverb states, "If you're out to beat a dog, you're sure to find a stick." If you are determined to be prejudiced, you will find a stick.

Constant Self-Focus

The Roman playwright Terence was correct when he told us, over two thousand years ago, something very basic about human nature: "My closest relation is myself." What he was referring to is something we talked about earlier in the chapter when we noted that most of us are primarily concerned with self. There are many reasons why seeing ourselves as the center of the universe interferes with listening, but we shall look at only two of them. First, our listening is obstructed when we adopt the "I must defend my position" attitude. In these instances, we stop listening in order to engage ourselves in mental debate. If someone says to us, "We don't need gun laws in this country," and to ourselves we say, "What is he talking about? Last year there were over six thousand people killed with handguns in the United States," clearly a barrier to listening has arisen, for we have stopped listening and are now mentally debating the speaker.

Second, many of us adopt the "I already know what you have to say" attitude. This barrier begins to form when we say to ourselves, for instance, "Oh no, not another speech on drug addiction." When we assume this position, we miss a great deal of life. Think of what a narrow view we have when we are so dogmatic as to believe we know all there is to know on any subject. Much of what we have learned has been acquired by listening, and we would be foolish to stop listening before we hear the speaker's entire position.

Message Overload

Earlier in this chapter, we talked about the importance of listening and how we use listening more than any other communication skill. We thus encounter a large number of words during a normal day. If you think about it, we most likely hear over one billion words each year. It is often this constant bombardment of words that creates yet another barrier to listening. It is not surprising that when we are faced with so much verbal input, we often just stop listening to everything. We simply shut down the brain to all outside noise. When this happens, the important words as well as the frivolous ones are not brought into consciousness. If you often suffer from message overload, you need to learn to concentrate on entire messages so that you can extract what is important and worthy of your energy. Being faced with message overload is a common occurrence; hence, learning how to be selective is crucial if you seek to improve your listening performance. In short, you must learn to pay careful attention to what is being said so that you can decide which messages are worth your time and which can be discarded. All we ask is that you learn to suspend judgment before you make that decision.

Thinking-Speaking Rate

It is estimated that we speak an average of 125 to 150 words per minute. Our minds, however, are able to cope with approximately 400 words per minute. This means that the mind has a great deal of idle time. This excess time forms one of the major barriers to proficient listening. In most instances, the extra time is spent mentally wandering away from the task of critical and careful listening. Many listeners use this listening-thinking gap for mental excursions ranging from daydreaming to thinking about the speaker's hairstyle. It would be far more beneficial to both sender and receiver if this time were spent analyzing the message.

Short Attention Span

❖ ❖ ❖ ❖

In many ways our final barrier is inherent in all the others, yet by giving it its own classification we can underscore its significance. We begin our discussion by asking you to spend a moment or two the next time you are listening to someone talk (or even reading this chapter) and to observe the manner in which your mind leaps from idea to idea. You will begin to notice at once the brevity of your attention span. There is something about the brain, and the human need for stimulation, that has us jumping from stimulus to stimulus. In many ways this characteristic of the brain (always seeking new data) works directly against our being good listeners. Perhaps the first step in overcoming our active brains is to simply admit that it is active. This recognition, if sincere, might well improve concentration.

Improving Listening

We have pursued two fundamental themes throughout this chapter. First, by listening carefully, you can reap countless benefits. As Plutarch noted, "Know how to listen and you will profit even from those who talk badly." Second, listening is a communication skill that can be improved with serious practice and training. If you genuinely desire to improve, your speech class offers an excellent arena for that improvement. You will have an opportunity to listen to a variety of speakers discussing a wide range of topics. I would recommend that you begin your efforts at improvement by incorporating some of the following suggestions into your listening behavior.

Identify Personal Listening Characteristics

Introspection, while often difficult, is crucial if you are going to improve the manner in which you listen. Therefore, your first step to enrichment is an analysis of your current listening habits. In a sense, I am advocating that you begin by heeding the maxim "Know thyself." This self-analysis should include both your outward and inward listening characteristics.

Outward Listening Characteristics. Your outward characteristics represent how others perceive you as a listener. Your posture, eye contact, and the like influence the kinds of messages speakers send you. The way in which people relate to you correlates with how you listen, or at least appear to listen, to them; hence, try to identify how you present yourself to others. Do you appear interested, enthusiastic, sincere, or bored? The answers to these and other such questions will help you understand your role as a listener.

Inward Listening Characteristics. Your inward listening characteristics relate to what is going on in your head. What are you thinking about while the speaker is talking? We have already discussed the importance of being objective and not jumping to conclusions too soon; now you can take this objectivity one step further and try to recognize the biases you carry around. For example, if you have a negative attitude toward homosexuals and a member of the Gay Students' Union speaks to you, your prejudice will affect how you listen.

If you find that you have some negative reactions to other people on the basis of their culture, you are apt to be engaging in ethnocentrism, where your culture becomes the prism through which you judge all other groups and cultures. If you start from this subjective position, it is easy to see how many of your conclusions about other cultures could be negative. How do you regard Japanese, Germans, African Americans, Mexicans, Arabs, or Jews? In most instances, we evaluate them by standards we have learned in our culture. How easy it is for all of us to say, "We do it this way; why don't they?" Feelings of "we are right" and "they are wrong" cover nearly all areas.

To overcome feelings of ethnocentrism, first try to identify your culture's role in how you perceive and listen to the remarks of people from different cultures. There is a saying that the time to repair the roof is when the sun is shining. The same point holds true with regard to listening—the time to think about listening is before the speaker begins. There are some specific ways you can prepare your communication profile before a listening experience. Let us look at four of them.

Learn all you can about the subject, speaker, and situation. This knowledge, much like an audience analysis, will help you understand and appraise what the speaker is saying. If you know that you will be listening to someone from Mexico talking to a college class in international business, you can make some predictions related to the subject, speaker, and setting.

Minimize physical barriers by placing yourself in a position where you can easily see and hear the speaker. Being in the back row of a noisy auditorium is hardly conducive to effective listening. Try to find a location where you can use the speaker's nonverbal cues to increase your understanding of the speech.

Eliminate all distractions in your environment that might call attention away from the speaker. For example, leave the school newspaper outside the classroom; it might become a distraction.

Bring the necessary materials to the communication event. This advice is intended to remind you that being prepared means that you do not search for paper and pen five minutes after the speaker has started. If you plan to use paper and a pen, or even a laptop computer, these items should be in front of you before the speaker begins.

Be Motivated to Listen

As a public speaker, you should know in advance what you hope to accomplish by the conclusion of your talk, the process called "selecting a specific purpose." What is true of speaking is also true of listening. As a listener you must also decide on a specific purpose. When you have been given the title of a talk, ask yourself what you want to know by the conclusion of the speaker's remarks. Obviously, your purpose will change radically from speaker to speaker and from situation to situation. On one occasion, you may decide that you want to know more about the stock market by the time a stockbroker finishes her talk. While listening to a politician, however, your goal might be to decide whether or not you wish to vote for the proposal being advanced. In either case, stockbroker or politician, *your comprehension and retention will be enhanced if you settle on a specific purpose or goal before the talk begins.*

One of the most important aspects of selecting a listening purpose is to make sure that you are motivated by that purpose. Efficient listening begins with motivation. Researchers in the area of listening have concluded that if you are motivated to listen, you are a more alert and active receiver. Ask yourself this simple yet important question: Do I learn more when I am interested or when I am bored? The answer is obvious. If you believe that the material affects you personally, you listen. What prompts you to listen might be something as pragmatic as making a sale if you listen carefully to what your customer is saying or as abstract as listening because the speaker deserves your attention. In either case, if you are motivated, if you have a purpose for listening, you will discover that you cannot be easily distracted. The English statesman Benjamin Disraeli said it best when he noted, "The secret to success is purpose."

Make Use of the Thinking-Speaking Time Difference

As noted earlier, we normally think at a pace about three times faster than our speaking pace. As good listeners, we can use this time to think about what the speaker is saying. We can ask ourselves: How does this item relate to the speaker's main purpose? How does this main point support that purpose? As alert listeners, we can make this time gap work for us instead of against us. By concentrating on what is being said, instead of mentally arguing with the speaker, we can put the time difference to efficient use. Later in the chapter we will talk about those situations that call for note-taking and how you can use your "free" time to engage in that specific activity.

You can also use the thinking-speaking time difference to observe clues to the meaning of the elements of the speaking situation. The setting, the staging of the event, and the program notes can give insight to what will be said. The speaker's inflection, rate, emphasis, voice quality, and bodily actions can offer clues to the meaning of what is being said and what the speaker feels is most important.

Clues naturally abound in the content and arrangement of the material. A vigilant listener takes note of the speaker's use of partitions, enumerations, transitions, topic sentences, and internal and final summaries. Clues common to writing, such as boldface type, italics, and quotation marks, are replaced with clues of voice, body, material, and arrangement.

Focus on Matter Rather Than Manner

Listening is concerned with a response to what people say. People talk to us so that they can share their internal state. Learn to focus on speech content, and not on the speaker's personality traits and extraneous considerations, so you can better understand what the speaker is trying to say. Try to imagine that the speaker is an information source and that you want to listen to that information. This is not to imply that nonverbal messages and the speaker's personality are not part of the communication process, but too much emphasis on these issues can de-emphasize the speaker's main mission. By forcing yourself to focus on content, you can avoid the tendency to make superfluous items seem more consequential than they are.

Be an Active Listener

Much of what we have discussed thus far implies that listening is an active process. What this means is that you cannot sit passively and expect to automatically receive the full impact of the speaker's message. As noted elsewhere, active listening requires that you consciously think about what the speaker is saying. There are some very specific mental responses you can choose that will improve your ability to be an active listener.

Recognize Patterns. Whenever possible try to recognize the various organizational patterns and sequences being used by the speaker. Is he or she speaking in terms of a linear time frame or talking about a problem that needs to be solved? If you cannot discern a pattern, then you must become even more active. This means mentally organizing the material so that it will be easier for you to discern which are the major and which are the minor points.

Regroup the Material. You might also find it helpful to regroup material under headings that are easy to remember. By being an active listener, you can compensate for speakers who offer long lists and expect the audience to remember 10 or 11 items. You, not the speaker, become responsible for sensible groupings.

When regrouping what the speaker is saying, you might use the following three-step sequence.

1. *Identify the speaker's primary point.* Ask yourself this question: What was the speaker's central thesis when he or she decided to give this talk? You should try to word the main thesis in a sentence or two.

2. *Identify the supporting ideas the speaker uses to clarify and/or prove the central thesis of the talk.* Did the speaker use illustrations, analogies, statistics, and the like to explain his or her basic purpose?

3. *Consider the adequacy and effectiveness of material used to explain the main ideas.* Was the material clear and relevant? Did the material support the main thesis?

Use Paraphrasing. Try to paraphrase the speaker's remarks. This means attempting to put the speaker's ideas into your own words as a "shorthand" summary of what has been said. For example, suppose someone says, "Today 80 percent of deforestation results from population growth; if the numbers keep rising until the year 2050, the U.N. estimates that an additional 2.3 million square miles of land will have to be turned over to farming, roads, and urban uses." You might paraphrase by saying to yourself, "Deforestation is growing at an alarming rate and will cause serious problems in the future if something is not done." The technique of paraphrasing represents yet another way of separating the main ideas from the minor ones, and the insignificant from the significant.

Take Notes. When appropriate, an active listener takes notes. Taking notes can have a number of positive results. You have a record of the most important points of the speech. Also, taking notes forces you to pay attention and strengthens your analytical skills. In taking notes, it is essential to remember a few important ideas.

1. *Start taking notes immediately.* That is, as soon as you identify the speaker's main thesis, you should immediately write it down.

2. *If you are the only person who is going to be using the notes, there is no need to use complete sentences.*

3. *Organize the notes in the same manner in which you would organize a speech.* This means showing major, minor, and subpoints by proper indentation.

4. *Good notes are brief and usually contain only the salient points and facts.* This means that you should write down only the key ideas.

Ask Questions

There is a German proverb that states, "To question is the beginning of wisdom." This advice relates directly to the point I shall try to make in this next section. Simply put, asking proper and appropriate questions is another skill that can improve listening. You might ask a question to clarify a key point, to gather additional information, or to help direct the flow of the conversation. Regardless of your purpose for asking questions, you need to keep the following points in mind.

Think about the timing of your question. You should wait until the speaker has finished the speech before you ask your question. Interrupting the speaker is both rude and disrespectful.

Know specifically what additional information you are seeking. You can usually obtain that information by using *closed-ended questions, open-ended questions,* or *probes.*

Closed-ended Questions. Closed-ended questions ask for a specific answer and narrow the options you offer the speaker. The response to the question is usually brief and, you hope, to the point:

Question: "Exactly how many students did you say would be affected by this change?"

Answer: "I said it should affect about 300 students."

Open-ended Questions. Open-ended questions encourage longer responses, as you are asking the speaker to explain some of the points that you did not understand.

Question: Why did you say we needed to take action on the proposal?'

Answer: 'There are a great many reasons why we need to act at this time. First . . .'

Probes. Although probes can take a variety of forms, they are primarily used after a question and encourage the speaker to develop in more detail the last answer he or she gave.

Question: 'Why did you say we needed to raise student fees at this time?'

Answer: 'The ruling came from the administration.'

Probe: 'Did you mention in your talk who you were referring to when you used the word "administration"?'

Remember that, even though you are asking a question, you are actually in the role of listener—you are not the principal speaker. Therefore, do not let your question turn into a long speech. You are seeking information, not pursuing a cause.

Use Vocal and Nonverbal Cues

The psychologist Sigmund Freud once noted that "No mortal can keep a secret, for betrayal oozes out of us at every pore." Freud was simply echoing an idea noted elsewhere in this chapter: an effective listener knows that people "speak" with their bodies and their voices in addition to their words. This idea is of such importance that we will now develop it in more detail.

Vocal Cues. Most discriminating listeners have learned to read meaning into a speaker's use of volume, pitch, and rate. For example, most people show enthusiasm and emphasis by increased volume. Nervousness is often reflected, because of a tightening of the vocal cords, by a high pitch. And increases in rate of speaking usually demonstrate excitement.

Nonverbal Cues. Research in the area of nonverbal communication suggests that many people are very good at accurately reading nonverbal messages. You should learn to read these messages so that you can gain insight into a speaker's meaning and mood. Although you might be familiar with most of the nonverbal behaviors people engage in, let us quickly review some of these actions and relate them to listening.

Facial expressions are one of the most reliable and available indicators of a person's attitude. By reading a person's face, we can often decide if the person is passive, intense, nervous, or enthusiastic. Eye contact, or a lack of it, reveals levels of intimacy, self-confidence, nervous states, and interest. Posture and body movements offer us clues into status, enthusiasm, the importance of the point being made, friendliness, and emotional states.

Practice

Proficiency in any skill results from a great deal of conscientious effort. You should, therefore, practice listening. A poor listener avoids difficult listening situations and evades tedious material. A case in point might be a college lecture on a highly abstract concept that defies the application of interest devices by even the most skillful speaker. In such cases, listeners must work along with the speaker at gaining meaning. It is a great temptation to stop listening when listening requires effort. Because of this, a weak listener never improves. Force yourself to practice; make yourself listen to music, speeches, and conversations that seem to hold no obvious interest value. If you practice this important skill, you will improve. Remember the words of the Greek playwright Euripides: "Much effort, much prosperity."

Evaluating Speeches

In most instances the act of listening ends with our response to what we have been exposed to. That is to say, every word and idea does something to us. To be aware of our response, and to have some control over it, is the hallmark of a good listener. People who are trained in listening know that after they perceive and comprehend the sender's message, they need to decide if they want to use or reject what the speaker has said. This final step is a complex one. It asks us to combine the best of our listening skills with some reasoned subjectivity. We must first understand what we have heard and then decide its merits. The need for such careful analysis should be obvious.

We are constantly besieged with requests to vote, give, buy, feel, and think in one way or another. A poor listener is easy prey for sophists, hucksters, shysters, and propagandists. Our major defense against those who attempt to influence or control our behavior is a combination of critical thinking and cautious evaluation. Both of these skills can be learned, and your speech class, by allowing you an opportunity to hear over a hundred speeches, is an excellent place to refine your listening ability. At the end of most classroom speeches, you will have an opportunity to present an informal critique, either oral or written. By evaluating and discussing the speeches in your classroom, you are not only helping your classmates improve their speaking ability, but you are developing a skill that can be transferred to situations outside the educational setting. As you critique the speeches of others, try to implement the broad principles discussed by your instructor. In addition to using the criteria your instructor suggests, you can evaluate speeches by applying the yardsticks offered in the next few pages.

Purpose

Whenever we speak, we occupy both the life and time of another individual. Therefore, all listeners have a right to ask whether the purpose of a speech justified the amount of time and energy they gave it (or were asked to give it). Was the purpose clear or were speaker and audience part of an ambiguous encounter? Aimless rambling touching on topics from pets to pollution serves no purpose and only contributes to confusion.

Following are a few questions listeners can ask themselves about a speaker's purpose:

1. Was the subject worthy of my time?

2. Was the purpose suited to this audience?

3. Were the values stressed justified by the speaker?

4. Was the purpose an ethical one?

5. Was the purpose clear and easily recognizable?

Substance

Closely related to the issue of purpose is the criterion of substance—whether or not a speech has something worthwhile to say. A number of questions can be asked with regard to the substance of a speech:

1. Was the speaker prepared? Did the speaker attempt to be objective and fair to himself or herself, to the audience, and to the subject? Did the speaker seem to care about communicating, or was he or she simply going through the motions of fulfilling an assignment? For example, did the speaker appear to have practiced the speech?

2. Were there indications that the speaker had analyzed the audience? Were factors such as the audience's age, sex, culture, education, and attitudes taken into consideration? Did the speaker indicate that the speech was being directed at the classroom audience or at a hypothetical audience?

3. Did the speech seem to be original and creative? A unique and imaginative effort should be noted, as should one that is mundane and dull.

Argument

The success of any attempt to influence beliefs or actions depends heavily on the merit of the arguments that the speaker offers. What claims did the speaker make and how did he or she support them? Listeners should be especially alert to the following:

1. Did the speaker separate facts from inferences? Was personal opinion identified and not confused with evidence?

2. Did the speaker make extravagant and exaggerated claims? Did his or her support and reasoning directly relate to these generalizations? Did the generalizations go beyond the confines of the speaker's purpose?

3. Did the speaker's illustrations, examples, statistics, testimony, and analogies meet the tests of evidence? Did the speaker use enough evidence to support each point?

4. Was the material varied?

5. Was the evidence suited to this audience?

Structure

The ingredients of a message may have great merit, but if they are not arranged in the proper order, they may not make much sense to the audience. Therefore, clear structure is an essential requirement for the successful communication of ideas. After you have listened to a speaker, apply the following tests of clear speech structure:

1. Was a central unifying theme made apparent?

2. Was the main theme of the speech easy to follow?

3. Was an organizational sequence clearly discernible?

4. Did the introduction of the speech set a tone that encouraged you to listen to the rest of it? Did the beginning of the speech offer a preview of what the rest of the speech would cover?

5. Were the major segments of the speech well balanced? (The speaker should not spend 80 percent of his or her time on only one point if the speech has six major ideas.)

6. Did the ending of the speech tie all the key points together?

Style

Style is concerned with the ways in which a speaker uses language. Remember, language represents our feelings and ideas. The way a speaker uses language is an important aspect of any communication encounter. The questions asked of a speaker's style might include some of the items in the following list:

1. Was the speaker's language comprehensible and clear? (Ambiguity and vagueness confuse the listening process.)

2. Did the speaker use words and phrases that were adequately defined?

3. Were imagery and word pictures used in a manner that made the speech colorful, vivid, and interesting?

4. Did the speaker avoid clichés, slang, and poor grammar? Was the speaker's language appropriate to the audience, the occasion, and the subject?

5. If English was the second language for some of the audience members, did the speaker attempt to paraphrase or explain words that might be misunderstood because of cultural and language differences?

Credibility

As a speech critic, you need to evaluate a speaker's credibility as well as his or her speech content. Credibility consists of the characteristics a speaker manifests during a speech that make listeners perceive him or her to be trustworthy and competent. Among the questions relating to speaker credibility are the following:

1. Did the speaker demonstrate a mastery of the subject matter?

2. Did the speaker show genuine concern for the listeners' welfare?

3. Did the speaker's words, actions, and dress contribute to the believability of the speech?

4. Did the speaker behave in ways that detracted from his or her credibility?

5. Did the speaker appear to be trustworthy?

6. Did the speaker present his or her material in an impartial and honest manner?

7. Did the speaker avoid making personal attacks against those individuals who held opposing positions?

Cultural differences play a part in the perception of credibility (discussed in detail in chapters 14 and 16). It is important to keep culture in mind as you assess a speaker's credibility. That is to say, not all cultures use the same guidelines for deciding who is a credible speaker. For example, in many Asian cultures, where silence and reflection are valued over talk and action, someone who is quiet, calm, and pensive would be perceived as having higher credibility than would a speaker who is enthusiastic and spirited. In most Mediterranean and Latin cultures, being credible means being verbal, displaying rhetorical skills, and being extremely animated. There are even different standards of dress that need to be considered in deciding what is credible attire. In short, make sure you take a speaker's culture into account as you judge his or her credibility.

Delivery

Recall that delivery is the way in which a speaker uses his or her voice and body to communicate a verbal message. It is important to consider the following questions when assessing a speaker's delivery:

1. How effectively did the speaker use the visual aspects of delivery? Did he or she maintain good eye contact? Did he or she have good posture and skillfully execute gestures and movements? Did the speaker use animated facial expressions? Did the physical dimensions of the speech detract from the message?

2. How effectively did the speaker use his or her voice? Was there sufficient variety in rate, pace, tone, intensity, pitch, and volume?

3. Were enunciation and articulation clear and was pronunciation correct?

4. Did the speaker appear to be familiar with the speech?

5. Was the overall delivery an aid or a hindrance to the speech?

Effects

One of the major themes of this book is that public speaking is a goal-directed activity, aimed at producing a response from listeners—a response that the speaker has decided on before beginning the speech. Therefore, an evaluation of any speech must include a discussion of how well the speaker accomplished his or her purpose. To examine the consequences of the speech, you should ask these questions:

1. Was the time you spent listening to the speech worthwhile, or was your time wasted?

2. Did the speaker add to your fund of knowledge, change your views on a topic, or entertain you?

3. Did the speech seem to have a long-range goal as well as an immediate goal?

4. What was the total impression left by the speech? As a listener, you should evaluate the main idea as well as the subpoints. At the end of every speech, you should ask yourself, What is the overall effect of the speech?

5. Was the speaker ethical in his or her overall treatment of the topic and the material?

Presenting Your Evaluation

One of the reasons to improve your listening habits is so you can evaluate the remarks of others. Some of those evaluations will be directed at your classmates when they conclude their speeches. Using the guidelines offered in the last few pages as the grounds for your remarks, I now offer some advice about the best ways to discuss a fellow student's speech.

First, personal experience tells you that no one enjoys being criticized, so *begin your evaluation with a positive observation.* You might say:

> Peter, I found that your talk taught me some things I did not know about the harmful effects of overexposure to the sun. You obviously did a great deal of research.

This is not a recommendation to make your comments insincere or artificial, but rather is a reminder of the powerful effects your harsh evaluation might have on someone who has just finished delivering a speech. Therefore, when delivering your assessment of someone's talk, please remember what is written in Ecclesiastes 28:17, "The blow of a whip raises a welt, but a blow of the tongue crushes bones."

Second, *be specific.* The speaker will not learn very much if you offer a generalization such as "That was a good speech," or "I did not pay attention during some of your talk." In place of these general comments, you should say, "Your speech was good because your use of current statistics and testimony helped prove your point about how dangerous it is to spend too much time in the sun without taking proper precautions." With regard to the comment pertaining to attention, it would have been more helpful to say:

> I found that my mind drifted from the talk when you reached your conclusion. You started repeating the idea of using sunscreen over and over again, even after you had mentioned this precaution at least four times earlier in your talk.

Third, *provide the speaker with some methods of improvement.* It is not enough to simply offer your view of the talk. What is needed, if your fellow student is going to improve her or his communication behavior, are some suggestions that can be applied the next time he or she delivers a talk. Therefore, instead of saying only "Your evidence was not very convincing," you might add, "I think your evidence would have been much more persuasive if you had had a larger variety of sources and those sources had been more current."

Listener and Speaker Responsibilities

A French proverb tells us that "The spoken word belongs half to him who speaks and half to him who hears." Which, of course, is yet another way to remind us that communication is a two-way process. That is to say, the speaker and listener are interrelated and need each other for a variety of reasons. If the communication encounter is to be successful, each must realize his or her obligation to the other. Let us examine this tandem relationship and some of the responsibilities each party should assume in an attempt to increase the likelihood that a communication event will be a rewarding one.

❖ ❖ ❖ ❖   ## Listener Responsibility

To be effective listeners, we must do more than listen: *we must assume some of the responsibility for the communication act.* Not only should we evaluate the messages we have received from the speaker, but we should also be aware of what messages we have given the speaker. What have we "told" the speaker by the manner in which we listened? Did we make the speaker feel we were interested or uninterested? Were we rude or attentive? Did we encourage or discourage clarity? Did we contribute to the speaker's sense of speech anxiety or did we help reduce it? The answers to these and countless other questions deal directly with the type of feedback given the speaker. You will recall from chapter 1 that feedback is the response you give to another person about his or her communication. Let us once again return to the topic of feedback and see how it can be used to facilitate communication and then briefly look at some ways that feedback can thwart communication.

Practice Good Manners. In this book we have talked a great deal about cultural differences. We now mention a cultural universal—good manners. While there are many reasons that all cultures teach their young children to be polite, perhaps the most important reason is that being civil usually makes all the parties involved feel more comfortable. As applied to the listening context, this comfort is brought about because people are looking attentive and are not acting in a rude manner. Hence, the first listener responsibility is simply to be courteous.

Offer Positive Feedback. Good manners can be channeled into specific action. All speakers not only feel better about themselves and others but they communicate more effectively when they receive positive feedback from listeners. How much incentive would you have to continue speaking if the persons before you were balancing their checkbooks, frowning, or reading newspapers? In short, our behavior as listeners affects the speaker.

Responding to what you hear is a form of feedback. As indicated earlier, your feedback is the way you "talk back" to the speaker. There are a number of general ideas that you should keep in mind when offering feedback. First, *the speaker must perceive the feedback you are sending.* Your requests for clarification cannot be acted upon if they are not received. Second, *the feedback should be specific, not ambiguous.* The feedback should be clear and should contain the information that tells the speaker how he or she is doing. As we indicated earlier, even the questions you ask of the speaker, as a form of feedback, should be clear and concise. Third, *the feedback you give the speaker should directly relate to what is going on at*

Listeners should use feedback to improve their listening skills. (Photo: indexstock.com)

the time. It is of little benefit to either party if your response is delayed to the point that it is no longer germane. Feedback is most effective when it is immediate. Waiting until after a speech to send positive messages to the speaker might help his or her ego, but offering that feedback immediately, through posture or facial expression, would encourage the speaker when he or she needs it most. Finally, *your feedback will help you get more from the encounter if it is descriptive, not evaluative*. Telling someone, "Your report was detailed and clear, but I still have one or two questions" is better feedback than saying, "The report was very weak and left a great many unanswered questions."

In addition to the general considerations just mentioned, you can take some specific actions to help both you and the speaker. Some of the following suggestions apply to platform speaking, while others are useful in group discussion, interviewing, and everyday conversation.

1. Eye contact establishes rapport between a sender and receiver and encourages communication. Research indicates that we seem to look at people more when we feel comfortable around them.

2. Nodding the head slightly also tells a speaker that the listener is part of the communication process and is tuned in to what is going on.

3. An act as simple as smiling can offer warmth and support to a speaker. It may be just what he or she needs to get over the nervous feeling that often confronts speakers.

4. Casual remarks such as "I see" and "Is that so?" involve listeners with a speaker. Even vocalizations such as "uh-huh" can be encouraging.

5. Asking relevant questions after the talk helps a speaker in two ways. First, your question may enable the speaker to clarify a point of confusion that might be troubling other members of the audience. Second, by asking your question, you are demonstrating your interest both in the speaker and in the topic.

6. There are times when you can help a speaker by remaining silent. Too often, we contaminate a communication encounter by talking when talking is highly inappropriate.

7. Try to lean your torso slightly forward in a natural manner. This nonverbal act makes a speaker feel that you are interested in what is being said.

8. Try to maintain a relaxed but involved posture. This tells the speaker that you are not tense, a message that should help put the speaker at ease.

Avoid Negative Feedback. Although the items mentioned thus far tend to help speakers, some listener behaviors can have the opposite effect. Let us suggest a few actions that you should avoid if you want to help a speaker perform at his or her optimum level. Notice as we move through this list how uncomfortable you would feel if your listeners sent you these negative messages:

1. Frequent shifting of your body position can be a signal to a speaker that you are uninterested in or bored with the talk. Think of the message conveyed by feedback such as bouncing a leg up and down, as

if the listener has an airplane to catch and might be late if the speaker does not speed up.

2. A slouching posture can give the impression that you would rather be someplace else. If you sit as if you are a candidate for a chiropractor, the speaker will surely feel that he or she is intruding on your time. This mental picture can impede the speaker's efforts.

3. Engaging in other activity while a speaker is talking not only is discourteous but can keep the speaker from relaxing and doing his or her best work.

4. Try to imagine how disconcerting it would be to have someone respond to your words with a long, loud sigh. We all know the meaning of a sigh in our culture, and it is not a positive one.

5. Facial expressions such as frowning, raising an eyebrow, scowling, and rolling the eyes all send negative messages.

6. Shaking your head in a negative fashion will also bruise a speaker's confidence.

7. In the United States, having your arms folded in front of your chest sends a rather negative message to a speaker.

Speaker Responsibility

As a speaker, if you hope to accomplish your purpose, you need to perform certain tasks, one of which is to hold audience interest and attention. The reason is obvious; if the listeners are not listening, they cannot respond to what you are saying. Let us examine a few of the more common techniques that speakers can use to encourage more effective listening. Many of these techniques are discussed in more detail later in the book.

Try to Empathize. In chapter 3 we spent some time discussing the place of empathy in human communication. Basically, we noted that empathy is the process of putting yourself in the place of someone else so that you can shape your messages to meet his or her needs.

What was said then applies to this chapter. As a speaker, you must understand your listeners and how they will react to you and your message. This is best accomplished by trying to hear your ideas and words as the listeners will. If you have not thought about your listeners in advance, you might talk on a subject that holds little or no interest for them. By using empathy, you can view your speech content as the listeners will, and you will not be asking them to listen to material that is inappropriate and uninteresting.

Adjust Your Delivery. In chapter 4, we talked about how a speaker's voice and body can aid listeners in understanding his or her verbal message. Always make sure you can be heard. It is very frustrating for a listener to strain in order to know what is being said. Moreover, delivery should be animated enough to arouse and maintain interest.

Another dimension of delivery adjustment can be found in the area of culture. You need to accommodate the listeners if they are from a culture different from your own. If English is their second language, you can help them listen by talking more slowly and paraphrasing extensively. If they are from a culture that values calmness, you can tone down your volume and level of animation.

Use Feedback. Listeners must use feedback to improve their listening skills; the same principle applies to speakers. As speakers, we should be sensitive to what our messages are doing to the people who receive them. Are they paying attention? Do they look interested? Do they look confused? Are they seeking more information? These are but a few of the questions that feedback may answer. Once we speakers secure this information via feedback, we are in a better position to make the necessary adjustments. If we sense apathy or that the audience is not listening, we can try to arouse attention and point the material directly to the needs of the audience.

As a speaker, you can do a number of things to improve the quality of the feedback you receive. First, although it may not be appropriate in all instances, *you can tell the audience that you want feedback.* This lets them know that you want them to keep you informed as to how they are reacting to your message. Second, *you can learn to be sensitive to nonverbal communication.* As you recall, nonverbal messages carry approximately 55 percent of the meaning of an utterance. Learning to read those meanings will tell you if the audience is listening. Be careful how you read this nonverbal feedback, however, when your audience represents a variety of cultures. As noted elsewhere, people from the Mediterranean area are likely to be very animated, while people from Eastern Asia might not outwardly show you what they think of your talk. Third, if the situation allows for it, *you can even ask questions of the audience* as a way of determining if they are listening. A Danish proverb offers the following advice: "Better ask twice than lose your way." As a speaker, you can modify this maxim to read, "Whenever appropriate, I should ask questions of my listeners." Their responses give you the opportunity to measure how well they understand you. By asking questions, the listeners are able to seek additional information in those areas that are not clear.

Be Clear. You know from your own experience that it is very difficult to listen to a speech that rambles aimlessly. As speakers, we can meet part of our responsibilities by being well organized. We will discuss much more about clarity and organization later in this book, but for now remember that it is unfair to ask a listener to make sense of disjointed wanderings. If the listeners represent dissimilar cultures, you might also want to make extensive use of transitions, previews, and other devices that contribute to clarity.

Be Interesting. If material lacks interest for us, it is difficult to listen; hence, as speakers we must strive to make our content lively, stimulating, and relevant. This means learning how to establish and maintain audience attention with techniques such as suspense, humor, and novelty. These, and many other attention devices, will be developed in detail later in this book, but for now we simply need to underscore the importance of enhancing the speaking process to avoid being colorless and dull.

Culture and Listening

One of the major themes of this book is that the ways in which we communicate, the circumstances of our communication, the language and language style we use, and nonverbal behaviors are primarily all a response to, and a function of, our culture. What is true about verbal and nonverbal communication is also true about listening. That is to say, listening, like most communication variables, is influenced by culture. That influence is seen in a number of different ways. To help you better understand the role of culture in listening, let us look at some of the specific links existing between a culture and listening.

First, in many cultures in the Far East, the amount of time spent talking, and the value placed on talking, is very different from what happens in those cultures that value conversation and public speaking (Middle East, Mexico, the United States). In Japan, for example, the culture is very homogeneous and most people share similar experiences. The commonality often allows them to know what the other person is thinking without the use of words. In fact, they often believe words get in the way of understanding. Think for a moment of the message contained in the Asian proverb, "By your mouth you will perish." Or what about the view toward silence versus talk in the Buddhist saying, "There is truth that words cannot ever reach." It is easy to see how these two orientations, one favoring talk and one preferring silence, could influence the listening process.

Second, when judging delivery as a clue to what is being said, remember to allow for cultural variations. That is to say, some cultures value active speakers and some value passive. For example, in Japan, Thailand, and Korea, speakers tend to talk in soft voices, while in the Mediterranean area, the appropriate volume is much more intense. Even the size and number of gestures are controlled by culture. You cannot expect people from a culture that values reserved behavior to engage in the same number of gestures as one that has a very energetic communication style.

Third, a person's culture will even be reflected in the question-and-answer period discussed earlier in the chapter. If the speaker was from the Chinese or Japanese culture, for example, they would not expect questions from the floor. Questioning a speaker would cause both the speaker and listener to lose "face"—or, by Western standards, be embarrassed and humiliated in front of other people. Questioning the speaker would bring discomfort because it would appear that the speaker was not clear in expressing his or her views—hence, the need for a question. The listener would lose "face" because having to ask a question would indicate she or he did not understand what was being said.

Fourth, as you listen you will experience the sway of culture as it affects accents and vocabulary. Accents by people trying to speak English as a second language and the confusion they may experience with vocabulary often make it more difficult for you to listen and comprehend what is being discussed. In these instances, my advice is rather simple and straightforward—be tolerant and practice being patient. You might also put yourself in the place of someone trying to speak a second language that is new and often complex. This attempt at empathy will usually increase your concentration and your compassion.

Finally, developing empathy as a listener is also influenced by culture. As you would suspect, it is very hard to develop empathy toward someone you do not know. If you are talking to your best friend and she has a look on her face that you have seen many times before, you are apt to be able to read that expression with a degree of accuracy. An expression on the face of a stranger might be more difficult to interpret. If you add the variable of culture, the process of reading internal states becomes even more difficult. For example, not all cultures display their emotions in the same manner. In cultures such as the Asian and Native American, outward signs of emotion are very uncommon. Members of these cultures are taught to "keep things inside." As you can imagine, it can be very perplexing to try to empathize without sufficient information about what a person is thinking and feeling.

You will even be confronted with situations in which the verbal information that listeners offer cannot be used to develop empathy. For example, in North American culture, you can ask people to respond verbally to what is going on at a particular moment and they will supply you with the data you need to determine if they understand what you are talking about. However, remember that people in some cultures will not answer your request for information on their feelings about what you are discussing. In the Japanese and Chinese cultures, people often say "yes" even when they mean "no," as a way of saving face. In many Latin cultures, where social harmony is important, people supply the response they think you want to hear rather than answering truthfully, which they believe might upset you. You need to approach the subject of empathy carefully if the audience is composed of people from diverse cultures.

Summary

Listening is one of our most important communication skills. Effective listening is an active process that demands conscientious effort. Virtually everyone can improve his or her listening ability simply by becoming aware of some of the problems of listening and their remedies.

A listener who is sincere about improvement should be alert to the major barriers to effective listening: poor listening habits (faking attention, listening only for facts, avoiding difficult material, avoiding the uninteresting, criticizing the speaker, yielding to distractions), defensive listening, prejudices, constant self-focus, message overload, the thinking-speaking rate, and short attention spans.

You can become a better listener if you identify your personal listening characteristics, prepare to listen, have a specific listening purpose, make use of the thinking-speaking time difference, focus on matter rather than on manner, be active, ask questions, use vocal and nonverbal cues, and practice listening.

Speech criticism and evaluation are also explored in this chapter. Listeners should question much of what they hear and, whenever possible, offer constructive criticism to the speaker. This criticism can be centered on questions of purpose, substance, argument, structure, style, credibility, delivery, and effects. When offering an evaluation, it is important to be positive and specific and to offer suggestions for improvement.

Both listeners and speakers have certain communication responsibilities that are built into each encounter. Listeners should create a positive psychological environment by adopting a listening attitude and posture that encourages the speaker to reach his or her full potential—the listeners should try to put the speaker at ease. The speaker can meet some of his or her obligations by (1) trying to empathize with the listeners, (2) making adjustments to the delivery, (3) using feedback, (4) being sure that the message is clear and well organized, and (5) seeing that content is interesting, lively, stimulating, and relevant.

Finally, to be an effective listener, you must adapt to the countless communication events that have you interacting with people from different cultures. On those occasions, it is important that you practice tolerance, patience, and empathy.

Concepts and Questions

1. Why is listening an important part of the communication process?

2. Explain the process of listening.

3. What are some common misconceptions about listening? How can those misconceptions create listening problems?

4. What are some major questions that a listener should ask if he or she is going to evaluate a speech?

5. What are some major barriers to effective listening? How can those barriers be overcome?

6. How can taking notes help the listening process?

7. What are the speaker's responsibilities in a speech situation?

8. What are the listener's responsibilities in a speech situation?

Activities and Exercise

1. Attend a public speaking event. Make a log of what distractions you experienced while trying to listen to the speaker.

2. Sit on a bench somewhere on campus. Close your eyes and try to take mental note of all the different sounds you hear.

3. Listen to a political speaker and evaluate his or her speech in light of the characteristics discussed in this chapter.

4. Write an essay in which you candidly evaluate your listening habits. Conclude the essay with a discussion of those areas you plan to work on during the course of the semester.

5. Try to locate two public-speaking situations that are basically the same. At the first event do not take notes. During the second speech take notes. Then write a short essay that discusses the differences in your listening behavior in the two situations. ✦

Part Two

Your Ideas

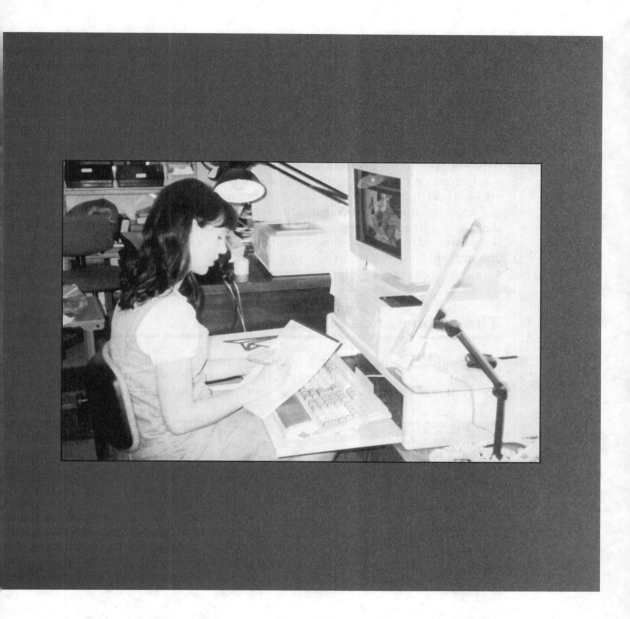

CHAPTER SIX

Evidence: The Foundation of Your Ideas

Comment is free, but the facts are sacred.

—*Charles Scott*

We begin this chapter with a simple yet important question: Why do you hold the attitudes and beliefs that you do? You were not born believing that capital punishment should be abolished, that the recycling of trash is one way to help save the environment, or that using animals for laboratory testing is cruel. The reason you have these views, and countless others, is that something in your life—a talk with your parents, a television program, a newspaper article, a conversation with a friend, a politician's remarks, a website you visited, or some other experience—gave you the data and rationale that enabled you to reach the personal view you now hold. What is important for our analysis is not the idea that attitudes and beliefs are personal but rather that these attitudes were prompted by ideas and materials that were, at one time, external to you. Someone, or something, contributed to your belief. This chapter will concentrate on how you can present ideas and materials to other people so that you can alter and change their beliefs and attitudes.

The Importance of Evidence

We all know that stating a point does not necessarily render it clear, believable, or true. There may be assertions that listeners will understand and accept at face value because the assertions are consistent with their existing

The evidence you offer your listeners not only helps to prove your claim, but it can make your speech more interesting and memorable.

beliefs and prejudices. Students who have difficulty finding a parking space each day when they drive to campus do not need much proof when you assert that "parking at this college is a serious problem." The "facts" for them are apparent and compelling, much like the quotation from Henry David Thoreau, "Some evidence is very strong, as when you find a trout in the milk." More frequently, however, our statements by themselves are not "strong"; therefore, listeners require that our assertions be supported and explained with evidence. For example, a speaker on a college campus advocated that the football team be disbanded on the grounds that it was a financial burden to the student body and that it benefited only a small number of students. Because this charge was merely asserted and not supported with proof, the speaker's plea was not heeded. The speaker needed evidence to support the assertion.

The evidence you offer your listeners not only helps prove your claim, but it serves some additional needs your audience may have. For example, when used effectively, forms of support can make a speech more interesting and help listeners remember your main points. Notice in the following example, from a speech on dog attacks against humans, how a speaker made her material compelling, persuasive, memorable, and interesting by using three different forms of evidence.

> See these scars on my arm; they were caused by a dog. Not my dog, but my neighbor's. Last month I was walking my dog around the block as I do every night. As I passed my neighbor's yard, I noticed that her guard dog was not barking at me and my dog. Even stranger was the fact that her dog was not in its normal location. I immediately knew that something was wrong. And I was right. From around the corner of the house, with teeth showing, came her dog. I knew that the dog would try to attack my dog, so I attempted to get between the two dogs. This turned out be a bad mistake, for instead of attacking my dog the guard dog attacked me. And you can see the results on my arm. I learned a few days later that according to the Center for Disease Control and Prevention I was just one out of 4.7 million Americans who get gnawed by dogs annually. With those types of numbers, you can easily see how you might be the next victim of an aggressive dog.

As you see from our previous discussion and the above example, evidence is a necessary component of successful communication because it helps prove and clarify the validity of our ideas. In this chapter we will talk about what supporting materials are and how you can use them to accomplish your specific purpose.

Verbal Support

Some of the things we say about a particular subject are incidental; we use them to get and hold listeners' attention. On the other hand, some points are fundamental and vital to the accomplishment of our speaking purpose. Therefore, one of our basic tasks as speakers is to study our subject until we recognize the elements in it that are essential to accomplishing our purpose. The essential components that help render our ideas understandable and believable are called **forms of support.** The word "support" accurately describes their function because the materials we select provide sustenance for the central theme of our speech. Just as a builder uses certain materials to construct a house, so you, as a speaker, have to supply the materials for developing and proving your ideas. Using supporting materials enables us to say to listeners, "Driving at 55 miles an hour was an excellent law, and we should all work to have Congress and the President reinstate it. And here is why. There is proof that the 55-mile-an-hour speed limit saves lives and fuel. Let me explain." The "whys" enable you to offer reasons that might make your opinions believable and acceptable to another person. They are your forms of support.

Let us consider some of the specific forms of support available to clarify and/or prove an important and fundamental assertion. Although our analysis discusses only one form of support at a time, in reality you will seldom be able to prove your point with a single piece of evidence. As Aristotle reminded us over two thousand years ago, "One swallow does not make a summer"; similarly, one form of support does not prove a point. The content of your speech is much like a jigsaw puzzle, for just as it takes many pieces to complete the picture, your forms of support must work in combination.

Illustrations

Regardless of the culture, storytelling has commanded and held attention since the beginning of recorded history. All teachers, preachers, lawyers, and writers know how important a good story can be. These narratives, whether on television, in books, on computer or movie screens, or transmitted face-to-face, are essential devices for proving and clarifying a point while at the same time maintaining interest. We are all curious as we listen to the story to hear why this or that happened or how the tale will end. The fact that a story or an example holds attention renders it an excellent tool in nearly all communication situations.

An **illustration** is the narration of an incident that amplifies, proves, or clarifies the point under consideration. It is, in a sense, a speaker saying to the audience, "Here is an example of what I mean." It can also be thought of as a story that supports the point the speaker is trying to make. Illustrations generally take one of two forms: (1) detailed, factual illustrations or (2) hypothetical illustrations.

Detailed, Factual Illustrations. Think of a **detailed, factual illustration** as a striking and vivid story that answers the questions *who? what? where? when?* and *how?* Because of the detail in the story, and because the story is true, a factual illustration can be both lifelike and meaningful to the audience. The knowledge that something actually occurred is a source of interest. Notice how interest is stirred when we hear someone say, "Let me tell you about this frightening thing that happened to me last week as I was walking to my car." We are now ready for the story—the details of what happened on that day. The popularity of biographies and "reality" television programs gives further credence to the idea that most of us like hearing about other people and events, and we like it best when the information comes in the form of a detailed, well-told story. The captivating nature of a true story was cleverly explained by English author Edward Stillingfleet: "The story should, to please, be true, be apropos, well told, concise, and new; and whensoe'er it deviates from these rules, the wise will sleep, and leave applause to fools."

Let us now look at a few examples of factual illustrations of a topic that aroused interest.

Trying to convince an audience that the drug called angel dust is dangerous, a student speaker used the following detailed, factual illustration to help *prove his assertion and gain support* for his idea:

> A friend of mine had heard so much about a street drug called angel dust that he decided to try some. Although I urged him not to experiment with this substance, he and a few friends went to a rock concert, and he thought it might be a good place to try out this new drug. He took the angel dust and waited for something to happen. And it did! At first, he became very irritable and anxious. He then started arguing with his friends for no apparent reason. The arguing quickly escalated to hostility and violence. The confrontation became so intense that the police had to be called to the section of the stadium where he was sitting. By then, my friend had become so violent and out of control that it took six police officers to subdue him and take him to jail. During the course of his thrashing around, he cut his head badly enough to need 17 stitches. When the drug finally left his system, he was still not fully recovered. For months afterwards, he had a paranoid tendency toward the police and believed that they were trying to capture him. It became so bad that he had to leave school and go to a hospital for treatment. For my friend, angel dust was indeed dangerous.

Factual illustrations are *useful for clarifying* as well as for proving a point. Notice in the following example how the speaker gives an illustration to explain what she is referring to when she talks about the problem of solid waste. The illustration lets the listeners see an actual case so that the concept will be clear:

> There it was—the ship called the *Good Dream* from port of New York. It was now bobbing down the Atlantic Coast and through the Caribbean. It was a 3,100-ton barge loaded with unwanted trash. After 41 days and more than 2,000 smelly miles at sea, the barge was still searching for a home. With an end to its odious odyssey nowhere in sight, the scow raised once again the dilemma of a throwaway society, quickly running out of room for all its solid waste.

Illustrations can also add a *touch of reality and personalize* the story by dealing with "real" people:

> Let me tell you about Molly, a typical victim of domestic violence. I first met Molly huddled on my front porch at six in the morning, when I was leaving for work. She was wearing only a bathrobe. Her hands were bleeding; she had cigarette burns on her arms and large, dark bruises on her neck. Molly told me that she and her husband had fought, and that he had tried to kill her. When he started to get a knife from the drawer, she decided to run, and that is how she ended up on my front porch. Molly told me that this was not the first time she had needed to flee for her life. It seems that Molly, like so many other women, was a victim of ongoing domestic violence.

A well-told story can *capture and focus attention*. In the following example, notice how the narrative attracts attention to the problem of carjacking:

> So you believe that carjacking is only a series of statistics? Not for my best friend, Janet. On a warm summer night last month, Janet was walking to her car after working in the library all day, when, without any warning, two teenagers stepped out from behind a pillar and accosted her. They forced her into the trunk of her 1996 Ford Mustang. Five hours later, after being tossed around in the trunk of her car, she was eventually hurled out onto the pave-

ment as her abductors drove away. She was comatose and suffering from dehydration as a result of the 130-degree heat in the trunk when the police found her, forty minutes later. After two weeks Janet finally regained some consciousness, but doctors fear she may have suffered irreversible brain damage. For Janet, carjacking was more than a statistic. Carjacking changed her entire life—forever and ever.

An illustration can *serve as the springboard for the presentation of additional and more specific evidence.* For instance, in the following example, a speaker is able to use his factual illustration as an introduction and transition for other pieces of evidence in a speech on the importance of recycling:

> The other day, while I was enjoying a walk along the beach, I noticed a number of shiny objects floating in the water. At first I thought they were fish, so I decided to walk closer and have a better look. Much to my surprise, my nose and eyes soon told me that what I was smelling and seeing was not fish but tin cans, plastic trash bags, and garbage sacks. I was seeing the negative effects of what is called ocean dumping—a waste disposal system that I have since discovered is bringing harm to those areas that have tried to dispose of their trash in this manner. The problem, however, seems to be that incineration and sanitary landfill methods also present serious problems. Let us look at those problems.

Notice in our next example, on a speech dealing with suicide, how a speaker is able to use a *factual illustration to prepare us for statistics:*

> I was touched by the sadness that suicide can bring last year when my roommate Scott killed himself during spring vacation. By all outward signs you would never suspect that Scott would be someone who would take his own life. He was a good student, well liked by his peers, had a winning smile, a delightful sense of humor, and appeared to have specific career goals. Yet on April 7, Scott took his father's handgun, held it up to his head, and pulled the trigger. I was shocked when I heard the news. I, like all of you, knew about suicide, but I thought it was one of those things that happened to other people, not to people I knew. But since Scott's death, I have discovered that suicide is not uncommon in the United States. In fact, in the United States there are approximately 30,000 suicide deaths annually, which averages to 17 Americans per day.

All the illustrations in the last few pages had some common characteristics that contributed to their overall effectiveness. Let us highlight these characteristics in terms of evidence:

Talk about concrete places and events.

Refer to familiar topics.

Use colorful and vivid language.

Be interesting.

Relate the story directly to the main point.

Try to personalize the story.

Hypothetical Illustrations. The **hypothetical illustration** is yet another effective illustration. *This type of illustration is a detailed, fictional illustration that allows the audience to see "what could be" or "what could be supposed."* Hypothetical illustrations are most often used to depict future events or to make the future seem graphically clear. In a speech dealing with a proposal to raise school taxes, you might offer a hypothetical illustration of how the proposal would affect the audience. If you were telling the audience that there are dangers associated with being a "latchkey child," you could ask the listeners to imagine a child coming home to an empty house and playing with matches. You might offer a detailed hypothetical illustration to convince the listeners that high school dropouts have a difficult time securing employment—as in the following:

> Suppose a friend of yours, who is still in high school, decides that he has had enough school. He is doing poorly in math and English and feels there is no real need to finish the semester. On Saturday, he asks the owner of a local market to give him a job. The market owner can pay only $5 an hour, but your friend, having never made that much money, decides to take the job instead of reporting back to school on Monday. After about two weeks on the job, he is dismissed. Business is off at the store and the owner can't afford any extra help. Your friend then goes from store to store and from factory to factory, looking for employment, but he soon discovers that employers are not interested in hiring someone without at least a high school education. Your friend, in essence, is unable to find work because he left school.

Depicting the future with an illustration can place listeners in a situation that affects them personally and emotionally. A question such as, What happens if you reject the idea of added security patrols on campus? affords the speaker an opportunity to place the audience in the center of a hypothetical picture. For example, the speaker, talking about campus security, could have the audience visualize the point he or she is trying to make by saying, "Imagine you are walking to your car late one night after studying in the library . . ."

In the following example, from a speech on cigarettes and lung cancer, we can see how the speaker let the listeners see themselves as the central figures in the illustration:

> Let us assume for a moment that you are a smoker, and as a smoker you find yourself in the following situation. You wake up one night and discover that your chest is burning. At breakfast, you seem to be coughing more and are having difficulty catching your breath. You decide it is just a cold, so you put off going to the doctor. As the day goes on, the pain and the cough get worse, so you make an appointment to see the doctor. As part of your examination, the doctor takes an x-ray of your lungs, which reveals grave damage. The doctor tells you what you already know—that if you had not smoked, this problem would most likely have never have happened.

When used effectively, hypothetical examples propel listeners into the future by telling what can happen if this or that proposal is not followed. In the next example, an effective hypothetical illustration shows what an earthquake would be like if we were not prepared:

> You now begin to feel the room rock back and forth. It is an earthquake, and now you must make some decisions. You can't decide if you should stay in one spot or try to locate a safe place. But, you ask yourself, what is a safe place? As the room shakes with even more force, you find yourself also wondering, Where is the first aid kit if I need it? How do I turn off the gas, water, and electricity? And what will I eat and drink? If you listen to my talk today, you will be able to answer these and other questions concerning what to do before, during, and after an earthquake.

As was the case with factual illustrations, the hypothetical illustration should be a story that is vivid and interesting. In the next example, from a speech dealing with the overcrowding at the Grand Canyon, a speaker uses a hypothetical example to make his point:

> Imagine that you and some friends have just arrived at the top rim of the Grand Canyon and you are ready to start a hike that you have been planning for over a year. After you park your car in a parking lot that reminds you of the lots at a large shopping mall, you approach what you believe to be the start of the trail. However, you suddenly stop. You can't believe your eyes. There in front of you is a line that is similar to those you experienced when you visited Disneyland. This line seems to run on for miles. It appears that all of the 5 million visitors to the Grand Canyon have decided to hike on the same day. As you and your friends slowly make your way down a well-worn path to the start of the trail, you notice that the ground is covered with trash. At that moment, you begin to realize that the large crowds will keep you from your dream. You have discovered what other people now know, that the Grand Canyon is too crowded to be enjoyed. But there is something we can do about it, and that is what I would like to talk about today.

In using a hypothetical illustration, a few key points need to be kept in mind.

1. *You should never present an imaginary story as being a true one.* Use phrases such as "imagine a situation such as this," "suppose you discover," or "what would happen if" to allow the audience to separate fact from fiction.

2. *If a hypothetical illustration is going to be effective, it must seem reasonable and capable of happening.* An obvious exaggeration will offend your listeners.

3. *An imaginary story, although very interesting, proves very little.* As a student of communication, you should try to locate other forms of evidence if you are trying to prove a point. This will let you rely on hypothetical illustrations to clarify a point or arouse emotions.

4. *When using a hypothetical example, make certain that it is appropriate and related directly to the point in question.* The story must not be in the speech for its own sake, but for the purpose of supporting or clarifying an idea.

Specific Instances

A **specific instance**, *although somewhat similar to an illustration, is actually a very specific example that omits much of the detail and development of an extended factual illustration.* In many cases specific instances are no longer than a sentence or two. As such, several condensed examples are advanced by the speaker as a means of indicating the widespread nature of a situation or of suggesting the frequency of an occurrence. Since a specific instance is short and takes little time to present, it allows the speaker to offer a great deal of material in a short amount of time. For instance, if you are asserting that college graduates are having very little trouble locating good teaching positions, you might establish your point by stating, "John Timmons, a friend of mine who majored in education, found an excellent teaching position after he graduated from college. Graduates from San Francisco State University and from UCLA are also reporting very little difficulty in locating good teaching jobs."

Speaking on the topic of new research on alternative fuels, a student recently told her audience that "Nissan was testing a methanol-fueled vehicle, BMW was working on a hydrogen-powered car, and Italy's Fiat was about to offer an electric car to interested buyers."

Still another example of a specific instance might appear in a talk about the value of the honor system. The case could be aided by saying, "The University of Indiana has found the honor system to be successful; Purdue University and the University of California at Davis have also reported satisfactory results from the honor system." By using actual people, places, events, and things, the speaker makes the material both meaningful and persuasive.

Some examples may require only a few words: "College tuition at state universities is so high that my friend Roger could not come to school this year, nor could my roommate from last semester." Other examples may call for a sentence or two:

> There are countless endangered species that are found all over the world. In North America, we see that the humpback whale has now been added to the list of animals in great peril. It is estimated that by the year 2000 the golden toad of Central America will disappear from the earth, and, in South America, the black lion tamarin also faces extinction.

Regardless of the length of the specific instances, they add strength and understanding to an idea. They provide excellent proof and are often *most effective when they directly follow a detailed, factual illustration.* For example, a student who wanted to prove that a recent strike had adversely affected the workers supported her position by relating a true story (factual illustration) of a worker who had to sell his home and relocate his family because of the strike. The speaker then bolstered the case by offering two undeveloped illustrations that showed how other families were touched by the strike:

> Because of the prolonged strike, Tom Gemhouse had to watch his car being repossessed, and Sally Peters, for the first time in her life, had to accept food stamps.

As is the case with so many of the forms of support, *specific instances often work best when they are used in combination with other pieces of evidence.* In the next extended example, notice how the speaker used specific instances along with statistics and expert testimony:

> Everywhere we look we see animals vanishing from the planet. In Asia, the Asiatic lion, snow leopard, giant panda, and kouprey are nearly extinct. Scientists now tell us that, at the rate we are going, we are eliminating 50 to 100 species every day. So rapid is this extermination that Thomas Lovejoy of the Smithsonian Institution recently noted that 'insects, birds, and mammals are vanishing at a rate much faster than we can calculate.'

Guidelines for Using Illustrations

When you use narratives to clarify or prove your point, it is important that they meet certain requirements. Remember, when you use an example or illustration, you may be asking the listener to draw a conclusion and believe your assertion from the illustration. For instance, someone might try to condemn all student athletes because of one football player who failed three classes. In drawing a generalization from that one example, the speaker is suggesting that the example supports the assertion. To avoid such errors, ask the following questions when you use or listen to illustrations presented as a justification for a specific hypothesis:

Is the illustration a typical case? There can be no absolute measure of "typical" in applying this test. The answer depends on many factors, but most importantly on the phenomenon being discussed. If the conclusion of the argument is controversial and primarily a value judgment, a listener should expect more than one or two illustrations. Just as you cannot indict all football players from a single example, you cannot prove that downtown Burbank is not a safe city because your friend was beaten and robbed there.

Is the example clearly relevant to the idea? When we talked about critical listening in chapter 5, we observed that a careful listener learns to ask, "So what?" of certain information. Checking the relevancy of examples is merely an extension of that idea. If we were to talk about the dangers of night driving and cite only an illustration of someone whose brakes had failed, we would be guilty of offering an irrelevant case.

Is there other evidence to support the conclusion being made by the generalization? This test should be applied to any evidence, whether it is presented in the form of an illustration, a statistic, testimony, or an analogy. Before you are satisfied that the example proves the point, you should ask for other facts and authoritative opinions that might suggest the falsity or validity of the generalization. Suppose, for example, that you are urging reforms in college registration procedures and have offered a single illustration to substantiate the need for reforms. Your position will be enhanced if you offer additional support, such as citing remarks of the dean of admissions, which adds believability to your thesis.

Statistics

While the use of narratives has a long history, dating back as far as people have been coming together, statistics is a relatively new science. The use of statistics can be traced back only to the Old Testament and to population records commingled by the Babylonians and the Romans. Even with this short history, scholars and social critics have had a love/hate relationship with numbers and statistics as a device used to prove a point. English writer Sir Thomas Browne was almost poetic when he wrote, "I have often admired the mystical way of Pythagoras, and the secret magic of numbers." However, the American author Mark Twain, disturbed by the misuse of statistics, had a very different view of numbers when he wrote the famous lines, "There are three kinds of lies, lies, damned lies, and statistics." In many ways, both men are correct. That is to say, statistics are a powerful and useful tool, but they must be used correctly.

It is best to view statistics as examples. They are a numerical method for proving or describing something. You will recall that this was the same function we attributed to narratives. However, with statistics you are not talking about one or two cases or instances, you are attempting to measure and

❖ ❖ ❖ ❖

define instances quantitatively. Because statistics are facts or occurrences represented numerically, they compare or show proportions as a means of helping a speaker develop and prove a point. Used in this way, statistics help compress, summarize, and simplify facts that relate to the issue in question. They are generalizations derived from comparisons of individual instances. For example, instead of talking about how alcoholism affects one person, a speaker can use statistics to examine how the disease harms many people. Notice how much more serious and widespread alcoholism appears as a speaker says, "There are an estimated 12 million alcoholics in the United States. They account for 50 percent of all auto fatalities, 80 percent of all home violence, 30 percent of all suicides, and 60 percent of all child abuse."

Although it is not our intent in this section on statistics to ask you to become an expert in statistical analysis, we believe that to use statistics effectively you need to understand a few basic terms that you find in the material you read and that you might want to use in your speech. Many of these ideas have most likely been introduced to you in your mathematics or psychology classes. Specifically, I will explain what is meant by *range, mean, median, mode,* and *percentages.*

Range. *The range is the extent and amount of variation of anything.* It is the difference between the highest and the lowest numbers that are being examined. It can be the high and low temperature during the month of December or the difference between the number of handgun accidents in 1996 and the number in 1998.

Mean. *The mean is the average that describes the central tendency of what is being examined.* As you might remember from your mathematics classes, the mean is obtained by adding up all the items and then dividing by the total number of items.

Median. Another useful descriptive statistic is the median. *The median is the middle point in a series of numbers arranged in order from highest to lowest.* The median number will then mean that half the numbers lie above that number and half fall below it (2, 5, 8, 10, 13—the median number is 8).

Mode. *The mode is the score (number) that occurs the greatest number of times* (2, 2, 5, 5, 5, 8, 10—5 is the mode).

Percentages. Finally, there are statistics discussed and shown in percentages. *Percentages show the relationship of a portion to a whole, expressed in hundredths.* For example, if you said "75 percent of the 852 students polled approved of this plan," you would be automatically saying that out of all the students in the survey (100 percent), three-quarters approved the plan.

Statistics, like illustrations, *may be either brief or detailed.* Let us look at just a few examples of how concise statistics can be. Speaking on the subject of heart problems, a speaker might simply say, "*Time* magazine noted that heart attacks claim about 550,000 lives each year." If the subject were the growing population of the elderly, a speaker could quickly say, "In 1990, 11 percent of the population was over sixty-five years of age; that figure in 1998 is 14 percent."

Even when they are short, *statistics can be tied together in a series.* Speaking on the topic of violence in public schools, a speaker noted the following:

According to the National Education Association, every school day sees at least 100,000 students toting guns to school. Forty students are hurt or killed by firearms, 6,250 teachers are threatened with bodily injury, and 260 teachers are physically assaulted.

Another speaker used a string of statistics to prove that family violence is a serious problem when she said, "At least 1.8 million women are battered every year. Twenty percent of the women seeking emergency surgical procedures are victims of domestic violence. More than 1200 children die each year through child abuse."

There are also occasions when statistics take a slightly longer form. Discussing the topic of waste disposal, a speaker used the following statistics to show just what people are trying to discard:

> What to do with waste material in this country is a very serious problem. In one year, we needed to find a place to dump 2 million tons of major appliances; 22 million tons of food; 10 million tons of newspapers; 3 million tons of plates, towels, and napkins; and 52 million tons of bottles and containers.

You should not assume that because statistics are numbers they are automatically uninteresting. A well-trained speaker can make them appealing. In the following example, notice how a speaker used statistics to make the topic of ecology interesting:

> Let us look at what could happen if just one typical office practiced measures to conserve and preserve the world's natural resources. For instance, if just one person were to use his or her own ceramic mug in the office each day, it would eliminate as many as 500 throwaway cups a year. The same office worker using a half-page cover sheet for a fax instead of a full page and sending five faxes a day would save about six rolls of paper each year. And if the other employees in that 50-person office used both sides of the paper just 10 percent of the time, the office could save ten trees and $750 a year just in reduced paper cost.

Statistics often enable a speaker to make quite *striking comparisons*. Note how a speaker who is opposing a petition that would have Congress and the President reconsider the 55-mile-per-hour speed limit used comparisons to make his point:

> According to the calculations of most economists, the 55-mile-per-hour speed limit causes enough of a traffic slowdown to waste about $6 billion worth of travel time per year. The National Highway Traffic Safety Administration says we save about 4500 lives per year because of the speed limit; hence, it costs about $1.5 million per life saved. Is this a bargain, or are there other social policies that might save more lives for less money? Well, it has been estimated that placing a smoke detector in every home in the United States would save about as many lives in total as the 55-mile-per-hour limit and would cost only $50,000 to $80,000 per life saved; more kidney dialysis machines could save lives for only about $2,000 per life saved; and there are even a number of highway improvements that could be made, through reducing roadside hazards, and would cost only about $20,000 to $100,000 per life saved. At a cost of $1.5 million per saved life, the 55-mile-per-hour speed limit is hardly a bargain.

The comparative nature of statistics was also evident when a speaker, trying to demonstrate how much we spend on the military compared with what we spend on social problems, offered the following comparisons:

> The United States is first in military spending, first in military technology, first in total global military bases and naval fleets, and first in the number of nuclear bombs and warheads. Yet we rank seventh in life expectancy, tenth in

spending for public education per student, fourteenth in proportion of population with access to safe water, and seventeenth in infant mortality rate.

Although we are treating each of the forms of support in separate units, they actually *work in combination*. In the following example, dealing with the government's increased interest in synthetic fuels, notice how the speaker used both statistics and expert testimony to help prove her point:

> The lure of getting in on the ground floor of new energy developments—with government help—is attracting applicants to synthetic fuels. Sixty-one companies in twenty-four states have applied for loan guarantees and price supports from the U.S. Synthetic Fuels Corporation, which was created by Congress to stimulate the development of commercial plants to produce liquid and gaseous fuels. The corporation has $17.5 billion in government subsidies to distribute over three years. According to Acting Chairman John J. McAtee, Jr., completion of the projects could enable the country to produce the equivalent of 2 million barrels of oil per day by 1997. That amount would represent one-third of the oil the nation now imports.

In the next example, dealing with one of the causes of high health-care costs, the speaker linked statistics with expert testimony as a way of further proving her point:

> For all its sophistication and ingenuity, the health-care industry has a low-tech problem—paper. Sorting, shuffling, and processing billions of pieces of paper cost at least $40 billion a year. Experts agree that paperwork is indeed part of the health-care dilemma. Richard Landen of the Health Insurance Association of America recently noted that 'people—the payers, patients, doctors, and hospitals—are drowning in paperwork.'

Guidelines for Using Statistics

Statistics are a strong form of proof and should be gathered and presented in the most effective manner possible. The following few rules may increase your competency when using statistics.

Whenever possible, *present your statistics as round numbers*, especially when offering several. It is much easier to remember the population of a city if we hear "one and a half million," instead of "1,512,653," and "8 million acres of Alaskan oil lease sales surround Native coastal villages" is preferable to dealing with numbers such as "7,987,898 acres." There are, of course, instances where exactness is essential.

Give specific and complete source citations for your statistics. Saying "these statistics prove that" or "quoting from a reliable source" does not tell your audience where you located your information. If the material is controversial, it is useful to cite the source magazine or book, specific pages, and the date. In most cases, however, the date and name of the magazine or book are sufficient—for example, "According to the June 14, 1998, issue of *Newsweek*, only 10 percent of the teachers in the United States believe that their training did a good job of preparing them for the classroom." You might cite your source by saying, "A few statistics from the Justice Department's recent *Report to the Nation on Crime and Justice* will illustrate my point." Documentation adds to the credibility and acceptability of your arguments.

Avoid presenting too many statistics at one time. A speech crammed with numbers can create confusion and boredom. Imagine a speaker who says, "Let us look at what happened in 1998. On January 14, the profits for IMT went up 3 percent, a rise of 1 percent over 1996. This is a dollar increase of $2,474,743.32. When compared to April of 1995, which had a 4 percent increase, we can see a net gain of over $3,499,812.79." Think of how difficult it would be to comprehend the following set of numbers from a speech on the economy: "Consumer confidence is down 0.08 percent, commodity prices down 0.17 percent, unfilled orders for durable goods down 0.12 percent, new plant equipment down 0.02 percent, manufacturing labor hours down 0.15 percent, and the index of leading indicators down 0.3 percent."

Make certain that your statistics relate directly to the point you are making. The relationship between your statistics and your assertion would be hard to discern if you were to say, "Last year the sale of riding horses increased by 100 percent, so we can see that most people are tired of paying for gasoline." Consider a speaker who fails to relate his statistics directly to his conclusion by saying, "A Roper survey reports that 57 percent of U.S. military personnel favor a no-combat policy for women. Hence, we should not let gays into the military service."

Make sure that your statistics are accurate. Remember the quotation by Mark Twain; he underscored many people's feelings regarding the use of numbers to prove a point. There are countless instances, whether intentional or unintentional, where statistics are presented in an inaccurate and misleading manner. A factual example will demonstrate how statistics can be vague and deceptive. The author of a widely quoted book on human sexuality sent out 100,000 questionnaires but collected only a few thousand responses. From this very limited and unrepresentative sample, which, of course, produced a highly distorted picture of sexual behavior, the researcher advanced what he called a "series of reports." You must be extremely careful when using statistics. Any kind of fraudulent activity is highly unethical and will greatly damage your credibility.

Whenever possible, *try to personalize your statistics.* Numbers are much more meaningful when the people hearing them can visualize their significance on a personal level. A speaker talking on the subject of illegal marijuana pointed his material directly at the audience when he said, "Last year, Americans used over 30 million pounds of marijuana. This quantity made over 30 billion cigarettes. This works out to about 125 marijuana cigarettes for each man, woman, and child in the nation." Another speaker pointed her statistics even more directly to the audience when she noted, "Each recycled beverage can you return to the store will save you the equivalent of six ounces of gasoline."

At times, *repeat and interpret the statistics in your own words.* As already noted, numbers are difficult to comprehend and remember. Therefore, a verbal elaboration of the statistics is normally very useful. For example, a speaker who was examining teenage drivers first said, "Automobile accidents account for almost half of the deaths of sixteen- to nineteen-year-olds in the United States." She followed this sentence with her own reading of the statistics: "This means about 50 percent of our teenagers will die needlessly." Another speaker, trying to point out the level of apathy among voters in the United States, made her point, and than repeated it in the following manner: "Voter indifference is a serious problem in our country. For example, in the last presidential election only 55 percent of the voting-age population turned out to vote. Just think about that. It means that almost half of the those who could vote decided not to exercise their constitutional right."

Make your statistics interesting. A speaker talking about the deadly effects of smoking offered the following appraisal of smoking:

> Just how harmful is smoking? The World Health Organization and the San Diego Cancer Research Group estimate that the number of people who die from smoking each year is now over 3 million. This number is equal to the entire populations of San Diego and San Francisco.

Another speaker, using statistics to try to get his audience to donate money to the United Way, made his numbers interesting in the following manner:

> The United Way provides medical benefits to over 4,000 children in our community. You can add to those benefits by a simple donation. For example, your gift of $5 per week would provide immunization for 200 children. If you give up just one fast-food lunch each week you will be replacing your Big Mac with the realization you are helping to immunize young children against numerous childhood diseases.

Your statistics should be *drawn from reliable sources*. Because statistics are so easy to generate, they can be produced by both credible sources and sources that have no expertise in the topic. They can also be produced by groups or individuals that have a bias toward the topic being discussed. For example, while side effects are possible in most abortion procedures, statistics on these side effects might be one-sided if they were provided by pro-life organizations. As a speaker, you must be aware of possible bias in how the statistics were gathered and who presented them.

Consider using visual aids to clarify your statistics. In chapter 7 we will, in great detail, discuss all types of visual aids. But for now we simply state the obvious—*seeing your statistics will clarify them for your audience and make them memorable.* Having someone tell you that 48,000 were killed in auto accidents and that 63 percent of those people were not wearing seat belts would be easier to understand if you also saw those numbers in in front of you.

Testimony

In our complex world, no individual can be an authority on all topics. We have become increasingly dependent on the testimony of experts to help us find the relevant facts of an issue or a concept. A public speaker must also, on many occasions, turn to an expert. An expert is someone who, because of his or her training, experience, and background, is an authority on the subject being discussed. **Testimony** *of an authority, as a form of support for a specific point, is often the most important type of evidence a speaker can use.* It can show that the opinions of persons of authority, or experts in the field, corroborate the speaker's own views. For example, if a speaker were trying to convince an audience that periodic chest x-rays could save lives, she might quote the testimony of the surgeon general of the United States: "Our office has long held the belief that systematic and regular chest x-rays could help save the lives of many cancer and TB victims."

A speaker giving a talk to convince an audience that former convicts have a difficult time reentering society used expert testimony in the following manner:

> Lester N. Smith, who served as head warden of Sing Sing Prison for 11 years, indicated the scope of the problem faced by former convicts when he stated that society rejects former convicts right down the line. It is hard for them to

locate a job, almost impossible for them to own a home, and difficult for them to lead a normal life. The labor unions often bar them and big companies fear them. In a very real sense, they find most roads back to a normal life filled with social and economic blocks.

In both examples, the persons quoted, because of their positions and expertise, knew a great deal about the topic under discussion. In the next two instances—one about drugs, the other about welfare—notice how the *persons cited echo the speaker's view while adding to their own credibility as experts*:

Dr. David Sanders, who is the head of the San Diego Drug Rehabilitation Center and a leading researcher into the effects of drugs on the brain, offered the following commentary as to the dangers of the street drug called angel dust: 'It's the most dangerous drug I've seen. And I've been in contact with every imaginable drug on the street for the past 20 years.'

As one of the commissioners of welfare in Erie County, May Edgar is well aware of the problems faced by most welfare workers. In a recent article in *Newsweek* magazine, she noted, 'Welfare workers do not have time to know their cases or to acquire the necessary skills in rendering services to people and preventing them from becoming permanently dependent on public aid.'

Earlier, we noted that on most occasions speakers use more than one form of support at a time. Notice in the following three examples how *testimony is linked with other pieces of evidence*:

We desperately need to do something or we will soon see the complete elimination of elephants in the world. Curtis Bohlen, who is senior vice-president of the World Wildlife Federation, recently stated that 'poachers are now killing off elephants at a faster rate than they are reproducing.' This dwindling population is clearly seen when we begin to realize that the elephant population went from 1.3 million in 1979 to around 500,000 in 1999.

Dr. David Baltimore, a Nobel-prize-winning biochemist at MIT, put it bluntly. 'AIDS is a problem for everyone—gay and straight, urban and rural. We are at a critical point in the progress of the epidemic, and we are quite honestly frightened by the future prospects.' Frightened is indeed the right word when you think that by 2000, 370,000 Americans will have been diagnosed as having AIDS, the death toll will have risen by 54,000 a year, and the virus, in all probability, will have spread to between 5 million and 10 million persons. How many of those 5 million to 10 million Americans will eventually die of AIDS? Perhaps half—but no one really knows.

In the next example, we see once again *how testimony can be used most effectively when combined with other forms of support*. In a speech dealing with the dangers of drinking and driving, the speaker was able to move from a factual illustration, to some statistics, and then to expert testimony:

There we were: some friends and I having a good time while driving down old Route 78. Then, without any warning, I noticed a driver coming the opposite direction in an extremely erratic manner. Within an instant, I saw the speeding car hit the guard rail, become airborne, and start veering toward our car. And that is the last thing I remember before waking up paralyzed in a hospital bed, paralyzed for life because of the intoxicated driver that happened to be on old Route 78 the same night I was there with my friends. But I am, of course, lucky to be alive. Last year alone, drunk drivers killed 2,700 young people between the ages of fifteen and nineteen. As Dr. Kenneth Lyons Jones of the University Medical Center noted, 'Our young people are being killed by drunk drivers at an alarming rate.'

Expert testimony can be used to support and clarify informative as well as persuasive material. In the following example, from a speech about the possible link between alcoholism and genetics, the speaker used testimony to inform the audience of the validity of asserting the existence of such a link:

> Dr. David Cendelsom, professor of psychiatry at Harvard University, noted there is now mounting research to bolster the claim that children of alcoholics inherit certain physiological traits that may indicate a tendency toward alcoholism.

Guidelines in Using Testimony

On most occasions the audience may not be familiar with the person you are using as the expert giving the testimony. You may have noticed that in all the examples offered in this section, the *source's credentials were offered as part of the evidence.* It is not enough to say that "Dr. Harrington stated that the number one cause of skin cancer is overexposure to the sun." You must say, "Dr. Harrington, head of the Dermatology Department at State University Medical Center and the author of the book *Skin Cancer: Causes and Cures*, stated that the number one cause of skin cancer is overexposure to the sun."

When using testimony, *you must guard against confusing lay opinion and celebrity testimonials with testimony of an expert.* Over two thousand years ago, the Roman playwright Terence warned that "there are as many opinions as there are people." You simply cannot gather a quotation from just anyone and assume that it is accurate or that it will carry any weight with your audience. You must also be careful not be fooled into believing that because Jay Leno and Michael Jordan are famous in one area (show business or sports), they are experts in all areas. For instance, Bill Cosby may be a good comedian, but that does not qualify him as an expert on tooth decay. In short, the views of lay people or the testimonials of famous individuals do not necessarily constitute expert testimony.

Cite complete sources when using testimony. Let the listeners know where you found your evidence, whether in a magazine, book, newspaper, television program, or personal interview. You will increase your personal credibility, as well as the credibility of your sources, if you say, "According to the Sunday, January 15, 1997, issue of the *New York Times*, the Supreme Court, after reviewing obscene material from the Internet case in Florida, concluded that . . ."

Select experts who will carry considerable weight with your audience. In all circumstances, you should establish the person's credibility and explain to your audience why he or she is an expert. That is, make it clear to your listeners that this particular person should be respected. The audience's acceptance of the expert will go a long way toward proving your point. A college professor may teach eighteenth-century English literature, but this does not qualify him or her as an expert in economic affairs.

Do not try to memorize your quotations. By reading your quotations directly, you can assure accuracy and avoid forgetting parts of them. Reading small portions of your speech, such as some of your evidence, will offer your audience a change of pace. Furthermore, the act of reading a particular quotation will enhance its credibility. A small card, if handled correctly, will not detract from your speech.

❖ ❖ ❖ ❖

Testimony should be relevant to the point being discussed. Speakers often cite an authority to prove a position, but, on closer examination, listeners discover that the expert is talking about another problem. Imagine how ineffective it would be if you were talking about mental health and quoted this testimony, "There are a great many people in hospitals today who would not be there if they were not rushing to keep an appointment." On some occasions, you might find it helpful to explain the relevance of a piece of testimony in your own words. You could say, "Police Chief Jones is telling us that . . ."

Whenever possible, use brief quotations. Long quotations are often quite difficult to follow and may hinder the audience's concentration. Even when paraphrasing, you should aim at brevity.

Carefully attend to the means of introducing quotations. Lead-ins, such as "In a speech last week the Secretary of State noted. . ." and "So we see, as Professor Jones pointed out, that overpopulation and food shortages present serious problems. . ." can help hold the audience's attention and, at the same time, reveal the source of the quotation and when it originated.

Indicate the beginning and end of any quotation so that the audience will be able to distinguish your opinions from those of the expert you are quoting. However, avoid the all-too-common practice of saying "quote" and "unquote." A change of voice, a pause, a move, or a certain phrase can better indicate the beginning and end of a quotation.

When reading lengthy testimony, make sure you maintain eye contact. On occasions when you must read to your audience, do not let your notes become more important than your listeners. This advice applies not only to reading testimony but to reading any material, whether it is a quotation, a set of statistics, or an example.

Analogy

All of us, whether in everyday conversation or on the public platform, use analogies to help explain and/or prove our points. Analogies are not only popular but they can also be powerful. The English writer James Colton alluded to this power when he wrote, "The analogy, although it is not infallible, is yet that telescope of the mind by which it is marvelously assisted in the discovery of both physical and moral truth." We are using **analogy** when we ask someone to compare one idea or item to another. In trying to make our ideas clear, interesting, and compelling, we suggest that item A "resembles," "is similar to," or "is not as good as" item B. By using comparisons, we try to support our main thesis and explain our principal ideas. For example, when a contemporary tennis champion says, "Trying to run my business affairs without a Silver-Reed computer would be like trying to win Wimbledon without my tennis racket," she is making a point by using analogy—comparing the known (the importance of a tennis racket) to the unknown (the importance of Silver-Reed computers).

Comparison frequently takes the form of analogy. In an analogy, *similarities are pointed out in regard to persons, ideas, experiences, projects, institutions, or data, and conclusions are drawn on the basis of those similarities.* Because analogies compare the unknown to the known, people find them easy to relate to. As Freud once remarked, "Analogies, it is true, often decide nothing, but they can make one feel more at home." Think of how much more "at home" we feel if someone is trying to explain the European game of rugby by comparing it to the American game of football.

As just indicated, the main function of an analogy is to point out similarities between what is already known, understood, or believed and something that is not. For example, in trying to make the point that the requirements for securing a marriage license are deficient, a speaker offered the following analogy, comparing the known to the point she was trying to make: "Why is it we place more demands on securing a license to drive than we do on obtaining a license to get married?" Using this technique as support or clarification, you show the listener that what he or she already believes or knows (that it is easy to get a driver's license) is similar to what you are trying to prove or explain. For example, if you suggest that it is dangerous to drive while intoxicated, you might offer the following analogy:

> We all know that driving a car at high speed during a foggy night is dangerous because of our impaired vision [known]. The same can be said of those who try to drive after consuming alcoholic beverages, for their vision is also obscured and their life is in peril [unknown].

In arguing that a basketball players' strike against the owners of the teams is detrimental to both parties, a speaker could use an analogy in the following manner: "Let us not have another players' strike. What we learned from the last strike was that it resembled a war that neither side could win. Both factions suffered heavy losses in dollars, fan support, and credibility."

A speaker recently used an analogy to gain acceptance for a proposal that would forbid children under the age of twelve from riding three-wheel off-road vehicles: "We don't let children play with real guns because they are dangerous, yet we have allowed 559 children to die since 1985 because we have let them play with three-wheel off-road vehicles."

Another speaker, trying to make the point that nurses are underpaid, made effective use of analogy by suggesting that a nurse makes in one year what some rock stars earn in the time it takes to sing two songs at a rock concert.

Analogies are usually divided into two types, *figurative* and *literal*. **Figurative analogies** *compare things of different classes*, such as the workings of a college library and the workings of the human circulatory system, smoking cigarettes and drinking poison, not wearing a helmet when driving a motorcycle and deep sea diving without oxygen tanks, growing teenage violence and cancer, or the theory of airplanes and the flight of birds. To say that writing a term paper is like learning to swim because both have certain basic rules that are difficult at first and get easier with time would be an example of a figurative analogy. A speaker comparing the growth of the number of millionaires in the United States with the growth of McDonald's fast-food outlets would also be using a figurative analogy. Figurative analogies are generally creative, vivid, and interesting, but, because they do not contain statistics or other facts, they often have limited value as proof when they are not used with other forms of support.

Figurative analogies can take the form of a single sentence or they can be lengthy. An excellent brief analogy was offered by Bill Gates, the founder of Microsoft. When responding to criticism that he did not include rival Netscape's Web browser in Windows 98, Gates stated the following analogy:

"It's a little like asking Coke to include three cans of Pepsi with every six-pick of Coke."

A much longer analogy was presented by a speaker trying to have his audience understand the effects of global warming on the environment:

> Think of the Earth as an oven set at 300 degrees. When you open the door just for a moment, not only do you let heat escape, but air from the outside leaks in. The air that enters the oven does not immediately cool the oven down to the outside temperature; it never does because the capacity of the oven is too large to be entirely influenced. However, certain parts of the oven cool down, certain parts remain the same, and certain parts even increase in temperature to compensate for heat loss. The Earth operates in a similar manner. The Earth is set at an average temperature. It fluctuates up and down, but this takes hundreds, if not thousands, of years to be noticed. Because of influences such as the burning of fossil fuels in the form of car exhausts or factory emissions and the continued burning of the rain forests, humans have been pumping more heat into the Earth's atmosphere.

In using the **literal analogy**, *you compare items, ideas, institutions, persons, projects, data, or experiences of the same class.* You might compare one instructor to another, one political creed to another, one city to another, similar historical events, or similar athletic teams. On the basis of the similarities, you build a theorem. You reason that if two or more things of the same class contain identical or nearly identical characteristics, certain conclusions that are true in one case may also be true in the other(s). For example, Winston Churchill used a literal analogy when he compared the turning point of the Civil War to what he believed to be the turning point in World War II.

Again, with literal analogies, it is the similarities of the ideas being discussed that gives the literal analogy its persuasive influence. A speaker recently made effective use of a literal analogy when she spoke to the Board of Supervisors about flooding in her community. Notice her strong use of comparison:

> Our city, just like El Cajon, suffers from dangerous flooding each time there are heavy rains. El Cajon recently solved this problem by rechanneling the water that flows from Sutherland Dam. We should do the same thing.

In a speech dealing with the unfair treatment of people suffering from AIDS, a speaker made effective use of a literal analogy with the following comparison:

> A hundred years ago, people with leprosy were sent off to remote islands and treated in the most inhuman manner. There was a prevailing belief, later proved wrong, that the general population would all contract leprosy if it had contact with lepers. We are now acting as if people who have AIDS were lepers. More and more, we are hearing suggestions that we isolate them from the population, just as we did with lepers.

Another example can be found in a speech trying to persuade an audience that the United Nations Charter should be obeyed by all member nations:

> We Americans take a great deal of pride in the Constitution and the Bill of Rights. We know that our country would not be as great and as strong as it is if we were to discontinue our obedience and allegiance to the laws and regulations contained in these documents. The same can be said of the United Nations Charter, for just as each of us, as individuals, must comply with the Constitution and its provisions, so must the members of the United Nations comply with its laws and rules. If the individual nations do not observe and

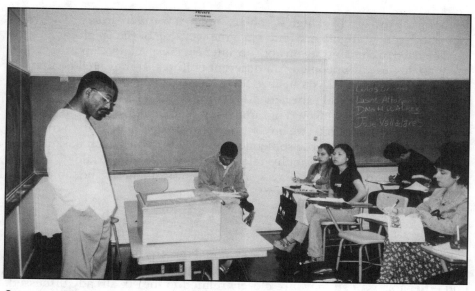

On occasions when you must read to your audience, do not let your notes become more important than your audience.

obey the laws of the Charter of the United Nations, it will not be an effective instrument for world peace.

The comparison and similarities are obvious: we are aware of the concepts behind the Constitution (known); the speaker suggests that the same concepts are inherent in the United Nations Charter (unknown). In summary, you believe and understand one; therefore, you should believe and understand the other, for they are basically the same.

Guidelines in the Use of Analogies

When selecting and using analogies, either figurative or literal, you need to apply the following guidelines.

Do the points of likeness outweigh the points of difference? If the differences between the essential features being compared outweigh the similarities, one can hardly establish a logical connection. If we compare a supermarket to a high school in order to make the point that each must keep its customers, we have overlooked some fundamental differences existing in the two cases.

Is the premise (generalization) on which the analogy is based accurate? Saying "just as a ship sinks without a captain, so will our club be destroyed without a president" is an example of a false circumstance being used as a basis for a generalization, because a ship does not necessarily sink without a captain. The premise for the entire analogy and conclusion is therefore inaccurate and invalid.

Is the analogy appropriate to the audience? It is important for the audience to clearly observe the likenesses and the essential characteristics of the analogy. If one-half of the comparison confuses your listeners, you may find that your analogy has hindered rather than aided your speech. It would probably

❖ ❖ ❖ ❖   be confusing to a group of high school freshmen if you were to say, "The workings of the rotary engine are much like the working of the epiglottis."

The need to concentrate on appropriateness is especially important when using analogies with people from different cultures. It may well be that the part of the analogy that you believe to be known by the audience is actually not part of their cultural experiences. A culture that does not have a concept for "window shopping" would not understand an analogy that said, "Just as we all window shop before we buy, we need to slow down before we rush into this decision." Think of how someone from a culture in which basketball is not played might have difficulty relating to the following analogy: "We all know that the more agile the player, the easier the slam dunk. The same is true of a person trying to master figure skating."

Other Forms of Verbal Support

At the beginning of this chapter, we noted that the forms of support occasionally overlap—that a factual illustration might well contain statistics. Certain other forms of support are closely related to the six already discussed. Many of these are further extensions and refinements of those just mentioned. A case in point is all the variations found in illustrations: an *anecdote* is an amusing story in which real-life characters are usually featured; *fables* use animal characters that speak and act as if they were human; and *parables* are fictitious stories from which a moral or religious lesson may be drawn. As you can see, all three of these are forms of illustration.

There are also forms of support, such as *explanations* and *descriptions* (which are discussed in detail in chapter 13), that serve more to clarify than to prove a point. For example, a speaker might explain in great detail the complicated role of the federal government in public welfare payments. Though this explanation might help support a premise dealing with the need for reorganizing our nation's welfare system, it does not, in and of itself, prove that there are major evils in the status quo. We shall return to some of these ancillary forms of support when we talk about informative speeches in chapter 13.

Other devices for developing and clarifying, such as restatement, repetition, and description, are also discussed in detail in chapter 13. The important point to keep in mind is that, in most situations, it is best to use a combination of devices. For example, you may have occasion to begin by defining what you are talking about, even before you offer an illustration of the point. You could follow this bit of evidence by quoting an expert who, in turn, cites statistics or uses an analogy. You then might move to a detailed description of the central point. What is important to remember is that any of the techniques discussed in this book should be used if they will aid in securing the desired response. The various classifications are a guide for specific occasions; the real communication situation must determine your final selection.

The Ethical Use of Evidence

One of the basic themes of this book has been the idea that the messages we send to another person have an effect on them. That is why every chapter to this point in the book has alerted you to the ethical responsibilities associated with communication. As you move through the remaining chapters, you will see how this important topic reemerges. The author's rationale, whether talking about the use of language (chapter 12) or about appearing on television (chapter 15), is the same—when you send a message to another human being, you are gaining access to their life space and therefore influencing how they might think and act in the future. This influence demands that you consider your actions. Let us examine those actions as they apply to the ethical use of statistics and testimony.

The Ethical Use of Statistics

Statistics can have a telling effect on an audience. Unfortunately, as we noted earlier, statistics are highly susceptible to error and abuse. An ethical and conscientious speaker, as well as a critical and careful listener, must be willing to apply certain criteria to the statistics they confront.

Are the units being compared actually comparable? Someone could say that Los Angeles has 2,500 more crimes per year than Dallas does but if Los Angeles counts all crime and Dallas counts only crimes against people and not those against property, the statistics cannot be compared. In addition, the city of Los Angeles may have a population of 4 million, while Dallas has only 1 million residents. In both of these cases, the units are not comparable. To present them as being equivalent would be an unethical act.

Do the statistics cover a sufficient number of cases? A statement that 50 percent of the voters polled favored Proposition II would be quite misleading if only 10 people (out of 40,000 eligible voters) were asked their opinion.

Do the statistics cover a sufficient period of time? There are two considerations in applying this test. First, if one is going to talk about the high cost of foreign aid, one must give current statistics. The foreign aid bill changes each year, and what was valid five years ago is likely to be outdated today. Second, if you wish to draw conclusions from your data, you must be sure that the period covered is not exceptional. The flow of mail in December, unemployment figures related to seasonal companies, and traffic after a football game are obviously exceptional cases.

Were the gatherers of the statistics strongly interested in the outcome? Whenever you gather and analyze evidence, it is crucial that you examine the biases and attitudes found within the special groups that originally compiled the data. For example, if you were considering the problems associated with the cutting down of the California redwoods, you might find different results when you approached the lumber industry than when you asked the Sierra Club. In these instances, the speaker should consider as many different sources as possible and try to locate a neutral source. Napoleon once remarked, "Neutrality consists of having the same weights and measures for each."

The Ethical Use of Testimony

In using and listening to testimony, remember that an expert's opinion may not be based on concrete and comprehensive data. There are some safeguards and ethical considerations you should observe whenever you use expert testimony:

Is the person an unbiased observer? Objectivity on the part of an expert is essential if we are to respect and believe her or his testimony. The chairperson of the Republican National Committee would hardly be qualified to give an objective account of a Democratic president's term in office. Nor could a chemist for a pesticide company offer unbiased testimony on the need to destroy the sawtoothed grain beetle to preserve U.S. food crops.

Is the reference to authority specific? Attributions such as "according to an eminent authority" or "an expert in the field concluded" are vague and misleading. The audience should know exactly who is being quoted and why he or she was selected.

When and where was the opinion expressed? Statistics, theories, and findings are soon outdated. What an expert said in 1986 may not accurately express his or her views today. In addition, the place where a statement is made may well influence what is said. The Secretary of Labor might state one view at the Teamsters' convention and expound another position, on the same theme, before the Chamber of Commerce.

Have you accurately recorded and presented the statements of the expert? This current ethical objective is self-evident. That is to say, it is obvious that to misquote someone, on purpose, is unprincipled and unethical. How would you as a listener like to be told that Dr. Jones said that "smoking during pregnancy is not dangerous" when, in reality, Dr. Jones never uttered those words?

Are you confusing expert testimony with lay testimonials? In this era of mass communication, we are often confronted with famous celebrities being presented as experts. Someone who has a successful situation comedy on television may not be qualified to evaluate and comment on the health benefits of ice cream.

What should be obvious by now is that an ethical speaker is truthful. This simple admonition is clearly articulated by the Swiss philosopher Henri Ameil: "Let us be true: this is the highest maxim of art and of life, the secret of eloquence and of virtue, and of all moral authority."

When to Use Verbal Support

Determining when the various forms of support are needed is no easy task. Every audience, occasion, and topic has special demands that make each communication encounter a unique and dynamic experience. There are, however, basic questions to ask when you are trying to decide where and when you should use support.

Are you making a statement that will be accepted as true simply because you assert it? For example, if you want to convince an audience that educational benefits for veterans should be increased, you must do more than say, "The meager grants now awarded under the GI Bill are so small that many veterans cannot attend college." Any intelligent listener would respond by saying, "What do you mean?" or "How do you know this is true?" You should use forms of support when you are making a statement that needs substantiation as a means of establishing its authenticity, believability, and plausibility.

How much substantiation is needed? There is no simple formula for deciding how much support any assertion will require. In most instances, you will have to depend on your own good judgment and common sense. View the assertion or statement from the perspective of your audience. Your audience analysis will let you see things from the listeners' point of view. Ask yourself this question: "Would *I* need and demand proof for the opinions being expressed?"

Are you making a statement that requires no further clarification? We have already mentioned the need to ask yourself if an idea needs proof; now the issue is one of clarity. As pointed out earlier, the forms of support are often used for clarification as well as for proof. Ask yourself, Is my idea clear? If the answer is no, support is needed. If you were to say, "There is often a stigma attached to persons who have been mentally ill," you would run the risk of the audience not knowing what you mean. However, you could clarify your point with an illustration about someone who actually was stigmatized because of confinement in an institution.

Are you making statements that might be attacked or refuted by other speakers? Evidence tends to operate as a neutralizing agent. If someone offers evidence, and you do not, the other person is more apt to be believed. However, if during your speech you buttress your arguments with proof, it will minimize the impact of the evidence your rival speaker offers.

How to Use Verbal Support

Nearly every speaker faces the problem of trying to decide what to do with the material he or she has gathered as part of the preparation process; learning how to use your supporting material takes practice and experience. Each time you give a speech, you will find that integrating your supports into your speech becomes smoother and easier. There are, however, some specific techniques that you can use. Many of these were mentioned earlier with the advice following each of the forms of support. However, a few of these suggestions warrant reexamination.

Direct Quotations and Paraphrases

First, *there will be times when, because of the nature of the evidence, you will want to present it as a direct quotation.* This is usually the case with statistics and expert testimony. In fact, your credibility is enhanced and the impact of the statistics or testimony is often greater when you present it in its original form. In offering testimony about the dangers of freebasing cocaine, a speaker might use a direct quotation in the following manner: "Dr. George R. Gray, director of emergency medicine at Bay View Free Medical Clinic, said, 'Freebasing is like putting your finger in an electric socket. It can only lead to your eventual collapse.'"

Second, there will be times when the technique of paraphrasing may be appropriate. When you paraphrase, you restate a passage in your own words. This restatement often helps clarify as well as support an assertion. It is not so much a summary of what has been said as it is a recasting of the original passage into a style that is more suited to the speaker and the audience. For example, notice the difference in style between the original source and the speaker's paraphrase:

Original: Although cocaine is not a leading cause of drug-related deaths, in a number of cities, including San Diego, San Francisco, and New York, it is now the fastest-growing source of serious drug-related medical problems, according to epidemiologists for the National Institute on Drug Abuse, who met last week in Washington.

Paraphrase: The increase in the number of deaths by cocaine is a serious matter. Although it is not yet the leading cause of drug-related deaths, epidemiologists for the National Institute on Drug Abuse say it is now the fastest-growing source of serious drug-related problems.

Original: The number of women inmates has almost tripled in the past 10 years. In 1987, there were 12,000 women behind bars; 20,000 in 1990; 28,000 in 1992; and 40,000 in 1997.

Paraphrase: From 1987 to 1997, the number of women inmates more than tripled, from 12,000 to 40,000.

You will recall from the previous chapter the importance of paraphrasing as it relates to listening and culture. We once again examine this idea, but this time in the context of asking your audience to understand the evidence you are offering. If your listeners, because of language problems, fail to interpret your evidence correctly, you will not accomplish your purpose. Hence, the need to paraphrase takes on added significance *when the listeners have English as their second language.*

Transitions

The correct use of transitions, which can be words, phrases, or sentences, is an essential ingredient in the correct use of evidence. Transitions serve several functions. Primarily, *they provide your speech with a smooth flow as you move from idea to idea.* As we shall see when we discuss the speech to inform (chapter 13), transitions make it easier for your audience to remember key ideas. When used with evidence, they show relationships between your ideas and your evidence. Transitions tell listeners you have completed one thought or piece of evidence and are about to move on to something else. ("Having spent the past few minutes talking about why college tuitions have been rising, we are now ready to discuss what we can do about this problem.")

Transitions can also link several items of support. ("There are other statistics that support the danger of passive smoke to one's health. Let us look at some of them.") They can lead the audience from one point to another. ("We have seen what the experts say about the dangers of passive smoke. Let us look at other evidence to substantiate their claims.") Notice in the examples thus far that the transition stated both the idea the speaker was finishing and the one that he or she was about to treat next.

A good transition can also highlight the importance of a specific piece of evidence while moving the audience on to other evidence. For example, after presenting a factual illustration, statistics, and testimony, a speaker used the following transition for both emphasis and clarity:

Mr. Miller's sad experience with escalating nursing home costs is not an isolated case. The number of uninsured elderly suffering the same fate as Mr. Miller grew from 25 million ten years ago to about 47 million in 1999. And, according to Mr. Fazlur Rahman, chief of hematology and oncology at Angelo Community Hospital in San Angelo, Texas, the problem is only going to get worse.

There are some occasions when the transition takes the form of a single word or phrase. Some of the more common transition words and phrases include:

in other words	moreover
in addition	for example
therefore	thus
finally	consequently
on the other hand	to be more specific
for instance	to illustrate this point

As you have observed, transitions can take a variety of forms. Let us look at a few additional types of transitions so that you can introduce your point and move from one piece of evidence to another.

Bridging. *Bridging, perhaps one of the most common transitions used in public speaking, directs your audience from what you are currently talking about to what you want to treat next.* For example, if you have been talking about the widespread incidence of crime in the United States and are now ready to offer some specific statistics to substantiate your assertion, you might introduce your statistics in the following manner:

> There are simply too many criminals in the United States. Let me show you what I mean. The best estimates suggest that 36 million to 40 million people, or 16 to 18 percent of the population, have arrest records for nontraffic offenses.

If you wanted to add to this idea, another bridge could be used:

> The statistics I just shared with you tell only part of the story. They don't tell us just how many criminals we have already identified. For example, we currently have 2.4 million people under correctional supervision, 412,000 of them locked away in cells.

Signposting. *Signposting* is also an effective transitional tool. *Not only does signposting enable you to direct the audience's attention to the point immediately ahead, but it also allows you to preview what lies beyond.* In the next example, notice the twin functions of signposting:

> Let me offer you some evidence showing just how much crime costs us in the United States. Then we can discuss what to do about this problem.

Good speakers can use signposting as a way of reminding their audience of a number of points at the same time. In the following example, the transition reviews what has been accomplished and highlights what is to come:

> So far, we have seen how easy access to handguns causes needless accidents among children and increases the rate of murder; also, handguns are used in most suicides. Now let us spend some time talking about why these handguns are so easy to secure. Once we have done that, we can examine some solutions to this serious problem.

There are many occasions when signposts simply take the form of numerical indicators. For example, if you are talking about the fact that Iran might be a major trouble spot in the near future, you could use signposting in the following manner as you move from point to point:

Today I want to talk about four reasons why I believe Iran continues to represent a major conflict area for the United States. First, Iran continues to support terrorism throughout the Middle East. Recently, Iran . . . Second, Iran is actively supporting Islamic revolutions that are highly anti-American. For example, the leaders of Jordan and Egypt are both saying . . . Third, Iran is working to undermine the Arab-Israeli peace process. Last week, for instance, . . . Finally, Iran continues to arm itself at an ever-increasing rate. In the past two years, Iran has spent an estimated . . .

Before we move on to other transitional devices, I will briefly summarize some words and phrases that can be used as signposts:

first	finally
second	in conclusion
one	next
let's now look at	in overview
lastly	in closing
to reiterate	in review

Spotlighting. *Spotlighting* is a transitional device that actually serves two purposes. First, like all transitions, *it tells the audience that you are moving on to another idea or piece of evidence.* In addition, *it signals the audience that what is coming next is important.* Notice in the examples that follow how the speaker alerted his listeners that something significant was about to be talked about:

I would urge you to think about this if you were to remember only one idea of this talk.

We now arrive at the most meaningful part of this speech.

I am now going to explain the single most important element in this entire debate.

The most significant thing I can tell you about this new proposal is that . . .

Summary as a Transition. *There may be times when you simply want to summarize your supporting materials.* We talked earlier about how statistics serve as a kind of summary of facts. In a sense, specific instances also constitute a type of abridgment. In both cases, you are eliminating some of the detail for the sake of time and clarity. The value of a good, concise summary may be seen in the following comparison:

Original Source: There are a great number of inmates on death row, waiting for the courts to decide their fate. For example, Florida has 294 prisoners on death row, Texas has 283, California 247, Illinois 120, Pennsylvania 115, and Georgia 102.

Summary: There are 1,161 prisoners on death row in the five states that have the largest number of inmates awaiting the results of various court decisions.

When we talk about summaries, we are referring to two different types of summaries—initial summaries (previews), and internal summaries (running). Although all of these devices are discussed in detail in the chapter on informing (chapter 13), they are introduced now so that you might be able to use them as you present your evidence to the audience.

Initial summaries are useful when you are about to introduce a series of forms of support.

So that you will fully understand just how serious the problem of air safety actually is, I will begin by offering you the views of experts in this area and, second, share with you some startling statistics that will substantiate their concerns.

Internal summaries, when used as transitions, move the audience from a set idea or piece of evidence to a new point.

Having seen what the experts believe about air safety, and how their views are supported by the facts, we are now ready to talk about what can done about this problem.

Nonverbal Transitions. *Transitions can be nonverbal as well as verbal.* Leaning forward, smiling, pausing, and moving in one direction or another all signal to the audience that a new idea or form of support is about to be introduced.

Because transitions are such an important tool, we will also discuss them elsewhere in the book. For now, however, make abundant use of them as you move your audience from one piece of evidence to another and from one point to another.

Visual Support

The importance and use of visual aids will be the subject of the chapter 7. However, because visual aids are a useful means of supporting and proving an idea, a principle, or a concept, we need to discuss them briefly at this time. By seeing what is talked about, the listener brings still another of his or her senses into play. In trying to convince a judge that a stop sign was blocked from view by a large tree, a lawyer displayed a photograph. On seeing the picture, the judge ruled the defendant could not have seen the sign from his car. The old adage "seeing is believing" made the point both real and believable. By using a chart, a model, a graphic, a demonstration, or an exhibit, you prove the assertion you are advancing. In addition, statistics that are detailed and confusing can be clarified and reinforced by a graph, table, or poster that highlights the main features. Notice how "seeing" the following statistics reinforces the assertion that sex education is needed in public schools:

IN ONE DAY
2,753 TEENAGERS GET PREGNANT
1,099 TEENAGERS HAVE ABORTIONS
367 TEENAGERS MISCARRY
1,287 TEENAGERS WHO ARE NOT MARRIED GIVE BIRTH

As you can see in this example, visualizing the statistics adds to the persuasiveness of the idea. Visual support is also useful when you are speaking to an audience of mixed cultural backgrounds, some of whom might have English as a second language. Comprehension and persuasion are enhanced when the audience can see as well as hear your important points. Therefore, do not hesitate to use visual support to aid your cause.

The Role Of Culture in the Use of Evidence

You must also take your audience into consideration when deciding how and when to use your evidence. It should not surprise you that there are cultural variations regarding the selection of forms of support. For example, cultures such as the Latin, Arabic, and African favor illustrations and stories over "facts," while most Germans, North Americans, and English demand statistics and the advice of experts if they are to be persuaded. There are even cultural differences as to who can be called an "expert." In one culture, it might be an elderly person; in another culture, it could be someone with impressive professional credentials. In short, a full audience analysis is needed before you decide on what evidence you will cite and how you will use it.

Summary

In this chapter, we were concerned with the topic of evidence, more specifically, the devices speakers use to support and clarify assertions and observations. The forms of support we examined were factual illustrations, hypothetical illustrations, specific instances, statistics, testimony, analogy, and visual support. We indicated that you need to be concerned with the ethical issues involved in evaluating, presenting, and listening to the various forms of support.

This chapter also offered advice as to when and how to use evidence. Techniques such as using direct quotations, paraphrasing, and transitions were discussed. It was noted that the most effective transitions take the form of bridging, signposting, spotlighting, nonverbal actions, and summarizing.

The chapter concluded by alerting you to the role of culture in the use of evidence.

Concepts and Questions

1. How do the forms of support assist you in accomplishing your speech purpose?

2. Identify and explain three kinds of support.

3. What are the tests you apply to examples and illustrations in order to ascertain their validity?

4. What factors should be kept in mind when using statistics?

5. What is the difference between literal and figurative analogies?

6. What are effective transitional devices?

7. What are some ethical considerations in the use of evidence?

Activities and Exercises

1. Write an assertion pertaining to a topic that is currently in the news. Then locate a factual illustration, two sets of statistics, and expert testimony to support your assertion.

2. Attend a political rally where the purpose of the speaker is to get you to vote for him or her. Try to locate the forms of support the speaker used to get your vote. Then analyze the quality of the support in light of the characteristics discussed in the book.

3. Read a detailed story in a newsmagazine. Locate as many forms of support as you can in the story.

4. Write a literal analogy on any subject you like. Then write a figurative analogy on the same topic.

5. Read a recent "State of the Union" address. Analyze the speech for the forms of support used by the President. Ask yourself if the evidence supported the various points made by the President. ✦

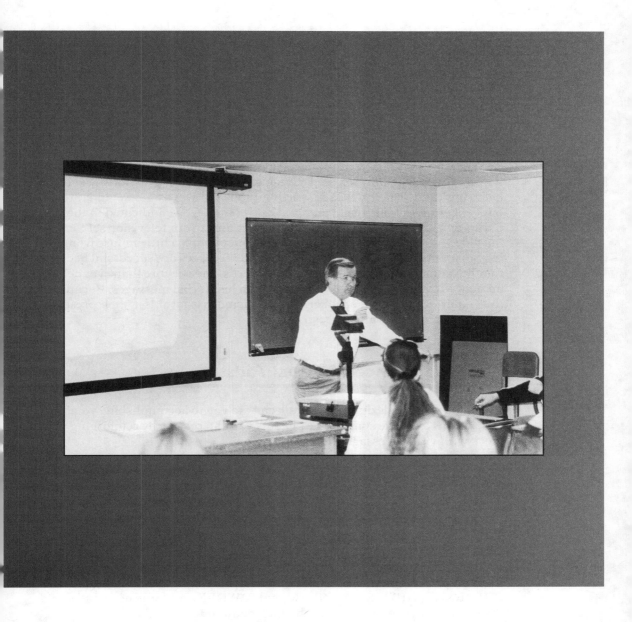

CHAPTER SEVEN

Visual Aids: Displaying Your Ideas

Our ears are less accurate than our eyes.

—*Greek proverb*

Ask yourself this simple question: Why do most of us enjoy going to the movies, watching television, going to sporting events, and playing computer games? The answer is obvious—we are all captivated by what our eyes behold. We are drawn to movement. This chapter is about how you can use the audience's desire to see as well as hear to help you accomplish your purpose.

The value of visual aids to speech making cannot be overstated. Although they might be trite phrases, there is some truth to the expressions "Seeing is believing" and "One picture is worth a thousand words." Like all cultures, ours encourages both visual and oral expression. As we indicated in the first paragraph, we all grow up seeing films, attending to our television sets, enjoying video games, watching music videos, and moving a little mouse from one icon to another. All of these action-oriented messages are successful because they have something happening besides words. Today, more than ever before, audiences expect speakers to use more than just verbal messages. Because of this requirement, public speakers should include visual aids in their presentations whenever they are appropriate.

The Importance of Visual Aids

Using visual aids during your talk can aid you in accomplishing your purpose. Let us examine some of the benefits you can receive by reinforcing your ideas with visual messages.

Retention

Visual aids can assist the audience with both *memory* and *recall*. When people see as well as hear a message, there is a much better chance that they will remember the point being made. By some estimates we retain only 20 percent of what we hear, yet when hearing is combined with seeing, the percentage jumps to nearly 50 percent. If you were talking about the early Plains Indians of North America, and put the names ARAPAHO, ARIKARA, CHEYENNE, HIDATSA, MANDAN, and PAWNEE on a large poster, it would assist the audience in retaining the information.

Support

In chapter 6, you saw the value of visual aids as a *means of support*. We noted how visual aids can make an idea concrete and persuasive. A picture of a child as a victim of a drunk driver has a greater impact than the citing of sta-

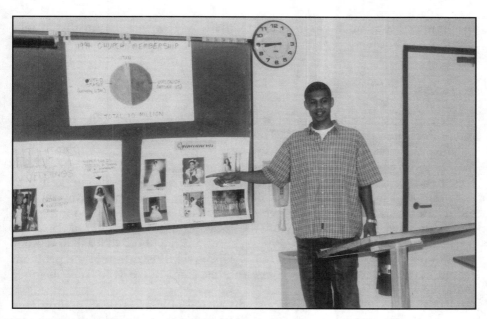

Visual aids can help the audience understand the point you are trying to make.

tistics on the same subject. Think of how you could support your assertion about the increased number of deaths due to handguns if you had a bar graph depicting the steep rise in deaths over the past five years. And recently a speaker, trying to convince the City Council that a certain intersection was dangerous, played a videotape that showed the obvious hazards associated with the intersection in question.

Clarity

Visual aids can *clarify* complex material. The word *larynx* might be unfamiliar to the listeners, but a model or diagram can offer a definition of the term. A common principle of teaching and learning maintains that it is worthwhile to use as many physical senses as possible: the more sensory associations one has with an idea, the better are one's chances of remembering the idea. If your audience sees a videotape, even one you have made yourself, of the pollution of a local lake, they will have a much clearer image than if they simply hear about the filth in the water. Consider how the complex boundaries and borders of the Middle East could be made less confusing by looking at a large map instead of hearing a speaker try to describe the territorial lines with only words. Also, you could even use large pictures of some bears feeding at Yellowstone National Park and buffalo roaming in a valley to illustrate the abundance of wildlife within the park's boundaries.

Organization

On many occasions *the structure and organizational sequence* of a speech can be enhanced by visual aids. The poster or overhead transparency could contain the major points of the speech or even a breakdown of one section of the talk. Imagine how easy it would be to follow the steps in a speech on how to change the oil in a car if accompanied by a poster listing the proper sequence of actions.

Attention

The English author Samuel Johnson once wrote that "The true art of memory is the art of attention." This advice certainly applies to visual aids, because their use helps memory by *arousing and maintaining attention and interest*. Although interest and attention are discussed in many other chapters, here the discussion centers on how the use of visual aids can gain and maintain that attention. A pretty picture, a shiny object, or a drawing provides listeners with an object on which to focus their attention, and the listeners are usually anxious to hear what the speaker has to say about the object. In a speech on water pollution, you might show a large photo of trash and other foreign matter found in a local stream. This vivid illustration of the problem would certainly get attention, focus interest, and make your speech more dynamic.

There are a number of reasons why visual aids are so compelling as a method of gaining and holding attention. These factors deal with the interplay between psychological processes and physical stimuli. A brief examination of two of these optical attention factors might help you decide which aids to select.

Intensity. As you know from experience, colorful lights and brilliant colors almost demand that you look at them. When you consider the concept of *intensity* in choosing your visual aids, you enhance the chances that your listeners will pay attention. A chart showing the projected rise in the number of Alzheimer's disease cases will take on added meaning if you can demonstrate that increase with a bright red graph that is moving in an upward flow. Think of the impact if you say, "We need to do something about this disease. Roughly 4 million Americans have it today, but that number is projected to grow to 14 million by 2050," while you are pointing to the bold red line that is making the same point.

Contrast. Contrast is yet another visual device that arouses attention. Try to use aids with a variety of patterns, shapes, colors, and the like. Imagine how clear and compelling your comments about the debris found on the beach would be if, while making this point, you were to place an assortment of this trash on a clean table.

Credibility

The use of visual aids not only helps with retention, persuasion, clarity, and interest, but it can also add to your *personal credibility*. Listeners will think well of you if you have put forth the energy and taken the time to prepare a clear and compelling learning aid. For example, an audience would surely be impressed if you located and printed some maps from the Internet and then took the time to make transparencies of the maps. Be aware, however, that your credibility might well be diminished if your aid is poorly displayed and/or constructed. In other words, simply having an aid is not enough; to have a positive effect it must be an effective aid.

Culture

Finally, visual aids are useful when speaking to people from cultures different from your own. The most obvious advantage would be for those who have English as a second language. Seeing what you are talking about might help them understand a difficult concept. For example, it might be easier for listeners from China to comprehend a speech on changes in American fashions if they could see pictures of the clothes being discussed instead of only hearing words such as *drape* and *pleat*. Even being able to *see*, in a visual way, some of the words in your speech might help nonnative speakers of English understand some of the concepts you are trying to explain. There are also cultures (Japanese, French) whose members are very cautious and deliberate in making decisions. They demand more proof than do North Americans. In these cases the visual aid becomes yet one more piece of proof.

Choosing the Appropriate Aid

Before taking a detailed look at the many visual aids you can use to assist you in your efforts, it might be useful to look at some general guidelines to apply when deciding what aid would be most appropriate for your presentation.

Specific Purpose

Begin thinking about your visual aids by asking the following question: *What is the purpose of my speech?* The supporting materials you would select for a persuasive speech differ from those you would choose for an informative talk. If your aim is to entertain, you might use posters that show whimsical cartoon characters depicting key points. This design, however, would be inappropriate for a speech on the plight of the homeless living in your city. In most instances, choosing the most appropriate medium is usually a matter of common sense.

Audience Size

The *number of people* who will hear your talk will influence the visual aids you eventually select. If you were to speak to one hundred people in a large auditorium, they would have a difficult time seeing photographs or flip charts. You would need to adapt to the size of the audience and thus would most likely use overhead transparencies, slides, or other devices that can be enlarged and projected over a long distance. Here again, common sense is your best advisor in matters of audience appropriateness.

Time, Money, Availability

Issues such as *time, money, and the availability* of certain equipment also affect your decision as to which aid to use. For example, slides take a few days to develop and can be expensive, and certain types of transparencies require

❖ ❖ ❖ ❖   special equipment. In short, try to select the medium through which you can produce the best visual aid with the resources at your disposal.

Audience Analysis

Remember to *think about your audience* when selecting your visual aid. This means considering everything from the abstract nature of your content to the attention span of your listeners. A group of young children you are trying to persuade to not start smoking would not be influenced by a graph showing the rise in teenage smoking. Yet a comical poster containing an easy to remember slogan would facilitate your cause. As emphasized throughout this book, try to put yourself in the place of your listeners—even if they are from another generation or culture. Ask yourself: Who are they? What are they interested in? How much do they know about this topic? All of these questions will help you select the appropriate aid.

Expertise

Finally, ask yourself if you have *the skills necessary to operate the visual aid you are considering.* On countless occasions I have observed speakers who, with the best of intentions, did not know how to use the equipment necessary to present their aid. Needless to say, they were extremely embarrassed when they could not locate the light source for the overhead transparency machine, or operate the "stop" switch on their friend's VCR. Our point is a simple one: either know how to use the aid you want or allow sufficient time to practice using the machinery you will employ during your talk.

Nonelectronic Visual Aids

The American philosopher George Santayana once noted that "Imagination is infinite." Although he was obviously not talking about visual aids, he was reminding us that our use and selection of aids is limited only by our imagination. Hence, we urge you to be creative as you adapt the aids we discuss to your particular speech. As you read the following lists, keep in mind that although we will examine each type of aid one at a time, *you will usually find them most effective when used in combination.* That is to say, if you are trying to explain how to tune up a car, you are well advised to show the tools and replacement parts needed. In addition, a poster showing the engine would be helpful, so the audience can see where the various parts are located. If your purpose is persuasive—you want to convince your audience to vote for placing a new traffic signal at a dangerous intersection—you could present a chart that shows statistically how the number of accidents has increased on this corner. You could also present your own videotape showing how hectic traffic is at peak hours. Let us now examine some of the visual aids that you should learn to use to help let others know what you think and how you feel.

People

❖ ❖ ❖ ❖

Although it might appear somewhat obvious, we will begin with an often overlooked visual aid—**people.** You, the speaker, automatically add a visual dimension to the presentation. You can turn that visual capacity to your advantage by using your own body to demonstrate various points. For example, if you are talking about the correct golf stroke to hit a "slice," you could demonstrate the correct movements by swinging the club yourself. If you are discussing the proper attire for backpacking, you can even wear that apparel.

You can also ask someone else to serve as a visual aid. To demonstrate the correct way to carry out artificial respiration, you might ask a friend to role-play a person having breathing problems. If you are trying to inform people about water safety, you might have someone lie on a table so you can demonstrate the correct form for holding a victim while swimming to shore. Usually it is not a good idea to call on a volunteer from the audience unless you have contacted the person in advance. You might find that a spontaneous volunteer is unpredictable. The volunteer might be nervous or even try to become "the star of the show."

Objects

Reality is usually more compelling than a mere representation of that reality. An **object** being talked about can be displayed to help explain an idea or a principle; the object captures and maintains attention. For example, in a speech dealing with how to develop film, you can demonstrate with the objects that are actually involved in the developing process. Audience members can better understand the process if they can see all of the essential articles, such as trays and solutions. Similarly, an audience can better understand a speech on football protective gear if it can view a football player's shoulder pads, hip pads, and helmet. Effective communicators are not satisfied to talk about an object or activity; they want the listeners to see the object or process in question. A dog by your side when talking about obedience training, flowers when explaining flower arrangements, puppets when discussing the history of puppet shows, rocks when demonstrating gem polishing, and a knife and block of wood when instructing how to carve are all useful in helping you accomplish your purpose.

Displaying an object can help explain an idea or principle. (Photo: Gloria Thomas)

Models

Because they are replicas of the real thing, **models** can serve three useful purposes. First, they can help explain a complex idea. For example, a three-dimensional model of the human heart could greatly simplify an explanation of this intricate organ without distorting any of the heart's main

Figure 7.1 Feedback Model

functions. Second, models can be made in any size or shape; therefore, they can be made to move from place to place. You could not bring an aircraft carrier to class, yet seeing a disassembled model of the ship would be helpful to any audience. Finally, because models have to be constructed, the model maker can emphasize whatever aspect of the process he or she wishes. Notice how in Figure 7.1 a speaker, wanting to emphasize feedback when communicating, constructed a model stressing messages and feedback while not even showing concepts such as encoding, decoding, and channels. In this visual aid, the speaker was able to accent what concerned her most—feedback.

When selecting and using objects and models, try to keep three points in mind.

1. Some items should be avoided because of their potential to create a negative response. For example, live snakes or guns might make members of your audience nervous.

2. Make sure you choose an aid that can be seen by everyone. We recall a student trying to demonstrate how to program a VCR by pushing actual buttons on a machine, but the buttons could not be seen by all members of the class.

3. In most instances it is not a good idea to circulate your visual aid throughout the audience. People are likely to find the object or specimen more entertaining than you. When we talked about listening in chapter 5, we stressed how easily people are distracted. Your aid could be a distraction.

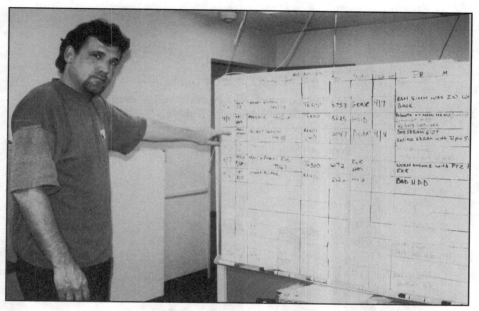

Make sure the material on your aid is clear and easy to see. (Photo: Gloria Thomas)

Posters

Posters are among the simplest of all visual aids to locate or construct. They can clarify and reinforce any idea or process you select. What is attractive about a poster is that it can be prepared ahead of time and tailored to your needs with very little effort, using only some colored pens and poster board. Figures 7.2, 7.3, and 7.4 show posters created to help the audience remember the key elements of three different presentations—statistical data, a set of directions, and a diagram of a garden. In each instance, the speaker, one on the United Nations, one on fire prevention, and another on vegetable gardens, is engaging the sense of sight as well as of hearing.

There are some principles to keep in mind when preparing posters.

1. While posters are effective for small audiences, you need to guard against posting numbers and images that are difficult to see. What may be large enough to see when constructed at home could look like little dots on a sheet of paper in a large room.

2. Many posters suffer from too much clutter and text, so be sure that all the important items are easy so see. This means not having too many words per line, not mixing and overusing print styles, not having enough spacing, and using too many colors.

Maps

Maps are very helpful in assisting the audience to locate various geographic points of reference. If, for example, you were giving a speech pointing out some of the reasons Israel is concerned about its security, you could display a map showing how Israel is surrounded by Egypt, Jordan, Syria, and Lebanon. The map would clearly indicate the location of these Arab countries

Figure 7.2 Poster

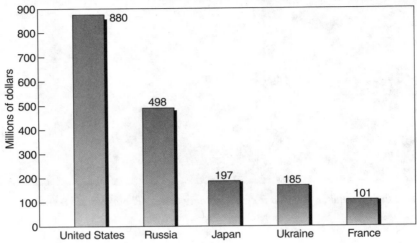

Figure 7.3 Poster

Home Fire Prevention Plan
1. Remove rubbish from halls and closets.
2. Use appropriate containers for storing flammable materials.
3. Check electrical wiring and appliances and make needed repairs

relative to the borders of Israel. A student recently made effective use of a map in an informative speech on the new countries in Africa. The map helped the audience see the exact location of the countries the speaker was talking about.

Their availability is yet another advantage of maps. In most instances, you should be able to secure a map from your local or campus library. Like books, maps can be checked out for short periods of time. The main problem in using maps is that most commercially prepared maps contain too much detail and that detail cannot be seen by everyone in the audience. Hence, the best maps are those you prepare specifically for your speech.

Let us offer a few guidelines to keep in mind when you are preparing a map:

1. Remember to use light on dark, black and white, or bright colors. This will not only make your aid easier to see, but it will also hold attention.

2. While it is somewhat obvious, make sure everyone can see the map. This means you must imagine the size of the room and the distance between the visual aid and the person in the last row. When considering the problems associated with size, you need to make sure that your important points, such as the lettering on a map, are not too small.

Paintings and Drawings

Paintings and drawings (also sketches and cartoons) are extremely helpful and are readily available to all speakers. You can make your own paintings or drawings, gather them from books and magazines, or use already prepared computer graphics packages from "clip art" files. Most copy centers can now enlarge any drawing or picture you bring them, for a small fee. Imagine how you could use paintings or drawings to help explain your point if you were speaking on the history of the American automobile, modern architecture, the life of a bug, or cultural differences in the portrayal of nature in art. Paintings would make your material more compelling, interesting, and memorable.

Photographs

Photographs, taken by the speaker or a professional photographer, can be tailored to any speech. The realism associated with photographs makes them a valuable tool. If you were speaking on the topic of tree identification in your community, you could take pictures of various trees, enlarge them, label

Figure 7.4 Diagram

My Vegetable Garden

them, and use them to help the audience see the distinguishing characteristics of each tree. These photographs may not have been available elsewhere, but with a camera you can create your own visual aids.

Photographs can also be used to support a persuasive assertion. If, for example, your purpose is to persuade an audience to give money to a relief fund to help flood victims in your community, you can show pictures of the flooding and of people left homeless by the disaster.

You need to follow some simple procedures when using photographs:

1. Remember that the *photographs you use must be large enough* to be seen by all members of the audience. Most photographs are developed in sizes that are too small to meet this criterion. Therefore, long before the speech, make the necessary arrangements to have your photographs enlarged. As already indicated, recent technology for enlarging has made the use of photographs, pictures, and paintings an even more attractive proposition. Through the use of color laser enlargement techniques, a small picture or photograph can be greatly amplified. For a very small fee, any copy center can amplify your photograph or picture so that the members of the audience will be able to see it.

2. Your *photographs should be of high technical quality.* Although it might be humorous to share your efforts as an amateur photographer, pictures that are out of focus or are cluttered with unnecessary detail detract from your speech.

3. When showing your photographs to your audience, it is *not a good idea to pass them around the room.* The combination of movement in the room and people looking at the pictures while you are talking creates a serious distraction.

Figure 7.5 Organizational Chart

Charts and Graphs   ❖ ❖ ❖ ❖

Most of us have a difficult time comprehending numbers or abstract and complicated ideas if we only hear them. **Charts** and **graphs**, which are pictorial representations of statistical or complex material, can often help with this problem by making issues more understandable. You can make your own charts and graphs, copy ones from secondary sources, or use many of the computer programs that now convert statistics into visual form. Charts and graphs also have the advantage of offering a visual summary that shows trends, processes, and relationships. Reflect for a moment on how easy it would be for an audience to see an increase in personal income taxes over the

Figure 7.6 Comparison Chart

Major U.S. Weapons Systems		
Item	Estimated Cost (millions)	Number to Be Produced
F-14 Tomcat	$10,564.0	580
F-15 Eagle	12,603.4	729
F-16 Condor	13,833.3	1,730
F-18 Hornet	12,815.8	811

past 20 years on a graph that shows, on the horizontal axis, the years involved and, on the vertical axis, the average amount of taxes paid by each individual.

The five most common charts and graphs are the **organizational chart**, which displays, by means of blocks and interconnecting lines, an organization's hierarchy of control and responsibility, or parts of a process (see Figure 7.5); the **comparison chart**, which compares or contrasts two or more quantities, usually of a statistical nature (see Figure 7.6); the **pie graph**, which is a circle divided into several "slices," each representing a classified item and its relationship to the other items (see Figure 7.7); and the **bar graph** and **line graph**, which are used to represent trends or compare variables at fixed times (see Figures 7.8 and 7.9).

Let us offer a few words of warning about using charts and graphs in speech making:

1. Many "homemade" visual aids suffer from too much clutter. Keep in mind that you will defeat the entire purpose of your chart or graph if it is not *clear, simple, legible, and accurate.* In short, to prevent chart and graph "overload," limit the data on the visual aid to what is absolutely necessary to make your point.

2. *Do not put the graph or chart up without reading or interpreting it for the audience.* I have seen speakers display elaborate charts in front of an audience and forget to talk about the material depicted on the chart.

3. Charts and graphs can often be rather dull. Whenever possible, try to *use bright colors or other creative ways of showing the points* you are trying to stress on the chart or graph. For example, you could show the blight of the world's rain forests by using green trees on your graph instead of numbers.

Figure 7.7 Pie Graph

Figure 7.8 Bar Graph

Figure 7.9 Line Graph

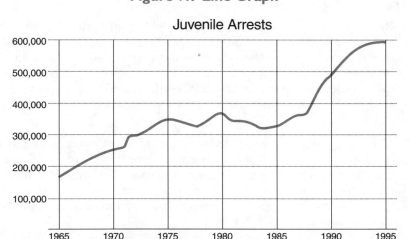

Juvenile Arrests

Chalkboards and Dry-Erase Boards

In this age of action and sophisticated technology, using a chalkboard or a dry-erase board might seem a rather dull type of visual aid, yet for many reasons it can help you accomplish your communication purpose. Let us look at some of the advantages of this aid so that you can decide when and how to use boards.

Convenience. The main advantage of boards as visual aids should be obvious to anyone who has attended school: *they are convenient*—items can easily be added or removed at any time. They are usually found in conference rooms and auditoriums, as well as in classrooms. A conscientious speaker should check the speaking environment beforehand to be sure that a chalkboard or white dry-erase board will be available. One speaker very casually said, "Now let me diagram how this system will work," only to turn around and find there was no chalkboard in the room. Both the speaker and the audience were greatly embarrassed.

Display of Steps in a Process. A board offers an opportunity to present a *step-by-step development of the process* being explained. Using chalk or special pens for the white dry surface, you can add material as you go along, to visually demonstrate, say, how a ship is built from the inside to the outside. Moreover, because chalk and marking pen can be erased, you can delete certain items as a means of clarifying your point.

Adaptability. Boards also *let you adapt* to specific and often unexpected situations. If you were speaking on the need to immunize children against life-threatening diseases, you might decide, on the spur of the moment, to turn to the board and write, "Five dollars can immunize a child against six life-threatening diseases." These words would add impact to your message and focus the listeners' attention on your main point.

Movement Facilitation. Finally, boards can help *facilitate your movement*. The act of walking to the board frees you from the constraints of the lectern.

Boards are handy and helpful, but some words of advice are in order concerning their use and abuse:

1. Because it takes time to write, you need to make sure that you do not lose the audience's attention while lettering and diagramming. Therefore, you should try to continue talking and maintaining *eye contact* while you are at the board. If you try to overcome this problem and put your material on the board before you speak, your audience may spend more time looking at your artwork than at you.

2. Although you can use a board in a spontaneous manner, in most instances you should plan the content and mechanics of your drawings well in advance of the presentation. This means rehearsing with *your drawings* as you practice your speech. Too often, speakers have turned to the board and written something on it without thinking of its impact.

3. *Print*; do not write. Handwriting is much harder to read than standard bold print. There is nothing more frustrating to an audience than trying to decipher unreadable material. This caution also applies to your artistic abilities. Because it is so easy to pick up a piece of chalk or a marking pen, many speakers start to draw without thinking about the audience. They end up cluttering the board with marks that make very little sense to anyone but themselves.

4. If at all possible, try to *secure a variety of colors* when selecting chalk and marking pens. The range of colors will add to both clarity and interest.

Flip Charts

Flip charts (sometimes referred to as "butcher paper"), which are large unlined tablets, combine some characteristics of posters and of chalkboards. Most of them are two feet wide and three feet high. They rest on an easel and are written on with broad-tipped felt pens. Because the pages can be turned, you can mark on some pages as you move through your talk.

Flip charts are useful for speeches that attempt to explain a progression or process. For example, a speech describing the ten steps in learning how to draw mountains could use each page of a flip chart to demonstrate a stage of the process. You can also mark pages in advance of your talk. Regardless of how you use a flip chart, remember to leave the first page blank unless you plan on using what is showing as part of your introduction. If your listeners see a figure on a chart before you start talking, they will try to anticipate what you plan to say.

Although they appear to be somewhat elementary, we need to examine a few additional guidelines for using flip charts:

1. Securely attach the flip chart to the easel.

2. Adjust the easel height before you start your presentation.

3. Grasp the chart in the middle to flip pages so that the paper moves with ease.

4. Remember to face your audience while you are using the flip chart.

Duplicated Material (Handouts)

Duplicated material (often referred to as "handouts") is another highly recommended type of visual aid for a number of reasons. Handouts can be used when the information cannot be explained by employing any other aid; when the audience needs time to carefully examine the material being discussed; or when you want the audience to take a copy of the information with them when you complete the speech. Duplicated material can be easily and quickly prepared and readily updated; it can provide a permanent record once the speech is over. With the popularity and availability of copy machines and computer printers, it is a rather simple matter to produce duplicated material. Handouts allow each member of the audience to have a copy of a long quotation, a diagram, a map, a chart, or an illustration. Many business meetings and educational settings call for materials to be in the audience's hands as part of the presentation.

When you want to use duplicated material (or even distribute blank sheets of paper), you may find the following suggestions profitable:

1. Unless you plan to use your handout at the very start of your talk, you should not distribute the material until you are ready to use it. Circulated material offers listeners an easy excuse to stop listening.

2. Make sure to give each person a copy of the material. Trying to read over someone's shoulder can confuse listeners.

3. Your material should be neat and readable. It is of little value if your words contribute to audience comprehension but, at the same time, the printed material is distracting and perplexing. One will counteract the other, and the result may be a lack of understanding.

4. When using handouts, keep talking while the listeners are looking at the material on the handout. This will enable you to remain the focus of their attention.

5. References to the handout should be very specific. Offer comments such as "notice the shape of the bird's wing on page two; this is one reason it can fly faster than birds even twice its size."

6. It is often helpful to put the same material contained in the handout onto a transparency. This will enable you to personally highlight the important material while the audience is looking at the printed material you have distributed.

Electronic Visual Aids

In addition to the nonelectronic visual aids just discussed, there are also a number of very effective electronic devices you can use. If you have a topic that lends itself to the electronic media and have access to an electrical outlet and a screen, you might want to consider some of the following aids.

Slides

Although they often require elaborate preparation, slides can benefit many speeches. In recent years, because slide projectors are so easy to operate, this aid has become extremely popular in business, government, and educational contexts. Like photographs, slides can be selected for a specific purpose or product. They are also useful in that many slide projectors are equipped with remote control units that can advance the slides while the speaker stands in front of the audience or moves around the room. With this device the speaker can control the rate of speed at which the slides appear. Because slides are often colorful and change quickly, they can hold attention while informing, persuading, and entertaining. Imagine how interesting it would be to listen to a speech on masks of different cultures while you were looking at a variety of masks being projected on the screen. Think of the persuasive impact of showing slides that allow your audience to see the plight of "homeless" dogs and cats being kept at the local animal shelter.

A major asset of slides is that if you have something that is too small for your audience to see, such as a photograph, chart, drawing, or article, you can make a slide of it. Another appealing attribute of slides is that you can get them from a variety of sources: media centers, libraries, and friends. It is possible to make slides with some personal computers. You can also take them from your personal archives. If you took pictures during a trip to China and now want to talk about the Great Wall of China, you can use your slides to help illustrate your points and also create interest.

You should keep a few ideas in mind if you plan to use slides:

1. Number and title all slides. This will keep them in correct order.

2. Rehearse your talk while using your slides—ideally, with the same slide projector you will use during the actual presentation.

3. Time your talk carefully so that you allow sufficient time for the audience to look at each slide.

4. Avoid movements in front of the projector's light beam so that you will not block out the picture temporarily or cast distracting shadows on the screen.

5. If you are converting a photograph to a slide, allow sufficient time before the speech for the slide to be produced.

6. Projector bulbs burn out without any warning. If at all possible have a spare bulb with you during your presentation. You might also make sure your extension cord is long enough to reach the electrical outlet.

7. If it is available, use a remote-control switch when presenting your slides. This will make possible some degree of movement during your talk.

8. Because the room will be darkened, you will not be able to have direct eye contact with your audience. Therefore, your voice and

material must remain active unless you want to turn on the lights at the end of your talk and find most of your audience fast asleep.

9. If you wish to remain in the front of the room, you might consider asking someone who knows how to operate a slide projector to show the slides for you.

Videotape

Videotape systems represent yet another audiovisual tool that has gained popularity in recent years. They can be used in a lighted room and are easy to transport. There are two types of videotapes that you can use—those that are prerecorded and those you make yourself. Many systems can be used with computer-generated graphics (which are discussed later in this chapter). Most college campuses and major business firms have audiovisual centers that catalog, store, and circulate thousands of prerecorded tapes. Nearly every topic has been explored on videotape. You can use these tapes to help clarify and explain various points in your speech. You will also find that many of these centers will let you borrow their equipment so that you can make your own tapes.

Making one's own videotapes represents one of the newest and most exciting phenomena in the communication field. The equipment for producing "programs" is relatively inexpensive, lightweight, and simple to use. Because of their portability, these systems enable creative speakers to make tapes that are highly individualistic. You could, for example, take a small video camera to your community's inner city and interview homeless people for a speech dealing with the need for homeless shelters. You could also make a video on cultural differences in gestures by filming people from various backgrounds engaged in communication encounters. And a speech on how to improve various swimming strokes would greatly benefit from a tape that demonstrated the strokes being discussed.

Most video units are simple to start and stop, so you can speak for a few minutes and then let your tape do some of the "talking" for you. You can, with the aid of a friend, even be the "star" of your own production. There is nothing that prohibits you from being on the screen and "live" in front of an audience at the same time. Think of how effective it would be if, while talking about the newest methods of water safety, you were to show a video of yourself demonstrating the correct methods of rescuing a drowning person from the ocean, a lake, and a swimming pool.

Making your own videotapes represents one of the newest and most exciting phenomena in the communication field.

Videocassette players also contain a number of features that can contribute to both interest and learning. For example, most machines will let you replay, "freeze-frame," and use slow motion. These techniques afford you an opportunity to stress particular parts of the videotape.

There are a few important points to keep in mind when using video equipment:

1. Remember to rehearse. As noted elsewhere, when using electronic equipment you are depending on "other sources" besides yourself. Hence, become familiar with those "sources" and even be prepared for breakdowns in the equipment should they occur.

2. The television screen is very small, so make sure that all the members of audience can clearly see your videotape.

We should note in closing that when you are photographing other people with any type of camera, you must get their permission to use the pictures. That is to say, it is against the law to randomly take pictures of other people and display them without the subject's written consent.

Computer Aids

Computer Graphics. In the past few years, **computer graphics** has become an increasingly useful vehicle for producing visuals for a presentation. Computer graphics can now supply a speaker with novel and effective means for visualizing material. The graphics produced are clear, readable, and interesting. Many home computers (and virtually all business computers) have the capability of producing line graphs, bar graphs, charts, and drawings in black and white or color. What is nice about most of these graphics programs is that you do not have to be a computer genius to "run" the programs. With the aid of programs such as PowerPoint, Freelance, and Persuasion, you can design creative graphics or select from hundreds of drawings (see Figure 7.10). When you are satisfied with the results displayed on the monitor, you can print out those same lines, graphs, shapes, or elaborate and colorful pictures. Once they are on paper, these computer-generated graphics can be displayed as easily as any traditional poster, painting, photograph, or object.

Your graphics can also be displayed using what is called an LCD (liquid crystal diode) projection unit. This device, which is connected to a computer and fits on top of an overhead projector, reproduces onto a larger screen what is on the computer monitor. This allows the audience to see a clear enlargement of the graphics you have created. If you so desire, you can use the LCD unit for immediate reproduction and reworking of your visuals while you are talking. Some display panels are even equipped for sound reproduction.

Word Processors. The most fundamental way to create visuals on your computer is to turn to your computer's writing program. Programs such as Microsoft Word, Microsoft Works, WordPerfect, WordStar, and PFS Professional Write allow you to use "bullets," a variety of typefaces, bold type, line spacing, and a choice of fonts. All these "tools" can make your visual aids informative and attractive, whether you make a transparency or poster.

When using computer graphics, you should remember the following advice:

1. Try to strike a balance between clarity and trying to be Pablo Picasso. Because some graphics programs and laser printers

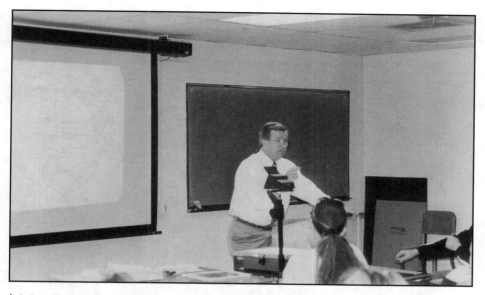

It is important to maintain eye contact with your audience when you use visual aids.

allow for detailed and dazzling artwork, there is a tendency on the part of novices to get carried away. Hence, try not to mix too many type styles or to add extra material simply because it is available.

2. Allow ample time to produce your graphics so that you will be able to practice with them long before you give the speech.

3. Remember, in most instances the material reproduced by the computer will not be large enough for all members of the audience to see. So set time aside to have your graphics enlarged at a copy center.

4. As is the case with all new technology, computer equipment is subject to imperfections and "crashes." Therefore, check all your equipment just a few hours before you begin your talk.

CD-ROM

The **CD-ROM** (Compact Disk—Read Only Memory) is one of the newest electronic innovations available to the public speaker. These compact disks include everything from words to complete video and audio clips. Whether you want to offer a review of space exploration or the history of American blues music, consider using CD-ROMs. When connected to a large video projector, or to the LCD panel mentioned earlier, the content on the disk can be shared with all the members of the audience. If you do not have disks in your personal collection, most campus media centers have a large collection of disks that they will check out to faculty and students.

Transparencies

Although they have been used for decades and are not as dramatic as some of the new technologies, **transparencies** remain one of the most popular

**Figure 7.10 PowerPoint® presentation gaphics
as seen on computer screen**

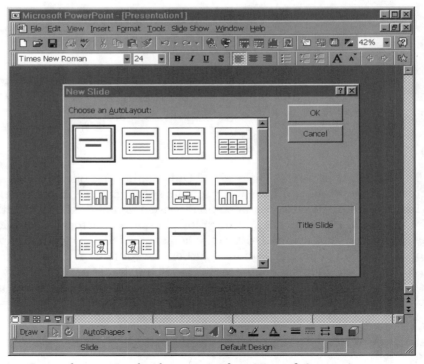

Source: Screen shots reprinted with permission from Microsoft Corporation.

Figure 7.11 Creating a PowerPoint® presentation

Using an Existing Outline
- Open an existing outline in your favorite word processor
- Save as text file
- Open Powerpoint
  - Select *blank presentation*, click *ok*
  - Click *ok* through default slide screen
- *Insert* menu, *Slides from Outline* option
  - Select appropriate file then insert
- Go to *View* Menu, *Outline* option
- Adjust hierarchy as needed, edit text as needed
- Go to *View* menu, select *Slides* to see content in slide format
- New slide can be added in this view:
  - *Insert* menu, *New Slide* option,
  - choose an appropriate *Autolayout*
  - enter text right on the slide

Add Some Zip
- *Format* menu, *presentation template* option
  - You might have to find the PowerPoint directory (folder) then Templates directory
  - Select appropriate directory for your output
  - Select desired look

Adjust Format
- *View* menu, *Master, Slide Master* options
  - drag and select text then change color, font, size, etc. Changes will be reflected in all slides when you return to slide view *(View* menu, *Slides* option)

Insert Graphics
- *Insert* menu, select *picture, clipart* or *movie* options
- Point to appropriate directory (folder) to find files

To Create a Powerpoint Presentation from Scratch
- *File* menu, *New* option
  - select *blank* or *template* for presentation
  - select appropriate *autolayout* style
- Select preferred view for entering text into slides, *View* menu, *Slides* or *Outline* option

Catherine Hays, Electronic Media Center, University of Maryland. Reprinted by permission.

and common visual aids used by speakers. The transparency is a thin, clear sheet of plastic (acetate) bearing an image from any book, magazine, or journal that contains material you would like your audience to see. Transparencies are useful because they are simple to construct and easy to move from location to location. Perhaps even more important, you can personalize your transparencies by placing any image you want on the sheet of plastic. By using a felt-tip pen to write or draw on the plastic sheet, you can stress any process, idea, or concept you deem significant.

Most campus audiovisual centers or copy centers can make transparencies for you, inexpensively. You can even insert a sheet of transparency plastic into your home computer printer and create your own transparency. The transparency is illuminated onto a screen by an overhead projector. These machines are found in nearly every classroom or business meeting room. Thus, a group of people can view material that is ordinarily visible to only one person at a time.

Transparencies can be made in advance of your talk, or they can be constructed while you are speaking. For example, you could trace the route of an oil spill while discussing each city that was touched by the spill.

Transparencies have the added advantage of letting you face your audience as you display the visual aid. Chalkboards force you to watch what you are writing; however, you can "load" the transparency projector while you look at the audience.

Many speakers find it useful to prepare a series of transparencies. By laying one piece of plastic over another, you can give your aid an overlay image. Each overlay after the first transparency shows a different and more detailed explanation of the point being made. As each overlay is added, a concept can be made more complete, a complex process simplified, sequential stages developed, or additional information presented. Remember, whatever use you make of transparencies, they allow you to control the amount of information your audience receives at any one time. For example, in a speech dealing with acid rain, you could begin by projecting an unadorned map of the United States and then, with each additional overlay, demonstrate the severity of the problem as the map grows darker and the rain spreads.

As is the case with all the aids discussed in this chapter, transparencies must be used with great care. If handled incorrectly, they can call attention to themselves, reduce your credibility, and reduce audience comprehension.

Let us examine a few guidelines you should follow when using transparencies:

1. Overhead transparencies have the potential to make you look clumsy. It takes a few seconds to change visuals as you lift a "gate" and drop each new transparency into place. If the new insert is not positioned correctly, or the gate is not opened smoothly, the image on the screen will leap around or appear off center. Therefore, be sure that your image on the screen is level and upright. Although it may give everyone a good laugh, you will be embarrassed, for example, if your picture of the Mississippi River shows the water running east to west instead of north to south. In short, you will be better off if you practice, practice, practice.

2. Too much clutter and detail on a single transparency will only confuse your audience. Because language is linear (you can say only

one word at a time), the audience must wait for you to complete one idea before you can start another. However, your aid has the potential to include a great many items all at the same time. Your visual on the Mississippi River would be very confusing if, when first projected on the screen, it showed major and minor ports, wildlife areas, all the streams that empty into the river, each city and town, and the main sections of pollution. In short, if there is too much for the audience to see, they will have difficulty finding the focal point.

3. Number your materials so that you will have them in order when you reach for them during your talk.

4. Make sure your images—numbers, letters, or drawings—are large enough for everyone to see. You are showing only a projected image. If the original image is small, the projection will be small. As a general rule, you should have only five to seven words per line when constructing your transparencies.

5. Turn the projector to "off" when you are not displaying an image. The bright light of the machine or a picture you are no longer talking about might well become a major distraction. In addition, remember to turn off the machine once you have displayed your last transparency.

6. The projector used to illuminate the transparency has a light bulb that needs to be cooled by a small fan. The fan produces a humming sound. Therefore, remember to increase your volume when the projector is displaying your transparency

7. Remember, all electronic aids have the potential to present mechanical problems. Hence, it behooves you to see that the machine is in good working order before your talk and that you know how to operate it. If it does break down during your speech, you should try to handle the "disaster" with wit and humor. Your audience will surely empathize with your situation.

Audio Aids

Although this chapter is titled "Visual Aids," we must briefly discuss the role of audio in speech making. Compact disks, tapes, and records can make your material more interesting and unforgettable. If you were presenting a speech on the history of jazz, it would be extremely beneficial for the audience to hear actual examples representing each musical period. You could also use audio aids if you were giving a speech about famous American orators and wanted your listeners to hear the Martin Luther King, Jr., speech "I Have a Dream."

Audio aids can also be used in conjunction with other aids. Recently, a speaker who was giving a speech on the cruelty of bull fighting played music from Ravel's *Bolero* as she moved the audience through a series of slides that concluded with the killing of the bull.

❖ ❖ ❖ ❖   ## Preparing Visual Aids

The philosopher Thomas Fuller once wrote that "A danger foreseen is half avoided." We would add that preparing your visual aids in advance of your presentation can not only avoid "danger" but can also add to the overall effectiveness of your speech. Hence, when you compose your aids, consider the following points:

1. *Conduct an audience analysis for your visual aids in much the same way you would for the verbal content of your speech.* Ask yourself these two important questions: First, Is this visual aid suited, in both content and form, for this audience? A visual aid that insults your audience's intelligence or one that is much too complex for their backgrounds will hinder, instead of help, your speech. It would be an affront to ask a group of third-year computer science students to look at a diagram showing a keyboard, monitor, and printer. Second, ask yourself, What visual aids would help me accomplish my purpose? Your aids should not be "window dressing," used to make your speech more attractive. They must be pertinent and serve a purpose. Many speakers, especially those preparing speeches to inform, use the occasion as an excuse to show their favorite pictures or slides. Try to avoid this fault. Remember, your aids should instruct, convince, and motivate or stimulate interest.

2. *Be sure that the lettering, artwork, or other main features are large, clear, and of sufficient contrast for everyone in the audience to see.* Too many visual aids force the audience to squint and strain as if they were reading the last line on an eye chart. The lettering should allow for sufficient spacing so each word can be easily read. The use of bold type and italics should also be employed to help with clarity and interest. The artwork should also be attractive and free of distracting elements. Try to use color, contrasting shapes, and other techniques to keep your aids from being dull and ordinary.

3. As noted elsewhere, *check the physical surroundings and furnishings before your talk.* By evaluating the setting in advance you will avoid discovering, when it is too late, that there is no place to put your chart or no electrical outlet for your tape recorder or VCR. Many speakers have had to hold their aids throughout their speech because they failed to investigate the accommodations. How awkward you would feel if you started to show a film in a room that could not be darkened.

   Part of evaluating the surroundings should include deciding how you will present your visual aids. For example, if you are using a poster, will the room have an easel or a bulletin board, and will you have to bring your own tacks or tape?

4. *Practice your speech with your audiovisual aid.* Rehearsing how to use your aid, so that you will be comfortable with it, is as impor-

tant as practicing the language and delivery of your talk. This practice will help you become familiar with your aid so that its use is not marked by an awkward break in the speech. Too many speakers fail to recognize the importance of this rehearsal and end up having to look at their aid to remember what it contains.

Using Visual Aids

Once you have prepared your visual aids, you must then decide how to use them most effectively. Following are some do's and don'ts that should help you plan the use of your visual aids:

1. *Remember the necessity of maintaining eye contact with your audience.* Too many speakers enjoy their visual aid so much that they forget their audience. They also neglect other aspects of delivery; some speakers move in front of their visual aid, blocking it from the view of the audience.

    Your eye contact will be enhanced if you can avoid passing an aid through the audience either just before your talk or while you are speaking. Should you want them to carry something away from the speech, pass it out at the end of your talk.

2. Unless circumstances demand otherwise, *you should keep your visual aid out of sight until you are ready to use it.* There are enough distractions pulling on your listeners; your aid should not provide another. When you are finished with your visual aid, remove it from the audience's line of vision.

3. In most instances, *it is best to display only one visual aid at a time.* To have more than one aid in front of the audience at one time encourages the listeners to divide their attention between the aids and perhaps miss certain important points about the one you happen to be discussing.

4. *Learn to expect and deal with the unexpected.* Although this might seem like a contradiction in terms, it is nevertheless a point worth remembering. The horror stories concerning the use of visual aids are legendary. Slides being placed into the projectors upside down, photographs sticking together, easels and tripods falling apart, colors that have run because they got wet while being transported, videotapes breaking during talks, and "live" subjects that upstage you are just a few of the problems that might beset your presentation. Learn to think about a contingency plan should you be faced with the unexpected. Perhaps the best advice is to stay calm, keep right on going, laugh at adversity, and let your audience know that you are aware that your visual aids conspired against you.

5. *Visit and prepare the room in advance.* Notice barriers that might obstruct the audience's view (desks, podiums, etc.). If you are going to project images on a screen, make sure you know the loca-

tion of the lights and how to draw the curtains. Thinking about these sorts of issues will help you avoid problems before they occur. Or as Shakespeare once told us, "To fear the worst oft cures the worse."

Summary

You should use visual aids whenever you believe they might assist you in accomplishing your purpose. Although it might be a slight exaggeration, Alfred Lord Tennyson was correct when he noted that "things seen are mightier than things heard." Visual aids let people "see."

Visual aids can help make your verbal message more interesting, more understandable, more persuasive, and more memorable. They also add to your personal credibility. In choosing the most appropriate aid, you need to analyze the purpose of your talk, the size of your audience, the availability of certain aids, and your expertise in using a particular aid. You should investigate a wide variety of visual aids, such as people, objects, specimens, models, posters, diagrams, maps, paintings, photographs, charts, graphs, chalkboards, flip charts, duplicated material, slides, videotape, computer art, CD-ROMs, transparencies, and audio aids.

Whatever form of visual aid you choose, you should select it for its appropriateness to the audience, the subject, and the purpose of the speech. It should be easily seen by the audience, it should be easy for the speaker to manipulate, it should accurately represent the concept being discussed, and it should be free of distracting elements. In short, a visual aid should aid. You are advised to practice using your visual aid before making your speech and then to observe certain cautions during the presentation. Remember to look at your audience, coordinate your visual aid with your words, avoid passing your aids through the audience, and display only one aid at a time.

Concepts and Questions

1. What are the major advantages of using visual aids when giving a speech?

2. What considerations should be taken into account when selecting a visual aid?

3. Name and describe five types of visual aids.

4. What drawbacks often accompany the use of visual aids? How can those problems be overcome?

5. When constructing your own visual aid, what are some problems you might face? How do you plan to overcome those problems?

6. As it relates to this chapter, explain the phrase "a picture is worth a thousand words."

Activities and Exercises   ❖ ❖ ❖ ❖

1. Bring four visual aids to class and explain each of them in light of the material discussed in this chapter.

2. Watch five television commercials. Make a list of the types of graphics and other visual aids the makers of the commercial employed to get their point across.

3. List five speech topics on a sheet of paper. Under each topic list the types of aids that could be used to help get attention and explain the topic.

4. Take a trip to the audiovisual center on your campus. During your visit examine the catalogues that list various films, videos, CD-ROMs, and the like. Also determine the type of equipment that students may check out.

5. Choose an informative topic that you would like to talk about. Give a speech on the topic without visual aids and then again with visuals aids.

6. Give a humorous speech that demonstrates some of the problems that might occur when using visual aids. ✦

CHAPTER EIGHT

Research:
The Content
of Your Ideas

Wisdom is not acquired, save as the result of investigation.

—Hindu Proverb

Clarence Darrow, a great American trial lawyer, lecturer, and writer of the early years of this century, offered this advice: "Anybody who speaks should spend a thousand days on trying to get ideas and knowledge to every one they spend on the way to tell it." Although Darrow's advice may be rather extreme, it nonetheless underlines the importance of engaging in thorough research before you begin to fashion a speech. Even though you may draw heavily on your personal experiences as you prepare your talk, the principal part of your supporting materials will come from a research effort that can be alternately exhilarating and tedious. But try to remember the advice contained in the Guinean proverb, "To prepare does not spoil the trip, it makes it better."

Many students are dismayed when they discover that doing research is part of the public-speaking experience; however, when they begin the process of probing and searching, they discover that the rewards of learning how to do research far outweigh the disadvantages. The elation that comes from discovering new information about a subject you are interested in will often prompt you to search still further. The English author Charles Dickens remarked, "There is a passion for hunting something deeply implanted in the human breast." The goal of this chapter is to urge you to tap into that passion.

Learning how to do research provides you with skills that you will need for lifelong learning. Once you master the techniques of digging out and using diverse sources of information, you can apply these talents to different situations as they arise. The payoff that comes from knowing how to perform research for a speech extends well beyond the limits of the classroom.

In chapters 1 and 2, we noted that effective speech making involves following a systematic series of steps. When you have selected your topic, determined your speech purpose, and conducted an analysis of the audience and occasion, your next step is to begin your research. You must locate the materials that will help you accomplish your main objective. As a starting point, you need to realize that doing research is not a random or haphazard activity; it is systematic and tedious. That is to say, although plunging into your research because you are enthused is a noble endeavor, you must also have a plan of action.

Having a Research Agenda

Ralph Waldo Emerson wrote that "there is always a right way of doing everything, even it be to boil an egg." This same wisdom applies to doing research; there is a correct way to approach researching any topic. Most experts agree that, regardless of the subject matter being sought or the questions being posed, successful research involves six interrelated steps.

Although many of these steps were mentioned when we discussed speech preparation in chapter 2, it is nevertheless useful for you to see all of them spelled out here again.

❖ ❖ ❖ ❖

Start Early

The importance of starting early cannot be overemphasized. The simple fact is that good research takes time—lots of time. Starting early is also essential if you hope to accomplish your communication purpose. The American poet Countee Cullen said the same thing far more lyrically: "And dilly-dalliers never yet/Have at the proper moment sallied/To where they were supposed to get." Starting early keeps you from rushing and allows time for a degree of trial and error.

Decide on a Specific Topic

Often, the most frustrating part of doing research is getting started. Part of the frustration comes from not deciding on a topic in advance of searching the Internet, going to the library, or telephoning someone for an interview. Whether your topic is carjacking or test tube babies, you need to know what you are interested in if you expect your time to be productive. Of course, there will be times when you choose your topic and there will be other occasions when your topic is selected for you. In either event, have a subject in mind *before* you start your research. The more specific your topic, the easier you will find your research assignment. You need to move from a general subject to a specific area within that subject. You cannot easily research a topic as immense as world religion, but you can locate information for a speech that compares the Ten Commandments with the Eightfold Path of Buddhism.

Use a Variety of Sources

Use independent sources. A good researcher quickly learns the difference between material that stresses a single point of view and that which is free from self-serving interests. Articles on cigarette smoking underwritten by the tobacco industry must be questioned as to the independence of their conclusions.

Select a Research Strategy

Deciding on a research strategy involves two interrelated issues. First, you must think about the various places you can find material on the subject you are researching. For example, should you interview professors in the Religion Department? Should you locate books on comparative religion? Should you visit a local Buddhist Temple? Second, a research strategy also means starting your research with some questions in mind. The famous Roman rhetorician Cicero, writing over two thousand years ago, offered some guidelines for developing a strategy that are still applicable today. Cicero maintained that to research a speech effectively, a speaker needed to ask the following research questions about the proposed topic:

- Who?

- What?

- Where?

- By which means?

- Why?

- How?

- When?

If the speech dealt with a comparison of the Ten Commandments with the Eightfold Path of Buddhism, some of the following research questions might be useful as a starting point:

- *Who* are the people I will be talking to?

- *Who* are the experts on this topic?

- *What* does the audience already know about the topic I will be discussing?

- *What* additional information should I supply them?

- *Where* are the locations that might have information about religion (specifically the Ten Commandments and Buddhism)?

- *By what means* can I access material on religious precepts?

- *Why* will the audience want to hear about this information?

- *How* much background information do I need to supply the audience?

- *When* will I need to complete my research so that I will have time to prepare my outline?

Keep Complete and Accurate Records

In addition to keeping a record of the material you find, it is essential that you keep track of the sources of that material. Your personal preferences will decide if you use cards or sheets of paper, or create files on your computer. In the next few pages, we will talk about how to list your bibliography and references (or computer file), but for now remember that these references tell you where you found your information.

Systematically Organize Your Material

Organize your material into specific headings. For example, if you are researching the Ten Commandments and the Eightfold Path, you could develop headings around the origins of these precepts, the writings that carried the messages, the people who introduced the religious precepts, early translations of the writings, and the like.

Finding Material

❖ ❖ ❖ ❖

Resource material is to be found in a number of places. You must learn to familiarize yourself with those places so that you can support your ideas with clear, believable evidence. What follows is a discussion of the sources that successful speakers use as part of their speech preparation.

It is essential that your material be recorded in an accurate manner and a usable form. (Photo: photodisc.com)

Personal Experience

Lawyer Owen Young remarked that, "Experience is wisdom's best friend." The natural starting point for the gathering of speech materials is your own storehouse of knowledge—the place that jurist Benjamin Cardozo referred to as "the archives of my memory." In all likelihood, you will choose to speak on a particular topic because it holds an attraction for you. Learn to draw on that attraction as a first step. In the course of your life, you have undergone countless experiences. Whether an experience was firsthand (undergoing extensive treatment for skin cancer) or vicarious (seeing a news clip on *NBC Nightly News*), it is still a part of your private "library." Some of the best speeches use personal experience as a major source of information. For example, a middle-aged man who left Vietnam at the end of the war as a boatperson vividly explained the horrifying trip in a manner that went well beyond any account that could be found in a book. Another speaker, who worked as a ski instructor, talked about survival techniques in the wilderness. A student who was born and raised in a town of only 500 people talked about how her school experiences prepared her for life at a major university. Thus, begin by writing down what you know about the topic. Not only will you start to build a supply of information for the speech, but you will place yourself in a position to identify the areas in which additional research is needed.

It is unwise, however, to rely solely on your personal background as a source of supportive material. All of us have perceptual limitations that can distort our view of reality. What we have learned and what we can recall are subject to our individual prejudices. A paratrooper who has participated in an invasion would most likely perceive the action very differently than a person who has only read about it or viewed clips of it on television. Personal experiences are useful and necessary, but when used to the exclusion of other sources they have limited value. As is the case with so many aspects of life, moderation and balance are the watchwords.

Interviews

Once you have "talked to yourself," you might find it very useful to talk to other people—people who are experts. This same advice, in slightly different

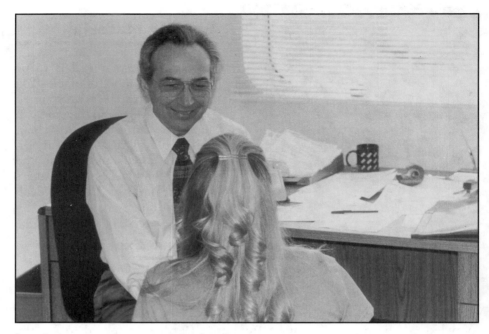

Interviews represent a strong research tool.

form, was offered by the French scholar and writer François Rabelais when he wrote, "What harm in getting knowledge even from a sot, a pot, a fool, a mitten, or an old slipper." We can add "other people" to that list. The experiences and observations of other persons who might know more about the subject than you are often excellent sources of information. To secure that information, you will most likely have to conduct an interview.

As a research tool, interviews have several strong points. First, *if you want the most current information, an interview can give you access to the person who is currently involved with your topic.* Books, magazines, and even CD and computer programs take time to write, print, and distribute; hence, they can be outdated. Interviews are timely; you can talk to someone about what is happening now. Second, *an interview allows you a certain degree of selectivity.* Instead of simply talking to someone who knows a little about the topic, you can gather data by going directly to an expert—someone with firsthand information. For example, if you were preparing a speech on the training program for Olympic skiers and a member of the Olympic team lived in your community, you could interview this person as a way of gathering firsthand information. Third, *there is a "give and take" with the interview process that allows you the freedom to probe a topic beyond a single response.* That is to say, if the person you are interviewing says something you do not understand, or something that you want to know more about, you can ask him or her right on the spot for more information. Fourth, *interviewing as a research tool is also useful in that it lets you gather information on fairly narrow topics.* For example, if your subject is the problem of rape on your campus, you can go directly to the campus chief of police and get his or her view of the topic, as well as some valuable facts and figures. Interviews also stimulate interest when they are reported in the speech. The audience wants to hear what you have to say because you have gone to an expert.

As a college student, you are in a position to make extensive use of interviews. Most professors, because of their teaching assignments and research programs, are experts in specific fields and can offer you valuable assistance. To illustrate, if you were going to give a speech dealing with the problems of interracial marriages, you might gain useful information and new ideas from interviews with professors of sociology, psychology, religion, and marriage and family relations. In addition, you might seek an appointment with some of the campus clergy. In all these instances, you are increasing your knowledge of the topic.

Information-gathering interviews, because they are a formal communication activity like a speech or group discussion, require a great deal of forethought and planning if they are to yield useful and relevant material. Let us look at some of the stages of that planning as a means of improving your interviews. After discussing the preparation phase of interviewing, we will examine some guidelines for conducting an interview. We will also see how to convert the interview material into something useful for a speech. The section ends with some special considerations to keep in mind when interviewing someone whose culture is different from your own.

Preparing for an Interview. *Determine the purpose.* As is the case with a speech, you must begin the interview process by deciding the purpose of your interview. Ask yourself this simple question—why am I considering an interview? The answer to this question will help you determine who you will seek out for an interview and the types of questions you might ask. For example, if your speech was going to deal with late-night campus security, your interview purpose would lead you to the campus chief of police, with a list of questions about current policy as to escorts, lighting, and the like.

Set up an interview. You should set up an interview well in advance, taking pains to arrange it at the convenience of the interviewee. He or she is granting you valuable time, so it is only a matter of simple courtesy to take his or her schedule into consideration. You should make your purpose very clear during this first contact. This means specifying the general nature of the content of the proposed interview and the amount of time that will be needed to conduct the interview. Identifying your purpose is not only important for the interviewee, but it will also enable you to focus on a specific goal. Knowing what you want from the outset keeps you from wasting time on irrelevant issues. If you want to find out how a person from Mexico views the United States' role in the Organization of American States, you would hardly prepare questions on how Mexican citizens perceive our electoral process.

Learn about the interviewee. Learn all you can about the person you will be interviewing. Specifically, what information does the person have, because of his or her position and experiences, that drew you to that individual? Being knowledgeable about the interviewee's expertise will enable you not only to ask good questions but to let him or her know you are serious about your task.

If the person you are interviewing is from a culture different from your own, it is important that you investigate any cultural "rules" that might have an impact on the interview. For example, many Muslims do not touch other people with their left hand. Hence, in greeting a Muslim, you need to be careful that you do not violate this cultural rule.

Develop some interview questions. Before the meeting, prepare a detailed, well-organized agenda of questions you want to ask. An information-gathering interview is a systematic and well-thought-out conversation. Although

❖ ❖ ❖ ❖   interviewers may give the impression of being spontaneous and do react to what the interviewee says and does, most successful interviewers know in advance the type of information they need from the other person.

In preparing your questions, you should decide not only the content of your inquiries but also their sequence. In most instances, you will find it useful to move from the general to the specific or from difficult to easy questions.

When preparing and asking questions, try to use *open, closed, mirror, and probing* questions.

1. *An open question invites a relatively unrestricted area of response.* When interviewing a Cambodian student about the dietary habits of her homeland, you might ask, "What kinds of foods are popular in your country?" This broad question allows the respondent to choose the approach she wishes to take in dealing with the question.

2. *A closed question, which is often the most effective in information-gathering interviews, severely restricts the choice of responses available to the interviewee.* "Do you think there is the likelihood of a presidential veto?" invites a yes or no answer. "How much money is available for school lunch programs in this district?" gives the respondent little room for anything except an answer involving some figures. As these examples indicate, closed questions are practical in that they are normally used to elicit brief and specific answers in a rapid-fire series. In this way, they can draw out a great deal of factual information, often in a short period of time.

3. *A mirror question, as its name suggests, reflects the answer just given by the respondent.* "You said that gang membership is likely to increase?" prompts the interviewee to elaborate on his or her previous answer. Interviewers ask mirror questions, then, to secure clarification of a point raised by the interviewee.

4. *A probing question serves somewhat the same function as a mirror question in that it seeks elaboration of a point already raised.* "What do you mean by that?" or "Can you explain in a little more detail?" directs the respondent to continue with the present theme. Even a simple "Oh?" or "I see" suggests that you want to know more. Your nonverbal behavior can also serve as a kind of probing question. A fixed gaze and a nodding head can tell the interviewee, "Go on."

When thinking about the questions you will ask, remember that there are certain types of questions that you should avoid. For example, there is no need to ask questions you can answer without the interview. To ask someone, "How long have you been in charge of the international studies office?" when the college catalog would supply the answer is a waste of everyone's time. Questions that are too vague should also be avoided.

Decide on recording equipment. During your planning stage you should consider whether or not to use a tape and/or video recorder (granting, of course, that the interviewee will allow it). There are advantages and disadvantages to the use of a tape recorder. One of the obvious advantages is that you can obtain an accurate record of the meeting. Also, you are freed from the task of taking notes. The major disadvantage is that a recording device can have an inhibiting effect on some interviewees; hence, you may not get the honesty and spontaneity you desire. In summary, you should consider the comfort of your interviewee, the setting for the interview, the topic to be discussed, and the pros and cons of taping.

Conducting the Interview. In conducting an interview, you would be wise to divide the meeting into three closely related parts— the opening, the body, and the closing.

The opening. The beginning of the interview, which should start on time, has two main purposes. *First, try to establish rapport with the interviewee by setting a relaxed and friendly mood.* Putting the interviewee at ease will increase the chances of securing accurate and complete answers to your questions. *Second, during the opening, you should preview the reason for the interview and what you hope to accomplish.* During this period, you should set up the tape or video recorder if you secured permission from the interviewee. Although a recorder assures the accurate quotation of the interviewee's remarks, many people feel uncomfortable having one in the room. If the interviewee does not want to be recorded, make sure you have paper and pen so that you can write down his or her answers.

The body. It is in the body of the interview that you cover the essential material of the meeting. That is to say, once you have established rapport and previewed the interview, you are ready to gather the information you need to prepare your speech. To aid you in that effort, you should attend to the following guidelines:

1. *Keep the interview moving and on track.* By asking salient questions, you can control the flow and tone of the meeting. This helps assure you that the key issues get covered.

2. *Remember that the interviewee has the information you need.* Therefore, let him or her do most of the talking. Although most of us like to be the center of attention, in an interview the respondent should be the focal point.

3. *Offer verbal reviews as you go.* By letting the interviewee see what has been accomplished, you can avoid repeating the same ideas throughout the meeting. These reviews also let you verify your findings as you go. By saying, as a review, "So you believe that these four exercises are crucial to all young skiers," you can check your conclusions.

4. *By your words and actions, try to make the interviewee feel comfortable.* Not only is this the polite thing to do, but it helps you maintain rapport and encourages the interviewee to talk freely.

5. *Listen carefully.* Remember, you will be quoting and paraphrasing what you heard the interviewee say. You must not misquote. When you detect a contradiction or fail to understand something the interviewee says, you should ask for clarification; however, you can do this only if you are listening.

6. *Be time conscious.* You are using the interviewee's time, so do not overstay your welcome.

The closing. In closing an interview, summarize what has taken place ("So today we have . . ."), discuss a follow-up meeting if one is necessary ("Perhaps we can meet again on Tuesday to finish our talk?"), and show your appreciation ("Thank you very much for your time. You have given me some valuable information.").

After the Interview. Immediately after the interview, you should review your notes and decide what material is best suited for your speech. When selecting what to use, it is best to concentrate on two types of information. *First, try to locate the main theme of the interview.* If the topic was campus crime and you interviewed the chief of police, the main theme might be how crime is increasing on campus. *Second, you will want to isolate specific points you can use as evidence.* This support can take a variety of forms: statistics ("Last year we had a 92 percent increase in campus crime"); examples ("Just last night someone attacked a student as she was walking to her car"); and testimony ("I really believe we are seeing an increase in crime on this campus").

In reviewing your notes, if something is unclear you should call the interviewee and ask for clarification. Asking others for information is an important part of doing research. As philosopher John Locke wrote, "I attribute the little I know to my not having been ashamed to ask for information, and to my rule of conversing with all descriptions of men on those topics that form their own peculiar professions and pursuits."

The Role of Culture in Interviewing. Throughout, this book has stressed the impact of culture in all aspects of human communication. The interview process is not immune from this influence. Therefore, should you decide to interview someone from a culture different from your own, I urge you to keep the following points in mind.

Differences in making contact. You will find that even the method you use to contact someone for an interview is affected by culture. For example, while most of us might feel it is highly appropriate to contact people by phone and ask for an interview on the next day, this process is not used in many Asian cultures. For these cultures a formal letter, allowing the other person to set the time of the interview, is what is expected.

Differences in greeting behavior. The initial greeting you offer the interviewee is yet another area of concern. When you greet Western Europeans, they, along with the Japanese, would expect you to be somewhat formal. First names are never used with cultures that value formality. You should also avoid any attempts at "small talk" when meeting someone from a formal culture.

Differences in the use of language. Be aware of problems associated with language when interviewing someone from another culture. Although cultural differences in the use of language are discussed in detail in chapter 12, one area of concern needs to be identified at this time: the manner in which questions are asked and answered during the interview. Simply put, the dominant culture of North America uses language in a direct manner, while many Asian cultures are indirect. Most Americans, for example, learn to say "yes" and "no" with great ease. Yet the Japanese and Chinese seldom use the word "no." They find it too harsh and direct. They would prefer to be vague and equivocal rather than offer a direct answer that might offend their communication partner. You can see how this attitude toward directness could affect the entire interview. I therefore urge you to use open questions instead of direct questions when interviewing someone from a culture that has language prescriptions.

Differences in the use of time. The time it takes to conduct the interview will also be affected by the culture of the participants. This variable of time shows itself in a variety of ways. For example, the time it takes for the interviewee to answer the questions you ask will indicate the influence of culture. In both the Mexican and Arab cultures, talk is highly valued. These cultures take great pleasure in conversation and in demonstrating their rhetorical skills. Hence, the response to your question might consume more time than you had allotted for the answer. The pace at which the interview is conducted is also influenced by culture. In the United States, we are raised to believe that "time is money" and that we should not waste it. We even have a tendency to rush through our communication encounters. However, in many cultures a slower pace is valued. The Asian and Latin cultures are two examples of people who do not like to hurry their conversations. Therefore, be prepared for many different time schedules as you move from culture to culture.

Writing, Phoning, Faxing, and E-Mailing

Gathering information from people and organizations can also be implemented by writing, phoning, faxing, or E-mailing the person or organization in question. These tools are simple and quick ways of gathering information on a particular topic. Writing letters has been used for centuries to make contact with other people; the widespread use of the other three devices clearly reflects major changes in our culture that justify the label "Information Age."

The use of these four tools is based on two interrelated premises. First, *people besides you are interested in your speech topic*, and, second, *these groups and individuals are eager to furnish you information on that topic.* Locating and contacting these organizations and agencies is a relatively easy task, as discussed in the next few pages.

Locating Sources

Organizations and Agencies. Countless organizations and agencies are especially designed to gather and disseminate information about certain topics—whether it is the budget deficit, drunk driving, drug abuse, Alzheimer's disease, backpacking, or organ transplants. These organizations can represent *commercial interests* (National Dairy Council, American Paper Institute, National Automobile Dealers Association, Aerospace Industries Association of America, Chemical Manufacturers Association, American Iron and Steel Institute, Association of American Railroads); *health issues* (American Lung Association, American Physical Therapy Association, National Rehabilitation Association, American Institute of Nutrition, United Cerebral Palsy Association, American Academy of Allergy and Immunology, National Society to Prevent Blindness, National Association of the Deaf, American Association on Mental Deficiency, Leukemia Society of America, American Institute of Nutrition); *environmental concerns* (National Audubon Society, Nature Conservancy, Water Pollution Control Federation, Air and Waste Management Association, Friends of the Earth, Greenpeace, National Parks and Conservation Association, Save-the-Redwoods League, Sierra Club, Soil and Water Conservation Society, National Wildlife Federation); or *specialized interest* *groups* (Aircraft Owners and Pilots Association, Women in Communications, National Council on Child Abuse/Family Violence, American Civil Liberties Union, Abortion Rights Action League, African-American Institute, Animal Protection Institute, American Council of Education, Handgun Control Inc., Planned Parenthood, National Space Society, National Investigators Committee on UFOs).

The extensive list of examples in the previous paragraph demonstrates the idea that there are literally thousands of groups that will forward you information upon request. You simply need to contact them via fax machines, letters, phone calls, or the Internet. Most of these organizations are listed in the *Encyclopedia of Associations*, a reference book found in most libraries. This helpful guide, which is constantly being updated, is made up of three separate volumes: *National Organizations of the United States; International Organizations*; and *Regional, State, and Local Organizations*. Each volume not only lists thousands of organizations but also includes addresses, telephone numbers, and descriptions. *The World Almanac*, a popular newsstand reference book, provides the names and addresses of over a thousand groups under the listing of "Associations and Societies."

Government Agencies. Government agencies, at all levels, are another source of information that can be gathered by writing letters, making phone calls, faxing, or using the Internet. Topics ranging from organic farming to state lottery revenues are treated in government publications. At the national level, these topics are listed in a resource guide provided free of charge by the U.S. Government Printing Office (Washington, DC, 20402). Libraries have this index in their reference section.

Foreign Governments. Many foreign governments will answer requests for various kinds of information. For example, if you wanted to know more about how mainland China provides for part-time work permits, you could contact the nearest Chinese embassy or consulate. In most instances, information requests are answered promptly by the appropriate party. If you live near an embassy or consular office, you may be able to pick up the information in person. It is good to remember that when you request information about any organization representing a specific cause or orientation, you may receive material that does not "tell the whole story." It is advisable to check other sources when using some of the facts and figures from these groups.

Contacting Sources

Using the Telephone. Thousands of the groups and organizations you may want to contact can be reached easily by telephone. Not only can you locate most of the phone numbers through "information," but, with the advent of the "800" number, you can reach these organizations in a rather simple and inexpensive way. Most libraries have a *Directory of 800 Numbers*.

Using Fax Machines. If you are willing to pay a small fee for some of the materials, organizations will gladly fax them to you. All you need to do is locate a fax machine and know its "number" (most colleges and stationery stores have these machines and numbers) and request that the material be sent to that number.

Using E-mail. In many ways the use of E-mail is one of the most exciting tools to grow out of modern computer technology. E-mail, with the simple stroke of a key or the clicking of an icon, gives someone the freedom to reach

80 to 90 million individuals in 170 countries—and to have that contact within seconds or minutes. If you have a computer, an Internet provider, and the address of the person or organization you want to contact, you can gather material on any subject you deem important.

E-mail must be addressed to a specific person or entity. E-mail addresses have a common form: for example, *samovar@mail.sdsu.edu*. E-mail contains a return address (usually that of the sender of the E-mail) and a subject heading. It now rather simple to locate someone's E-mail address. Most search engines (Yahoo!, Excite, Lycos, Alta Vista, Magellan, etc.) have a feature that not only lists worldwide Yellow Pages but also contains a directory for locating E-mail addresses.

Once you locate the person or organization via E-mail, it is important that you are very specific regarding your request. Since most E-mail messages tend to be shorter than most other forms of correspondence, try to avoid being vague or too wordy. Most people like E-mail because there seems to be a built-in "get to the point" attitude associated with it, so get to the point when using E-mail as a research tool.

Visual Electronic Media

During the last 20 years visual communication has been one of the fastest-growing industries in the world. One of outgrowths of that industry has been the tremendous number of television programs, video productions, and films that have been stored and catalogued. Most colleges and universities have media centers, where they catalog and store films, commercial and noncommercial videotapes, audiocassettes, and even student media projects. Learning to use such sources, whether a videotape of a *National Geographic* special on rain forests, a student project on earthquake preparedness, a film on world religion, or an interview with a famous scientist, can add another valuable research tool to your collection.

Using electronic media as research instruments has become even more attractive in the past decade, as more and more material has been cataloged and indexed. For instance, in addition to the extensive media listings in your campus media catalogue, you can now find visual media listings in some of the following collections: *CBS News Index, Television News Resources: A Guide to Collections, Film Review Index, International Index of Multimedia Information, Public Television Transcripts, Television Index,* and *Transcript Video Index: A Comprehensive Guide to Television News and Public Affairs Programming.*

Using the Library

Donald C. Bryant and Karl R. Wallace, in their text on oral communication, noted, "The library is to the speech maker what the laboratory is to the scientist. It is a place of search and research." Although today many computers permit a great deal of the searching and research to be done at home, it is nevertheless still true that the library, whether on campus or a public facility, remains a wonderful place to conduct research and to gather material.

To make your visits to the library more productive, this section focuses on how to access (1) basic material in the library, (2) electronic databases in the library, and (3) traditional printed material in the library.

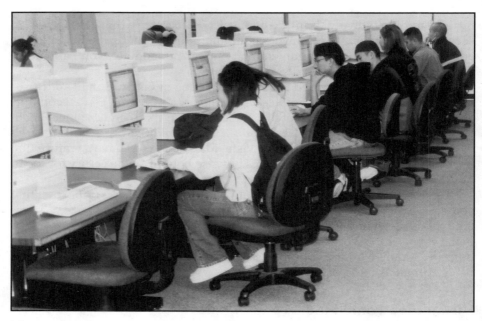

Libraries now have extensive electronic databases.

Accessing Material in the Library

First, *know your library and librarians*. Although similarities exist, no two libraries are alike. Regarding the library you will primarily be using, you should try to learn the following aspects:

- The library catalog system, whether in card form or computer format, which is the heart of any library.

- The interlibrary loan system.

- Basic procedures for using library material.

- The location of indexes, abstracts, reference books, government documents, special collections, nonprint media archives, and the like.

When using the library, you should feel free to ask questions of those who work there. Timidity may cost you access to valuable information. Remember the Malay proverb, "If you are reluctant to ask the way, you will be lost." In addition to asking questions, you should consider taking a tour of the library. Most libraries offer detailed tours of both the facilities and the procedures of the library. Sign up for one of these "expeditions" as part of your speech training.

Most public libraries, and virtually all college and university libraries, currently have the electronic equipment necessary to search through indexed files from journals, magazines, and research reports. In fact, many personal computers are now "programmed" to conduct these searches so that the researcher can access material from home. When you use computers in this fashion, you are conducting on-line searches, and the indexed files that are being scanned are referred to as databases.

You are most likely already familiar with, or at least have seen, the computer search system being used by your public, college, or university library. A very popular system to locate material within a library is LUIS (Library User Information Service). Because most systems are alike, we need only to discuss LUIS for you to get a feel for how computer searches function.

As you approach the system, you will see a keyboard and a terminal screen containing the following information:

Search	*Options Commands*
To search by	Title: = T
	Author: = A
	Subject: = S

If you are looking for a specific book and you know the title, you would type on the screen, following the prompt T =, *Oral Communication: Speaking Across Cultures*. If the book is in the library, you will immediately see the author's name, the title of the book, the date of publication, and the call number. If you know only the name of the author but not the title of the book, you would type on the screen A = Samovar. All of the books in your library written by that author would appear on the screen. If you were interested in a specific topic, such as public speaking, you would type S = Public speaking. All the books in your library on this subject would appear on the terminal screen.

Many computer search systems have printers. Hence, once you have selected the books you are interested in, you simply tap the "print" button on the keyboard, and you will get a printed listing of these books. You need only stroll to the stacks, list in hand, and locate your materials.

Accessing Electronic Databases

In addition to locating books, magazines, and journals within the individual library, computerized databases have now become popular tools for anyone doing research. These databases are fast and easy to use. The most widely used database for general use is *Info Trac*. This is an index to more than 400 magazines. This computer search is available at no cost at many college libraries. Information is stored on microfilm or laser disc in *InfoTrac* and can be accessed by using methods similar to those in using the *Reader's Guide*. The main differences between *InfoTrac* and traditional indexes is (1) the use of a monitor instead of a book, (2) the availability of a printed copy of the appropriate sources, and (3) the speediness of a computer search over the manual use of indexes.

Other useful indexes are *ProQuest* (over 1,000 general-interest, business, and scholarly publications), *Academic Search FullTEXT* (provides the full text of articles for over 1,000 periodicals), and *Public Affairs Information Service* (a compendium of journal articles, government documents, statistical data, etc.). Depending on the library and computer, these databases can be accessed through CD-ROM players, on-line searches, or mainframe computers.

The number of companies that now retrieve information for researchers is growing so rapidly that any "complete listing" is bound to become obsolete in a short time. Nonetheless, a sampling of the available services follows.

One of the earliest and most popular systems used by college students is the Educational Resources Information Center, or ERIC. ERIC is composed of a series of clearinghouses that gather, organize, and catalog unpublished materials, such as project reports, conference reports, and other research findings. The ERIC service is especially helpful if your topic falls into one of the following subject areas: career education; counseling and personnel services; early childhood education; educational management; handicapped and gifted children; higher education; information resources; junior colleges; languages and linguistics; reading and communication skills; rural education and small schools; science, mathematics, and environmental education; social studies and social science education; teacher education; tests, measurement, and evaluation; and urban education.

Bibliographic Retrieval Services (BRS) enables you to gain access to bibliographic and full-text databases on subjects as diverse as dentistry, agriculture, social sciences, chemistry, mental health, medicine, and books in print.

The DIALOG (Dialog Information Services) retrieval service can search over hundreds of databases containing more than a million references. DIALOG organizes its many databases by headings such as business; science and medicine; law; news; energy and environment; humanities; and people. You simply identify your specific subject area and ask the computer to show you what it has. It will search thousands of newspapers, magazines, and other publications in a few seconds. Among its databases are those compiled by Dun and Bradstreet, Harvard Business Review, UPI News, Historical Abstracts, Standard and Poor's, Moody's Investor's Service, and many others.

WILSONLINE has on-line access to *The Reader's Guide to Periodical Literature* (an important index mentioned earlier), the *Business Periodicals Index*, the *Education Index*, and many other periodical resources. More than three thousand periodicals and half a million books are covered by its databases.

Dow Jones News/Retrieval is an on-line computer service offering the latest financial information on request. Articles appearing in the Wall Street Journal, Barron's, and Dow Jones News Service go back as far as three months.

ORBIT search service is a bibliographic database focusing on scientific and technological data. You can obtain copies of full-text documents from any of the available services.

An excellent commercial source of stored data is *LEXIS/NEXIS*. This server contains government documents, periodicals, law journals, and newspapers.

Regardless of what index you use or the system you employ to access that index, you should keep three points in mind. *First*, as mentioned throughout this chapter, *seek the aid of the people in your library who operate the various computer services*. They will be glad to offer you some tips on how to use the system. It does not take a computer science major to use these systems, but you might need some instruction.

Second, remember that computers do not think for you—they are only an aid. In some instances, they are an aid that costs money to use. Therefore, you must do some creative work before you ask the machine to offer you what it has stored in its memory bank. While a printed index is created with one heading at a time, computer searches can examine many requests simultaneously. This is why you should request information carefully. If you are lackadaisical in your requests, the bibliography produced by the computer may not access the information you need. Many students have wasted time, energy, and money because they were vague in what they asked of the computer. In short, be specific and know what you are looking for before you use the computer.

Third, most computer databases have stored information only for the past 15 or 20 years. Therefore, if you are looking for information published before the 1970s, you may have to bypass the computer search.

Printed Material in the Library

Although our focus now moves to the printed material available, in most instances, as pointed out later in this chapter, these same materials can be accessed via the Internet.

Reference Books. When we think of reference books, most of us draw a mental picture of long rows of *Encyclopedia Britannica* and *Encyclopedia Americana*. In many cases, researchers start the library portion of their work by turning to **encyclopedias**. They are easy to use in that they are arranged alphabetically, and they are usually kept updated by means of annual supplements. In addition to general encyclopedias, there are a number of specialized encyclopedias. Depending on your subject, you might find some of the following works especially helpful: *Encyclopedia of Education, International Encyclopedia of the Social Sciences, Encyclopedia of Philosophy, Encyclopedia of Psychology, Asian American Encyclopedia, Encyclopedia of Religion and Ethics, Encyclopedia of Black America, Encyclopedia of Religion, Encyclopedia of American and Foreign Policy, Encyclopedia of World Art, Encyclopedia of Educational Media Communications and Technology, Latino Encyclopedia, Encyclopedia of Information Systems and Services, Encyclopedia of Associations,* and *The McGraw-Hill Encyclopedia of Science and Technology*.

As you might suspect, there are now entire encyclopedias available on **CD-ROM.** These interactive encyclopedias can display thousands of photos (many of which move), maps, and illustrations along with sound and text. A request for material on Mozart offers the user pictures of the composer, numerous selections of music, and written information about the composer. These new disks even come with a "print feature," so you can have a copy of any information you might find useful. The three most popular CD-ROM interactive encyclopedias are *New Grollier Encyclopedia, Compton's Multimedia Encyclopedia,* and *Microsoft Encarta.*

Beyond encyclopedias, there are many other useful references. *The World Almanac, The Statesman's Year Book, The New York Public Library Desk Reference, Information Please Almanac, Guinness Book of Records, Statistical Abstract of the United States, Facts on File,* and *Commerce Reports* all furnish facts and figures that speakers may find useful.

For information about people, it is always advisable to consult **biographical guides.** A few of the more useful guides are *Current Biography, Who's Who in America, International Who's Who, Webster's Biographical Dictionary, Who's Who,* and *Who's Who of American Women*. Some guides are more oriented toward prominent persons of the past, such as *Dictionary of American Biography,* which profiles persons from American history, and its British counterpart, *Dictionary of National Biography.* Still another work, *Chamber's Biographical Dictionary,* contains more than fifteen thousand biographies, dating from ancient history to the present.

Literary References, Anecdotes, Humor, and famous **quotations** can be found in books such as *International Thesaurus of Quotations; Macmillan Book of Proverbs, Maxims and Famous Sayings; Sourcebook for Speakers; Famous Last Words; A Treasury of Jewish Quotations; Bartlett's Familiar Quotations; Oxford Dictionary of Quotations; The Home Book of Quotations*; and *The Little, Brown Book of Anecdotes*. For information about poets, playwrights, novelists, and major characters in literature, you can consult Benet's *Reader's Encyclopedia*.

The list of reference works in this section is but a glimpse of the sources available. There are guides to reference books that can put you in touch with other possibilities. For example, *Guide to Reference Books* lists works in medicine, technology, and science; history and area studies; social and behavioral sciences; humanities; and general reference works. *American Reference Books Annual* has an updated list of works in many disciplines.

Finally, *Books in Print* contains a list of books currently in print or scheduled for publication by January 31 of the following year. As you would suspect, *Books in Print* can also be accessed through a computer.

Magazines, Journals and Pamphlets. There are hundreds of international and national **magazines** available to assist you in your research efforts. Many of them can be accessed via your computer. It would be impossible to list all of them. However, several publications contain articles on a wide range of subjects. *Time, Newsweek, U.S. News & World Report, Business Week, Fortune, New Republic, Forbes, Reporter, Nation, Atlantic Monthly, Harper's Magazine, Current History, National Geographic, Foreign Affairs, Yale Review, Saturday Evening Post, Vital Speeches of the Day, Aviation Week and Space Technology, Kiplinger's Personal Finance Magazine, Congressional Digest, Consumer Reports, Ebony, Harvard Business Review, New Yorker*, and *Smithsonian*.

In addition to the countless magazines written for the general public, there are thousands of very **specialized journals and trade magazines** written for specific audiences. Whether the topic is advertising, broadcasting, health, recreation, public relations, world affairs, religion, law, psychology, education, political science, sociology, communication, or engineering, there are academic and trade publications available. Most of these materials are indexed. If you cannot locate a specific journal or trade publication, ask any library assistant to help you locate it.

Most libraries have the *Magazine Index* and its monthly supplements, which lists over four hundred magazines you can use to locate material to augment the information you gather from your other sources.

Most libraries also have a large collection of **pamphlets**, which are hard to catalog and index because of their size and subject. These pamphlets, which are printed and circulated by various groups and organizations such as the American Medical Association and automobile clubs, cover a wide range of topics. Normally, this material can be secured from the library's vertical file or by asking the librarian for the location of the college's pamphlet collection. The Vertical File Service Catalog also lists pamphlets published and distributed by various organizations and agencies.

Atlases and Gazetteers. Intercultural interaction is a fact of life. With so many political and social changes taking place throughout the world, we are seeing alterations in geographic boundaries and the renaming of many countries and regions. Part of a good research program is to be aware of these changes, for what happens in one part of the world affects the entire planet. This intercultural interdependence demands not only that we know about other cultures but that we are knowledgeable about the location of those cultures. Atlases and gazetteers help us obtain that knowledge.

Atlases, of course, are books that contain maps; however, they also contain much more. Most have charts, tables, plates, and even statistical information about the regions, countries, and states. The most widely used atlases of the world are *Rand McNally Cosmopolitan World Atlas*, *Times Atlas of the World*, and *National Geographic Atlas of the World*. Useful atlases of North America are the *Rand McNally Atlas of the United States* and the *National Geographic Atlas of North America*.

Gazetteers are a type of geographical dictionary. They are arranged by alphabetical headings and can help you with spelling and pronunciation. They also contain a great deal of information related to population, natural resources, elevations, manufacturing, weather, and the like. The most widely used gazetteers are *Webster's New Geographical Dictionary* and the *Longman Dictionary of Geography*.

Newspapers. Information on almost any topic can be secured from newspapers. While books normally take years to be written and published, newspapers are an excellent source of current happenings and information. Most influential newspapers can either be read via the Internet or located in the library. Several major U.S. newspapers are now indexed, making it much easier to locate specific information. Some of the leading newspapers that are indexed are the *New York Times, Wall Street Journal, Christian Science Monitor, Los Angeles Times, Chicago Tribune, Washington Post (D.C.), New Orleans Times-Picayune*, and *Atlanta Journal/Atlanta Constitution*. Two highly regarded foreign newspapers are the *London Times* and the *Manchester Guardian*. When you are investigating a regional issue, you will find it helpful to consult local newspapers.

Because of the large ethnic population in the United States, most libraries carry a number of newspapers from other countries and cultures. Many of these newspapers are printed in English. I urge you to peruse international and ethnic newspapers if you are planning a speech involving topics or people from other cultures.

Government Publications. Students are often surprised to learn that various local, state, and federal agencies produce thousands of reports, books, and pamphlets each year and that these materials are housed in libraries. Any librarian can show you where these sources are kept and how they are indexed. The most workable indexes for federal publications are the *Congressional Record* (the daily accounts of the workings of Congress), *Monthly Catalog of U.S. Government Publications* (the main listing of federal government reports), *American Statistical Index* (government statistical reports), and *National Journal* (a weekly index concerning executive, Congressional, and judicial decisions). Various government agencies such as the departments of Commerce, Health and Human Services, Transportation, Housing, and Labor also produce countless reports.

Subject Abstracts. As you explore the sources available to a researcher, you will undoubtedly come in contact with subject abstracts. These abstracts offer concise summaries of articles, books, and other publications that can be consulted. If you read the abstract, you can then decide whether or not the entire work justifies further consideration.

While there are many such abstracts, the following are a few you might find helpful: *Communication Abstracts* (advertising, broadcasting, interpersonal communication, journalism, public relations); *Criminology and Penology Abstracts* (criminal behavior, delinquency, treatment of offenders, criminal procedures); *Environmental Abstracts* (air pollution, ecology, wildlife); *Psychological Abstracts* (all areas of psychology); and *Sociological Abstracts* (social control, group behavior, mass phenomena). Again, I urge you to consult a librarian as to the location and availability of these and other subject abstracts in your library.

Indexes. Any person who has ever conducted library research knows how fortunate we are to have indexes. They save us countless hours of tedious drudgery by cataloging and listing materials on nearly every subject imaginable. Some examples are the *Biological and Agricultural Index, International Index, Applied Science and Technology Index, Art Index, Biography Index, Education Index, Criminal Justice Periodical Index, General Science Index, Psychological Index, Psychological Abstracts, Business Periodicals Index, Index of Legal Periodicals, American Statistical Index, Statistical Reference Index, Business Periodicals Index, Humanities Index, Public Affairs Information Index*, and *Social Sciences Index*.

Microfilms, Microfiche, and Ultramicrofiche. In the interest of saving space and facilitating speedy access to printed materials, libraries have turned to the use of film in several forms, collectively known as microfilms. Virtually all the kinds of printed material we have been discussing for the past few pages can be found on microfilm, microfiche, or ultramicrofiche. Microfilms are reels of film on which printed matter is photographed in greatly reduced size. Newspapers are often put onto microfilm. A microfiche is a microfilm sheet about the size of an index card that contains rows of printed or written pages. Ultramicrofiche, although less than half as large as a microfiche, contains many more pages of materials. All these microfilms use projection devices for the readout. Assistance in the operation of any of these devices is available from members of the library staff.

Using the Internet

Most students of college age grew up playing computer games, "surfing the net," and using computers in a variety of ways. Therefore, most know the essentials of using a personal computer. What we will now suggest is that the combination of a phone and a computer can also be a worthwhile research tool. That tool is called the **Internet.** Although the Internet consists of many components (E-mail, etc.), we are most concerned with the **World Wide Web.** It is this aspect of the Internet that allows users to access information, graphics, and audio from the Internet. To help you appreciate the Web as a tool for conducting research, we attempt to answer the following four questions: (1) What is the World Wide Web? (2) How do you use the Web to find general information? (3) How do you narrow your Web search? and (4) What precautions should you take when using the Web?

What Is the World Wide Web? In simple terms it might be best to think of the Web as one part of the Internet. It is a global collection of computer networks that allows you the freedom to access millions of pieces of information. That information is "housed" in computers all over the world. You can gain access to that information in one of three ways: direct linkage to your college,

The World Wide Web allows users to access information, graphics, and audio material to use in speeches. (Photo: Gloria Thomas)

university, or telephone; access via a phone modem to the university network; or telephone or cable access via a modem to a local or national commercial "provider." For anyone using the Web for research, resources for information can include such things as on-line journals, magazines, and newspapers; professional and governmental archives and databases; access to academic and public libraries; access to commercial databases and abstract services; and an endless supply of commercial and private websites.

How Do You Use the Web to Find General Information? The easiest, and in some ways the most efficient, way to use the Web as a research tool is through one of the many *search engines* that are now available. These search engines have simply done a great deal of organizing for you. That is, instead of your aimlessly wandering from topic to topic, the search engine attempts to catalogue thousands of subjects into various categories. Think of this catalogue as an enormous table of contents. All you need to do is "ask" your computer to locate one of the commercial search engines (listed below) and then type in the subject you are interested in. Or you can "click" on a subject if there is one you find interesting. On your screen you will then see numerous locations to go to for information.

Here are some of the popular search engines:

Yahoo!	Alta Vista	Magellan
Excite	Infoseek	My Virtual Reference Desk
Lycos	HotBot	Beaucoup
Looksmart	AOL Net Find	Netscape Search

In addition to the general search engines listed above, there are some other *general sites* that often contain information helpful in researching a speech.

Here are some of these sites:

Britannica Internet Guide	New Century Net Work
CNN	Time
ABC News	U.S. News and World Report
New York Times	Mercury Center
USA Today	CNBC
Library of Congress	Virtual Reference Desk at Purdue University

How Do You Narrow Your Web Search? Because search engines cannot provide a complete and comprehensive catalogue of everything that is on the Web, you will find it very useful to search material by employing what is called *key-word* or *phrase searches*. Key-word or phrase searches are particularly useful as a starting point for conducting your research on the Web. All the Web sites mentioned earlier have a blank "window" on the screen that is located at the top of the site. This window allows you to type in any word or phrase you want. For example, if you were doing research for a speech dealing with weather problems associated with *hurricanes*, you would simply type the word *hurricane* into the blank window and then hit the "enter" key on your keyboard. You would then be given a list of all the specific sites dealing with hurricanes. You can then view all the sites you deem appropriate to your topic.

Because of the popularity of the Web, in recent years it has become "cluttered" with information that is often only tangentially related to the subject in question. Therefore, you need to learn how to narrow your "request" from a specific site. Following are a few guidelines when searching the Web by using a key word or phrase:

1. Because not all search programs use the same databases, you should use more than one search engine when employing key words or phrases to locate material.

2. The six best search programs for conducting key-word searches are *Alta Vista, Excite, Magellan, Yahoo!, Lycos,* and *Dejanews Research Served.*

3. Be as specific as you can when typing in a word or phrase. If you are interested in material on hurricanes, do not type in the word "weather." That would most likely produce a yield of 20,000 sites.

4. To narrow your search it is often a good idea to type in your topic with quotation marks. For example, if you type "Hurricane Irene" with quotation marks, it makes a phrase out of the words instead having the engine search for each individual word.

5. Most searches yield better results if you use lower-case letters instead of capitals.

6. If you have a phrase with more than one word, and you want to make sure that all sites include that word, place a plus sign (+) before the word. If, for example, you were researching hate crimes against Jews and did not want all hate crimes, you would type "hate crimes + Jews".

7. If the topic is too broad and you want to exclude some references from your search, add a minus sign (–) before the word you wanted excluded. For example, if you wanted sites that could yield information about hate crimes but you did not want material on hate crimes against gays, you would type "hate crimes – gays".

While most search engines use the same coding system and follow the same procedures, there are slight variations. I therefore urge you to practice with a variety of engines before you start your actual search.

   What Precautions Need to Be Taken When Using the Web? Many people hold the opinion that if something is on the Web, it must be both truthful and reliable. This notion is simply false. We have already alluded to the fact that the Web is full of a great deal of superfluous and inaccurate information. Remember, the Web cannot decide, if you ask "it" a question, the difference between the *National Observer* and the *New York Times*. Hence, anyone using the Web as an aid for conducting research needs to be careful when deciding what is valid and what is fallacious. I urge you to quickly review chapter 6 and note the observations there regarding the tests you should apply to the use of evidence. In addition to that advice, a word or two regarding the use of *primary* and *secondary* research data is in order.

   Primary data is usually considered to be material directly from the original source. Such data can include original manuscripts, laws, direct quotations from individuals, and results of scientific studies and surveys. If you were investigating violence in children's television programs, and wanted the results of important studies on the subject, you would go directly to those studies if you were consulting primary sources. Simply reading about what someone had to say about the studies would mean you were using **secondary** research. Secondary data is not only "second hand," but it is often characterized by an interpretative dimension. That is, someone might be commenting on violence on television and mention a few studies. As someone using the Web, you need to make sure you do not confuse someone's evaluation of a Federal Communications Commission ruling (secondary source) with the actual ruling (primary source).

Recording Your Material

Over two thousand years ago the Greek philosopher Sophocles noted that "It is terrible to speak well and be wrong." It would also be terrible to have conducted a great deal of research and be unable to use it because you had not kept track of your research. Many beginning speakers find that it is difficult to keep records of everything that they have read and heard. You should not attempt to keep facts, figures, and quotations in your head. Unless you have a phenomenal memory, you will need to record your information for further use.

Ensuring that the information is usable should be one of your primary concerns when recording your data. Hence, you should try to develop a research and recording style with which you feel comfortable. Following are some guidelines for selecting a methodology for recording and using your research.

Photocopying Material

There are two ways to photocopy the material you would like to consider using—you can use a photocopy machine or print directly from your computer. Since most libraries have photocopy equipment, the recording process often begins with your making copies of the material you deem most useful. You can make copies of selected portions from books, newspapers, magazines, or periodicals.

If you are using a computer that is attached to a printer, you simply have to press the "PRINT" button or move the mouse to the appropriate spot. With today's technology you can even print directly from most websites.

Being Accurate

Whether you copy, print, record your material on index cards, or create files in your computer, there are some guidelines that will aid you in making the most efficient use of your research:

1. Take complete and accurate notes on what you read. It is important, for ethical as well as practical reasons, that you keep a record of exactly where your material comes from. For example, if your material is from a magazine, you should write down the name of the author, title of the article, name of the magazine, volume, date, and page, and you should cite this material in your speech, outline, and bibliography. Use quotation marks when quoting directly, and avoid plagiarism at all times.

2. There will be some occasions when your note-taking is in the form of a paraphrase. In these instances, you will be putting the author's main idea into your own words, so you can summarize and clarify someone else's findings and conclusions. You might develop the practice of putting your paraphrases in brackets ([ ]) as a way of differentiating them from direct quotations (shown in your notes with quotation marks).

3. When copying notes from your resource material (books, journals), you should use a separate card or notation on your computer for each entry. Your material will be much easier to review and organize if each fact is by itself. This will let you sort your material under the appropriate heading until you are ready to use it.

4. Your research cards or computer notations should include not only the correct citations and quoted material but also your personal evaluations of the material. Notes to yourself will come in handy as you begin to piece the speech into the organizational scheme you eventually select. In short, each card should include

(a) the complete citation, (b) the quoted material, and (c) your personal comments. Following is a typical card or computer evaluation.

❖ ❖ ❖ ❖

> Crewdson, John. "AIDS: A Million Cases Feared by End of Century." San Diego Union-Tribune, 14 June 1998, sec.C, p. 5, col. 2-5.
>
> "Earlier this year, when more than 50 prominent American scientists were ask by a pharmaceutical company to chart the future of the AIDS epidemic, they predicted that by the turn of the century more than one million Americans will have fallen ill from the disease."
>
> GOOD GENERAL QUOTATION SHOWING THE SCOPE OF THE PROBLEM.

Citing Traditional Sources

Although there are numerous methods for citing research data, two of the most popular bibliographic formats are those of the Modern Language Association (MLA) and the American Psychological Association (APA). What follows are some examples on how to use these two classification systems.

Using MLA

Book with one author: Brownell, Judi. *Listening: Attitudes, Principles, and Skills.* Boston, MA.: Allyn and Bacon, 1996.

Book with two authors: Andereck, Paul A., and Richard A. Pence. *Computer Genealogy: A Guide to Research Through High Technology.* New York: Ancestry, 1985.

Article from a journal: Zimmerman, Stephanie. "Perceptions of Intercultural Communication Competence and International Student Adaptation to an American Campus." *Communication Education* 44 (1959):321-335.

Article from a monthly magazine: Rodriguez, Richard. "Late Victorians: San Francisco, AIDS, and the Homosexual Stereotype." *Harper's* 281 (October 1995): 57.

Article from a weekly magazine: Adler, Constance. "Foul Ball." *TV Time* I (13 October 1990): 20.

Article from a daily newspaper: Stein, Mark. "Quake Solemnly Remembered in Bay Area." *Los Angeles Times.* 18 October 1990. Sec. 1, P. 1, Col. 4.

Television program: *The Civil War.* Writers, Geoffrey C. Ward, Ric Burns, and Ken Burns. Producers, Ken Burns and Ric Burns. PBS Miniseries Event, September 23, 24, 25, 26, 27, 1990.

Personal and telephone interviews: Day, Thomas. Telephone interview. 3:30 P.M., 7 May 1995. Sagan, Carl. Personal interview. 5:00 P.M., 10 October 1992.

Compact disc: Trzetrzelewska, Basia. *Time and Tide.* Epic, EK40767, 1994.

Anonymous article: "The Dawn of the Laptop Computer." *Consumer Reports.* 55, No. 6 (June 1990): 377.

Encyclopedia: "Reconstruction." *The New Columbia Encyclopedia.* 4th ed. 1975, pp. 2286-7.

❖ ❖ ❖ ❖   *Using APA*

Books with one author: Bernstein, T. M. (1965). *The careful writer: A modern guide to English usage.* New York: Atheneum.

Chapter in a book: Zarefsky, D. (1992). The great society as a rhetorical proposition. In T. Windt & B. Ingold (Eds.). *Essays in presidential rhetoric* (3rd ed., pp. 129–147). Dubuque, IA: Kendall/Hunt.

Journal article: Gregg, R. B. (1994). Rhetorical strategies for a culture war: Abortion in the 1992 campaign. *Communication Quarterly*, 42, 229–243.

Edited book: Sommerville, J., & Santoni, R. E., (Eds.). (1963). *Social and political philosophy.* Garden, NY: Anchor Books.

Convention paper: Hellweg, S. A., & Steven, M. D. (1990, November). *Argumentation strategies in the vice-presidential debates: 1976, 1984, and 1988.*

Magazine article: Fineman, H. (1995, January 6). Citizen Bill. *Newsweek*, 125, 17–18.

Newspaper article: Stern, M. (1995, January 28). White house inflated data on migrants. *San Diego Union-Tribune*, p. A14.

Interview: Smith, C. (1998, February 13). Telephone interview.

Citing Internet Sources

Because the Internet is relatively new, deciding how to cite sources is still somewhat problematic. Therefore, instead of offering you examples for each type of Internet reference, we shall simply recommend some Web sites that explain how to correctly document material from the Web.

MLA Style for Internet Sources:
http://www.lib.berkeley.edu/TeachingLib/Guides/Internet/MLAStyle-Sheet.html

APA Style for Internet Sources:
http://fur.rscc.cctn.us/OWL/UsingSources_APA.html

Ethical Considerations in Conducting Research

Now that we have considered some of the skills necessary for productive research, we need to pause and return to one of the major themes of this book—the ethical responsibilities associated with human communication. Nowhere is this topic more relevant than when you are conducting research. As you have seen, doing research demands a delicate balance between your own creativity and the work of others. In this final section, we offer some advice as to how you can achieve that balance.

Evaluating Your Sources

Begin by asking yourself if you have conducted a meticulous and careful search of all the available materials. Too often speakers consult only materials that are easy to locate or that buttress their own thesis. The weakness of this position is that they may not be obtaining an accurate representation of the question they are investigating. For example, to research and use material on the topic of abortion only from the National Organization for Women might greatly limit your findings on this topic. To be ethical, you should try to control bias and be eclectic in your search for material.

There are, of course, some other questions you must ask yourself regarding your research findings: Is the source current? Is the source credible? Do other sources agree with findings of the source I plan to use?

Using of Copyrighted Material

With the advent of copy machines and computer printers, it has become relatively easy to make copies of someone else's material. There are, however, certain ethical and legal issues involved when we reproduce material from another source. Let us briefly look at some of those issues.

Current law, both domestic and international, maintains that all printed and audiovisual matter, including computer software, is automatically copyrighted and owned by the creator of the material—even if no copyright notices are attached. Copyright implies that permission or a royalty fee would be necessary before the material in question could be reproduced. Although these rules are often enforced, there are some major exceptions that allow you to use a great deal of material that has been generated by other sources. Let us mention three of the most common exceptions.

First, there is the waiver inherent in *public domain laws*. This simply means that all published or created material that is over 75 years old is no longer subject to copyright laws. Hence, you could reproduce a picture of an early attempt at flying from a 1905 magazine without having to worry about copyright infractions. Second, there are some materials that are considered *royalty-free*. For example, publications generated by the federal (not state and local) government can be used without permission. This means that if you were gathering material on food supplements, you could consult and use material from pamphlets and booklets produced by various Federal departments and agencies.

Third, because of something referred to as the *fair use doctrine*, scholars and researchers have been able to use information if they follow certain guidelines. While the actual doctrine is somewhat complex, the message for the researcher who is trying to comply to the fair use doctrine is contained in the following advice:

1. Use only limited portions of the copyrighted material.

2. Do not cause economic harm to the copyright holder.

3. Use the material for educational and not commercial purposes.

Avoiding Plagiarism

As noted in chapter 1, you must always avoid plagiarism in both written and oral presentations. As you know, plagiarism occurs when a writer or speaker offers the words of someone else as if they were her or his own. This practice is a form of intellectual thievery, for you are stealing from someone else. To be ethical and to avoid ever giving the slightest appearance of plagiarism, follow these guidelines when finding and using research material:

1. Never use another person's exact words without giving proper acknowledgment. In written form, this means showing the entire source. When delivering the talk, you cite the complete reference.

2. When conducting your research, take careful notes so that you can always identify which comments and findings are yours and which belong to someone else.

3. If you are going to paraphrase, either in your outline or your talk, you should nevertheless follow the rules of honesty and tell your audience that the remarks are not yours.

4. If you have any doubts about whether you should assign credit to someone else, do so! The key is always to be truthful. The Swiss philosopher Henri Frédéric Amiel said it with shining prose when he wrote, "Let us be true: this is the highest maxim of art and of life, the secret of eloquence and of virtue."

Summary

In this chapter, our main concern was with ways of locating the material you will need in order to accomplish your purpose. You should begin by developing a research agenda. This means starting early, deciding on a specific topic, consulting a variety of sources, keeping accurate records, and systematically organizing your material. Once you have decided what you know and do not know about the subject in question, you can find what you need via electronic media; you can write and telephone for information or fax material; conduct interviews; use visual electronic media, electronic databases, reference books, magazines and pamphlets, academic journals, newspapers, subject abstracts, and subject indexes. You can also use the Internet to find material.

We also discussed how to record your material so that you can use it when your research is completed. We examined the importance of using notes, of being accurate when reproducing material, of being complete with regard to content and source citation, and of jotting down some personal evaluations on your card. We concluded by asking you to always be ethical in carrying out all of your research projects.

Concepts and Questions

1. What are the steps in establishing an effective research agenda?

2. Why is the interview a good source of information?

3. What are some printed sources of information that can be useful in preparing a speech?

4. List three sources of electronic databases that might be useful in conducting research.

5. What are the advantages and disadvantages to using the Internet as a
    research tool?

6. Why is it a good idea to include your own experiences as a starting point
    in conducting research?

7. What are some ethical considerations that should be followed when con-
    ducting research?

Activities and Exercises

1. Plan a trip to the campus library. During the course of your visit make
    note of the various locations for all the research sources discussed in this
    chapter.

2. Prepare a short speech that reflects your views on the role of ethics in
    gathering and presenting information to an audience.

3. Go to the World Wide Web and try to locate information on any two of the
    following topics:

    a. Problems associated with an increasing world population.

    b. Teenage smoking.

    c. Ethics in government.

    d. Dog training.

    e. Financial investments.

4. Go to reference books that contain proverbs or quotations and locate
    material on the following topics:

    a. Children.

    b. Family.

    c. Freedom.

    d. Fate.

    e. Hard work. ✦

CHAPTER NINE

Critical Thinking: The Appraisal of Your Ideas

Common sense is not so common.

—*Voltaire*

French philosopher Rémy de Gourmont may have been correct when he noted that "thinking is hard work." Because thinking is as natural a process as breathing, we assume that it is a simple activity. It is not! At least critical thinking is not. It is the purpose of this chapter to help you become a more critical thinker so that you can accomplish your communication goals as both a speaker and a listener.

It is only fitting that we pause at this juncture in the book to examine the topic of critical thinking, for the manner in which you approach data from the outside world touches every aspect of speechmaking. The material you select for your speech will be influenced by your ability to make sound judgments. In addition, the way you use that material is affected by critical thinking. Even how you listen to the words of others is partially controlled by the important skill of analytical and judicious thinking. As noted in chapter 1, in a democracy this skill is essential if we are to be free from the manipulations of those who wish to control us.

In chapter 6 we talked about the need to use evidence to strengthen your ideas, and in chapter 8, the places to locate that evidence. Thus far, however, we have not discussed in detail the various ways you can think about your ideas and evidence. That is to say, although systematic research can help you locate speech materials, you need to analyze those materials before using them in your speech. As you appraise the materials you have gathered through reading, listening, and observing, you need to make a conscious effort to think critically—to distinguish fact from opinion, knowledge from belief, sound reasoning from fallacious reasoning. Critical thinking enables you to avoid errors in reasoning as you collect the material for your talk. It also contributes to the accuracy with which that material is presented. Critical thinking, as noted in the chapter on listening (chapter 5), even affects the manner in which you receive messages. *The very word "critical" implies learning how to discriminate between reasoning that is reliable and reasoning that is marked by omission and inaccuracies.* People with these analytical skills can isolate weak and harmful assumptions and dismantle them.

Before talking about ways to evaluate a piece of material, you should ask yourself if you have any tendencies of thought that might impair your ability to judge that material fairly. All of us are subject to lapses of good judgment from time to time. We fall into habits of thinking that make objectivity hard to attain. Therefore, in the early part of this chapter, we will look at some of the habits people develop that can become barriers to critical thinking.

The second part of the chapter deals with flaws that may appear in the materials gathered through research. Patent attempts to mislead as well as innocent blunders will be examined as we investigate a variety of fallacies. In particular, we will look at fallacies that stem from (1) the misleading use of words, (2) the use of materials that are not truly relevant, and (3) violations of logical consistency.

Personal Barriers to Critical Thinking

Chapter 5 included a discussion of some of the personal factors that reduce our efficiency as listeners. Such barriers as constant self-focus, defensiveness, and avoidance of difficult and uninteresting material were mentioned. There are, however, other personal barriers that often impede critical thinking. Some of these barriers are discussed in what follows, so you can learn to hold them in check as you gather material, present that material, or listen to the remarks of other speakers.

Frozen Evaluations

Over two thousand years ago, Greek philosopher Heraclitus observed that "nothing is permanent but change"; however, when it comes to our personal beliefs, change is difficult. Once we have made up our minds about something, it is annoying to have to reconsider our decision. It is more comfortable to hold fast to our original conclusion. Because of this universal tendency, we are apt to harbor frozen evaluations about everything from events to people to ideas. For example, once a person has labeled another a "feminist," "born-again Christian," "liberal," or "conservative," with all the associations those labels bring to mind, the person tends to freeze and solidify this view of the other, rejecting any data suggesting he or she is more than those labels. Maybe you can recall some of the foods you tried once as child and found you disliked. You then refused to eat those foods until adulthood, when you finally gave in and tried them again, and much to your surprise, you liked them. This simple example about foods can be applied to other things, including ideas and people. You need to learn to suspend such frozen evaluations and look for evidence of change. If, after you have reconsidered the material in question, you still adhere to your original belief, at least you know that you have been open-minded and fair. You might also find that you have learned something new, even if you do not agree with it. There is a famous saying that creates the same idea in slightly different words: "Minds are like parachutes. They only function when they remain open."

Self-Interest

It is not surprising that most people are concerned with those things in life that affect them on a personal level. The degree to which we are personally involved in something even affects our perception of it. The problem is that self-interest often causes us to refuse to look for evidence that we do not want to face. Ostrichlike, we ignore the facts. We build false expectations on wishful thinking. On other occasions, we are even unwilling to identify our self-interests. For example, coastal residents who have homes along the beach are apt to be more concerned with proposals for offshore oil drilling than are inland residents, yet because of self-interest, they do not listen to all sides of the issue. If a piece of legislation means money in our pockets, we tend to view it with favor; if it means money out of our pockets, we tend to dislike it. Self-interest, then, is a powerful determinant of the way we look, or fail to look, at things. To achieve a greater degree of objectivity in making judgments, we need to be aware of the role that our self-interest is playing and then make allowances. For example, when you encounter a magazine article telling you that you will suffer financially if a certain measure is passed by the legislature, you need to ask yourself, Am I opposed to this measure because it lacks all merit, or am I just concerned about holding onto my money?

Ego-Defense

Although the source of the following commentary is anonymous, the observation is one worth considering:

> It is a curious fact that of all the illusions that beset us, none is quite so curious as that tendency to suppose that we are mentally and morally superior to those who differ from us in opinion.

It is only human nature to want to protect both our physical and emotional well-being, and one way we do this is by rejecting the ideas of other people. Much like the barrier of frozen evaluations, in ego-defense we reject another person or even a piece of valid evidence if we feel that our personal beliefs are under attack. We usually engage in a series of mental activities that keep us from systematically evaluating the concept under investigation. We often resort to excuses and self-delusion in order to preserve our self-esteem. This face-saving behavior can lead us to ignore evidence that runs counter to our beliefs, no matter how substantial that evidence might be. It can cause us to shift the blame for our conduct onto others. It can cause us to invent rational explanations for irrational actions. Of all of our bad habits of thinking, the practice of ego-defense poses one of the greatest barriers to objectivity. It is not by chance that almost one hundred years ago philosopher Gilbert Chesterton wrote, "One may understand the cosmos, but never the ego; the self is more distant than any star."

Ethnocentrism

As just indicated, it is difficult to avoid judging others and their ideas without thrusting ourselves into the equation. It is particularly hard to be open and tolerant of the customs, beliefs, and values of other groups and cultures when they run counter to those of one's native culture. All of us are molded and shaped by the experiences of our culture and automatically develop the habit of evaluating all other cultures by these experiences. We talked about this concept in chapter 1 and noted that it was so common that anthropologists have given it a name: **ethnocentrism.** In effect, when practicing ethnocentrism, what we are doing is placing our own culture in the central position of priority and worth. Ethnocentrism can induce an attitude that says, either consciously or unconsciously, "our way is not only the right way, it is the only way." If our culture calls for dating rituals to include flowers or tickets to a rock concert and somewhere else in the world the suitor offers a handful of raw fish, is one right and one wrong? Christians and Muslims speak to a single God, the Hindu speaks to many gods, and the Buddhist has no god; is one right and one wrong? Of course not, they are only different

Knowledge does not know color, gender, nationality, or boundaries.

views of the world that have developed over a long period of time and for specific cultural reasons.

The danger of ethnocentrism is that it produces a type of perceptual blindness that greatly limits what a person takes in and uses. It limits true knowledge. I am not advocating that you arrive for your next date with a handful of fish but rather that you develop the view that Euro-American principles are not the only principles, even though many great ideas are founded on them. This new receptiveness will let you seek out the writings, philosophies, and world views stressed in other cultures. It is a provincial and naive belief that the Western world is the exclusive creator of wisdom and information. People need to broaden their perceptions and not limit their thinking to one point of view. Knowledge does not know color, gender, nationality, or boundaries. Hence, be alert to the dangers of narrowness and dogmatism in your thinking. St. Thomas Aquinas said much the same thing two thousand years ago: "Beware of the man of one book."

Stereotyping

The word **stereotype** was originally a printer's term, referring to a metal printing plate made by casting metal in a mold. *The word has taken on a figurative meaning, referring to a long-standing, oversimplified, exaggerated, inflexible judgment* (one cast in a mold). A stereotype is actually two things. First, it is a special kind of frozen evaluation—a prejudgment of another's religion, race, profession, sexual preference, affiliation, or the like. Second, stereotypes are an outgrowth of selective perception in that we let ourselves see only a small slice of the world. More often than not, we acquire these prejudgments from the media, our friends, or our relatives. We accept them uncritically and make them our own. Thus, we may harbor stereotypes of college professors, Asians, hairdressers, environmentalists, used-car salespeople, the elderly, Southerners, Democrats, preachers, and rock musicians. Even if we have never met a person from Iraq, we have our ready-made judgment on hand in case we do, and that stereotype will bias the way we perceive that person. If, in our research, we find an article written by a person we have prejudged, our reading of that article is not likely to be objective.

Not all stereotypes are acquired from media, friends, and relatives. Sometimes an individual manufactures his or her own. For example, a single bad encounter with a person from another country might lead someone to an unfavorable prejudgment of the next person she or he encounters from that country. This act of attributing to all members of a group the qualities of a single member is an example of hasty generalization, one of the fallacies discussed later in this chapter.

Stereotypes contaminate our thinking in a number of ways. First, *when applied to people, ideas, or cultures, they cause us to conclude that a belief is true when, in reality, it is not.* To conclude that all Germans only care about hard work is to engage in a damaging and misleading stereotype. Germans have a long history of loving the arts, being outdoors, enjoying fine foods, and the like. To stereotype them as being obsessed with only work limits one's ability to accurately think about Germans and the ideas they produce. Second, *stereotypes hamper critical thinking because when they are repeated often enough, they are difficult to overcome.* Think for a moment about the myths associated with women, Arabs, or the elderly. From a host of sources, the stereotypes are repeated with such regularity that it takes constant vigilance if we are to confront and analyze them. Stereotyping results in our lumping each of these groups into a rigid category. It is this type of classification that limits our thinking process.

Prejudice

We need to thank the French philosopher and dramatist Voltaire for offering the perfect introduction to our final barrier to critical thinking. In 1756 he wrote, "Prejudices are what fools use for reason." His reason for writing these words is obvious—prejudices are an obstacle to obtaining the truth on any subject. **Prejudice** refers to an unfair and biased attitude toward another individual or group. Prejudice can take a variety of forms. Regardless of the form or target, all prejudice harms both the speaker and the listener. Knowing how prejudice is manifested will help your critical thinking skills by allowing you to observe the manner in which you perceive, approach, and communicate with other people. Therefore, let us look at two specific ways prejudices are reflected in human communication.

Negative Comments. People with a prejudice may talk about the object of their prejudice in **negative** and **stereotypic** terms. Someone would be engaging in this form of prejudice if he or she said, "Those Germans did it once, so we can never trust any of them again." Another example of a lack of critical thinking would be "We can move our plants and factories to Mexico. Those people work for almost nothing."

Avoidance. People also act out prejudice when they **avoid** contact with the individual or group that they dislike. You can easily see how this behavior would hamper critical thinking. How do you ever get to test your prejudice if you never interact or communicate with its object? Avoidance of such people engenders an avoidance of critical thinking.

So far, six of the major barriers to critical thinking have been discussed. As you would suspect, there are many more. However, this section has singled out some of the most destructive ones. Overcome these and your ability to think critically will be greatly enhanced.

❖ ❖ ❖ ❖

Detecting Fallacies

Now that you have attempted to identify some potential flaws in your own thinking process, you are ready to take the next step and critically examine the evidence, reasoning, and ideas you encounter in your research. Such critical thinking can also be applied to your presentations. Richard Whately, a nineteenth-century logician, classified as a **fallacy** "any unsound mode of arguing which appears to demand our conviction, and to be decisive of the question in hand, when in fairness it is not."

Logicians, social psychologists, and rhetoricians make repeated attempts to classify types of fallacies, but no one has been successful in devising a system that has won universal support. Not only is there a problem of classification and division, but there is also a question as to what to include and what to exclude. Discussions of fallacies often contain lists with as many as 50 or 60 kinds of fallacies. This chapter will not attempt to investigate all possible fallacies but will examine those that you are most likely to encounter as you assess and present your materials and ideas. For the sake of convenience, fallacies are grouped under three principal headings: language deceptions, extraneous appeals, and faulty logic.

In discussing the fallacies, the focus is twofold. First, as *a listener* an awareness of fallacies should assist you in detecting errors in thinking as you confront the ideas of others. Second, you should also find yourself scrutinizing your own *thinking* and *speaking* more carefully as you become familiar with these intentional and unintentional deceptions.

Language Deceptions

What the author T. S. Eliot called "the intolerable wrestle with words and meanings" is a problem that constantly confronts a speaker, reader, or listener. The reason that language can be so troublesome is that language has power. It shapes our perceptions and helps direct our behavior. Therefore, we need to be on guard against words, phrases, and sentences used in a way that obscures or distorts meaning, produces confusion, or misleads us in our use or appraisal of a message. The next few pages explore some of the more common fallacies of word management: semantic ambiguity, syntactical ambiguity, equivocation, innuendo, separation from context, and infusion of emphasis.

Semantic Ambiguity. Richard Sheridan, the famous Irish playwright and witty parliamentary orator, was once asked to apologize for insulting a fellow member of Parliament. "Mr. Speaker," replied Sheridan, "I said the honorable member was a liar it is true and I am sorry for it. The honorable member may place the punctuation where he pleases." Language can be ambiguous.

In everyday speech, it is not unusual for a word or phrase to suggest a variety of different meanings. The fallacy of *semantic ambiguity* occurs when the context of the statement (word or phrase) does not make clear which of several meanings of a word is intended. If the context does not help clarify the intended meaning of the term in question, it is quite possible that the listener might interpret the word in a way not intended and thus arrive at a false conclusion. Think for a moment of the built-in ambiguity if someone says, "The shooting was terrible," and you failed to know the context. Did a friend have a poor hunting trip? Did the makers of the movie have a bad production day? Were two police officers discussing a murder? Even the simple sentence, "Honey, please get my coffee" changes meaning depending on whether the words are uttered to wife, stranger, or secretary.

Examples of the fallacy of semantic ambiguity abound. If someone were to say, "He is a liberal talker," we might interpret liberal as a label for that person's political stance, or we might take it to mean that he or she is very talkative. Unless the user of the word offered a clue as to the intended interpretation, we would have to rely on mere guesswork. If we were to hear a movie critic say, "Brad Pitt's role was better than most," we would be left to speculate about whether the allusion to Brad Pitt's role referred to the character part he was asked to play or referred to his acting. Moreover, the claim that the role was better than most might be construed to mean that it was better than the majority of the parts Pitt has been given in films or that his performance excelled that of most of the other performers in the film.

Although it is probable that many semantic ambiguities are merely the result of sloppy wording, it is not unusual for advertisers, salespeople, and politicians to use them deliberately. A TV commercial that trumpets a product as "new and improved" is depending on the vagueness of the terms for its effectiveness. The advertiser has a belief that we will attach favorable associations to the terms. *New* becomes *fresh, pristine, radically different*, and *youthful*, while *improved* becomes *decidedly better, without rival*, and *flawless*.

As a speaker, it is important for you to give the listener a clear indication of which meaning is intended. As a listener, you might be able to ask the speaker for the meaning he or she had in mind. If it is not possible to make such a request, use your own knowledge of the subject and what you might know about the speaker to decide on the meaning. It is important however, that your conclusion be tentative, because you were confronted with semantic ambiguity.

Syntactical Ambiguity. *Syntactical ambiguity* involves the use of a word or phrase that is liable to more than one interpretation because of its unique placement within the structure of a sentence. The problem, then, is not one of word selection, as is the case with semantic ambiguity; it is the position that the word or phrase occupies within the grammatical structure of the sentence that is the source of confusion. The result of this confusion is that an incorrect conclusion can be drawn.

Consider, for a moment, the following statement: "The principal scolded the custodian because she was angry." Does it mean that the principal, in a fit of anger, scolded the custodian, or does it mean that the principal scolded the custodian because the custodian had exhibited anger? Just who is "she"? How would you rewrite the sentence to make it clear? What about a sentence that says, "During my four years of college I had about thirty odd professors"? Is "odd" being used to indicate an imprecise number of professors or is it a description of personality traits?

Suppose you are a prospective home buyer and you encounter an advertisement in the realty section of the newspaper: "Large home and ten acres needing attention." What needs attention? The large home? The ten acres? Both? For the advertisement to be clear, some restructuring of the wording is necessary.

Unlike semantic ambiguity, syntactical ambiguity is seldom intended. Writers and speakers simply become careless in the way they put sentences together. After all, the meaning is clear to them. Why should it not be clear to others?

It should be noted that the fallacy of syntactical ambiguity most frequently occurs when a writer or speaker fails to indicate the referent of words such as "his," "hers," "its," and "this" or does not make clear what a word or phrase modifies.

Syntactical ambiguity also occurs in the attempt to translate material from one language to another. Difficulties can arise for a variety of reasons. There might not be an equivalent part of speech in the language into which a message is being translated. For example, in the Urdu language (the official language of Pakistan), there are no gerunds (a verbal noun ending in "ing"), and it is difficult to find an equivalent form for an English gerund. Even the placement of nouns and verbs varies from language to language. In Japanese, for instance, the verb usually comes at the end of a sentence. It is easy to see how such variations could cause ambiguity.

Equivocation. The fallacy of **equivocation** is committed when a speaker makes a word or phrase appear to have only one meaning, when, in fact, he or she is using it in two different senses.

Let us suppose that a high-ranking public official made the following statement:

> This great nation of ours has a record of lending assistance whenever and wherever it is needed. If we are lending funds to any nation, however, we should have a reasonable expectation of being repaid.

Note the shift in meaning of the word "lending." The context in which it first appears is typical of those where lending means "giving." Thus, we "give assistance" to those in need. In the second sentence, however, the context would suggest that lending means "loaning." When we loan funds, we expect to be repaid (with interest). Perhaps the speaker wants the connotation of unselfishness that surrounds the first use of "lending" to preclude the connotation of greed that might be evoked by the second use of the word.

Those who commit the fallacy of equivocation may not be aware of their error. For example, it is conceivable that a person might be unaware that the word *rational* can mean "logical" or "sane." That person might observe:

> The psychiatrist says that rational people don't act the way Bill's been acting, but I was in a discussion with Bill just yesterday and found his arguments to be very rational. He backed up every one of his arguments with lots of good evidence.

It might well be that the person does not understand that the psychiatrist is making a judgment about Bill's sanity, not his ability to construct a logical argument. Whether the equivocation is intentional or unintentional is not particularly important. What is important is that the equivocation is detected and taken into account as part of the appraisal of the message. This fallacy is not always easy to detect, especially when the two different usages of the word or phrase are separated by several sentences, as they might be in a complex argument.

If you believe, as part of your research efforts, that the material you are reading is an equivocal message, or if you are listening to a speaker who is engaging in the fallacy of equivocation, you should try to identify the problematic word or phrase. Although precise definitions are never possible, focusing on the culprit is the first step to avoid becoming a victim of this common fallacy.

Innuendo. Equivocation and ambiguity are fallacies that stem from what is actually stated. *Innuendo*, on the other hand, is a matter of what is hinted at rather than explicitly stated. We see this fallacy when a writer or speaker, often through a skillful choice of words, brings us to the brink of a conclusion that would put someone or something in a bad light. Yet, as we indicated, the person committing this fallacy usually stops just short of asserting that conclusion. Because the fallacy of innuendo relies on suggestion instead of proof, innuendo is particularly insidious.

If someone were to state, "These street people may eventually get around to looking for a job," he or she would seem to be implying that the street people have not yet started a job search. Since no overt claim to that effect has been made, the speaker escapes the responsibility of providing any proof. In like fashion, if someone were to state, "These college kids may get around to doing something worthwhile someday," he or she would be implying that college students presently are doing nothing worthwhile. By hinting at something rather than making an outright claim, the speaker avoids having to offer proof.

As you can see, innuendo enables an unscrupulous writer or speaker to attack someone or something while maintaining an avenue of escape. If a salesperson wanted to undermine a prospective customer's favorable opinion of a competitor's product, he or she might say, "Of course, if you're satisfied with that level of quality, I can see why you might want their product." The implication is that the competitor's product is of inferior quality, even though no such claim has been made. Should the customer challenge the implied attack on the competitor's product, the salesperson could always say, "I didn't say their product was of inferior quality. I was simply noting that you are the ultimate judge of what you want." Thus, the salesperson can attack and then deny that he or she is attacking.

Although argument by innuendo can be encountered in many communication contexts, it is particularly noticeable in situations in which character attacks are a popular method of combat. In political campaigns, candidates try to undermine public trust of opponents; in courtrooms, lawyers try to shake jury confidence in the reliability of witnesses; in editorials and commentaries dealing with emotionally charged issues, exponents of competing ideologies try to impugn the motives of one another. In gathering supporting material for a speech, if you collect evidence from campaign speeches, trial transcripts, editorials, or commentaries, be especially alert to the possible presence of innuendo. If you hear innuendo in a speech, ask the speaker to spell out the evidence that led him or her to the conclusion. In no case should you blindly accept an implicit claim without being satisfied that the logic and support justify the claim.

Separation from Context. *Separation from context* takes place when we take words, phrases, sentences, or even paragraphs out of the larger work of which they are a part. When this happens, it can suggest meanings that were not intended. Thus, a person encountering something quoted out of context may make a judgment about the material that he or she would not make if seeing it in its original context. A few examples may illustrate this point.

Let us assume that you turn to the entertainment section of the newspaper in search of information about movies playing in your area. You see one advertised with the following testimonials:

'. . . something great.' *Evening Sun*

'. . . overwhelmingly beautiful.' *Morning Post*

'This film takes the prize. . . .' *Freeway Weekly*

You might conclude that the critics recommend the movie; however, the ellipses, which tell you that something has been omitted, are danger signals. Perhaps you ultimately discover that the *Evening Sun* said: "This modest little film pretends to be something great." The *Morning Post* may have stated: "Although the plot is absurd and the acting is abysmal, the scenery is overwhelmingly beautiful." The *Freeway Weekly* could have observed: "This film takes the prize for movies that will never make it to the video rental shelves."

A more serious example might be encountered on the editorial page, where a writer is giving reasons for opposing the confirmation of a presidential appointee:

> The candidate's own words convict him of partiality to the interests of the tobacco industry. How can we expect a fair ruling on legislation curtailing the sale of cigarettes in hospitals receiving federal subsidies from a man who has stated publicly, 'My right to smoke cannot be abridged at the mere whim of those who happen to prefer a smoke-free environment'?

It is possible that the candidate may have made that remark in the context of an abstract discussion of the rule of law. He might well have said,

> Our legal system ensures that our rights cannot arbitrarily be abridged, however repugnant to others the exercise of our rights might be. Until their repugnance is translated into laws that meet the tests of constitutionality, our rights remain unfettered. My right to drink myself into a drunken stupor in the privacy of my home cannot be abridged at the mere whim of a neighbor who hates to see me self-destruct. My right to smoke cannot be abridged at the mere whim of those who happen to prefer a smoke-free environment. My right to do any number of equally irrational things cannot be abridged arbitrarily. There must be a law in place that, in principle, restricts the exercise of those rights.

Viewed in context, the quoted sentence suggests quite another meaning than the one assigned by the writer who quoted it out of context. Quoting out of context is not necessarily motivated by a desire to twist the meaning to suit the speaker's argument. Our perceptions are highly selective, so it is possible that the speaker sees only what he or she wants or expects to see and may not have even read the entire paragraph. Noticing that one sentence, the speaker may have assumed that the rest of the material was in harmony with his or her preconceived notions.

Infusion of Emphasis. It was once said of a famous actor that he could read the telephone book aloud and make it sound like Shakespeare. By reading names, addresses, and numbers in a certain cadence and in a particular tone of voice, he could create the illusion of someone reading a sonnet or soliloquy. Although the illusion the actor created could hardly be classified as a fallacy, the practice of placing emphasis on another's words, phrases, or ideas that were never intended to be emphasized can constitute a fallacy if it misleads the reader or hearer. An example might be observed in a jury trial. Suppose the defendant, in replying to a question about his reason for striking the victim with a blunt instrument, replied, "I didn't mean to hurt him." The prosecutor, in his summation speech, might say to the jury,

> Let me remind you of the defendant's own words: 'I didn't mean to hurt him.'
> No, he had something much more lethal in mind. He wanted to kill him.

The defendant's emphasis on the words suggests that he had no intention of inflicting harm. The prosecutor's emphasis on the word "hurt" suggests that the defendant had a sinister motive.

Another example might be afforded by news reports of a political candidate announcing her decision to quit the race for office. In a letter to the press, the candidate states,

> Nothing is more important to me than the welfare of my family. The prospect of a long and bitter campaign and the toll it would exact upon my family has made me reconsider my priorities. Accordingly, I am removing myself from consideration for the nomination.

Let us suppose that three different newspapers print the candidate's letter, but each provides a different headline for the story. One newspaper emphasizes the coming campaign in its headline: "Candidate sees bitter campaign and quits." Another headlines the matter of priorities: "Candidate shuffles priorities and deals herself out." The third newspaper has a headline that calls attention to the candidate's devotion to her family: "Candidate chooses family over nomination." All three newspapers have, in some measure, distorted the candidate's message by emphasizing only a small portion of the ideas contained in the letter.

Constant vigilance is necessary on the part of anyone who is listening to a speech or is sorting through the evidence to be used in a speech. If you have encountered evidence through the spoken word, remember that vocal shadings can change the points of emphasis within a message. If you are looking at headlines for clues to the content of a printed message, remember that headlines are selective in their content and may not fairly represent the information to follow.

Extraneous Appeals

In addition to being sensitive to the various word deceptions just examined, a critical thinker should be on the lookout for extraneous and irrelevant appeals that may be used to cloud issues and hide inadequacies of evidence and reasoning. Such appeals can have a telling effect on an unwary researcher or listener, diverting attention from the real issues by the strong allure of emotionally charged material.

Of the fallacies involving the introduction of extraneous and irrelevant matter, perhaps the most common are character attacks, emotional appeals, and appeals to authority. Let us look at each of these fallacies so that you can be aware of their impact on the communication process.

Character Attacks. Called the *argumentum ad hominem* fallacy, this tactic involves discrediting an opponent's character instead of dealing with the relevant issues at hand. Thus, the arguments are transferred from principles to personalities in an attempt to negate the other person's testimony or evidence. Such arguments seem to suggest that truth can be forthcoming only from persons of good character; hence, one should reject anything said by a person whose character is suspect. Many *ad hominem* attacks are directly related to the writer's or speaker's prejudices. That is, the personal characteristics being questioned are often those of race, gender, age, economic class, national origin, or level of education.

You would encounter this fallacy in listening to a speaker say, "Professor Jones says cleaning up the environment should be this nation's top priority, but what does he know about cleanliness? He teaches at a school in the dirtiest part of town." An *ad hominem* fallacy was also evident when a speaker recently noted, "The city's new highway program should be vetoed. The highway commissioner is a notorious troublemaker and philanderer." In another example, a columnist, in expressing opposition to a proposed trade agreement with a foreign nation, impugned the character of that nation's representative rather than addressing the trade agreement itself:

> So we have a proposal brought to us by a man who lied to his fellow citizens about his personal wealth, who spent his official salary on caviar and cars while others starved from want of bread, who made pious declarations of his devotion to the ending of world hunger while feeding his kennel of dogs the most expensive meat to be found anywhere.

Ask yourself whether the person's alleged character flaws are germane to the issue being discussed.

Reference to another's personal circumstances or lifestyle is often made in an effort to detract from the merit of what that person is saying. For example, suppose that a millionaire member of Congress sponsors a bill to aid the homeless. An opponent of the bill might make this observation: "How can a wealthy person like my distinguished colleague here possibly understand the plight of the street people? She has never been cold or hungry." In another instance, a priest's argument for salary increases for schoolteachers may be met with the reply, "It's easy for Father Dawson to ask us to raise our own taxes. He doesn't have a houseful of kids to raise." The person's lifestyle is hardly relevant in either instance, yet every day views are questioned simply because they emanate from someone whose circumstances are unlike those of the majority of people.

When you are confronted with *ad hominem* thinking, it is often a good technique to ask the creator of the fallacy to offer you other good reasons, apart from those related to the personal attacks, for believing as he or she does. In most instances, you are apt to be confronted with even more fallacies, for people who argue *ad hominem* are usually unaware that they are using such appeals.

Emotional Appeals. Playing upon the emotions of people to color a cause and/or distract from the merits of that cause is one of the most common of all fallacies. I am not trying to suggest that there is something inherently wrong with asking people to become emotionally involved with an issue; what I am saying is that the use of emotion should not be a substitute for sound logic and appropriate evidence. When emotion is used as a substitute, it becomes an error in reasoning and thinking. Appealing to the emotions and prejudices of readers or listeners is called *argumentum ad populum*. As we just noted, instead of presenting empirical evidence and logical argument, an *ad populum* speaker or writer attempts to win support for his or her point of view by enlisting our nonrational impulses. There is no denying the fact that emotional appeals can be very persuasive. It is up to us as consumers of persuasion to be on our guard against any attempt by others to bypass the rational grounds for belief or action. Fortunately, appeals to passions and prejudices become less successful as individuals learn to recognize such appeals.

This section samples three specific forms of fallacies resulting from unwarranted appeals to emotions and prejudices. Bear in mind, however, that the possibilities for fallacious *ad populum* appeals extend far beyond the range that our samples suggest.

Fear. The English philosopher Bertrand Russell once wrote "To conquer fear is the beginning of wisdom." He was, of course, alluding to the kind of fear that is ill founded because it lacks a rational basis. It is an appeal to this kind of fear that inhibits critical thinking.

You have probably seen advertisements for home security systems that depict a shadowy, menacing figure slipping through a window that has been forced open or standing silhouetted in the doorway of a dark bedroom. These manufactured threats may have their counterparts in the real world, but the point is that the advertiser wants you to use your imagination as a substitute for tangible evidence of a threat. Unless the advertiser can couple the imagined threat with hard evidence of a real threat, the advertisement is nonrational.

Fear arising out of presumed threats to our physical safety and well-being can exert a coercive force on our judgment. Equally coercive in its effect is fear of scorn or rejection. A publisher who touts a beauty book with the slogan "Learn how to hang onto your mate" is hinting that the permanency of a relationship is threatened by ignorance of the information contained in the book, yet no evidence is produced to show the likelihood of such a consequence. To take another example, note that some fitness salons seldom sell fitness in their advertising. They sell freedom from the fear of being ostracized; nowhere do they offer any evidence that one is in danger of being ostracized.

Naturally, there are times when it is perfectly logical to experience fear. If someone offers you evidence of an imminent threat to your personal safety, you ought to feel fearful; however, you should be skeptical of appeals to fear that fail to provide evidence of the reality of a threat.

Sentimental attachment. All of us have numerous *sentimental attachments* and a strong desire to preserve these highly personal things that we cherish. Love of our family, friends, nation, and traditions are sentiments that are deeply ingrained and exercise a strong influence on the way we see the world.

Appeals to these sentiments are, in many cases, fully justified. The abuse occurs when they are used as a shortcut to persuasion. A politician urges us to support a particular policy because "I know you love this country as much as I do," yet she fails to explain why support of the policy is necessarily the best way to demonstrate that love. "Loyal opposition" might be an even better way. Witness the plea of a ruler who calls on his neighbors to join him in a "holy war," even though his private agenda is anything but holy. History affords numerous examples of the misuse of appeals to sentiment.

Prominently displayed symbols of things we cherish are often used in connection with messages. The "halo effect" of the flag displayed behind a political candidate supposedly lends credibility to his or her message. The picture of a happy family seated at the Thanksgiving table in a grocery advertisement suggests that the purchase of turkey, at this particular market, is a demonstration of love for your family.

A critical thinker must be on guard against subtle applications of the tactic. Whenever you feel yourself warming to an argument, pause for a moment and consider whether sentiment is an influential factor. If it is, then you would do well to reexamine the argument to see if there are logical elements that support the sentiment.

Vanity. The English essayist Sir Richard Steele, writing in the *Spectator* in 1711, stated, "Among all the diseases of the mind there is not one more epidemical or more pernicious than the love of flattery." We all enjoy a compliment, especially when it is well deserved, but many of us have learned, often through bitter experience, that compliments can blind us to factors that may be detrimental to our welfare.

Persuaders have long recognized the power that flattery can exert. When used with subtlety and seeming sincerity, it disarms the flattered person and predisposes him or her to be more receptive to the flatterer. Therein lies the danger. Once the critical faculty is put on hold, the flattered person becomes more susceptible to suggestion without any proof.

A common ploy used by speakers is to pay a compliment, perhaps praising the community, the auditorium, a local hero, or something that evokes civic pride. Then the speaker may compliment the audience itself for its generosity, open-mindedness, or maturity. Having done so, the speaker moves into his or her message with the presumed good will of the audience. Then comes the mischief. An assertion is made, but, instead of offering proof for the assertion, the speaker says:

> I know you folks are well read enough to be familiar with the facts, so I won't bore you with reciting them here tonight. Needless to say, they demonstrate the magnitude of the problem.

You do not need to become cynical of every compliment you receive, but remind yourself of its irrelevance to the matter you are supposed to be judging.

Appeals to Authority. The educator Robert Lindner wrote that "authority has every reason to fear the skeptic, for authority can rarely survive in the face of doubt." What is true about accepting authority applies to all cases when we embrace ideas and beliefs without questioning the person advancing the argument or appeal. It is easy to engage in blind compliance, for as children we are taught, and rightly so, to respect authority. The problem arises when we become adults and are faced with many "authorities" who do not deserve our respect. Every day we are confronted with advertisements that are misleading and politicians who withhold information or "shave the truth." History is full of striking examples of how even the most educated of listeners are remiss in their duty and obligation to question authority. From the demoniacal rhetoric of Hitler to the pronouncements of suicide cult leaders, we can see the serious dangers of not seeking and demanding the truth of authority

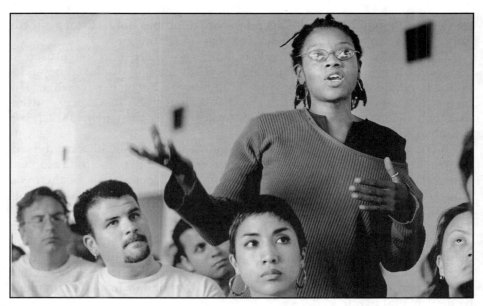

Developing a questioning mind is essential for becoming a critical thinker. (Photo: Justin Warren/Daily Bruin)

figures. If we do not develop a questioning mind, we are not being critical thinkers. Instead, we are allowing noncredible sources to control our belief systems and our actions.

The fallacy of appeals to authority is known as *argumentum ad vercundiam*. As we indicated, this fallacy often shows itself when a speaker, instead of presenting valid evidence, offers proof for a position by only making an appeal to a "name," to an institution, or to an authority. For example, a speaker would be engaging in this fallacy if he or she said, "George Washington, the father of our country, warned us against the danger of foreign alliances; therefore, I maintain that we should withdraw from the United Nations." Granted, George Washington was well qualified to offer sound advice on American policy in the context of his time, but the needs of modern foreign affairs are quite different from the needs expressed in Washington's time.

To avoid becoming a victim of this fallacy, I urge you to do three things. First, if the speaker or writer is invoking an unidentified source, you should immediately ask that the authority be identified. Second, try to determine if the authority is biased. Someone from PETA (People for the Ethical Treatment of Animals), while well meaning, may not be the best person to comment on the use of horses for rodeos. Third, and most importantly, don't be intimidated when someone with a famous name is improperly used to support an argument. An expert in one area is not automatically an expert in all other areas. William Shakespeare, Mark Twain, and Carl Sandburg are great writers, but they should not be used to support an argument for a balanced budget. Learn to approach experts with a degree of skepticism.

Faulty Logic

What the French writer Jean de la Bruyère said over two hundred years ago is still true today: "Logic is the art of making truth prevail." In the next few pages, let us look at some ways that this search for truth might be hindered.

Violations of logical consistency, whether intentional or unintentional, are to be found in the messages of saints and sinners alike. Their capacity for misleading should be a matter of great concern to anyone who wishes to make sound judgments and employ critical thinking.

Hasty Generalizations. Snap judgments, jumping to conclusions, stereotypes, and generalizations based on insufficient evidence are all examples of the *hasty generalization fallacy*. In this fallacy, a speaker draws a universal conclusion from evidence warranting only a restricted conclusion. An example of a hasty generalization is saying that marijuana has great health benefits because you know of a person who feels better since he started smoking marijuana on a regular basis. We also see the hasty generalization when we hear someone say, "Doberman pinschers are dangerous dogs. My neighbor has a Doberman pinscher and it once barked at me in a very menacing manner."

This fallacy is common in daily life. Most of us can recall instances in which tourists have experienced one or two unpleasant situations and then reached conclusions concerning the honesty and character of all the people in that particular city. Another example is a speaker who concluded that all supporters of the Libertarian party are rich. The speaker stated, "Eric Foresman supported the Libertarian party and he is a millionaire; Scott Allen supported them and he is very rich; so, you see that all supporters of the Libertarian party are rich."

One of the reasons it is so difficult to deal with hasty generalizations is that the people who present them are usually sincere in their belief, believing the conclusion reached by the generalization. In addition, most generalizations do not stem from the facts but rather from personal experience. Because these experiences are meaningful and real to the people offering the generalizations, they usually do not realize that their conclusions are mistaken. In some instances, you might simply say to the person, "That is an interesting illustration; do you know of any other cases?"

Begging the Question. The fallacy of *begging the question* can take many different forms. But what they all have in common is that the person committing this fallacy is assuming at the outset of an argument the very point that is to be established in the conclusion. Put in slightly different terms, the conclusion appears as a premise in this fallacy. In addition, begging the question is a serious fallacy because a speaker often assumes the truth or falsity of a statement without proof. If someone making a speech were to state that "the widespread cheating among our students is bad and therefore should be abolished," he or she would be begging the question. In this example, the speaker is taking for granted that cheating exists, when the statement cannot justify such a conclusion.

Begging the question normally appears in the form of "arguing in a circle." If you use one proposition to prove another proposition, you are engaging in this fallacy. Arguing in a circle usually appears in the following form: "Medical Plan X is best because the experts say so. How do we know who the experts are? They are the persons who prefer Medical Plan X." In this case, begging the question is illustrated by taking as a premise what is true only if the conclusion has been granted to be correct. In another example, a speaker also assumed the conclusion at the outset when he said, "The deterioration and corruption in government, which we all see every day, is the direct result of the fact that we have too many Democrats in the Senate."

We suggest two defenses against begging the question. First, *keep track of the logical structure of the argument.* This will help you discover if the main premise and the conclusion are exactly the same. Second, *you can directly confront the person engaging in this fallacy.* Ask her or him why the conclusion should be assumed without evidence.

Card Stacking. *Card stacking* is one of the most reprehensible of all the fallacies discussed. This fallacy usually occurs when the argument is painted as much more extreme than it really is. It depends upon exaggerations, false evidence, misstatements of facts, and often outright lies. Notice in the following few sentences how extreme positions are advanced as a means of advancing the speaker's position:

> 'Once the gun law is passed, all our guns will be taken from us by the federal government.

> 'Opposing the death penalty would allow all those killers to walk our streets.'

> 'If we listen to the animal rights people, all medical progress in the United States will be halted.'

As you can see, card stacking involves the use of exaggerations, distractions, and/or illogical statements in order to give the best or the worst possible case for an idea, a program, a person, or a product. The speaker selects only the items that support his or her position, regardless of the distortion they produce. Listing a few of the accomplishments of one's administration while leaving out all the failures is an example of this technique. This one-sided presentation often passes as the truth if the recipients of this fallacy fail to ask themselves, and eventually the speaker, if there is another side to the issue. Aesop, the Greek fabulist, reminds us that "Every truth has two sides; it is well to look at both before we commit ourselves to either."

Half-Truth. A *half-truth*, as a fallacy, is much like card stacking. In this case, a speaker tells only part of the story or offers a small portion of the facts. Notice the half-truth in the following example:

> In selecting an area hospital for our trauma center, we ought to rule out Rosewood Hospital because it has a higher death rate among patients than any other hospital in the county.

What the speaker is neglecting to mention is that Rosewood Hospital accommodates three times as many geriatric patients as any other hospital and would naturally have a higher death rate. Hence, what is happening is that the speaker is leaving out evidence and offering half-truths by only presenting us with half the facts. Learn to demand the *whole* truth. As a speaker and listener, remember the advice of the Greek philosopher and playwright Sophocles: "The truth is always the strongest argument."

Fallacy of Division. Applying to the part what may be true of the whole is known as the *fallacy of division*—for example, "His home state is called the 'Land of Lakes,' so he probably has a lake, or at least a pond, on his property." What we see in this fallacy is someone trying to tell us that what is true for one instance is true in all instances. The speaker would be committing the fallacy of division if he said, "John belongs to the fraternity that was just suspended from campus. Therefore, I would conclude that John cannot be trusted." Here is a clear example of taking a part of a larger premise and misapplying it to an individual case. Earlier, when we talked about stereotyping, we were dealing with notions that probably had their origin in fallacies of division.

Fallacy of Composition. The opposite of the fallacy of division is the *fallacy of composition*, in which properties of the part are assumed to be properties of the whole. That is, the speaker asks us to infer that what is true of some parts or members of something can also be true of the entire classification. Thus, if one house in a subdivision is contaminated by radon, a person might say, "I sure wouldn't live in that contaminated subdivision." We would also be seeing this fallacy if someone said, "Since Tom is a great football player, the team he plays for must be a great team." Again, someone is asking us to assume that a characteristic automatically passes from the parts to the whole.

Non Sequitur. In a broad sense, any argument that fails to establish its conclusion may be said to be *non sequitur* because the meaning of the phrase is simply "it does not follow." More specifically, the fallacy of *non sequitur* means that a conclusion is drawn from premises that provide no adequate logical ground for it or that have no relevant connection with it. Notice in the following two examples that the points being linked do not make much sense, yet the speaker, employing weak or counterfeit reasoning, asks us to connect them.

> 'Because Jones is a good husband and a fine father, he ought to be elected mayor.'

> 'Since only a few people are smart enough to handle complex problems, the wealth of this country should be in the hands of the very rich.'

It is obvious in both examples that a logical cause-effect relationship cannot be made. Still other statements point out how speakers reach false conclusions as they try to establish cause-effect connections.

> 'Since only men can run a mile in under four minutes, they should be the only ones flying jet airplanes.'

> 'The child is unhappy, beautiful, and a college freshman; she must therefore come from an average American family.'

One of the most common and insidious forms of this fallacy is *post hoc, ergo propter hoc*—"after this, therefore because of this." This fallacy assumes that because one occurrence precedes another in time, the one is the cause of the other. Superstitions belong here. If you walk under a ladder on your way to class, receive an A that same day, and then conclude that walking under a ladder gives a person high grades, you are guilty of *post hoc, ergo propter hoc*. A speaker noted, "Since minority groups have been given more educational opportunity, we have had an increase in the crime rate throughout the United States. I would conclude, therefore, that the growth in crime is directly related to education." Here again, it is not sufficient to say there is a connection simply because one thing followed the other. In short, because two things happen in sequence does not mean that they are logically or causally connected.

Either/or Thinking. Either/or thinking, often called *polarization*, is when we see issues only in terms of two extreme positions and therefore polarize the arguments. Polarization is a problem because the English language has many words that are extremes and therefore speakers are tempted to use these words to make their speeches startling and dramatic. Think for a moment of the countless words that represent two ends of a continuum: hot/cold, tall/short, relaxed/nervous, friendly/unfriendly, legal/illegal, good/bad, and so forth. The problem is that in reality very few issues and questions actually involve extremes. Most problems and solutions are located in the gray areas. That is to say, most of the challenges we face are not as simple as good or bad, right or wrong, yes or no. When a speaker says to you, "One has to believe that capital punishment is the only way to stop the crime on our streets," he or she is using the simplistic logic found in either/or thinking. You should learn to avoid polarization, both in perception and language. In viewing the world, speakers should realize that people are seldom one thing or another. You can also learn to describe the world with words that are less extreme if you increase your vocabulary.

Summary

In making a fair assessment of the materials discovered through research, one has to use critical thinking. In order to improve our ability to think critically, we must first take an inventory of our present way of thinking. Some of the bad habits people can acquire include not questioning authority, relying on frozen evaluations, seeing matters in terms of their own self-interest, practicing ego-defense, getting involved in ethnocentrism, and harboring stereotypes and prejudices. Once we are aware of our own thinking habits, we can make corrections where needed.

As we turn to an examination of the thinking of others, we need to be sensitive to the presence of unsound modes of arguing, called fallacies. Fallacies involving verbal flaws include semantic ambiguity, syntactical ambiguity, equivocation, innuendo, isolating words from their context, and adding undue emphasis to certain words or phrases.

Fallacies involving the use of irrelevant matters include character attacks and emotional appeals.

Fallacies of reasoning include hasty generalization, begging the question, card stacking, half-truths, fallacy of division, fallacy of composition, and either/or thinking.

Concepts and Questions

1. According to your experiences, what are the greatest obstacles to critical thinking? How can these obstacles be overcome?

2. What is the link between critical thinking and one's ethical responsibilities?

3. What is the danger to listeners if they are asked to reach decisions via extraneous appeals?

4. What are five types of faulty logic? Give an example of each.

5. What are five types of semantic deceptions? Give an example of each.

6. What is ethnocentrism? How might it show itself during a communication encounter?

Activities and Exercises

❖ ❖ ❖ ❖

1. Bring two examples of faulty reasoning to class. Explain in detail why these examples reflect weaknesses in critical thinking.

2. Select three ethnic groups. Write down all the negative stereotypes associated with these groups. In addition, write a paragraph discussing how these stereotypes could hamper intercultural communication.

3. Collect two advertisements from a newspaper or magazine. Analyze these advertisements to see if you can discover any of the errors in critical thinking and deception discussed in this chapter.

4. Give a four-minute speech in which you use three of the barriers to critical thinking discussed in this chapter.

5. Locate a letter to the editor in a newspaper that contains some of the errors in critical thinking discussed in this chapter. ✦

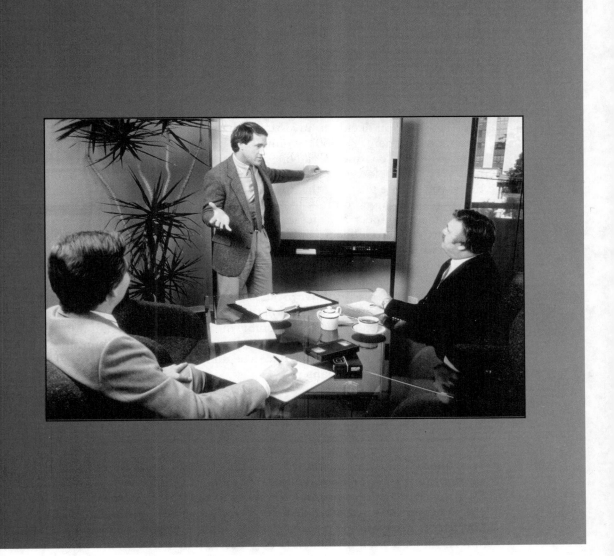

CHAPTER TEN

Organization: The Assembling of Your Ideas

Order is half of life.

—*German proverb*

Let us suppose that you have been assigned to make a 10-minute informational presentation in your speech class. You are free to choose your own topic. You know that various areas of the country are in the midst of a prolonged drought, while some regions are experiencing severe flooding. You begin to wonder if anything can be done about these disparities in nature. You ask yourself, What about water conservation, cloud seeding, dams, channels, and the like? You decide to investigate the topic of water conservation and water management. You look at numerous books and magazines and conduct a computer search for material on water conservation. After locating eight or nine very good references concerning the problem and some suggested solutions, you decide to solicit the opinion of a representative of the community water agency. Then you talk to a professional politician, a farmer, a plant manager, an engineer, a professor of geography, and several homeowners. By this time, you have collected some information about the subject—probably enough for 10 speeches. Now what? Obviously, you have to narrow the subject and decide on a specific purpose for your talk. You review your materials and decide to limit the subject to conserving water in the home. You phrase your specific purpose: "To have my listeners understand ways to reduce water usage in the home." You put aside all the materials not directly related to that purpose. You are ready at last to assemble the remaining materials into a form suitable for communication to your audience. This process of putting it all together so that your speech will have a beginning, a middle, and an end is the central concern of this chapter.

The Importance of Organization

Putting your ideas and information into a logical sequence is an essential step in successful communication. The famous Russian mystic Madam Swetchine said it far more eloquently when she wrote, "To have ideas is to gather flowers, to put them in order is to weave them into garlands." Knowing how to organize your ideas and materials can benefit you in any kind of communication encounter, whether it be a casual conversation, an interview, a group discussion, or a formal public speech. The specific advantages of being well organized are numerous. First, *the organizational process enables you to put your material together in a variety of ways to help you determine the sequence of ideas best suited to your listeners and to your purpose.* In this way, it enables you to detect the places where more evidence is needed to support a point or where logical flaws might be present.

Second, *clear organization helps both you and your audience retain ideas with greater ease during the presentation.* You benefit because, during the pres-

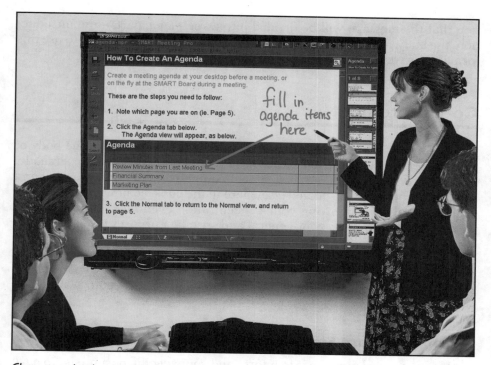

Clear organization promotes greater understanding and encourages listeners to remain attentive. (Photo: Courtesy of SMART Technologies, Inc.)

sure of delivering the speech, you do not have to search for a sequence or an order; these decisions have already been made deliberately and systematically. The audience is rewarded in that the material "makes sense." You know from your own experiences that it is easier to comprehend and retain information if its flow and arrangement is self-evident and vivid rather than murky and disjointed. Clarity of organization adds to that flow. Remember, your listeners must understand your message at first utterance, for, unlike reading, they cannot go back and reread it.

Third, *by organizing your material into a meaningful sequence you can see the relationship between the main ideas and subordinate ones.* This process of sorting everything out before the talk also enables you, very early on, to observe both gaps and redundancies in your material.

Fourth, *if what you say is well ordered, your listeners will assign it greater credibility.* They will, of course, also perceive you in a more credible light if your material is well sequenced and free from distracting verbal excursions. On many occasions, we deem a speaker to be poorly prepared if we have a difficult time following what he or she has to say; yet, if that speaker is clear, we see him or her as credible. In short, clear organization promotes greater understanding and encourages listeners to remain attentive.

Although there are a variety of approaches to speech organization, we shall concentrate on the method that involves (1) formulating a core statement that expresses the central idea of the speech, (2) phrasing main points and subpoints that support the core statement, and (3) choosing appropriate patterns to show how the main points relate to one another. We will talk about how to devise an overall speech plan and discuss the mechanics of outlining. The approach to speech organization presented here is based on the assump-

❖ ❖ ❖ ❖ tion that the message will be divided into three major parts—the introduction, the body, and the conclusion. Although not all messages need to use this format, it is workable in the majority of cases.

Core Statement

As you begin to put together the materials that will go into the body of your speech, you will find it useful to have your general purpose (to persuade, inform, or entertain) and a specific focal point always in mind. General and specific purposes are discussed elsewhere in the book, so now let us examine some methods of narrowing your concentration even more precisely. One way to further compress your general and specific purposes is to compose a **core statement.** *The core statement crystallizes your speech into one sentence.* A core statement serves as the unifying element around which you can assemble the materials that will help you accomplish your general and specific purposes. It is, in short, a specific declaration of what you expect to accomplish with your speech.

Informative Core Statements

If your general purpose is to inform and your specific purpose is "to have the audience understand ways to reduce water usage in the home," your core statement might be "There are seven things you can do to reduce water usage in the bathroom, kitchen, and laundry." With that core statement as a focal point, you can arrange your materials into those that concern water usage in each of the separate areas indicated. If your general goal is to inform and your specific purpose is "to have the audience understand the features to look for when buying a laptop computer," your core statement might be "The principal features to look for when buying a laptop computer are display clarity, keyboard adequacy, speed, and portability." Again, you can see how the core statement suggests the ways in which the materials can be put into orderly groups.

The core statement of an informative speech might suggest the steps in a process, such as "Cheese making involves coagulation, compression, and curing." It may suggest the parts of a whole, such as, "The principal parts of a sailboat rudder are the tiller, the head, and the blade." It may suggest the characteristics that distinguish the subject from other closely related subjects, such as this definition of stage fright: "Stage fright is a form of communication apprehension specific to a given communication encounter." As you can see from the examples cited in this and the preceding paragraph, the core statement calls for development by supporting material in order to carry its intended meaning to the audience.

Persuasive Core Statements

If your speech is designed to persuade, your core statement might be phrased as a declaration of policy, such as "Off-shore oil drilling should be prohibited along the southern California coastline." Or it might be worded as a value judgment, such as "Air travel is safer than rail travel." Perhaps it takes the form of a statement alleging something to be true, such as "Loud music has caused hearing loss in many teenagers."

When do you formulate your core statement? Ideally, just as soon as you have completed your investigation and analysis of the subject. With the results of your research before you, you will be in a position to ask yourself, What does all this add up to? Your answer should provide you with the elements necessary to compose your core statement.

In wording your core statement, be careful to phrase it in terms broad enough to cover all the major areas to be included in your speech yet specific enough to suggest what will not be included. Compare the phrasing of the following statements:

Core Statement A: Successful weight loss involves several considerations.

Core Statement B: Successful weight loss involves a proper diet, proper exercise, and a proper mental attitude.

Statement A suffers from the ambiguity of "several considerations." Statement B indicates precisely what will be discussed.

One of the benefits of composing a core statement at the outset of the organizational process is that it provides you with a way to test the relevance of any material you expect to introduce into the speech. If any proposed main point, subpoint, or piece of supporting material doesn't relate to the core statement, then you can discard it as irrelevant. In this way, the unity of the speech is maintained.

Remember, a core statement should (1) have but one central idea, (2) be worded in very specific language, (3) be a complete sentence, and (4) be audience centered.

Formulating Main Points and Subpoints

Once you have formulated your core statement, you can lay out the main points that will clarify, reinforce, or prove the core statement. These main points serve as the principal units of the body of the speech. Even though it is your introduction that will begin the speech, in the preparation stages it is far more beneficial to plan your body before you worry about the introduction and conclusion. Hence, you begin the organizational process by translating your core statement into main points and subpoints.

Most speeches have two to five main points. Like the core statement, the main points are also worded as statements, but each point deals with only one aspect of the core statement—for example:

Core Statement: The key factors in selecting a room air conditioner are ease of installation, cooling efficiency, and energy consumption.
Main Point: I. Ease of installation depends on the size of the window opening, the weight of the cabinet, and the type of mounting hardware.
Main Point: II. Cooling efficiency is dependent on the unit's BTU rating, the thermostat, and the size and condition of the room to be cooled.
Main Point: III. Energy consumption is directly related to the size of the motor.

The following guidelines may assist you as you select and phrase the main points of your speech:

1. Make certain that each main point has a direct *relationship* to the core statement.

2. See that each main point is clearly distinguishable *(separated)* from the other main points.

3. Be sure that the main points, taken *collectively*, develop the core statement completely.

Let us now examine each of these three guidelines in detail.

Relationship to the Core Statement

To be considered a main point, a statement must contribute directly to the proof, explanation, or illustration of the core statement. One way to determine whether or not a statement is a main point of a persuasive or argumentative speech is to place such connectives as "because" and "for" between the core statement and the main point in question. Following is an example:

Core Statement: You should buy term insurance, *because*

   I. It provides sufficient coverage at less cost than whole-life.

   II. It is convertible to whole-life.

   III. It is usually renewable.

The relationship between the core statement and the main points of an expository speech may be checked by using expressions such as *namely, for example,* and *in that.*

Core Statement: Synthetic cooking oil has attractive features, *namely,*

   I. It has no cholesterol.

   II. It has no calories.

   III. It tastes the same as vegetable oil.

Can you tell which of the following main points is not clearly related to the core statement?

Core Statement: There are myths regarding the effectiveness of some vitamins.

   I. Vitamin C does not prevent colds.

   II. Vitamin B6 is not useful in treating premenstrual syndrome.

   III. Vitamin C is not found in all four food groups.

   IV. Vitamin E does not help women with mammary dysplasia.

Separation From Other Main Points

Although the main points have a common kinship to the core statement, they should nonetheless *be separate from one another.* Which of the following points seem to overlap each other?

Core Statement: You should buy generic drugs.

I. They are just as effective as brand-name drugs.

II. They are cheaper than brand-name drugs.

III. They are often more easily available than brand-name drugs.

IV. They are a godsend to people on a tight budget.

Points I and III are apparently dealing with separate issues, but point II sounds more like a subhead of point IV. Unless the main points are clearly distinguishable from one another, listeners are apt to become confused by the developmental pattern.

Collective Completeness of the Main Points

How can we tell when we have formulated all the potential main points of a speech? Only when every facet of the core statement has been indicated for development somewhere. We do not consider an airplane complete if one of its wings is missing. Similarly, if one aspect of the core statement does not find a place in the main points already formulated, then another main point is called for.

Determining all the essential parts is seldom easy. If you are selling automobiles and want to convince a customer that a particular model is the best one to buy, you should determine what constitutes a "best" car, not from your own personal view, but from the probable vantage point of the customer. To your customer, the "best" car might be the most stylish or the most powerful or the most economical to operate, so try to look at your core statement through the eyes of your listeners and ask, What points will the speech have to cover before winning audience agreement? or What points will the speech have to clarify before listeners fully understand?

Although the discussion in this section has centered on the selection and phrasing of main points, all the principles discussed are equally applicable to the selection and phrasing of subpoints. A subpoint bears the same relationship to a main point that a main point bears to the core statement.

When deciding on and arranging your main points, and subpoints, ask yourself the following:

1. Can some main points and subpoints be combined?

2. Are the main points and subpoints clear?

3. Do the main points and subpoints directly relate to the main assertion being advanced?

4. Are all the main points and subpoints of equal weight?

Organizational Patterns

We have all had the experience of recognizing a familiar face but then finding it almost impossible to remember just where we have seen that face before. We struggle to remember the occasion or the surroundings in which we have seen the person. Sometimes we give up in exasperation; at other times, we remember that the face belongs to the person who sat next to us on a flight from New York to Atlanta, to the supermarket checker, or to the mail carrier. Psychologists tell us that things perceived in isolation do not have as much meaning as when they are seen in relationship to other things, which give them meaning. We develop habits of organizing our perceptions into meaningful contexts. Some things we perceive within a time frame, others in terms of their spatial placement, and still others in terms of logical parts, components, or divisions. We organize our perceptions of argumentative and nonargumentative relationships in special ways.

A list of organizational patterns would be endless, so we will concentrate on those that have proved to be particularly serviceable to speakers over the years. Keep in mind that no one pattern is suitable for all topics and purposes. Therefore, an organizational scheme must be selected with great care. *Your ultimate plan should take into account certain predictions you have made about your potential listeners.* Your audience analysis should have told you about their probable level of acquaintance with the topic, their probable attitude toward your specific purpose, and their probable attitude toward you as a spokesperson on the topic.

One more introductory observation is called for before we explore some of the more widely used organizational patterns. *Please keep in mind that we will reexamine most of these patterns later in the book, when we discuss the speeches to inform, persuade, and entertain.* Our purpose at this point is simply to look at the various patterns so that you can use them to prepare outlines and speeches early in the course.

Chronological Pattern

Many subjects can be developed in terms of a chronological (time) sequence. Most obvious are speeches that deal with the steps in a logical progression; speeches on how to do something or make something, or speeches that treat historical matters. For example, in autumn, speeches about the origin of holidays, such as Halloween and Thanksgiving, are popular. If you were asked about the origin of one of the later holidays, such as St. Valentine's Day, you would probably devise a speech pattern that would start with the first known traces of the celebration and then work forward to the present time. The design of your main points might resemble the following:

Core Statement: St. Valentine's Day has a long history.

    I. The annual Roman feast of Lupercalia, held in February, most likely was its predecessor.

    II. The feast was Christianized in A.D. 270 to commemorate the martyrdom of Saint Valentine.

    III. The holiday was celebrated thereafter by west European Christians on February 14.

    IV. In the 1840s, the first commercial Valentine greeting cards were sold in the United States.

The chronological pattern is also effective when examining a person's life. Notice the time sequence in the example shown following:

I. The life of Martin Luther King, Jr., clearly reflects the many influences on his nonviolent philosophy.

   A. The influence of his family.

   B. The influence of his education.

   C. The influence of his meeting with Mahatma Gandhi.

Historical events organized in the chronological pattern do not necessarily have to be old to be effective. For instance, a student talking about how various Presidents have proposed programs for health care reform looked at the plans advanced by Presidents Reagan, Bush, and Clinton.

As indicated earlier, historical time sequencing is just one of many topics that can fit into the chronological pattern. When someone offers instructions or describes a process, he or she is using a step-by-step method, which is a kind of time pattern. The following example illustrates how the time pattern applies to a speech describing the manufacture of soap:

Core Statement: The manufacture of soap involves four basic procedures.

   I. Fats, oils, alkali, and salt are boiled.

   II. The resulting curd is washed and allowed to settle.

   III. The upper layer of the curd is churned.

   IV. The resulting product is cut, shaped, and stamped.

Often more than one pattern is used in a speech. That is to say, you may be employing the overall scheme of topical pattern (described later in this section) and yet have chronological as one of your subsets. For example, a speaker recently gave a talk using a problem-solution pattern to talk about environmental waste disposal. Within that talk she used a chronological pattern when talking about some of the problems the world faces if it does not learn to recycle waste products:

I. It takes a very long time for most trash to decompose.

   A. A glass bottle takes 1 million years to decompose.

   B. An aluminum can takes 80–100 years to decompose.

   C. A rubber boot sole takes 50 years to decompose.

   D. A plastic bag takes 10–20 years to decompose.

It is a good idea to keep the number of main points in a time pattern to no more than five—three to five is the ideal range—for ease of understanding and retention. Consequently, you will find it convenient to group a number of chronological details under general headings, such as "The first era was ...," "The first decade was characterized by ...," or "The ancient Greeks were the first to systematize the study of public speaking."

The chronological pattern is a popular organizational scheme in that nearly everyone perceives events and processes in this linear fashion. The weakness of this pattern is that it does not easily lend itself to complex discussions or issues related to causes and effects.

Spatial Pattern

As the name implies, spatial patterns organize main points around how various parts connect to each other. *Geographical topics fit neatly into this pattern.* If, for example, you were talking about population growth around the world, you could discuss various regions of the world:

Core Statement: The increase in the world's population is a serious problem.

   I. Population growth in Africa.

   II. Population growth in Asia.

   III. Population growth in Latin America.

Speeches involving *locations or tours usually lend themselves to the spatial pattern:*

Core Statement: There are many special sites to see when visiting Yosemite Valley.

   I. As you enter the park, you see a magnificent view as you descend into the valley.

   II. Once you reach the bottom of the valley you experience the beauty of Yosemite Falls.

   III. From the middle of the valley you will be able to see Half Dome.

Speeches about the spread of an empire, the encroachment of a disease, or the location of natural resources are all examples of how one might use a spatial pattern with a geographical topic. If you want your listeners to visualize the layout of a proposed passenger station on a new suburban trolley line, for example, you might arrange your materials in terms of a familiar configuration:

Core Statement: The trolley stop will be laid out in an L-shaped configuration.

   I. The vertical axis of the L will be a 50-foot-long waiting platform at trackside.

   II. The short horizontal axis of the L will contain ticket-vending machines.

   III. The open space to the right will be a one-acre parking lot.

If you are describing a building, you might arrange the details from basement to attic, from east wing to west wing, from entrance to exit, or from front to rear:

Core Statement: The Campus Center Building will have four levels.

   I. The basement level will house a snack bar, bowling alley, and game room.

   II. The ground level will have shops, a restaurant, and reception lounges.

III. The next level will have a small library, facilities for using audio-visual material, and office space.

IV. The top level will house guest rooms for visiting dignitaries.

Sometimes *you can combine a spatial pattern with a time pattern* if the subject is suitable—for example:

Core Statement: During the last hundred years museums devoted to children have been opened in a number of locations throughout the United States.

I. The Brooklyn Children's Museum was founded in 1899.

II. The Children's Museum of Boston was founded in 1913.

III. The Eugene Field House and Toy Museum in St. Louis was founded in 1913.

IV. The Exploratorium in the Palace of Fine Arts in San Francisco was founded in 1969.

V. The Please Touch Museum in Philadelphia was founded in 1976.

VI. The Interactive Space Museum was opened in Washington, D.C. in 1996.

When you use a spatial pattern, you are "telling" the audience that there is a specific reason you are arranging your material in this order. For example, if you are explaining a proposed Community Plan to the Board of Supervisors, your main points might look like the following:

Core Statement: Ramona's New Community Plan touches all portions of the area.

I. The effect of the plan on the valley.

II. The effect of the plan on the lower foothills.

III. The effect of the plan on the upper mountains.

Notice that, in the last example, even within the pattern, the sequencing made sense in that we moved from low to high. Space patterns often go from left to right, top to bottom, bottom to top, or front to back. They can also move in a descending order of importance. For example, if your topic is preparing your home for an earthquake, you could divide the house into the sections that are most dangerous (the garage area because of oil and gasoline) and those that are least dangerous (making sure there will be enough food in the pantry).

Topical Pattern

Topical patterns are among the most widely used sequences in speech making. If you want to *call attention to natural divisions and categories of a topic,* you will find that the topical pattern is very effective. With this pattern you are suggesting that there is a classification and/or relationship among the parts of your subject. That classification can relate to such things as roles, functions, component parts, qualities, features, and levels of hierarchy. Some examples may illustrate the wide array of speech subjects that can be treated topically.

> **Core Statement:** Cigarette smoking affects many parts of the body in negative ways.
>
>   I. In your lungs cigarette smoke can cause bronchitis.
>
> II. In the reproductive system of women, cigarette smoke causes miscarriages.
>
> III. Your cigarette smoking increases the heart rate by as many as 33 beats per minute.

> **Core Statement:** We send nonverbal messages with many parts of our body.
>
>   I. Our eyes send messages.
>
> II. The way we move sends messages.
>
> III. Our facial expressions send messages.
>
> IV. Our posture sends messages.

> **Core Statement:** Automotive trouble is most likely to occur in one of three systems.
>
>   I. It may occur in the electrical system.
>
> II. It may occur in the fuel system.
>
> III. It may occur somewhere within the transmission.

> **Core Statement:** The Ramona Community Plan is environmentally sound.
>
>   I. The plan protects the lakes from pollution.
>
> II. The plan protects the wildlife.
>
> III. The plan protects endangered plants.

Patterns of topical time and space relationships are especially useful in presenting nonargumentative material, such as speeches of exposition, description, and narration. Moreover, it is possible to combine a variety of these patterns within the same speech. The main points, for example, might follow a spatial pattern; the subheads developing a main point might follow a topical pattern; and the subheads developing still another main point might use the time pattern.

One final observation is needed before we conclude our discussion of the topical pattern. Be careful that the topical pattern does not become a formless sequence where you can deposit any topics that fail to make sense anywhere else. Students often make the mistake of calling anything a "topic" and therefore end up tossing in items that fail to relate. An example of calling anything a topic is to discuss solutions to sleep disorders by examining prescription drugs, herbs, and the history of sleep disorders. Keep in mind that regardless of the pattern you select, the link between major and minor topics must be obvious to the audience.

Cause-Effect Pattern

The cause-effect pattern organizes the content of the speech around a set of conditions represented as the cause of an event or a phenomenon. What you are suggesting in this organizational sequence is why a particular "thing" occurred (causes) and that it is instrumental in bringing about certain results (effects). Notice in the following arrangements how each main point (the cause) resulted in certain consequences: (effects).

> **Core Statement:** The reduction of funds for after-school programs has brought about (cause) serious problems.
>
> I. The remedial reading program has been eliminated. (effect)
>
> II. Free hot lunches have been eliminated. (effect)
>
> III. Street crossing guards have been eliminated. (effect)

> **Core Statement:** Not getting enough vitamins in your diet has serious consequences for your health. (cause)
>
> I. A lack of vitamin K can produce increased blood hemorrhaging. (effect)
>
> II. A lack of vitamin C can produce scurvy. (effect)
>
> III. A lack of vitamin B6 can produce anemia. (effect)

> **Core Statement:** There are many reasons (causes) why trial by jury is ineffective.

Problem-Solution Pattern

The problem-solution pattern is often conceived of as a longer and more elaborate version of the causal pattern. Many persuasive speeches lend themselves to the problem-solution pattern. In these situations, you are urging the adoption of a new policy or plan. It involves (1) presenting a problem area, (2) proposing a solution to the problem, and (3) defending the proposed solution.

Let us see how a problem-solution outline might look. Suppose, for example, that the houses in your neighborhood have been defaced by graffiti that you suspect has been applied by youngsters with cans of spray paint. You think the best solution to the problem is to ban the sale of spray paint to minors. You might arrange the main points of your speech as follows:

> **Core Statement:** The sale of spray paint to minors should be prohibited by law.
>
> **Problem:**
>
> I. Some minors use spray paint destructively.
>
>   A. They deface public buildings.
>
>   B. They deface private residences.
>
>   C. They deface pavement and sidewalks.

Solution:

    II. A ban on sales of spray paint to minors represents a solution to this problem.

        A. It would make access to spray paint much more difficult for minors.

        B. It would make minors more fully aware of community feeling about defacement of property.

Defense:

    III. Such a ban is feasible.

        A. It is legally feasible.

        B. It is administratively feasible.

Defense:

    IV. Disadvantages of a ban are minor.

        A. Stores selling spray paint would experience little decline in sales.

        B. Minors needing spray paint for legitimate use could obtain it through parents.

Defense:

    V. Banning sales is the best solution.

        A. It is less costly than surveillance systems.

        B. It is a better deterrent than the threat of harsh punishment.

You will notice that both main heads and subheads are topical groupings. The main heads involve the topics of problem, solution, and defense of solution. The subheads are groupings of such topics as defacement, accessibility, awareness, and legal and administrative feasibility.

The problem-solution pattern can take a number of forms. Obviously, the number of problems you isolate and the solutions you propose will depend on the complexity of the problem and the amount of time you have been allocated. For example, your pattern might be as simple as the following:

Core Statement: We need an evening security escort service on campus.

Problem:

    I. The incidence of rape has grown significantly on our campus.

        A. Statistics show the increase.

        B. Experts confirm the increase.

Solution:

    II. An escort service would provide students protection as they walk on campus at night.

   A. The escort could walk students to their dormitories.

   B. The escort could walk students to their automobiles.

One of the major advantages of the problem-solution sequence is simplicity. By convincing the audience that there is something wrong with the status quo (too many car alarms going off during school hours), they will be receptive to your solution (having car alarms turned off during school hours).

Level-of-Acceptance Pattern

The level-of-acceptance pattern, sometimes referred to as the withheld proposal or indirect sequence, moves the audience through a succession of points that gradually lead to a conclusion. This pattern is usually used when audience analysis reveals that the speaker is likely to encounter strong listener resistance to his or her point of view. In these cases, it is wise to start with ideas that are acceptable to the listeners and then work progressively toward less acceptable ideas until the least acceptable idea (perhaps your solution) is reached. In the early stages of this sequence, then, you would be using the "common ground" technique. An example of this strategy is seen in the following outline:

Most acceptable idea: (common ground)

   I. Every person values his or her job security.

  II. All of us are concerned about how our jobs are threatened by foreign competition.

 III. All of us want steps taken to preserve our jobs.

  IV. Any equitable solution requires the participation of every person in the firm.

Least acceptable idea:

   V. The most equitable solution is an across-the-board 10 percent salary reduction.

Core Statement: All employees of the firm should take a 10 percent salary reduction.

The first point is a statement of common ground. The presumption is that most listeners will not challenge this idea. The second and third points may require some demonstration, although they, too, are likely to be areas of common ground. The fourth point may be more difficult to establish, particularly if the prevailing attitude is to "let Joe do it." The fifth point would most likely receive the greatest resistance. However, if the speaker succeeds in establishing these points in order, the core statement is more likely to be heard with favor than if it were announced at the outset.

Motivated Sequence

For over fifty years, Professor Alan H. Monroe's motivated sequence has been a very popular method of organizing speeches. In his book, *Principles and Types of Speech Communication*, he divided the motivated sequence into five steps. When applied to persuasive speeches, this format involves: (1) the attention step, wherein the speaker secures initial audience attention; (2) the need step, wherein the audience is made aware of the existence of a problem; (3) the satisfaction step, wherein a solution to that problem is explained and defended; (4) the visualization step, wherein the speaker envisions what the future will be like if the recommended solution is (or is not) put into practice; and (5) the action step, wherein the audience is given directions for implementing the solution. Note the similarity between the problem-solution sequence described earlier and the need and satisfaction steps of the motivated sequence.

Professor Monroe indicated that when this sequence is applied to informational speeches, the visualization and action steps could be omitted. The attention step would serve the same function as in a persuasive speech, while the need step would be aimed at making the audience feel a need for the information to be presented. The satisfaction step would, of course, provide the needed information.

Because the motivated sequence is such an effective organizational scheme, it is discussed in much greater detail in chapter 13, when we look at the informative speech, and in chapter 14, when we examine speeches to persuade.

Organizational Patterns and Culture

Throughout this chapter, we have talked about the organizational patterns that are most effective if your audience is composed primarily of members from the dominant North American culture. Our cultural experiences have taught us to string ideas together in a manner that, while common for us, is not universal. Four examples will help us clarify this idea. First, in North America the deductive organizational pattern is very common because it is highly structured and rigid—characteristics admired in our culture. Hence, we often introduce broad categories and then move to specifics to explain the assertions. As we shall see in a moment, not all cultures employ this pattern. Second, because people in our culture normally look for causes behind events, the cause-effect pattern is a popular method of organization. This pattern assumes there are reasons (causes) for all actions. Again, this is not the approach taken by many cultures. Third, as we have previously discussed, much of the thinking in the Western world is linear—direct and straightforward. The connection between each point when we organize our thoughts, prose, or speaking is clear and easy to see. We often hear people praise someone because their "ideas flowed together." Like so many mental processes, this form of organization is not used by all cultures. Finally, and this may simply be a corollary of the first three, we often introduce broad categories and then move to specifics to explain assertions. Throughout school, we are taught to "make a point and then subordinate it."

It would be easy to assume that everyone in the world organizes her or his thoughts in the same manner. This is simply not the case. The mental processes of reasoning (discussed in the previous chapter) and ways of organizing ideas are influenced by culture. In many Eastern cultures, such as the Korean, the pattern is to start with specific observations and then extract generalizations. In Asian cultures the main point is often not clearly called out but rather contained within a story, illustration, or parable. In addition, many cultures employ configural logic instead of linear methods. In configural schemes, often used by Asians and Native Americans, the association between each point is not direct and spelled out. This type of pattern assumes that the listener will make the connection on his or her own. Gaining this type of information from audience analysis will help you select the most appropriate organizational pattern. I do not suggest that you completely abandon the Western organizational patterns that you are comfortable with but rather that you make some attempt at understanding and, when appropriate, incorporating other organizational patterns.

When talking to people from cultures different from your own, the technique of establishing "common ground" in the level-of-acceptance pattern also takes on added significance. That is to say, what is believed in one culture may not be "common" to another culture. In our last example, the common ground approach was very North American. However, the Japanese have a very different view of the workplace and employment. They believe in great loyalty to their companies and would not necessarily agree with the premises being advanced by the speaker in the example. Speeches dealing with women's issues need to be given special attention if you are using the indirect approach to diverse cultural groups. In much of Latin America and the Arab world, women are perceived quite differently than in the United States. If your starting point is faulty, at least from the Latin or Arab point of view, your entire organizational sequence will suffer.

Outlining the Message

Benjamin Franklin wrote, "A place for everything, and everything in its place." The truth of his adage is perhaps most evident in the preparation of a speech outline. It is here that all the pieces begin to fit together. However, outlining is usually misunderstood and often dreaded by most students. One common misconception is that outlining is something you do after you have composed a speech—a frivolous requirement instructors impose on students. Those who entertain such a view of outlining are depriving themselves of one of the most valuable tools for ensuring that their speeches are organized in a clear and unified manner.

Importance of Outlining

An outline is essentially a visual representation of the cognitive process you go through as you put a speech together. There are a number of advantages to constructing a detailed outline before your speech is actually delivered. First, because the process is visualized, *you are better able to tell where gaps exist, where reasoning is faulty, where illustrations are needed*—in short, where revisions will make your ideas easier for the listener to absorb (and for you to remember). Second, *a good outline enables you to see the interrelationships of the parts of your message, their proportions, the adequacy of their development, and how well they function as a whole.* Finally, *an outline serves as the first step in the process of constructing the notes you will use to deliver your talk.* As

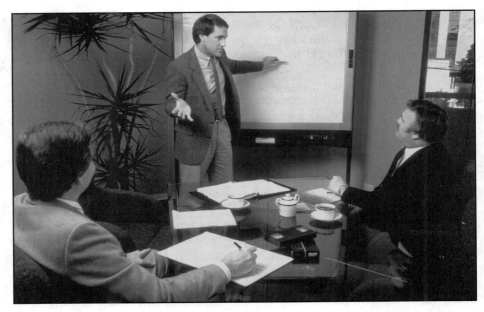

A good outline enables you to see the interrelationships of the parts of the messages. (Photo: corbisimages.com)

noted in chapter 2, you begin learning your speech from the full outline and then move the key points of the outline to your notecards.

A speaker making optimum use of the outlining process *first assembles a* **master outline** *(sometimes called a brief) designed to promote understanding of a subject in all its dimensions.* Such an outline contains far more material than ever reaches the presentation stage. It serves as the warehouse from which to draw materials for a presentation outline. The **presentation outline**—the one with which we will be primarily concerned—*is designed with the audience in mind; thus, it is much more selective than the master outline, or brief.*

Although experienced speakers may use an abbreviated outline made up of key words or phrases, beginning speakers profit more from using a complete-sentence outline. It is especially important to use the complete-sentence form when outlining argumentative speeches because logical relationships cannot be clearly expressed through the use of key words or phrases. Moreover, the extra effort required to construct a complete-sentence outline helps you remember your ideas more readily during your speech.

Characteristics of Effective Outlines

It is difficult to say just how much of your actual speech should appear on your outline. Many variables affect this decision. They range from how familiar you are with the topic to the amount of time you have been allotted. However, as a general rule of thumb, the total number of words in your outline should equal no more than one-third to one-half of the words you think you will say during your talk. Regardless of the formula that meets your needs, observe the following principles as you prepare your outline:

1. *Assign only one idea or statement to each unit of the outline.* In this way, you will be able to ensure that your material is clear and free from auxiliary points. Notice in the following two illustrations of this point how Example B is much more explicit than Example A.

Example A (Incorrect)

   I. Because it is cleaner and cheaper, solar power is preferable to fossil-fuel power; moreover, it has unlimited availability.

Example B (Correct)

   I. Solar power is preferable to fossil-fuel power, for

     A. It is cleaner.

     B. It is cheaper.

     C. It has unlimited availability.

Example A (Incorrect)

   I. The proposed development is bad for everyone in that it takes away greenbelt areas and opens up the park regions to commercial development.

Example B (Correct)

   I. The proposed development would harm our community.

     A. It takes away greenbelt areas.

     B. It opens up park regions to commercial development.

2. *Do not allow points to overlap.* The following example represents an infraction of this rule:

   I. Poisonous snakes are found in all regions of the United States.

     A. They are found in the East.

     B. They are found in the West.

     C. They are found in the North.

     D. They are found in the South.

     E. They are particularly numerous in California.

The inclusion of E throws the pattern into confusion, since a single state is not equivalent to a region.

3. *Maintain consistent levels of importance among coordinate points.* Units that are labeled as main points, for example, should share common elements. The inclusion of a unit of greater or lesser magnitude will destroy the consistency of the pattern—for example:

   I. Consumption of meat is declining in the USA.

     A. Sales of beef are down.

     B. Sales of pork are down.

     C. Sales of lamb are down.

     D. Sales of fish have increased.

The inclusion of D breaks the consistency of the pattern and introduces an annoying element of disproportion.

4. *Maintain clear levels of subordination.* Through the proper use of symbols and indentation, the hierarchy of points is indicated. Compare Examples A and B that follow:

Example A

   I. Advantages of paper packaging are

     A. Light weight

     B. Strength

     C. Biodegradable nature

     D. An important export item for many years

       1. In the early twentieth century

       2. At mid-twentieth century

       3. In the past decade

Example B

   I. Advantages of paper packaging are

     A. Light weight

     B. Strength

     C. Biodegradable nature

  II. It has been an important export item

     A. In the early twentieth century

     B. At mid-twentieth century

     C. In the past decade

Notice that in Example B, Roman numeral II should not be a main point but rather should be part of the subordination to Roman numeral I.

5. *Use a consistent set of symbols and indentations to indicate relationships among main headings and subheadings.* The usual system is

   I. Main heading _____

     A. Subheading _____

       1. _____

         a. _____

           (1) _____

           (2)_____

    b. _____   ❖ ❖ ❖ ❖

  2. _____

 B. _____

II. _____

Note that main headings are consistently designated by Roman numerals; that subheadings that explain, illustrate, or prove the main headings to which they are immediately subordinated are designated by capital letters; that the level that is subordinate to the subheadings is designated by Arabic numerals; and so on down the scale of importance.

6. *Supporting points, whenever possible, should be worded in parallel sentence form.* By using corresponding structure and language, you test the logic of your material and make it clear for your audience. Notice how Example B is much clearer than Example A in that each point in B begins with a common and consistent vocabulary:

Example A

 I. Vitamins in your diet might be essential to good health.

  A. Some people say that niacin might be a possible cancer inhibitor.

  B. It has been suggested that folic acid may help protect against heart disease.

  C. It could be that vitamin D is related to some kidney diseases.

Example B

 I. Vitamins in your diet might be essential to good health.

  A. Niacin may inhibit certain kinds of cancer.

  B. Folic acid may help protect against heart attack.

  C. Vitamin D may help prevent certain kidney diseases.

7. *Your outline should have an introduction, body, and conclusion.* Including these three elements in your outline can help you visualize how all the parts of the speech fit together.

Introduction

 I. Be careful the next time you approach that cute little boy playing with a toy gun—it may not be a toy.

Body

II. Juvenile crime is on the increase.

  A. Murder is on the increase among juveniles.

   1. Evidence

   2. Evidence

B. Armed robbery is on the increase among juveniles.

    1. Evidence

    2. Evidence

C. Aggravated assault is on the increase among juveniles.

    1. Evidence

    2. Evidence

Conclusion

III. Juvenile crime is on the increase.

A Sample Outline

As indicated elsewhere, an outline for an entire speech would probably be divided into four parts: introduction, core statement, body, and conclusion. In some speech classes, the instructor may require a statement of general and specific purposes and a bibliography of sources consulted. In some instances even a title will be assigned. The following is a brief outline of an informational speech.

Title: A Vacation Afloat

General Purpose: To Inform

Specific Purpose: To have my audience learn about houseboating as a summer vacation.

Introduction

I. The English essayist Kenneth Grahame once wrote, "Believe me, my young friend, there is nothing, absolutely nothing, half so much worth doing as simply messing about in a boat."

A. Having just returned from a wonderful vacation spent on a boat, I would agree with Mr. Grahame's conclusion.

B. My idea of relaxation is to sit in a little boat in the middle of a lake, with a fish on the line and some lemonade in the ice chest.

C. My boyfriend's idea of relaxation on a boat is to be somewhere next to nature, but he wants most of the creature comforts still available.

II. Today, I want to tell you how both kinds of boating vacations can be achieved simultaneously in the same location.

Preview

I. Specifically, I would like to talk to you about how houseboating on Lake Powell is a vacation that, first, allows you to be outdoors; second, is very comfortable; and, third, is very affordable.

Body

I. Houseboating offers something for the person who likes outdoor camping.

   A. There is the change from everyday urban life.

      1. There is no freeway traffic to fight.

      2. There is no time clock to punch.

   B. There is solitude in a beautiful setting.

      1. There are many secluded coves where you can anchor your boat.

      2. The water is blue and clear.

II. It offers something for the person who wants to fish in great comfort.

   A. You can fish and still have the so-called creature comforts.

      1. Because there is water all around, you don't have to get up at 4 A.M. to drive somewhere to start fishing.

      2. You can fish right from your own front porch.

   B. Lake Powell is well stocked with fish.

      1. There is a large variety of fish in the lake.

      2. Here is a picture of a fish we caught during my last trip on a houseboat. (*Visual Aid*)

III. Houseboating offers something for those on a budget.

   A. The cost can be shared.

      1. A group of four can share the cost of a 35-foot houseboat.

      2. A group of 10 can share the cost of a 50-foot boat.

   B. Special rates are available.

      1. Three-day rentals during weekdays are 40 percent less than on weekends.

      2. Weekly rentals during off-season are less than half the rate of peak-season rentals.

Conclusion

I. For fun in the sun, I recommend a vacation on a houseboat.

   A. It offers seclusion.

   B. It offers good fishing.

   C. It is not very expensive.

❖ ❖ ❖ ❖   ## Using Transitions

In chapter 6, we looked at a number of different kinds of transitions and talked about how they link your forms of support into a cohesive unit. Let us briefly return to the topic of transitions so that you can learn how to include them as part of your outline.

You will recall that transitions are words, phrases, and sentences that connect your ideas to one another. Their major function is to tell your listeners what you have done ("The statistics we have just looked at clearly demonstrate the widespread nature of this problem") and where you are going next ("Let us see if the experts agree with the numbers I have just presented").

As noted in chapter 6, a transition can take a number of specific forms. Four of the more common ones are the (1) *preview* ("Now would be a good time for me to talk about the reasons our college does not have a suitable student health plan"), (2) *summary* ("Having looked at the major funding programs on campus, you can see why we do not have a suitable student health plan"), (3) *summary-preview* ("We now know what is wrong with the student health plan, but what can we do about it?"), and (4) *enumeration* ("There are three reasons our health plan is not working. First, . . .").

As a general rule, transitions are not absorbed into the same system of symbolization and indentation that are part of a normal outline. They are usually shown in the following manner:

I. _____.

    A. _____.

    B. _____.

        1. _____.

        2. _____.

*(Transition)*_____.

II. _____.

    A. _____.

    B. _____.

*(Transition)*_____.

III. _____.

You may want to review chapter 6, where you will be able to find a much more detailed discussion of this important communication tool.

Summary

The process of assembling a speech usually begins with the formulation of a core statement embodying the central idea of the speech. Growing out of the core statement are the main points, subpoints, and supporting materials. Coordinate points should (1) relate to the core statement, (2) relate to one another yet be separable from one another, and (3) collectively develop the statement under which they stand. Material should be meaningfully organized around a logical sequence. Among the most common patterns of grouping are chronological, spatial, topical, cause-effect, problem-solution, level-of-acceptance, and the motivated sequence.

An outline is a tool for arranging constituent parts of a message into an orderly sequence. Good outline form features the use of a consistent set of symbols to show proper subordination of ideas. Each unit of the outline should contain only one idea; points should not be allowed to overlap; and coordinate points should be parallel.

Concepts and Questions

1. What are the benefits of good organization?

2. What are core statements, main points, and subpoints, and how are they related?

3. Differentiate between chronological, spatial, topical, problem-solving, level-of-acceptance, and the motivated sequence.

4. What is a complete sentence outline?

5. Why is it important for speakers to prepare outlines?

Activities and Exercises

1. Listen to a speaker in your class. As you listen to his or her speech, try to outline the main point and subpoints.

2. Explain how you might use a chronological pattern when preparing a speech dealing with the Olympic Games.

3. Select any topic suited for a speech to inform. Explain how you would use any three of the patterns discussed in this chapter to outline the topic.

4. Listen to a speaker from a culture different from your own. Make an outline of the talk. Compare the method of that speaker's organization to the common organizational patterns found in your culture. ✦

CHAPTER ELEVEN

Introduction and Conclusions: Connecting Your Ideas

All's well that ends well; still this finis is the crown.

—*Shakespeare*

Our focus in chapter 10 was on ways of arranging materials so that they would be clear and directly support the core statement. In this chapter we deal with the materials that precede and follow the body of your talk. How do you capture interest and attention? How do you lead up to the central portion of the speech? How do you make a graceful exit? Our goal in this chapter is to answer these questions.

Preparing the Introduction

An old English proverb states, "A good beginning makes a good ending." Also, a good beginning helps makes a good speech. Remember that your introduction is your first exposure to your audience. You know from your own experience how quickly people form first impressions and just how important these images can be. Research in interpersonal relationships suggests that when we meet someone, we decide within the first 14 seconds whether they are friendly, likable, educated, attractive, or trustworthy. Although such decisions may not be accurate, they nevertheless are conclusions about the other person that influence our response to what they say and do. What is true in

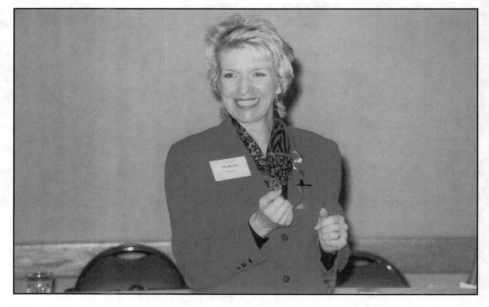

A good beginning is crucial if you are going to establish a positive image and begin the process of accomplishing your purpose. (Photo: Randall Reeder)

informal interaction also applies to public speaking. Therefore, a good beginning is crucial if you are going to establish a positive image and begin the process of accomplishing your purpose.

Some experts and many students believe that, in addition to being important, the introduction is often difficult to prepare. It must be relatively short but must accomplish a number of purposes. For instance, an effective introduction should (1) *secure the listeners' attention*, (2) *motivate them to want to listen to the entire speech*, (3) *establish the speaker's goodwill and credibility*, and (4) *prepare the listeners for what is to follow*. Although these four purposes are often combined, they all set the tone for the remainder of the talk. In the first part of this chapter, we will examine how you can achieve all of these purposes at the beginning of your speech. We should point out that we will return to the topic of introductions in chapters 13 (speeches to inform), 14 (persuasive speeches), and 15 (special occasion speeches), when we examine specific types of speeches. However, for now we will explore some of the more popular approaches to beginning a speech.

Gaining Attention

The kind of attention a speaker should seek is not the momentary, fleeting attention that inevitably occurs when the speaker appears on the platform. Rather, it is the kind of attention that attracts and holds the audience. In order to do so, the speech has to provide a stimulus that overrides all the other stimuli competing for the audience's attention. In every communication situation there are countless distractions that often keep the audience from listening. Perhaps the audience is more concerned with the discomfort of sitting in a hot, stuffy classroom. Maybe a number of the listeners are engaged in animated conversations, while others are enjoying private daydreams. Whether you confront one of these situations or you face the kind of captive audience found in required speech classes, you may have to use ingenious ways to gain favorable attention. Let us look at some of the best methods to gain and maintain attention at the outset of your talk.

Quotations. A favorite device for opening many speeches is a thought-provoking or curiosity-arousing quotation. The interest value of this technique is that someone else has made a striking observation about the issue you plan to discuss. For example, a speaker giving an anti-hunting speech began with the following quotation:

> Hunting man. Fire you little gun. Bang! Now the animal is dead and gone. Nevermore to peep again, creep again, leap again, eat or sleep or drink again. Oh what fun.

If your speech is aimed at explaining ways of building self-esteem, you could start out with this quotation:

> 'No one can make you feel inferior without your consent.' This observation, made by former first lady Eleanor Roosevelt, strikes directly at one of the reasons so many of us hold low opinions of ourselves.

A speaker discussing the popularity of magazines that feature sensationalism and gossip opened with this quotation from Alice Longworth:

> 'If you can't say anything good about someone, sit right here next to me.' Alice Longworth, who had these words embroidered on a pillow in her sitting

room, could have been describing the allure of those gaudy magazines that you find next to the checkout stand in the local supermarket.

Recently a speaker, talking on the topic of cultural differences in doing business, started with the following introduction:

> There is an Arab proverb that states, 'Live together like brothers, and do business like strangers.' This seemingly simple proverb offers great insight into how each culture perceives the business arena.

And still another speaker, whose topic centered on the contributions of Martin Luther King, Jr. to American culture, started with the following famous quotation:

> How many of you have heard these famous lines before? 'I have a dream that one day this nation will rise up and live out the true meaning of its creed: "We hold these truths to be self-evident: that all men are created equal." . . . I have a dream that my four children will one day live in a nation where they will be judged not by the color of their skin but the content of their character: I have a dream today.'

Quotations can be brief or long. Notice in the next two examples, both dealing with the freedom of the press, how attention is aroused in just a few words or in an entire paragraph:

> (Short) The free press is the foe of rhetoric but the friend of reason.

> (Long) The invention of the printing press added a new element of power to our race. From that hour, the brain and not the gun, the thinker and not the soldier, words and not kings, were to rule the world; and weapons, forged in the mind, keen-edged and brighter than the sunbeam, were to supplant the sword and the battle-ax.

In selecting an opening quotation, you should be guided by three criteria: *relevance*, *provocativeness*, and *good taste*. If you cannot build on a quotation, then the listeners may feel resentment when they realize you have cited it simply to gain attention. It must bear a connection to your subject. A quotation that is not provocative simply fails to attract the audience's attention in the first place. A quotation that is in poor taste will get the wrong kind of attention and will work to your disadvantage. Recently a speaker, talking about American buying habits, alienated most of the women in the audience by using a quotation that reinforced a common and insulting stereotype when he said, "Edgar Howe was right when he noted that a woman does not spend all her time in buying things; she spends part of it in taking them back."

Chapter 8 mentioned a number of excellent books of sayings and quotations you could consult as part of a research program for a particular speech. The Internet also has numerous websites that offer collections of quotations on every subject. You might also start the practice of collecting interesting quotations on your own, to create your own personal storehouse of quotations.

Illustrations and Anecdotes. As noted in chapter 6, everyone enjoys a good story. Hence, if properly handled, stories, anecdotes, and illustrations can be among the most effective openings you can use. Illustrations give you an opportunity to be creative. These narratives cause the audience to listen effortlessly. Illustrations can be factual or hypothetical. Let us begin by examining how *factual illustrations* can arouse attention.

In a speech focusing on the dangers of some commonly prescribed drugs the speaker used the following factual illustration to arouse interest and direct the talk the central point of the speech:

> It was to have been a very happy occasion for this young, newly married couple—their first New Year's Eve together. But on New Year's Eve morning last year, says Jerry Thomas, 'I awoke to hear my wife Mary gasping for air. As Mary's entire body throbbed out of control, I dialed 911 and then began frantically blowing air into her lungs, but it was too late.' At first the death of the healthy 22-year-old woman was a mystery. But just last month the mystery was solved. Mary's death certificate was stamped with the following words: Death due to a Toxic Level of the Antihistamine Hismanal.

As mentioned, illustrations can call attention to an event that both captures attention and points to your topic. A student gave a speech to inform on some of the overlooked personality traits of Abraham Lincoln. To stress Lincoln's sense of humor, she started with the following story:

> When the Confederate forces were attacking Fort Stevens, Lincoln made a tour of inspection of the Union troops. He was shown around by the general's aide, Oliver Wendell Holmes, Jr. As Holmes pointed out the enemy lines, Lincoln, wearing his customary tall hat, stood up to get a better view. At once, there was a crackle of musketry fire from the opposing trenches. 'Get down, you fool!' shouted Holmes. An instant later, he realized what he had said and wondered what kind of disciplinary action would be taken against him. As Lincoln was leaving, he said good-bye to the young officer and added, 'I am glad you know how to talk to a foolish civilian.'

Illustrations are also useful if you can personalize them by making yourself the main character. Notice the impact in the following incident because the person in the story is the speaker:

> My name is Kevin Kirk. On April 17, 1998, a beautiful spring night in Ramona, California, I was a passenger with six of my best friends in a van that was headed for a camping trip in the mountains. We were laughing, joking, sharing stories, and getting more and more excited as we approached our destination. But we never reached our destination. We were struck by a drunk driver. I remember being thrown from the van. It seemed like hours before I was moved into an ambulance. Once they started loading us, I began to realize that some people were missing. The reason for their absence became obvious within the next few minutes. Four of my friends were killed in the crash. I am here to tell you my life has never been the same because of that drunk driver.

A good factual illustration not only awakens attention and directs the audience to the main topic, but it can also motivate listeners to want to hear what will follow. A speaker recently combined attention with motivation by starting a talk on how gang violence is a problem of small as well as large communities in the following manner:

> The car screeched to a halt at the corner of 34th Street and 17th Avenue and someone inside the car fired two shots at point-blank range. Hit in the arm and back, 13-year-old Kevin Franks, an innocent bystander, ran half a block before he collapsed and died. The murder was a classic drive-by large city shooting. However, the shooting did not take place in Los Angeles, Chicago, Detroit, or New York, but rather in a small town in Ohio that is about the same size as our town.

In chapter 6, we noted that illustrations can also be *hypothetical*. These represent the accounts you offer to listeners that place them in key positions of the story. One student started her speech on the need to spay or neuter pets with the following hypothetical illustration:

> Please come with me as we take a tour of the county Humane Society. As we approach the first outdoor enclosure, we see four cute little puppies wagging their tails. They are, of course, anticipating the attention they know we will give them. Next to the puppies, we see a full-grown German Shepherd. He is as beautiful as any dog we have ever seen in a movie. From the inside cages, we hear the cats demanding that we pay them a visit. As we enter the cat area, we quickly notice two things. First, how sweet and engaging they all look. And, second, how many of them there are in the kennel. You are even more surprised when I tell you that there are more dogs and cats in areas we have not even visited. But the real shock and astonishment arrives when I tell you that these cats and dogs will soon be killed. It seems our county has a serious animal overpopulation problem.

In a speech about preparing for earthquakes a speaker stimulated interest by using a hypothetical illustration that made the members of the audience the central characters of the story:

> Imagine you were sitting at home one night and you felt a strange rocking sensation coming from your chair—a sensation strong enough that it forced to you to stop what you were doing. As you began to concentrate on what was happening you began to notice two extraordinary occurrences—the pictures on the wall were moving, and your dog was howling in a manner you had never heard before. All at once it hit you—the movement and the howling were related. You were experiencing an earthquake. As you looked around the home and started to see objects flying in many directions, it quickly became clear that this was a very serious earthquake. One question seemed to be repeating itself in your head: 'What should I do?' And now I ask you that question: 'Would you know what to do if you were caught in a major earthquake?'

Before you decide to open a speech with a story or an illustration, take pains to see that (1) it is fresh (old stories told from a new slant are as fresh as brand-new stories), (2) it is pertinent to the main theme of the speech, (3) it can be effectively related (your limitations as a storyteller should be considered), and (4) it is not offensive. The importance of this last quality cannot be overemphasized, especially if the story is a humorous one. In your audience analysis, look for any information that would alert you to matters of taste. Generally speaking, it is wise to avoid stories that derive their humor from the ridicule of religion, racial origin, culture, or gender. Self-directed ridicule is, perhaps, the safest form of humor in a story or an illustration. (See the treatment of illustrations in chapter 6 for additional guidelines.)

Reference to Recent Event or Occasion. Associating the theme of your speech with something currently in the news is another good way to make the audience attentive. For example, if you wanted to discuss the plight of migrant workers, you might refer to a newspaper article dealing with a local ordinance affecting hiring:

> Yesterday, the *Times* reported that the City Council is on the verge of passing an ordinance that would make it illegal to try to hire migrant workers off the streets. This kind of action will deprive a large number of migrant workers of their principal means of support.

By associating your theme with a recent happening, you impart an air of freshness and immediacy to your ideas that is likely to make the audience want to listen further. Notice in the next example that the student captured attention by directly linking her introduction to a common and current event:

> I would suspect all of you were appalled last week when you saw your television screens filled with pictures of the riot that took place at the local amusement park.

Referring to the occasion is often an excellent technique if you have to make a speech at a formal occasion, such as a banquet, a graduation ceremony, a dedication, an induction of club members, a special lecture, or any situation where the occasion is the central reason people have gathered. In your core speech, a formal reference to the occasion would seem "stuffy" and affected. However, if your sailing club or the debate team were gathering to hand out awards, it would be highly appropriate to open with a reference to the occasion. For example, "You are here today because you are the best! You have worked hard every day for over a year, and tonight we are to recognize your efforts."

Rhetorical Question. At this moment, try not to think of your first roller coaster ride. Whatever you do, make sure you do not picture that ride. You are probably unable to keep that experience from your mind at this moment. The reason is simple; the brain has a mind of its own, and it does not take much to activate it. This concept is the idea behind rhetorical questions.

A rhetorical question "forces" the listener to want the answer to the question the speaker poses. A skillfully phrased question creates a feeling of suspense that makes the audience want to "stay tuned." However, not just any question will do; it must make the audience eager for an answer. Lacking that element, a rhetorical question is ineffectual as an attention device. Naturally, what makes an audience curious for an answer depends on the nature of that particular group of listeners. A group of entering freshmen would probably be attentive to a dean of admissions who asked this rhetorical question at an orientation meeting: "How many of you will still be in college next year to start your sophomore year?" However, a group of chemistry majors would hardly come to attention on hearing a speaker ask them, "Where can you buy a first edition of Hugh Blair's *Lectures on Rhetoric and Belles Lettres* for only 48 cents?" Their unspoken answer probably would be, "I don't know and I don't care." However, if that question were addressed to an audience of graduate students of rhetoric or to a group of dedicated bibliophiles, it might have an electrifying effect. It is evident, then, that you need to know something of your listeners' interests before you plan your strategy.

In using rhetorical questions, you can begin with just one ("Ever wonder what it would be like to work alongside a robot?" "Do you know who was the only American President to win the Pulitzer Prize?"), or you can ask a series of questions:

> What would you do if, at this very second, the person sitting next to you fainted? Would you just sit there? Would you try to help? What kind of help would you offer? Would you wonder if you were doing the right thing?

Startling Statement or Fact.Perhaps your audience analysis will reveal that your listeners are likely to feel apathetic about your topic. In that case, you can usually make them attentive by saying something about your subject that is startling. A speaker wanting to talk about the ease with which someone can secure a handgun started with the following startling statement: "I could, at this moment, take a gun out of my pocket and point it directly at any of you. This is how easy it is to secure a weapon in our city."

A startling statement can be very useful when you have to introduce a speech on a familiar theme, such as asking for contributions to the American Cancer Society or urging people to wear seat belts or stop smoking. In such cases, you can refer to audience members in a startling statement—for instance:

> Isn't it too bad about these three people sitting in the front row? They are going to be hospitalized for quite a while—probably long enough to exhaust all their savings. They may have to sell everything they own—car, furniture, even their homes.

Undoubtedly, the "three people" would be startled by this introduction, and it is likely that the remainder of the audience would find their curiosity aroused. To be effective, the startling statement or fact, like all attention-seeking devices, should be relevant to the topic and should be based on an understanding of the audience. It is easy to see that indiscriminate use of this device could be self-defeating.

Unusual facts related to the topic of a speech can also arouse interest. In a speech dealing with how to identify counterfeit money, a speaker started with this fact: "Did you ever notice that all 50 states are listed across the top of the Lincoln Memorial on the back of a five-dollar bill?" Yet another speaker, talking on how to improve spelling habits, began her talk with the following fact: "Did you know that there are only four words in the English language that end in 'dous'—they are tremendous, horrendous, stupendous, and hazardous."

As you recall, many introductions work in combination. Therefore, you might find many occasions when your startling statement takes the form of a rhetorical question: "How many of you realize that the United States, with only 5 percent of the world's population, has more greenhouse emissions than any other country on earth?"

Humor. In chapter 15, when we examine special occasion speeches, we will deal with the topic of humor in great detail. However, because it is an effective attention-getting device, we need to touch briefly on humor at this time.

Humor, if relevant to the topic and done in good taste, can get a speech off to an excellent start. The following humorous anecdote was used to open a speech about the importance of being able to adapt to any situation:

> A doctor at the health service office for our university had an urgent call from a student. The student told the doctor his roommate had accidentally swallowed his fountain pen. The doctor told the student to bring his roommate to the office. The doctor then asked the student what he had been doing since the accident. The student replied, 'Using a pencil.'

It is important that the humor point the audience in the direction of the topic. In the next example, the speaker planned to talk about cultural differences in the use of language. To arouse attention while introducing the topic, she used the following humorous opening:

> A Frenchman learning English said his teacher noted that English is a strange language. He asked, 'What does this mean—"Should Ms. Noble, who

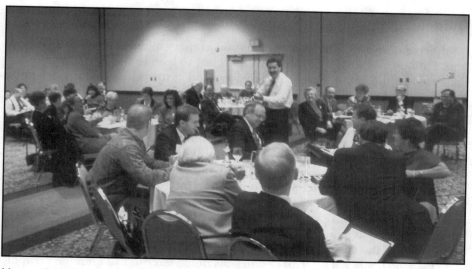

Humor, if relevant to the topic and done in good taste, can get a speech off to an excellent start. (Photo: Randall Reeder)

sits for this constituency, consent to stand again, she will in all probability have a walkover"?'

Humor, as an introduction, may even take the form of a joke. In a speech dealing with exercising, a student told the following joke she had heard at an Ellen DeGeneres concert:

> The comedian Ellen DeGeneres knows about exercising first-hand. She recently noted that her grandmother started walking five miles a day when she was 60. And today she is about 97 and they don't know where she is.

For a speech before a group of science teachers a speaker started with the following joke:

> Two atoms are walking down the street and they run into each other. One says to the other, 'Are you all right?' 'No, I lost an electron!' 'Are you sure?' 'Yes, I am positive.'

In using humor, make sure that you are not offensive and that your humor relates to the topic you will be discussing.

Visual and Audio Aids. In chapter 7, we discussed how visual aids can both clarify an idea and arouse interest. This twofold advantage makes visual aids excellent devices for starting a speech. A few examples from recent student speeches using visual aids will demonstrate the utility of these tools.

To create interest in a speech on animal abuse, a speaker simply started by turning on a VCR that showed a tape of lions and bears being kept in extremely small quarters. For a speech dealing with the earliest stages of organized culture, another student had a transparency projected on a screen of a mural from a subterranean cave in France that dated back 40,000 years. To persuade an audience that schools need to teach more geography, a student had a map on the board and asked the audience if they could identify the 10 major countries outlined on the map. Finally, in a speech dealing with the history of jazz, another student began her talk simply by having the audience listen to some music. As you might suspect, this approach captured everyone's attention.

Guidelines in Using Introductions

Keep a number of ideas in mind as you prepare and deliver your introduction. First, *be creative.* What this means is not to leap to the first introduction that crosses your mind, but instead put yourself in the position of the listeners. Ask yourself if the introduction you have selected will make them stop whatever they are doing and focus on you and your message. If your truthful answer is "yes," you have a good and innovative introduction.

Second, *put off preparing your introduction until you have worked on the body of your talk.* You will usually find that an idea for a compelling and interesting introduction will emerge from the body of your speech. We fear that too many novice speakers start their preparation by deciding on an introduction simply because it is the first words an audience will hear. Again, this is a bad plan of action in that it forces you to think about an introduction before you have been exposed to all aspects of your topic—aspects that will be developed in the body of the speech.

Third, *do not begin with an apology.* As noted later in this chapter, an apology is appropriate in cultures such as the Japanese, but it is not a useful device in the United States. You lower your credibility, and will not get much sympathy, if you start by telling your audience that you did not have much time to prepare or that you do not know much about the subject. It is better to find the time to prepare and learn about the subject rather than having to apologize. The American author Ralph Waldo Emerson offered much the same advice when he wrote, "No sensible person has ever had to make an apology." I would add— a well-prepared speaker does not have to begin with an apology.

Fourth, *plan on spending a great deal of time preparing your introduction.* As I stated at the outset of this chapter, first impressions are important, and the introduction is part of that first impression.

Fifth, *do not make the introduction too brief.* While there is a natural tendency to want to get to the main points of the speech, you need to remember that a good introduction is not only intended to arouse attention, but is also a period that allows the audience to cease what they were doing and begin to focus in on you. This redirection of attention may take some time; the introduction furnishes that time. You also need to guard against taking an extreme position with regard to advice and offering your listeners an introduction that is too long.

Finally, *avoid using a senseless or tasteless gimmick to open your talk.* There is a big difference between a creative introduction and one that is pointless and inane. The audience will be offended if you try to get their attention by pointing a weapon at them, pulling a rattlesnake out of a burlap sack, wearing ridiculous clothing, or screaming out in a terrifying manner for no apparent reason.

Preparing Your Audience for the Speech

Once you have obtained the favorable attention of your audience, then you need to get them ready for what is to come. On many occasions they will, of course, have an idea of your topic by the material you included in your opening remarks. If you tell a story of a drunk driving accident or show a video of abused animals, the audience will know the general nature of what you plan to discuss. However, under normal circumstances, one or more of the following things will need to be done in order to prepare your audience adequately: (1) justify the topic, (2) delimit the topic, (3) present your speaking credentials, (4) define your terms, (5) provide background information, and (6) establish a common ground with the audience. Again, depending on the time you are allotted, the type of speech you are presenting, the composition of your audience, and the topic, you might combine some of these tasks.

Justify the Topic

When your listeners have not gathered for the express purpose of hearing you talk about a given topic, you need to offer them a reason for listening.

> Having listened to me for the last few minutes you are aware that I am going to talk about the demise of many local newspapers in the United States. Perhaps you are now saying, Why should I listen? Well, let me tell you why this topic concerns you.

What the speaker will now do is demonstrate why this topic is relevant to this audience.

In speeches to inform, the justification of the topic usually deals with the question, "Why do you need this information?" In a speech to persuade, it answers questions such as "How does this issue affect you?" and "Why should you be concerned about this problem and its solution?" If traffic around the campus was causing severe delays, you could easily justify the topic of plans for remedies of the traffic problem.

Sometimes the device used for gaining attention can also justify the topic. For example, a rhetorical question may provoke attention and instill a need for information—"How many of you realize that a lack of exercise can adversely affect nearly every part of your body?"

Delimit the Topic

You may find it necessary to draw the boundaries of your discussion when approaching certain topics. If you were to say, "Today I'm going to talk about AIDS," you might cause the audience to anticipate any number of possibilities. Will you be discussing treatment methods? Future research directions? Legislative efforts to require universal testing for AIDS? Where AIDS is most frequently encountered? In such cases, it may be good for you to point out what you are going to exclude as well as what you are going to include in your discussion. By doing so, you enable your listeners to adjust their expectations accordingly. If listeners know the boundaries of your discussion, they can listen more efficiently.

There are occasions when it is unwise to indicate the boundaries of your discussion, especially if the creation of suspense is essential to the accomplishment of your purpose. (Be sure this is not a rationalization resulting from confusion in your own mind about the boundaries of your discussion.)

Presenting Your Speaking Credentials (Establishing Credibility)

If your authority (credibility) to speak on a subject is not known to your listeners, you may need to establish it during the early part of the speech. On some occasions this would be done for you by the person introducing you to the audience, but, if the introducer fails to do so (or if there is no introduction), the task falls on you. How shall you make your credentials known? This can usually be accomplished without creating the impression of immodesty. Following are a few examples:

> I want to share with you some information about human nutritional needs that I learned in my health science class last semester.

> I know you are all familiar with the jokes about the preacher's son. As a preacher's son, I'd like to set the record straight about what it is really like to be a member of a minister's family.

> I've long been intrigued by the story of the duel between Alexander Hamilton and Aaron Burr. What series of events led to the duel? Could it have been avoided? What might have been the consequences of a peaceful solution to their differences? Speculation about these matters has been one of the subjects of a history seminar I'm taking. Today, I want to give you the results of my inquiry into this famous incident in our nation's early history.

> You have read and heard about the dangerous aspects of street gangs. From second- and third-hand sources, you have been exposed to the violence associated with gangs. Well, I was a gang member in junior and senior high school, so I can tell you first-hand about this lifestyle. I know from my own experiences why people join gangs and how they can get out of them. Let me share some of these observations with you during the next 10 minutes.

> For 40 days last summer, I was with a group of other students who hiked through the mountains of Tibet. I visited many places so far removed from civilization that some villagers had never seen outsiders. The villages had no electricity, no running water, and no roads for vehicles. Today, I would like to share some of my experiences with you.

If your authority to speak on a subject is not known to your listeners, you may need to establish it during the speech.

Defining Your Terms   ❖ ❖ ❖ ❖

On some occasions, your subject might involve special terminology, jargon, or technical vocabulary that should be defined early in the speech. If your subject is dealing with computers, you may want to define words such as *interface, integrated circuit, megabyte,* and *microprocessor* early in your talk. One student, speaking on the importance of proper eye care, defined *myopia, hyperopia, astigmatism, cataracts,* and *glaucoma* during the introductory portion of her talk. You can set aside part of the introduction to define all the terms to be used, or you can define each term when it first appears in the speech.

Remember that defining terms and concepts takes on added significance when you are talking to a culturally diverse audience. For example, if your subject is drugs in the workplace and your audience is composed of people new to the United States, you may need to explain such things as the differences between depressants and stimulants. For people from countries other than the United States, even differences between "over-the-counter" and "prescription" drugs might need clarification.

We should add that on many occasions speakers often find it useful to define terms as they are introduced to the audience for the first time.

Providing Background Information

Sometimes your listeners cannot gain a full appreciation or understanding of your subject unless they are familiar with certain background information, often in the form of historical details. To discuss a great event without indicating the historical context in which it occurred is to deny listeners an important dimension for understanding this event.

Supplying background information is an important consideration if the audience members are not familiar with the major premises of your speech. For example, a student talked about the historical aspects of African-American culture before she moved to the main sections of her speech, which dealt with the differences between forced and selected immigration. She contended that this information had to be given early in the speech so that the audience could clearly understand the points she wanted to make later in her talk.

Other background materials may be physical in nature. For example, if you want the audience to sense the magnitude of the Grand Canyon, you have to put it in a physical context. How does it compare to the size of other topographical features with which the audience might be familiar? To give an audience a notion of the grandeur of the Lincoln Memorial, you have to put it in a physical context. An architect's genius cannot be fully appreciated by simply examining the building he or she designed. One has to see how the building integrates with its physical environment.

Establishing Common Ground

Occasionally, you are forced to take an unpopular stand on a controversial issue. If you wish to win audience support for your position, you must pave the way carefully. One method is the establishment of a common ground of belief between you and the audience. Essentially, it means that you will take pains to stress the areas in which you and the audience agree before you turn to the issues on which you and your audience hold divergent viewpoints. For instance, if you are eventually going to advocate that certain areas of a park should no longer be used by people on motorcycles, you might want to begin by talking about what is happening to the plants and animals in the park. By establishing an interest in plants and animals, you might be building common ground.

Conceivably, if the audience is from a culture vastly different from your own, this act of establishing a common ground could occupy a major share of your speech. For example, if a speaker from Japan wanted to talk on how quality circles are useful in problem solving, he might have to demonstrate how the organization of these groups is much like groups the audience is already familiar with.

Introductions and Culture

A major theme of this book is that not all cultures approach communication in the same manner, nor do they necessarily have the same communication patterns. The topic of introductions is a clear example of how culture and communication are interrelated. As noted earlier, the whole idea of a speech having an introduction, a body, and a conclusion is a Western concept. In many cultures, people simply start talking without any concern for having to gain attention and interest. Let us look at three cultural variations in starting a speech so that you will be able to appreciate the role of culture in forming introductions.

First, it is not uncommon for people from Japan to start their talk with an apology. Being modest and humble is highly valued in their culture. Therefore, to reflect that deferential attitude, a speaker may start by implying that she wishes she could have had more time to prepare or that she hopes the speech will benefit the listeners. If your audience is composed of many people from Japan, you might attempt to offer a mild apology as part of your introduction:

> I know all of you are familiar with my topic, so I don't want to tell you what you already know, but, if you are patient with me, I might be able to add to what you have already learned about this important subject.

Second, in Latin American cultures, establishing rapport and feeling comfortable with the people you are around is very important. Hence, if you were talking to people from Mexico or any other Latin culture, it would be wise to spend some time putting everyone in a relaxed and amiable mood before you go to the body of your talk.

Third, in Western cultures, people often admire the speaker who is witty and clever, has a keen sense of humor, and can begin a speech with a joke. This book has recommended that you use humor as a method of gaining attention. However, I must alert you to the fact that while laughing is universal, many cultures believe that the telling of jokes is the domain of the professional comedian, not the public speaker. They believe that people get paid for telling jokes and that the occasion of speechmaking is a serious matter.

Preparing the Conclusion

All too often, speeches end with these words: "Well, I guess that's about all." Judge for yourself whether this ending accomplishes the desired functions of a speech conclusion: (1) Does it redirect the audience's attention to the central point of the speech and tie together the main content of the speech? (2) Does it conduct the listener into the frame of mind that should be dominant at the end? (3) Does it leave the listener with a sense of completeness?

There is a tendency for beginning speakers to give less thought to the preparation of the conclusion than to any other portion of the speech, yet the conclusion can be a critical part of the speech. A poor conclusion can undermine all the speaker has accomplished to that point. It is in order, then, to examine some of the possible means of ending a speech effectively.

Summary

A brief recapitulation, or summary, of the main points of the speech is a common device used in concluding. It is particularly valuable in instructional speeches because it reinforces the instructions that the speaker wishes the audience to recall. For example, in concluding a speech on the fundamentals of tennis, a speaker could use a summary in the following manner: "Today you learned some of the elementary techniques of tennis; when you're on the court, try to remember that (1) you should always keep your eye on the ball, (2) you should keep your arm firm, and (3) your swing should follow through." In another informative speech, offering smokers some tips on how to discontinue the habit, the speaker used a summary in the following manner:

> During the last 15 minutes, five important points were made concerning how you could quit smoking. First, I suggested that you set a specific date to quit; second, consider some of the healthy alternatives I recommended; third, remove reminders of smoking; fourth, avoid settings that you associate with smoking; and finally, drink plenty of water. Good luck. I am sure you will be successful.

Yet another speaker, informing her audience about Buddha's notion of Right Speech, ended with this summary:

> So today we learned about what the Buddha meant by Right Speech. For Buddha, Right Speech meant no deceit, false witness, gossip, or slander.

In persuasive speeches, a summary can remind listeners that sound reasons have been advanced for the belief the speaker wishes them to hold or for the action he or she wishes them to take. In the following example, from a speech on trial by jury, the speaker reminded the listeners of a point she had stressed throughout the speech:

> Today, we have seen that trial by jury is costly and time consuming, and it often produces unfair decisions. This is why I urge you to support the plan that would replace all jury trials with a panel of three experts.

Usually, a summary is used in conjunction with other concluding devices, because by itself it may not accomplish all the purposes of a conclusion that we have discussed. For instance, the student in the previous example added the following lines to her speech as a means of intensifying her main thesis:

> If we don't change this antiquated system of justice, we will all be guilty of sending innocent people to jail because we let their fate be decided by twelve people who had absolutely no expertise in dealing with legal matters. If you thought you needed surgery, you would want a doctor to decide the seriousness of your problem. Why, then, do we allow untrained 'strangers' to decide legal problems?

Quotations

The journalist Hendrik Van Loon once wrote that "somewhere in the world there is a quotation for everything." We have already seen that a quotation can serve as an effective opening of a speech; it can, with equal effectiveness, serve as part of the conclusion.

In a speech dealing with the need for ethical standards in government, a student used to following quotation to end his speech:

> The Civil War Senator Henry Clay knew the importance of moral character in government when he said, over one hundred years ago, 'Of all the properties which belong to honorable men, not one is so highly prized as that of character.'

Another speaker, talking about the difficulties in understanding other cultures, ended with the following quotation by the English author Rudyard Kipling:

> Oh East is East, and West is West, and never the twain shall meet, Till Earth and Sky stand presently at God's great Judgment Seat.

At times it is an effective technique to have two quotations from the same person, citing one quotation at the outset of the speech and the other at the end. In a speech on the topic of ecology, a student was able to use two excellent quotations by Walt Whitman, the first to open the talk and the second to end the speech:

Introduction

> I believe a leaf of grass is no less than the journey-work of the stars, And the pismire is equally perfect, and a grain of sand, and the egg of the wren, And the tree toad is chef-d'oeuvre for the highest, And the running blackberry would adorn the parlors of heaven.

Conclusion

> The earth does not argue, Is not pathetic, has no arrangements, Does not scream, haste, persuade, threaten, promise, Makes no discriminations, has no conceivable failures, Closes nothing, refuses nothing, shuts none out.

You might find that an opening quotation could be repeated at the end of the speech. This is often a very effective rhetorical technique. Whatever quotation you choose, it should meet the tests of relevance, good taste, and impact.

Illustration or Story   ❖ ❖ ❖ ❖

An illustration, like a quotation, can be used as effectively in the conclusion as it can be in the introduction. You will find it particularly useful as a means of visualizing for your listeners the importance of the ideas you have discussed in the body of your speech. A hypothetical illustration works well in that the characters in the story are the members of the audience. In a speech on the topic of government-sponsored immunization for young children, a speaker ended her talk with the following hypothetical illustration:

> As I said during my speech, it would cost the government only five dollars per child to immunize the children of this country against six diseases that threaten all of them. Should the government refuse to be part of such a program, you might see the day when your child comes down with a crippling disease that could have been avoided by a simple vaccination. Imagine how you would feel if your little boy or girl was the one lying in a hospital bed because our government did not grant the funds necessary for this program.

Illustrations distill the essence of your message and present it in a form that makes it memorable to listeners. If the prevailing mood of your speech has been very sober, then you might find that an illustration or a story in a light vein can provide the touch needed to leave the audience in the right frame of mind. A student concluded a speech dealing with cultural differences in the perception of death with the following humorous anecdote:

> One of the main points of my speech is that cultures do not agree as to what happens at the end of life. Well, cultures are not alone; most individuals don't know for sure about an afterlife. Comedian George Burns worked for over thirty years with his wife, Gracie Allen. After her death, he visited her grave regularly. Someone once asked him if he told Gracie what was going on in his life. 'Sure, why not?' was his reply. 'I don't know whether she hears me, I have never been dead, but I've nothing to lose and it gives me a chance to break in new material.'

We recently heard a speaker use a story about Henry David Thoreau to end her speech on the importance of standing up for your beliefs:

> Today I have urged you to be true to your convictions. We can use the American author Thoreau as our model. When Thoreau was languishing in jail after he had refused to pay the Massachusetts poll tax because he believed it was unjust, his friend Ralph Waldo Emerson came to visit him. During the conversation Emerson asked Thoreau why he was in jail. Thoreau answered by saying, 'Why are you *not* here?'

Challenge

Speeches designed to stimulate the audience to greater efforts or stronger devotion to a cause or an ideal often end with a challenge: "If we all work together, we can stop the land developers from making our city one large parking lot and shopping mall. I implore you to help me preserve the little bit of open space we have left in our town." Occasionally, an informative speech can also use this kind of ending if the speaker wishes the audience to seek more information about the subject that was discussed in the body of the speech. In any case, the challenge should be worded so as to encourage a spirit of confidence in the audience's capacity to meet the challenge. The earlier example concerning smoking could have ended in a challenge and with encouragement if the speaker had elected to say, "I have no doubts that, with willpower, determination, and a strong resolve, you will stop this unhealthy habit and join the millions of others who have said 'no' to smoking."

One of the most famous uses of the challenge was that issued by John F. Kennedy in his inaugural address, the much quoted "Ask not what your country can do for you—ask what you can do for your country."

Declaration of Intent

Speeches intended to induce action can be concluded effectively when the speaker sets an example for the audience by declaring what he or she personally plans to do. "I will be the first one. I have now fastened a donor tack to my driver's license. Please join me in this action so that other people can enjoy life after you are gone." Patrick Henry's famous closing remarks in his "Liberty or Death" speech are a well-known example of this concluding device.

Recently a student used declaration of intent when she said the following:

> I will not stop working for the homeless in our community until every single person on the street has a warm place to sleep and hot food to eat. To do less would be closing my eyes to the suffering of those who live but a few miles from where we are sitting at this very instant.

Alluding to the Introduction

Returning to the introduction of your speech is often an effective method of concluding your talk. You can reestablish your introduction in a variety of ways. For example, if you start with a rhetorical question, you might end by restating the same question, but now you can offer the answer:

> I asked you 10 minutes ago if you knew what to do if an earthquake were to take place at this instant. Now, when I ask that question, the answer should be 'yes.'

You can also return to the introduction by finishing an illustration you started at the beginning of the talk:

> We now know we have to do something about domestic violence. We may not have faced situations like the one that confronted Susan. Remember, she had no place to go and no one to turn to. The new downtown center for battered women will now give people like Susan somewhere to go and people to comfort and protect her.

Guidelines in Using Conclusions

In planning your conclusion, keep some of the following ideas in mind. First, *practice the conclusion so that it does not wander aimlessly*. Too many speakers fail to develop an incisive conclusion and thus end up dragging it out for a long period of time as they drone on about insignificant issues. Second, having just asked you not to elongate your conclusion I now suggest that you *avoid ending too abruptly*. Because some speakers have failed to prepare an effective conclusion, they end without giving the audience any warning.

Again, balance and moderation are the keys. Third, *try not to add any new points to the conclusion of your talk.* If something is simply tossed in at the end, it will only confuse the audience and detract from your specific purpose. Fourth, *regardless of the form your conclusion takes, it should stress your strongest ideas.* Remember that it will be the last thing your audience hears before you sit down. Finally, just as you should not begin with an apology, you should also avoid ending by apologizing. Apologies, at least in the culture of the United States, have the appearance of reducing one's credibility.

Summary

After designing the body of the speech, the speaker must give considerable thought to the introduction and conclusion. An introduction gains attention and prepares the audience for the remainder of the speech. Among the methods of gaining attention are quotations, illustrations or stories, references to recent events or occasions, rhetorical questions, startling statements, humor, and visual aids. An introduction also justifies and delimits the topic, offers an opportunity to present your speaking credentials, defines key terms, provides background information, and establishes common ground.

The conclusion redirects the audience's attention to the core statement and tries to give the audience a sense of completeness. Some methods of concluding are summary, quotation, illustration or story, challenge, declaration of intent, and allusion to the introduction.

Concepts and Questions

1. What should the introduction accomplish?

2. Why is it important to have a good introduction?

3. Why is it important to have a good conclusion?

4. What is the purpose behind using the introduction to prepare the audience for the body of the speech?

5. What is the rationale behind using rhetorical questions as a device for starting a speech?

6. Why is restating your main points one of the purposes of a summary?

Activities and Exercises

1. Locate three quotations for a speech dealing with "patience."

2. Write three rhetorical questions for any of the following topics:
   a. Study habits.
   b. Exercise.
   c. Donor cards.

3. Listen to a political speaker. Write a short essay discussing the speaker's introduction and conclusion.

4. Select any subject that interests you. Try to think of as many ways as possible to introduce that topic to a group of people who have no interest in the topic.

5. Give a two-minute speech to your classmates that begins with some form of humor. ✦

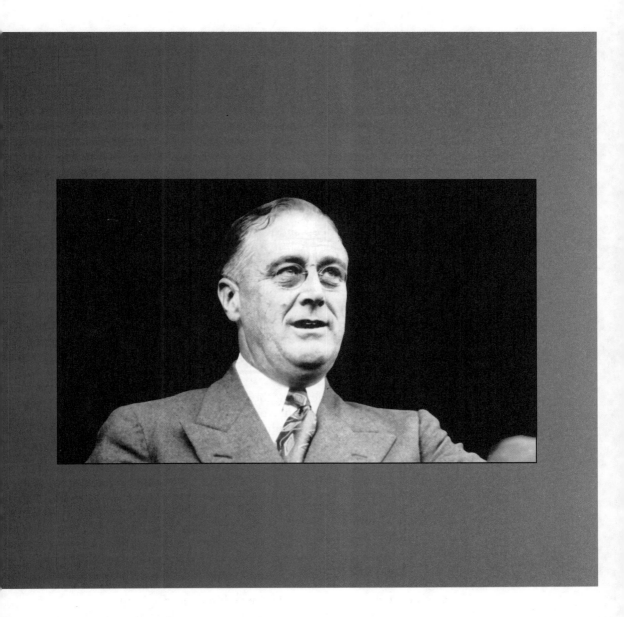

CHAPTER TWELVE

Language:
The Medium
of Your Ideas

> Why does language provide such a fascinating
> object of study? Perhaps because of its unique role in
> capturing the breadth of human thought and endeavor.
>
> —*David Crystal*

A Yiddish proverb states, "Words should be weighed and not counted." There is no better way to start this chapter on language than with the wisdom contained in those seven words, because they alert us to the importance of the words we select. However, because words come so easily to most of us, we have a tendency to forget both their importance and their force on human behavior. To underestimate the power of language is a mistake, for words can call up vivid mental images; they can change the way we think and even the way we act. Depending on how we use them, they are capable of bringing other people great joy or deep sadness. Words are indeed magisterial and must be used with great care. As the American philosopher Tryon Edwards wrote, "Words are both better and worse than thoughts; they express them, and add to them; they give them power for good or evil; they start them on an endless flight, for instruction and comfort and blessing, or for injury and sorrow and ruin."

The Importance of Language

For students of communication, there can be no topic of greater importance than language, for with your words you express your ideas and share your internal states. You would be living a solitary life if you could not tell others what you know and what you want to know. One of the charming aspects of language is that you can make choices as to what words to use. With practice, you can learn to choose words consciously and purposefully—words that help you accomplish your purpose and let you exercise some control over your environment. This chapter is about making the proper choices. However, at the outset remember to be ever vigilant and meticulous when you make those choices. Words are powerful and once they are received they have a commanding effect on people. The words of the English writer Robert Burton said it even more eloquently, "A blow with a word strikes deeper than a blow with a sword."

Have you ever stopped to consider just what language is and what its possibilities and limitations might be? Have you seriously examined the way in which you use this valuable gift? Are you making the most of your ability to use words or are you, like most people, content to use only three to four thousand words from a potential "list" of nearly a million? These are some of the matters addressed in this chapter. First, we will talk about the need to be aware of some general characteristics of language in order to use language to your advantage, and, second, we will discuss some techniques of language use that you need to develop in order to become an effective speaker. And finally, we will offer some advice as to how you might be able to improve your use of language.

Understanding How Language Works

If you understand something about how language operates, you are able to make intelligent decisions concerning which words to select and which to reject as you seek to accomplish your speaking purpose. For example, if you know that your listeners' backgrounds and cultures influence the meaning they attach to words, you will choose words that are commensurate with their experiences.

Let us start with a definition of language. **Language** *may be thought of as an organized system of symbols, both verbal and nonverbal, used in a common and uniform way by persons who are able to manipulate these symbols to express and communicate their thoughts and feelings.* Words are the symbols used in verbal language, just as certain gestures, movements, and facial expressions are the symbols of nonverbal language. (We examined nonverbal symbols in chapter 4, when we discussed the topic of delivery.)

Words Are Only Symbols

The English philosopher John Locke once noted that "Words, their primary or immediate signification, stand for nothing but the ideas in the mind of him who uses them." We begin by offering this quotation because it clearly identifies the most important idea concerning language and symbols. In rather unadorned terms, we can say that symbols stand for something else—and what they stand for is in the head of the person who uses them or hears them. In short, *words, the symbols used in verbal communication, are substitutes for "the real things."* Try as you will, you cannot eat the word *apple* or drive the word *car*. Words only represent the things—in this case, *apple* and *car*. It is important to remember that there is no necessary relationship between a word and the thing it symbolizes. In reality, words are only sounds or scratches on paper that we use to talk about the one that is in our heads. In this sense, you need to appreciate that we actually live in two different

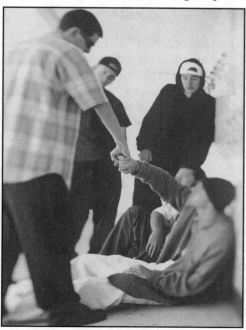

Private codes refer to the language whose meanings are agreed upon by a specialized segment of the community. (Photo: indexstock.com)

worlds: the one made up of words and the one composed of what the words stand for. In short, words are arbitrary symbols. People who share the same culture and language have simply agreed that a certain sound or combination of sounds stands for a given thing, concept, or experience. The word "elephant" could just as easily represent a winged creature if people were to agree to that meaning.

As a speaker, it is important to always remember this simple yet profound notion that language is symbolic and that words have no meaning in themselves. They only mean what people think they mean. This realization should guide you in your selection of the words you finally decide upon. Words are the tools you use as you attempt to share your reality, but because they are only symbols they can, as the English novelist Joseph Conrad reminds us, "be the great foe of reality."

Words Have Many Uses

A common problem encountered in our use of language involves the belief that every word has but one meaning. This, of course, is simply not true. In fact, the 2,000 words most frequently used have approximately 14,000 different meanings. In your vocabulary, you probably have countless words with multiple meanings and uses. The word *cat*, for example, can refer to a jazz musician, a form of tractor, a type of fish, a type of boat, or a whip. In similar fashion, the word *lap* can represent the distance around a track, a portion of one's anatomy, the drinking method of a cat or dog, or the sound of water washing gently against the side of a boat. And the simple word *flush* can mean becoming red in the face, water rushing and flowing, chasing an animal out from a hiding place, being level with another surface, or a hand of cards in poker. A quick glance at any page of the dictionary will yield thousands of words with multiple meanings.

Thus far, our examples of multiple meanings have been rather unostentatious and plain (cat, lap, and flush). What happens when the words you select are complex and controversial? Do the meanings for the following words and phrases have a single, one-to-one relationship: *human rights, obscene, sexuality, gay, liberal, conservative,* and *right to life?* The answer to the question is "no." There is indeed more than one meaning and interpretation for each of these words, and when you add the variable of culture, the meanings become even more confounded and ambiguous. How would you express a meaning for the phrases *laptop computer, affirmative action, cellular phone,* and *car jacking* to someone from a culture that does not have these experiences or expressions as part of its working vocabulary?

We conclude this section on a word's multiple meaning by asking that you reflect on the wisdom contained in the following quotation offered by former Chief Justice Oliver Wendell Holmes, Jr.: "A word is not a crystal, transparent and unchanged, it is the skin of a living thought and may vary greatly in color and content according to the circumstances and the time in which it is used."

Words Evoke Denotative and Connotative Meanings

We have already explored the idea that when someone selects a particular word, he or she is not using it in precisely the same way someone else might use it. Because meanings exist only in the mind, not in the object, thing, or concept being described, people possess different meanings for the same word. Meanings are also affected by the denotative and connotative aspects of words. Let us look at each of these dimensions of meaning and see how they affect communication.

Denotative Meaning. When someone asks the meaning of a word you have just used, he or she is usually seeking its denotative meaning. *The denotative meaning is the one that society has sanctioned as the "official" or literal meaning of a word, the meaning furnished by the dictionary.* It is often referred to as the "core" meaning of a word. Denotative meanings are somewhat impartial and neutral, and seldom contain emotional overtones. There can be general agreement as to what is a car, tree, chair, table, and the like. As we discussed earlier, however, the dictionary may furnish several "official" meanings for a given word. The word "land, for example, is variously defined as the solid portion of the earth's surface, as a country or nation, as a piece of real estate, as the act of arriving at a destination, and as the act of catching a quarry such as a fish or gaining a prize such as a job.

The context in which a person uses a word usually suggests its intended denotative meaning. Dictionary definitions ordinarily are phrased in nonjudgmental language. They tend to be factual and concrete. These denotative meanings normally cause public speakers very little trouble. It is in the second category of meaning, connotative, where problems arise.

Connotative Meaning. *Connotative meaning is the private, emotional meaning that the word evokes.* It is the meaning that reflects your personal experiences and feelings with the thing or event the word represents. The connotations you have for a word are more likely to determine your response than the denotations, because you learned most of your connotative meanings through subjective experiences. For example, when you hear the word *plumber,* you may think of the quiet little man who solved your drain problem in five minutes and charged you less than half the usual amount for a service call, or you may be reminded of the fast-talking con artist who discovered that you had 20 other problems with your plumbing that needed immediate attention. Even the word *dog* can elicit powerful connotative meanings. Imagine your response to this word if you were badly bitten by a dog when you were a child. However, if you were raised around dogs, and had fond memories of dogs, your connotative meaning for the word would be positive.

Because connotations are more subtle and varied than denotations, they often cause confusion in intercultural transactions. Words such as *love, hate,* and *democracy* have a great number of connotations. For example, you may "love good food," "love your mate," "love your parents," and "love your country." The word *love* is the same in each instance, but the connotations are very different. Understanding the subtlety of these differences requires familiarity with a culture, which often take time to develop.

Words Convey a Partial Picture of Reality

Each of us sees the world in a restricted way because we perceive things selectively. Looking at the same city, many people might well observe different characteristics. One person might look at the city's buildings, while another notices its traffic, and a third observes the pollution in the sky. What is common with our example of a city applies to all the things in our surroundings—we notice some features of the outside world, and others we ignore.

What is true about perception is also true about language. That is to say, *at any one instant, we can talk about only a portion of reality*. This notion, often referred to as **allness**, is based on the assumption that when we say something about a "thing" or an idea, we are not saying all there is to say on the subject. In most instances, a great deal is being left out. This notion of "language leaving things out" can create numerous communication problems. Let us mention just of few of these obstacles.

What Have We Omitted? One problem with language is that on many occasions we are forced to omit accounts that may well be more important than the accounts included. If a friend tells you about her history class, she can tell you about only a small portion of that class. Most of what happened and what she saw and experienced must be left out. You may hear about the lectures, but what about the textbook? You may hear about the examinations, but what about the class activities? What you are always going to get will be but a small slice of her total reality, and that portion will be difficult to describe because she has to decide what to include and exclude. If someone asks you about your new car, you must select what to say. From your total impression of your car, you might say, "It is a black Ford." You have abstracted only part of your impression. Think for a moment of all the things you could have said. You could have said it was a 1997 truck with four-wheel drive and a cab on the back. Even with the added words, you could not say all there was to say about the truck. What is true of the simple examples of the truck and the history class is characteristic of all words. The concept is simple—no single word captures the total essence of what the word is trying to describe. The English poet Tennyson said much the same thing when he wrote, "Words, like Nature, half reveal / And half conceal the Soul within."

What Can We and What Can We Not Talk About? The details we can include in our verbal accounts of reality are limited by our vocabularies and our experiences. If we do not have a label (word) for something we perceive, it is very difficult to talk about it with any degree of clarity. A speaker would have a difficult time explaining a hospital's computerized axial topmography (CAT) scanner if his or her vocabulary did not contain the words necessary to talk about its essential processes and components. What we choose to say about a topic is also influenced by our personal experiences. If someone holds biased and prejudiced views toward African Americans, and you ask that person about the famous "I Have a Dream" speech by Martin Luther King, Jr., what he or she decides to tell you will be influenced by bigotry. As the German philosopher Friedrich Nietzsche observed, "Every word is a preconceived judgment." It is important, then, for us to remember that what we say is a reflection of our vocabulary and background and that we can never say everything about anything. What is equally important is that we realize that the limiting nature of language demands that we be exact when we select our symbols. Knowing that we will be leaving things out obliges us to choose the best possible words and phrases.

Words and Their Meanings Are Learned

Simply stated, *our meaning for any word is determined by our experiences with that word*. Put in slightly different terms, the meaning for any word grows out of the meaning we have learned for the word. As children, most of us asked our parents from time to time, "What does that word mean?" However, in most cases children learn the thousands of words they know simply by being exposed to those words. Because people often have different experiences, they will also have different words and meanings for those words. We hear the word *dog* and see a domesticated pet that is often a member of the family and might even sleep on the new furniture. In other parts of the world, however, *dog* elicits a different image and definition. In Hong Kong, China, and Korea, dogs are often considered to be food. Different personal and cultural experiences produce different definitions. It is important to remember that what is true with our elementary example of *dog* applies to ideas and concepts that are much more involved. Think for a moment of how people from different backgrounds and experiences might define words such as *abortion, AIDS, affirmative action, sexual harassment, free choice,* and *manifest destiny.*

Words Reflect Our Experiences

Because our experiences vary so will the words we use and our meaning for those words produces what are called *shared and private codes.*

Shared Codes. *Shared codes designate those aspects of language whose meanings are generally agreed upon by most members of the language community.* The words that fall under this category seldom evoke emotional responses. These words are somewhat like those we discussed when we examined denotative meanings. In public speaking, these words seldom cause problems.

Private Codes. *Private codes refer to the aspects of language whose meanings are agreed upon by a specialized segment of the language community.* These words can create problems for the speaker who has not thought about his or her audience. Private codes can take a variety of forms. For example, they may consist of both specialized words (RAM, memory cache) or specialized meanings for common words. See if you can determine the meaning of the following private code:

> There we were, we thought we were tanked. Sure to be a pickle boat when along come the black gasser. What a smooch. Three turkeys in front of us bottled immediately.

Taken from the community of sailboat racing, the foregoing prose is simply a description of how a poorly skippered boat almost sank the boat in question before a strong gust of wind came along and saved the day.

Private codes are common in professions and co-cultures. Horse trainers might know about a bug boy (apprentice jockey), chalk (the horse expected to win the race), and being rank (running down the racetrack in an erratic manner). In the same way, prostitutes would know the private meanings for terms such as date (a client), outlaw (a prostitute working with a pimp), COYOTE (a union of prostitutes), and "the life" (the world of prostitutes).

The last few paragraphs have emphasized that you must think about the other person during all stages of the preparation and communication process. Ask yourself these simple questions: What are the experiences of my audience, and how will these experiences influence the meaning they give to the words I use?

Language and Intercultural Communication

One of the major themes of this book has been that most of us now speak before audiences that are composed of people from a variety of cultures. Therefore, it behooves you to understand the role of language when speaking to these diverse audiences. Let me mention a few language variables that should be taken into consideration.

Idioms

When speaking to people who are not completely familiar with your language code, you could cause confusion. And often that confusion is compounded when you employ idioms. By definition, idioms are not capable of literal translation. Try to imagine how people who have English as a second language would interpret the following expressions:

There are people all over this world who are born with two strikes against them.

I will put this plan to the acid test by seeing how it deals with the nuts and bolts of the problem.

If we stop being wimps and adopt this plan, we will be able to stop beating our heads against a brick wall.

We need to be careful that the tail does not wag the dog.

Do not listen to John; he has an ax to grind.

The use of humor was so bad, Janet laid an egg.

Jane dropped the ball this time and is she ticked off.

What we need to do with this proposal is go tell David to take a hike.

He split a gut laughing to the point I thought he would have a cow.

If you don't think we are on the same wavelength, just give me a buzz.

We can no longer dilly dally; it is time to get off the dime.

After reading these examples, you should see the need to be aware of the language principle that words have many uses, some of which are tied directly to culture.

Ambiguity

Ambiguous language, which we will discuss in detail later this chapter, can also be troublesome when people have English as their second language. The word **ambiguity** actually means being able to be interpreted in more than one way. As you read some the examples cited below, try to put yourself in the place of listeners who are decoding what they hear by trying to give meaning to each word:

Today you need to consider that it is red tape that is holding up the new bridge.

Our local hospital is being sued by seven foot doctors.

Due to the new program high school dropouts are being cut in half.

Chef throws his heart into helping to feed the needy.

The stolen painting was found by the tree.

Mating of the panda has failed—the veterinarian will take over.

The police will now begin their campaign to run down jaywalkers.

Although these examples may have a humorous tone to them, they nevertheless demonstrate potential problems when one uses ambiguous language in intercultural communication.

Directness

It has been said that nothing distinguishes one culture from another better than how each uses language. Knowing some of those "uses" will help you when talking to people from cultures different from your own. Perhaps the major difference is in whose cultures use *direct* language and whose use indirect.

Direct. Most Americans are familiar with language that is direct because it is the style most common in the United Sates. This use of language is characterized by bluntness, explicit expressions, specific words, and a desire to be exact.

Indirect. Indirect language, which is found in most of the Southeast Asian cultures, is very different from direct language. Indirect language is less blunt and explicit than direct language. It is valued in these cultures because its use enables the speaker to maintain harmonious relationships. There is a belief in many cultures that follow the teachings of Buddhism and Confucianism that harmony in human relationships is crucial and that harmony is encouraged by speech that is not "acrimonious." In fact, Buddha actually talked about avoiding "harsh speech." This meant using language that not only was polite but was not curt. Even today Asian and East Asian cultures avoid using the word "no" whenever possible, because they believe the word "no" is too blunt and harsh.

Loquacity

The value placed on rhetorical eloquence must also be taken into consideration. For example, Arabic culture places a very high value on language. Members of this culture believe that the Arabic language is "God's language." Because of this high regard for language, speaking well is an important value among Arabs. We see this value reflected in the way Arabs speak. For instance, Arab language is often marked by embellishment, effective use of analogies and similes, repetition, and extended illustrations.

The Greek culture is yet another collection of people who place a high value on a person's use of language. Greeks have a long tradition that glorifies rhetorical techniques. The Greeks use a variety of key sayings and proverbs to express many feelings and ideas.

Formality

There are many cultures, such as the German and English, in which formality is a primary value in the use of language. When talking to audiences composed of people from these cultures, you need to avoid slang and other types of casual language patterns. If the culture values simplicity in the use of language (for example, Japanese, Chinese, Korean), you should not overstate your points. If the culture you are talking to values rhetorical artistry (for example, Arab and Mexican), you should aim for a grander and more commanding style. In all these instances, what is called for is a careful assessment of your audience, coupled with a sense of good taste.

There are also times when cultural attempts at adapting can backfire. This is especially true when speakers attempt to "speak the language" of certain co-cultures. An excellent example can be found in the engaging language used by African Americans. Many African Americans use a specialized vocabulary called **argot** to produce group solidarity. This unique language, composed of hundreds of words, grows out of the experiences found in the African American community. It would be folly and embarrassing if a European-American speaker tried to adapt to an African-American audience by using words such as *shucking, jiving, hussling, woofing, Charlie, bad*, and *oreo*. Such a speaker would not demonstrate an ability to "speak the language" but, instead, would display a lack of tact. The same is true of a middle-aged person who thinks he or she is being inspirational by telling a teenage audience to "take it to the max!" or saying "let's jam." Trying to make another culture's unique expressions one's own generally results in transparent artificiality. This sham is usually obvious and puts both the speaker and the audience in an awkward situation. Be yourself; to do otherwise is inappropriate and artificial.

One more word of caution is warranted if you are speaking to an audience composed of people who are not familiar with the North American culture. Your language should not make reference to examples that are rooted in the American experience. When you talk about the Hollywood Freeway, Plymouth Rock, or the Super Bowl, you are asking the listeners to know these expressions and what they refer to.

Now that you have an idea how words work, let us turn our attention to what constitutes the effective use of language.

Characteristics of Effective Style

Over 250 years ago, English author Jonathan Swift wrote, "Style may be defined as proper words in proper places." What was true then is true now. **Style** still means the manner in which someone chooses his or her words and strings them together. This selection process also takes into consideration the manner in which the words fit the audience and occasion. Saying the right thing, in the right way, at the right occasion is not a simple task. Therefore, we spend much of this chapter discussing how you can improve your style.

Effective Style Is Clear

Having just read about all the problems associated with language, you can see why clarity is perhaps the most indispensable of all the qualities of good style. It is especially important for a speaker's words to be understood by the listeners at the moment of encounter, because listeners, unlike readers, cannot stop to consult a dictionary and, in many instances, cannot even ask the speaker for clarification. Let us examine some of the ways you can make your message clear.

Oral Style Promotes Clarity. In chapter 1 we talked about how public speaking differs from the essay and from casual conversation. We will return to that earlier discussion and explore some specific ways an oral style can contribute to clarity.

Use rhetorical questions. You will recall that rhetorical questions are an excellent device to arouse attention. In addition, rhetorical questions, when phrased correctly, can point the material *directly* at the audience. These questions force your listeners to become mentally involved in the speech. If you were speaking on the subject of recycling, you would be using good oral style if you asked, "What percentage of your tax dollar would you estimate our city spends each year to dispose of our trash?" If your topic were violent behavior in our society, you could even ask a series of rhetorical questions to bring about a clear, interesting, and lively style: "Just how violent are we? How do we rank against the rest of the world in violent behavior? Why are we so violent?" As you can see from the example, rhetorical questions bring listeners into the communication process by offering language that is concise, compact, and clear.

Use repetition. Oral style uses more repetitions than does written style. In chapter 6, we talked about making your evidence clear by the generous use of transitions. You will recall the techniques of bridging and signposting as two methods of repeating your main ideas. In chapter 13, we examine even more formulas for effective repetition. In both chapters, the message is the same—in written communication, the audience can reread a paragraph or page and then move on; in public speaking, the speaker "turns the pages." Therefore, it is important that the audience understands what is going on at all times. Repetition is yet another way to ensure that understanding. If you had just made an important point regarding the overcrowding of prisons, you would further your cause by uttering the following words as a way of clarifying that point: "Having just seen that the prison population in the United States is now approaching the 900,000 mark, we can better appreciate just how serious the problem really is." The stylistic technique of repetition adds to clarity while reminding your listeners of what you deem important.

Parallel wording is a type of repetition that can add to clarity at the same time it makes an idea compelling. For example, if he or she says the following there can be little doubt as to the speaker's position on the death penalty:

> The death penalty was inhuman when it was conceived hundreds of years ago. The death penalty is inhuman as it is applied today. And the death penalty will continue to be inhuman if we use it in the future.

Use personal pronouns. Oral style is usually more personal than written style. Talking directly to someone and looking into his or her eyes enhance intimacy. So do the words you use. As we pointed out in the chapter on audience analysis, you "connect" with your audience when you use pronouns such as *you, we, us, our,* and *I*. Think about the impact of the following two sentences:

> One has to be very careful when deciding to take that final drink before getting into one's car.

❖ ❖ ❖ ❖   You need to be very careful when deciding to take that final drink before getting into your car.

To further personalize your material, you can use specific names from your audience: "John was telling me just the other day about his friend Robert, who got arrested for drunk driving during spring vacation."

Natural Language Promotes Clarity. We begin this section with advice from someone whose credibility on the use of language cannot be questioned—William Shakespeare. Over three hundred years ago, Shakespeare wrote, "When words are scarce they're seldom spent in vain." What he was telling us is that, whenever possible, use one word instead of two, a word with a clear meaning, and one sentence instead of two. Which is the clearer word in each of the following pairs?

Prevarication or lie?	Ennui or boredom?
Risible or laughable?	Sanguine or optimistic?
Betrothal or engagement?	Edifice or building?
Recapitulate or summarize?	Denouement or end?
Eschew or avoid?	Commence or begin?

Is the user of the first word in each pair really aiming for clarity, or is he or she trying to exhibit an impressive vocabulary? Simpler words generally increase understanding and reduce ambiguity.

There might be times when even what appears to be a natural or simple word can cause confusion. Think for a moment of the ambiguity in the next two sentences: "These minks were harvested in California." "Our chickens are grown in Iowa." The words *harvested* and *grown,* because they are used in a context that actually doesn't apply, are not very clear.

The purpose of communication is to share ideas, information, and feelings. If the language you use does not convey your meaning to your audience, then your communication purpose cannot be achieved. You may fear that using simple language makes you appear infantile or dull. That is not the case. However, there are many occasions when the appropriate word should be ceremonial and formal. You should use the literary word for those occasions. In most instances though, vague, complicated, showy words and too many words can cause serious communication breakdowns. As the English writer John Ray advised, "Those that use too many words for explaining any subject, doth, like the cuttlefish, hide themselves from others."

Concrete Language Promotes Clarity. As noted elsewhere in this book, an audience listening to a speaker cannot, as they can with a book or videotape, go back and reread or replay the words they were exposed to. Therefore, as a speaker you need to be clear. Yet most of us are guilty of expressing ourselves rather vaguely at times. We may say, "I saw this person crossing the street," without any further identification of the "person" or the street or the method of crossing the street. A friend might tell us, "I watched this program the other night," with no indication of the program's name, the night of the week it was seen, or whether it was a televised or in-person program. Someone may allude to "that neat little thing" without indicating precisely which "thing" he or she is talking about or whether "neat" is descriptive of its appearance or function. Or think about how often people talk about "that stuff" with no indication of what the word "stuff" is referring to. In all of these cases, word

Precision

choice falls short of precision because it is not concrete and/or it lacks specificity.

As a speaker, *if you learn to use names, dates, places, and other details,* your listeners are apt to get a much clearer mental picture of what is being discussed. For example, "Fred and Ann went to the science fiction and comic book convention at Golden Hall last Saturday afternoon" is certainly more specific than "They went to something not long ago." We hear general statements such as, "A lot of the people got sick from eating at the fair." A person concerned with communicating a clear picture would say, "Twenty-five first-graders from Polk Elementary School suffered severe stomach cramps after eating candy apples purchased from the concession stand located at the west entrance to the fairgrounds." Here we can see the value of being specific so that the listeners have a reasonably clear indication of what transpired.

In many instances, only a word or two can make the difference between being vague and being clear. Think about how much more apparent your meaning is if you say, "On October 6" instead of "some time next month," or if you say, "Gail gets all A's" instead of "Gail does well in school."

In the following general and specific comparisons, notice how a more specific word helps a speaker produce a clearer meaning:

General	*Specific*
animal	dog, horse, elephant, camel, cat
vehicle	car, bike, coach, motorcycle
worker	plumber, painter, carpenter, mason
color	blue, red, green, violet, yellow
move	crawl, creep, glide, run, waddle
sports	baseball, basketball, football
vegetables	carrots, broccoli, green beans
exercise	walking, swimming, running
residence	house, apartment, condominium
doctor	surgeon, pediatrician, urologist
educator	principal, teacher, professor
reading material	magazine, book, journal
automobile	Ford, Dodge, Jeep, Porsche

Using the specific and concrete examples in the right-hand column will clarify the discussion for the audience. In short, it is easier to visualize a dog being abused than an animal being mistreated.

Effective Style Observes the Rules of Grammar

Ask yourself this question: What would you think if you were listening to someone and during the course of the conversation he was to say, "The School Board is about to give *ourselves* a large pay raise." If you are like most people, two things would happen. First, the person would lose your respect and, second, the error in grammar would call your attention away from the point the person was trying to make. Effective style, including correct grammar, keeps a listener's attention on the subject matter of the speech, not on the manner of

Distractions of grammar

expression. Thus, a speaker should try to avoid the distractions that can accompany errors in syntax and grammar. *Grammatical errors damage a speaker's credibility* and also confuse the listener. For example, "His voice fits him perfect" may appear to be an understandable statement at first glance, but the listener might pay more attention to the grammatical inaccuracy than to the sense of the statement. Note the degree of distraction inherent in these common grammatically incorrect statements:

I need your help, give me them votes.

I had wrote this petition after think about this issue for a long time.

There wasn't no easy way out for any prisoner which hoped to escape.

She has went there many times in the past.

He hadn't ought to give to this here charity.

I had went to this college once before.

Our college's graduate school has a difficult job before them.

Having studied them before, the rocks was of a limestone variety.

Me and my friend are going to the show.

John can't hardly follow the instructions.

That there plan ain't going to work.

I think he done it.

They was going to do the same thing we did.

If we do not put a new light at that corner of Main and Second, someone will be hurt bad.

They was going to stop the petition even before it was circulated.

Me and my group will not back this plan.

Often what is considered improper speech becomes so commonplace that it creeps into our vocabulary without our even being aware of it. The phrases "Tell it like it is," "None of them is going," "It was a real difficult decision," "Solutionwise, this is a good plan," and "She gave 120 percent to this project" are all examples of words and phrases being used incorrectly.

Effective Style Is Vivid

Throughout this chapter, both in latent and in manifest ways, the power of language is accentuated. Nowhere is that power more evident than in the area of picturesque and vivid language. As important as clarity and correctness are, these qualities alone may not be sufficient to hold attention, maintain interest, and create a favorable impression. Effective style also needs the assistance of a third quality—vividness. The importance of vividness to effective style is made evident by the words of the American writer Logan Pearsall Smith: "Style is a magic wand, and turns everything to gold that it touches."

To achieve vividness, successful speakers have relied on two fundamental methods: (1) imagery and (2) figures of speech. What follows is a discussion of how each method makes your ideas come alive in a memorable fashion.

Picturesque and vivid language help to hold attention and maintain interest. (Photo: indexstock.com)

Imagery Promotes Vividness. A philosopher noted that we speak so that others can see what we mean. The wisdom of that simple observation can be underscored by my asking you to take part in the following experiment. Stop for a moment and ask yourself what happens when you tell yourself to picture a small white polar bear sleeping peacefully on a drifting block of ice. You know exactly what happens. You picture that bear. This unadorned example demonstrates that, when using imagery, we are asking our listeners to see a prior event or to experience a new situation that we paint for them. In either case, the objective is to have the audience vicariously experience the sensation we describe. The forms that imagery takes, then, correspond to the human senses. Through language, we can evoke sensations of sight, smell, taste, touch, organic sensation, and kinesthetic sensation. Consider, for example, the various senses aroused by the following descriptions:

1. As I lay awake in the darkness, I could hear the muffled sound of footsteps on the gravel pathway that led past my bedroom window.

2. When I stepped inside the abandoned miner's cabin, I saw a shaft of sunlight coming through a hole in the roof and falling on a rusty metal basin that lay on the bare wooden floor.

3. The plastic quart bottle slipped from my grasp and the ammonia poured out onto the kitchen floor, filling the room with fumes that made me gasp for breath.

4. Running my fingertips across the smooth lacquered finish of the tabletop, I suddenly encountered a small indentation made by an object apparently dropped by accident.

5. Grasping the dangling vine firmly, I swung out over the water, then released my grasp to plunge feetfirst into the refreshing depths of the river.

6. In great anticipation, I raised a spoonful of the gumbo to my lips, only to discover that someone had emptied what seemed like half a bottle of red pepper sauce into the mixture.

7. Sandpipers darted out into the receding surf to find tiny minnows.

8. After spending all morning tossing bales of hay from the truck to the cattle standing huddled on the frozen ground, I was one mass of aching bones and muscles.

9. As my eyes were fixed on the Yellowstone fire, I had the feeling I was looking directly into the midday sun.

10. If you were there with me, you, too, would remember the outlandish red color of the clamoring birds as they moved from the murky marsh into the enormous trees that gave them asylum from the wandering tourists.

11. I could not force my gaze directly into the eyes of the small, brown puppy, paws against the cage, appealing to me to take it home.

On many occasions, the impression to be communicated takes more detail and development than one can put into a single sentence. In these instances, the singleness of impression might be expressed by an extended illustration. In the following example, the speaker wanted her audience to understand how cruel it is to keep elephants in small cages or in the back of a truck, moving from town to town as part of a traveling circus:

> Elephants, like humans, grieve, cry from frustration and sadness, and help one another. They have a long childhood and remain with their mothers for 15 years. They are sensitive, intelligent, and affectionate, and they long for social relationships. Now try to imagine one of these magnificent creatures in complete isolation, spending its entire life in either a small cage or the back of a truck, being moved from city to city. Confined, chained, and caged, the elephant quickly learns the futility and brutal repercussion of protesting. Picture this dignified and social animal responding to this isolation and lack of space. Pacing, weaving, rocking, sucking, or chewing on the steel bars of the cage are the animal's response to monotony and loneliness. Many, of course, simply go mad.

Another speaker, trying to encourage a group of smokers to stop smoking, used imagery in the following manner:

> Let us imagine for a moment that you are feeling good as you take a long, deep puff on your cigarette. But let us also add a touch of realism to this scene by asking you to also picture what your body is doing with this invisible and sinister chemical as it invades your body. Your gums and teeth are the first recipients of the poisonous chemical. While the smoke pays but a short visit to your mouth it is leaving enough pollution to increase the risk of painful gum diseases and the agony of mouth and throat cancer. But this is just the beginning. As the smoke continues its journey into your unsuspecting lungs, you will soon find that your breathing is shallow and impaired, for now the smoke deposits insidious toxins that, after a period of time, will increase your chances of crippling and deadly cancer. Your stomach too will experience the corrupt and silent killer of cigarettes. While you cannot see them, small bits of acid are coating your stomach, adding to the chances that you will develop

lacerated ulcers. Think about all this the next time you decide that it is okay to take one little puff of this cleverly concealed stick of dynamite.

In some instances, even a single word can make your material more vivid, colorful, and lively:

horse	mount, nag, equine, bronco
hot	scorching, torrid, blazing
walk	stroll, plod, shuffle, slink
violent	turbulent, raging, explosive
cheap	frugal, prudent, scrimping
fast	rapid, nimble, brisk
poor	destitute, impoverished, insolvent
small	diminutive, paltry, scanty
loud	boisterous, deafening, resounding
silent	hushed, muted, quiescent
soft	malleable, delicate, mushy
hungry	famished, ravenous, voracious
painful	agonizing, throbbing, excruciating

Obviously, the context, as well as your analysis of the audience and occasion, will determine which words and phrases you utter. However, regardless of what factors you take into consideration, your language must not be inanimate, dull, or mundane.

Figures of Speech Promote Vividness. On many occasions, you might find it useful to enhance and elevate your speaking style so that it rises above ordinary and everyday speech. When you want to use variations from literal or common forms of expression, figures of speech are highly effective. They impart vividness to your language usage. Moreover, figures of speech can greatly increase a speech's vigor, clarity, and beauty. In addition, they add to your credibility. Among the most popular figures of speech used by experienced communicators are *simile, metaphor, antithesis, personification, hyperbole, climax, onomatopoeia, rhetorical questions, parallelism, and alliteration.*

Simile. **Simile** *is an expression of the figurative resemblance of one person or thing to another, put in the form of an explicit comparison.* A simile normally uses "like" or "as" to compare and link similar ideas. One is using a simile when saying, "At times, finding a gasoline station that services cars is like hunting for a place to camp on the Hollywood Freeway." A simile involving the importance of child rearing might well state, "A strong tree is like a strong family—both need deep roots." A speaker talking about the poor attendance at a town meeting also used a simile when he said, "The auditorium was as desolate as a cemetery at midnight." Another speaker noted, "He was so thorough that he examined the book as if he were a customs inspector." Perhaps one of the most famous of all similes is the one that noted, "Requesting the television industry to police itself is like asking the fox to guard the henhouse."

Metaphor. Closely related to simile is **metaphor,** *the comparison of unlike things that allows us to say a great deal with very few words.* The comparison is implied and built into a metaphor. Hence, the speaker can omit the words *like* or *as*. A simile says that one thing is like another; a metaphor says that one thing is another. Thus, the simile "He is like the Rock of Gibraltar" becomes a metaphor when expressed as "He is the Rock of Gibraltar." Abraham Lincoln, discussing the danger of two Americas, used the metaphor, "A house divided against itself cannot stand." In both these instances, the speakers created a figurative comparison suggesting that two dissimilar things are alike. To say, for example, that "the two approaching headlights reminded me of two flickering candles just before they burn out" is to imply that the approaching headlights were actually similar to a candle. A speaker talking about campus violence would be using a metaphor if she were to say, "The hallways in our high schools have become war zones."

Antithesis. Style can also be made more vivid by using antithesis. *In this figure of speech, contrast is emphasized by the position of words.* That is to say, strongly opposed notions are put side by side in parallel construction—for example, "The homeless want employment not welfare checks, dignity not pity." When John F. Kennedy uttered the words "Ask not what your country can do for you—ask what you can do for your country," he gave an antithesis that has now become a classic figure of speech. It is often the cadence of the antithesis that gives it added power. In this sense, many speakers use an antithesis to end their talk. Imagine the impact of the speech that ends with these words: "We will not simply get by, we will excel. We will not simply accept, we will demand. We will not simply wait, we will act."

Personification. *A figure of speech in which life and personality traits are attributed to inanimate objects or abstract ideas* is **personification**. The following are some examples of this excellent figure of speech:

The old house just shuts its eyes to the ugliness springing up around it.

That piece of cake was begging me to come and taste it.

The problem has been with us so long that it is a member of the family.

The trees, knowing they would be spared the power of the chain saw, seemed to be dancing in the wind.

The cat was so humorous that it, too, seemed to laugh out loud.

My car had taken such good care of me for 10 years that last week I decided to give it a birthday party.

Even the stately faces on Mt. Rushmore looked a little sadder the day our astronauts perished in that tragic explosion.

Hyperbole. *Based on exaggeration,* **hyperbole** is a figure of speech that magnifies objects beyond their natural boundaries in order to make them more impressive and more vivid. Some examples:

He stood there, tall and proud—taller than Mount Everest and prouder than Denver on the day the Broncos won the Super Bowl.

It took Susan so long to enroll in the required classes that she was now able to be in the same graduation class as her daughter.

There was so much hot air coming from those politicians that I thought the convention hall would become airborne.

He had been living in the back of his truck so long he had to give it an address.

This dog training method is so effective that one dog became so smart that he trained his master to bring him his dinner at exactly five o'clock each night.

Climax. **Climax** *is a figure of speech that presents a series of thoughts or statements arranged in order of increasing importance.* It is the building effect of climax that gives impact of this figure to speech:

First the government takes your apple, then it takes your tree, and before long it takes your whole orchard.

The first fee increase saw me taking a part-time job. The second addition forced me to take full-time employment so I could stay in school. Now, with the additional charge, I must leave school and abandon my education.

Onomatopoeia. Another figure of speech is **onomatopoeia**. While this is often thought of as a vocal device, it can be thought of as a language tool. *It is a figure of speech in which the sound of a word or group of words imitates the sound it names or describes.* The following words fall into this category: *rumble, crash, splash, boom, buzz, snarl, cackle, hiss, smack, chatter, thud, slither, bang,* and *fizzle.*

Rhetorical questions. Even though treated elsewhere in the book, rhetorical questions are also an effective linguistic device. You will recall that a rhetorical question is a query intended to produce a mental response on the part of your listeners. When rhetorical questions are used as a figure of speech, it is often effective to ask a series of questions. Notice the verbal impact in the following examples:

Do you believe you are receiving the best education possible? Ask yourself these questions: How crowded are my classes? Do my professors know my name? Am I being challenged to do my best work?

Why is suicide one of the fastest-growing causes of death among young people in the United States? And do you know someone who is manifesting suicidal tendencies? Is it your brother, sister, best friend?

Parallelism. *Mentioned earlier in this chapter,* **parallelism** *is the figure of speech in which two or more clauses or sentences are stated in the same manner.* The result is a rhythmic pattern that can be captivating and interesting. Notice the parallel structure in the following example:

We will not give up this fight until every homeless child has a safe place to sleep. We will not give up this fight until every homeless child receives three meals a day. We will not give up this fight until every homeless child moves from the streets to the classroom. And we will not give up this fight until every homeless child has adequate medical care. The battle may be arduous, but we will not give up the fight.

Another speaker, challenging the audience to be motivated about animal rights, noted:

Be committed to animal rights for all animals. Care about the cats that suffer because they are overbred. Care about the dogs that languish in small pens because we do not have enough space in our animal shelters. Care about the rabbits that get chemicals put into their eyes in the name of animal testing. Care about the tigers that pace all day in small cages because zoos are inadequately funded. Care about the elephants that travel in circus trucks that are so small they can hardly move around. Care for all the animals. Care. Care. Care.

Alliteration. The final figure of speech, **alliteration**, *is much like parallelism, except that it is the repetition of a sound that adds interest to the point being made.* Notice the vividness in the following examples:

> When we entered the cave for the first time, we could sense the approaching perils, pitfalls, and problems we would face.

> I can assure you she will make an excellent candidate. She has both character and charisma.

> This program was doomed to fail. It was too costly, too chaotic, and too complex.

> This law is important for our community. We must persuade, prod, and push our legislature to adopt the proposal.

Effective Style Is Appropriate

There is an Italian proverb that says, "Since the house is on fire, let us warm our hands." This advice, although sublime in its words, underscores the importance of fashioning one's remarks to the situation and circumstance. Adaptability is indeed one of the hallmarks of a successful communicator. When you move from one communication situation to another, you will find it necessary to adjust your language style to meet the unique demands of each encounter. Thus, your style will be appropriate because you have geared it to (1) *the specific audience* and (2) the *occasion*.

Appropriate to the Audience. As one aspect of adaptation, your language may be the most crucial. You know from experience that you often change words and phrases as you move from person to person and place to place. If a professor calls on you in class, you respond with one type of language, yet if a friend asks you a question, even the same question, your remarks are far less formal. *You are making your language appropriate to the receiver.*

You run the risk of not accomplishing your purpose when you use language that is not suited to your listeners. Imagine how you would feel if you had gone to hear a lecture entitled "An Introduction to Perception" and heard a speaker say, "Once we know that we can see electromagnetic radiation with wavelengths of 380 to 760 millimicrons, we should find out what the subjective experience is at each point between the upper and lower thresholds." If the entire audience were composed of persons with very little background in perception, this would be a blatant example of inappropriate language. Suppose you tuned in a television "household hints" program and heard the host say, "So whatever you do, don't put a neutral sulphated monoglyceride detergent on your woolens."

Appropriate to Women. In recent years, there has been an increasing awareness of the sexist character of some of our everyday language. Much of this language is perceived as belittling others because of their gender. A speaker who is sensitive to the feelings of the listeners avoids words and phrases that might be viewed as demeaning or offensive. Let us examine three aspects of sexist language that are inappropriate.

The use of "he." Our first area of concern is the use of "he." Traditional grammar has conditioned most of us to use the pronoun "he" to represent the entire class of humans, whether they are male or female. Saying "each voting member of this community should exercise his right to vote" completely excludes over half the population and even suggests a subtle bias. In the same manner, to say "The average student is worried about his grade" is to imply that women are not concerned about their grades. Let us suggest a few ways that you can avoid masculine pronouns and use language that is more generic, and less offensive:

1. In the example above, it would be better to say, "All persons should exercise their right to vote."

2. The misuse of "he" can also be avoided if you learn to pair the pronouns and use constructions such as "he or she," "women and men," and "her or his."

3. The use of "they" is yet another effective nonsexist device: "As voters learn about the issues, they will make the correct choices."

4. Using the second person ("you") can help overcome the use of masculine pronouns: "As you mark your ballot, think about the importance of today's topic."

5. The masculine emphasis can also be avoided with the use of the word "one." "When failing to vote, one is failing to exercise a powerful and basic gift of a free democracy."

Omitting women. Sexist language often omits women from the culture by making maleness the norm. That is to say, language regarding occupations should not exclude recognizing that women can hold those positions. Let us offer just a few examples to clarify the point:

fireman	firefighter
mailman	mail carrier
chairman	chairperson
salesman	sales representative
workman	worker
congressman	member of congress
weatherman	weathercaster
city fathers	city leaders

Sexist overtones. A great many words, phrases, and references are inappropriate because they possess strong sexist overtones. A speaker attempting to use humor in a speech on vocabulary building offered the following joke that many in the audience found both a stereotype and highly inappropriate: "An average woman's vocabulary is said to be about 500 words. Small inventory, but think of the turnover." There are many other instances where remarks with sexist overtones would be inappropriate. For example, it would be insulting to most women in your audience to use the word *girl* if you were talking about an adult. Think of the image associated with words and phrases such as *spinster, little old lady, the weaker sex, libber, his better half, chick, sexy, buns, broad,* and *little woman.*

Appropriate to the Occasion. As noted in chapter 3, the speaking occasion is a very important determinant of what constitutes appropriate style. Religious ceremonies, eulogies, appeals for charity, and the like usually preclude the use of facetious expressions, slang, or obscenity. A small informal meeting of friends might call for casual language, while a college commencement address demands a more serious tone. For example, a commencement speaker might say, "May the doors of learning, now open to you and your fellow students, remain wide for the future generations of this great state," but, in a small group, that same statement might be perceived as pompous and out of place.

Effective Style Is Free From Distractions

Effective style benefits you on two counts. It enables you to explain your internal states (what you are thinking about) in a way that other people might better understand them, and it adds to your perceived credibility. However, if your language habits are deficient, clarity is lost and your prestige is lowered. As you would suspect, there are patterns of expression that can interfere with your overall communication effectiveness. People inadvertently choose words and phrases that divert attention from their main ideas. Let us examine some of the types of words and phrases that can lower your credibility and cause your audience to become distracted from your main idea.

Slang. It may be acceptable under certain circumstances to use slang words and expressions, but, more often than not, they lessen a speaker's status and distract from the purpose of the speech. Speakers who use slang usually do so because of laziness. Words and phrases such as *nerd, macho man, bummer, freaked out, ticked off, jazzed, turn off, pad, stoked, kick it, awesome, turkey, rip-off, wiped out, humongous, the pits, outta sight, real awesome, blow your cool, bread, cop out, go for it, uptight, dude, gross, radical,* and *booze* are all examples of slang. Because slang is often regional and changes with each generation, many of these words may not be used in your community today. Yet when they were used, they did little to clarify an idea, make an image more vivid, or raise a speaker's credibility.

Triteness (Clichés). Some words and phrases, which are refreshingly novel for a time, lose their novelty through overuse and thus become trite. They lack originality and impact because of their commonness. The Unicorn Hunters of Lake Superior State College annually publish a list of words and expressions that they propose for extinction because of their overuse—words and expressions such as the *bottom line, state of the art, networking, play it by ear, time frame, world-class, cutting edge, input, interfacing, empowerment,* and *meaningful dialogue.*

If the previous expressions of relatively recent vintage are already regarded as trite, think how much more so are the following expressions: *high on the hog, madder than a hornet, to each his own, busy as a bee, behind the eight ball, it takes one to know one, it takes two to tango, green with envy, leave no stone unturned, the straight and narrow path, cold as ice, keep a stiff upper lip, happy as a lark, a legend in her own time, light at the end of the tunnel, can of worms, unaccustomed as I am to public speaking, bit the bullet, moment of truth, fresh as a daisy, dime a dozen, talk is cheap, ax to grind, few and far between, dead as a door nail, it goes without saying, last but not least,* and *beyond a shadow of a doubt.*

It is easy to let many of the clichés in the previous paragraph creep into your vocabulary. The very nature of a trite expression implies that it is commonplace. However, you can be more creative than simply returning to the overused expressions of other people.

Jargon. During the Olympics a speaker on television, who was a professional horse trainer, attempted to explain some parts of a horse's anatomy by saying "The stifle, gaskin, hock, and cannon help the horse gain power for its jump." Obviously, those were terms specific to a profession but not common to a general audience. This sort of language problem occurs often. It seem that each profession has its own language. Therefore, as a speaker you must remember that what is clear to a bureaucrat ("social entitlements") may not be clear to a voter, just as what is clear to a nuclear physicist ("quantum gravity") may be very confusing to a lay audience. Someone without a medical background might have trouble with words such as *xerophthalmia, retrolental fibroplasia, cervical dysplasia,* and *pellagra*. It would also be hard for a heterogeneous audience to decide the meaning of the sentence, "The new technology uses synchronized digital time phase projections."

When addressing a general audience, a speaker must avoid jargon and highly technical language. It would be very difficult for someone without a computer background to understand the jargon words and phrases *RAM, DOS, mainframe, menu, file, scroll lock, data base management,* and *downloading*. And think about how confusing it would be if you were not an organizational manager for a major corporation and heard someone using words and phrases such as *benchmaking, replexity, broadbanding, re-engineering,* and *rightsizing*.

Loaded Words. Loaded words often seem descriptive, but actually they are communicating the speaker's attitude toward the subject matter. They are expressing likes and dislikes on issues that are often very emotional. Think of how very different the image created by language is if one person, speaking on the abortion controversy, talks of the "unborn child," while another person uses the words "undeveloped fetus" to describe the same circumstance. By playing on emotionalism, both sets of words, implicitly and explicitly, ask listeners to respond on a purely emotional basis.

Notice the images called forth by phrases such as *fat cats, stingy, selfish tightwads, health nuts, welfare chiselers, do-gooders, big conglomerates, bureaucrats, male chauvinist pigs, extremists, bleeding heart liberal, nonfeeling spinster, demagogue, queer, religious fanatic,* and *barbaric approach*. Are these words really consistent with the facts in your context? If a colorful expression can be selected that does not distort reality, it should be used; if the appeal is strictly irrational, the speaker is guilty of a violation of ethical responsibility.

Empty Words. A philosopher once noted that "some so speak in exaggeration and superlatives that we need to make a large discount from their statements before we can come at their real meaning." He might well have been talking about "empty words." In this day of mass appeal, we are barraged by superlatives and exaggerations. This overexposure may condition an unsuspecting communicator to lean heavily on overworked and meaningless terms. Notice the empty quality of the following words and phrases: *super, colossal, deluxe, monumental, monstrous, new and improved, really great, magnificent, terrific, very good, fantastic, extra special,* and *a whole lot*. Many persons have been so bombarded with empty words that they are tempted to discount them and pay little attention to the person using them.

Contractions. It has become popular to use shortened forms of certain words. Although such contractions are derived from words in good use, they often lower the prestige of the speaker and indicate a lack of concern for language. Some common contractions are *exam* for examination, *y'know* for you know, *didn't* for did not, *condo* for condominium, *prop* for proposition, *prof* for professor, *caf* for cafeteria, *auto* for automobile, *letter of rec* for letter of recommendation, *ad building* for administration building, *grad school* for graduate school, *sub* for substitute, and *lab* for laboratory. *Frisco*, *Vegas*, and *DC* are poor substitutes for San Francisco, Las Vegas, and Washington, D.C., and their use by visitors to those cities is particularly irritating to local residents. Perhaps the public-speaking situation also calls for *should not* instead of *shouldn't*, *we will* instead of *we'll*, and *will not* instead of *won't*.

Taboo Words. The topic of taboo words as a verbal distraction is a difficult one, for every audience and every occasion is different. While one person might consider a certain word a profanity, such as *damn* or *hell*, another person might not be offended by these words. The same, of course, is true of most curse words. Some people view swearing as offensive, while others see it as part of everyday life. Most people, though, find profanity inappropriate in the public-speaking environment.

Derogatory Language. There is yet another category of taboo words that should not be part of the vocabulary of a competent speaker. These are words that are degrading and repugnant to an entire class of people. It would be callous, tasteless, and a sign of ignorance to use words such as *Hymie, Dago, Jap, Spic, Chink, Chinaman, Nigger, Hebe, Frog, Wop, Kraut, Kike,* and *Polack* when referring to people from different ethnic backgrounds. These kinds of taboo words are the mark of verbal bigotry and an insensitive speaker.

It is also insensitive not to respect the wishes of your culturally diverse audience if, as a group, they would prefer words such as *Asian* for *Oriental*, *gay* for *homosexual*, *Native American* for *Indian*, *African American* for *black*, and *person with a disability* for *handicapped*.

Ethics and Language

It is perhaps fitting that we move from a section on derogatory and hyper-critical language to one dealing with the ethical issues surrounding your use of language. To begin our discussion of the ethical responsibilities of language, we need to return to a theme woven in and out of every chapter. Simply stated, the words we use and the actions we take have an influence on other people. Our messages create change. Therefore, in selecting your words, I urge you to follow some ethical guidelines.

Be Accurate in Your Use of Words

When you are presenting facts or describing a scene, you should use language that correctly and carefully represents reality. In the following example, a speaker distorted the facts when, in giving a speech opposing the United Nations, she said, "The United Nations does not even respect the United States, because its official languages are Russian and French." The inaccuracy is that the United Nations has six official languages (English, French, Spanish, Russian, Arabic, and Chinese), not only the two selected by the speaker. It would be unethical to use language in this imprecise manner simply to make your case. Language should properly represent the facts. The

English author Walter Savage Landor said much the same thing when he wrote, "I hate false words, and seek with care, difficulty, and moroseness, those that fit the thing."

❖ ❖ ❖ ❖

Be Aware of the Emotional Impact of Your Use of Words

Knowing the emotional impact of some words could help you avoid language that touches the passions of your audience in an unethical manner. We are not suggesting that you avoid animated and passionate language but rather that when you employ a style to arouse the emotions, you do so in a way that does not exaggerate or falsely embellish the point you are trying to make. Overstated appeals to fear represent a vivid example of language use that is unethical.

Do Not Be Hateful in Your Use of Words

It is unethical to use language that is hateful. Words that are racist, anti-Semitic, or speak maliciously of a person or group of people are examples of hateful language. There is nothing wrong in speaking out when you see evil in the world; in fact, as a citizen in a democracy, it is your duty to speak out against injustice. However, your language should not lower you to the same level as your bigoted adversaries. Rise above character attacks and the language of demagogues. History is full of too many examples of how hateful words only produced more hateful words. Therefore, let your language be forceful, honest, and free of hatred.

Perhaps the best advice that can be offered concerning the ethical use of language is what was said at the beginning of this chapter: Words have power, so you should respect and use them with great care, for, as the Greek poet Homer said, "Once a word has been allowed to escape, it can never be recalled." Reflect on their force before you let them escape.

Improving Your Language Habits

Some people believe that effective speakers are born, that the ability to speak well is given to some but not others. This is simply not true. Even though language habits and vocabulary develop early in life, they are constantly open to change, and this change can be in the direction of improvement. However, improvement requires more than memorizing a few rules or formulas. It demands practice and hard work over a long period of time. The English philosopher Charles Spurgeon suggested that this practice should last a lifetime: "To acquire a few tongues is the task of a few years; to be eloquent in one is the labor of a life." If you are willing to labor, much of your effort should be channeled into the following activities:

1. *Learn to use a dictionary and a book of synonyms.* These two sources provide clues to new words that are often more accurate and vivid than the ones you have been using. For example, *Roget's Thesaurus* and *The Synonym Finder* can help you widen your vocabulary while increasing your choices when you are searching

❖ ❖ ❖ ❖   for the right words with which to share an experience. In addition to books, most computer writing programs now contain a "built-in" thesaurus. You should learn to use these sources, so instead of having to say, "It was good," you could be more specific by using one of the choices afforded by a thesaurus, such as *beneficial, edifying, salutary, capital,* or *valuable.*

2. *Be alert to new words as you listen, write, and read.* Listening is an excellent method of improvement, for it allows you to perceive the overall impact of a word. Hearing someone say "glistening" instead of "bright" may persuade you that one strikes the ear more pleasingly than the other. Novels, plays, speeches, poetry, and essays illustrate how knowledgeable persons use language. In the correct context, a writer might avoid "the road was dangerous," preferring, instead, something like "the road was hazardous," or "treacherous" or "perilous."

3. *Be sensitive to the difference between oral style and written style.* Language generated to be heard is somewhat different from language written to be read. Speechmaking tends to contain more personal pronouns; more repetition of words, phrases, and sentences; shorter sentences; words and phrases that are easy to understand at first encounter; and more colloquial expressions. As you create your speech, then, remember to compose for the ear rather than the eye.

Summary

Keep these general language principles in mind as you engage in both public and private communication: (1) words are symbols used to represent objects, ideas, concepts, experiences, and feelings; (2) one word can have many meanings and many uses; (3) words can have denotative and connotative meanings; (4) words convey only a partial view of reality; (5) words and their meanings are learned; and (6) words reflect our experiences.

It is important to remember that cultures often use language in ways that vary from those in the mainstream culture in the United States. These differences can be seen in the use of idioms, ambiguity, directness, loquacity, and formality.

Clarity, correctness, vividness, and appropriateness characterize effective language usage. Clarity is the product of using oral style, simple words, current words, and concrete and specific words. Correctness results from observing the grammatical standards expected of you by your audience. Vividness is obtained through imagery and figures of speech. Appropriate language is that which is suited to the audience's background, culture, and gender. Appropriate language also is adapted to the occasion. Effective style avoids distractions such as slang, triteness, jargon, loaded words, empty words, contractions, taboo words, and derogatory language. Remember the power of language and strive to be ethical in your selection of words and phrases. And finally, language can be improved by sincere study and conscientious practice.

Concepts and Questions   ❖ ❖ ❖ ❖

1.   What are some differences between speaking style and writing style?

2.   What types of verbal distractions should you try to avoid?

3.   What specific verbal devices can make your language more vivid?

4.   What is the difference between connotative and denotative meanings?

5.   How can you improve your speaking habits? Try to be specific.

6.   What does it mean when we say "language reflects our experiences"?

7.   Why is it important to avoid sexist language when you communicate?

Activities and Exercises

1.   Give a short speech in class in which you explain and offer examples for any three of the following figures of speech:
     a. simile
     b. metaphor
     c. antithesis
     d. climax
     e. personification

2.   Listen to a speech given by someone from a culture different from your own. Make note of how the speaker used language in ways that differ from how you use language.

3.   Go to a thesaurus and find five synonyms for the following words:
     a. fast
     b. dangerous
     c. silent
     d. creative
     e. clarity

4.   Give a short humorous speech that contains at least three of the distractions that were discussed in this chapter.

5.   Interview someone from a very specific profession. During the course of the interview ask the person to give you some specific jargon words that are part of her or his training, experience, and occupation. Write a short essay that discusses how those words might cause problems during a speech to a lay audience.

6.   List some common idioms in your culture that you believe might not be clear to people for whom English is a second language. ✦

Part Three

Having an Influence

Informative Speaking: Being Understood

The American educator Norbert Wiener once wrote that "To live effectively is to live with adequate information." What Wiener is telling us is that all human beings, if they are to flourish in family, culture, and society, need to share ideas and information with other human beings. Think of the frustration we would experience if we were deprived of the faculty of transferring or receiving knowledge. We would be unable to pass along what we know individually, as well as what our culture knows collectively. Progress would be halted, mistakes would be perpetuated, traditions would be nonexistent. *One of the primary functions of speech is to provide us with a means of disseminating knowledge.*

The ability to render an idea clear and comprehensible is one of the most highly prized skills a person can possess in our complex and ever-changing society. Being able to tell others, in a clear and interesting manner, how this or that functions or operates is often a measure of someone who is educated. Regardless of the culture, individuals who have knowledge, and can share it, are perceived as being productive and credible. There is even a belief among many cultures that it is wrong to have knowledge and not share it. The Persian poet Saadi once wrote, "Whoever acquires knowledge and does not share it resembles him who ploughs his land and leaves it unsown."

Situations calling for the use of informative discourse are numerous. Virtually all teaching can be labeled informative speaking. Instructing and training workforce and office and sales staffs likewise involve informative speaking. Even directing a stranger toward a particular destination in your city calls for informative discourse. At all levels of communication, both formal and informal, people engage in informative speaking, and in this "Information Age" it is used with accelerating frequency. We are now experiencing an unprecedented explosion of ideas and information; new concepts are emerging from every direction and from every discipline. As noted earlier, knowing how to organize, clarify, and transmit those concepts is one of the hallmarks of an educated person.

An informative speech imparts materials that increase a listener's knowledge of a given subject. If you know a great deal about fraudulent practices in mail order businesses and give a speech on that topic, you expect your listeners to know more about that subject when you complete your talk. Therefore, *the primary objective of informative speaking is to present information so that it will be easily understood, remembered, and perhaps even applied by your audience.* Hence, the informative topic is usually noncontroversial and is not intended to change someone's attitude. As you would suspect, it is difficult to draw a rigid distinction between speeches to inform and speeches to persuade and entertain. As observed in chapter 2, what a speaker intends to be a speech to inform may have a persuasive effect on the listeners and may be very entertaining. It is difficult to say that a speech has but a single clear-cut

Giving instructions in a clear and concise manner is an important communication skill. (Photo: Gloria Thomas)

end or purpose. It is more realistic to view discourse on a continuum, with many gradations and variations running from informing to persuading. The English writer Charles Colton must have been writing about the difficulty of a single purpose when he wrote, "A windmill is eternally at work to accomplish one end, although it shifts with every variation of the weathercock, and assumes 10 different positions in a day." In the final analysis, it is the receiver's response that determines whether a message is informative, persuasive, or entertaining; in most instances, it is a bit of each.

Basic Assumptions About Learning

Regardless of the type of informative speech you will be giving, if your aim is to increase audience understanding of a subject, you should be aware of the important principles that contribute to both short-range and long-range learning. Educators and psychologists have suggested some basic assumptions about how persons learn and retain information. These assumptions should help you select a topic, as well as prepare and present your material. Therefore, once these principles concerning learning have been identified in the following paragraphs, they are woven into the entire chapter, so you can see how theory can be turned into practice.

Motivation

Learning is facilitated when we are motivated. The results of many experiments to determine how people learn have validated Aristotle's claim that "all that we do is done with an eye to something else." We learn more and retain it longer when we see a reason for listening. If, for example, you have been experiencing difficulty in setting your VCR to record programs during your absence and a speaker says that he is going to remove some of the mystery from VCR operation, you are apt to pay close attention to his talk. Think about your motivational level if you live near a nuclear power plant and hear that a speaker's topic is "reevaluating the risk of living near a nuclear reactor." You can see from these examples that one of the principles of effective motivation is that it points the topic directly at the audience; it makes the subject personal.

Curiosity and interest, as well as anxiety, can motivate people. A speaker once encouraged her audience to listen to a speech on the Japanese yen by declaring that the yen and the U.S. dollar are interrelated. She did what every effective informative speaker is able to do—she made the material interesting.

It is important to remember the role of culture in motivation as you think about your speech to inform. Not all cultures are motivated by the same propositions. While many North Americans are motivated to listen to a speech on the stock market so that they can add to their material wealth, members of other cultures might not find this appeal as challenging. In much of the world spiritual goals far outweigh material possessions. Later, this chapter presents some techniques you can employ that will motivate your audience to learn from your presentation.

Coupling the Known With the Unknown

Learning is facilitated when the unknown is coupled with the known. This concept reminds us of the simple idea that we can learn new ideas if they are linked to what we already know.

If you have never ridden horseback but can visualize the relationship between steering a car and reining a horse, you might couple these experiences and be able to understand something of elementary horsemanship. Having people visualize how a computer disk is much like an enormous filing cabinet can help them see the basic function of computer disks. As noted in chapter 6, analogies point out similarities between what is already known and what is not, making these forms of support particularly useful in informative discourse.

Logical Sequence

Learning is facilitated when information is encountered in a logical sequence. Most of us have suffered through speeches that lacked clear direction and seemed to leap from point to point at random. Perhaps we tried to reorganize the speaker's rambling ideas, but more often we simply stopped listening out of frustration. Part of this chapter capitalizes on what researchers now know about the constituents of successful organization. Simply stated, people tend to learn faster and retain material longer if the material is arranged in an order that is clearly identified and easy to follow. Various organizational schemes as well as some transitional devices that contribute to learning are examined later in this chapter.

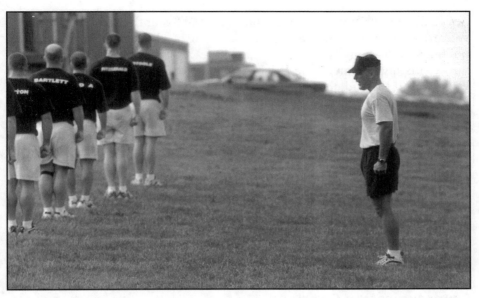

Listeners remember a fact or an idea much longer if it is repeated and reinforced. (Photo: Mark C. Ide)

Repetition

Learning is facilitated when key ideas are repeated. A typical television commercial makes certain you don't miss the main point; it is repeated or restated over and over. You most likely can sing the McDonald's commercial because it has been repeated so many times, but can you name the state capitals for all 50 states? A person who places a hand on your shoulder while saying, "I'm very fond of you," is nonverbally repeating a verbal point. This same principle of frequency applies to learning theory and, hence, to informative speaking. We have all heard the advice, "Tell them what you are going to tell them, tell them, tell them what you told them." Do not let the fact that this expression has become a cliché deter you from heeding the message. Listeners do remember a fact or an idea much longer if it is repeated and reinforced. These two principles often take on added significance when you are speaking to people who do not share your cultural background. For example, if you are explaining how to prepare a résumé to people who have no such item in their country, repeating and reinforcing would help them learn about this new procedure. Later in the chapter, in the discussion of previews, transitions, and summaries, I will offer some specific advice on how to use the learning tools of repetition and reinforcement.

Multisensory Stimulation

Learning is facilitated when multisensory stimulation is used. As pointed out in chapter 7, educators have known for a long time that learning is fostered when a stimulus is presented in a way that involves as many of the senses as possible. This principle has been reinforced since we entered the television and computer age. These pieces of equipment rely heavily on visual perception. Hence, think about including aids if your goal is to have people learn. For example, if you use a visual aid depicting the topography of the Los

Angeles basin while you discuss conditions that foster the formation of smog, you are apt to produce a clearer understanding of why the Los Angeles metropolitan area is so prone to experience this form of air pollution. A speech on how to distinguish an edible mushroom from a deadly one obviously needs visual aids if the audience is going to be able to make such a distinction long after the speech is over.

Being able to call on a variety of senses is extremely important if you are speaking to people from another culture who are not familiar with all aspects of the North American culture. Imagine how much easier it would be to learn about traffic signs and signals if you had posters and pictures so people could actually see what you were talking about.

Throughout this chapter, as you study techniques that contribute to learning, you will see the value of returning to chapter 7 in order to reexamine the visual aids discussed there. Without doubt, you will find visual aids to be helpful when giving a speech to inform.

Communication Overload

Learning is facilitated when the learner is not subjected to communication overload. The human brain, amazing as it is, can process only a certain amount of new material at any given time. Speakers who offer too many pieces of information run the risk of confusing rather than enlightening their listeners. All of us have encountered speeches so filled with information that we were unable to recall even a fraction of it. Trying to explain all the causes of world hunger or how to outfit an army for desert conditions in an eight-minute speech are two examples of topics that could produce overload. Thinking about your audience and narrowing your topic are perhaps the most meaningful steps you can take to avoid problems of excess and overload before they arise. Techniques for reducing overload during a speech presentation are examined later in the chapter.

Depth

Learning is facilitated when the content is perceived as having some depth. At first glance, the principle of depth might seem to contradict what you have just learned about overload, but they are really two different ideas. The principle of overload says that people can remember only so much at one time; therefore, you should not offer too much or be too technical. The principle of depth maintains that people will learn very little if they are offered very little. You know from your own experiences that once you decide that material you are listening to is inconsequential and trivial, you cease to pay attention—and learning stops. And, of course, the opposite is true—people pay attention when they find the material intellectually stimulating. In planning the depth level of your speech, you need to be especially sensitive to the make-up of your audience. Some key questions you should ask are, Who are they? What do they already know about the topic? What do they expect of me? Will they be able to understand all that I have to say in the amount of time I am allotted?

Central Focus

❖ ❖ ❖ ❖

Learning is facilitated when the learner is provided with a central focus. Put another way, we tend to learn more when we know what we are expected to learn. Although your audience is likely to remember any number of things from your speech, you want them to be especially aware of your main idea and main purpose. If your purpose is clear, and you stay with that single purpose, it can serve as a unifying thread that holds everything else together. All the details you introduce will make more sense if they can be placed into a single context. Having a central focus helps you as well as your audience. It reminds you that every piece of information in your speech should relate directly to the central purpose. As Benjamin Disraeli wrote, "The secret of success is constancy to purpose."

Types of Informative Speeches

All informative speeches have a common goal—*to increase the fund of knowledge of the audience.* Nonetheless, those speeches take different forms as they pursue that common goal. Speech teachers have attempted to classify informative discourse into four basic types. Although in some instances the categories may overlap, it is useful for speakers to be aware of the distinguishing characteristics of each type.

Instructions

The most frequently occurring type of informative talk is the one that provides an audience with instructions or directions. This type of speaking is often called the "how to" speech or the speech of demonstration. In these instances, the speaker is telling others how to perform a task, such as how to replace a sealed-beam headlight on an automobile or how to administer first aid to a burn victim. Employers use instructional speeches to show new employees how to perform their job assignments.

Here are some possible "how to" subjects:

1. How to stock supplies in a home for an earthquake emergency.

2. How to compose an effective job résumé.

3. How to organize a Neighborhood Watch program.

4. How to construct effective overhead transparencies.

5. How to administer CPR to someone who is having breathing problems.

6. How to draw cartoon animals.

❖ ❖ ❖ ❖   **Descriptions**

Another common type of informative discourse offers a description of something. Engineers, teachers, sales managers, and supervisors are often called on to describe a new model, a layout, a display, a location, an event, or even an attitude. If you want your listeners to have a greater insight into the life of Buddha, you might describe his family, his education, and his early interest in religion.

The following are some sample topics that would use description:

1. The effects of sleep deprivation on the human body.

2. A horseback-riding tour of the Grand Canyon.

3. Food markets in rural India.

4. The floor plan of the White House.

5. The underwater sea animals off the coast of San Diego.

6. A typical day for an ambulance paramedic.

Explanations

The third general type of informative speech is explanation—sometimes called exposition. Speeches that attempt to explain how and why an object, a process, or a procedure operates as it does fit into this category of information sharing. A speech that discusses the principles involved in the manufacture of soft bifocal contact lenses is an example of explanation.

Below are some sample speeches of explanation:

1. To explain the action of acid rain on ancient marble statuary.

2. To explain how a hurricane forms.

3. To explain how the federal deficit is calculated.

4. To explain how seawater is converted into drinking water.

5. To explain how electric cars differ from gasoline-powered cars.

6. To explain how fax machines operate.

Reports

Most college students have been asked to present a report at some point in their schooling. Perhaps it was a book report, a committee report, or a report on a survey or project. At any rate, you were faced with the responsibility of transmitting to others the substance of what you had read, discovered, or deliberated on.

Here are some sample report speeches:

1. To report on efforts to overcome community resistance to a proposed landfill site.

2. To report on plans for your city's participation in a cultural exchange program with a Japanese city.

3. To report on Larry McMurtry's latest novel.

❖ ❖ ❖ ❖

4. To report on the new requirements in the General Education program at your university.

5. To report on efforts to secure legislative approval of a budgetary increase for a campus building program.

6. To report on the scandal faced by the 2002 Olympic Games.

Preparing a Speech to Inform

There is a Spanish proverb that offers the following advice: "A forward person is worth two." The message is sound, simple, and consistent with what has been said throughout this book—being prepared is a useful trait for any effective communicator. Before any behavior can be changed or any response secured, there must be both analysis and preparation. Several general principles of preparing informative speeches bear closer examination.

Determining a Purpose

If your goal is to make ideas clear to others, you must first determine what you want them to know about those ideas at the conclusion of your talk. The specific purpose of any given informative speech is a statement of exactly what the speaker wants the audience to understand. Here are some examples:

1. To have the audience understand how summer internships operate.

2. To have the audience understand the medical procedures for treating rattlesnake bites.

3. To have the audience understand how to select drought-resistant ornamental plants.

4. To have the audience understand how Hispanic cultures view the role of the elderly in a family.

5. To have the audience understand how to reduce grocery bills by using free coupons.

6. To have the audience understand how to find bargain air fares on the Internet.

7. To have the audience understand how to request documents under the Freedom of Information Act.

8. To have the audience understand the best methods to begin a meditation program.

Please notice that all these specific purposes tell precisely what the speaker wants the audience to understand.

❖ ❖ ❖ ❖ ## Choosing and Narrowing the Topic

In choosing and narrowing a topic for an informative speech, you should look to many of the criteria presented earlier in the book. Let us briefly review some of them as they apply to the speech to inform.

First, in most instances, *you should know more about the topic than do the members of the audience.* During the course of the speech, and in a manner that does not border on boasting, you should tell them how you came to know as much as you do about your subject. For example, you might say, "Having worked as a page in the legal department of a national magazine. . ."

Second, *the topic should be relevant.* Intelligent people would not like to hear you talk about how to put frosting on cookies or your favorite ride at the amusement park. A comprehensive audience analysis (coupled with common sense) is perhaps your best guide to determining relevance. As always, try to view the topic from the position of your receivers. This listener-centered approach will help you avoid trite and uninteresting subjects.

Third, *the topic should be stimulating as well as timely.* Remember, in most instances you have selected the topic because it interests you. Therefore, it must be a topic that also arouses curiosity at the same time that it holds attention. It is an exciting challenge to take what appears to be a dull subject and give it life and vitality.

Finally, *locating sufficient material is yet another consideration in selecting and narrowing a topic.* Think how frustrating it would be if you wanted to discuss the types of wildflowers found in your region but could not find any information. Be assured that your frustrations would be shared by your audience, for they would not hear anything new.

Gathering and Selecting Material

Interest and Clarity. If you are to secure understanding, *your speech must contain materials that are interesting, clear, and comprehensible.* In order to accomplish this objective, you should begin by making an inventory of what you already know and the material you have available to you. You will then be in a position to determine what additional materials you need. If you are going to talk about how to manage stocks and bonds and you have been a stockbroker, you already have a starting point. After the inventory, you are ready to locate and gather the necessary information. By realizing your aims, personal resources, and limitations, you can select the illustrations, examples, comparisons, definitions, statistical data, interest factors, forms of restatement, and visual aids that will accomplish your specific purpose.

Audience Involvement. *Select material that will encourage the audience to interact mentally with your material.* Think, for example, of how a rhetorical question requires the listeners to respond mentally to the question even if they do not want to. Imagine your own reaction when someone says to you, "How many times have you started to open the hood of your car, only to realize you don't know the difference between a spark plug and a fire plug?" The speaker can then move to material that answers this question. You cannot help but become involved with the material if someone says, "What would you do if a person you love came running into the house, screaming, 'I've just been bitten by a black widow spider'?" In each of these examples, you are forced to take part in the communication process, because the speaker selected material and rhetorical questions to encourage your interaction.

Audience Analysis. Be sure to keep the knowledge level and cultural backgrounds of your audience in mind when you select material. The main reason audience analysis is crucial to informative speaking is that the speaker knows something that the audience does not and therefore must constantly adjust to this fact. However, that adjustment can take place only if the speaker knows the make-up of the audience. Remember, you are the expert and therefore know the distinctive vocabulary of the subject and all other specialized aspects. Many beginning speakers mistakenly assume that since they know about the subject, their listeners do also. Try to overcome this shortcoming by selecting material that is aimed at your specific audience.

In these days of culturally mixed audiences, the importance of doing a thorough investigation of your listeners takes on added meaning. Think of how embarrassing it would be, and the wasted time involved, if you were to spend 10 minutes talking about the life of Muhammad to a group that includes a large number of Muslims. What about the folly of talking about how to dress for success to people who believe they should always wear the traditional attire of their country? In short, remember the cultural make-up of your audience when selecting material.

Visual Aids. Select materials that allow your audience to see as well as hear your main points. Chapter 7 listed a number of visual aids that you could use to make your material clearer and more interesting. (As stated earlier in this chapter, it would be helpful to return to chapter 7 to review those devices.) All visual aids contribute to increased understanding and retention. Therefore, some of them should be integrated into your speech. Imagine what a good idea it would be if, for a speech dealing with acupuncture, you could show the actual needles used in acupuncture and a poster indicating where the needles are inserted into the body.

Variety in Materials. Select material that is varied. By using a variety of materials, you can accomplish two important goals of informative speaking at the same time. First, you increase the chances that you will be understood. If your statistics fail to explain your point, then perhaps your quotation or example will. Second, by using various kinds of data, you can keep the audience's attention. As we discussed in the listening chapter, people have short listening spans; hence, they need to be able to transfer their focus while still understanding the point you are trying to make. Examples that are mixed with visual aids and definitions can both arouse and maintain interest.

The Materials of Informative Speaking

Although increased understanding is the foremost concern of informative discourse, speakers must realize that information alone does not necessarily capture or hold attention. As mentioned in the preceding paragraph, the mind constantly seeks new stimuli and quickly darts from idea to idea. Hence, listeners need a reason for listening—they must be motivated throughout the speech. Therefore, the materials of an informative speech must serve a dual purpose; *they must increase comprehension while holding attention.*

The features of a speech that hold attention overlap those that contribute to learning. What we might label an attention factor might also help explain a key point. For purposes of analysis, however, informative materials are separated into two categories. First, we will begin by examining the kinds of content you can use to facilitate understanding. Next, we will explore some techniques that can help you gain and hold the attention of your listeners.

Contributing to Clarity

It is impossible to overemphasize the importance of clarity to informative speaking. And as you might suspect, clarity begins with your selection of material. Writing on the subject of clarity, the French poet Nicolas Boileau commented on the need to select appropriate material when he noted that "What is conceived well is expressed clearly, / And the words to say it with arrive with ease." Scholars in the fields of education, psychology, and speech communication have isolated a number of devices that promote clarity. You will notice that all of these techniques are linked directly to the basic principles of learning we examined earlier in the chapter.

Definitions

What sound advice Shakespeare gave us when he wrote, "Define, define, well-educated infant." He know that many mistakes are made when people are confused about meanings. A speaker may neglect *to define* some of the basic and important terms, phrases, or concepts of the subject because they are so much a part of the speaker's everyday thinking. We must always be mindful of the fact that words are symbols, usually interpreted differently by different persons. Thus, a listener may attach meanings to words or phrases that are unintended by the speaker.

This entire problem of offering definitions takes on added significance in this age of cultural diversity. As noted in the chapter on language, we learn our meanings from our cultural experiences. If a particular culture does not have a specific experience, the people of that culture do not have a word for it. For example, imagine if you were from a small non-Western culture and were asked to define (understand) the words and phrases for *skywriting, bungee-jumping, affirmative action, sexual dysfunction*, or *low-cholesterol cooking*. Although all these terms have meaning to members of the North American culture, they may not be phrases that are used in other cultures. Therefore, you need to give special attention to definitions when your audience is composed of people from different cultures.

When trying to decide which words need definition, begin by examining those that are abstract or unfamiliar. If you are talking about *multiculturalism, educational dropouts, welfare reforms*, and *career retooling*, you should define what you mean by these abstract terms. These terms, because they are often misused, are so abstract that they may evoke any number of meanings. Simply put, by defining such words, we tell our listeners exactly what we mean when we use them.

Confusion also results when a speaker uses words or phrases unfamiliar to the listeners. If you were talking about alternative fuel sources for automobiles and you mentioned methanol, compressed natural gas, and ethanol without defining these terms, the audience might become confused. A speaker might also add to the confusion if, in talking to a lay audience, she were to say, "The congruity theory of persuasion is an effective tool for advertisers." However, if she were to define *congruity*, the unfamiliar might become clear.

In defining words or phrases, speakers should observe the following guidelines:

1. *Define the unknown in terms of the known.* Using language that is simpler than the original expression is an application of this principle. Going from the known to the unknown establishes a common frame of reference and allows the audience to see what you mean. For example, a veteran Navy radar operator defined radar by comparing it to the action of a tennis ball being bounced off a garage door.

2. *Define a word by placing it in the context in which it will be used.* For example, you might say, "In discussing the problem of school dropouts, we shall concern ourselves with the student who leaves school, for whatever reason, before graduation or before the age of eighteen." In this way, the audience knows whom you are talking about when you use the term *dropout*.

3. *Define according to the knowledge level of your audience.* If you were talking to a group of electronics experts and used the simple radar analogy just cited, you might insult them, yet the same radar analogy might be very effective for a group of liberal arts majors.

4. *When defining words, terms, or phrases, try to combine formal definitions with informal definitions.* By combining a formal definition with one of your own, you give the audience a clearer idea of what you are talking about. Notice in the following example how the formal and informal definitions contribute to increased understanding:

   > Archaeology is the systematic recovery and study of material evidence of human life and culture in past ages. That is to say, an archaeologist tries to locate any type of material, be it animal fossils or clay pots, that will give some insight into how our culture has evolved through the ages.

5. *Defining by synonyms is one of the most common forms of definition.* A synonym is a word that has almost the same meaning as another word. When defining by synonym, you are actually incorporating many learning techniques into one device. You are using comparison and linking the unknown to the known. It is important to select synonyms that are familiar to the listeners. It does not make much sense to define one word with a word that is even more confusing. A speaker would be using synonyms if he or she were talking about primitive cultures and used words such as *instruments, tools, implements, utensils*, and *appliances* to help explain what primitive kitchens were like. Also, the notion of *dogmatic* would be easier to understand if a speaker used synonyms such as *opinionated, arrogant, bigoted*, and *closed-minded* to supplement the definition.

6. *Anticipate cultural differences in the way certain terms are understood.* In a multicultural society such as in the United States, there is always a possibility that certain words or expressions common to one cultural group may have no equivalent words or expressions in the culture of another group. This is particularly true of colloquial expressions and technical terms. If you were giving a speech about skiing and used the expression "hot-dogging," it might perplex a listener from Belize or Malaysia, who might be familiar with the usual meaning of hot dog. If you were to refer to a tachometer when talking about automobiles, a person from an area where bicycles are the most common form of transportation might not have the slightest idea of that word's meaning. If you must use such words, show consideration to those of other cultures by offering definitions that fit within their frame of reference.

7. *Definitions can explain a concept or word by telling how it is used or how it functions.* When trying to explain mime theater, a speaker defined by function when she said, "Mime is a form of acting with only gestures and facial expressions. A mime performs without the use of words."

Examples and Illustrations

The value of *examples and illustrations* as means of clarification cannot be overemphasized. Examples are the simplest and most common of all the devices, and they are the easiest to use. Examples allow you to say, "This is what I mean." A speaker using examples to clarify an assertion might proceed as follows:

I. This university has a number of programs to help individuals with disabilities secure a college education.
  Example A. It has an "outreach" program that goes into various special education classes and explains admission requirements.
  Example B. It offers numerous scholarships to individuals with disabilities.

Thus far, we have talked only about brief examples. However, you should remember that many examples can become detailed narratives and, as such, these illustrations can also clarify. If you were talking about the plight of our national park system, you might use what is happening to Yosemite as an illustration:

Although Yosemite National Park is one of our most magnificent parks, with its sheer granite peaks, lush Sequoia groves, and magnificent waterfalls, it is also one that is experiencing the effects of too many people trying to live in harmony with nature. For example, an exposed sewer line feeds into the park's drinking water; the historic Ahwahnee Hotel is a potential fire hazard; and three bridges in the park have cracks in their foundations from the increased traffic.

The most important criterion for using examples is that they prove or clarify the generalization being made. For instance, if you were speaking of the roles played by contemporary first ladies, you could give explicit examples of the activities of Pat Nixon, Betty Ford, Rosalyn Carter, Nancy Reagan,

Barbara Bush, and Hillary Rodham Clinton. These examples would explain your point in a vivid and concrete form while holding the attention of your listeners. Your illustrations do not always have to come from first-hand experience. Being able to read about first ladies can supply you with the examples you need. In short, membership in a street gang is not the only way you can gather illustrations on gang graffiti.

Comparison and Contrast

You can improve clarity through the use of *comparison and contrast*. Comparison shows how two things are alike; contrast shows how they differ. These devices are useful in leading listeners from the known to the unknown. In explaining the functions of the United States Senate, you might use comparison to explain the similarities between the Senate and your student council. By pointing out the duties and functions of the council (known), you would show the likeness in the Senate (unknown). As we have said elsewhere, *analogy* is a good form of comparison because it also compares the known with the unknown. For example, a speaker trying to explain why digital systems are more accurate than analog systems begins with a simple yet clear analogy, using a concept that everyone is familiar with—watches:

> Consider watches: an analog watch uses a big hand and a little hand to represent information, while a digital watch uses numbers to convey the same information. Look at an analog watch and it will say that it's about 20 minutes to 11, while a digital watch tells you it's exactly 10:42.

Analogies and comparisons also have the added advantage of being interesting at the same time they contribute to comprehension. Imagine how attention would be heightened if you were talking about the problems related to drunk driving and said:

> Every year, more than 345,000 people are injured in alcohol-related crashes. Spread over each of our lifetimes, this translates into two out of every five people in the United States. Put into slightly different terms, this can be compared to seeing four of the people seated here in the front row being involved with a drunk driver.

When using comparison, it is important to remember that the items being compared should be similar. Think of how confusing it would be if you were to compare New York City to Billings, Montana, in a speech concerned with subway travel or ethnic restaurants.

In some cases, contrast may be more helpful than comparison. If the audience knows the point from which the contrast originates, the contrast will be particularly meaningful. A famous newsman discussing the relative freedom of speech enjoyed by journalists today noted that when he started out as a reporter in the late 1950s, the newspaper would not print the words *rape*, *abortion*, and *condom*. Another speaker, discussing the financial woes of a nationally prominent banking company, pointed out that "shares sold today at 48 dollars sold at 87 dollars just a year ago." This stark differentiation helped the speaker underscore the magnitude of the company's difficulties.

Statistics. Statistics are frequently useful to explain an idea in terms of quantity or size. For example, if you were talking about income tax in the United States, it would be useful to offer statistics on how much money is generated by this tax form and what percentage of the total budget this figure represents. If you were trying to explain the increased number of visitors to the national park system, you might say, "Use of the parks has steadily increased, from 100 million visitors in 1980 to over 360 million last year." You could highlight the size of Central Park by noting that it occupies 840 acres, or about one and one-third square miles. The statistics could take on added meaning if you would say, "This is about the size of our entire campus—from the parking structure to the football field."

A few guidelines should be kept in mind when using statistics to clarify a point:

1. *To be useful, statistics must be compared or contrasted with something else to show how many, how few, how large, or how small an idea or a thing really is.* If you were offering statistics on the number of light-years to the nearest star, you might make such figures meaningful by explaining a light-year in terms of how many trips that would involve between campus and the downtown area.

2. *Try to make your statistics as interesting as possible.* For example, a speaker discussing how much money North Americans spend on taxes made the numbers interesting by saying, "The average North American spends two hours and 45 minutes of every eight-hour work day earning enough to pay taxes."

3. *In a speech to inform, you must be careful not to use too many statistics at one time or to use statistics that are not clear.* You want people to remember the key elements of your speech, not minor subpoints. If you assault them with too many numbers, they will not absorb anything. What would you remember from the following statistics dealing with the relationship of modes of travel to death? "Your chance of dying in a bicycle crash is one in 96,000. In an automobile, it is one chance in only 5,300. And in drowning it is one chance in 37,000." Here we see not only too many numbers but also numbers that do not make much sense.

Description

Descriptions represent some of the best ways to clarify and explain a concept or idea. Description enables you to picture, or portray, an object, an event, or a person by stimulating the listeners' senses of sight, sound, smell, taste, or touch. A listener's mind is focused on the object by means of vivid word pictures. A speech on an ethnic neighborhood might describe homes, markets, children at play, musical sounds, traffic noises, overheard conversations, food aromas, and so on. For instance, an audience might be made to "see" a food market by including details such as these: "Strung like Christmas garlands are strands of chili peppers, some bright red, others green or yellow, and even some that are black. Hanging over the meat counter are long chains of plump chorizo, the spicy Mexican sausage—as many as eight or 10 different varieties."

At times, descriptions are much longer than a sentence or two. When describing what a meteor looks like, a speaker noted the following:

> The luminous streak appeared in the sky all at once. It seemed to be about half the diameter of the full moon and much like a street arc light. Its tail, of brilliant orange, with a sharp blue flame fading out at the extreme end, looked to

be 10 or 12 times as long and fully as broad as the body. The downward course was leisurely, as if in slow motion.

Another speaker used description when trying to inform her audience about the various clues that can be used when trying to select the winning racehorse by examining the horses in the paddock (walking ring) before the race:

> Watch the way the horses look in the paddock and how they are behaving. They should be prancing and alert. Their skin should have a bright shine to it. If they are feeling well the coat should actually glow. They should get very excited as the jockey mounts them. And as they leave the walking arena they should have a spring and bounce to their gait. They are saying they want to run!

It is important when using description to include as many details as possible so that the image or thing being discussed is clear. Discuss the event, person, place, or thing with vivid language. It is through these details that listeners visualize purpose, function, size, shape, and color. You should have noted that in all our examples the speakers sought to incorporate size, weight, amount, density, color, form, arrangement, texture, and composition. All these verbal characteristics add to the picture the audience "sees."

Demonstrations

Clarity can also be enhanced through *demonstrations* of an act or a process while you are discussing it. Showing the correct arm and shoulder movements for jogging would enable your audience to see and hear the point you are trying to make. You can also demonstrate with an object. Imagine how clear your lesson would be if you were assembling an aquarium at the same time you were giving a speech on that topic.

Demonstrations can be quite useful when many members of your audience are from cultures that might not be familiar with the point you are trying to make. Seeing what you are talking about would help clarify your words. For instance, if you were trying to explain some of the differences between football and soccer to a group of people who were from a culture in which only soccer is played, you could show one major difference by demonstrating how each sport kicks the ball. You would be enacting the words of the English poet George Herbert when he wrote "The eyes have one language everywhere."

In most instances, it takes time to display and exhibit while you are talking. Therefore, allow a few extra minutes when you are practicing for a speech that uses demonstrations. Also, as stressed elsewhere in this book, do not let your demonstration or visual aid get in the way of your eye contact. Your audience must remain your focus, not your demonstration or the object in front of you.

Reinforcement and Emphasis

We can never retain all that we hear. Therefore, by means of *reinforcement and emphasis*, a successful speaker underscores the materials he or she deems most important and compelling. Reinforcement and emphasis take on added significance when you are speaking to culturally diverse audiences that may not be familiar with some of your content. By reinforcing and stressing specific points, you are making it clear to your audience what ideas are

❖ ❖ ❖ ❖   most important. Four of the most common reinforcement techniques are discussed in what follows.

Restatement. Restatement is more than simple repetition; **restatement** *uses new words to convey and echo an idea already discussed in a speech.* After speaking on the dangers of cigarette smoking, you might want to restate your main thesis as "cigarette smoking can cause great physical harm to many parts of the body." In this way, the listeners hear the idea again but expressed differently.

Repetition. *Repetition is the use of identical wording in presenting an idea again.* Through repetition, the main point is better remembered. You might say, "Cigarette smoke is responsible for 150,000 to 300,000 cases of bronchitis and pneumonia; just think about it, 150,000 to 300,000 cases of bronchitis and pneumonia."

Both restatement and repetition have their roots in learning theory and should be used frequently in communication. Perhaps the author H. G. Wells was correct when he noted, "After people have repeated a phrase a great number of times, others begin to realize its meaning."

Focusing attention. *Calling attention directly to an idea you wish to stress is yet another device available to speakers.* Simply saying "this is important" or "please listen to this" can focus attention on the point you wish to emphasize. These two phrases tell the audience that they are about to receive some significant information. Imagine how your attention would be arrested if, while you were daydreaming, someone looked directly at you and said, "It is important that you understand this issue."

Nonverbal emphasis. *The way you use your voice and body can also help reinforce and emphasize the aspects of your speech you would like listeners to retain.* For example, you can reinforce an important idea by changing the loudness of your voice or by pausing. You can also add emphasis by moving toward your listeners. This activity accents the verbal elements of your talk. Even gestures, such as pointing, can stress an important aspect of the message.

Partition, Enumeration, and Summaries

As a speaker moves through a speech, the listeners can lose track of the main thesis unless their memories are refreshed occasionally. Therefore, it is of prime importance for the speaker to enlist devices that help the audience remember the main ideas as they are developed throughout the speech. In chapter 6, we talked about using transitions as a way of encouraging clarity and retention. We examined bridging and signposting as two such transitional devices. Four other techniques are added to that list here: *partition, enumeration, internal summary,* and *final summary.*

Partition. *A partition (often referred to as an initial summary or preview) is a list offered early in a speech of the points that will be covered.* You simply tell your audience what main ideas you plan to treat in the body of your speech—for example, "In talking about the special vocabulary associated with computers, I want to talk about bits, bytes, and chips." Having highlighted what you plan to cover, you are now ready to move to the body of your talk.

Enumeration. *Enumeration, which occurs during the body of your speech, is the numbering of each point as it is introduced*: "First . . ., second . . ., and third . . ." This technique is helpful in increasing clarity by alerting the audience to movements from one idea to another. If you had three main points concerning the unanswered questions regarding Mars, you could use enumeration in the following manner as you introduced each new point: "First, let us ask if living organisms ever existed on Mars." "Second, now that we have explored the issue of living organisms, we can ask what kind of organisms these were." "Third, knowing about the living organisms of Mars, we will now try to decide if the life we have been talking about looked anything like us."

Internal Summary. *An internal summary can appear periodically during the body of the speech.* It is a summary that reminds your listeners of the main points or subordinate points that you presented earlier. An internal summary not only underscores key ideas, but it also is an excellent transitional device. Notice the twin uses of summary and transition in the following speech on satellite broadcasting:

> Thus far, we have examined the launching and positioning of the satellite, the transmission process, and the role of the transponders. Let us now turn our attention to the final phase—reception.

Final Summary. *Final summary is the reiteration of main items at the close of the speech*—for example, "In trying to explain computers, I looked at bits, bytes, and chips." The speaker who was talking about Mars concluded with the following summary:

> Today we looked at three questions concerning the mysteries surrounding Mars. First, we examined the question of whether there are living organisms on Mars. Second, we attempted to discuss what those organisms might be like. And finally, we compared those organisms to ones found here on earth.

Contributing to Interest and Attention

The English author Wilmot once wrote that "Attention makes the genius; all learning, fancy, science, and skill depend on it." Wilmot is saying that without attention, concentration, and focus, the mind fails to completely grasp what is transpiring at the moment. Whether we are trying to persuade or inform, interest and attention are crucial.

For our analysis, think of attention and interest as interchangeable; they have interlocking and overlapping meanings. Human behavior proves that what interests us commands our attention; likewise, what we attend to interests us. As important as interest and attention are to communication, gaining control of someone's consciousness is no simple matter. The brain must attend to something, but a little self-reflection reveals that attention darts from idea to idea. Attention rises and falls and is always changing in both intensity and direction. As a speaker, you must gain some command over audience attention so that you can focus it on yourself and your topic. The next few pages contain some suggestions to help you steer your listeners' attention toward you and your message.

There is no magic formula that will transform a dull message into a scintillating experience for an audience. Each speaking situation makes unique demands. However, we can profit from the findings of psychologists who have probed the nature of attention and interest. These findings have yielded guidelines for minimizing the effort listeners must exert in order to stay attentive to our ideas.

Noting That Which Is Imminent. Most of us, while trying to live in the present, find that we are interested in that which is soon to happen: what is *imminent and impending*. We all find the future exciting. The American essayist Joseph Krutch said, "The most prevalent opinion among all of us seems to be that tomorrow will be wonderful." Appealing to the notion of "tomorrow," a speaker wanting to discuss recent improvements in the safety features of automobiles said, "I heard on the radio this morning that the first of the new model cars are due to arrive at dealers' showrooms within the next ten days. It will be interesting to see how they measure up to the safety standards that I'd like to discuss with you today." Yet another speaker, talking about new communication systems, aroused interest by saying, "People in the twenty-first century will wear their telephones like jewelry, with microphones hidden in necklaces or lapel pins and miniature speakers tucked behind each ear."

A speaker giving a talk on a ballot proposition used "the impending" to arouse and maintain attention:

> In just two weeks, we shall be asked to decide the fate of this city's hiking trails. On Tuesday, November 7, the voters of this community are going to have an opportunity, by means of a ballot proposition, to decide if the State of California should use tax money to purchase several wilderness areas from the federal government. This issue has been debated for years, and now it appears that the time for action has arrived. Because you will be affected by the outcome, and because you will help determine that outcome, it might be helpful if I take a few minutes today and explain the proposition in detail.

You have probably noticed how much more interested in college registration students become on the eve of the opening term or how prognostications about conference football standings take on greater interest closer to the start of the football season. All these examples are telling you to look for ways of linking your subject to the near future.

Appealing to Proximity. Just as ideas involving temporal nearness catch interest more readily than those in the distant past or distant future, so are *ideas involving physical proximity more compelling than those that are remote*. A story involving the neighborhood that you and your listener live in will probably capture attention faster than one concerned with another city. News organizations know that their listeners are more interested in local news than national or world news.

The immediate physical surroundings in which the communication act takes place also offer possibilities for applying this interest factor. For example, if you are trying to give your audience a conception of the size of a cantina in which you had worked during a summer in Baja California, you might compare its dimensions with the size of the room (or building) in which the audience is situated. If you are describing a pagoda in Formosa, you might say, "See that carillon tower on the old library building? The pagoda I'm describing was about that height." A speaker who wishes to use a hypothetical illustration to explain a principle of boating safety might say, "This weekend, two of your colleagues here—Nancy and Sara—are going out to Mission Bay to rent one of those small sailboats for a cruise around the bay." Give your listeners someone close to identify with and they will likely be more interested in following the illustration. Every teacher has learned the attention value of a student's name in promoting the student's interest in what is being said.

Referring to the Familiar. A female student whose hobby is skydiving used this analogy: "Jumping out of a plane gives you somewhat the same sensation you experience when you unexpectedly reach the top step of a dark stairway. You raise your foot for another step, then discover it isn't there." By relating the unfamiliar (jumping out of a plane) to the familiar (reaching for a step that is not there), she enabled her listeners to experience vicariously a small part of her favorite pastime.

This *technique of relating the unfamiliar to the familiar is basic to effective speaking*, whether persuasive or informative. The listeners' frame of reference must always be considered when attempting to explain a new idea or concept. Reference to the familiar, however, does not mean simply telling the audience what they already know. Instead, tell the audience what they do not know in terms of what they do know. If you were attempting to explain to a college audience the game of *jai alai*, you might liken it to handball played on a larger court, with scooplike baskets substituting for the gloves worn by handball players. Describing the bureaucratic levels through which a welfare payment application must travel by referring to the steps and complexities of registering for classes would be another application of the principle of familiarity. You could also use familiarity if you were talking about anxiety to a speech class and asked them to remember the nervousness they felt in the hours and minutes preceding their first presentation to the class.

When creating interest by means of a reference to what is familiar, always make sure that all members of the audience are familiar with your reference. For instance, in the example used earlier involving handball, if there were people of another culture who were not familiar with handball, your attempt at securing interest would be wasted.

Invoking the Listener's Personal Needs. Who is the most important person in the world to a listener? Without being critical to any of us, you would have to agree that it is probably the listener, as well as the *things that directly affect him or her*. Always ask yourself if your message has any bearing on the listeners' self-interest. Does it concern, directly or indirectly, the listeners' health, safety, family, pocketbook, status, personal comforts, or any of a long list of needs and wants? Subconsciously, every listener may be asking the speaker, "How does this concern me?" One speaker capitalized on the audience's personal needs when he tried to interest a group of college students in a speech on "making effective use of study time":

> Each one of us in this room has given up something to be here. We have given up activities ranging from making money on a job to playing tennis during this lovely sunny day. So why are we here in college instead of doing something else with these four years? If we reflect on it, the answer is very simple—we came here because we believe that a college education has both immediate and long-range rewards that we deem important. However, to be the recipient of these rewards, we not only give up certain things, but we have to attend classes and spend a great many hours studying. This study time comes from time when we could be socializing or engaging in other leisure activities. Knowing that we all want more time for various occasions, I would like to talk to you today about how you can improve your grades and, at the same time, have more freedom to have fun—specifically, how to make more effective use of your existing study time.

A speech concerning a nuclear power plant might be prefaced by remarks concerning possible cuts in the listeners' light bills or new conveniences to enjoy as a result of cheaper electricity. Allusions to new food additives that will cut cooking time drastically might enhance listener interest in an explanation of chemical compounds. A discussion of a proposed state budget takes on added impact when the speaker suggests that the listeners' children might not enjoy "free" public education if certain amendments are adopted. In short, never overlook the possibility of relating your message to the personal concerns of the audience.

Imparting Activity. Chapter 4 discussed how a speaker who uses meaningful bodily action and vocal variety holds attention more readily than a speaker who does not. The content of a speech can also be infused with activity. If a speaker arranges ideas in a logical, easy-to-follow sequence, those ideas seem to move for the listener. A jumbled, helter-skelter lack of arrangement is one of the surest ways to lose audience interest.

Speakers should use words that suggest action. "He staggered out of the woods" is more compelling than "He walked home." "The old pickup truck was doing 75 when it drifted over the divider strip into the oncoming lane" is more meaningful and interesting than "She was going too fast in that truck."

During a classroom speech on memory improvement, one speaker demonstrated a technique for memorizing a list of items. Among other things, the speaker asked the audience to visualize each item in motion—the more absurd and exaggerated the motion, the better. He explained that we tend to remember moving objects more readily than stationary ones.

Varying your supporting materials also imparts a feeling of activity to your message. We all like action. Blaise Pascal wrote, "Our nature consists of motions." Give your listeners that motion. Rather than dwelling at length on sets of statistics, add variety by inserting appropriate examples, analogies, and quotations from authorities.

Using Reality. A student speaker was discussing how free enterprise was now being practiced in Moscow by small entrepreneurs. "I bought this T-shirt I'm wearing from a sidewalk vendor who was operating right under the noses of the authorities," she said. "I can't translate the Russian lettering on it, but I think it's fun to keep people guessing," she continued. In another, more somber speech, the sister of a North American student being held prisoner in Turkey for alleged possession of illegal drugs recounted the anguish of her brother's confinement. "This envelope brought the first letter he was allowed to write from prison." Another speaker, discussing the famous ocean liner the *Queen Mary*, held up a soiled logbook from the engine room of that vessel: "This is the chief engineer's log of the last transatlantic voyage of the *Queen Mary*," he said. The first student did not need to wear the T-shirt with Russian lettering in order to discuss free enterprise in Moscow. The sister of the jailed student did not need to hold up the envelope from her brother to make clear his ordeal. The man talking about the *Queen Mary* did not have to use the logbook to recount the ship's history. In all three cases, however, use of an actual object heightened interest in the topic. The real item is almost always more compelling than the best verbal description, pictorial representation, or mock-up that can be devised. By the same token, a reference to an actual example tends to be more compelling than a reference to a hypothetical example.

Naturally, it is not always possible or practical to produce "the real thing," whether it is an object or an example. In such cases, you have to substitute that which is realistic for that which is real. For example, if you are trying to get an audience to visualize a circumstance in the future, you obviously cannot produce the actual circumstance, but you can provide lifelike details that will cause the listener to respond, "Yes, that could very well happen." Putting real persons in hypothetical circumstances or hypothetical people into an actual setting lends credibility and interest to such examples. You will recall our example in which a speaker said, "This weekend, two of your colleagues here—Nancy and Sara—are going out to Mission Bay to rent one of those small sailboats for a cruise around the bay." Although the event depicted was hypothetical, the persons and places were real. Thus, the event bore a resemblance to reality.

Pointing Out Conflict. From talk shows that are in poor taste, to soap operas, to sporting events, we are all drawn into examples of conflict. There is something captivating about disagreements, whether they are major or minor. Therefore, a speaker should be aware of the value of conflict in examples, illustrations, and the like as a means of holding audience interest on a subject.

Perhaps conflict is implicit in the subject itself. A speech opposing a proposed course of action has built-in conflict, as does a problem-solving speech. On the other hand, subjects in which conflict is not implicit require that the speaker superimpose it. A speech explaining what happens to a letter from the time it is mailed to the time it reaches its destination does not seem to have a built-in element of conflict, but by the skillful use of a hypothetical illustration, a postal worker did introduce conflict into that subject. He asked the audience to imagine that a listener in the front row was carrying in his suit pocket an insurance premium he had forgotten to mail. To keep his insurance in effect, he would have to see that the premium reached the home office 1200 miles away within 36 hours. Would mailing the premium at this moment enable it to reach the company in time? For the remainder of the speech, he followed the progress of that particular piece of mail until it reached its destination in the nick of time. The twin ingredients of conflict and suspense kept the audience interested throughout the speech.

Although it was part of a lengthy introduction, conflict was used by a speaker to direct attention while discussing the issue of a clean environment:

> For the past ten years, our nation has developed a towering environmental ethic—a recognition that people must learn to live in harmony with nature rather than to exercise a professed inalienable right to use and misuse limited resources, to poison and pollute, to ruin our landscape, and to run from the consequences. Yet there is another view that argues that runaway inflation, unemployment, and a sluggish economy have been brought about by environmental regulations. Who is right? Do we need government mandates and environmental regulations to keep from having polluted water, fouled air, and scarred land? Or do these regulations harm us? And what are these regulations?

Using Humor. The English poet and essayist Joseph Addison wrote, "I shall endeavor to enliven morality with wit, and to temper wit with morality." Although Addison was referring to his journalistic intention, his declaration might serve as a guide for speakers. Throughout this book, I have made a case for the use of humor, and chapter 15 will develop the topic in great detail. We have observed that unless the subject you are talking about is extremely serious, the judicious use of humor can have a series of benefits. It can be an effective means of securing and holding audience interest; it encourages people to enjoy themselves while learning; and it can even help you be accepted by the audience. However, using humor requires skill. Because the audience's response to a speaker's use of humor is so unpredictable, it is best to use it sparingly and with propriety. Sometimes it succeeds too well, so that the audience's attention becomes focused on the humor as an end in itself rather than as a means of making the larger message more interesting.

Remember that the audience's reactions to your attempts at humor are apt to take a variety of forms. Humor can be successful without your listeners falling off their chairs in wild abandon. They may simply smile or take inward pleasure from your statements. Because humor can aid you in making your informative presentation more interesting, a few positive suggestions and possible dangers inherent in using humor are explored in what follows.

When using humor as an attention device, think of something novel and original. Look to the possibilities offered by *exaggeration, incongruity,* and *sarcasm.*

Exaggeration. A student informing his listeners how they could improve the value of their automobiles should they decide to sell them used exaggeration as a form of humor when he told the following joke:

> I had a friend whose car looked so bad that, when a toll bridge operator said, 'Three dollars,' my friend responded, 'Sold.'

Another speaker, who was talking about credit card interest rates, said "If you must borrow money, borrow it from pessimists—they never expect it back."

Incongruity. Incongruity, presenting the familiar in an unfamiliar manner, has humorous overtones. Speaking on the topic "What is the P.T.A.?" a student offered the following bit of humor: "My mother used to visit my teacher so often that the other kids elected her class president."

Sarcasm. Sarcasm, if used carefully, can also be an effective humorous technique. While informing a class about Women's Rights, a speaker told the following story as a means of recapturing attention:

> A feminist who was giving a speech in support of Equal Pay for Women was interrupted by the deep voice of a heckler from the crowd: 'Don't you wish you were a man?' 'No,' she replied without missing a beat. 'How about you?"

Talking about some of the thrills of skydiving a speaker told his audience, "If you believe in the saying if at first you don't succeed, then skydiving is definitely not for you."

When using humor in an informative speech, it is important to remember that your main purpose is still increased understanding. Stringing a series of unrelated jokes together would be highly inappropriate. In addition, an analysis of both your audience and your occasion are crucial. Because humor can be offensive, you must carefully consider how your efforts will be received. As Aesop wrote almost two thousand years ago, "Clumsy jesting is no joke."

Using Illustrations. Illustrations, stories, and anecdotes represent yet another technique of speech making that we have discussed in this book. In chapter 6, we saw how factual and hypothetical illustrations can be used to prove or clarify a point. In chapter 11 we also noted how useful illustrations can be in introductions and conclusions of a speech. Earlier in this chapter, we discussed how illustrations and examples increase understanding and aid retention. In each instance, we noted that all people, regardless of their culture, enjoy listening to stories. Now we will examine illustrations as a way of stimulating audience interest.

A speaker gave a speech on the topic of the history of manners. To demonstrate the various ways people respond to correct manners, she offered the following humorous illustration:

> Mark Twain, often careless about his dress and manners, one day called on Harriet Beecher Stowe without his necktie. On his return, Twain's wife noticed the omission and scolded him. A little later, a messenger turned up on Mrs. Stowe's doorstep and handed her a small package. Inside was a black necktie and a note that read, 'Here is a necktie. Take it out and look at it. I think I stayed half an hour this morning without this necktie. At the end of that time, will you kindly return it, as it is the only one I have. Sincerely, Mark Twain.'

Keep in mind that listeners not only enjoy illustrations and stories, but they expect them. Notice how the evening television news, which is basically informative, uses human interest stories to hold audience attention. Statistics on unemployment are more meaningful and vivid when the newscaster presents them in combination with an illustration of how one family is experiencing the effects of unemployment. Notice in the following example how Bruce Barton, a famous advertising agency executive, made the rationale for advertising both clear and interesting when he told the story of an advertising agent:

> Coming one day to a crossroads town, our friend found that there was only one store. The proprietor did not receive him enthusiastically. 'Why should I advertise?' he demanded. 'I have been here for 20 years. There isn't a man, woman, or child around these parts that doesn't know where I am and what I sell.' The advertising man answered very promptly (because, in our business, if we hesitate we are lost), and he said to the proprietor, pointing across the street, 'What is that building over there?' The proprietor answered, 'That is the Methodist Episcopal Church.' The advertising man said, 'How long has that been there?' The proprietor said, 'Oh, I don't know, 75 years probably.' 'And yet,' exclaimed the advertising man, 'they ring the church bell every Sunday morning.'

In another informative speech, dealing with some of the little-known facts about the life of the Greek philosopher Socrates, a student offered the following illustration to demonstrate how much the philosopher attempted to live a spartan life:

> Knowing the frugality of Socrates' way of life, a friend was surprised to discover the philosopher studying with rapt attention some flashy wares on display in the marketplace. He inquired why Socrates came to the market since he never bought anything. 'I am always amazed to see just how many things there are that I don't need,' replied Socrates.

Physically Involving Your Audience. Attention and interest can also be aroused and sustained by securing the audience's physical involvement in your speech. We have already discussed the need to secure the listeners' mental involvement; there might be occasions when your purpose can be served by having the audience perform an action. Think of how interesting a speech on meditation techniques would be if you actually had the audience practice some of these techniques. Or think of the interest created if your topic were how to draw simple landscapes and you had the audience look out the window and practice drawing while you discussed various stages of the artwork.

If the speech subject matter lends itself to activity, you can use the following three recommendations.

First, *there might be occasions when you ask your audience to take notes or engage in another writing exercise.* Your listeners actively participate in the communication process. The specific action can range from taking notes to filling out forms.

Second, *you can physically involve your listeners by asking them questions that they should answer aloud or by raising their hands.* Here again, personalizing your speech will give listeners the feeling that they are part of the communication experience. It is hard not to think that the speaker is interested in you when he or she says, "Please raise your hand when I point to one of the national parks on this map that you would like to visit."

Finally, *there are certain subjects that literally demand audience participation.* How could you teach golf, dance, CPR, drawing, or swimming without having people engage in some activity? Even a speech on the problems of blindness would be aided by asking the audience to close their eyes and try to walk around the room. In all these examples, audience participation and interest work together.

Organizing a Speech to Inform

Almost two hundred years ago, Napoleon Bonaparte wrote what might well serve as both an introduction and a metaphor for this section when he observed, "Unhappy the general who comes on the field of battle without a system." The same is true for public speakers. They must speak with a plan. The systematic arrangement of material is crucial in informative speaking if the listeners are to retain the information presented. Listen carefully the next time you hear an informative talk, and you will discover that there are occasions when the educated, as well as the uneducated, forget the importance of organization and clarity. Speeches that seem to bound from point to point without offering internal or external clues seldom leave the listeners with anything meaningful. Therefore, in this next section, we shall examine the basic steps of organizing a speech to inform.

Introduction

The introduction to a speech to inform has four interrelated purposes: (1) to arouse attention, (2) to create a desire for the detailed information contained in the body of the speech, (3) to establish your right to inform, and (4) to preview the main points of the speech.

Arouse Attention. Chapter 11 discussed in detail the methods of starting a speech. At that time we highlighted the advantages of beginning a speech with a quotation, illustration, reference to a recent event, rhetorical question, startling statement, promise of reward, reference to the subject, reference to the occasion, humor, or visual aids. I urge you to review some of these devices as you think about starting your speech to inform. Keep in mind that you should review your topic, the audience's interest, the audience's knowledge level, the speaking time available, and the speaking occasion before deciding on a specific method for starting your talk.

When listeners are not vitally concerned with a topic, it is often profitable to begin with a *factual or hypothetical illustration, a startling statement or example, or an interesting quotation*. These devices arouse apathetic and disinterested listeners.

Illustrations. To stimulate audience interest in a speech on hang gliding, a speaker used the following *factual illustration* as an introduction:

> The other day, while I was driving home from school, I noticed an extremely large bird gliding gracefully through the sky. As I looked again, I realized that this was truly the largest bird I had ever seen. I pulled my car over to the side of the road so that I could get a closer look. As I gazed into the sky this third time, I thought I must be dreaming, for what was flying over my head was not a bird, but a person—a person with wings.

Recently a student whose specific purpose was to inform the audience about the personality of H. Ross Perot offered the following story as a means of capturing attention:

> H. Ross Perot once decided that he would give a Christmas present to every American prisoner of war in Vietnam. Accordingly, thousands of parcels were wrapped and packed, and a fleet of Boeing 707's was chartered for the trip to Vietnam. Then the message came from the government of Vietnam— no such gesture could be considered during the time of war. Perot continued the correspondence. The Vietnamese replied each time saying any charity was impossible as long as Americans were devastating Vietnamese villages. As Christmas drew closer, the parcels remained undelivered. Finally, Perot had an idea. He took off in a chartered fleet of aircraft and headed for Moscow. The Russians were not at war with Vietnam. In Moscow, Perot and his associates posted each parcel one at a time at the Moscow main post office. The packages were delivered to Vietnam intact.

Hypothetical illustrations represent yet another attention-getting device that is very useful if your general purpose is a speech to inform. Notice how, in the following example from a speech on how to prevent some heart attacks, the speaker aroused attention by using the members of the audience as the main characters of the story:

> Imagine you are sitting at home watching your favorite television program when suddenly you feel a sharp heavy pain beneath your breastbone. You also feel massive pressure running down your abdomen. All of these feelings are accompanied by a numbness in your neck, shoulders, and down your arms. Now you begin to experience shortness of breath. You try to get up but are struck with sudden light-headedness and nausea. What is happening to you can best be defined as a coronary heart attack.

Startling statements. Speaking on the subject of solid waste disposal, the speaker began by trying to secure attention with a series of startling statistics:

> In the next year, we have to decide what to do with 2 million tons of major appliances; 22 million tons of food; 10 million tons of newspapers; 3 million tons of paper plates, towels, and napkins; and 52 million tons of bottles and containers. Do you have any ideas where we can put all this? Suggestions now range from putting it all in satellites and sending it into outer space to making a large island out of it and calling it Son of Big Mac.

Quotations. Attention is also aroused by using interesting *quotations*. A speaker who was about to discuss some of the features of the Mojave Desert opened his speech this way:

J. B. Priestley said of the desert, 'This country is geology by day and astronomy by night.' I suspect that most people who try to cross the desert as quickly as possible would agree with Priestley's observation.

One speaker used the following quotation as a means of starting a speech dealing with the plight of the inner cities: "Author James Baldwin wrote that 'a ghetto can be improved in one way only: out of existence.' "

Yet another speaker, who was presenting a the history of string instruments, began his speech with the following quotation by English playwright Richard Steele:

> Violins are the lively, forward, importunate wits, that distinguish themselves by the flourishes of imagination, sharpness of repartee, glances of satire, and bear away the upper part in every concert.

In selecting any introductory device, it is important to remember that if you fail to arouse interest at the outset, you are apt to deliver the entire speech to an audience whose attention is focused elsewhere.

Create a Desire to Listen. In all communication situations, it is to your advantage to stimulate a desire in the audience to want to listen to your presentation. In the introduction of an informative speech, make it clear to your audience that your topic holds significance for them and that they will benefit by listening. For instance, a speaker used an introduction to demonstrate that paying attention to her speech could save the listeners a great deal of money. The topic was gasoline conservation, and the speaker said, "By following the few simple suggestions I will discuss today, you should be able to save enough money on your gas bill each month to treat yourself to a nice dinner at an elegant restaurant."

There are many informative situations when "the reason to listen" is even more compelling. Shortly after a major earthquake in the region, a student pointed the material toward the audience:

In all communication situations, it is to your advantage to stimulate a desire in the audience to want to listen to your presentation. (Photo: corbisimages.com)

Where were you when the earthquake hit last month? Did you panic? Did you stay calm? Did you know what to do? Well, regardless of your answer, experts say you will most likely get another chance to think about the rhetorical questions I just asked, for it is very probable that our city will experience another quake before too long. Today, I think I can offer you some information that will assist you in coping with that experience.

Other methods of stimulating interest in your topic can be much more elaborate. A student trying to explain how to take better photographs showed the audience some prints that were obviously examples of poor photography. While thumbing through the enlarged photos, she asked her listeners, "How many of you take photographs that turn out like these?" The audience laughed. She then said, "How many of you would like to take photos that look like this?" Then she displayed some beautiful specimens of outstanding photography. She added, "You can all take photographs similar to these if you follow a few simple steps. I have been an amateur photographer for six years and would like to share some of these steps with you now."

There are also occasions when the listeners' curiosity is appealed to as a way of arousing interest in what is to follow. Notice how intrigued we become if a speaker tells us a story of how the Masai dispose of their dead in ways that are very different from Western methods. Our interest would also be aroused by a speaker who asked us if we know where and how the AIDS epidemic began. When speaking on the philosophy of Francis Bacon, a student read the following paragraph as a way of pointing the audience to the body of the speech:

> Reading maketh a full man, conference a ready man, and writing an exact man, and, therefore, if a man write little, he had need have a great memory; if he confer little he had need have a present wit; and if he read little, he had need have much cunning, to seem to know that he doth not. Histories make men wise; poems witty; the mathematics subtle; natural philosophy deep; moral grave; logic and rhetoric, able to contend.

The student then added, in his own words, "What does this mean for us 350 years later?" You can better hold attention during the body of your speech if you have already created an atmosphere where the audience wants the information you are going to offer because you have created curiosity, awakened interest, or convinced them that they need the material. By motivating the audience early in the speech, you also increase the probability that they will learn something by the conclusion.

On some occasions, you can combine arousing attention and creating interest within a single example. For instance, a speaker talking about the great white shark combined attention and interest with the following introduction:

> What animal can you think of that is 21 feet long, has eyes seven times more powerful than humans', has a sixth sense that enables it to detect even the slightest of muscle movements produced by other animals, and has jaws that open to three feet? If you said the great white shark you are right.

Establish Your Right to Inform. The third task of the introduction is to establish your personal credibility on the subject you will be addressing. The objective of an informative speech is to increase listeners' knowledge of a particular topic. The assumption is that you know something they do not and that, by listening to you, they will learn more about this subject. In some cases, the audience will know about your expertise in the area and readily accept you as an authority. The chief of campus security talking about an escort service for women who are on campus late at night would be just such an example. However, there will be many occasions when the audience will not be aware of your knowledge of a topic. When this happens, you should offer some information to help establish your credibility.

If your specific purpose is to inform the audience of how to stop a victim's bleeding at the scene of an accident, you might mention your experiences as a paramedic. One student from Haiti established her "right to inform" by telling her audience that she had recently left that country and wanted to offer a firsthand report of what the new government was trying to accomplish. Yet another speaker, wanting to explain the inner workings of a mental institution, established her credibility in the following manner:

> As a psychology major, I have had three courses in abnormal psychology. This past summer, I also served as an intern at the Union Hill mental hospital.

Recently, another student whose specific purpose was to have the audience understand the difference between purchasing a single stock and investing in mutual funds told the class that before returning to college, she had had a ten-year career as a stockbroker.

When you are demonstrating your expertise, make sure you do not sound boastful. For instance, you can tell your audience that you have been taking pictures and studying photography for eight years without implying that you are the greatest outdoor photographer since Ansel Adams.

Preview Main Points. Early in this chapter, we saw that people learn more when they know what they are being asked to learn. Therefore, the final part of your introduction should provide a brief initial summary (preview) of the main points to be taken up in the body of your speech. The speaker mentioned earlier who was interested in the topic of AIDS used the following preview to tell the audience what the speech would focus on: "Today, to better understand the issue of AIDS, I would like to begin by talking about the early cases of AIDS, then discuss the location of these early instances, and finally mention how AIDS has traveled throughout the world." By giving the audience a glimpse of the speech's organizational pattern, the speaker let the listeners know what to look for as the speech progressed. If you prepare the listeners for what is coming, they will find it much simpler to locate your main ideas. In the example of the amateur photographer, the speaker previewed her speech with, "In looking at these simple steps for improved photography, I will talk about composition, lighting, and equipment." On some occasions, it might even be useful to say the numbers "first," "second," and "third" as you offer your initial summary. For example, the speaker talking about photography could have said, "I will talk first about composition, second about lighting, and third about the necessary equipment."

Initial summaries can also be lengthy. Some speakers use their previews as a bridge to link what they have been talking about to what they will talk about. Notice how these two purposes are served in the following example:

> We all seem to agree that we want good grades but have very little time to study. How do we resolve this dilemma? Let me suggest a solution called 'time management,' but also let me warn you that time management is no simple matter. It takes goal setting, motivation, and evaluation. Let's look at

these three in detail and try to figure out how we can accomplish more in the same amount of time.

Previews are also useful in that they lay the foundation for reinforcement and repetition—two processes that are important to learning. The preview is the initial step in that process. It is the first time you introduce your audience to your main points. As you move through the body of your speech and sign-post each main idea, the audience will hear the key points for a second time. Finally, at the conclusion, you will once again tell the listeners what you have tried to do during your allotted time. Hence, on three occasions, you will highlight your main points.

You should follow the same order in presenting information in the introduction, body, and conclusion of the speech. That is to say, if you tell the audience in the preview that you plan to look at the advantages and then the disadvantages of contact lenses, you must not reverse the order in either the body or the conclusion. This change, while seeming insignificant, can confuse your listeners.

Body

As a speaker, once you have (1) *captured the listeners' attention*, (2) *aroused their interest in the information to come*, (3) *established your expertise, or right to inform*, and (4) *previewed your main points*, you are ready to present the information itself. Earlier the chapter noted what you could do to promote the listeners' comprehension of your ideas and to maintain their attention at a high level. You must also organize the body of your speech into meaningful groupings. The division of the whole into its parts is an essential step in explaining any complex concept. No one, for example, can understand all the aspects of public welfare, but most persons could assimilate certain features if they were presented and explained separately. In most instances, the division of a speech is inevitable in light of the subject matter. Such groupings are more easily remembered if they can be worded in a logical pattern. Reexamine some of the patterns of arrangement discussed in chapter 10 in light of their application to informative speaking.

Chronological Pattern. The *chronological pattern* has its greatest utility in presenting historical events, explaining processes, and relating personal experiences. To discuss the history of phonograph recording, you might develop your material under these headings:

I. Cylinder recordings of the late nineteen century.

II. Disk recordings of the early twentieth century.

III. Long-play recordings of the mid-twentieth century.

IV. Compact disc recordings of today.

To discuss a medical procedure, you might use these headings:

I. Preoperative procedures.

II. The operation.

III. Postoperative procedures.

The speaker mentioned earlier who talked about earthquakes used time as an organizational scheme:

    I. How to prepare for an earthquake.

    II. What to do once an earthquake occurs.

    III. What to do after an earthquake.

Spatial Pattern. Spatial order is especially effective in speeches describing a scene, location, or geographical distribution. For instance, your material could be arranged directionally from north to south, top to bottom, or center to outside. Weather patterns could be described according to those affecting the East Coast, Midwest, and West Coast. For a speech on sea life, you might select the following order:

    I. Surface sea life.

    II. Sea life 20 feet below the ocean surface.

    III. Sea life on the ocean floor.

If your topic is how to enjoy the local zoo, you could use the following sequence:

    I. Animal exhibits when you first enter the zoo.

    II. The enclosures in the middle of the zoo.

    III. The displays that ring the outer perimeter of the zoo.

If your topic is how to avoid serious hazards in the home, you could use the following pattern:

    I. Hazards found in the garage.

    II. Hazards found in the kitchen.

    III. Hazards found in the bathroom.

Problem-Solution Pattern. The *problem-solution* sequence is a common organizational pattern for speeches to inform. It moves the listeners from an obstacle (problem) to a remedy (solution). If you are dealing with the topic of first aid, you could organize your presentation around two serious problems (bleeding and shock) and then discuss the solution to these problems (treating bleeding and shock):

    I. The problem of excessive bleeding.

    II. The victim in shock.

    III. Treating bleeding and shock.

If your topic is carjacking, you might use the problem-solution pattern in the following manner:

    I. The rise in carjacking instances.

    II. Methods to avoid being a casualty of carjacking.

Another speaker used the problem-solution sequence to inform about the subject of illegal immigration:

I. What happens when people enter the United States illegally?

II. What is being done to deal with the problem of illegal immigration?

Ascending-Descending Pattern. The *ascending-descending sequence* takes listeners from the simple to the complex or from the less important to the more important. A speech about how to execute a series of dives from the high platform could effectively use an ascending-descending order (less complex-more complex):

I. The basic platform dive.

II. The swan dive.

III. The pike dive.

IV. The somersault dive.

A speaker trying to teach the audience how to meditate used the ascending-descending order:

I. Novice meditation techniques.

II. Moderate meditation techniques.

III. Advanced meditation techniques.

Causal Pattern. Causal order tells of the causes of certain effects or tells of the effects resulting from various causes. In giving a talk entitled "The Sun and Our Health," your pattern might be:

I. The effects of the sun on the skin.

II. The effects of the sun on the eyes.

III. The effects of the sun on the hair.

When treating the topic "Why World War II?" you might select the following arrangement:

I. United States and German relations before 1941.

II. United States and Italian relations before 1941.

III. United States and Japanese relations before 1941.

By examining the relationship of the United States to each of these countries, you would be able to point out some possible causes of World War II.

Topical Pattern. The *topical pattern* is probably the most frequently used of all patterns. This arrangement sets out several facets of a topic that are obviously related and consistent. If you are talking about the financial structure of your university, you might include this pattern:

I. The university's assets.

II. The university's liabilities.

III. The university's endowments.

In speaking on the subject of giant pandas, you could use the following topical sequence:

❖ ❖ ❖ ❖

     I. The pandas' diet.

    II. The pandas' breeding patterns.

   III. The pandas' natural habitat.

In speaking on the subject of the Islamic religion, you could use the following topical pattern:

     I. The history of Islam.

    II. The role of the prophet Muhammad in Islam.

   III. The Five Pillars of Islam.

The key to the topical pattern is that the arrangement is rather apparent and is the one an audience most likely expects. For example, if you were going to talk about the mechanics of sight, the audience would expect your topics to include the optic nerve, retina, cornea, pupil, iris, and lens. You may wish to order the material so that it moves from the simplest to the most complex, the most familiar to the least familiar, the least important to the most important, or the most acceptable to the least acceptable. When deciding on an organizational pattern, review the suggestions offered in chapter 10.

Conclusion

The methods of concluding a speech are explained in detail in chapter 11. However, certain concluding techniques are especially valuable for speeches to inform. For example, it may be helpful to restate your message and summarize its main points: "Today, we have seen that your grades can be improved if you select the correct location to study, learn how to determine the key points in your textbooks, and know how to prepare for objective examinations."

The most popular concluding technique is a *final summary (or reiteration)*. Listeners tend to pay close attention when they feel the end of the speech is near. The final summary takes advantage of this captured attention by reviewing the main ideas in the same order they were presented in the initial summary and in the body of the speech. In speaking on the topic of college registration, you might conclude by saying, "We have seen that you can register for classes in three ways. First, you can register by mail; second, you can make special arrangements with each instructor; and, finally, you can sign up in the registration office on the first day of classes."

Another speaker, when talking about handicapping horse races, ended her speech with two types of conclusion—a quotation and a summary:

> Knowing how difficult it is to make money at the races, most of us can agree with George Gissing's observation that 'horse racing is carried on mainly for the delight and profit of fools, ruffians, and thieves.' Yet, we also know that horse racing is fun, and we continue to go, so, to feel less like a fool, I urge you to follow the four steps of handicapping that I presented in my talk. First, examine the type of race you will be betting on; second, the 'class' of each horse in the race; third, the potential pace of the race; and, finally, the speed rating of each horse. Good luck—it's only money.

Once again, remember that your final summary should simply repeat your introduction and the main points of the body of your speech. If your initial summary said that you would teach the audience (1) how to prepare for an earthquake, (2) how to deal with the quake while it is going on, and (3) what to do once the quake is over, you should simply repeat these three ideas in your conclusion: "We should now know what to do before, during, and after an earthquake."

Sample Outline

Now that we have discussed the parts of an informative speech, we can look at a sample outline to review the relationship among those parts.

Title: Who Pays?

General Purpose: To inform

Specific Purpose: To have the audience understand the major arguments for and against state aid to parochial schools.

Introduction

(Rhetorical Question)

I. How many of you realize that one of the crucial battles that raged during the founding of this country remains an unresolved issue today?

   A. The early colonists were determined to separate church and state.

   B. Yet compulsory school attendance laws meant that parents who desired private schools were forced to finance two separate institutions.

(Motivation Toward Topic)

II. This highly emotional issue affects us today as much as it did over two hundred years ago.

   A. If the state were to pay tuition fees for private schools, millions of additional dollars would have to be found.

      1. Some of the money would come from our taxes.

      2. Money now being used to pay for public education would be rechanneled into parochial schools.

   B. If the state were to support parochial schools, some say it would bring church and state closer together.

   C. Yet what about the people who believe that, under the First Amendment, we can educate a child in any way we deem appropriate?

      1. Is it not a denial of our freedom to be forced to pay dual taxation?

      2. What if you believe that our public schools are "Godless"?

III. I have just completed a major research paper for my senior project in history on this topic.

     A. This paper focused on the specific issues involved in the separation of church and state.

     B. I plan to continue working on this project while attending graduate school.

(Preview)

  IV. To better understand this important issue of state aid to parochial schools, I will examine the arguments frequently made in favor of tax support for these schools and then examine the arguments advanced by those who oppose such aid.

Core Statement: Opinion is strongly divided on the issue of state aid to parochial schools.

Body

  I. Arguments that support tax aid for parochial schools are twofold.

     A. Denominational schools offer an important religious, spiritual, and ethical element not found in public schools.

       1. Only religious schools can teach Christian values.

       2. Public schools are Godless.

     B. The right of parents to determine the education and religious instruction of their children is a fundamental one.

       1. Failure to provide public funds for denominational schools is a partial denial of that right.

       2. This denial may well make some families second-class citizens, who are not benefiting from their taxes.

  II. Arguments advanced by those who oppose tax support for parochial schools are threefold.

     A. The appropriation of public funds for denominational schools would be a long step toward breaking down the unique North American policy of separation of church and state.

       1. It was part of an early colonial policy.

       2. It was an idea contained in the First Amendment to the Constitution.

     B. The organization of North American public schools along denominational lines would make education a divisive rather than a unifying factor in our lives.

       1. Schools now teach a variety of opinions and views.

2. Denominational schools would tend to teach dogma and one-dimensional attitudes.

C. The present arrangements promote healthy growth among various religions.

Conclusion

(Summary)

I. Today, by looking at both sides of an important issue, we have gained some insight into the pros and cons of tax support for parochial schools.

A. Those in favor of tax support suggest the following:

1. Denominational schools can do a better job of teaching values and ethics.

2. It is unfair to deny a basic right to persons who select parochial schools.

B. Those opposed counter by saying the following:

1. Granting funds for these schools would bring church and state closer together.

2. Denominational education is divisive.

3. The status quo is beneficial to both church and state.

II. In the final analysis, you must seek additional information before deciding how you feel about this important historical and religious problem.

Summary

This chapter examined speeches to inform, which are intended to increase an audience's knowledge of a subject. To achieve that end, you should be aware of some basic characteristics of learning—motivation, coupling, organization, frequency, multisensory stimulation, overload, depth, and central focus.

There are basically four types of speeches to inform: instructions, descriptions, explanations, and reports. In preparing a speech to inform, make sure that your specific purpose focuses on a worthwhile topic. You can then gather and select the materials of your speech. To help the audience learn and retain that material, you should use some of the following techniques: definitions; examples and illustrations; comparison and contrast; statistics; description; demonstration; reinforcement and emphasis; and partition, enumeration, and summaries.

To make your material more interesting, use some of the following attention-getting devices: noting that which is impending, alluding to that which is physically near, referring to the familiar, invoking personal needs, imparting activity, using reality, pointing out conflict, using humor, creating illustrations, and physically involving the audience.

When organizing a speech to inform, you should prepare an introduction that arouses attention, creates interest, establishes your expertise or right to inform, and previews your main points.

In selecting an organizational sequence, you can select from a number of patterns: chronological, spatial, problem-solution, ascending-descending, causal, and topical.

The most effective way to close an informative speech is to conclude with a summary.

Concepts and Questions

1. What is the primary objective of informative speeches?

2. What are six basic assumptions of learning and how do they relate to informative speaking?

3. What are the four basic types of informative speaking?

4. What should the introduction in the informative speech accomplish?

5. What devices help to maintain audience interest?

6. What are some problems that often make a speech too technical for a lay audience?

7. Why is establishing your credibility important in informative speaking?

Activities and Exercises

1. Attend one of your college or university classes and analyze the professor's presentation in light of the material discussed in this chapter.

2. Prepare a four-minute informative speech on one of the basic assumptions of learning. Use examples in your presentation.

3. Select a very technical topic and recount how you would explain some of the complicated aspects of the topic.

4. Select a topic and word your specific purpose in light of the four types of informative speeches:
    a. instructions
    b. descriptions
    c. explanations
    d. reports

5. Write a short essay that discusses why the following factors are important to informative speeches:
    a. basic assumptions of learning
    b. being clear
    c. being interesting ✦

CHAPTER FOURTEEN

Persuasive Speaking: Changing Beliefs, Attitudes, Values, and Behavior

> Every thought which genius and piety
> throw into the world alters the world.
>
> —*Emerson*

The Importance of Persuasion

It is a fact of life that people we know and those we hardly know, are constantly asking us to change our minds on a variety of topics. Have we not all heard some of the following appeals?

Our elementary school should adopt a multicultural curriculum.'

Casino gambling on Indian Reservations should be made illegal.

You should volunteer your services to the Big Brother or Big Sister Program.

Affirmative Action laws should be applied.

You should adopt a vegetarian diet.

The campus bookstore should be student run.

The United States should recognize the Cuban government.

Three new trauma centers should be established in our city.

The government should prohibit the sale of disposable diapers.

Racism is one of the most serious problems facing the United States.

We should all work to establish a viable third party in the United States.

Our campus needs an evening police escort service.

Whether we are the receiver or the sender, messages such as these are part of daily life. Persuasion, of course, also takes place during our interpersonal interactions. For example, you might advise a friend to stop smoking, try to "sell" yourself during an important job interview, attempt to convince a professor to change your grade, or ask someone to buy your used car. In each of these instances, as well as those listed above, we are asking others to agree with a particular point of view, feel a certain way, or carry out an action.

Examples of the utility of persuasion abound. You can see it at all levels of human communication, from the dialogues of high-level diplomats to the simple pleas of children seeking favors from their parents. Advertisers urge us to buy their products; politicians solicit our votes; friends try to get us to stop smoking; medical experts advise us to limit our intake of fat; parents try to win our cooperation in keeping the phone bill within reason. In short, whenever change is desired, people tend to choose persuasion as the means of bringing about that change.

Defining Persuasion

In chapter 13, we observed that the purpose of informative speaking is to increase the listeners' understanding of a particular topic by being clear and interesting. And even though listeners may act in a different manner because of the information that the speaker provided, the goal of the informative speech is learning. This is not the case with persuasion. *In persuasive speaking the speaker, with conscious intent, seeks to modify and/or change the beliefs, attitudes, values, or behavior of his or her audience.* The key phrase in this definition is *conscious intent.* That is, the speaker knows exactly what he or she wants from the audience before the preparation process begins. This awareness of intent allows the speaker to employ the best logical and emotional appeals available. A wise and ethical persuader knows that changes induced by coercive tactics and unsupported assertions are apt to be short-lived and grudgingly endured, while changes that are willingly undertaken may last indefinitely.

This chapter, then, aims to examine some of the ways in which you, as a persuader, can ethically influence changes in the beliefs, attitudes, values, or behavior of your listeners.

Types of Persuasive Speeches

Persuasive speeches can be classified according to the kinds of audience response being sought. The three most general categories are speeches (1) to convince, (2) to actuate, and (3) to stimulate. While these types often overlap, knowing what type of speech you will be giving is the necessary first step in selecting your arguments and appeals.

Speech to Convince

If your aim is to secure audience agreement with your position, then you are making a speech to convince. You might want the audience to agree that there is too much violence in children's cartoons, or that the library charges too high a fee for overdue books. Examples of a speech to convince would also be the argument that term limits should be imposed on all publicly elected officials, or that exit polls during national elections often keep some people from voting. You might be concerned about domestic violence and hope to convince your audience that it is a serious and growing problem in the United States. In all five of these examples, you are trying to convince your audience of the validity of your assertion. You are not asking them to take action but only trying to get them to agree with your position.

Speech to Actuate

If your objective is to get audience action on a matter, then you are making a speech to actuate. Your emphasis is on an overt behavior. Notice the action dimension when you urge your audience to donate to a charity, sign up for the campus mentor program, write to a legislator, buy an insurance policy, take a specific college course, get a pet from an animal shelter, or sign an organ

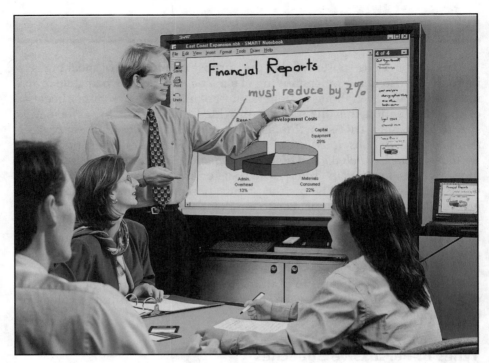

Factual evidence is a crucial part of any speech to persuade. (Photo: Courtesy of SMART Technologies, Inc.)

donor card. In all of these instances you are asking for them to do something that involves action.

Speech to Stimulate

If your aim is to reinforce, intensify, or rejuvenate listeners' existing attitudes or beliefs, you are making a speech to stimulate. You are giving inspirational messages, arousing emotions, and inciting pride. Telling a group of college freshman to study hard or asking an audience to value the life of all animals represents speeches that try to arouse basic beliefs. Talking about the need to overcome ethnocentrism is yet another topic that falls into the category of a speech to stimulate. Your goal in each of these instances is to remind the audience of a basic value they most likely already hold. You are "stimulating" them to once again think about that value. Some occasions for stimulating speeches range from sermons to company pep talks to commencement addresses.

The Goals of Persuasive Speaking

Persuasive speaking, like all the forms of communication discussed in this book, is not a random and aimless activity. Rather, it is motivated by a speaker having a *conscious set of goals. More specifically, in persuasive discourse, a speaker seeks to accomplish a specific, predetermined purpose by bringing about changes in belief, attitudes, values, or behavior.* Therefore, as a persuasive speaker, you need to be concerned with these four variables if you are to accomplish your persuasive purpose. You need to ask yourself this simple yet complex question: *How must my audience change or modify their beliefs, attitudes, values, or behaviors if they are going to respond favorably to my recommendations?* To help you answer this question, let us pause and examine the key components of these four variables.

Beliefs

The Spanish poet Antonio Machado eloquently underscored the importance of values when he stated, "Under all that we think, lives all we believe, like the ultimate veil of our spirits." What is a belief? *A **belief** is commonly defined as a personally held conviction in the truth of a statement or in the existence of something.* In a sense, it is a way for people to structure their reality. Such convictions can be held with or without proof. We have beliefs about religion ("Muhammad was a messenger from Allah"), events ("NATO troops intervening in Bosnia was necessary"), other people ("Senator Smith would make an excellent president"), actions ("It is beneficial to take one aspirin each day"), and even ourselves ("I am very witty").

Beliefs may be founded on direct experience, on the word of someone you trust, or on your own reasoning. You might believe that aspirin alleviates headache pain because you have experienced relief after taking aspirin. You might believe that a certain treatment will arrest the spread of a malignant growth because a physician you respect claims it has done so in the past. You might believe that a particular restaurant poses health hazards because you saw a dead cat next to the restaurant's garbage cans.

Beliefs are also strongly affected by culture. We are not born with our beliefs; they are learned, and culture is the teacher. Americans might acknowledge that *CBS Evening News* or the *New York Times* is a good place to learn about what we should believe. In the Islamic tradition, however, there is a belief that the writings in the Koran are an infallible source of what to believe in. Whether we trust the *Times*, the Bible, the Koran, the entrails of a goat, tea leaves, the visions induced by peyote, or the Taoist I Ching depends on our cultural background—and any successful speaker needs to remember that. People who have grown up in China, part of the African plain, or Cuba may believe that business and the means of production should belong to the state or to the people collectively. On the other hand, someone born in the United States or Canada most likely grew up believing that an individual "deserves what he or she earns" and would be reluctant to share profits.

If you plan to persuade another person, you need to know his or her beliefs on the topic in question. This information will help you select your arguments and emotional appeals. If, for example, you predict that your audience believes that exercise is crucial for good health, you could appeal to this belief as you ask your listeners to support a new bike trail in the park.

Attitudes

*An **attitude** can be defined as a state of mind or an emotion toward a person or situation.* An attitudes might also be thought of as a *tendency* to behave in one way or another. They reflect our likes and dislikes toward persons, places, and things. They are usually easier to change than are beliefs. You may feel a certain way about youth gangs, the police, military service, talk shows on television, labor unions, beauty pageants, and the use of animals in medical research. Your attitudes tend to guide you in your responses to these and countless other subjects and orientations. These predispositions to act one way or another are learned from our family, the media, schools, religious affiliations, and the like. They are important to persuasion in that most persuasive efforts seek to change or reinforce existing attitudes. As a speaker, you need to predict your audience's attitudes because those attitudes will determine whether your listeners will respond favorably or unfavorably to your specific purpose. For example, if the audience members have a positive attitude toward the German culture, they might easily support your speech about a plan to put a German car company in their city. In this case; your arguments are simple. However, if their attitude is that the Germans are already too influential in the economy of the United States, you would have to muster an entirely different set of arguments so that your position is consistent with some positive attitudes they do hold. Attitudes are so powerful that they can sway many decisions and actions.

When thinking about your audience, it is important to remember the role of culture in shaping and maintaining attitudes. As noted in chapter 3, cultures have varying attitudes on a host of subjects. These cultural attitudes, whether about the elderly, gays, guns, individualism, work, women, or the future, need to be taken into account.

Values

Values represent yet another variable that influences what people are apt to think or feel about a particular subject. Many of our most important beliefs and attitudes are grounded in our basic value system. **Values** *have been called the evaluative components of our beliefs and attitudes.* Evaluative qualities include what is good or bad, right or wrong; what ought to be or ought not to be; and what is useful or useless, appropriate or inappropriate. It is also important to keep in mind that values are arranged in a hierarchical order—some values are more important than others. In short, values serve as a sort of "guiding light" that assists us in making choices and resolving conflicts.

As indicated, what is important about values is that they underpin most of our attitudes, beliefs, and actions. The value placed on a woman's right to choose influences an attitude toward abortion. Someone who highly values education might find it easier to support a plan to increase taxes for a new university. Someone who values the sanctity of all life might support a suggestion to stop using animals for medical experiments. A person who places a high priority on physical appearance might find it easier to stop smoking if someone was to tell him or her that prolonged smoking causes lips to wrinkle badly as one gets older.

Although each of us has a unique set of values, some values tend to permeate a culture and are called cultural values. Most cultural values are derived from the larger philosophical issues that are part of a culture's milieu. Cultural values define what is worthwhile for members of a culture to die for, what is worth protecting, what frightens people, what are proper subjects for study and for ridicule, and what types of circumstances lead to happiness.

Cultural values include views of such topics as age, privacy, time, responsibility, change, equality, honesty, status, and work.

Behavior

Behavior *refers to an audience's observable activity.* Behavior change represents the action component of persuasion. You are asking people to do something that can be observed. That observable state ranges from total inactivity to hyperactivity. Changes in behavior can take a person from action to inaction or the reverse; the change may involve an increase or decrease in the intensity, duration, or magnitude of an action. For example, if you were to urge your best friend to discontinue jogging as a form of exercise, you might observe one of these changes in behavior: your friend might jog more than ever out of defiance, might ignore your advice and continue to jog as usual, might cut down on the amount of time spent jogging, or might choose walking or another form of exercise. Behavior changes are sometimes immediate (persuading people to sign a petition that you circulate after your talk), sometimes delayed (persuading people to buy healthier foods next time they go to the market), and sometimes lasting (persuading people to stop eating meat). The acid test for the speech that stresses behavior change is that you are asking the audience to act (behave) differently than they did before you started speaking.

Concerns of Persuasion

Once you have decided that your reason for speaking is persuasive, your next step is to narrow your focus. Whether you seek to bring about changes in belief, attitude, value, or behavior, you must think of your goal in terms of a specific **proposition.** A proposition describes the way you want you listeners to believe or act. *Most propositions for persuasive speaking deal with questions related to facts, values, and/or policies.* Before examining these three types of questions, you should keep in mind that a single speech might contain one, two, or all three of these questions.

Questions of Fact

When a speaker is asserting that something actually exists or is true or that something happened or did not happen, the issue involved is a question of fact. In these instances the speaker's central point is termed a **proposition of fact**; he or she is attempting to prove or disprove the existence of something. The goal of the speaker is to persuade the audience that the proposition being asserted is true. Following are a few examples of propositions of fact:

Overworked traffic controllers present serious risks to airline travelers.

Tap water in our town contains many impurities.

The county's landfill facilities are now at capacity.

Boxing causes brain damage.

A national health insurance program will greatly increase taxes.

❖ ❖ ❖ ❖

A vegetarian diet reduces the risk of colon cancer.

The jury system often produces decisions that are unfair.

Television talk shows often encourage violent behavior.

Notice that in each of these examples the speaker is asserting the "fact" as if it were true. He or she will then have to offer evidence and sound reasoning to persuade the audience that the assertion is a fact. Three additional observations regarding issues of fact are in order before we move on. First, it is important to note that propositions of fact deal with alleged facts—matters whose reality can be disputed. Second, they may deal with past, present, or future circumstances. "Last year's tax bill undermined voter confidence in the administration" alleges the existence of a circumstance in the past. "Water rationing is causing an increase in the insect population of the Central Valley" asserts a present condition. "Most Americans will be unable to afford a home by the year 2005" alleges a future condition. Finally, remember that propositions of fact set the stage for the other two propositions. Proving that overexposure to the sun can cause skin cancer (fact) allows you to then persuade your audience to use sunscreen lotions when going into the sun (policy).

Questions of Value

If a speaker and a listener differ over the merit of a value judgment, the issue involved is a question of value, and the speaker's central point is termed a **proposition of value**. In other words, the speaker is placing an estimate of worth on something, alleging that it is good or bad, better or worse than something else, right or wrong, justified or unjustified. Words such as *moral, corrupt, worthwhile, unjust,* and *virtuous* are often heard in propositions of value. All these types of questions deal with propositions that tend to be subjective, personal, and even private. The following are examples of propositions of value:

State prisons are inhuman.

Abortion is immoral.

Capital punishment is incongruous with Christian values.

Sex education has a place in health classes.

Helping the homeless is our moral responsibility.

Our culture puts too much emphasis on physical appearance.

The use of animals for testing purposes is cruel.

Our treatment of the homeless is irresponsible.

Like propositions of fact, propositions of value may deal with matters in the past (the United States mistreated Native Americans), present (elderly people are ridiculed on most television programs), or future (the Internet should be strictly regulated to protect children).

Questions of Policy   ❖ ❖ ❖ ❖

Differences between a speaker and a listener over the advisability of pursuing a specific course of action falls under the category of a **proposition of policy**. The speaker argues that something should or should not be done. That is to say, questions of policy ask for a specific action and/or a new policy to be taken. That policy or action can be personal ("Cigarettes should not fbe sold on our campus") or general ("The Federal government should double the tax rate on cigarettes"). Here are some sample propositions of policy:

Films rated X should not be shown on campus.

A lifeguard station should be installed at South Beach.

The cigarette tax should be raised by 50 cents a pack.

The insurance industry should be regulated.

The proposed student center should not be built with student funds.

Our college should provide a free child-care center for students with young children.

You should sign up for a volunteer program to aid the elderly.

The death penalty should be abolished.

As noted elsewhere, it is not unusual for a speaker to defend all three kinds of propositions (fact, value, and policy) within a single speech. For example, a speaker trying to win support for a proposed policy usually has to prove several propositions:

Something is wrong with the current system—proposition of fact: "There is too much violence on prime-time television."

The proposed plan will help solve the problem—proposition of policy: "Prime-time television needs to enact a stricter rating system."

The proposed policy is better than other proposals advanced—proposition of value: "Our children will not be exposed to harmful messages."

We have talked about changes in listener beliefs, attitudes, values, or actions as the aim of a persuader advocating propositions of fact, value, and policy. However, remember that it is not the persuader or the persuasive speech that changes those beliefs, attitudes, or actions—it is the listener who changes them. The persuader's job is to present the listener with a choice between an existing belief, attitude, or action and one that the speaker recommends. Then it is up to the listener to make a choice. If the speaker's recommendations prove to be sufficiently attractive, the listener will choose to make the desired change. Presenting an attractive alternative, then, lies at the heart of persuasion.

Preparing a Persuasive Speech

Preparing a persuasive speech involves a process similar to that used in preparing an informative speech. A speaker (1) chooses a topic, (2) formulates a specific purpose, (3) analyzes the audience, (4) finds the materials for achieving that purpose, (5) organizes the speech, and then (6) practices it. Although all six of these steps have been discussed in detail elsewhere in this book, their application to persuasion requires certain unique procedures.

Choosing a Topic

Ideally, the choice of a topic for a persuasive speech should arise from the speaker's recognition of a condition that requires change. That change can take the form of individual change ("You should never drink and drive") or it can be a change that requires the help of others ("We all need to support House Bill #253, which requires an automatic jail term for anyone driving under the influence of alcohol"). Occasions that call for persuasive speaking are nearly endless. Perhaps you feel that student activity fees at your school are too high, but also believe that you may never see a reduction until students get together to put pressure on those responsible for setting the fees. Such a situation calls for a persuasive speech. Perhaps you live near a pulp mill and suffer from the odor of its operation. You want the odor reduced but know that such a reduction will not take place until people unite to put pressure on the management. Again, the need for a persuasive speech arises. In each case, you become aware of a disturbing element. Then you take a stance with regard to the correction of that disturbing element.

There may be times when the topic and position are chosen for you. Perhaps a friend asks you to solicit for a worthy cause. Perhaps you become a salesperson and are told what to sell. Regardless of whether you originate the subject or someone else does, you should not undertake a persuasive task unless you are interested in the topic and are motivated to persuade.

Formulating a Specific Purpose

In a persuasive speech, the statement of your specific purpose indicates exactly what you want the audience to believe, feel, or do:

> For my audience to believe that the act of poaching in parts of Africa is endangering many rare animals.

> For my audience to volunteer one hour each weekend to help clear a firebreak around the campus.

> For my audience to believe that all employees working in the transportation industry should be tested for drugs.

> For my audience to support a boycott of the campus bookstore.

> For my audience to believe that tanning booths are dangerous.

> For my audience to agree that violence directed at gays is increasing at a rapid rate.

> For my audience to donate money for the flood victims in the southern portion of our states.

When you have formulated your specific purpose, you can begin analysis your of audience.

Analyzing an Audience

Although chapter 3 dealt with the topic of audience analysis, we need to return to this crucial phase of communication here because the majority of failures in persuasive speaking can probably be traced to an insufficient or inaccurate analysis of those whom the speaker wishes to influence. Perhaps the speaker has taken pains to find out about the listeners as individuals but has failed to take into account what they are like when they become members of a group. The group imposes codes of behavior that do not necessarily operate on individuals removed from the group. A salesperson accustomed to dealing with one person at a time sometimes finds it difficult to deal with a group, so different are persons in their public and private behaviors. On the other hand, some speakers find it easier to deal with a group than with an individual because most people tend to think less critically as members of a group. Whatever the case, a speaker should become familiar with what motivates each listener as an individual and as a member of a group.

In analyzing your listeners, you should seek answers to the following questions: (1) What attitudes, beliefs, and values do they hold about my topic? (2) What has influenced them to take their present positions on the topic? (3) What is their attitude toward me as a spokesperson? Let us examine each of these questions in detail so that you will have a greater appreciation of the link between audience analysis and persuasive speaking.

Determine Attitudes, Beliefs, and Values Toward the Subject. You may discover that there are many different individual and group attitudes toward your topic and your position on that topic. Generally, those attitudes may be clustered under the following heads: *apathetic, hostile, interested but undecided,* and *favorable.* It is important that you make an effort to determine which attitude is most representative of your audience. This will let you select the arguments and appeals that directly relate to the audience's beliefs, attitudes, and values.

Apathetic. Individual listeners, or perhaps the entire audience, may have a "don't care" attitude. For example, if you are trying to enlist the support of a group of white-collar workers for legislation governing the wages and hours of farm workers, their attitude might be, What do the wages and hours of farm workers have to do with us? To help your listeners overcome their apathy, you might decide to place particular stress on the link between your proposal and the listeners' self-interests. If you are trying to persuade a group of land developers that a specific project should not be supported, you might use the argument that the new project would lower the property value of vacant and undeveloped land in the area.

Hostile. Individual listeners, or the audience as a whole, may be strongly opposed to the point of view you wish to urge. For example, imagine the attitude of a group of produce truckers toward your proposal to reduce the speed limit of all commercial vehicles to 50 miles per hour. In such a situation, you might commence with ideas on which you and the truckers agree before you turn to those areas in which you disagree. Maybe you would point out that you can understand their concern about possible produce spoilage if transit time is prolonged, but then you could show them that lower vehicle insurance premiums, occasioned by a safer speed limit, would enable them to purchase refrigeration units for their trucks. When dealing with hostile audiences, you can approach the topic indirectly and/or demonstrate to the audience that they already agree with the basic assumption behind your position.

Interested but undecided. If your audience analysis shows that some or all of your listeners are interested in but undecided about what you are advocating, you might decide to emphasize the factual evidence supporting your position. No doubt you have noticed that salespeople are quick to offer information about their products when they detect a sign of customer interest. In such cases, persuasion may be effected through information.

Favorable. If you know that your audience favors the point of view you intend to uphold, you might want to reaffirm your listeners' basis for agreeing with your position. This is especially so in situations calling for a "pep talk." Sometimes beliefs have to be rejuvenated; listeners have to be reminded of the merits of their grounds for belief. There is nothing wrong with trying to persuade people of what often appears to be common knowledge. We all know that smoking is harmful to one's health, that drinking and driving is dangerous, and that seat belts should be worn at all times, yet think of the millions of people who need to be reminded of these three "facts."

Once you have thought about the type of audience you will be addressing, you can begin to ask some very precise and specific questions as they directly relate to the topic:

- Does the audience know that a problem exists? Do they doubt or deny that a problem exists?

- Are they aware of the seriousness of the problem? Do they doubt or deny the seriousness of the problem?

- Are they aware of the causes of the problem? Are they likely to doubt my interpretation of the causes?

- Are they aware of the possibility of solving the problem? Do they doubt or deny that a solution can be found?

- Are they aware of the various solutions that have been advanced? Are they aware of the advantages and disadvantages of some or all of the proposed solutions?

- Do they doubt the workability of my proposed solution?

- Do they doubt the superiority of my proposed solution over other proposed solutions?

- Are there cultural differences that will influence how they perceive the problem and the solution?

In all these questions you are attempting to discover whether your audience has criteria to measure the truth of the facts you are alleging or the value judgment you are urging.

Any analysis of the audience must include an evaluation of their perception of you as a speaker. The topic of credibility is so important to the persuasive speaker that it is discussed it in great detail later in the chapter. This chapter offers some ways to assist you in having the audience perceive you as a highly credible source. But for now you must remember to involve all dimensions of credibility early in your preparation. For example, discover if the audience perceives you as having a good reputation before you give your speech. If your prespeech image is negative, you will have to exert great effort during your speech to supplant it with a favorable reputation. If the audience has no prior opinion of you, your job will be to create a good impression through the speech itself.

Finding Material

Theories of persuasion date back to the times of the ancient Greeks. Perhaps the definitive statement of the principal ways in which persuasion occurs was made by Aristotle, 24 centuries ago, when he wrote in his *Rhetoric*: "Persuasion is effected by the arguments, when we demonstrate the truth, real or apparent, by such means as inhere in particular cases ... Persuasion is effected through the audience, when they are brought by the speech into a state of emotion . . . The character of the speaker is a cause of persuasion when the speech is so uttered as to make him worthy of belief . . ." A glance at the various treatments of persuasion since that time demonstrates the durability of Aristotle's classification of the modes of persuasion. That is to say, current research in the field of persuasion supports Aristotle's conclusion that *to change the mind or behavior of other people, we must have a sound argument, appeal to their emotions, and be perceived as a highly credible source.* Therefore, in this section, we shall explore (1) convincing arguments, (2) impelling psychological appeals, and (3) personal credibility.

Convincing Arguments

In *Henry V*, Shakespeare wrote, "There is occasion and causes for the why and wherefore of all things." He is saying that from the simplest to the most complex of acts, whenever we take an action or entertain a given belief or attitude, we like to think we have good reasons for doing so. In fact, we human beings search for reasons to justify our behavior, whether it is past behavior ("I voted for Nancy because I was tired of student fees going up each semester"), present behavior ("I wear seat belts because I am concerned about automobile safety"), or intended behavior ("When I graduate, I plan to work for the Sierra Club so that I can concentrate on environmental issues"). You will notice that, in all three of our examples, the person has a reason for his or her action (a dislike of higher fees, a concern about safety, a desire for a certain type of career).

The two key requirements for a reasonable argument are *reasoning* (how we organize our thinking and material) and *concrete evidence*. In a sense we have touched on these two ingredients in other contexts, when we dealt with evidence in chapter 6 and critical thinking in chapter 9. However, let us now examine these concepts from a persuasive speaking perspective. We will look at evidence here and examine sound reasoning later, in the chapter when we treat organization.

Most evidence falls into one of two categories: evidence of fact or evidence of opinion. Let us now look at each of these types and apply them to persuasive speaking.

Evidence of Fact. *Factual evidence is a crucial part of any speech to persuade.* Remember, in persuasive speaking you are usually asking people to change their beliefs. Factual evidence may be drawn from your personal observations or from external sources. You may have witnessed an event and then reported to others what you saw. Perhaps you saw an automobile accident at an intersection and then recounted the details to an investigating officer. Maybe you argued with a friend over which subcompact car gets the best gas mileage and cited figures compiled from your own driving experience in one of the cars.

The validity of factual evidence drawn from your own personal observation is dependent on how you answer the following questions:

- How well equipped am I to be a good witness of the "facts" I reported?
- Are my perceptions colored by an emotional state?
- Did I see only what I wanted to see?
- How well equipped am I to report what I have seen?
- Do I alter the story to make it more interesting?
- Do I possess the vocabulary necessary for relatively objective reporting?

Factual evidence (examples, illustrations, and statistics) that you draw from outside sources must meet these same tests plus some additional tests of validity:

- Is the fact being reported by the person who observed it?
- Is the fact being reported by a secondary source?
- What is the secondary source's reputation for reliability?
- When was the fact observed, and when was it reported?
- Is the fact represented out of context? Do other sources report the same fact?

Persuasive arguments need factual evidence if listeners are to believe your assertions and observations. For example, if you were trying to prove the extent of "downsizing" in the military, you might use the following facts to support your point:

> The cutting ax has been deep. According to the Department of Defense, 165 facilities are to be shut or slimmed down, 43 of them major bases. More than 60,000 civilian jobs will be eliminated.

If you are persuading an audience that waste disposal is a serious problem in the United States, you could offer the following fact: "Half of our 6,000 landfills will be full or closed by the year 2002." In this and the previous example, you can see how the persuasive speaker used facts to help convince the listeners that they should believe the validity of the assertion being advanced.

Evidence of Opinion. We once again ask you to return to chapter 6 and review our detailed discussion of expert testimony as part of your preparing for persuasive speaking. You will be reminded that opinion evidence has two sources also—your own personal opinions based on your direct experience and the opinions of others who, presumably, are experts. The acceptability of an "educated guess" is, of course, dependent on whether the audience views you as a person qualified to express an informed opinion. If, by reason of your occupation or your major field of study, you do possess the necessary qualifications for expertise—and if your audience recognizes these qualifications as adequate—you may use yourself as a source of opinion. By and large, however, student speakers should use the testimony of a recognized authority. Your arguments would have a persuasive tone if you were to say, "The Surgeon General of the United States recently said that secondhand smoke represents a serious health hazard for nonsmokers." Think of the added weight of your position on the destruction of the world's forests if you were to offer the following testimony: "Professor Daniel Wilson of the University of California Environmental Biology Department said that three plants that might help cure AIDS are currently being bulldozed over in the forests of Panama, Brazil, and Costa Rica."

Impelling Psychological Appeals

French writer Joseph Roux observed, "Reason guides but a small part of us, and that the least interesting. The rest obeys feeling, true or false, and passion, good or bad." In the context of this the chapter, he is saying that people are not computers or machines, that on most occasions evidence alone is not sufficient to induce the desired response from an audience. This is particularly true when that response calls for a behavioral change, such as taking (or refraining from taking) an action. You can probably think of a time when someone convinced you that you ought to take a certain action, but you never got around to doing so. Perhaps the person used faultless reasoning and unimpeachable evidence to convince you that a problem existed and that there was an ideal solution to that problem, yet you failed to take the steps necessary to implement that solution. Why? Because they failed to touch you on a personal and intimate level.

What are the forces that motivate and impel us to act? As you would suspect, these forces are multiple and complex—too complex to be analyzed in a few pages of a textbook. Philosophers, pastors, and psychologists nevertheless seem to have agreed on three general forces that can exert an influence on actions: *(a) our desire to satisfy a personal need, (b) our desire to maintain consistency*, and *(c) our susceptibility to suggestion*. What is interesting about these three characteristics is that they are found in all cultures. Let us look at each and see how it can be used by a persuasive speaker to accomplish a purpose.

Our Desire to Satisfy Personal Needs. In his renowned study of human needs and motivations, A. H. Maslow supplied a classification system that lists five human needs in their order of urgency. Knowing something about these needs will enable you to link them to your specific purpose and to your material.

1. *Physiological needs.* The most basic of our needs are physiological. These are needs for food, water, air, and rest. These biological needs have to be met before we are inclined to attend to other, less urgent needs. If your audience is in a hot, stuffy room, they might be receptive to signing a petition that would urge the college administration to add a new air conditioning system to the campus classroom building.

2. *Safety needs.* Second in importance, according to Maslow, are our safety needs. A strong need in all of us is the desire to feel free from harm in the present and future: safe and secure in our homes, jobs, and play. Speeches

dealing with life insurance, seat belts, drunk driving, smoking, health, crime, and the like can make effective use of this important need. One speaker appealed to this need in a talk on the advantages of a vegetarian diet. Among other things, she told her audience that when compared to nonvegetarians, people who do not eat any animal products have a lower incidence of heart attack and colon cancer. Another speaker who was urging the city to add more police officers to the local parks used the need for safety when he talked about the increased number of violent crimes against children taking place in the parks. He not only offered statistics, but he also told the story of a little boy attacked by two other youths who wanted his money.

3. *Social needs*. Once physiological and safety needs have been met, we are ready to turn to social needs. These are needs that Maslow maintains relate to our need to be loved and valued. We all need a sense of belonging to or being a part of someone else's life. Families, friends, and lovers help us satisfy this need. Ethical appeals to family, religion, and culture are powerful persuasive tools. A speaker who appeals to social needs may show audience members how his or her proposal will offer their parents a complete health plan without depleting their parents' savings accounts. A speaker appealing to college spirit, love of country, or the welfare of loved ones is also tapping into this basic need.

4. *Needs for self-esteem*. Maslow suggests that each of us wants to experience a feeling of self-respect as well as recognition from others; thus, we take many paths to satisfy these yearnings. Telling listeners how, by adhering to your message, they can achieve a specific goal, gain respect, be accepted, or raise their status and credibility appeal to this need. As you would suspect, this is a very popular allure if your topic deals with having your listeners purchase a product. To tell a group of students that by purchasing a study guide, their grades will go up and their professors will think better of them is an example of using the esteem need.

5. *Self-actualization needs*. These center on our desire to realize the full potential within us. Thus, we turn to creative acts in whatever areas our interests dictate. You are appealing to this highest of motives when you show your audience that, by adopting your proposal, they will "enrich their lives and reach their full potential."

All these five classifications have implications for persuasion. For one thing, a person with an unfulfilled need would probably be amenable to recommendations about how to fulfill that need. Consequently, a persuader is well advised to discover the listeners' needs and then plan a strategy of persuasion based on fulfilling those needs. By showing listeners that the speaker's proposal will satisfy a felt need, he or she increases the chances of achieving a specific purpose.

How does a speaker invoke the listeners' needs? Perhaps an examination of some motivational appeals used by persuaders over the years can help answer that question.

Self-preservation. Safety devices, physical fitness courses, and life-prolonging medications are examples of goods and services that provide a partial answer to our need to stay alive and enjoy physical well-being. Construction workers who wear hard hats and buy shoes with steel-reinforced toes are acting out of a desire for self-preservation. We buy smoke alarms for our homes in response to that desire. The familiar tactic of those soliciting support for an

❖ ❖ ❖ ❖

increase in military expenditures is to use self-preservation as the appeal: "With more and more small countries developing nuclear weapons, we'd better move fast in our own program of weapons development if we want to avoid a war in a remote area of the world." Self-preservation is also the obvious motive when a speaker asks for added campus security by telling the story of a couple "mugged" and seriously injured after a college basketball game. By simply adding the phrase, "Just think about it, you could have been the one who was sent to the hospital," the speaker points the example directly at the audience.

Sexual attraction. A quick glance at almost any magazine, newspaper, billboard, or television advertisement confirms the power of sex attraction as a motive to buy an astonishingly wide range of goods and services. Advertisements that urge you to buy an airline ticket to Cancun conjure up images of a sun-bronzed lover. Even the purchase of a microwave oven is supposed to leave you more time for the one you love. While an advertiser can flaunt sex appeal freely, a public speaker is well advised to use this motive more discreetly.

Acquisition of property. In the dominant North American culture, the acquisition of material goods is a basic value. Advertisers and public speakers know of this value and make great use of appeals to our wallets and purses. Bargain sales, "giant economy sizes," higher rates of return on investments, and various speculative ventures are manifestations of the nearly universal desire of persons to acquire property. For instance, a spokesperson for a school bond drive points out that a better-educated citizenry will be a more prosperous citizenry, suggesting that money spent now will be returned many times over as a result of a healthier economy.

Fear. Over two thousand years ago the Greek playwright Aeschylus invoked the power of fear when he wrote, "Fear is stronger than arms." Much of our behavior is motivated by fear. We fear the loss of our money, loved ones, health, job, and in fact all those things we deem important. Speakers who tell us to wear seat belts, get flu shots, and eat healthy foods are all appealing to fear of consequences that await us if we do not heed their assertion.

Self-esteem. At times, we will sacrifice personal safety, sublimate sex attraction, and disdain the acquisition of property if it means that our self-esteem can be increased. The desire to be "looked up to," to be well regarded by our peers or superiors, to be perceived as responsible and reliable is a powerful motivating force. It may show up in such diverse actions as donating a large sum to charity, enrolling in night school, climbing the Matterhorn, skydiving, "standing up for our rights," or driving an expensive sports car. Extended to groups, self-esteem takes the form of civic pride, a desire to be "number one," a wish to be the host of the Super Bowl, or a desire to have the world's finest medical research laboratory.

Personal enjoyment. Our love of cars containing all the options, of exotic food and drink, of luxurious accommodations, of remote-controlled appliances, of all the so-called good things in life becomes a more dominant motive once our basic needs for food, clothing, and shelter have been satisfied. We do not buy cream cheese for its life-sustaining qualities but for its power to bring pleasure to our taste buds. We do not buy a $200,000 home just to keep out the elements but to satisfy our love of the good things. Portable compact disc players, holographic art, catamarans, hang gliders, and motor homes are acquired primarily to satisfy our need for personal enjoyment.

Loyalty. Whether our allegiance and loyalty be directed at country, state, community, or campus, we are all proud of our affiliations. A speaker who is aware of this devotion to country or club can effectively use it to motivate an audience. An example of using loyalty as a motive appeal is telling a group of students that, unless we get the money for the new library, our university will become a second-rate institution.

Individualism. Although it is a very Western trait, a call to individualism is an effective motive appeal. In the North American culture, individualism is the belief that the interest and welfare of the individual is paramount. It stresses individual initiative and encourages free expression. If speakers can link their central themes to these characteristics, they can greatly improve the chances of accomplishing their persuasive purposes. Recently, we heard a speaker justify the need to spend more money on police protection by suggesting that when burglars enter your home illegally, they are violating your private domain.

Curiosity. People undertake many things not simply for tangible benefit but to satisfy their sense of curiosity. We flock to a balloon-launching event, patronize a wax museum, buy a paperback book with an enticing cover, or try a "new taste sensation" because we find the unusual and the novel so alluring.

Imitation. The desire to "be just like" a person we admire may prompt us to buy the breakfast food recommended by an Olympic gold medalist, to acquire the same kind of large-screen color television set as our neighbor, or to vote for the political candidate recommended by our favorite movie actor. A speaker must be cautious, however, in appealing to imitative instincts. Pains should be taken to discover whether or not the listeners really admire the model. If the listeners envy the model instead, they may go to great lengths to avoid imitation.

Altruism. We like to think that we are compassionate and that most of our actions are not selfishly motivated. We make anonymous donations to charity, we send CARE packages abroad, and we volunteer to read to the blind. A successful persuasive speaker is well aware of altruism in all of us and uses this appeal when asking help for victims as diverse as abandoned animals and neglected children. Notice in the example that follows (on the subject of the laboratory testing of animals) how the speaker connects compassion to her topic while describing a cosmetic testing laboratory:

> They had over one hundred rabbits in a large crate. They then shot the rabbits with a chemical. Regardless of whether or not the rabbit was dead they would throw it 10 feet onto a pile in the middle of the floor. Many rabbits would still be crawling around on the floor and on top of the other dead and dying rabbits. I could tell that the main objective in the laboratory was not killing the rabbits humanely and painlessly, it was speed and efficiency. Many of the rabbits had blood coming out of their mouths, others were convulsing and having spasms. It got to the point where I could no longer stand to watch their suffering. I literally became ill and had to leave the laboratory.

Using Motive Appeals

A speaker should keep some of the following ideas in mind when using motive appeals.

1. *Try to consider using as many appropriate appeals as possible, because not all members of an audience are motivated by the same appeal.* Needs and

wants differ from individual to individual and from culture to culture. For example, if you oppose the construction of a new state prison near a residential area, you might be addressing citizens who live in the affected area, others who live in the same city but not close to the affected area, and still others who are residents of other cities hundreds of miles away from the prison. Moreover, you might find them to be of diverse ages, financial means, social classes, and value systems. With such a heterogeneous audience, it would be folly to rely on a single type of motive appeal. Although a fear appeal (threat to self-preservation) might motivate those who live in the affected area, it would hardly be applicable to those from another city. You might have to inform those people of the threat to their pocketbooks (need for acquisition of property) posed by expenditures of tax dollars for the building and operation of the proposed prison. Pointing out to other segments of the audience that their personal enjoyment of the natural beauty of the area is threatened by the construction of a new prison might be appropriate. Conceivably, you might use the "fight city hall" appeal if some of your listeners believe that government has too much power and is forcing an unwanted prison on the community.

There are many more categories and appeals available to creative speakers than the ones highlighted earlier in the chapter. You might want to attract interest in your topic by using hope, power, control, independence, or conformity. Always consult your audience analysis when considering which appeal may have the best results.

2. *Always combine emotional appeals with logical appeals.* This blending allows an audience to see the wisdom of your proposal at the same time as they are "moved" by it. Notice in the following example, dealing with stricter drunk driving laws, how a motive appeal (in the form of a factual illustration) is fused with statistics:

> The holiday season was special to nine-year-old Carla and her family. Carla's birthday was five days before Christmas, and her grandmother's birthday was Christmas Eve. The family was going to celebrate both birthdays and Christmas that night. So, for this young girl, as the family headed down the highway, a very special night was awaiting her. However, one thing went dreadfully wrong. On the way to the family gathering, a drunk driver, with three times the legal limit of alcohol in his blood, crashed into the side of the car where Carla's head was resting. The bright, cheerful, loving child was killed instantly. Carla would not get to open presents on Christmas morning with her family. In fact, like the other 2,000 people killed by alcohol-related crashes between Thanksgiving and New Year's Eve, Carla would never get to celebrate another Christmas. Instead, Christmas will always remain for Carla's family a tragic remembrance of the cruelty of drinking and driving.

3. *Whenever possible, use specific and personal examples when employing motive appeals.* It is easier for all of us to visualize a single case than an abstract number. As professor Clifford Orwin once noted, "Compassion depends on imagination." Think about the hurt and impact we feel if one of our best friends dies of AIDS as compared to how we would respond to statistics that tell us that over 200,000 deaths have been reported from AIDS in the last 10 years. Again, I urge you to personalize your motive appeals.

❖ ❖ ❖ ❖   Our Desire to Maintain Consistency

There are a number of theories of attitude change based on the hypothesis that people attempt to keep their thoughts and actions consistent. Although there are some minor variations among their approaches, scholars such as Fritz Heider (balance theory), Leon Festinger (cognitive dissonance theory), and Charles Osgood and Percy Tannenbaum (congruity theory) have all been concerned with people's apparent need to maintain consistency and balance among their beliefs, attitudes, and knowledge—their cognitions. If something introduces an element of inconsistency (imbalance, incongruity, or dissonance), according to these theories, we make adjustments necessary to restore a state of consistency.

When applied to human communication, the balance theories tell us that if we receive information that causes us discomfort ("We need to raise taxes"), we lose our sense of balance and harmony. If you believe, for example, that a secret organization is a "hate" group that preaches one ethnic group's supremacy over all others and then you are told that your childhood idol, your late grandfather, was a member of that organization, an element of inconsistency has been introduced into your cognitions. You have warm memories of your grandfather's gentle, caring ways, his efforts in charitable drives, his friendliness to everyone, and his staunch defense of anyone who was considered an underdog. How do you resolve this inconsistency? Perhaps you will resolve it by changing your belief about the secret organization or your attitude toward its members. You might transform your unfavorable predisposition toward them into a neutral or (conceivably) favorable one. Perhaps you will resolve it by telling yourself that the organization was not a hate group at the time your grandfather was one of its members. Maybe you will speculate that your grandfather was a "double agent" who had infiltrated the organization in order to keep authorities informed of the group's activities. You might resolve the inconsistency by simply refusing to believe the news of his alleged membership. You might say to your informant, "You are mistaken," or "You are lying!" Conceivably, you might try to banish the memory of your grandfather or be filled with disgust or hatred for him or a deep sense of betrayal.

The application of the consistency principle to persuasion can readily be seen in selling. Much selling is rooted in the introduction of a dissonant note to a prospective buyer. Let us say that Susan is happy with the set of tires on her car because she believes them to be safe. Into this picture of contentment intrudes a salesperson who raises serious questions about the durability of the tires. Susan's cognitions, thus, are thrown out of balance. The salesperson has the answer that will restore the balance (or at least hopes so).

Sometimes a persuader's job is to help listeners live with an existing inconsistency by offering a means of reducing its intensity or rationalizing its existence. Wartime propaganda furnishes an example. The people of a peace-loving nation are besieged with a sense of guilt at becoming involved in a war. They are offered the palliatives, "This is the war to end all wars," "We must not desert the cause for which so many of our people have died," "We must fight so that our children can live in peace," and "If we don't stop them here, we'll have to stop them somewhere else." In these instances, the persuaders have attempted to offset the severity of the listeners' cognitive dissonance—"I don't believe in war, but here I am supporting a war"—by reminding the listeners of other beliefs or attitudes they hold that are consistent with supporting the war—"I believe in safeguarding our children," "I believe in honoring our dead," "I believe that the achievement of peace is worth any price," and "A stitch in time saves nine."

The apparent need of human beings to maintain consistency offers a well-spring of opportunities for a person engaged in persuasive speaking. Let us look at some of those opportunities and some guidelines in the use of dissonance theory:

1. *Remember that people may hold several attitudes on the same topic.* A person might believe in the separation of church and state but accept the idea that young children need to learn spiritual values while attending school. Knowing that attitudes are likely to be diverse enables persuasive speakers to select from a host of appeals instead of feeling that they are tied to only one argument.

2. *Realizing that the existence of dissonance makes people psychologically uncomfortable should allow you to seek ways within your speech to abate that frustration.* For example, if you are asking an audience of hunters to reduce the number of deer they can hunt in a single season (creating dissonance), you might lessen that dissonance by telling them that if they do not curtail their activity, they will deplete the deer population within the next two years.

3. *There might be competing values and attitudes at work within the same individual.* That is to say, attitudes are situational and contextual. Someone might believe that spotted owls should be protected in the redwoods but, because he or she dislikes the petition process, might balk when you ask him or her to sign a petition putting the issue on the state ballot.

Our Susceptibility to Suggestion

Our final inducement to action centers on our vulnerability to suggestion. Do you find yourself wanting to yawn when you see another person doing so? Do you develop a sudden yearning for a bag of peanuts when you see someone at the ballpark eating peanuts? Are you tempted to join a growing crowd around a sidewalk musician? If so, you are probably yielding to the power of suggestion.

Suggestion is the arousal of a response by either indirect or direct means. In the public-speaking arena, it may operate through channels external to a speech's message, such as the decor of the surroundings, flags, paintings, posters, comfortable seating arrangements, proper lighting, giant photographs, acts of ritual music, and prominently displayed collection plates or canisters. These factors may condition listeners to respond positively to a speaker's message. When your goal is persuasion, you should be aware of these external contingencies. Creating the proper atmosphere is often as powerful as the words you utter.

Suggestion also operates through your message. If you stress positive ideas, if you are fair when mentioning ideas contrary to your position, if you avoid name calling, and if you acknowledge controversy when it exists, you condition the audience to respond favorably to your point of view (or at least you condition them against a negative response).

There is also a power of suggestion that audience members exercise on one another. If we see others laughing, we often find it easier to do so. If the non-verbal behavior of others signals apathy or interest, disagreement or agreement, hostility or enthusiastic support, we may be affected in surprising ways. Carnival "barkers" recognize the influence of decoys to draw customers to their sideshows and concession stands.

Personal Credibility

You hear two speakers arguing the same cause but on separate occasions. Both use essentially the same lines of reasoning and similar evidence. Nevertheless, you want to agree with one speaker, while the other fails to budge your convictions. Something about that one speaker inspires believability. What is the difference? There are many words that might describe this phenomenon—for example, "image," "credibility," "charisma," and "character." Regardless of the words used, the point is that often, despite the evidence you cite and the motive appeals you employ, all your efforts will be wasted if the audience does not perceive you in a positive light. *Your character touches the audience as much as your content.* The American author Josiah Holland wrote, "Character must stand behind and back up everything—the sermon, the poem, the picture, the play. None of them is worth a straw without it."

In human communication, the word **credibility** is most often used to discuss this important and complex personality trait. It is generally how the audience perceives you and the causes you represent. Before we discuss the constituents of personal credibility, and ways to increase credibility, it might be useful to pause and offer two important introductory observations.

First, *in most instances an audience decides on your credibility in four stages.* They (1) may know something about you before you talk, (2) will have an initial impression, (3) make alterations as you speak, and (4) have a final impression. Second, *the components of credibility are multidimensional.* This simply means that the data the audience uses to decide if you are a credible source are varied and detailed. It is seldom a single factor they use, but rather a combination of factors. Later in this section, a long list of techniques that can enhance your credibility is presented.

Up to this point, credibility has been referred to in rather general terms. Let us now be a little more specific and ask this question: *What are the constituents of personal credibility*—that "something special about the speaker" that affects us so profoundly? Ever since Aristotle, speech theorists have attempted to isolate those elements. Aristotle maintained that if a listener perceives a speaker to have good character, good sense, and goodwill, then the speaker's arguments are more apt to be believed. Aristotle treated personal credibility, or ethos, in terms of how it derives from a speaker's verbal message. Contemporary theorists now also take into account a speaker's nonverbal behavior in discussing personal credibility. In addition, they point out that credibility is partly a product of a speaker's reputation. The theorists use terms such as (1) *competence* (being knowledgeable), (2) *trustworthiness* (having integrity), and (3) *dynamism* (displaying attractiveness) in discussing personal credibility. **Competence** seems to be somewhat like Aristotle's good sense, since both deal with the speaker's apparent level of knowledge and fitness to speak on a topic. **Trustworthiness** and Aristotle's good character seem to be closely akin, since both name traits of character that the audience finds reassuring. **Dynamism** is closely related to a speaker's presentational traits—

those nonverbal signals of competence, trustworthiness, and amiability or goodwill. The popular term "image" is a composite of all these factors.

The three components of credibility are examined more closely in the following paragraphs, which suggest some facets of speaker behavior to which North American audiences respond favorably. (People from other cultures may not use the same traits to judge credibility as do members of the dominant culture of North America.)

Competence. Demonstrating competence takes a number of forms. For example, a speaker can manifest competence through intelligence. The extent to which a speaker seems to have mastery of the subject matter is a determinant of an audience's response. In general, the speaker's credibility is enhanced if he or she has conducted extensive research and marshals an impressive amount of diverse evidence, shows insight into all aspects of the question, uses reasoning that meets the tests of logical validity, and displays "common sense."

There are some very specific behaviors that can contribute to a speaker's level of competence:

1. *Use proper language.* Nothing lowers credibility faster than a poor vocabulary, mispronunciation, and the misuse of language. It might be helpful if you were to return briefly to chapter 12 and reexamine language distractions.

2. *Creating clear and original visual aids also helps establish a high level of competence.* The audience will feel that you are serious about your topic if they perceive that you have taken the time to prepare audiovisual aids.

3. *Credibility is enhanced when a speaker uses credible sources and cites those sources.* If the audience knows that you have contacted responsible and reliable sources, they will often link the high-credibility source to your credibility. For example, your credibility would be enhanced if you were talking about the number of false convictions associated with the death penalty and said, "According to the November 9, 1998, issue of *Newsweek*, there have been 75 known cases of people wrongly sentenced to die."

4. *You should start your speech on time.* All of us assign meaning to the way in which someone uses the clock. The assumption is that a person is not very conscientious if he or she is tardy.

5. *An image of competence can be projected by appearing to be poised.* A speaker who is in command of himself or herself inspires confidence. Not becoming unsettled by distractions, handling interruptions gracefully, and coping with hostile questions calmly are all signs of a temperament that inspires confidence.

6. *Using a variety of forms of support would assist the audience in believing you are competent.* Remember that this component of credibility is the one that shows the audience that you know what you are talking about. Admittedly, you cannot be an expert on all subjects, but you can show the audience that, by your supporting evidence, you are at least knowledgeable on the subject being discussed.

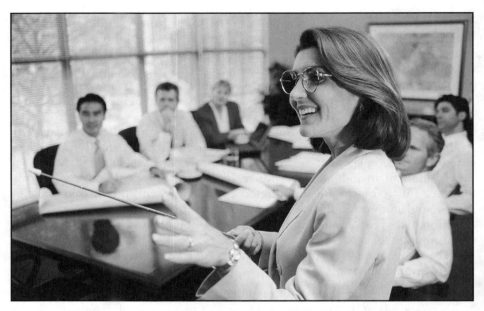

An image of competence can be projected by appearing to be poised. (Photo: indexstock.com)

7. *If done in good taste, you can also inform the audience of any distinguished experiences you have had that would qualify you as an "expert."* For example, a speaker who was talking about the workings of the United States Senate told the audience that he had had an internship one year to work on the floor of the Senate.

8. *If you are going to be introduced to the audience by another speaker, make sure he or she imparts information that clearly demonstrates your qualifications.* The person introducing you should have access to all the data pertaining to your accomplishments, training, background, expertise, and the like.

Trustworthiness. It is often referred to as integrity, honor, altruism, goodwill, and ethical character. Benjamin Franklin even referred to it as "heart" when he wrote, "The heart of a fool is in his mouth, but the mouth of a wise man is in his heart." Regardless of its label, an audience's perception of you as a sincere, honest person is one of the most important aspects of successful public speaking. What makes this component so intriguing is that people tend to show their character in many different ways. Ralph Waldo Emerson noted that "if you act, you show character; if you sit still, you show it; if you sleep, you show it." The question for us is how to show it in your speech. Some actions that often convey integrity are listed here:

1. *Moderation is usually equated with reasonableness.* Although intellectual enthusiasm and commitment are admirable traits, most people are fearful of an extremist. Hence, moderation should be your guide. People tend to be wary of those who indulge in overstatement, in personal abuse, or in unseemly emotional displays.

2. *Closely associated with moderation is tact.* Tact is the ability to deal with others without giving offense. Applied to persuasion, it means such things as disagreeing without being disagreeable, admonishing without scolding, and enlightening without insulting the audience's intelligence.

3. *Objectivity contributes to high levels of personal credibility.* If your material and the sources for that material are fair and unbiased, the audience will feel that you have been honest in your approach to the topic.

4. *Sincerity is greatly admired in all cultures.* A salesperson tells a customer, "I'd like to sell you this car because, quite frankly, I stand to earn a good commission. Furthermore, you are going to get a good car in the process." The salesperson's sincerity and candid disclosure of her real motives may have a disarming effect on the customer because most of us place credence in the remarks of those we regard as sincere and open in their dealings with others. None of us likes being duped. Emerson was right when he noted, "Sincerity is the highest compliment you can pay."

5. *People tend to trust speakers who they believe share many of their own traits and attributes.* In the study of credibility, this concept is called homophily; it is also referred to as "establishing common ground." It means the degree to which the individuals involved in a communication act believe they are similar. As a persuasive speaker, you need to convince your audience that you share some of their concerns, values, attitudes, and beliefs. If possible, you should also indicate how your backgrounds might be comparable. For example, if you are an honor student talking to a group of potential high school dropouts about the need for them to stay in school, your credibility would be aided if you were to mention that, at one time, you were a poor student and had even thought about leaving high school.

6. *Credibility is also linked to reliability.* Someone who "stands by their convictions," even if such a position is unpopular, is admired by most audiences. We admire the person who is not swayed by public opinion and fads, but instead can be counted on to follow his or her beliefs. Such a person is reliable and thus is appreciated.

7. *Honesty contributes to an image of being trustworthy.* Honesty can be reflected by such things as granting the existence of opposing views, not withholding evidence that the audience should have, and admitting that there might be some legitimate drawbacks to your proposal that need to be examined. Your audience will respect such actions on your part. Remember the good advice regarding honesty supplied by Shakespeare: "No legacy is so rich as honesty."

Dynamism. The final ingredient of credibility is harder to describe than were the first two. Dynamism is a rather abstract term referring to such things as how a speaker presents him- or herself and how attractive the audience perceives him or her to be. Words associated with dynamism might be *energetic, enthusiastic, compassionate, strong,* and *confident*. Research has isolated specific behaviors that help a speaker project an image of dynamism:

1. *Eye contact is crucial if you plan to "tell" the audience you are interested in them.* By looking at your listeners, you are making an effort to "connect" with them. This combining of personalities through gaze is part of dynamism.

2. *We all tend to like people whose appearance is suited to the occasion.* We would not have much confidence in a doctor whose lab coat is covered with grime and whose hands are dirty. In the same vein, although wearing jeans, an untucked shirt, and sandals might be appropriate in many places, it is impertinent to wear such attire in a formal situation. In most public-speaking situations, credibility is directly linked to a neatly dressed and well-groomed speaker.

3. *Facial expressions are another important measure of credibility.* A great deal of research indicates that a smile is a powerful communication tool. Ask yourself how much more comfortable you feel when someone is wearing a pleasant face instead of a frown.

4. *Enthusiasm in voice and body is perhaps one of the most vivid signs of a speaker who is dynamic.* If your outward expressions are passive, dull, indifferent, and listless, the audience might assume that you are not interested in them or in the topic you are discussing. They ask themselves, If you do not believe in yourself or in your arguments, why should I? Enthusiasm also tends to be contagious. If you feel good about yourself, you might even make the audience experience similar feelings about themselves. Appreciation of this connection could add yet another dimension to your credibility.

5. *Appearing relaxed also helps create a favorable impression.* If you are tense and nervous, the audience is apt to infer that you are not comfortable with your arguments or are not well prepared. As you recall, mannerisms tend to be contagious. If you are uncomfortable, you might make your audience uncomfortable.

Organizing a Persuasive Speech

As far back as the eighth century B.C., the Greek poet Hesiod offered the advice that "it is best to do things systematically, since we are only human, and disorder is our worst enemy." To keep you from having "disorder," let us now talk about organizing the persuasive speech—more specifically, the principal functions of the introduction, body, and conclusion as they apply to a persuasive speech.

Introduction

As you know from previous chapters, the basic functions of an introduction are to get attention and to prepare the audience for what is to follow. In a persuasive speech, these two functions have to be accomplished in a way that creates a climate of acceptance. If you are going to ask an audience to change or alter a belief ("Dumping of nuclear waste is a serious problem for our city"), or to behave in a different manner ("You should carry a donor card in your wallet"), you must make sure that you establish rapport with the audience at the same time you are arousing interest. It is also wise for a speaker to refrain from assertiveness in the early stages of a persuasive speech, because such behavior may generate suspicion and hostility. Opening in a spirit of inquiry is much less likely to erect barriers. It is also important to affirm your credibility early in your speech, so that you can begin to establish some common ground. If you decide to announce your central point, or core statement, some time during the introduction, you should consider phrasing it in the form of a question. Compare these two ways of orienting your audience to the nature of your talk:

> Today, I would like to discuss with you the question, Are prisons justified in a modern society?

> Today I will attempt to demonstrate that prisons are not justified in a modern society.

Many experienced speakers find that illustrations (hypothetical or factual), rhetorical questions, and/or startling statements are effective when giving a persuasive speech. Before deciding on an introduction, I urge you to return to chapter 11 and review some of the techniques discussed in there.

Body

The body of a persuasive speech contains the defense of the persuasive proposition. For example, if you are defending a proposition of policy, you will probably offer arguments to show the need for a policy and demonstrate the capacity of your policy to satisfy that need. If you are defending a proposition of fact or value, you will probably offer criteria to measure the truth of the fact or value judgment in question and then apply those criteria. Regardless of the type of persuasive speech you are giving, it is important that you design a strategy that allows you to present your best case. Some of those strategies are presented in detail, after discussion of the basic outline of the persuasive speech.

Conclusion

The conclusion of a persuasive speech should place the audience in the state of mind most conducive to the accomplishment of the speaker's purpose. For example, if your purpose is to actuate, the audience should be ready to act. If your purpose is to convince, the audience should be ready to assent. As was the case with the introduction, it would behoove you to return to chapter 11 and review some of the suggestions offered there regarding these conclusions.

❖ ❖ ❖ ❖   ## Designing the Persuasive Speech

Chapter 10 presented a number of organizational patterns that can be used when preparing a speech. Let us return to some of these sequences and place them in the context of the persuasive speech.

Problem-Solution Pattern

If you are interested in persuading an audience to implement a specific policy, the problem-solution pattern is very useful. This pattern is one of the simplest outline forms and is based on dividing the body of a speech into three parts. After an introduction designed to gain attention and orient the listeners, the speaker moves into the body of the speech, where he or she (1) presents the problem area, (2) explains the solution to the problem, and (3) defends the solution. The speech concludes with a call for the appropriate belief or action. An example of a proposition of policy structured around the problem-solution order follows:

Introduction

I. While driving home from work last Tuesday, I saw a Lincoln Continental plow into a Ford, which spun into a BMW, which ended up halfway underneath a garbage truck.

   A. I stopped my car and went over to help the injured people.

   B. One of those hurt in the accident was our classmate Brenda.

II. The locale of that pileup was Grand and Main, an intersection that has experienced many such accidents.

Core Statement: A left-turn traffic light should be installed at the intersection of Grand and Main.

Body

Problem:

I. The intersection presents the worst traffic problem in town.

Support:

   A. It is the scene of numerous collisions.

      1. Evidence.

      2. Evidence.

Support:

   B. It is a bottleneck during morning and afternoon rush hours.

      1. Evidence.

      2. Evidence.

Cause:

  II. The cause of this problem is the lack of a left-turn traffic light at the intersection.

Support:

   A. Cars attempting left turns from Grand onto westbound Main are targets of cars southbound on Grand.

Support:

   B. Cars waiting to turn left produce a backup of homebound traffic on Grand.

Solution:

  III. A left-turn traffic light would correct the existing problem.

Support:

   A. It would minimize collisions.

Support:

   B. It would speed northbound traffic on Grand.

Defense:

  IV. A left-turn traffic light would be practical to install.

Support:

   A. It would be practical from an engineering standpoint.
      1. Evidence.
      2. Evidence.

Support:

   B. It would be practical from a financial standpoint.
      1. Evidence.
      2. Evidence.

Defense:

   V. A left-turn light would not introduce disadvantages.

Support:

   A. It would not introduce hazards.

Support:

   B. It would not be aesthetically unpleasing.

Defense:

  VI. A left-turn light is the best solution to the problem.

Support:

   A. It would be less costly than an overpass.

Support:

   B. It would be more convenient than rerouting northbound traffic onto Cisco Avenue.

Conclusion

   I. I have attempted to show that a solution to this dangerous traffic condition does exist.

   II. You can help this proposal become a reality by signing the petition that I am about to circulate.

   III. Perhaps if we had this light a month ago, Brenda might be in class today.

Monroe's Motivated Sequence

This organizational strategy is a variant of the problem-solution order, and as such is useful for speeches that ask the audience to take a specific action. As its name suggests, the motivated sequence has a psychological orientation and therefore attempts to fuse concrete evidence with motive appeals. That is to say, the motivated sequence seeks to move listeners through a succession of psychological steps that is both logical and emotional. Let us look at the five steps in the sequence (attention, need, satisfaction, visualization, action) by examining a skeleton outline the includes all five steps.

General End: To Persuade

Specific Purpose: To convince my audience that severe punishment is need to solve the rape problem.

Attention must be a speaker's first concern. Unless the speaker can get the audience to pay attention early in the speech, most attempts at persuasion will fail. Interest and curiosity must be aroused. A preview is often offered during this stage of the talk. All of the methods discussed elsewhere in the book can be applied to the persuasive speech.

   I. During this class period today, over 80 women will be raped in the United States.

   A. This means that approximately 700,000 adult women are raped each year.

   B. In our small town alone we had over one hundred rapes reported.

   C. Called by the American Medical Association the "silent violent epidemic," many rapes go unreported.

Transition: Let me begin by mentioning some of the effects of rape and than move to what we can do about this problem.

II. The problem of rape is very serious.

   A. Many victims develop a post-traumatic stress syndrome.

     1. Symptoms can include fear, humiliation, anger, flashbacks of the rape and shock.

     2. I friend of mine who was raped was so upset she had to withdraw from the university.

   B. Medical problems resulting from rape can include everything from acute injury to unwanted pregnancies.

   C. The consequences of being raped can be long lasting.

     1. Many rape victims avoid all contact with family members and friends.

     2. Many rape victims find it difficult to have any intimate sexual relationships long after the rape has occurred.

   D. According to the American Medical Association, the seriousness of rape is often felt by very young people.

     1. The AMA reports that 61 percent of all rape victims are under the age of eighteen.

     2. Some victims are as young as eleven.

III. The serious problem of rape in our culture could be greatly reduced if the judicial system would mandate harsher sentences.

   A. A recent *Newsweek* article noted that only one in 100 rapists is sentenced to more than one year in prison.

   B. Twenty-five percent of convicted rapists are put on probation and do not serve time in prison.

   C. Many rapists are repeat offenders.

     1. According to Dianne Cruz, of the Crime Victims Association, "Rapists have such a high rate of recidivism that we often find that many of them have been arrested for rape before."

   D. What we all need to do is support legislation that mandates more severe punishments than is now the case.

     1. Rape convictions should carry a mandatory five-year jail sentence.

     2. A person convicted of rape for a second time should face a 20-year jail sentence.

The main purpose of the *need step* is to have the audience see that the problem is serious. It is in this portion of the speech that evidence and motive appeals are employed. By pointing out that a problem exists, you build the case for the solution you will offer in the satisfaction step.

In the *satisfaction step,* you offer, explain, and defend your solution to the problem.

❖ ❖ ❖ ❖

The visualization step asks the listeners to visualize the impact of adopting or not adopting the solution. The visualization can be positive or negative—or both.

The action step (your conclusion) calls on the listeners to implement the solution.

IV. If we fail to act, rapists will continue to find that the judicial system does not impede them from performing their cruel acts.

   A. After raping a fifteen-year-old, James Adams was sentenced to jail for only six months.

   B. His short term allowed him to rape again.

      1. He lured a thirteen-year-old girl into his house.

      2. He then tied her down with his belt and raped her.

V. Our legal system must reexamine the current approach it is taking toward rapists.

   A. We must remove them so they cannot repeat their callous acts on innocent women.

   B. As you leave class today, remember the 80 who were raped while you and I were safe in this room.

Deduction

Earlier in this chapter, we discussed the importance of having "convincing arguments" as part of your persuasive strategy. It is no accident, then, that the patterns of deduction and induction are commonly used in the development of persuasive speeches.

The means of persuasion involve logical appeals, psychological appeals, and the listeners' perception of the speaker's personal credibility. (Photo: indexstock.com)

When we ask an audience to follow a **deductive** reasoning pattern to believe in our position, we are suggesting that what is true of a general class can be applied to specific cases. This is a powerful form of reasoning and a sound organizational scheme. In persuasive speaking, it is usually wise to begin with an assertion that most people will accept, for, later in the speech, you will ask them to believe that what is true with regard to one case is true of an entire case. For instance, if your speech deals with the treatment of gays in the military, the first leg of your argument could state that all members of the military forces should be treated equally. Second, you could develop the idea that Thomas Jackson is gay, is in the military, and therefore (conclusion) should be treated fairly. Although this example is somewhat stilted, it nevertheless shows the need to have a believable premise so that you can support the remainder of the argument.

Deductive arguments are seldom presented in the formal style used in the preceding example. Normally, one of the premises or the conclusion is obvious and can therefore be omitted to give the speech a smoother flow.

In deduction, the proposition is disclosed prior to the presentation of the materials that support the proposition. For example, if a speaker wishes the audience to agree with the proposition, "Our selling used books would be a better fund-raiser for our club than a car wash," the speech might be organized in this order:

Introduction

I. By the end of this month, we have to make a decision about our annual fund-raiser.

II. There are two alternative fund-raisers available to us, a used book sale and a car wash.

Body

Core Statement: A used-book sale would be a better fund-raiser than a car wash.

I. It would involve very little expense because we can all donate books.

II. It would be easier to prepare because we would only have to display the books in front of the fraternity house.

III. It would yield a great profit because both the product and the labor would be free.

Conclusion

I. I hope you will give careful consideration to a used-book sale.

When you are moving the audience through your talk by using the deductive process you need to keep three things in mind. *First, is the general rule really true?* Should all people in the military be treated equally? *Second, is the minor premise true?* Is Thomas Jackson gay and in the military?

 **Induction**

Constructing an **inductive** argument is the opposite of constructing a deductive one. With induction, the analysis moves from the specific to the general. This type of organizational scheme is often called moving from the particular to the general. To say that violence against teachers has increased in New York, Los Angeles, Chicago, and Cleveland, and therefore violence against teachers is a serious problem in many cities, is an example of reasoning by means of the inductive process.

When using induction as a mode of organization, a speaker withholds disclosure of the proposition (core statement) until after presenting the materials supporting the proposition. Using the same proposition just used, "A used-book sale would be a better fund-raiser than a car wash," a speaker's inductive order of presentation might appear this way:

Introduction

   I. By the end of this month, we have to make a decision about our annual fund-raiser.

Body

   I. The fund-raiser we choose should have these qualities:

      A. It should involve minimal expense.

      B. It should be easy to prepare.

      C. It should yield a profit.

  II. We have two alternatives from which to choose.

      A. A used-book sale.

      B. A car wash.

 III. A used-book sale has these merits:

      A. It involves less expense.

      B. It is easier to prepare.

      C. It yields a greater profit.

Core Statement: A used-book sale would be a better fund-raiser than a car wash.

Conclusion

   I. I hope you will give careful consideration to a used-book sale.

Induction is most useful when your audience is skeptical or even hostile to what you are going to propose. You can build a very effective case for your cause if you start by offering solid evidence that is hard to refute and then draw a conclusion from that evidence. Observe this technique in the following speech on polluted water systems:

> Last month, Banner Beach was closed because of contamination from the city sewer system. Three weeks ago, Paradise Cove had to be closed when poisonous chemicals were found in the fish that people were catching. And just

yesterday, lifeguards told swimmers to stay out of the water at North Beach because of an oily substance floating near the surface. I think we can all agree that something needs to be done at once about the amount of pollution on our beaches.

When moving the audience through your analysis via the induction sequence, you should remember that the examples from which you draw your generalizations must meet certain tests:

1. Are there enough examples to justify the generalization? How many cities must have experienced classroom violence before you can conclude that it is a serious problem?

2. Are the examples representative of the class of things about which you are generalizing? While the first test relates to the quantity of evidence, the second test relates to their quality.

When choosing between deductive order and inductive order, a speaker should be guided by his or her knowledge of the audience's predispositions. If the speaker feels that the direct approach exemplified by the deductive order would make the audience defensive, then the speaker should choose the inductive order. However, there are occasions when the direct approach is preferred. For example, if two speakers were debating a proposition of fact or value, the audience might view a late disclosure of position as ridiculous.

Persuasive Strategies

Behavioral scientists have attempted to answer persistent questions regarding various persuasive strategies. Of particular interest to students of persuasion are these scientists' tentative answers to the following issues.

Placing Ideas

Does an argument exert a more lasting influence if it is heard first or heard last in a series of arguments? If the audience is familiar with the issue or if they are involved in the controversy, say scientists, they are influenced more by the argument heard first. If the audience is disinterested or if they are relatively uninformed about the issue prior to hearing the arguments, they are influenced more by the argument heard last. Regardless of where you place your strongest arguments, it is absolutely essential that you conclude your speech by reminding your audience of the specific action you wish it to take.

Deciding Which Argument to Place First

When both sides of a controversy are presented in succession, will the side presented first or the side presented last be in the more advantageous position? Some studies have concluded that the side presented first has the "natural" advantage. Other studies, however, have been inconclusive. Therefore, what is needed, as always, is detailed audience analysis.

Presenting Both Sides of the Argument

Are attempts to persuade helped or hindered when "the other side" is presented as well as the speaker's own side? It is usually a good idea to discuss opposing views. In most instances, the listeners will have these assessments in their minds and you might as well treat them as part of your approach. In addition, if the listeners are initially opposed to the speaker's position, the stratagem exerts a persuasive effect.

Making Your Position Clear

Is it more effective to imply the conclusion one wishes the audience to accept or to state it explicitly? Research indicates that an explicit statement exerts a more persuasive effect on the majority of listeners. In short, you should not keep the audience guessing about your solution to the problem you have outlined.

Combining Evidence With Emotional Appeals

Is it best to use evidence or motive appeals when trying to persuade people to take action? The answer to this question is simple: if the topic in question lends itself to both logical argument and motive appeals, then use both. Because human behavior is complex, most people need a variety of reasons to change their minds or to take a specific action. In short, a fusion of objective data and motivational appeals will help you accomplish your persuasive purpose.

Remember that the foregoing advice is tentative. Many variables operate in any communication situation; it is virtually impossible to design an answer that will take all people and situations into account.

Persuasion and Culture

Although we have alluded to the issue of culture throughout this chapter, it is now time to examine this important topic in more detail. Specifically, let us explore the ways in which culture influences the three dimensions of persuasion that we discussed earlier in the chapter: (1) convincing arguments, (2) impelling psychological appeals, and (3) personal credibility.

Culture and Convincing Arguments

Cultural Variations in the Use of Evidence. In the West there has for centuries been a long history of public debate. Many of the early democracies of Greece and Rome were built on the traditions of argumentation and persuasion. Even today, Western cultures believe that the best methods for persuasion demand the use of sound arguments and the application of reliable evidence. Both of these areas (reasoning and evidence) have an intercultural element. In chapter 6, when we examined the forms of support, we noted that there were no agreed-upon standards across cultures for what was considered concrete evidence. You will recall that some cultures favor stories, allegories, analogies, and parables (Latin American, Arab, Native American). Members of these cultures have long believed that stories are a powerful form of evidence. In other cultures, the people prefer concrete data (German, English, North American). There are also cultural idiosyncrasies with regard to what constitutes a reliable source. In one culture, an authority is someone associated with religion, while in another the authority is the oldest person or the one with the most education. In cultures that do not have a long tradition of a free and open press (Chinese, African, Russian), even the citing of so-called reliable sources does not have the impact it does with an audience composed of only members of the North American culture.

The Quantity of Evidence Used. There are also differences in the amount of evidence that people from various cultures expect. Cultures that emphasize logic (European, North American), and de-emphasize feelings and emotions, anticipate that a persuasive speaker will offer a great deal of evidence to support his or her claims. In cultures that show feelings and are more emotional (Latin, African, Arab), less evidence and more motive appeals might be the rule.

Cultural Variations in Reasoning. The mental processes of reasoning prevalent in a community is another major characteristic of culture that often influences the persuasive process. If you are a North American speaker and you use the deductive method of reasoning to make your case, and you are interacting with someone who usually uses the inductive method (as in the case of the Korean culture), you are apt to have a major misunderstanding when you finally reach your conclusion. You are moving from broad categories to specific examples that most likely rely on "facts," while many people from Korea start with specific observations and eventually extract generalizations.

There are also differences in the use of deduction and induction in North America and their use in much of the Arab world. Because the Arab language tends to combine ideas with the use of conjunctions, speakers using this language do not always place their main points where non-Arabs would expect them. And conversely, Arabs often have difficulty with Western forms of linear thinking.

Western thought and reasoning patterns are often difficult for other cultures in that they assume a direct relationship between mental concepts and the concrete world of reality. This orientation places great stock in logic and rationality. Most Westerners believe that truth is "out there" and that it can be discovered by following scientific methods and engaging in logical, linear calculations. The Eastern view, best illustrated by Taoist, Buddhist, and Zen thought, holds that reasoning works quite differently. To begin with, people are not granted instant rationality. In fact, there is even a strong belief that intuition transcends the data of the senses. People who hold this view do not believe that one finds truth through active searching, talk, and the application of Aristotelian modes of reasoning. On the contrary, one had better wait and be patient, and if truth is to be known, it will make itself apparent.

Culture and Psychological Appeals

Cultures differ in both the number of emotional appeals they find appropriate and the content of those appeals. As just noted, some cultures rely on linear logic and "facts," while others are more comfortable focusing on people and their feelings. Italians, Portuguese, Arabs, and Mexicans believe that sincere and emotional feelings transcend rigid syllogisms and tangible facts.

❖ ❖ ❖ ❖   Conversely, some people in the Western culture believe that persuasion rooted only in emotional appeals should be avoided. In fact, since the time of the early Greek and Roman philosophers, people have been warned to be leery of the sophist. This view often clashes with cultures that appreciate a speaker with a rhetorical flair. Therefore, in selecting your specific motive appeals, you must analyze your audience to discover its cultural composition.

As you saw when we discussed attitudes, beliefs, and values earlier in this chapter, not all cultures perceive the world in the same manner. What appeals to one culture may not inspire another. For one culture, appeals that center on material possessions might be effective, yet that same plea would not work with cultures that value a spiritual life over the acquisition of property. Some cultures value modesty (Japan, China, etc.) and would find your resorting to sexual appeals somewhat offensive. Even linking your message to fear should be carefully analyzed if your audience is culturally mixed. Some cultures tend to be apprehensive about the future and the uncertainty of life (Japanese, Greek, French), while others usually do not find the ambiguity of life the least bit frightening (North American, Danish, Swedish, English). You need to learn all you can about the cultural characteristics of the members of your audience when deciding if you should use motive appeals and how to make the appeals you select compelling and forceful.

Culture and Personal Credibility

The chapter's earlier discussion of credibility was based solely on what affects North American listeners. Other types of behavior are prized by listeners of other cultures. The people of Japan, China, and other Asian cultures tend to look favorably on the speaker of few words, since such behavior is taken to indicate that the speaker is reflective. There is a Japanese proverb that says, "He who speaks has no knowledge and he who has knowledge does not speak." The Chinese have an aphorism, "Fear the dog that is not barking." Most Asian listeners are leery of speakers who are wordy, direct, impulsive, or assertive. Although self-disclosure is regarded favorably by North American listeners, it is viewed as a breach of good taste by German and Japanese audiences. Jewish, Mexican, and Greek cultures expect speakers to be very animated and emotional in their visual and vocal mannerisms. To be otherwise is to be suspected of lack of conviction. As pointed out in chapter 12, Arab cultures deem it important for speakers to use a great deal of embellishment in their language, so a speaker addressing an Arab audience would probably make greater use of metaphors and similes than would a speaker addressing an American audience. In many cultures (Latin America, Asia, Germany, etc.), a speaker's status and reputation influence the development of credibility.

Persuasion and Ethics

Never forget the link between communication and ethical behavior. Your actions produce serious results—they modify the thinking and behavior of other people. Or as a West African proverb notes, "If it rains on the mountaintop, it is the valley below that gets flooded."

Because change is at the very core of persuasion, we now return to the important subject of ethics. Let me suggest six questions you should ask yourself as a way of determining if you are being ethical in your treatment of your material.

1. *Who will benefit from my persuasive speech?* The implications of this question are obvious. Are you the only one who will profit from the changes you are asking of your listeners, or will they also benefit if you accomplish your specific purpose? Asking someone to buy a product that they do not need but will make you a great deal of money is an example of persuasion with selfish ends. Consider how much you would resent a speaker who led you to think that you would benefit from signing a petition against a new walking trail, when in reality the speaker only wanted your signature because the public trail would pass directly in front of his or her house. Concealing your persuasive intent is both insulting and unethical. The ethical speaker makes his or her motives very clear. The speaker will even tell the audience that there might be a second side to the issues being discussed.

2. *Am I using inflammatory language to help accomplish my purpose?* Inflammatory language is defined in chapter 12. Here, I simply remind you that language is a powerful tool that can be used for good or for evil. So ask yourself if you are avoiding the real issues in the case and appealing to a lower level of reasoning by using emotional words and phrases such as *male chauvinist pig, right winger, red-neck racist,* or *practicing feminist.* We should never, as the French essayist Voltaire advised us, "use words to hide our thoughts."

3. *Am I misusing fear appeals?* The improper use of fear appeals can take a variety of forms. In many persuasive situations, speakers use fear appeals to replace rather than augment concrete evidence. There is nothing inherently wrong with legitimately using fear to accomplish your purpose. Showing people, through the use of vivid word pictures, the dangers of smoking, the hazards of drinking and driving, or the results of unsafe sex is not an unethical act if such fear appeals are accompanied by other material (statistics, expert testimony, and the like). In addition, you must be careful that your fear appeals do not involve exaggerated claims. For example, to tell people that everyone who smokes dies a horrible and painful death would be a major exaggeration.

4. *Am I cognizant of the specific composition of my audience?* If a speaker knows the make-up of the audience but ignores the information, he or she chooses to be unethical. For example, if you are talking to very young children, who might be impressionable, it would be unethical to ask them to make decisions that demand maturity beyond their years. Every Christmas, dishonest advertisers encourage children, when their parents are not at home, to call

a 900 number and "talk to Santa Claus." Such persuasion attempts are both dishonest and unethical.

5. *Have I been ethical in the gathering of my information?* It is not enough to worry about ethics when you are presenting the speech; you must ensure that your listeners have access, through you, to fair and truthful material. The concealing and omitting of information that the listeners should have is also a violation of high ethical standards. As the "carrier" of the message, you have a responsibility to carry a message that is complete and comprehensive.

6. Perhaps in deciding on your ethical stance you might ask yourself this final question: *Would I like to be treated in the same manner I am going to treat my audience?* For most of us that sentence has a familiar ring to it. It is a paraphrase of one of the most quoted passages from the Bible. Actually, the admonition is, "Do to others what you would have them do to you." What is so intriguing about this ethical decree is that it is found in every religious tradition. Whether it be Hinduism, Buddhism, Islam, Judaism, or Christianity, the message is the same, and one worth repeating as we conclude our section on ethics—**regard others as you would like to be regarded.**

Summary

Persuasion is the process of inducing willing changes in a listener's beliefs, attitudes, values, and behavior. Successful persuasion rests on a thorough knowledge of the audience and its attitudes toward the speech topic, the speech purpose, and the speaker. The objects of change are the listeners' learned predispositions, convictions, and manifest behavior—particularly with respect to issues of policy, fact, and value. A speaker's position should rest on a knowledge of the audience's thinking about the subject.

The means of persuasion, according to rhetorical tradition and modern social psychology, lie in logical appeals, psychological appeals, and the listeners' perception of the speaker's personal credibility. The constituents of logical persuasion are evidence and reasoning. Evidence should be derived from an authoritative source and should be fairly presented, recent, and capable of corroboration.

Persuasion through psychological appeals traditionally is thought to involve the use of motivation and suggestion. The needs and wants to which the speaker may link the message include self-preservation, sex attraction, acquisition of property, fear, self-esteem, personal enjoyment, loyalty, individualism, curiosity, imitation, and altruism. Suggestion is the arousal of a response by indirect means. It may operate through channels external to the speaker, through the speaker's delivery, and through the verbal message.

Persuasion through personal credibility is possible when a speaker manifests poise, modesty, moderation, tact, goodwill, common sense, reliability, honesty, friendliness, sincerity, enthusiasm, and genuine concern for the listeners' welfare—provided they perceive these factors.

Although a persuasive speech can be organized in a variety of ways, certain methods seem to enjoy high popularity. The problem-solution order and the motivated sequence are particularly appropriate for developing propositions of policy. Deductive order and inductive order are among the patterns well suited to developing propositions of fact and value.

To be successful as a persuasive speaker, it is essential for you to understand the role of culture in persuasion. Culture will influence the arguments you use, your selection of motive appeals, and how the audience perceives your credibility.

Finally, you must consider the ethical ramifications each time you appeal to audience members to change their belief systems and/or the way they behave. The best, and in some ways the simplest, ethical rule to apply is the one that asks you to put yourself in the place of the audience. Would you be willing to have someone persuade you by using the same techniques you are applying to your audience?

Concepts and Questions

1. Differentiate between beliefs, attitudes, values, and behaviors.

2. What is the importance of audience analysis in preparing a persuasive speech? What types of audiences should be considered?

3. List seven motive appeals.

4. What is the major difference between deduction and induction?

5. What are the major components of personal credibility?

6. Why should motive appeals be used in combination with logical appeals?

Activities and Exercises

1. Make a list of five specific ways you could establish your credibility with an audience.

2. Select any three motive appeals and use those appeals in a short talk on any persuasive topic.

3. Write three specific purposes for a persuasive speech. Use propositions of fact, value, and policy.

4. Write a short essay that reflects your personal views on the role of ethics in persuasive speaking.

5. Attend a political rally. Listen to the speakers and record their logical arguments and their motive appeals. Write a short essay that evaluates the effectiveness of their efforts.

6. Write a short essay on considerations you would have to take into account if you were giving a speech to a culturally diverse audience.

7. Listen to a talk radio program and analyze how the people calling into the program use logical arguments and motive appeals. ✦

Part Four

Changing Environments

CHAPTER FIFTEEN

Special Occasions: The Unique Communication Situation

> Every tale can be told in a different way.
>
> —*Greek Saying*

A Spanish proverb notes, "I dance to the tune that is played." This adage serves to introduce this chapter about the need to adapt to the unique speaking situation. Although the principles of oral communication discussed in previous chapters apply to virtually every kind of circumstance, additional demands must be addressed when preparing and presenting talks that depart from the usual settings and from the traditional classifications of informative and persuasive speaking. In addition, some occasions do not provide "lead time" for preparation and you must therefore speak in an impromptu manner. And there are also situations where it is not feasible to use an extemporaneous mode of delivery and you will need a detailed manuscript. There are even events that call for a question-and-answer period between a speaker and listeners. And because of the electronic age, you might even find yourself in front of a television camera. Such unique and special occasions are the focus of this chapter.

One of the attributes of a highly successful public speaker is an ability to adjust to any predicament. There is a story of how Teddy Roosevelt was shot in the chest in an assassination attempt and uttered the words, "I will deliver this speech or die, one or the other." This story, although somewhat theatrical, does make the point that adapting and modifying your message and your manner of presentation is important if you are to be an effective speaker. Any successful communicator must be prepared when called upon, to deal with the following six speaking occasions: (1) *impromptu speeches*, (2) *manuscript speeches*, (3) *entertaining speeches*, (4) *speeches before television cameras*, (5)

The requirements of good oral communications apply even in unusual speaking environments. (Photo: Gloria Thomas)

speeches of introduction, and (6) *occasions when questions from the audience are solicited during or after the speech.* We shall now examine each of these unique communication situations.

Impromptu Speeches

One of the questions that students tend to ask on the first day of speech class is, "Will there be any impromptu speeches?" Although there are probably some students who actually hope for impromptu speeches, falsely believing that this sort of speech does not involve preparation, there are more who fear being called on suddenly to "make a few remarks." To be asked to give a speech on the spur of the moment is often unnerving, in spite of the fact that all of us do a great deal of impromptu talking every day and are not troubled about it. If you were to analyze your normal conversations, you would probably find that they are spontaneous responses to another person's equally spontaneous remarks. Why is it that we fear making an impromptu speech? Probably because we think people expect more from a public speaker than they do from a private conversation. How, then, do we cope with that dreaded, "Why don't you come up here and tell us what you think about . . .?"

Preparing an Impromptu Speech

Consult Your Memory. Perhaps it seems somewhat strange to have a heading referring to preparation after the impromptu speech has just been referred to as a "spur of the moment" experience. However, preparation, although somewhat limited, is a crucial part of successful impromptu speaking. Preparing for impromptu speaking includes both long-range and short-range preparation. One example of what is meant by long-term preparation comes from the great statesman and orator Winston Churchill, who once noted that he had devoted the best years of his life to preparing his impromptu speeches. This simply means that, like all good speakers, he knew that his past experiences had prepared him to talk on almost any topic. Hence, *the first thing that should cross your mind when confronted with an impromptu event is that your memory contains countless pieces of knowledge and millions of experiences that can serve as the keystone of an impromptu talk.* You are your own private storehouse of information; look inside and you are apt to be surprised and pleased with what you find. As the playwright Oscar Wilde wrote, "Memory is the diary we all carry about with us." So I urge you to pause and open up this "diary."

Develop a Positive Attitude. The second step in preparing for an impromptu situation is *to adopt a positive mental attitude toward the impromptu event.* Keep in mind that those who ask you to speak impromptu do not really expect a polished oration; your listeners' expectations are not as demanding as they would be under different circumstances. Your listeners are probably more concerned with hearing your off-the-cuff remarks about the subject than they are about watching a display of oratorical brilliance. I should add that the term "positive mental attitude" also means staying relaxed and calm.

Try to Anticipate the Topic. Third, *try to anticipate what might be asked of you.* Pay close attention to what is going on at a conference, dinner, or meeting you are attending. Listen to what is being said by others. Often, you can build on their remarks when you are called on to speak. Avoid daydreaming so that you can spare yourself the embarrassment that can occur when you are unexpectedly asked to speak. Listening is a part of the preparation for any speech and especially so for an impromptu speech.

Use Your Time to Organize Your Talk. Fourth, *once you are called on to speak, make good use of the time interval prior to your first words.* Although this time may range only from a few seconds to a much longer period of time, it can still be put to good use. The brain is a marvelous instrument and works at extremely high speed when it has to. Therefore, use your time to engage in some of the following activities.

1. *Try to formulate a central point around which you can build your remarks.* Perhaps you can build on what a previous speaker has said—for instance, "Tom is absolutely right, and I'd like to add a few observations of my own." Perhaps you disagree with remarks that have been made and can build your speech around the reasons for disagreement: "I'm afraid I'm going to have to take issue with my friend's arguments on at least three counts." If you happen to be the first speaker (or the only speaker), then you might design a speech that answers one or more of the following questions about the topic you have been given: What is it? Who is connected with it? Where can it be found? When did it come into being? Why should I be concerned about it? How can I deal with it? Needless to say, many other questions might apply, each of which could provide a central point around which to build your speech. The important thing is to try to find a unifying theme and then stick to it.

2. *Once you have arrived at a central point for your speech, select an organizational pattern that will let you develop that central point.* Following are six commonly used patterns:

> **Refer to what has been said by a previous speaker. State your position on the issue. Develop your position by an illustration, an analogy, or any appropriate form of support. Summarize what you have said and sit down.**

    I. John said that there is no solution to the high cost of medical bills in our country.

   II. I believe he is wrong.

        A. We need only look at what Hawaii, Oregon, and California have done to control cost.

            1. Hawaii

            2. Oregon

            3. California

  III. In short, although I respect John's views, we have seen that there are some possible solutions to the health-care problem if we just turn to what some states have done.

Start with an illustration. Draw a central point out of that illustration. Add additional support to your central point and conclude.

    I. Last week, I drove home in the rain.

        A. A car came directly at me.

        B. As I started to move out of the way, my brakes locked.

        C. I started to skid out of control.

        D. Luckily, I hit a soft embankment.

   II. When I later talked to people, I discovered that skidding is a common problem.

 III. I also discovered that skidding in the rain can be avoided with an antilock braking system.

State a proposal. Tell your audience why it is important. Then explain the proposal.

    I. I believe that organ transplants are important.

   II. They give people who are ill a chance to live.

 III. The deceased body can produce many essential body parts.

        A. One heart

        B. Two lungs

        C. Two kidneys

        D. One pancreas

Develop your theme chronologically.

    I. Glycol ether exposure on the job first became known as a serious problem in 1996, when a study showed that 900 painters at a plant in Connecticut developed serious blood disorders.

   II. Two years later in another plant in New York 400 painters exposed to glycol ether developed the same blood disorder.

 III. And last year a study showed a 40 percent increase in miscarriages among women exposed to glycol ether on the job.

Develop your theme according to spatial or geographical considerations.

    I. The war against drugs has an impact in Mexico.

   II. The war against drugs has an impact in Colombia.

 III. The war against drugs has an impact in the United States.

Divide the topic into components, such as economic, social, and political aspects or mental, moral, and physical aspects.

    I. What are the implications of breast implants?

        A. Emotional implications

❖ ❖ ❖ ❖
    B. Physical implications

    C. Cultural implications

A review of the organizational patterns presented in chapter 10, as well as the informative and persuasive patterns discussed in chapters 13 and 14, will suggest a variety of ways to put together a coherent message.

Delivering an Impromptu Speech

Be brief! Your listeners realize you did not have long to prepare and are therefore not expecting a long dissertation. Remember the sound advice offered by a French philosopher over two hundred years ago: "All pleasantry should be short; and it might even be as well were the serious short as well."

Try to have an introduction so you do not have to hurry into the main part of your presentation. This will give you valuable time to think of what to say and will help you relax and gain your composure.

Do not apologize. Although an apology might be appropriate in the Japanese culture, in the North American culture it often seems insincere and lowers a speaker's credibility.

Do not rush your presentation. Many impromptu speakers feel they need to hurry through their talks. All speaking, in public or private, is most effective when it is characterized by a lively conversational delivery, not a rapid presentation that make paying attention a difficult job.

Do not prolong your conclusion. Too many impromptu speeches end on a note of apology or embarrassment. Why not simply summarize what you have said, restate your central point, and sit down? You might even find it helpful to plan your last line before you start talking. This will keep you from having an awkward moment as you attempt to end your remarks.

Because impromptu speaking is such an important activity, I urge you to practice making impromptu speeches. The ability to cope with an impromptu speaking situation can be greatly improved if you are willing to practice. One good method is to read the editorial page of your local paper and frame a reaction to each editorial or letter on subjects about which you feel strongly. Valuable, too, are speeches you can build around a word or phrase such as sexism, integrity in public office, consumerism, business ethics, global economy, and military alliances.

Other tools of improvement are books of quotations and anecdotes. Try to master a few interesting and generic citations and stories that can be used on almost any occasion. Not only will having a storehouse of engrossing material help your speech, but knowing that you have tucked away some good information will help you relax when you are called on to give an impromptu talk.

Manuscript Speeches

In chapter 2, we discussed speaking from a manuscript and examined some of the disadvantages of this form of public speaking. There are many cases, however, in which a manuscript speech is highly useful. If you watch the president delivering the annual "State of the Union" address, you will be aware that the speech is being read through a teleprompter, but read none the less. And while not all of you will be President, you will likely attend professional conventions and have to present important reports. In instances like these the material will be read aloud. If you have observed the proceedings of a local government agency, you have seen people read their written responses to an important issue being considered by the elected officials. Manuscript speeches are also useful when the exact timing of the speech is important. In fact, there are many occasions when a speaker can benefit from a "polished" speech, in which every word is carefully crafted and selected for accuracy and effect. In addition, many people who have English as a second language feel more comfortable reading their speeches instead of having to think about selecting the right word on the spur of the moment. To derive the optimal benefit from a manuscript speech, certain considerations of preparation and presentation need to be taken into account.

Preparing a Manuscript Speech

An occasion that calls for a manuscript speech is usually a very special one. Accordingly, most speakers are willing to put a great deal of energy into the preparation of their manuscripts. The following sequence, although somewhat time consuming, is helpful in preparing a manuscript.

First, begin by going through many of the same steps discussed in chapter 1 in the section titled "Organizing Ideas." After addressing questions of purpose, audience analysis, and analysis of the occasion, begin developing an outline. An outline for a manuscript speech, like an outline for an extemporaneous speech, should be concerned with organizing to produce an introduction, a body, and a conclusion. The content of the manuscript should be well researched, interesting, and accurate.

Second, once you have gathered your material and have completed an outline, you are ready to write your first draft of the manuscript. In your writing, you should keep some of the following ideas in mind so that your manuscript will sound more like spoken language than written. Use language that is simple and clear. This does not mean that you should avoid eloquent vocabulary. It means that you must keep in mind that you are writing a speech, not an essay. Use transitions, internal summaries, and other techniques that contribute to clarity. Use personal pronouns to draw your listeners into the speech. In writing, people often remove the personal aspect of the communication event. Don't let this happen. Again, you need to realize that you will be engaged in an oral exchange, even though you are reading.

Third, after reading the first draft aloud, you will want to make changes. Many sections that would be acceptable in an essay are ineffective when read aloud. Recording your talk or having a friend listen to an early draft of the speech is also valuable.

Fourth, once you have made the necessary corrections and additions, you should have a well-written and highly polished speech. The manuscript from which you read can be made even more useful by following a few simple guidelines: (1) use stiff paper; (2) write on only one side of the paper; (3) number the pages; (4) type the manuscript, using triple spacing; (5) use short paragraphs—they are easier to locate when you return to the manuscript after establishing and maintaining eye contact; and (6) use a fresh ribbon or cartridge in your typewriter or computer printer; dull or faded print is difficult to read.

Finally, practice speaking from the final draft a number of times so that you become familiar with the material and develop dexterity in handling the paper. You might also find it helpful to mark the manuscript where you want to pause or add vocal emphasis and variety. You should also add a note or two on the manuscript that simply says **EYE CONTACT.** This will remind you to look at the audience as well as at your manuscript.

Delivering a Manuscript Speech

The principles of good delivery discussed in chapter 4 also apply to manuscript delivery. The practices listed below are unique to manuscript delivery:

1. *Do not try to conceal the manuscript.* Many speakers have tried to feign total spontaneity, only to discover that such deception works against them. In addition to having trouble locating their places in the speech, they incur audience displeasure at being deceived.

2. *Establish and maintain eye contact.* The fact that you are speaking from a manuscript should in no way detract from your initiating and maintaining rapport with the audience. Eye contact can be fostered by becoming very familiar with your speech.

3. *Concentrate on ideas rather than words.* Keep in mind that it is a speech you are delivering. If you start to read every word and forget the influence of ideas, you will no longer have the unique effect of speech communication.

4. *Be animated in both voice and body.* There is nothing inherent in a manuscript that stifles delivery. From correct posture, to vocal variety, to sincere and enthusiastic gestures, the manuscript speech demands good delivery.

Entertaining Speeches

We need only look at the TV evening news or the daily newspaper to know that life is full of troubling and complex issues. Our personal life can also offer countless examples of the often difficult nature of modern existence. It is no wonder that people like entertainment and humor to relieve some of the tensions of life and to add pleasure to daily activity. This was true even in ancient Greece; as Plato once noted: "Even the gods love their jokes." It is often a public speaker who supplies the jokes and the entertainment.

Many occasions call for a speech to entertain. You may be familiar with after-dinner speeches (although they are often after breakfast or lunch), in which the objective is to help the audience relax and get in a light-hearted mood. Possibly, you belong to a club or an organization that has occasional meetings of a purely social nature, where speeches provide part of the entertainment. Maybe you will be asked to talk about an interesting experience you have had, to tell about a celebrity you have met, or to take part in "roasting" a fellow club member. Perhaps you will be allowed to choose your own entertaining topic, or you might decide that your speech to persuade or inform would be more effective if you were to incorporate some entertaining aspects.

Regardless of the specific circumstance, the speech to entertain is a common form of public and private address.

Characteristics of the Entertaining Speech

A speech to entertain can be humorous, but not all speeches to entertain need to be funny. The one basic requirement for all speeches of entertainment is that they must hold attention and interest in themselves. A speaker can best accomplish this objective by incorporating into the speech many of the factors of attention and interest discussed in chapter 13. Attention can be gained and held by imparting action and using illustrations and humor. Some additional characteristics of a speech to entertain are as follows:

1. *The delivery should be lively, enthusiastic, and animated.* Both your voice and your body should reflect the pleasure associated with a casual and relaxed atmosphere. Even your content should be exhilarating. In short, the general mood of an entertaining speech should be "upbeat" and genial. Pessimism, bitterness, gloom, and denunciation are out of place in a speech to entertain.

2. *Stories, illustrations, and humorous anecdotes should be liberally used.* A fully developed example is often so vivid that it captures and maintains attention. Remember, these illustrations should be fresh and make a particular point. Notice in the famous example that follows how the speaker uses the humorous narrative to make a point about the importance of being able to think on your feet when confronted with a problem:

> When Albert Einstein was making the rounds of the speaker's circuit, he usually found himself eagerly longing to get back to his laboratory work. One night as they were driving to yet another rubber-chicken dinner, Einstein mentioned to his chauffeur (a man who somewhat resembled Einstein in looks and manner) that he was tired of speech-making. 'I have an idea, boss,' his chauffeur said. 'I've heard you give this speech so many times. I'll bet I could give it for you.' Einstein laughed loudly and said, 'Why not? Let's do it!' When they arrived at the dinner, Einstein donned the chauffeur's cap and jacket and sat in the back of the room. The chauffeur gave a beautiful rendition of Einstein's speech and even answered a few questions expertly. Then a supremely pompous professor asked an extremely esoteric question about anti-matter formation, digressing here and there to let everyone in the audience know that he was nobody's fool. Without missing a beat, the chauffeur fixed the professor with a steely stare and said, 'Sir, the answer to that question is so simple that I will let my chauffeur, who is sitting in the back, answer it for me.'

3. *Like all speeches, a speech to entertain is well organized, easy to follow, and usually constructed around a central theme or idea.* The theme often deals with a common topic in a novel manner. For example, the problems of eating three meals a day while orbiting the earth in a space shuttle would make a good entertaining speech. People would also find it entertaining if someone used the theme of bungled and botched practical jokes.

4. *The response sought is usually immediate and momentary.* The audience may remember some of the information long after the speech, but the speaker's primary concern is the audience's response at the time of the talk.

Using Humor. The French philosopher Sébastien Roch Nicolas Chamfort wrote that "the most wasted day of all is that on which we have not laughed." Although this counsel might be slightly overstated, it nevertheless reminds us of the important role humor and laughter play in our lives. Although this section of the book examines speeches to entertain, much of the advice about using humor can be applied to all forms of speech making. That is to say, regardless of the type of speech you are giving, humor can be very useful.

As noted elsewhere, laughter is universal—it is a common language; the whole world likes to smile. Humor is the mainstay of the majority of entertaining speeches. It holds our attention and, if properly used, creates an enjoyable and friendly atmosphere. In some respects, however, it is one of the most unpredictable devices a speaker can use because a favorable audience response depends on so many variables. If the humor depends on adroit timing, then woe to a speaker whose timing is off. If the humor is topical and the audience is not up-to-date in its knowledge of current happenings, then the humor backfires. All of us have had experience with telling a joke that "went over like a lead balloon." We are confronted with the same problem that has faced speakers for centuries: what makes audiences laugh? Even though the question is difficult to answer, there are a number of ways you can create humor. Let us look at some of those devices so that you might be able to incorporate one or two of them into your speech to entertain.

Exaggeration (overstatement). A circumstance deliberately overstated is a potentially humorous situation. As long as the exaggeration maintains a semblance of reality, then the audience can enjoy what it knows is an obvious, intentional distortion. To describe an egg fight in terms usually reserved for describing an epic battle between mighty nations would be perceived as obvious exaggeration (and, if all goes well, as something humorous). Whole speeches have been devoted to recounting a mundane event as though it were a major moment in history. You can even take a common occurrence, such as automobile traffic, and make it humorous. Think for a moment of the potential for exaggeration as you talk about, in detail, the traffic congestion in your town by noting that the situation is so bad that most people have not only car phones, but also cooking and toilet facilities in their cars. Exaggeration as humor can even be concise. One speaker, talking about people being bored during his speech, said: "I do not object to people looking at their watches when I am speaking—but I strongly object when they all start shaking them to make certain they are still running." Another speaker used exaggeration when she remarked that "Lottery prizes were getting out of sight. First prize in the California lottery is now Arizona." And the comedian Bruce Baum used exaggeration when he said the following: "I don't know what's wrong with my television set. I was getting C-Span and the Home Shopping Network on the same station. I actually bought a congressman." If you have ever watched any of the celebrity "roasts" on television, you probably recall that one of the tactics used by the roasters is to embellish a minor failing of the roastee and make it sound downright calamitous.

Incongruity. A piece of chocolate cake topped with anchovies makes a ludicrous combination; the two foods are hardly "right for each other." In a literal sense, incongruity is present in any situation in which the parts do not fit together. The unusual, the sudden, an unexpected twist, and the inconsistent are all potential sources of humor. The notion that England's Queen Mother might say to a royal gathering, "Hey, let's party!" strikes one as incongruous. Similarly, a speaker would use incongruity if he or she were to describe the courtship of a buzzard and a bird of paradise. The casual mixing of the exotic and the ordinary, the timid and the boisterous, the vulgar and the refined is always incongruous and usually amusing.

Often a series of incongruities are strung together to make a succession of humorous examples. Notice in the example below how a speaker used incongruities to make the point about some strange behaviors of Americans.

Only in America can a pizza get to your house faster than an ambulance.

Only in America do banks leave both doors open and then chain the pens to the counter.

Only in America do we leave cars worth thousand of dollars in the driveway and leave useless junk in boxes locked in the garage.

Only in America do we use answering machines to screen calls and then have call waiting so we won't miss a call from someone we didn't want to talk to in the first place.

Only in America do we buy hot dogs in packages of 10 and buns in packages of eight.

Affronting authority. If it is carried out in jest, and without malice, poking fun at authority figures is also a source of humor. Bosses, political leaders, bureaucrats, and teachers are popular choices for a good-natured "assault." Think for a moment of the subtle humor contained in the simple line, "It is good we have four years between elections; it takes us that long to forget the promises the politicians made and forgot to keep." Even good-natured jokes about ministers and priests are examples of having fun at the expense of someone or something normally regarded with respect and reverence. Most of your audience could relate to the following joke because it has fun at the expense of an authority figure:

A preacher observed a young boy sleeping during his sermon, so he asked the boy's mother to please wake him. The boy's mother replied, 'Sir, it would be fitting if you were to wake him up yourself; you put him to sleep.'

Sarcasm. Following is a joke that some say was first told in 413 B.C.: A barber, talkative like the rest of his profession, asked King Archelaus how he would like his hair cut. "In silence," replied the king.

One reason this joke might have lasted so long is because, if handled with tact, sarcasm is an excellent source of humor. Think of the wit and sarcasm if someone was to offer the following story of one of their professors:

My history professor really trusted us not to cheat on examinations. Once he came into class and announced that the exam would be conducted on the honor system, so we should all take seats five seats apart from each other and in alternate rows.

Sarcasm has the added advantage of being able to make a point while it entertains. Notice in the following example how the speaker, talking to a women's group, used humor and sarcasm to deal with a common misconception:

Famous British actress Beatrice Campbell was once asked by a rather pompous gentleman why some women were so devoid of any sense of humor. She replied, without skipping a beat, 'God did it on purpose so that we may try to love men instead of spending our life laughing at them.'

Yet another speaker made effective use of sarcasm when called on to introduce a friend at the end of his after-dinner speech. He told the audience, "We have been eating and giving our full attention to a turkey stuffed with sage; now it is time to listen to a sage stuffed with turkey."

Again, although sarcasm is often a good source of humor, be sure that it is gentle, not cruel.

Human predicament. Experiences that are common to all of us can also be a reference point for humor. A speaker gave an entertaining speech with the theme of how poor service has become in the United States. To make one of her points, she told the following joke:

> Good service is so hard to get now that a friend of mine sent a collection agency only half of a ripped check for payment on his newspaper subscription renewal. He also included a note that said, 'The other half of this check is somewhere in the bushes in my yard, where half of my papers end up each month.'

Another speaker used common predicaments in a speech to stress how we are all becoming victims of the electronic age. Specifically, she told the following story to demonstrate one of the curses of electronic phone systems:

> Recently, I was on the phone for what seemed like an eternity, while this electronic voice moved me through countless recordings and numerous push-button assignments. I became so frustrated with the entire procedure that, when a real voice finally arrived on the phone and asked for my account number, I responded by saying, 'Please press one.' I hope they got my message.

Don't be afraid to laugh at yourself. Using ourselves as the point of humor often establishes rapport with the audience.

Unusual facts. People often find strange, bizarre, and novel facts to be both humorous and entertaining. For example, think of the interest level that can be generated with the following off-beat facts taken from the Internet:

> Coca-Cola was originally green.

> Each king in a deck of playing cards represents a great king from history: Spades—King David, Clubs—Alexander the Great, Hearts—Charlemagne, and Diamonds—Julius Caesar.

> Every day more money is printed for Monopoly than is printed by the United States Treasury.

It is easy to see how these examples might well serve as a springboard to a much longer speech.

Humor and Culture. The author Virginia Woolf wrote, "Humor is the first of the gifts to perish in a foreign tongue." Her astute observation might well serve as a warning to all of us who attempt humor when speaking to a culturally diverse audience. Laughter is universal, so do not avoid using humor when your listeners come from dissimilar backgrounds; however, do become aware of two cultural issues that can affect your attempts at being entertaining.

First, as we have discussed elsewhere, there might be language problems that affect the impact of your joke. For example, much of North American humor uses idioms. Imagine what would happen if you were speaking to an audience in which most of the members had English as a second language and, at the end of your joke, you were to say, "So you can see he was a real couch potato." And what do you think the reaction would be if, as part of your humor, you were to say, "They just didn't stop bugging me"?

A second potential problem in cross-cultural humor relates to our earlier discussion of what is deemed an appropriate topic for humor in each culture. In one culture, jokes about the elderly, status differences, and religion might not be offensive, yet to many cultures these are sacred subjects. Even using animals as sources of humor shifts from culture to culture. What is most important is that you do a thorough audience analysis before you select your jokes or humorous examples.

Guidelines in the Use of Humor. First, the audience needs to be considered during all phases of an entertaining speech. It is easy when using humor to forget that not all people see a situation in exactly the same way. Hence, audience analysis takes on special meaning when you are preparing and delivering an entertaining talk. Try to remember the importance of being tactful. Don't embarrass or ridicule any segment of the audience. Jokes about body functions are really not very funny, nor is humor that is sexist or racist. And as noted elsewhere, a careful analysis of your listeners is necessary before you launch a humorous attack against a person of authority. You do not want to trespass your audience's boundaries of good taste or offend their morals or standards by your choice of a humorous subject. You are not a nightclub performer or a professional comedian. Therefore, there is no need for personal attacks, vulgarity, or obscenity.

Second, if you are telling a joke that you read or heard on television, it is important that you identify the source of the joke. A famous newspaper writer was recently disciplined by his newspaper for writing jokes in his daily column that were actually the work of a comedian and not the columnist. In short, ethical standards apply to the use of humor to the same degree they are used in presenting evidence.

Finally, should you find it necessary to use humor that makes someone a buffoon, I recommend that you use yourself. That is to say, there is nothing wrong with telling a joke that has you on the receiving end of the punch line. A story about how you got lost while camping with some friends, and some embarrassing results of your misadventure, can be an excellent source of humor without making someone else out to be a fool.

Developing an Entertaining Speech

Now that we have talked about humor as one of the major components of the speech to entertain, we are ready to discuss how one goes about organizing this type of speech.

The primary consideration in developing an entertaining speech is knowing the exact make-up of the audience. In addition, your audience analysis should include some information on the occasion. It is important to know if the audience came only to listen to you, if they came to laugh, or if they expect some concrete information to take home. Once these questions have been answered, you are ready to determine the central theme and to decide on an introduction, an organizational pattern for the body, and a conclusion.

Introduction. Your opening remarks in an entertaining speech have the task of arousing attention, setting the mood, and establishing the main point. In a speech to entertain, you must make it clear that you do not plan to develop any profound concepts, for, if the audience expects you to "get some-where," they will be confused as you continue to provide only entertainment.

The rhetorical question is often a good technique to start a speech that seeks to entertain. If it is startling enough, it can readily capture attention. Imagine how your attention would be aroused if you heard an introduction that asked this rhetorical question: "How many of you realize that someone has been following your every move this week and recording it with a video camera?" A humorous quotation is a also a quick method of getting attention. In an entertaining speech dealing with "How I Overcame Stage Fright" a speaker started with the following Woody Allen quotation: "I'm a really timid person—I was beaten up by Quakers."

Body. When choosing your speech plan, or approach, you must keep in mind the nature of the audience, the occasion, and your speaking talent and limitations. There are endless varieties in the organization of a speech to entertain. A *topical order* ("Ten Ways to Tell You Are Not Ready to Graduate From College") or a *chronological order* ("My Donkey Trip Down the Grand Canyon") is especially appropriate.

A single, long narrative is a popular device in entertaining. As noted in chapter 6, a narrative, when presented as an illustration, holds attention, makes a point, and is interesting. A good narrative tells a story; for an entertaining speech, the story should be humorous. One student told the story of how her wedding was plagued by one unforeseen disaster after another.

You can use a series of short narratives developed around a central theme. A series illustrating interviewing problems when looking for a good job is an example of this approach. In any case, a speech to entertain should not lead in many different directions but should be built around a central theme. Remember also that interest may be derived from associating your ideas with things that are recent, impending, physically near, familiar, vital, active, unusual, suspenseful, concrete, real, humorous, or conflicting.

Descriptions can also be used in the body of the speech to entertain. A student who had worked as a chef at a famous restaurant described, in rather humorous terms, what went on "behind the scenes" in the kitchen.

Conclusion. The conclusion is usually very brief and continues to carry the robust and cheerful mood that was maintained throughout the speech. Specific devices for concluding were discussed in chapter 11 and should be reviewed as a means of determining which technique best applies to the specific communication situation you face.

Television Speeches

The *Wall Street Journal* noted that "if you are 30 years in business or the professions, the chances of your avoiding an appearance on television are nearly zero." Appearing on television is no longer the exclusive domain of professional broadcasters. For a long time, people tended to think of themselves primarily as receivers of televised messages. We used to believe that we simply would sit and have television do something to us. However, the role and use of television in our culture have changed drastically. We are becoming senders as well as receivers. In short, regardless of our professions, we are becoming users of television as well as its consumers. In both our private

Inexpensive, portable video equipment makes it possible for people to produce, direct, and even "star" in their own productions. (Photo: Gloria Thomas)

and professional lives, we are finding ourselves in front of television cameras. We will all engage in mediated events sooner or later, such as videotaped events in classrooms or courtrooms, or perhaps a videoconference that is televised to 20 campuses.

In part, technological advances in the medium of television are responsible for the increased likelihood that you will appear on camera. With the invention of cable and satellite systems, the number of people needed to fill the added stations and channels began to grow at a rapid rate. With the advent of fiber optics, channel capacity will continue to grow, as will the need for people to fill these channels. In a brief period of time, the number of TV channels in the United States increased from 1,000 to a potential of 350,000. In short, cable systems have accelerated the need for people in the professions to be effective communicators in front of television cameras. It is not only Dan Rather, Larry King, and Barbara Walters doing the talking; it is now all of us.

Television's new impact on our daily interactions does not stop with commercial, educational, and cable television. Inexpensive, portable video equipment makes it possible for people to produce and play back their own television programs. We can all produce, direct, and even "star" in our own shows.

Teleconferencing, both in the United States and internationally, is yet another example of how more and more people are using television in noncommercial ways. People in New York can now interact with people in Iowa, Tokyo, Moscow, and Indiana at the same time.

Business executives are now finding numerous uses for television. A full-page advertisement showing executives on television appeared in *Time* and *Newsweek* with the following caption: "Getting together by satellite—the world's largest privately owned earth station network lets you hold videoconference meetings at hundreds of Holiday Inn hotels at the same

❖ ❖ ❖ ❖ time." In addition, most large corporations now have their own in-house "mini-private networks."

If you are going to be an educator, you will also be using television, because "distance learning" will be used more frequently in the near future. Educators are now using closed-circuit systems, some with interactive units, to teach many of their classes. Other teachers are supplementing their instruction by making specific tapes tailored to various topics.

The medical field, at all levels, is finding countless uses for television. For example, health care professionals are appearing before the camera to give information on the Hospital Satellite Network or to diagnose patients thousands of miles away.

Judges, lawyers, and defendants are also seeing the need to understand this important medium. They must learn to present themselves in the best possible manner.

Politics is a field whose participants are already aware of the power of television. The politician who knows how to manipulate the television audience is usually elected.

As pervasive and widespread as television is, however, most people are still horrified at the thought of appearing before a camera. Why do they become extremely self-conscious and nervous when the camera is turned on? The answer is quite simple—most people do not understand the medium. A lack of understanding regarding television's uniqueness contributes to performance anxiety and on-camera failure. Hence, it is the purpose of this section of the chapter to dispel some of the myths of television and to assist you in overcoming the feelings of apprehension associated with this medium. Try to remember the advice of Antoine de Saint Exupéry: "Only the unknown frightens us."

We can begin to feel comfortable with television and overcome our dread of it if we keep two basic ideas in mind. First, speaking on television is fundamentally an act of communication. Therefore, everything we have discussed in preceding chapters applies to television speaking—with some minor modifications. For example, regardless of the medium or the setting, you should strive to be prepared, organized, logical, and interesting. Second, although television is basically a communication activity, it possesses certain unique characteristics that set it apart from face-to-face interaction. Once these features are identified and understood, they can help rather than hinder you. In the pages that follow, we will (1) discuss some of the special features of television that need to be taken into consideration, (2) examine how speech preparation is slightly altered by television, (3) offer some suggestions that apply to your television performance, (4) provide some hints for practicing your television performance, and (5) consider some ethical considerations when using television as a communication medium.

Television's Unique Features

Your first step toward improving your communication skills on television, whether you produce your own program or are interviewed on a professionally produced program, requires you to understand how television differs from face-to-face interaction. Let us begin our analysis by looking at eight features that are unique to television speaking. By comparing these to nontelevised events, you can learn to adapt your preparation and presentation to this special medium.

Feedback. Appearing on television, in most instances, differs from face-to-face interaction in terms of feedback. Throughout this book, I have stressed that you should be sensitive to how your listeners are responding to you and your messages. I urged you to notice if they seemed interested, confused, or irritable, and suggested that you make adjustments to your delivery and content as audience feedback dictates. As you would suspect, speaking before a camera, whether it is a personal hand-held unit or a large expensive studio camera, does not allow for the same levels of feedback. To begin with, the people who will receive your message are not in front of you, and will most likely see and hear you at a later date. Therefore, you must anticipate and speculate about the responses you are apt to produce. In this sense, audience analysis takes on added significance when a speaker is using mediated devices.

Distractions. Although public speakers can face occasional hecklers or people walking in late while they are talking, they seldom are confronted with the host of distractions that the television speaker encounters. Try to imagine how hard it would be to concentrate on your presentation during the hustle and bustle that takes place in a television studio. While you are trying your best to look relaxed and at ease, camera crews are adjusting microphones and cameras, technicians are working with equipment, and producers and directors are giving cues and signals. Even the simplest home video has activity and movement that is not found in most public-speaking situations. Being able to cope with all this activity is yet another ability that separates the advanced television speaker from the novice. The key, of course, is concentration.

Heterogeneity. Although there might be some occasions when your audience is composed of co-workers or classmates, in most instances television viewers, because of the "mass media" dimension of the medium, are more heterogeneous. This diversity of backgrounds and interests places special demands on each phase of the communication process. When the event is an international teleconference, the necessity for insightful adaptation is even more significant. Your preparation, content, and presentation must all be altered to meet the cosmopolitan make-up of your audience. Throughout this book, we have emphasized the importance of adaptation. We can all learn to adapt if we remember the words of the English novelist George Gissing: "Human creatures have a marvelous power of adapting themselves to necessity."

The Television Screen. The size of the television screen is yet another variable that must be taken into account. The ramifications of the small screen are numerous. For example, although it is obvious, people often overlook the idea that you do not look the same on television as you do in person. Even your movements look different on a screen than they do in "real life." In addition, the television camera can focus on certain parts of the body while avoiding others. The public speaker is in full view of his or her audience, while the televised speaker may be only partially in view. Even when you are in front of the simplest home video unit, you may not be aware of what part of your body is going to be captured on the screen. You can regulate your delivery if you know the impact of the small screen and the "selective process" of the camera. Later in this section we shall discuss television delivery in more detail.

Time Restraints. Television places specific time restraints on the speaker. There are, of course, a number of reasons why the clock holds sway over television. Speakers and programs are assigned specific time slots in all commercial, educational, and private facilities. The "show" is over when the time allowed for the program has expired. If you are being videotaped and the tape runs out, you are off the screen, whether you like it or not. Contrast this with the public speaker who simply smiles and announces that he or she has a few more things to say. You can clearly see how time restraints would influence your preparation, practice, organization, and content.

Collaborative Effort. The public speaker in face-to-face situations requires no intervening parties to establish a bond of communication with the audience—he or she is usually a free agent. Using television for simple or elaborate productions is a collaborative effort. You must use the time and energy of other people in order to be seen and heard. You cannot get on the screen or on the air by yourself. You need other people, who are cooperating with each other, in order to have a successful "program." Just as the Malay proverb tells us that "clapping with one hand will not produce noise," so too, working alone will not produce good television. You cannot simply talk and in some magic way appear on the screen; at least one other person must be involved to operate the camera.

Action. Although we encourage you to be relaxed and conversational while on television, we must also point out that television thrives on action. Viewers can be easily distracted because of the size and privacy of the screen. In addition, people are conditioned to expect activity when they watch either a movie or a television screen. You must be prepared to deal with these expectations. Your speech material must be interesting and tightly organized. I even recommend that you talk a little faster than usual in order to blend with the speed of the medium. Some studies suggest that people comprehend more words per minute watching television than they do in face-to-face encounters. Visual aids must be used whenever possible, because they involve activity and movement. Refer to chapter 7 for more information on visual aids.

Control. When you deliver a speech in person, what you say and what you do at that moment are what the "live" audience sees and hears. The cliché "what you see is what you get" certainly applies to public speaking. This is not the case with television speaking. In television, the speaker has a much greater degree of control over the program that the audience eventually receives. Camera angles, videotaping procedures, editing devices, and the like enable the speaker, either working alone or with technicians, to manipulate and control what the audience sees. Learning how to use this control is one of the attributes of a successful television speaker.

Preparing for Television

Teachers, business executives, doctors, lawyers, political leaders, and laypeople have all had problems with television that can be clearly traced to their lack of preparation. Regardless of the situation or type of speech, thorough preparation enables you to anticipate potential problems and to adapt your material to your specific audience. Chapter 3 devoted a considerable amount of time to the important topic of audience analysis. You might want to reread that chapter whenever you need to analyze your television audience. However, some of the distinct characteristics of television that we just finished discussing demand special consideration. Let us return to some of these features and see how they affect your audience analysis.

1. *When speaking to a "mass audience," your supporting material and emotional appeals should be kept somewhat general.* Imagine the countless backgrounds and value systems you face when you talk to thousands, or even millions, of people at the same time. Appealing to only one segment of this audience does not usually attract support from all the others. Telling a mass audience that they should donate funds to your college tennis team so that it can attend the national championships does not have the same appeal as a request for donations to the Red Cross right after a national disaster.

2. *Your organizational pattern should also consider the general nature of the audience.* This means you should use a simple, clear pattern. If you believe that those who might be viewing your presentation are from diverse educational and cultural backgrounds, you need to make abundant use of transitions, previews, and summaries.

3. *Because the audience is going to represent a variety of interests, you should arouse attention quickly, then maintain that attention level.* Notice how many television programs use techniques such as color and motion to capture your interest. Producers and directors are well aware of the short attention span most of us have. When you find yourself preparing for a television appearance, try to work with the technical staff so that they can offer you some help in this area. For your part, you should use the factors of attention discussed in chapter 13 and the types of visual aids highlighted in chapter 7.

4. *The fact that your presentation is designed for a mass medium should be considered as you choose your language.* While a group of classmates might understand the words "immune system," a multicultural audience might contain people who do not even have those words in their language. When addressing a heterogeneous audience, where some of the listeners might have English as a second language, your language should be simple, clear, direct, free of jargon, and devoid of confusing idioms.

Presenting Yourself on Television

Although the delivery requirements of a televised speech are in many respects identical to those of any other public speech, the acuity of the camera's eye requires that certain modifications be made. The following is a discussion of the factors that must be modified when you appear on television.

General Appearance. Over two hundred years ago, the philosopher Thomas Fuller wrote, "By the husk you may guess at the nut." He was, of course, alluding to the importance of appearance. Your own experiences tell you that looking good on television is not only important but expected. However, for a host of reasons, dressing appropriately for television is more complicated than selecting clothes and accessories for face-to-face speech making. Not only must you be guided by good taste and cultural constraints, but you must also consider the impact of the camera, microphone, and screen. Your attire must be pleasing and yet free of distractions. To help achieve these goals, study the guidelines in the following discussion.

First, *the resolution limitations of the camera tend to distort certain colors and patterns.* For example, thin stripes, pronounced checks, and sharply contrasting patterns tend to jump around the screen. Even clashing or loud colors, such as reds, cause distortion. Thus, in addition to wearing comfortable and attractive clothing, try to wear medium tones of gray, brown, and blue. Never wear just black and white on camera—the combination tends to photograph in a rather strange manner.

Second, *avoid wearing baggy blouses, shirts, suits, and dresses.* On television, these loosely fitting clothes will make you look 10 pounds heavier.

Third, *although jewelry can lend variety to and even enhance your wardrobe, beware of its impact on your televised appearance.* Highly polished gold and silver and large diamonds or rhinestones reflect studio lights and tend to "flare" and distort the picture. These items also attract attention and may take the focus away from you. Eyeglasses can also cause glare and should be worn only when necessary. This does not mean that you should deprive yourself of the means to read the Teleprompter, but you and the lighting crew may have to make some minor readjustments in the placement of the lights.

Fourth, *avoid wearing clothing and accessories that make noise.* Microphones are highly sensitive and will broadcast the rattle of jewelry and the squeak of shoes.

Fifth, *do not smoke on television.* Your image can suffer from the effect of this somewhat messy and unhealthy activity. In addition, viewers find it very distracting to see wisps of smoke floating across the screen while someone is talking.

Sixth, *some skin colors look washed out and "ghostly" on television.* Therefore, make-up is almost invariably used to enhance the video image. One way to determine how much and what kind of make-up you need is to do a video test. Seek some help in determining the results of that test. You might not be your own best critic. While a bald Caucasian may need his head "touched up" or darkened a little, a dark-complexioned speaker may need the skin lightened somewhat. These applications of makeup are for technical reasons; they are not intended to have you appear to be something other than what you are.

Eye Contact. Eye contact seems to be an aspect of television delivery that causes people the greatest amount of apprehension. However, by following a few simple suggestions, your visual rapport with the audience can be improved.

In a pamphlet called "So You're Going on TV," published by the National Association of Broadcasters, the following advice is offered: "Remember that although you are talking to a large audience, you should pretend you are speaking to a few friends who are comfortably seated in their homes." Although this suggestion seems somewhat self-evident, it is often ignored. Most beginning television performers do not know what to do with their eyes. Some look down at the ground or seem to enjoy viewing themselves on a monitor situated off-camera.

When to look at the camera, or how often to look, is yet another issue facing novices. The answer to this question is contingent on a number of factors. For example, if you are speaking to a live audience (people in front of you), you should treat the camera as if it were simply another pair of eyes watching you. This means the camera is no more or no less important than the rest of the audience. If, on the other hand, you are aiming your message to television viewers only, you should speak directly to the camera and disregard the studio audience. If you are being interviewed on television, you should look at the interviewer as if he or she were the camera. This will give your presentation a much more natural look.

Remember, the camera that is "seeing" you at any given moment is the one whose red light is lit. With practice and experience, you will be able to transfer your gaze as the red light shifts from camera to camera. In addition, your floor director will signal you when a camera change is imminent. This will help you avoid sudden and jerky movements as you alter your eye contact.

The use of notes is yet another matter that faces most television speakers. If you need notes in order to remember certain main points or an exact wording you do not want to forget, you will find that television usually allows you three options. First, *you can use notecards just as you would for a public speech.* Do not try to conceal your cards from the audience. Some people believe that these cards even add to your professional look. In using your cards, remember to refer to them only as you need them; do not let them become more important than the television audience. Make sure you can see them easily. Using stiff paper, double-spacing your copy, and numbering your pages will aid you in your efforts.

Second, *you can put your notes on large poster board cards and ask a member of the studio crew to hold them next to the camera.* With this method, make sure the printing on the cards is large and clear enough so that you find them easy to read from a distance.

Finally, *you can use a Teleprompter to help you remember your message.* This device, which is positioned next to the camera, shows either your entire speech or brief notes as you look toward the camera. Like the other two forms of using notes, this one also has some potential problems. Many Teleprompter users can be identified by their obvious left-to-right eye movements as they read their speech from the screen. In a personal conversation, such eye movement would be taken as an indication of a malady. You should learn the material on the Teleprompter so that you will be able to read the contents in a natural manner. Once you learn how to use the Teleprompter, you will find it quite useful.

Having talked about a number of factors that influence eye contact, we are now ready to examine a few specific suggestions:

1. *Look directly at the camera that has the red tally light turned on.* Look at the activated camera 100 percent of the time you are talking. Breaking your gaze, at least on television, gives the impression that you have lost your place or are being shifty or dishonest. If the red "tally light" changes or if the floor manager points to another camera, simply redirect your eyes to the other camera as smoothly as possible. With practice, these transitions will become graceful. For now, remember to imagine that the person you are talking to is inside the camera.

2. *Try not to yield to the distractions that draw your eyes away from the camera.* These distractions range from looking at yourself on the studio monitors to watching the stage crew move from job to job.

3. *Do not stare at the camera as if you have been hypnotized.* Countless performers have become transfixed by the camera; they gape, unblinking, at it. You would not do this in a face-to-face conversation, and you should not do it on television.

Facial Expressions. The advice with regard to facial expressions while appearing on television is similar to that offered for nontelevised speeches: be yourself. Remember, you are not acting but are trying to appear natural and spontaneous. Of course, you should try to avoid looking deadpan or too serious. Experienced television speakers tell us the obvious—that people enjoy seeing a smile. This does not mean you grin while talking about a major earthquake, but it does mean that, whenever possible, you smile at the people you are trying to relate to.

Because you can never know for certain when a close-up shot is being broadcast, you should act as if the camera were on your face at all times. This means that you should be concerned with how you look for as long as the red tally light is on, even if the camera is not pointed directly at you. Many first-time performers have been caught off guard because they thought the camera was focused elsewhere.

Movement. The requirements of movement, posture, and gestures on television are somewhat different from those for traditional public speaking. Let us explore a few of the differences that might affect your overall performance.

Ordinarily, the camera moves more frequently than you do. Not only does it move from side to side and back and forth, but the lens zooms in and out on you, making you appear close up even when the camera is some distance away. This means that there are many shots of which you are not aware. During the broadcast itself, angles and distances are always changing. Because you do not always know what is on the air, your gestures should be limited and controlled. You should avoid sweeping and rapid gestures so that the camera does not lose you or get out of focus. Gesturing directly toward the camera can also cause considerable distortion on the screen. Crossing your legs is yet another movement that can photograph awkwardly.

When you are using props or referring to maps or other graphics, you may need to move around and to point. If this is the case, arrive at the studio early enough to rehearse these movements before the taping of the program.

Even the most subtle of mannerisms become greatly magnified on camera. Scratching the top of your head, rubbing your arm, or playing with your glasses appears to be an irritating habit when performed on screen.

Try to adapt your posture and movement to the constraints imposed by the studio or setting. Your physical distance from other people, the social conventions that are operative, the number of people on the set, and the props (or lack of them) all influence your posture and movement.

Finally, be prepared to change posture quickly if the need should arise. Camera movements, microphone placement, and signals from your director may force you to shift positions on very short notice. You may have to move from giving a speech to being a member of a panel discussion. The first is likely to be formal, the latter informal. In addition, the equipment you use in the studio will demand that you adapt to or make changes in the environment. For example, a microphone on a table should not cause you to lean forward in an awkward position, an overhead boom should not make you look up, and a friend carrying a small portable camera with a built-in microphone should not force you to chase after him or her.

Vocal Aspects. An interesting phenomenon of television technology is its ability to alter the human voice. It can, for example, control volume, rate, and tone, but this electronic manipulation does not exonerate you from being aware of these and other aspects of vocal delivery. The same electronic systems that can help you sound better also have the capacity to hamper your delivery. For instance, a microphone tends to attract more attention to pauses and unpleasant qualities than does unmediated speech. Microphones are so sensitive that they can pick up and broadcast poor inflection, incorrect pronunciation, sound omissions, slurred sounds, and misplaced accents. Therefore, when speaking on television, be aware of your voice: be natural, enthusiastic, relaxed, and conversational.

You might also consider increasing your rate of speaking slightly when you are before the camera. What often appears to be reasonably paced discourse in face-to-face situations seems dull and slow on television. You might want to move from 120 to 130 words per minute, the normal rate, to 130 to 140 words per minute. A fast rate connotes action, and television thrives on action.

Using Microphones

The presence of a microphone is one of the differences between electronic presentations and face-to-face communication. In what follows, we look at some of the general do's and don'ts concerning the use of microphones, whether you are speaking on television, on radio, in an auditorium, or at an outdoor rally.

1. *When taking your sound check, use a normal voice.* Do not mumble, yell, or try to imitate a professional newscaster—be yourself. Do not take your sound check by saying, "Testing one, two, three." That is the way you count, not the way you talk. Finally, when taking a check, sit or stand in the same place you will occupy during the actual performance. Taking the check sitting down and then giving your talk standing up will not provide an accurate voice-level reading.

2. *Do not alter your pitch or volume range too much from the original volume check.* Distortion may occur if you increase or decrease your volume, pitch, or rate without the control room knowing about it, although a good sound technician can usually compensate for such variations.

3. *Remember to stay within microphone range so that your voice can be broadcast to your audience.* The correct range is usually determined by the audio engineer. Your responsibility is to make sure you do not walk or turn away from the microphone unless you know for certain you can be heard. This means knowing the range of a boom or how much cord you have left on your lavaliere microphone. If you run out of cord, do

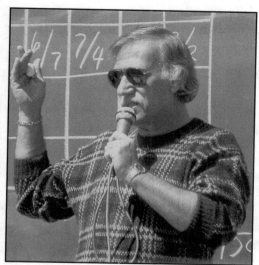

Microphones are highly sensitive instruments, engineered to pick up all sound, not just your voice. (Photo: Gloria Thomas)

❖ ❖ ❖ ❖

not pull on the cord out of frustration—you might unplug your microphone.

4. *Do not place the microphone too close to your mouth.* A good distance for a hand-held microphone is approximately one foot below and slightly in front of your mouth. A lavaliere microphone goes approximately six inches below the chin.

5. *Do not speak directly into the microphone.* Try to visualize yourself speaking across it instead of into it. This will give your voice a more natural sound.

6. *Be careful with "s," "ch," and "sh" sounds.* A microphone exaggerates these sibilant (hissing) sounds. Spend some time learning to "swallow" these sounds and concentrating on the sound that precedes or follows them. For example, focus on *ga* in *gas*, and *ould* in *should*. You might also be wary of "p," "v," "t," and "b" sounds. If they are stressed, they create a "popping" sound. Also, microphones magnify asthmatic or heavy breathing, so be careful not to breathe directly into them.

7. *Remember that a microphone is a highly sensitive instrument, engineered to pick up all sound, not just your voice.* The rattling of your jewelry can sound like a full orchestra if it is broadcast. You should also refrain from moving paper too near a microphone or tapping a microphone with your finger or pencil.

Controlling Nervousness

In chapter 4, we talked about speech fright and some ways to overcome it. As you might suspect, speech fright is often more serious when you visualize yourself in front of a camera.

Although some nervousness and apprehension can be beneficial, most of it impedes your delivery. The following are a few simple techniques that can reduce some of the harmful effects of too much nervousness:

1. *Yawn excessively before you go on camera.* This not only gives you more oxygen, it relaxes your throat muscles.

2. *Stretch as many parts of your body as you can without calling attention to your strange performance acrobatics.* Stretching relaxes the muscles that are apt to tense up as you wait for the program to begin.

3. *Have some water available so you can avoid the dry mouth feeling that makes talking seem impossible.* Be careful of too much water, however; you need to be on television, not in the restroom.

4. *Develop a good mental attitude.* This means being prepared for and actually looking forward to your television appearance. The experience will not hurt; in fact, you might actually enjoy being a "television star." This positive attitude will help you accomplish your purpose while adding to your self-confidence.

Practicing Your Television Presentation

❖ ❖ ❖ ❖

Throughout this book, we have stressed the importance of practice for successful speech making. This advice also applies to television. Let us therefore suggest three steps you should follow as you try to make your television appearance as productive as possible.

Practice Aloud. First, *practice your presentation aloud, and during these practice sessions make sure you time your speech.* If your talk is too long, you are apt to find yourself offering your conclusion to the stage crew but not to the people viewing their televisions. If you are making your own tape and you fail to time your talk, you might discover that you will run out of tape before you run out of words.

The availability of television equipment should offer you the opportunity to practice your speech before a camera. By using a playback system, you can see and hear your speech in about the same way your audience will be receiving it. Hence, you will be able to make the necessary adjustments in both delivery and content. As you view your tape, you should ask yourself some of the following questions:

- Did I have enough vocal variety to hold attention?

- Was my eye contact focused in the right direction? At the correct camera?

- Did my wardrobe and accessories detract from my message?

- Did my voice add to or detract from my presentation?

- Did I engage in any distracting mannerisms?

- Will I need makeup?

- Did I appear nervous?

- Were my movements (gesturing, walking) natural?

- What overall impression did I give?

Solicit Advice. *The second part of your practice session should include the soliciting of advice from people who have successfully used the medium.* For example, someone who has been on many interview programs can tell you whether to use a clipboard for your notes or have them printed on cards. You might also have some of your friends view your videotape and ask them what they think of your presentation. Keep in mind that this entire book has been filled with advice. Now I am simply asking you to look to other places for that assistance. As Shakespeare once wrote, "Friendly counsel cuts off many foes." Or put another way, good advice can eliminate some potential problems.

Locate and Develop Models. Third, *locate and develop models.* In ancient Rome, students had to memorize great speeches and deliver them as they were said to have been delivered originally. While we are not suggesting you mimic people you have seen on television, we are suggesting you observe people who use the medium well to discover some reasons for their success. By isolating what makes them effective, you can evaluate your own television personality. Again, we are advocating not the cloning of television performers

❖ ❖ ❖ ❖   but rather the finding of models who can offer you some specific clues as to what works and what does not work on television.

Ethical Considerations and Television

Throughout this book, we have directly and indirectly discussed the ethical responsibilities facing anyone who sends a message to another human being. When one person receives a message from another, the speaker is, in one degree or another, changing the other. While some changes might be significant and others subtle, it is change nevertheless. Nowhere is the import of this notion more meaningful than in our use of television. For there is power and influence associated with television that is not found in most other communication environments. This point was clearly made by the Pilkington Report on television when it concluded that "Unless and until there is unmistakable proof to the contrary, the presumption must be that television is and will be a main factor in influencing the values and moral standards of our society."

Your own experiences will also verify the power of television and the influence of the people who appear on this medium. Notice how many times you listen to a person on a talk show and find yourself responding differently than if you were talking to that person informally. A guest on a national talk show suggested that powdered vitamin C was healthier than the tablet form. In three days, most health food stores were completely sold out of powdered vitamin C.

We have been trying to suggest that the personal use of television involves personal responsibility. That responsibility can best be examined by looking at how you deal with (1) objectives and (2) values.

Objectives. Having objectives is one of the more distinctly human characteristics of television communication. Electronic hardware does not have objectives beyond those imbued by its human masters. It is simply a conduit delivering your ideas and values. Therefore, when we talk about objectives in television communication, we are talking about your objectives. Make sure you identify and understand them so that you can prepare and participate in an intelligent, ethical, and effective manner. A course that you might be teaching via a closed-circuit system has a different set of objectives than does a group of your friends making a home video to be played back at a birthday party. How well you identify your own objectives—whether to inform, persuade, or entertain—and how well you take the audience's objectives into account will determine how successful you are when using television to communicate. As the American author Norbert Wiener reminds us, "We need to determine not only how to accomplish our purposes, but what our purposes are to be."

Values. As you attempt to accomplish your objectives, you must develop a code of ethics. All individuals who step in front of a camera must be aware of the potential impact they are having on other people. The corporate executive videotaping a message for employees regarding the treatment of clients, as well as the person being interviewed on a talk show, must accept their ethical responsibility. Am I being truthful? Am I withholding information? Am I bowing to popular tastes? Do my objectives reflect the best interests of my receivers? These and other ethical questions must be confronted before you appear on television. As we have said repeatedly, whether you want to acknowledge the responsibility or not, what people see and hear on television can reshape the way they perceive reality. The communication scholar Richard Weaver made much the same point when he observed, "We are all of us preachers in private and public capacities. We have no sooner uttered words than we have given impulse to other people to look at the world, or some part of it, in our way."

Because television is a mass medium, being on television can often give you power, influence, and stature that may not have ever been available in face-to-face encounters. Therefore, you can see why I recommend that you ponder your ethical responsibilities when appearing on television. In short, ask yourself these two crucial questions: First, have the ideas and values I discussed diminished the individual and human potential of my viewers? Second, have I contributed to my viewers' emotional, spiritual, intellectual, or mental well-being?

Speeches of Introduction

A common practice on most public-speaking occasions is for someone to offer a brief introduction to the principal speaker. This assignment should be relatively easy in that in many ways it is similar to introducing a very close friend to a stranger. However, speeches of introduction are often poorly done. Let us mention a few ideas that can improve the manner in which you carry out speeches of introduction when you are faced with such an assignment.

First, *remember that the speaker you are introducing is the center of attention—not you.* On too many occasions the person making the introduction either fails to take the assignment seriously or uses the occasion to demonstrate his or her cleverness or "superior knowledge." Regardless of the reason, the introducer fails to focus on the speaker and the topic to be discussed.

Second, *keep in mind that a speech of introduction has three main purposes:* (1) to get the audience interested in the guest speaker, (2) to arouse audience interest in the speaker's subject, and (3) to establish a warm and friendly climate.

Third, *be brief.* As was already mentioned, an introducer subordinates his or her own speech for the sake of the main talk; he or she is only an emissary linking the speaker to the audience. In most instances, one to five minutes is the time allotted to a person making an introduction. This should allow ample time to get attention, point the audience toward the topic, and establish the speaker's credibility.

Fourth, *make sure your information concerning the speaker and his or her background and topic is accurate.* Errors in pronunciation should always be avoided. Contact the speaker in advance if you have any doubts regarding how the speaker pronounces his or her name. The issue of correct pronunciation is even more crucial in this age of cultural diversity. Often you will be asked to introduce someone whose foreign name is one you have never seen before. You should also have accurate information about the speaker's personal and professional background. Inaccurate information can cause a great deal of embarrassment to you, the speaker, and the audience. Secure the essential and personal information from the speaker well in advance of your formal introduction.

❖ ❖ ❖ ❖   Fifth, *it is often effective to begin an introduction with a brief reference to the nature of the occasion.* This may serve as a bond between the speaker and the listeners. Also, there may be occasions when it will be valuable to emphasize the importance of the subject.

Sixth, *once you have established rapport with the audience by humor, a reference to the occasion, or any other form of motivation, you are ready to give the biographical data necessary to identify the speaker and to make that person sound interesting and authoritative.* The biography, in most instances, should include (a) the speaker's place of residence, (b) his or her achievements (publications, honors, and awards), (c) the speaker's background in the topic (professional and educational), (d) the speaker's relationship to the audience, and (e) the reason this person was selected to deliver the talk. It is very important that all the data contained in the introduction be completely accurate.

Seventh, *if the occasion allows, hold the speaker's full name and subject until the end.* In this way, the speaker's name and topic can be presented as a climax: "Now that we know just how important it is to talk to someone who has actually done business in Japan, let me introduce Mr. James Ray, who will speak to us today on the topic of how to make contact with Japanese corporations."

Eighth, *refrain from excessive exaggeration.* On many occasions, I have seen introductions that embarrassed the person being introduced because of the amount of extreme admiration heaped on the speaker. In short, be flattering but not artificial.

Ninth, *avoid hackneyed words and phrases.* Introductions such as "Our speaker needs no introduction," "I am indeed honored," "I consider it a rare privilege," and "without further ado" are too common.

Tenth, *try to place the audience into a state of anticipation.* By the time you finish your comments, the audience should want to hear what the speaker has to say. As you mentioned earlier, this is done to arouse curiosity about the topic at the same time you are establishing the speaker's credibility.

Finally, *pay close attention to the speech so that, at its close, you can refer to the ideas and their value to the audience as you thank the speaker.*

Question-and-Answer Sessions

Student Cynthia Connors has just completed a classroom speech about half-human, half-beast legends. Someone in the audience poses this question to her: "Why do you say it is biologically impossible for such creatures to exist?"

Tom Fernandez is urging the city council to approve plans for the construction of a 160-unit condominium project adjacent to the municipal stadium. A councilman interrupts Tom to ask, "Have you considered the impact that stadium traffic on game days is going to have on the residents' access to their homes?"

George Thurmond is demonstrating the features of a food processor to a group of interested spectators in a department store. One of the spectators asks, "Why is this product so expensive?"

Answering both general and specific questions from the audience is a routine part of most communication encounters. A speaker seeking to

Answering both general and specific questions from the audience is a routine part of most communication encounters. (Photo: Randall Reeder)

instruct often invites the audience to pose questions whenever appropriate as a way of clarifying points that might not be self-evident when they were first explained. A speaker attempting to persuade is likely to be questioned or challenged by some listeners who disagree with the speaker's arguments or conclusions. A speaker who stimulates the audience's curiosity with unusual subject matter may be bombarded by questions after the address. A politician who takes part in a town meeting expects questions from the floor. With interactive television systems, people can ask each other questions even if they find themselves at different locations. In short, almost all speech situations lend themselves to a question-and-answer session. Because the audience's impression of a speaker is based not only on what happens during the speech but also on the speaker's prespeech and postspeech behavior, it is important to examine the ways in which a question-and-answer session can promote a favorable impression of the speaker.

Ways to Formulate an Effective Reply

In a question-and-answer session, remember that the people who ask the questions may not all have the same motives. That is to say, some members of the audience might be very sincere when they pose their questions. However, you might also be faced with people who want to give their own speeches and use the question-and-answer period as an opportunity to do so. You are even apt to hear a question from an individual who enjoys verbal confrontation. Regardless of a questioner's motive, you need to learn the characteristics of an effective reply, for, as the journalist Sydney J. Harris noted, "More trouble is caused in this world by indiscreet answers than by indiscreet questions."

It is easy to find yourself nervous or believing you will get caught off guard when you face questions from your audience. Nevertheless, it is important that you remain calm so that you can think of an intelligent response to the questions you are asked. Part of staying calm is making sure you start listening from the outset. You will recall that when we discussed listening in chapter 5, we told you that one of the most common errors in listening is not being

❖ ❖ ❖ ❖   prepared to listen. Remember, just a few words can alter the entire idea behind the question. Being asked about a specific 1998 court ruling on capital punishment is not the same as being asked to comment on capital punishment in general.

Stay Calm. Listening and staying calm is complicated if the question is a hostile one, yet, even in these situations, it is crucial that you keep your senses about you. In fact, remaining composed when facing a difficult predicament can aid your credibility and even astonish the person asking the unfair question. A classic example of disarming an aggressive skeptic is found in the following story concerning Buddha:

> A man interrupted Buddha's preaching with a flood of abusive questions. Buddha stayed calm and waited until the man had finished. He then asked him, 'If a man offered a gift to another but the gift was declined, to whom would the gift belong?' 'To the one who offered it,' said the man. 'Then,' said Buddha, 'I decline to accept your abuse and request you keep it for yourself.'

Buddha's advice is valid today. Be patient and stay calm when you are asked a question.

Repeat the Question. Repeating a question from the floor is one of the chief characteristics of an effective response: "You asked which animals are most endangered by the logging industry in the Pacific Northwest. It is the spotted owl." This technique is useful with both large and small audiences.

There are a number of reasons why your repeating the question is a good idea. First, there might be people in the audience who failed to hear the question you are being asked. This could be caused by room noise, or the person asking the question may have a soft voice. Second, the question may be poorly phrased, too wordy, ambiguous, or one-sided. By repeating the question, you are in a much better position to answer it. Third, the time it takes to repeat the question may afford you valuable time in which to formulate an answer. Finally, repeating the question allows you and the person asking the question to make sure that you have identified the main point of the question.

Rephrase the Question. On some occasions it might be useful to rephrase the question. Rephrasing is most useful when the question is complicated or when the person asking the question added superfluous information and took a long time.

You should begin by asking the person who posed the question if they mind your rephrasing it. Once they agree, as most people do, you need to be as accurate as possible as you interpret their original question. And, of course, you should verify that your rephrasing has not distorted their question. "As I understand your question, you seemed to concerned about the exact distance of the new housing development from the country park. Is that basically your question?"

Be Polite. Put yourself in the role of a questioner for a moment and think about the kind of reply you would appreciate from a speaker—probably one that is polite. Politeness is taught in every culture, and people have come to expect certain rules of politeness to be followed when they interact with other people, including when they ask a question. Usually, when someone asks a question, it is because he or she believes that question is important. Regardless of how naive, irrelevant, or poorly worded a question seems, the speaker should treat the questioner with dignity. If members of the audience laugh in derision at a poor question, it is wise for the speaker to refrain from joining in that laughter. A speaker who shows respect for a questioner's feelings deserves the goodwill that almost inevitably follows from such a gesture. As indicated earlier, even hostile questions should be answered without rancor. There is great wisdom in the proverb, "A soft answer turneth away wrath." One can disagree politely with a questioner, especially if the focus of the reply is on issues, not on personalities. Moreover, meeting hostility with politeness can disarm a hostile questioner while minimizing that person's influence on the other listeners. Let your answer be logical enough to satisfy a cynic and congenial enough to satisfy a friend.

Be Honest. Straightforwardness is another desirable feature in answering questions. Audiences are usually quick to sense evasiveness; sometimes, the favorable impression left by a speech can be negated by a shifty answer to a question asked afterward. If you do not know the answer to a question, it is better to say so than to try to divert the issue elsewhere. Likewise, if you do not wish to answer a question, then say so, adding an explanation for declining. In addition, be prepared to admit "I do not know" if such a response is true and appropriate. If you bluff, the audience will know it and will resent you for trying to deceive them. And in most instances that deception will be obvious. As the Chinese philosopher Mencius noted, "Listen to a man's words and look at the pupil of his eye. How can a man conceal his character?" In short, when a question is asked, come directly to grips with it and avoid diversionary tactics.

Eye contact and speaking directly to the person asking the question can also manifest a straightforward and candid image. By looking at the person posing the question, you are nonverbally saying, Here is my sincere and honest response to your question.

Be Brief. William Shakespeare remarked that "brevity is the soul of wit." Brevity should also characterize your answers—that is, brevity consistent with completeness. Some speakers are guilty of overkill in their answers. Not only do they use a question as an excuse to give another long speech, but they get sidetracked, answering questions that have not even been asked. In addition, taking a long time to answer a question often leads to vocal fillers such as "well . . . ," "um . . . ," and "er . . ." If there appears to be a number of questions forthcoming from the audience, brevity is a necessity.

Be Prepared. An answer that reflects preparation is another hallmark of a competent reply. Put yourself in the listeners' place and try to imagine what they might ask. Preparation also means researching the material for your reply and practicing it aloud. This rehearsal period is very common among public figures who find themselves facing press conferences. Being prepared not only makes your response more acceptable, but it also adds to your credibility. It is yet another way to show the audience that you know the material.

Organizing a Reply

The organizational format most appropriate for a reply is dictated by the nature and scope of the question itself and the amount of time allowed for the question-and-answer period. However, some organizational schemes seem to fit most occasions. Next, we will examine four of those formats.

Request for Clarification.

1. Refer to the section of your speech requiring clarification.

2. Use the appropriate clarifying devices—such as definition, restatement, example, illustration, analogy, diagram, and demonstration.

3. Ask the questioner if the point is sufficiently clarified.

An example of clarification might appear as the following:

I've been asked to define the word 'resistor,' which I used earlier in telling you about controlling power surges that can impede the electrical outlets in your home. In simple terms, a resistor is something that resists. In the case of electrical circuitry, it resists the flow of electricity. It enables just the right amount of voltage to be supplied to other components in the circuit. In a sense, a resistor acts somewhat like a water faucet valve that resists, or controls, the flow of water coming from the supply line. Does that explain it clearly enough?

Request for More Information.

1. Refer to the point on which you have been requested to offer further information.

2. Relate the information using an appropriate sequence—such as chronological, spatial, topical, or logical order.

3. Ask the questioner if you have answered the request sufficiently.

Consider the following example:

Sarah asked where the blood bank is located in relation to the park. 'As you know, Sarah, the western boundary of the park is along Sixth Avenue, from about Fir Street on the south to Upas Street on the north. Using the northern-most intersection—Sixth and Upas—as our reference point, the blood bank is located one block west at 440 Upas Street. Can you visualize that location now?'

Challenge to Your Position.

1. Refer to the point that has been challenged.

2. State the nature of the challenge.

3. Answer the challenge by offering additional evidence in support of your position and by showing the fallacious character of the questioner's objections.

Following is an example and a challenge:

The source of my data relating to the high prison population of California has been challenged by the gentleman in the front row. If he questions the syndicated columnist I quoted, let me refer him to the latest publication of the Bureau of Justice Statistics, United States Justice Department. He will find, and I am now reading from that publication, that California has more prison inmates than either New York or Texas. In fact, it has more prisoners than the combined prison populations of Washington, Oregon, Idaho, Montana, Colorado, Utah, Arizona, New Mexico, Nevada, Wyoming, Alaska, and Hawaii.

Redirect the Question.

1. Repeat the question so that the questioner knows you heard the request.

2. Refer the question back to the person asking the question.

3. Ask the questioner for a specific response.

Consider the following example of redirect:

> You are wondering why I am asking the paint company to remove the residue of their product. This is a very good question. I am curious as to what you would do with the waste material coming from the new paint factory.

Regardless of how you decide to organize your response, you must always keep in mind that the real key to replying to questions can be found in two simple words—*stay calm.*

Summary

In this chapter, we dealt with special communication situations. Although, in a sense, all communication is special and therefore has similarities in form and style, certain situations demand a different degree of proficiency if a speaker is to accomplish a specific purpose. The situations dealt with were those calling for impromptu speeches, manuscript speeches, entertaining speeches, television speeches, speeches of introduction, and question-and-answer sessions.

An impromptu speech is given on the spur of the moment or when a speaker has had little time to prepare. To keep from being completely overwhelmed, a speaker can call forth a few simple techniques such as remembering what was said just before he or she was asked to speak, thinking about past reading and speaking experiences, and working out a suitable organizational pattern.

A manuscript speech is unique in offering a speaker an opportunity to write out a speech in detail before delivering it. In preparing this type of speech, it is important to remember that it is a speech and not an essay. Once an outline is completed, the speaker is in a position to start the manuscript. Rewriting is always beneficial. The final draft should be highly polished. In presenting a speech, the essentials of good delivery must be kept in mind. Eye contact, vocal variety, and gestures are as important to good manuscript speaking as they are to good extemporaneous speaking.

The major purpose of a speech to entertain is to have the listeners enjoy themselves. A speaker, by using the concepts of attention and interest, has the audience relax in an enjoyable atmosphere. Humor is often a trademark of entertaining speaking; a successful speaker must learn to use humorous illustrations, exaggeration, incongruity, the affronting of authority, sarcasm, human predicaments, and unusual facts.

Changes in commercial and public television, new cable systems, and low-cost portable sending units have created a situation in which more and more people are finding themselves in front of a television camera. For these appearances to be successful, a television speaker should understand some of the unique features of television, conduct an audience analysis, adapt his or her delivery to the medium of television, and accept the ethical responsibilities associated with television speaking.

The main task of a speech of introduction is to create a rapport among the speaker, subject, and audience. By stimulating interest in both the speaker and the topic, you create a friendly climate, in which the audience is interested in hearing what the guest speaker has to say.

A question-and-answer session is a common part of communication encounters. Calmness, repetition, politeness, straightforwardness, and brevity are desirable qualities in replying to questions. The nature and specificity of the question, as well as the perceived motive of the questioner, affect the speaker's strategy for reply.

Concepts and Questions

1. What are some steps to follow when "preparing" an impromptu speech?

2. Discuss how to organize an effective reply when you are asked questions by members of an audience.

3. Explain the techniques for delivering a manuscript speech.

4. What are the purposes of the speech of introduction?

5. What are some of the characteristics of humor?

6. What are some ethical considerations when speaking on television?

7. In what ways should culture be considered when using humor?

Activities and Exercises

1. Give a three-minute impromptu speech on one of the following topics:
   a. Successful study habits.
   b. Plastic surgery.
   c. Gun control.
   d. Abortion.
   e. Separation of church and state.
   f. Fashion trends.
   g. Censorship.

2. Conduct a question-and-answer period after one of your classroom speeches.

3. Watch a television talk show and evaluate how well the guests employed the delivery techniques discussed in this chapter.

4. Your instructor will bring in all of the video equipment necessary for you to give a television speech. Once you have delivered that talk, your instructor and your classmates will evaluate your presentation in light of the material discussed in this chapter. You should also write an evaluation of your own performance.

5. Introduce a friend to the members of your speech class. Use the techniques of speeches of introduction discussed in this chapter.

6. Listen to a successful comedian and write a short essay that discusses the types of humor he or she employed.

7. Imagine that a famous television news anchorperson is coming to your campus and that you have asked her or him to your class. Give a speech of introduction to the class that reflects your preparation for this special occasion. ✦

❖ ❖ ❖ ❖

CHAPTER SIXTEEN

Discussion: Group Communication

> We are never so likely to settle a question
> rightly, as when we discuss it freely.
>
> —*Dame Rose Macaulay*

Each one of us is very special and unique. Yet, although we live our lives as individuals, we spend great amounts of time communicating as members of a group. Whether at work, school, or social functions, we constantly meet with others to discuss items of business or to solve mutual problems. Although, at times, these meetings are frustrating, numerous rewards can grow out of working with others. As an Ethiopian proverb says, "When spider webs unite they can tie up a lion." We all know the feelings of cohesiveness and solidarity associated with being part of a group that has successfully "shared a web" and resolved a mutual problem.

The Importance of Group Communication

Being a member of a group is an essential part of life. We are born into a group called "our family." This primary group teaches us everything from language to manners to what goals to pursue. Our success in life is often directly linked to how well we function in this group.

The concept of group involvement is also fundamental to the democratic process. In a democratic society, it is only natural that decisions should be made after considerable deliberation and discussion. The philosopher John Dewey said much the same thing when he wrote, "Democracy begins in conversation." We pride ourselves on being fair—that various points of view are presented and considered before a judgment is given or a decision rendered. As part of our democratic philosophy, each person counts and has the right and responsibility to contribute to the resolution of both individual and public problems through group discussion.

The uses of discussion are obvious when we reflect on the occasions and situations when we are in a position to exchange ideas and information with others. Group contacts are so common in our culture that an estimated 20 million meetings a day are held in the United States. Upper-level managers and technical professionals, for example, spend 60 to 70 percent of their time in meetings. Most professionals attend eight to 11 meetings per week. How well people function in these meetings helps determine both the accomplishments of the group and the success of the individual within the organization. That is to say, if you are a skillful member of a group, both you and the group will benefit.

The importance of group activity is not unique to North American culture. Group interaction is found in nearly all cultures. In fact, in many cultures, it is the preferred method of conducting life and business. In Japan, for example, it is very common for major decisions to be made by the people involved instead of by one individual called "the boss." For centuries, Native Americans have used tribal councils and meetings to make most of their major decisions. Improving your discussion skills should enable you to be more competent when you are with members of these and other cultures that stress collective communication.

In education, many classes function by means of the discussion process. In countless educational situations, we meet with others to resolve problems, share feelings, and gather information. In most Latin American cultures, nearly all classroom activities are conducted in groups.

In sum, while *working in groups* often consumes large amounts of time and can create conformity, it nevertheless *allows for a pooling of information and ideas, creates high levels of involvement, and usually produces better solutions.*

Speech Communication and Group Communication

Before embarking on a detailed exploration of group communication, it will be valuable to examine the relationship between speech communication and group communication. The following definition of group discussion shows the link between speech communication and being a member of a group: **Group communication** *is the systematic and objective sharing of ideas and information by two or more persons who work together in an effort to solve a problem or to gain a better understanding of a problem.*

Although the units of speech presented by any discussant might, by necessity, be shorter and more fragmented than in solitary public speaking, much of what is being done still uses the skills, principles, and techniques of oral communication. On the platform or sitting with others in a group, one must pay attention to such matters as audience adaptation, feedback, preparation and research, the expression of concrete ideas and their support in an organized manner, and language usage. Let us now return to these communication principles and see how they can be applied to the group situation.

Types of Group Discussion

We have seen the importance of group communication, or discussion, and that it is an extension of speech communication. Besides understanding these two ideas, it would be useful for you to appreciate some of the forms of small-group communication. By knowing some of the types of groups you may be affiliated with, you will be able to make the minor adjustments needed to be an effective speaker.

Although most classifications are not hard and fast, discussion groups are normally categorized as either public or private—with subclassifications within each of these two major categories.

Public Discussion

Public discussions are group experiences held before an audience. They are often formal and generally very structured. Public discussions usually follow one of the following three patterns:

Symposium. *In a symposium, each of several speakers, generally two to five, is introduced by a moderator and then delivers a talk.* These speeches center on one topic, theme, or issue. Each speaker may explain his or her position and thoughts on the subject as a whole or be limited to one phase of the subject. Frequently, the audience is allowed to ask questions at the conclusion of all the talks.

Panel. A panel is a discussion within a discussion. *In panel discussions a limited number of persons, usually four to seven, sit before an audience and discuss a topic.* There are no planned speeches; all the remarks are short and spontaneous. When the panel finishes its discussion, the members answer questions from the audience. During the past few years, the panel has become a very popular method of group discussion. Advancements in electronic media have allowed panel discussions to take place before a television camera, and the viewing audience can call in questions and comments.

Informal Group Discussion (Round Table). The informal group discussion, or round table, is the most common form of discussion. It is frequently a nonaudience discussion and tends to be more informal than the other methods. It consists of a small group seated around a table. *In this setting, group members exchange their views and information freely and spontaneously.* The stimulus-response pattern constantly changes as attention shifts from one person to another. This pattern is well suited for either decision making or information sharing.

You will notice that some public discussions demand interaction among the members of the group and the members of the audience. Often, oral reports or short speeches are given as part of the format. Thus, many group discussions have a public-speaking component.

Private Discussion

We also often engage in more personal exchanges, called private discussions. These may have overlapping purposes, but, as a means of classification, we will examine three of the most common types.

Therapy Groups. Therapy group discussions have many different names—support groups, encounter groups, sensitivity sessions, experiential groups, consciousness-raising groups, and T-group training. *Therapy groups are composed of persons who meet to gain personal insights from the advice and feedback provided by the other members of the group.* These groups examine issues ranging from drug rehabilitation to management training problems. No group solution is sought; rather, the aim is to learn about oneself and to offer encouragement and support to others.

Educational Groups. *Educational groups have one basic purpose—to help group members learn more about a subject by allowing them to pool their thoughts and information.* The content of such knowledge shifts from group to group. A group of teachers might want to learn the best ways to teach their students the metric system, tax accountants might be interested in knowing the ramifications of new federal tax laws, and executives about to be sent overseas might get together to learn about the German culture and language.

Problem-Solving Groups. Problem-solving groups are often called task-oriented groups. This is by far the most common of all group discussions. *In problem-solving groups people participate in order to get something done.* Problem-solving groups can take the form of a committee, a conference, or simply a group of individuals who share a problem and join together as a means of solving it. One group of business managers, facing lower profits, might meet to decide on the best ways to generate income for their company; another group of people might gather to discover how they can keep a landfill from coming to their town.

Because problem-solving groups are so widespread, this group activity is the focus of the remainder of the chapter.

Characteristics of Problem-Solving Groups

Although problem-solving groups share many features with other kinds of groups, they have several distinguishing characteristics, which can be translated into guidelines for participating in a group. That is to say, *knowing these features enables you to have a clearer picture of what discussion is, how discussion operates, and what your role is within the group.*

Cooperation

Cooperation is stressed in group discussion. It is important to remember that members of any problem-solving group have come together because they share a common purpose and have the same goal—the resolution of a mutual problem. Therefore, cooperation, not competition, is an important attribute of a good problem-solving discussion. Although arguments and disagreement occur, they focus on ideas and content, not on personalities.

Striking a balance between the goals of the individual and the goals of the group is often a difficult assignment. For example, there are apt to be occasions when the group's goals differ from individual members' goals. When this happens, there is often antagonism and resentment. The key to overcoming this problem is to remember that it is a common goal that has brought the group together. By keeping this essential idea in mind, the group can often discover complementary goals that can satisfy both the individual and the group.

Analysis and Investigation

Analysis and investigation are part of the discussion process. As we have seen, group members join together because they are vexed by the same problem. To find the best solution to that problem, they must be willing to analyze and investigate all sides of the issues involved. Members should be open-minded and not fearful of giving all points a fair hearing. A person who already has all the answers does not help the group, for it is the analytic, systematic search for those answers that gives a problem-solving group its investigative spirit. The philosopher John Stuart Mill wrote, "He who knows only his own side of the case, knows little of that." Problem-solving discussion demands that the group examine all sides.

Reflective Thinking

Discussion is a method of reflective thinking. Think for a moment of all the discussions that you have been a part of that ended with nothing being accomplished. How frustrated you felt as the group leaped from point to point in a random and aimless fashion. This should not have happened. Purposeful problem-solving groups follow a thoughtful process that is structured, systematic, and organized. The most common pattern of group reflective thinking is one developed from the phases of reflective thought described by the American educator and philosopher John Dewey. These phases, which are discussed in detail later in the chapter, consist of (1) defining and limiting the problem, (2) analyzing evidence for the causes and effects of the problem, (3) proposing solutions for the problem, (4) evaluating and analyzing all the solutions, and (5) deciding on ways to put the chosen solution into operation.

Subjectivity and Objectivity

Discussion groups attempt to strike a balance between subjectivity and objectivity. This balancing of emotional and personal feelings with logical arguments is essential if a group is working toward the resolution of real-life problems. Imagine how difficult it would be to talk about problems such as capital punishment, birth control, abortion, gays in the military, or censorship without having personal feelings fuse with rational research. This blending of what you feel and what the research reveals is one of the essential components of successful problem solving.

Skepticism

Skepticism is encouraged. Although a group strives for a high degree of solidarity, individuals should feel free to question and criticize ideas they believe are weak or insubstantial. Communication must be open and honest. A group that spends all its time simply nodding heads in agreement produces rather shallow conclusions. Therefore, phrases such as "I'm not sure that is a very good plan" and "Are you certain of that?" should be encouraged by all members. Later in this chapter, when we examine cultural variations in group participation, we will discuss the need to adapt attempts at skepticism to fit with cultural norms. For example, the Japanese tend to value group harmony over the final product and may say "yes" even when they mean "no." For now, it is important to remember the excellent advice offered by the French philosopher Denis Diderot: "What has not been examined impartially has not been well examined. Skepticism is therefore the first step toward truth."

Group Cohesion

Group cohesion is an important element of group discussion. Although group cohesion may appear to be only an extension of cooperation, it is much more complicated than simply trying to cooperate. Cohesion is the special ingredient that molds a group of individuals into a unit. Group cohesion, once it is established, offers each member a sense of belonging and a feeling of pride that they are affiliated with the group. It tends to be contagious, and, once trust is established, cohesiveness permeates all the group's activities. This bond, which is so important to the group, is encouraged when members share a concern. Reflect on your own motivations in a group, and you will realize that you feel enthusiastic when you believe that other persons share your concerns and your involvement. It is on those occasions that cohesiveness is strongest, and openness and high productivity characterize the group.

Group Norms

Group norms form the basic standards of behavior for the group. Norms tell the participants how to act. As communication patterns evolve, each group establishes various rules of conduct. These guidelines are both formal (a specific person will start the meeting) and informal (people talk whenever they have something to say). Norms are parameters that all group members should clearly perceive and follow as a means of reducing uncertainty. Norms also contribute to cohesiveness and increased productivity. However, norms are not always as transparent as they should be; when there is uncertainty about norms, frustration, tension, and anxiety become part of the group's experience. Hence, it is important to work toward realistic norms and to see that all members recognize them.

Democratic Process

Problem-solving discussion stresses the democratic process. One point that should be clear by now is the idea that group discussion is a highly democratic process. In a problem-solving group, all persons have mutual influence. Each individual member is offering her or his time and energy because the member is disturbed by something in the status quo. Whether it is a parking problem or worldwide pollution, everyone is seeking a solution and therefore has a right to be heard. In this sense, discussion is acting out the words of the Swiss novelist Friedrich Dürrenmatt: "What concerns everyone can only be resolved by everyone."

Preparing for Discussion

The philosopher Sir Thomas Buxton wrote, "In life, as in chess, forethought wins." This notion of forethought has been one of the major themes of this book. In each and every chapter, the importance of preparation has been stressed. Unless you prepare in advance, discussion will be an aimless, purposeless activity. Preparing for discussion involves three closely related activities: (1) *selecting a subject*, (2) *wording the subject*, and (3) *gathering material*.

Selecting a Subject

On most occasions, members of a private discussion group are in a position to select their own subjects ("How can we control excessive noise in the dormitory?") or at least have a major influence over what aspects of the sub-

Cooperation is stressed in group discussion. (Photo: corbisimages.com)

ject should be examined ("How can we help the college administration recruit more minorities?"). In deciding what to talk about and what problem to investigate, participants will find it helpful to follow a few guidelines:

1. *Decide early whether you will be dealing with a proposition of fact, value, or policy.* In chapter 14, when we examined the issue of persuasion, you were introduced to questions of fact, value, and policy. Propositions of fact are those that are concerned with the truth of a question or statement. Such questions are concerned with the existence of things, the occurrence of acts, the classification of data, and the sequence of events. A group asking "What is the current status of the world's rain forests?" would be investigating a question of fact. If the question centers on a proposition of value, the group would be discussing an issue that involves a subjective judgment: "What is the best community college in our city?" It is probably safe to say that most discussions focus on questions of policy. These are issues that are concerned with future actions and solutions. The word "should" is the key to these questions. "What should our university do about recent affirmative action rulings?"

2. *Select problems in which the participants are interested.* If the members of the group feel personally involved and are committed to a subject, they will be active in both research and participation. If you were living in a dormitory and found that the noise kept you from studying, which in turn was lowering your grades, you would want the problem resolved.

3. *Select problems that can be investigated prior to the discussion and that can be discussed in the time allotted to the group.* A group that is rushed, both before and during the discussion, usually produces a solution that reflects just such a hasty analysis and lack of deliberation.

4. *The subject should present a problem.* If the group is going to be motivated in a problem-solving discussion, its members should feel a common need to find a solution. The topic should provide at least two sides for investigation. If the solution is obvious at the outset, there is no valid reason to engage in the time-consuming steps of the reflective process.

Wording the Subject

The correct statement of the problem area is as important as the problem itself, for, if the group formulates the problem in a way that distorts the issue, confusion and misunderstanding will result. A poorly worded subject can also cost the group valuable time. The group will thrash around, trying to decide what interests it. In addition, the general subject area must be worded into a workable topic if all group members are to deal with the same problem. Consider the following suggestions for wording the subject:

1. *Phrase the subject or problem as a question.* A question highlights a specific problem while it motivates persons to seek answers to the problem. Subjects such as "price fixing," "how to be happy," and "war and peace" are so general that they cannot be discussed in a specific manner. On the other hand, a question such as "What should be the role of the federal government in regulating children's television?" or "What can our college do to improve the registration process for entering freshmen?" calls for an answer; hence, discussion can take place.

2. *Phrase the question clearly.* If the wording is ambiguous, the group may have to spend long periods of time trying to decide what to talk about. A question such as "What should be the current status of business?" is an example of ambiguity. The group must stop and decide what *business* and *current status* mean before it can even start working on the problem. Careful wording of the problem, even before the group begins discussion, also serves the dual functions of limiting and restricting the scope of the problem. A topic worded "How can we best secure an additional $100,000 for graduate fellowships at our university?" indicates precisely what the group will talk about.

3. *Whenever possible, avoid wording the problem/question in a yes-or-no form.* A yes-or-no response limits the available solutions and leads to debate instead of cooperation. Questions such as "Should our school adopt a year-round session?" place restrictions on the group and limit the responses participants can make. To provide the group with more than two answers, the question could have been phrased "What is the most effective way to use the facilities of the university?" This wording allows the group to examine a host of options, including year-round sessions.

4. *Word the topic impartially.* We all know that one can state a topic in such a way that it favors one side. One can also word a topic so that the conclusion appears obvious at the start. Both of these evils should be avoided. "Since all students would like a Democrat to be

elected president, how can we raise money for the campaign of our Democratic governor?" This example reflects partiality, states the conclusion at the start, and therefore greatly limits the group's latitude.

Gathering Material

Depth of preparation is as vital in a discussion as in a speech. Each member of a group depends on the other members for fresh ideas; if one member fails to gather concrete data, the entire group suffers.

In chapter 8, we discussed the steps and techniques of gathering and preparing material for a speech. Because these procedures are also essential for successful group discussion, they are worth reviewing.

1. *Think carefully about the subject before you begin your research.* To start researching a topic before you know specifically what problem you are trying to solve wastes a great deal of time and contributes to a high degree of frustration. For example, knowing that you are concerned with prison reforms, and not the entire criminal justice system in the United States, could save you both time and energy.

2. *Decide what you already know about the subject and what areas you should investigate in more detail.* If you have a part-time position in a maximum security prison, you would likely have some excellent firsthand knowledge of the inmates' daily activities. However, you might find that you need more research on areas such as prison budgets, training programs for the guards, and visitation rights.

3. *After you have identified your research strengths and weaknesses, gather your information.* As you recall, this information can take the form of illustrations, examples, expert testimony, or statistics drawn from interviews, printed material, and electronic media.

It is important to gather information before the group begins. (Photo: indexstock.com)

4. *Record and organize your material in a purposeful and meaningful pattern.* For a group to be successful, its planning must be as organized as a speech. Hence, your material and your group must be organized around a sequence that will make sense to all the members. This means that you should arrange your materials in the same general order that the group deliberations will follow. You would not start with the solution; therefore, your notes should not begin with the solution. Most problem-solving groups use the **reflective pattern** advanced by the American educator and philosopher John Dewey. If you are going to be in a group whose basic aim is problem solving, it will be helpful to organize your research around Dewey's general categories:

I. Define and limit the problem.

    A. Define important words and phrases found in the problem.

    B. Find materials that help limit the scope and range of the problem area.

II. Analyze the problem.

    A. Research material related to the history of the problem and place it next in your outline.

    B. Provide information and evidence to highlight specific facets of the problem. (These are usually called effects or symptoms of the problem.)

    C. Gather evidence that reveals and explains the causes of the problem.

III. List all possible solutions.

IV. Evaluate and analyze the solutions.

    A. Exploring the advantages and disadvantages is often helpful.

    B. Evidence that examines the effects of all the solutions is normally treated in this portion of the outline.

V. Treat evidence and research that discusses the best method of putting the solution into practice.

Organizing a Discussion

The famous British orator Edmund Burke once remarked, "Good order is the foundation of all good things." With regard to group problem solving, organization is essential. As we have seen, successful groups and the individuals within those groups do not simply jump from point to point as they attempt to solve their problem. Rather, if a group and its members are to accomplish a specific purpose, organization is crucial.

Most problem-solving groups can derive numerous benefits from using the steps of reflective thinking just listed. There are certain advantages built into this pattern. First, *by performing the five steps systematically, a group will*

❖ ❖ ❖ ❖ *progress logically from a problem to a solution.* By analyzing the key issues step by step, the group eliminates the haphazard decision-making processes characteristic of many deliberations. Think of all the occasions on which you were in a group that chose the first solution proposed, only to find later that the decision would have been much better if judgment had been suspended until all alternatives had been examined.

A *second* advantage of Dewey's five steps is manifest within the group itself. *If the entire group is concerned with the same step of the reflective thinking process at any given moment, then all the participants are talking about the same issues at the same time.* The person who begins a discussion by saying, "Now, the best way to solve this problem—" is stopped, because each person knows what phase the group is in at every instance. It is a simple matter to tell a person who is out of order that he or she has bypassed the first step of the problem-solving process, the defining of terms.

Recognizing and Defining the Problem

Before people can solve a problem, they must be aware that one exists. Therefore, *the first step in trying to resolve or understand a problem is defining and limiting it.* By stating and defining the problem early in the discussion, the group can set limits if the topic is too broad for the amount of time allotted. Defining terms early also lets the group set its goals ("We need to make sure we find a solution to the problem of pollution at our local beach"). This early portion of the meeting should define words and phrases that might be confusing. "What are we referring to when we use words such as 'pollution' and 'local beach'?" By analyzing crucial terms and key concepts at the beginning of the discussion, a group is in a better position to comprehend the problem's scope and seriousness. For example, if a group were to discuss the topic of high school dropouts, it should use the initial period of its discussion to define "high school dropout." Is it anyone under sixteen years old, or is the age to be eighteen and younger? Deciding issues such as these early in a discussion helps a group avoid the all-too-common problem of nearing the end of a discussion only to discover that no common definition was agreed on.

Description of the Problem

After group members have recognized, stated, defined, and limited the problem, they are ready to analyze the nature of the problem. Such analysis and evaluation normally demand that the participants exchange ideas and information on three topics: (1) *the history of the problem,* (2) *the effects of the problem,* and (3) *the causes of the problem.*

History. Adlai Stevenson offered sound advice when he wrote, "We can chart our future clearly and wisely only when we know the path which has led to the present." Knowing what has led to a problem and the duration of the problem helps discover how that situation can be remedied. For instance, if a group is discussing increases in student tuition, it might be helpful to explore the history of these fees to find out when they were first initiated and the rationale behind the proposed increase. If the topic is the worldwide dwindling elephant population, the group would want to look at facts and figures that demonstrate historically that the elephant population was 1.3 million in 1979, 650,000 in 1991, 600,000 in 1993, 555,000 in 1995, and 450,000 in

1997. A group discussing television censorship would be aided if they could historically trace how censorship was applied to this medium in the past.

Effects. Using the various forms of support mentioned in chapter 6, the group should discuss how serious the problem is, who is being affected, and how large the problem is. By some members reporting observed effects (what is happening?), all can see the outward manifestations of the problem and how widespread it is. For example, if the group is discussing "What can be done about the increased crime rate among teenagers?" someone might ask if the problem is serious; in response, another participant might attempt to substantiate the seriousness of the problem by stating that "the governor indicated that the crime rate among teenagers has doubled in the past ten years." A group trying to solve a problem related to AIDS would benefit by knowing the number of current AIDS cases and who is affected by AIDS. By knowing these facts the group can see what is transpiring at this time. If the problem is rain forest depletion, someone in the group could look up the effects and point out, "As of July 1996, rain forests were being burned and cleared at a rate of 42 million acres a year." By knowing what is happening (amount of rain forest being destroyed) and how widespread it is (effects of the problem), the group can later decide how to remedy the situation.

Causes. The group, having investigated and verified the effects of the problem, then turns its attention to an examination of the conditions that produced those effects. For example, in deciding what caused the increased crime rate (effect), someone might offer, with support, teenage unemployment as a possible cause. A group studying highway safety could examine the causes of accidents by noting that "well over 50 percent of all traffic deaths and injuries have been caused by people not wearing their seat belts." They could offer yet another cause by looking at the evidence that says "500 people are killed each week in alcohol-related crashes." By knowing what created the problem (not wearing seat belts, alcohol), the group can later propose solutions that directly relate to the problem.

Discovery of Possible Solutions

First, *before a group recommends any solutions to a problem, the members should decide what criteria are most appropriate in judging those solutions. Criteria are the standards that the group applies to any solution they might propose.* For example, a group might decide that any solution to teenage crime should (1) not violate the constitutional rights of the person arrested, (2) not be too costly, and (3) not add to the overcrowded conditions now facing most juvenile detention facilities. A group deciding on which fast-food outlets should be allowed on campus might establish that any solution should (1) ensure fair hiring practices, (2) not violate existing campus laws, and (3) not result in increased food costs. If a group were focusing on alternative fuel sources, it could say that any solution should (1) not be costly, (2) not create serious pollution problems, and (3) not make the United States dependent on other countries for fuel.

After the group has determined the specific problem to be solved, examined the effects and causes of the problem, and listed the criteria the solution(s) must meet, the group is ready to suggest possible solutions.

Groups can suggest either singular solutions ("The courts should be stricter with teenage offenders") or multiple solutions ("Stricter courts, better probation procedures, and parent counseling programs are needed"). At this stage of the discussion, it is important to list as many solutions as possible—if they meet the criteria. If the topic is alternative fuel sources for automobiles, the group might list and consider methanol gases (natural gas, coal, wood), compressed natural gas, ethanol (corn, sugar), and electricity (solar, nuclear, fossil fuel).

When discovering possible solutions a few guidelines should be followed:

- List all possible solutions.

- Allow all members an opportunity to contribute possible solutions.

- Do not evaluate the solutions when they are first presented.

Evaluation of Solutions and Acceptance of the Best Solution

Once all the solutions have been put forth, the participants should talk about each solution in detail, backing their remarks with concrete evidence and analyzing their conclusions in light of logical reasoning. In this deliberation, the advantages and disadvantages of each solution should be discussed and evaluated. For example, a group dealing with alternative fuel sources for automobiles might present evidence and discuss how methanol has fewer hydrocarbons than petroleum but, on the negative side, has only half the energy content of gasoline and is fatal if ingested or absorbed. They could note how electricity has almost no emission but has a range limited to about one hundred miles per charging period.

In this phase of the discussion, some of the following questions should be asked:

- How will the solution solve the problem?

- What will the solution do to the causes and effects mentioned earlier in the discussion?

- What will the solution do to the status quo?

- How does the solution meet the criteria?

Once these questions have been answered, and all the advantages and disadvantages have been discussed, the group is ready to decide which of the solutions will best solve, or at least minimize, the problem. The acceptance of the best solution is tentative and related only to the problem mentioned in the discussion.

Plan of Action

As a final step, the group must decide whether or not its preferred solution can be put into effect. If the solution seems workable, desirable, and practical, the group should determine the most effective means of implementing its findings and conclusions.

Specific plans for implementation are influenced by factors such as the topic, the time, and the power of the group. For example, a group discussing a local campus problem might present its solution to the college administration or to the student council. By contrast, a group dealing with an international topic might write a letter to representatives in Washington.

Some additional considerations for implementing the solution might include:

- Who will implement the solution? What person? What agency?

- Where and when will the solution be implemented?

- How will the success of the implementation process be measured?

Often, solutions are presented in a symposium format. On these occasions, each member of the group gives a five- or ten-minute speech that summarizes the conclusions reached during the discussion process.

Brainstorming as an Organizational Pattern

As indicated earlier, the reflective process, although it is the most widely used discussion pattern, is by no means the only organizational scheme available to group participants. Another pattern is *brainstorming*.

In its simplest form, **brainstorming** *is a technique that generates the free expression of ideas within a group setting.* Those who favor this discussion style maintain that it has two major advantages over some of the other discussion formats. First, it fosters creativity because it is not as rigid and structured as the other patterns. Group members are urged to string their ideas onto the ideas of others. Members are encouraged to make contributions as rapidly as possible, and no ideas are barred. In fact, there are certain "brainstorming rules" that a group adopts as a way of supporting this open and loosely structured orientation. The second advantage of brainstorming is that it advocates equal participation. Since the goal is to produce as many ideas as possible—no matter how bizarre they may seem—people feel free to take an active role.

The two benefits of brainstorming can be translated into the following five "rules":

1. *All adverse criticism is prohibited during the early stages of the brainstorming session.* One is not to criticize ideas or personalities until all ideas have been suggested.

2. *"Freewheeling" is welcomed.* Members are urged to submit even the most bizarre and remote ideas and suggestions. The assumption is that it is better to reject an idea than to not even hear that idea.

3. *Quantity of ideas is encouraged.* Members are asked to submit long lists of ideas, the theory being "the more the better."

4. *Combination and improvement of ideas is one of the chief goals of brainstorming;* therefore, each member feels free to add to any idea being discussed, because one idea can trigger another.

5. *All ideas should be recorded so that they can be evaluated.* The cataloging of ideas means that the group will be able to eventually slow

down and talk about those ideas that, at first glance, were generated with great dispatch.

Although brainstorming is loosely structured and at times appears cha-
otic, it often has the effect of getting the group moving at the same time the
group is generating ideas. As noted for the pattern previously discussed, some
groups insert a brief brainstorming session into their regular discussion.

Participating in Small Groups

Although to this point we have been talking about organization, structure, and procedure in groups, this book is about all forms of human communication. It is about the ways we send and receive messages. Therefore, the
remainder of this chapter will be concerned with how you can become a competent communicator whenever you find yourself in a group.

Group interaction and interpersonal relations are highly complex and
cannot be taught effectively in a single session or by reading a few pages of
techniques. However, most writers in the area of small-group communication agree that there are certain requirements for successful small-group
communication and that these behaviors can be learned and practiced by
motivated participants. These behaviors are usually divided into two interrelated categories: (1) *functional and task roles* and (2) *maintenance and supportive roles*. The first set of roles, or behaviors, centers on the communication functions that must be performed if the group is to achieve its desired
purpose and accomplish its goals. These roles primarily concentrate on the
"duties and responsibilities" of group members to get a discussion started and
keep it moving toward its goal. The second set, the maintenance and supportive roles, have a more personal dimension. These are the roles we play in an
attempt to establish and preserve group and individual harmony; they are
intended to build group cohesiveness and solidarity.

Placing communicative behavior into two categories is a very subjective
assignment. Inevitably, categories overlap, and in some instances a single
sentence might serve in both functional and supportive roles. For example,
you might be performing both kinds of roles if you were to say, "John, your
ideas always help us over difficult periods (supportive role). What do you
think we should do about the amount of money this plan will cost (task role)?"

Functional and Task Roles

Performing the following functional and task roles, whenever they are
needed, will profit both you and the group:

1. *Your participation should adhere to the logical pattern the group
   selects.* If the group chooses Dewey's reflective pattern, see to it
   that the group stays on track. Jumping from effects to solutions
   and back to definitions of terms not only wastes time but frustrates
   the participants.

2. *Make your presence known throughout the discussion.* Take it upon
   yourself to be an active member of the group. The amount of time

the group has and the number of participants obviously influence the frequency and length of your contributions, but you should feel free to participate as often as you have something to say. However, when possible, you should keep your contributions and exchanges brief and precise. Long and detailed contributions, although sometimes needed, frequently bore the other participants and keep others from getting their turn to talk.

3. *Ask questions of the other participants.* A lack of understanding about what is said by any of the participants hampers the reflective process. By asking questions of one another whenever there is a basic misunderstanding or a need for information, the group can overcome many obstacles. Many times, groups move ahead in a discussion only to discover later that they did not understand the earlier premises that led to the current stage of the discussion. By raising questions, the group can locate errors in reasoning. For example, someone might say, "Roger, my readings made it look as if the administration was completely at fault. Is that what you found out?" Asking Roger this question encourages further deliberation on the topic before the group moves on.

4. *Supply leadership for the group whenever needed.* Many participants rely solely on the judgment of the leader for decisions that should be the responsibility of all participants. Many leadership functions can be performed easily by any alert member of the group. For example, any participant can offer summaries whenever he or she feels they are appropriate and would aid the group. Do not make the mistake of assuming that the leader, because of the title, has all the answers. If you perceive that there is a task that needs to be performed, you should perform it. If the group appears fatigued, you should feel free to say, "Why don't we think about stopping for tonight?"

5. *Speak to the point being discussed and stay on that point when you speak.* One of the most common errors made by participants in a group is that they stray off the subject being discussed. During that fraction of a second before you get ready to speak, ask yourself if what you plan to say is directly related to the topic currently on the table.

Maintenance and Supportive Roles

Having discussed functional and task roles, we will examine six maintenance and supportive roles that also contribute to successful group discussion:

1. *Be tolerant of individual and cultural differences that will appear in the group.* Each of us is unique; we come from different backgrounds and, therefore, bring different personal histories to a group. These individual and cultural differences will be manifest in countless ways. What one person finds humorous, another may consider offensive. What is "planned growth" to you may appear to be "stifling of free enterprise" to the person sitting next to you.

From judgments of beauty to issues of truth, our decisions are influenced by our experiences, and, thus, having had different experiences, we often reach different conclusions. Effective participants are aware that perceptual differences are a natural outgrowth of individual and cultural diversity and that, in most cases, this diversity can benefit the group.

2. *All participants should provide clear, concise feedback.* Respond directly, verbally and nonverbally, to the remarks of others. We all know how frustrating it is when we make a statement to someone and receive only silence. In a group, the problem is compounded, for there are eight or ten persons who are not responding to what is being said. By nodding, smiling, or talking, we let our colleagues know our reactions to what they present. Feedback not only keeps the group moving, but it allows the speaker and other group members to know we are interested in them and their ideas.

3. *Communication is a two-way process; listeners also play a key role in discussion.* It is unfair to place the burden for understanding completely on the speaker. Participants in a discussion cannot sit back and contentedly assume they have nothing to do but wait for their turns to talk. Each listener must pay close attention to what is being said. Participants must ask questions and attempt to narrow and define all ambiguous concepts.

4. *Be prepared to play a variety of roles.* A competent group member is not tied to a single mode of behavior but, rather, can adapt to people and events. Gerald L. Wilson and Michael S. Hanna, in their book *Groups in Context: Leadership and Participation in Small Groups*, recommend some roles that can have a positive influence on the group. Perform some of these roles if it will help the group accomplish its purpose:

Evaluator role: "I am not sure we have spent enough time looking at this issue. I suggest we don't move on until we have examined this idea in a little more detail."

Initiator role: "I think the time might be right for us to establish some standards by which we can judge our solutions. What do the rest of you think?"

Opinion seeker role: "Do any of you have some evidence that would tell us how long this has been a problem?"

Coordinator role: "It seems that Robert and Susan are saying about the same thing. Perhaps we now have some agreement on this idea."

Energizer role: "We have accomplished a great deal so far. Why don't we keep going so we can finish this project by tonight?"

Presenting Your Ideas

Regardless of the role you play or the contributions you make in a small-group discussion, it is important that your comments be timely and presented clearly and concisely. If you do not speak well, you damage your chances for accomplishing your purpose. Therefore, in concluding this section on participation, I need to remind you that your remarks should (a) relate, (b) state, (c) support, and (d) integrate.

First, when offering an idea, *you should relate it to what is being discussed at that moment or to something that has been talked about earlier.* Remarks that are simply submitted to the group without being placed into a context often result in confusion or force the group to depart from the established agenda. Think of how frustrating it is for the entire group when someone begins to recount a personal experience related to the causes of the problem while the group is trying to work on specific solutions to a problem. Therefore, try to begin your contribution by linking it to what is going on at the moment: "Pat, you are right about the administration not facing the problem, but I think there are other reasons for the lack of support for this proposed clinic."

Second, *once you have used what was being discussed as a transition to your comments, you are ready to state your position or offer some new information.* "My research revealed that there was also a lack of interest among the students for this new clinic." It is important that you make your statements clearly and concisely.

Third, *once you have tied your comments to what is going on and have stated your position clearly, you should offer support for your assertion.* "A recent poll in the school paper showed that only 13 percent of the student body wanted the new clinic. Most felt they did not want their funds used on a project that would not be completed until after they had graduated."

Fourth, *you should conclude your comments by integrating them into the flow of the meeting.* This can be done by ending your contribution with a question: "Do the rest of you feel that the lack of progress is caused by both the administration and the students?"

Leadership in Small Groups

Having examined the characteristics of participation, we are now ready to move to the topic of leadership. *Leadership is exercising influence over a group to help it achieve its goal.* What is interesting about our definition of leadership is that it can apply to all the members of a group. In most instances, the person called "the leader" is also a participant. Therefore, our division of skills and techniques is not as inflexible as it first appears. What is important is that you learn both roles—leader and participant—to become an effective group member. By knowing the characteristics of participants and leaders, you can function in either role whenever necessary.

Leadership Tasks

Research in group discussion and group dynamics has revealed that the so-called born leader is a myth. Leadership is composed of traits and characteristics that can be learned and cultivated. In an ideal group, everyone possesses those traits, and there would be no worry about appointing someone to serve as the leader. In this model situation, all the participants would monitor the group's behavior as well as their own, the roles of leadership would be diffused throughout the group, and the leadership tasks would be performed by any person who believed that a particular task would benefit the group.

There are, however, occasions when shared leadership does not work or is inappropriate. For example, the principal of a school would most likely lead a faculty meeting. In such instances, the group must rely on a single leader to guide it and to stimulate participation. Even in these cases, though, numerous leadership functions can be shared.

Because leadership duties can be shared by all members or can be vested in one person, the suggestions that follow apply both to an appointed leader and to any participant who perceives a need for leadership in the group and attempts to fill that need.

Start the Meeting. *The leader has the responsibility to see that the discussion gets started in a systematic manner.* This assignment actually has a number of components. Knowing these duties will enable the leader, or any member of the group, to carry them out.

1. *The phrase "getting started" often involves having group members get acquainted.* We have all experienced an uneasy silence when forced to interact with strangers. The leader should help us over these periods by making sure there are some introductions and social conversation before the group begins its serious deliberations.

2. *Part of getting started means setting the tentative agenda for the meeting.* This might mean everything from explaining what the group hopes to accomplish down to deciding at what point the meeting should end.

3. *The leader should also state the purpose of the meeting and mention the problem to be discussed.* As the philosopher Irving Kristol has noted, "Part of every solution is to state the problem correctly."

4. *The leader needs to make arrangements for the proceedings to be recorded.* Having someone take notes during the discussion is beneficial for the entire group. For example, there will be many occasions when the members will want to know what they accomplished earlier in the discussion. Reviewing the group's notes can provide that summary. By having previous decisions at their disposal, the group can avoid needless duplication.

5. *These early duties should also include taking care of some mechanical and personal chores,* such as making sure that there is a place for the group to meet, that the necessary furniture is available (arranged in a circle if possible), and that the participants will be made to feel comfortable in the setting.

Stress Cooperation. *The leader should create a cooperative, democratic climate.* A group atmosphere characterized by demagoguery is not very creative and is often filled with discontent. You know from your own experience that if you feel uncomfortable as a result of the actions of an authoritarian leader, you do not do your best work. On the other hand, imagine how you would be encouraged to talk if a leader were to say to you, "Peter, you seem to understand what happened last year. What do you think we should do?" Part of being a democratic leader means getting participation from all members. It may mean changing the communication behavior of the monopolist as well as of the shy member of the group.

Remain Impartial. *The leader should try to remain impartial whenever possible.* Among group members, a tendency exists to view the leader as a boss or someone of superior rank. Viewed in this way, a leader who states his or her personal conclusions at the beginning of a discussion tends to close the door on free and open deliberation. This does not mean that, as leader, you cannot take part, simply that you must see that all sides are presented and that you do not become a spokesperson for one point of view too early in the discussion.

Follow the Organizational Pattern. *The leader should see that an agenda, or an organizational pattern, is followed and that the main phases of the problem are considered.* If the group uses an agenda, the leader should become its guardian. The leader must always be asking, "Where have we been?" "Where are we now?" and "Where are we going?" By using these phrases, the leader can keep the discussion organized and also keep everyone informed of the group's progress. Imagine how helpful it would be to have someone say, "Now that we have seen the effects of overpopulation, it might be to our advantage to examine some of the causes of this problem." Although personal stories can be interesting, they often take the group away from its task. When this happens, the leader should help the group return to the issue being discussed before the irrelevant comment was made ("Mary, that was helpful, but I think we should be talking about what has caused this problem").

Clarify Issues. *The leader should try to clarify details and contributions whenever possible.* If necessary, contributions should be rephrased. Asking appropriate questions is one of the most effective ways of clarifying ideas and information. These questions can take a variety of forms. First, a question can probe for additional information to clarify the point being made: "That idea seems unique. Did any of the rest of you come across a similar plan?" Second, a question can refocus the conversation on the topic: "Mary, how do you think those statistics relate to the point Tom was making?" Third, a question can help clarify the issue to move the group forward: "Okay, we seem to know what caused the fee increase; what can we do about it?" Finally, a question can deal with an interpersonal problem: "Tom, you and Susan seem to have conflicting interpretations of this event. Why do you think that is the case?"

Intervene When Appropriate. *A leader should know the appropriate times to intervene.* As we have said elsewhere, personal hostilities and pettiness have no place in a problem-solving group discussion. A group of this kind cannot waste its time on therapy; it has too much to do. Therefore, the leader must set a tone that does not allow destructive behavior to develop. If, by chance, conflicts do emerge, the leader must resolve them. The leader may have to change the behavior of a troublesome participant, settle an argument, and at times even offer friendly reprimands.

Part of intervening might take the form of the leader discouraging side conversations between some members of the group. It is rude and disconcerting to have two or more participants engaging in a private conversation while the group is conducting its business. On these occasions, the leader might very tactfully ask the discourteous members to direct their comments to the entire group.

Offer Summaries. *The leader should offer periodic summaries throughout the proceedings and also bring the discussion to a satisfactory conclusion.*

❖ ❖ ❖ ❖   Internal summaries allow the group to see what they have accomplished during various phases of the deliberations. The solution can also be summarized if one has been reached, or a summary can highlight the points of agreement. The discussion can also be concluded by reviewing the questions and problems that still remain unanswered.

Leadership and Culture

Later in this chapter, we will examine the role of culture in group communication in some detail. However, for now let us mention just a few cultural variations in how people perceive and respond to leadership.

Power Distance. As part of our culture, *each of us has learned how to define, perceive, and, respond to rank, status and power.* We have also learned how close or far away we are from the sources of power. This idea is called **power distance.** *It basically refers to whether or not status differences among people are minimized or maximized.* People who are from high power distance cultures (India, China, Mexico, Philippines) have learned to live with rigid status differences, hierarchical definitions of assigned roles, and a strong line of authority. People from these cultures often find it easier to work with leaders who are domineering and arbitrary. In the North American and many Scandinavian cultures, people often oppose leadership that is too rigid and controlling. As you move in and out of various groups, you will find people who like autocratic leaders and those who do their best work with a democratic leader.

Decision Making. There are also cultural differences in what is called **"participatory decision making,"** which can influence the variable of leadership. For example, in Japan, where quality circles are popular, workers and managers work jointly on many projects. Ideas and information flow freely during meetings and discussions. However, this style of leadership would not work in Latin America, India, or most Arab cultures. Most members of these cultures expect "the boss" to decide and are not prepared to function as leader.

Comply to Rules. There are even cultural disparities in the amount of comfort people experience both with leaders who ask for an abundance of rules and regula-

Leadership is exercising influence over a group to help it achieve its goal. (Photo: corbisimages.com)

tions and with those who have a minimum of guidelines. In the Chinese culture, in which the ordering of relationships goes back to the time of Confucius, most people feel comfortable with dictums and canons of behavior. Such is not the case in most Western cultures. Individuality is so strong that most North Americans dislike having to follow rules and challenge all attempts to regulate their actions.

Expectations. As we have seen, *cultures vary in what they expect from their leaders.* In cultures that have a strong work ethic, such as the German culture, group accomplishments are more important than group satisfaction. Hence, people in those cultures expect their leaders to get things done. Your personal experiences probably tell you that in North America it is also important for people to feel good about their group affiliations. Leaders are counted on to create an atmosphere that contributes to those feelings of satisfaction.

Formality. *Perception of formality is yet another approach to leadership that is reflected in culture.* The Western notion of informality is in sharp contrast with the formality found in much of the world. In the cultures of Germany, Japan, Egypt, Turkey, Korea, Mexico, and Iran, people have been raised to respect rank and status. When members of these cultures are in groups, they will treat the leader as a very high status person. They will not contradict the leader and, in most instances, will not take an active role unless the leader urges them to do so.

Gender Roles. Finally, *there are cultural differences in the perception of gender, which can influence leadership.* In cultures that highly value masculine traits (Indian, Japanese, German, Mediterranean), it is very difficult for a woman to function as leader. However, in cultures with a more fluid distribution of sex roles (North American, Norwegian, Swedish), gender is less of a consideration.

Dealing with Conflict

On many occasions, the behaviors described in the previous section do not resolve every problem that a group encounters. Human nature being what it is, most groups face some conflict during their existence. In spite of people's best intentions, the potential for interpersonal controversy seems to shadow most of our relationships. Because we are all unique, we bring our originality to every group. When we add the influence of culture to this mix, these differences are bound to create some tension and even conflict. Because conflict is so common, it is important that we understand it and learn to treat it in ways that are constructive instead of destructive. If animosity and anger fester, the group will suffer. A Chinese proverb says it even better: "The fire you kindle for your enemies often burns yourself." Why is it that interpersonal and group conflicts flare with such regularity? What can we do about them when they arise?

Definition of Conflict

In its simplest form, **conflict** *is a disagreement over an opinion or a course of action facing members of a group.* This normally happens when two or more participants perceive obstacles interfering with their own or the group's goals. What is interesting about conflict is that it can revolve around trivial matters ("Why does Ann always get the chair at the head of the table?"), or it can have its roots in more significant issues ("I don't want to be around people who believe the way you do about abortion").

There is a West African proverb that states "Every tree has a thick end, and every quarrel has a cause." When applied to conflict, the proverb is reminding us that not all conflict is bad. On many occasions, rewards can be gained from group conflict. For example, conflict can defuse more serious problems if the conflict is dealt with when it first arises. In this sense, conflict is used to stimulate rather than to stifle discussion. Conflict can also lead to the acquisition of concealed information if the conflict encourages people to expose their hidden agendas. Everyone feels better when things are out in the open. If handled effectively, conflict can even give us a better understanding of the problem because it often forces us to look at new information. Finally, group solidarity can be strengthened as members realize that they have overcome a serious problem.

Causes of Conflict

In most instances conflicts appear because people perceive incompatible goals or threats to their egos. In short, a person is frustrated or believes he or she is about to be frustrated by the behavior of someone else in the group. When this happens, negative emotions appear and conflict emerges in the group. Conflicts can usually be traced to four interrelated causes.

Individual Personalities. Our **individual personality** *(introvert, argumentative, extrovert, aggressive, passive, and so on) has conditioned us to respond to events in ways that often appear to be habitual.* Without much forethought, we seem to gravitate to our basic personality. Often that personality creates behavior that is negatively perceived by other people. Ask yourself if you are creating the conflict because you are acting in an attacking, boasting, or dominating manner. In short, be careful that you do not become a cause of the conflict. As the great philosopher Pogo once remarked in the comic strip, "We have met the enemy, and he is us."

Rigid Perceptions. Our perceived, and often rigid, relationships with the other group members can also cause controversy. If a person responds to someone else only in reference to the role the other person occupies (boss, leader, fellow student), that perception limits options when disagreements arise. A narrowing of behavioral choices is frustrating and can produce conflict.

Word Meanings. The meanings people attach to words during the group's deliberations can be a primary cause of conflict. We can never fully know someone else's meaning for a particular word. Simple words such as "gay," "conservative," "sexual harassment," and "affirmative action" may cause some group members to react emotionally. Be aware of the power of words.

Withdrawal. Finally, conflicts often occur because certain people mentally withdraw from the group. When someone in the group, regardless of the reason, draws away from the group, it can make the other members very angry. They infer that the "departed" person is disloyal because he or she has abandoned the group.

Managing Conflict   ❖ ❖ ❖ ❖

For anyone who has been involved in a group, the four preceding causes of conflict are obvious. They can keep a group from accomplishing its purpose, produce tension that interferes with the quality of the discussion, and even destroy the group by pushing it to its extreme. Therefore, it behooves you to know the signs of group conflict and how to manage it when it appears. Let us examine a few strategies you might find helpful as you attempt to guide a group over these difficult periods.

Identifying the Conflict. Identifying the conflict means having the group define exactly what is troubling the participants. Be as specific as possible as you urge the participants, including yourself, to focus on the issue that it causing the problem—whether it is an issue of content ("I know from my reading that approximately 25 percent of all babies born in the United States are born to unwed mothers") or an issue of personality ("John, like all men, you don't care about unwed mothers"). To help mediate the conflict, you could say, "It seems to me, Tom, that you and Mary are arguing over two issues: first, the exact number of people who are affected by this problem and, second, Mary's comments regarding your attitude about the consequences of the problem. Would you both agree?"

Once you have clarified the issues of the conflict, all parties can begin to focus on solutions to the controversy. If you are too vague, the conflict may never be identified or resolved. By being specific, you let all parties check their perceptions and give them a place to begin.

Avoid Win or Lose Positions. Avoid putting the participants into a win or lose position. The solution to a conflict need not mean that someone wins and someone loses. If you were to say, "Mary, you are wrong when you say Tom is not interested in the problems facing unwed mothers," you would be placing Mary in a losing situation. The key is to have people focus on the common interest that brought them together rather than individual positions. The notion of separating people from problems and issues is at the heart of successful conflict resolution.

Try to Mediate the Conflict. Try to negotiate and mediate the direction and tone of the conversation. You could say, "Mary, why don't you give Tom a chance to explain his point again, and then we can see if the two of you are disagreeing or just expressing the same idea with different words." Part of playing the role of the mediator is slowing down the discussion during the conflict. Conflict episodes often move so fast that they can get out of control before anyone realizes what is happening.

Respect All Views. You need to respect people who do not like confrontations or any form of conflict. Many people avoid conflict at any cost. These people tend to withdraw from the group when conflict occurs. Once they mentally leave, it is hard to recapture their interest. Therefore, work to establish an atmosphere that keeps people focused on issues, not personalities.

Use Collective Pronouns. Although at times you may have to refer to people by name, you should *try to develop the practice of using group pronouns as a way of centering on content instead of people.* Notice how words such as *we* and *our* focus the discussion on the group, while pronouns such as *I, me,* and *you* and specific names (Tom and Ann) can pit members against each other. This technique has all parties seeing themselves as attacking the problem instead of each other.

Seek Compromise. *Seek a position of compromise whenever possible.* We already noted the importance of avoiding a win-or-lose position; getting members to give a little is often a good way out of the either/or dilemma. Notice how compromise is used in the following example:

> There seems to be two different proposals on the floor. Some believe that we should give the men's golf team $1,000, while others would like the money to go to the debate team. Perhaps we might give each team $500. What do you think of that idea?

We all need to get over the notion that compromise is a form of appeasement. A healthier view is the one expressed by the British statesman Edmund Burke: "Every human benefit and enjoyment, every virtue and every prudent act, is founded on compromise and barter."

Stay Calm. If you are the target of the conflict, *it is important that you try to stay calm.* This advice, of course, falls into the category of counsel that is easier to state than to act out. We all know how difficult it is to remain composed when we feel we are under siege. Yet, by remaining patient, we can calm the entire group and perhaps get them to resolve the conflict.

Conflict and Culture

Although interpersonal conflict is part of every culture, each culture's ways of perceiving and dealing with conflict are influenced by its values. More specifically, our culture helps us define conflict and determine how it can be managed.

Not all cultures agree on what constitutes discord and conflict. In North America, there is a general belief that we can experience controversy over issues and not perceive the debate in personal terms. That is to say, most people are able to distinguish between conflicts based on tasks and those related to personalities. This is not the case with many East Asian and Latin cultures. Members of these cultures believe people, ideas, and issues cannot be separated; they are one and the same. Hence, members of these cultures are not likely to engage in direct hostility, even over tasks or assignments. Interpersonal harmony is highly valued, so people in these cultures seek to "save face" for themselves, as well as for others.

In many Mediterranean cultures, the view of conflict is very different from the one found in East Asia and Latin America. People in the Mediterranean area perceive conflict as a natural way of life. They expect people to have intense feelings on many issues. In a group, the expectation is one of debate, argument, direct confrontation, and controversy. It is also anticipated that the combatants will be extremely animated and boisterous when dealing with conflict. To the English and Japanese, however, who value a calm and reserved demeanor, this vigorous approach to group conflict would be considered rude and even vulgar. For them, a more indirect approach to conflict would be the proper method.

Finally, *there are cultural differences regarding the conflicting participants.* In cultures that stress the equality of all people and seek to avoid distinctions based on class, caste, rank, and superior and subordinate roles, there is apt to be more group and interpersonal conflict. These cultures encourage people to speak up and have their say in the matter ("The squeaky wheel gets the grease"). However, in cultures in which roles and status are clearly defined

(Japan, Mexico), people are less likely to challenge the thinking of someone of higher standing.

Barriers to Successful Group Discussion

The most common barriers to successful group discussion are violations of the guidelines offered for participation and leadership. There are, however, some additional barriers worth noting. Because they affect everyone in a group, a common effort must be made to overcome these barriers whenever they surface.

Apathy

Apathy among group members is perhaps the most common barrier to successful group discussion. Apathy is a complex phenomenon. It can be brought to the group by a single member or it can be generated during the life of the group. Apathy can be reflected in a variety of ways. A member might withdraw from the group, or the entire group could surrender any vitality or spirit it had at the outset of the meeting. In any case, apathy, and all of its external and internal manifestations, can destroy a group. When a group appears apathetic, you should not be reluctant to ask the participants to pause and examine their indifference. Although the following quotation is from an anonymous source, I nevertheless exhort you to remember the wisdom of these words the next time you drift toward being apathetic or see it in your group:

> Indifference never wrote great works, nor thought out striking inventions, nor reared the solemn architecture that awes the soul, nor breathed sublime music, nor painted glorious pictures, nor undertook heroic philanthropies. All these grandeurs are born of enthusiasms, and done heartily.

Excessive Formality

Although some cultures are comfortable with high levels of formality (German, Mexico, English, Japanese), in most instances *people from Western cultures do not like excessive formality.* Whether through rules or attitudes, an inordinate amount of formality hampers participation and increases tension in a group. Whereas some rules might be helpful, too many rules appear restrictive and can keep the members stiff in both mind and communication.

Control

Closely related to formality is the problem of control. *A lack of freedom and spontaneity destroys the free flow of ideas, feelings, and information.* Control, like apathy, can take many forms. One person may try to monopolize a conversation as a means of control, while another may exercise control by only calling on certain people to talk. Regardless of how control shows itself, it is a barrier to successful group communication.

Dogmatism

Dogmatism, although a corollary to the idea of control, is also a barrier that plagues many discussion groups. *If a group or any of its members is dogmatic and asserts principles and opinions as if they were gospel, the entire discussion suffers.* Dogmatism is characterized by narrow-mindedness and authoritarianism, both of which have no place in group discussion.

Lack of Patience

A lack of patience is another communication barrier that must be overcome if a group is to reach its full potential. In our culture, dispatch is valued, yet, as we have seen, the group process takes time. Sharing opinion and research is often tedious. Without patience, the group process is rushed and characterized by jumping to conclusions. Do not let this happen to your group. Remember the words of the Persian poet Saadi, "Whoever has no patience has no wisdom."

Groupthink

The final barrier, groupthink, is a concept that grew out of the work of Irving L. Janis. **Groupthink** *is a type of conformity that is directed at ideas as well as at people.* Group members perceive that cooperation is crucial and that everyone must work together toward a common goal. However, some groups, because of peer pressure and a desire to appear confident, take this position to the extreme. They become closed-minded and refuse even to look at contrary views and opinions. People and ideas that fail to conform are discouraged and even ignored. Groups can overcome groupthink if they grant that it is a potential barrier and work to eliminate the causes of individual and group conformity.

There are a number of steps that can be taken to overcome the barrier of groupthink. First, the group must encourage free and open discussion of all issues. Second, alternatives must be welcomed during the entire course of the discussion. Third, the consequences of all decisions must be considered, even if they may be negative. Finally, what has been decided should be periodically reviewed to determine if earlier decisions are still valid in light of newer findings. Perhaps the best way to survive groupthink is to heed the good advice of the humorist Thomas Haliburton, "Hear one side and you will be in the dark; hear both sides, and all will be clear."

The Role of Culture in Group Communication

It seems only fitting that we move from a discussion of communication barriers to an examination of the role of culture in group discussion. For if the group members fail to have an appreciation of how culture might influence group communication, a group might experience some serious interpersonal problems. Small-group communication settings involve intercultural communication when a group is composed of people from diverse cultural backgrounds. This occurs *in international settings*, when people from various countries and cultures meet to discuss international politics, economics, or business, and *in domestic areas,* when civic bodies attempt to solve problems within the community or *when students representing numerous ethnic backgrounds* meet to recommend school policies and actions. Some of the ways that cultural differences may be manifested during the course of the discussion process are detailed in what follows.

Individualism or Collectivism

Culture influences whether or not we value a group or an individual. In cultures that have a strong group orientation (East Asian, Latin American), collectivism rather than individualism is stressed; cooperation is emphasized over competition. People raised in these cultures find it natural to work for a common goal. However, people from cultures that place the individual ahead of the group (North American, Australian, French, Danish) usually find it difficult to adapt individual goals to collective goals. Think of the strong message of individualism in the phrases "God helps those who help themselves" or "Pull yourself up by your own boot straps." This type of orientation stresses an "I'll do it myself" attitude instead of a cooperative set of values. The individual is also expected to accept blame for decisions that lead to bad consequences ("You made your bed; now lie in it"). In a sense, North Americans want to know who to castigate when things go wrong. Asian and Latin cultures, however, have a strong group orientation rather than an individual orientation; decisions result from group interaction and group loyalty. The group, not the individual, is responsible for the consequences of its action, and when something goes wrong, the group, not the individual, is held responsible.

Conformity

Cultural differences can be found in how cultures perceive and value conformity—a topic discussed in the preceding section on barriers. This aspect of group behavior is somewhat related to the idea of collective versus individualistic cultures. Cultures that place a high value on individualism (North American, Australian, English, Israeli) encourage and tolerate independence, initiative, and self-reliance. These traits nourish nonconformity. On the other hand, people from collective cultures (Latin American, East Asian) seldom violate group norms. This desire to agree with others and conform shows itself in a number of ways that directly affect group interaction. For example, people from cultures that stress accord and harmony over deviation usually do not express their feelings if they sense that what they say will offend another person. They remain silent and use indirect speech. For example, Native Americans do not like to humiliate or embarrass other people; hence, they are apt to agree with what is being discussed even if they internally hold the opposite view. Asian and Filipino members of a group might even smile and nod politely to show they are conforming when in reality they may disagree with what is transpiring. Being aware of cultural differences as they apply to conformity will help you understand the messages, or lack of them, you get from other people.

❖ ❖ ❖ ❖   ## Use of Language

The influence of culture in groups can be seen in how participants use language. In cultures that have a strong verbal tradition (North American, Arab, Jewish), many people use words with great ease. Members of these cultures value talk, rely heavily on verbal language to express their feelings, and tend to be very direct. However, in many Asian cultures, where politeness is highly valued, people are less direct. They also hold the view that in many instances the strongest and most important emotions and feelings cannot be expressed with words. Because verbal language is often held in check, people from these cultures "read" other people by their nonverbal actions. Individuals from these cultures believe that people often understand each other without words. In fact, in the writings of Buddhism, one line notes that "there is a supreme truth that words can neither reach nor express." When in a group, people with this point of view might not talk as much as others would like them to. You need to appreciate the role of silence in certain cultures and not push too hard when people from Asian cultures wish to remain silent. They are taking part in their own way. For them, silence speaks. Not only do these cultures value silence and deliberation, but they also value process over product. These Eastern cultures want the participants to enjoy the group. For them, the final product is less important than harmony among the group members. According to this orientation, silence contributes to that sense of harmony.

Use of Time

A culture's perception of time can also be revealed during group discussion. In our culture, we learn that "time is money" and should not be wasted. Like the Germans and Swiss, we value time and try not to squander it. This often forces us to rush, be impulsive, and make quick decisions when we are in a group. People from Mexico, Japan, China, and Korea have an entirely different view of time. They believe one should give full attention to the moment and not act as if one is just "passing through." In a group, they tend to be more reflective and resist moving too quickly. A Korean proverb says, "Even if a bridge is made of stone it may not be safe." The meaning is obvious—proceed with caution. People with this outlook will often want to take time when considering all phases of a problem.

The desire to go slowly is also seen in the amount of time various cultures set aside to establish relationships. In North American culture, people are often valued because they are open and friendly. In North America, there is a belief that it does not take long to get to know someone. An outgrowth of this orientation is found in the speed with which a group of North Americans is ready to focus on the work at hand. Many cultures take an opposing view when it comes to developing social and working relationships. The Japanese and the Mexicans, for example, believe in establishing rapport with their associates before they conduct business. In a group situation, this value is translated into a slower pace and a desire to postpone focusing on the problem before the members of the group know each other.

Compromise

❖ ❖ ❖ ❖

Culture can also govern the processes by which the group negotiates and reaches compromise. For instance, in the Persian language, the word for "compromise" does not mean a midway solution that both sides can accept, as it does in English. Instead, it means surrendering one's principles. Also, a mediator is seen as a meddler, someone who is bargaining uninvited. In India, Mexico, and the Middle East, the process of negotiation is enjoyed. It is seen as an act of bargaining, in which there is give and take. Each person sets out to obtain the best possible deal, and everyone enjoys the process. However, this sense of pleasure in negotiation is not found in most Asian cultures. Many people from these cultures find the entire act of direct negotiation rather awkward. They prefer compromise over conflict. To be an effective group member, you need to discover if the background of the other participants makes them either willing to compromise or delighted with the prospects of a good argument.

Group Norms

Most group norms grow out of people's cultural experiences with groups, and as cultures differ, so do norms. For example, in North American culture, we have been raised to say what is on our minds. The proverb "the squeaky wheel gets the grease" tells us to be assertive. However, in many other cultures, the message is quite the opposite. In Japan, for example, there is an adage that "the nail that sticks up is the first to feel the blow of the hammer." Hence, in these, and other Asian cultures, group norms call for a different level of participation than do norms in North America.

Decision Making

There are also cultural differences with regard to decision making. Although some of these ideas might have been hinted at earlier, they are worth underscoring at this time. In the Japanese culture, where consensus is valued, decision making that does not have "winners" or "losers" is the norm rather than the exception. Not only is consent the rule, everyone in the group is expected to support the decision even if they do not agree with it. The Chinese, because they also value outward signs of harmony and consensus, hold much the same view as the Japanese toward decision making. In Latin America, decision making is often autocratic. People are socialized in these cultures to respect authority and not to question superiors. Hence, when working in groups, they will often look to the "leader" for all decisions. This same approach toward decision making is also found in Germany and France, where authority means "top-down" decisions.

Uncertainty and Ambiguity

Decision making is also influenced by a culture's view of uncertainty. That is to say, how do members of a particular culture cope with ambiguous and equivocal situations? In many cultures (Japanese, Greek, Mexican, French), uncertainty and the unpredictable make people anxious. They function more effectively when there is structure and specific rules to follow. People who dislike uncertainty also avoid taking too many chances. Cultures that socialized their members to be less apprehensive of the uncertainty of life (American, British, Canadian) have a higher tolerance for ambiguity, tend to dislike too many rules, and are willing to take risks. You can imagine the potential for communication problems when members from these two orientations are in the same group. The clash of cultural values would influence everything from the pace of the meeting to the amount of control given to the leader. Being aware of these differences can help you be a better group member when you are in a culturally diverse group.

Nonverbal Communication

As a member of a group, *you will observe cultural differences in nonverbal communication.* Let us look at some of these differences so that you will be able to understand your own nonverbal behavior in a group and also adapt to the nonverbal actions of others.

Clothing and Appearance. *Cultures have differing views toward clothing and appearance.* An Arab wearing a robe called a dishdasha or thobe and a headpiece can cause some people to feel strange because they do not understand the significance of the person's appearance. If some members of a group are from cultures that value formality, such as Germany and Japan, they are apt to dress in what appears to be formal attire. On the other hand, in the North American culture being relaxed is valued; hence, we usually attend meetings in casual clothing. Try to remember that one mode of dress is not superior to another; rather, it expresses a different attitude toward clothing and general appearance.

Gestures. *The use we make of our body is also a reflection of our culture.* As we noted in chapter 4, most people from the Mediterranean cultures use large gestures and are more animated than most people from England and Southeast Asia. You should not allow the size or ferocity of another member's gestures to represent his or her level of interest or commitment to the group. Rather, you should realize that differences in movement and gestures are but another cultural difference found in small-group behavior.

Emotional Expression. *Because emotional expressions are culturally learned, the members of your group might use facial expressions in a unique way.* The Chinese and Japanese, for example, do not readily show emotion in public. These cultures even use the face to conceal rather than reveal emotions. However, in Latin American and Mediterranean cultures, signs of emotion are not only shown but often exaggerated.

Eye Contact. *The amount and type of eye contact in a group are still other aspects of culture that you need to understand.* In our culture, eye contact is used to show interest and to indicate that the channels of communication are open. However, in many Asian, Native American, and Latin cultures, too much direct eye contact creates feelings of discomfort. Exactly the opposite orientation toward gaze is found in Arab cultures, in which one expects to stare directly into the eyes of one's communication partners.

Touch. *You should also be aware of cultural differences with regard to touch.* It might seem very natural in the group setting to reach over and touch someone as a way of making a point or offering comfort, yet cultural variations in this form of communication must be considered. For example, Muslims eat and do happy things with the right hand, but to touch another person with the left hand is a social insult; the left hand is reserved for toilet functions. People in cultures such as the Jewish, Italian, and French touch a great deal, but less touching is found among the English, Chinese, and Japanese. In short, be careful of using touch as a form of communication if you don't know all the group members' views of physical contact.

Use of Voice. *There are also cultural differences in the use of the voice.* Be prepared for people who use a great deal of volume, such as Italians, Greeks, and Arabs, as well as those who speak in hushed tones (Thai, Japanese).

Use of Space. *There are also cultural variations in the use of space.* Eastern European, Arab, and Latin cultures consider it normal for people to sit very close to each other. The North American culture regards this lack of space as a violation of its cultural norm regarding privacy. There are also cultures, such as the Chinese, who prefer side-by-side seating to face-to-face arrangements. Be prepared for these disparities as you interact with people from different cultures.

Taking Part in a Videoconference

In chapter 15 we talked about using television as a device for giving speeches. We now turn our attention to the use of television as it applies to group interaction, more specifically, videoconferencing. *The videoconference, often referred to as an electronic meeting, electronically links people who are physically separated.* For people living and working in the electronic age, knowing how to participate in a teleconference is almost as much a necessity as knowing how to use a computer or a fax machine.

The practice of holding videoconferences has grown so popular in the last few years that now many organizations, universities, and corporations own the required equipment. The benefits of such meetings are obvious. The expense of travel is eliminated, and electronic meetings take less time and can be arranged quickly. They also foster cooperation among geographically separated employees; the office in Mexico City can know what the office in Seattle is thinking. The videoconference also allows more people to participate. There is even some research suggesting that electronic meetings are more orderly and productive than traditional face-to-face discussions.

Educational uses of teleconferencing are also increasing. Basically, there is a need to reach learners who cannot travel to the classroom. The teleconference provides an effective way for the teacher and class to interact as if they were in a single setting.

As a professional, you will most likely be a member of a group that is using television to conduct your company's business. To assure that your appearance will be a successful one, let me offer you some information on (a) the characteristics of videoconferences, (b) preparing for a videoconference, and (c) participating in a videoconference.

The Characteristics of a Videoconference

The videoconference is basically a group communication experience conducted via television. Therefore, much of what was proposed in chapter 15 concerning televised speech and the material on group discussion already

Videoconferences now link people together. (Photo: corbisimages.com)

presented in this chapter applies to the videoconference. However, there are two general characteristics of the videoconference that make it different from face-to-face exchanges. You should be aware of those differences so that you can make the necessary adjustments to your preparation and participation.

Physical Separation. *There is the obvious physical separation in electronic meetings and classes that is not found in face-to-face groups.* This separation brings with it specific needs to modify some of your communication behaviors. For example, you will not be able to touch your colleagues or even exchange objects. A certain amount of intimacy will be lost. The physical separation may also mean a separation in time, as the exchange crosses time zones both in the United States and abroad. One group could want a short break for morning coffee while another set of participants is ready for a long lunch. Because of these and other limitations, you need to develop a new outlook toward interpersonal distance. Simply stated, although you will be expected to talk to your video partner or television instructor, you will not be able to sit near him or her.

Even the premeeting chitchat that is so much a part of the classroom and group experience is influenced by the fact that the participants are at different locations. The imposed separation also has an impact on the kinds of feedback you will use. Later in this section ways of adapting your feedback to the limitations brought about by physical separation are discussed.

Electronic Components. *The electronic components of television (sight and sound) also control interaction.* Who is on camera, the angle of the camera, volume control, and the like influence who and what is being seen and heard. Even the clock plays a unique role in this medium. Television time is expensive, valuable, and usually in short supply.

Preparing for a Videoconference   ❖ ❖ ❖ ❖

To be an active participant in a videoconference, you must be prepared. Many of the steps of preparation have been discussed throughout this book. However, as you learned in the last chapter, television does call for some additional planning.

Know the Purpose of the Meeting. Make sure you and everyone concerned with the conference knows the purpose of the meeting. Because the participants most likely do not have daily contact, it becomes crucial that they know exactly what is going to be discussed. Whenever possible, the purpose, much like the specific purpose of a speech, should be stated in one clear, concise sentence. For example: "The purpose of the May 8 videoconference is to have all members of the sales force discuss what can be done to improve intercultural communication within the organization."

Learn About the Other Participants. Try to find out all you can about the other participants. Who are they? Why have they been asked to participate in the conference? Who will the leader be? If it is an educational setting, who is the instructor? How much will he or she know about the topic? Will there be a guest? Will all the participants be of equal status? How much participation is expected of each member? Are there going to be people involved that use English as a second language? What countries and cultures will be represented?

Analyze the Technical Aspects. Prepare by analyzing the technical aspects of the meeting. Here are a few questions you should ask in this category: Where will the participants be located? Hotels? Television studios? Classrooms? The company conference room? How many people will be at each site? How long will the conference last? How many cameras will be employed? What time zones will be involved?

Establish Rapport. While you cannot establish much rapport with the people at separate sites, *try to create a relaxed and friendly atmosphere with the participants at your site.* Getting to know each other and feeling at ease will help overcome some of the fear associated with appearing on television.

Participating in a Videoconference

Your effectiveness as a participant in a videoconference can be enhanced if you follow the advice offered earlier in this chapter. In addition, much of what was said about group processes earlier in this chapter directly relates to videoconferencing. However, there are a few other communication behaviors that will make your appearance much more rewarding.

Follow the Teleconference Schedule. It is important that you comply with the teleconference schedule and encourage others to do the same. This means that contributions should be brief and relevant so time is not wasted. We have seen some students dominate an instructor's time during a videoconference. When this happens, they tend to be on camera more than the professor. To make television more interesting, it is a good idea to change speakers as often as possible.

Emphasize Good Communication. People expect more of you if you are on television—this also includes the way you communicate. Therefore, eye contact, body language, vocal variety, appearance, and the like must be given special attention. It might be helpful to review the advice we offered in chapter 15 on television presentations so that you understand all the nonverbal actions, from attire to posture.

Identify Yourself When You Speak. You should identify yourself as you begin your contribution—even if that contribution is in the form of a simple question. For example, "This is Mike Smith in El Cajon. Carol, I wonder if you could explain what you mean by the term 'participatory decision making'?"

Do Not Succumb To Distractions. Because you are not on camera all the time, or not even being seen by all the other participants, it is easy to lose concentration. Paying attention to the "hardware" of television can also be distracting. Make yourself listen to all of the proceedings. In this way, you will be able to take an active role during all of the meeting.

Adapt Your Feedback to the Situation. You must adjust your feedback to the electronic medium. This means using verbal feedback even though you are on television. You may not always know what is "on the screen," but your microphone, or one near you, will always be turned on. We have seen many participants embarrass themselves by talking to each other without realizing their microphones were transmitting every word they were saying to over fifty other people.

Evaluating a Discussion

For centuries, philosophers have told all who would listen, "Know thyself." You should also seek to "improve thyself." One way this can be accomplished is through group evaluation and self-evaluation. In fact, most groups find it useful to evaluate the process they use and the effectiveness of their techniques. This evaluation provides useful information that can be used in subsequent groups. It also affords members of the group valuable feedback concerning their participation in the group.

Many groups find it helpful to evaluate periodically as they move through the discussion process. They simply stop and ask questions concerning what is happening, why it is happening, what the results are, and what should be done. Evaluation that takes place at the conclusion of a particular meeting is also a popular method of assessment.

Evaluation can examine a host of variables. Members can evaluate group processes, participation, leadership, communication patterns and problems, interaction, tasks, and final products. These evaluations can be made by individual participants or by the group as a whole.

A large number of forms can be used in group and individual evaluations. We have included one such form at the end of this chapter. Many groups enjoy developing their own evaluation forms.

Summary

Whether to exchange information in a learning situation or to solve problems, we all find ourselves participating in group deliberations. As discussants, we may find ourselves participating in symposiums, panels, group discussions, support groups, educational groups, and problem-solving groups.

Figure 16.1 Discussion Grade Sheet   ❖ ❖ ❖ ❖

Name_____

Date_____

1. How well-prepared did the discussant appear to be? In what ways might he or she have been better prepared?

2. Did the discussant locate the real issues and avoid irrelevant matters? Did the discussion progress systematically from problem to solution?

3. Did the discussant have adequate knowledge concerning the topic? Was there breadth to the information? Was the information accurate?

4. What was the attitude of the discussant?

5. Were communication skills (adapting voice, action and language to the occasion, clearly stating ideas, listening actively) effectively used?

6. Was the discussant able to state and qualify conclusions and to synthesize the contributions of others?

7. Did the discussant adequately participate without dominating?

8. Did discussant assume a leadership role by initiating discussion. regulating participation. or summarizing?

9. Did the discussant take on functional. task. maintenance, and supportive roles?

Grade_____

Figure 16.2 Evaluation of Group Process

NAME_____

PROBLEM:

Circle with a pencil one segment of each rating scale below to indicate how you would characterize the discussion as a whole with reference to the ten dimensions noted.

EMOTIONAL CLIMATE

Listless	1	2	3	4	5	Animated
Tension, hostility	1	2	3	4	5	Friendly atmosphere
Dogmatic, unco-operative	1	2	3	4	5	Very cooperative

THOUGHT

Little use of information	1	2	3	4	5	Adequate information available and used
Frequently off the subject	1	2	3	4	5	Relevant discussion
Superficial discussion	1	2	3	4	5	Thoughtful discussion
Aimless, confused discussion	1	2	3	4	5	Methodical discussion; group has sense of direction

LANGUAGE

Often interrupt each other	1	2	3	4	5	Orderly discussion
Long contributions	1	2	3	4	5	Brief contributions
Provocative language	1	2	3	4	5	Courteous, temperate language

ADDITIONAL COMMENTS:

Name of Evaluator_____

Regardless of the context, it is important that we be well informed and follow an organizational scheme that leads us through the important phases of the problem. If the purpose of the group is to solve a problem, it is useful to observe the five steps of reflective thinking developed by John Dewey: (1) define the problem, (2) analyze the causes and effects, (3) identify all possible solutions, (4) select the best solution, and (5) put the solution into operation.

When participating in or leading a group, each person should adhere to a logical pattern, be prepared, take an active role, ask questions, supply leadership, be tolerant of diverse views, use feedback, create a friendly atmosphere, listen carefully, allow for deviant behavior, be willing to play a variety of roles, relate comments to what is transpiring at the moment, deal with conflict constructively, work to overcome barriers, and evaluate the group's progress.

When interacting with people from a cultural different from one's own it is useful to understand the influence of power distance, decision making, expectations, formality, and gender roles on group discussion.

Finally, if you find yourself in a group that is using videoconferencing, you should know some of the characteristics of this medium, how to prepare for videoconferencing, and some steps of successful participation.

Concepts and Questions

1. Define two types of groups. How are they alike? How do they differ?

2. Identify the characteristics of group discussion and explain how these characteristics might help to make group discussion an effective problem-solving tool.

3. List the steps of reflective thinking.

4. What are the major steps in preparing for a group discussion?

5. What are the major steps associated with brainstorming?

6. What cultural factors should be taken into consideration when communicating in a group composed of people from diverse cultural backgrounds?

7. What roles should the leader attempt to carry out?

8. What are some major considerations when taking part in a videoconference?

Activities and Exercises

1. Attend a panel discussion and evaluate the organizational structure and participation of the members.

2. Take part in a group that uses Dewey's five steps of reflective thinking and another group that employs the brainstorming sequence. At the conclusion of both experiences write an essay that reflects your reactions to both patterns.

3. Write a short essay describing how you would discourage a talkative member from dominating the group. Write another essay that discusses the methods you would employ to encourage a silent member to take part in the deliberations.

4. Discuss in class how a problem-solving discussion is related to the notion of participatory government.

5. Identify three groups to which you belong, and then write a short essay that examines how those groups use the discussion process. Include in your essay your evaluation of how successful the groups are—and if they are not successful, mention some of the problems these groups encounter.

6. Make arrangements to have one of your discussion sessions videotaped. At the conclusion of the session, play back the discussion and have the members of the group evaluate the group's effectiveness in light of the concepts discussed in this chapter. ✦

Bibliography

Burke, K. 1950. *Rhetoric of Motives* (Englewood Cliffs, NJ).

Monroe, A. H. 1962. *Principles and Types of Speech*, Fifth Edition (Chicago, IL: Scott, Foresman, & Company).

Nichols, R. G. and L. A. Stevens. 1957. *Are You Listening?* (New York: McGraw-Hill Book Company).

Tead, O. 1959. *Administration: Its Purpose and Performance*, (New York: Harper and Row).

Index

PowerPoint, 198, 200–201
Practice, 28, 34, 46, 48–49, 51, 52–55, 110, 112, 127, 132, 133, 199, 202, 204–205, 353, 384, 424, 426
Prediction, 67
Prejudice, 244–245, 251, 252
Preparation, 15, 26, 27, 34, 35, 45, 47, 49, 50, 52, 53, 58, 59, 171, 196, 204, 449, 457
  being prepared, 29
  level of, 68
  steps of, 38
Presentation (*see also* delivery), 20, 45, 92, 93–104, 180, 185, 187, 196, 245, 262, 425
  aural dimensions, 110
  oral aspects, 93
  visual aspects, 92
Presenting ideas, 28–30, 92–113, 148, 473
Preview, 282, 284, 354, 366–367, 437
Private codes, 313
Private discussions, 458–489
Problem-solving groups
  analysis, 459–461
  characteristics of, 459–461
  democratic process, 461
  investigation, 459–460
  plan of action, 468–469
  possible solutions, 467–468
  recognizing and defining, 466
  reflective thinking, 460
Procrastination, 53
Profanity, 330
Progress, 71
Pronouns, (*see also* Personal pronouns), 327
Pronunciation, 104, 107–108, 111, 136, 445
Propositions, 381–382
  of fact, 381–382, 383, 401
  of policy, 383, 401
  of value, 382, 383, 401
Proxemics, 101
Psychological appeals, 387, 389–392, 410–411
  and culture, 411–412
Public discussion, 458
Public speaking (*see also* Communication), 9, 12, 15, 17, 34, 108
  attitudes toward, 55
  and conversation, 14–17
  ethical responsibility, 16
Puerto Rican culture, 103
"Punctuation" devices, 14
Purpose, 15, 34, 37, 94, 95, 129, 133, 134, 149, 172, 180, 211, 262, 309, 343, 360, 425
  determining, 345
  formulating, 40–42

  general, 26, 34, 42, 43, 44, 264, 282, 363
  specific, 34, 42–45, 128, 183, 264, 268, 282, 345, 346, 378, 380, 384, 389, 466
  speech, 25–26, 210

Q

Quakers, 74
Question-and-answer period, 142, 446–451
Questionnaires, 82
Questions, 120, 138, 139, 362, 446, 458, 463
  asking, 131–132
  close-ended, 131, 216
  general, 446
  mirror, 216
  open-ended, 131, 216, 218
  probes, 131–132, 216
  yes-or-no, 463
Questions of fact, 381, 382, 462
Questions of policy, 383, 462
Questions of value, 382, 462
Quintilian, 19
Quotations, 50, 51, 163, 164, 195, 217, 231, 232, 249, 289–290, 302, 358, 362, 363–364, 370, 401, 424
  direct, 171–172
  humorous, 432
  opening, 290
  as primary research, 231

R

Rabelais, François, 214
Radio, 18, 46, 442
Rapport, 46, 49, 69, 99, 101, 139, 217, 300, 401, 430, 438, 446, 485
Ray, John, 318
Receiver, (*see also* Audience; Listener), 11, 18, 126, 186
  responsibility of, 21–22
References, 212
  books, 225
  literary, 226
Rehearsing, 59, 198, 205
Reinforcement, 353–354, 367
Relaxing techniques, (*see also* Tension-relieving techniques), 59–60
Reliability, 399
Repetition, 168, 315, 318, 332, 341, 354, 367
Reports, 222, 458
Research, 48, 49, 52, 92, 210–237, 240, 245, 397, 462
  agenda, 210–212

505